The Wiley Blackwell Encyclopedia of Gender and Sexuality Studies

Wiley Blackwell Encyclopedias in Social Science
Consulting Editor: George Ritzer

Published

The Wiley Blackwell Encyclopedia of Globalization
Edited by George Ritzer

The Wiley Blackwell Encyclopedia of Social and Political Movements
Edited by David A. Snow, Donatella della Porta, Bert Klandermans, and Doug McAdam

The Wiley Blackwell Encyclopedia of Health, Illness, Behavior, and Society
Edited by William C. Cockerham, Robert Dingwall, and Stella Quah

The Wiley Blackwell Encyclopedia of Consumption and Consumer Studies
Edited by Daniel Thomas Cook and J. Michael Ryan

The Wiley Blackwell Encyclopedia of Family Studies
Edited by Constance L. Shehan

The Wiley Blackwell Encyclopedia of Race, Ethnicity, and Nationalism
Edited by John Stone, Rutledge M. Dennis, Polly S. Rizova, Anthony D. Smith, and Xiaoshuo Hou

The Wiley Blackwell Encyclopedia of Gender and Sexuality Studies
Editor-in-Chief: Nancy A. Naples, Associate Editors: renée c. hoogland, Maithree Wickramasinghe, and Wai Ching Angela Wong

Forthcoming

The Wiley Blackwell Encyclopedia of Social Theory
Edited by Bryan S. Turner, Chang Kyung-Sup, Cynthia Epstein, Peter Kivisto, William Outhwaite, and J. Michael Ryan

The Wiley Blackwell Encyclopedia of Urban and Regional Studies
Edited by Anthony M. Orum, Marisol Garcia, Dennis Judd, Bryan Roberts, and Pow Choon-Piew

The Wiley Blackwell Encyclopedia of Environment and Society
Edited by Dorceta E. Taylor, Kozo Mayumi, Jun Bi, Paul Burton, and Tor A. Benjaminsen

Related titles

The Blackwell Encyclopedia of Sociology
Edited by George Ritzer

The Concise Encyclopedia of Sociology
Edited by George Ritzer and J. Michael Ryan

The Wiley Blackwell Encyclopedia of Gender and Sexuality Studies

Editor-in-Chief

Nancy A. Naples

Associate Editors

renée c. hoogland
Maithree Wickramasinghe
Wai Ching Angela Wong

Volume II
E–F

WILEY Blackwell

This edition first published 2016
© 2016 John Wiley & Sons, Ltd.

Registered Office
John Wiley & Sons Ltd, The Atrium, Southern Gate, Chichester, West Sussex, PO19 8SQ, UK

Editorial Offices
350 Main Street, Malden, MA 02148-5020, USA
9600 Garsington Road, Oxford, OX4 2DQ, UK
The Atrium, Southern Gate, Chichester, West Sussex, PO19 8SQ, UK

For details of our global editorial offices, for customer services, and for information about how to apply for permission to reuse the copyright material in this book please see our website at www.wiley.com/wiley-blackwell.

The right of Nancy A. Naples to be identified as the author of the editorial material in this work has been asserted in accordance with the UK Copyright, Designs and Patents Act 1988.

All rights reserved. No part of this publication may be reproduced, stored in a retrieval system, or transmitted, in any form or by any means, electronic, mechanical, photocopying, recording or otherwise, except as permitted by the UK Copyright, Designs and Patents Act 1988, without the prior permission of the publisher.

Wiley also publishes its books in a variety of electronic formats. Some content that appears in print may not be available in electronic books.

Designations used by companies to distinguish their products are often claimed as trademarks. All brand names and product names used in this book are trade names, service marks, trademarks or registered trademarks of their respective owners. The publisher is not associated with any product or vendor mentioned in this book.

Limit of Liability/Disclaimer of Warranty: While the publisher and author have used their best efforts in preparing this book, they make no representations or warranties with respect to the accuracy or completeness of the contents of this book and specifically disclaim any implied warranties of merchantability or fitness for a particular purpose. It is sold on the understanding that the publisher is not engaged in rendering professional services and neither the publisher nor the author shall be liable for damages arising herefrom. If professional advice or other expert assistance is required, the services of a competent professional should be sought.

Library of Congress Cataloging-in-Publication data is available for this book.

ISBN 9781405196949 (hardback)

Cover image: Clockwise from top left: Artists of street theater group ASSA (Ankara Cinema and Art Atelier) during a demonstration on International Women's Day © Piero Castellano/Pacific Press/LightRocket via Getty Images; Banyana beat Mali, Women's Championship match, South Africa, 2010 © Gallo Images/Alamy; Young girl from Oaxaca © Jennifer Bickham Mendez; Demonstration over same-sex marriages, Taipei, Taiwan, 2015 © Sam Yeh/AFP/Getty Images

Set in 10/12pt Minion by SPi Global, Chennai, India
Printed and bound in Singapore by Markono Print Media Pte Ltd

1 2016

Contents

Volume I

Editors	vii
Contributors	ix
Lexicon	xxxvii
Introduction and Acknowledgments	xlix
Gender and Sexuality Studies A–D	1

Volume II

Gender and Sexuality Studies E–F	497

Volume III

Gender and Sexuality Studies G–I	931

Volume IV

Gender and Sexuality Studies J–R	1471

Volume V

Gender and Sexuality Studies S–Y	2051
Index of Names	*2619*
Index of Subjects	*2633*

E

Earner–Carer Model

BRITT-INGER KEISU
Umeå University, Sweden

The earner–carer model is a welfare state approach based on the ideological, gender-egalitarian premise that men and women are equally involved in both paid labor and unpaid care work (Korpi, Ferrarini, and Englund 2013). The model is sometimes expressed differently, i.e., as the dual earner/dual carer model. Different welfare state policy structures divide into those that support either women's paid work within the labor market or the traditional division of male breadwinner/female homemaker. Hence, policy measures produce different incentives for families to divide up paid work and unpaid care work.

During the 1990s, many feminists studying welfare state issues criticized the overlooking of gendered aspects; as Grönlund and Öun (2010, 182) summarize it, "the unpaid work that is carried out in the family is part of the welfare production in society and […] for women, the important welfare state policies are not only those providing de-commodification, but also policies such as childcare and parental leave that contribute to women's integration into the labour market; that is, to their commodification." The critiques of feminist scholars have thus had an impact on welfare state theory and, in addition to the inclusion of care work, there also seems to be a growing consensus to include all socially constructed categories in the analysis, such as gender, class, ethnicity, and race (Korpi 2000).

Throughout the twentieth century, the traditional male breadwinner/female full-time homemaker ideal of family life was dominant in the Western welfare states, but during the second half of the century it became less pronounced, along with women's increased participation in the labor market. The model obliges men to earn enough for all members of the family; by the late twentieth century this ideal was no longer tenable even for middle-class families, and it has never been a reality for the working class (Fraser 1994). One example is the Swedish case, where both men and women were expected to do agricultural work and the ideal was that women should work all the time (Nyberg 1989, 2010). Women did not spend a lot of time caring for their children; looking after siblings was a task for older brothers and sisters.

An empirical study from the early twenty-first century shows the significance of the welfare state to family life. Korpi (2000; see also Esping-Andersen 1999) measures

The Wiley Blackwell Encyclopedia of Gender and Sexuality Studies, First Edition. Edited by Nancy A. Naples.
© 2016 John Wiley & Sons, Ltd. Published 2016 by John Wiley & Sons, Ltd.

three welfare state policy models from the 18 OECD countries that were examined: dual-earner support, traditional family support, and market-oriented policies. The third model allows market forces to shape gender relations and leaves private solutions for individuals and their families. The study used a two-dimensional classification of institutions, enabling either dual-earner families or traditional female homemaker families. The dual-earner index measures public day-care services for children aged 0–2 years, full-time day care for children 3 years and older, and the extent to which earning-related parental insurance is provided. The traditional family index measures cash child allowances to minor children, family tax benefits to minor children for families with only one economic provider, and finally part-time public day-care services for children of 3 years up to school age. In this empirical study, countries with high scores on the first dimension and low scores on the second are classified as dual-earner countries (Denmark, Finland, Sweden, and Norway) and countries with high scores on the second dimension and low on the first are labeled as traditional countries (Austria, Belgium, France, Germany, and the Netherlands). Finally, if they show low scores on both dimensions the countries are classified as market oriented, because mainly markets and families provide childcare (Ireland, Switzerland, and the United Kingdom). Hence, this empirical study shows how different welfare state models affect work and family arrangements. Additional research explores their impact on work–family conflicts (for further reading see Öun 2012).

If scholars such as Esping-Andersen (1999) and Korpi (2000) are frontrunners with their empirical studies based on models that include the dual-earner and female homemaker/male breadwinner families, feminists' critique has eventually had an influence, hence the inclusion of care work, and a dual-carer classification has been developed. This is shown in another empirical investigation in which the welfare state policy for dual-carer support is included in the theoretical framework (Korpi, Ferrarini, and Englund 2013, 28). The results indicate that "In most countries women with tertiary education have very high labour force participation rates irrespective of family policies: women most likely to have individual resources enabling them to make real choices thus tend to choose paid work." For those countries where women to a large extent lack university-level education, the effects of family policies are most visible. Earner–carer policies seem to have significantly higher impact on the number of employed women with low and medium levels of formal education in comparison with welfare state policies that are market oriented or those that support a traditional family model.

In scholarly debates, the Nordic countries are often considered to be frontrunners in their policy support for the earner–carer model. The policy orientation during the 1970s led to expansions in areas that affected unpaid care work such as parental leave, public day care, and the individualization of income taxation. This increased men's involvement in household work and childcare, and provided women with greater employment opportunities and career possibilities. The earner–carer policies developed in the Nordic countries have also had an impact on class equality simultaneously with gender egalitarianism (see Korpi, Ferrarini, and Englund 2013). Despite these efforts, men still take less substantial parts of the parental leave, and fewer men than women work part-time to take care of children (Statistics Sweden 2012). This asymmetry contributes to upholding the gender imbalance in certain higher-paying professions. Overall, this historical sketch shows the importance of feminist scholarly analysis for theory development, welfare state policy measures, and, in the long run, gender egalitarianism, here by means of families' division of paid work and unpaid care work.

SEE ALSO: Family Wage; Feminist Theories of the Welfare State; Gender Wage Gap; Parental Leave in Comparative Perspective; Work–Family Balance

REFERENCES

Esping-Andersen, Gøsta. 1999. *Social Foundations of Post-Industrial Economies*. Oxford: Oxford University Press.

Fraser, Nancy. 1994. "After the Family Wage: Gender Equity and the Welfare State." *Political Theory*, 22(4): 591–618. DOI: 10.1177/0090591794022004003.

Grönlund, Ann, and Ida Öun. 2010. "Rethinking Work–Family Conflict: Dual-Earner Policies, Role Conflict and Role Expansion in Western Europe." *Journal of European Social Policy*, 20(3): 179–195. DOI: 10.1177/0958928710364431.

Korpi, Walter. 2000. "Faces of Inequality: Gender, Class and Patterns of Inequalities in Different Types of Welfare States." *Social Politics*, 7(2): 127–191. DOI: 10.1093/sp/7.2.127.

Korpi, Walter, Tommy Ferrarini, and Stefan Englund. 2013. "Women's Opportunities under Different Family Policy Constellations: Gender, Class, and Inequality Tradeoffs in Western Countries Re-Examined." *Social Politics*, 20(1): 1–40. DOI: 10.1093/sp/jxs028.

Nyberg, Anita. 1989. *Tekniken – kvinnornas befriare? Hushållsteknik, köpevaror, gifta kvinnors hushållsarbetstid och förvärvsdeltagande 1930-talet-1980-talet*. Linköping: Tema Teknik och Social förändring.

Nyberg, Anita. 2010. "From Foster Mothers to Child Care Centers: A History of Working Mothers and Child Care in Sweden." *Feminist Economics*, 6(1): 5–20. DOI: 10.1080/135457000337642.

Öun, Ida. 2012. "Work–Family Conflict in the Nordic Countries: A Comparative Analysis." *Journal of Comparative Family Studies*, 43(2): 165–184.

Statistics Sweden. 2012. *Women and Men in Sweden: Facts and Figures 2012*. Örebro: Statistics Sweden. Accessed August 10, 2015, at http://www.scb.se/statistik/_publikationer/le0201_2012A01_Br_X10Br1201eNg.pdf.

FURTHER READING

Crompton, Rosemary. 1999. "Discussion and Conclusions." In *Restructuring Gender Relations and Employment: The Decline of the Male Breadwinner*, edited by Rosemary Crompton, 202–203. Oxford: Oxford University Press.

Ferrarini, Tommy, and Ann-Zofie Duvander. 2010. "Earner–Carer Model at the Cross-Roads: Reforms and Outcomes of Sweden's Family Policy in Comparative Perspective." *Social Policy and Quality of Life*, 1(17): 373–398.

Gornick, Janet, and Marcia Meyers. 2008. "Creating Gender Egalitarian Societies: An Agenda for Reform." *Politics & Society*, 36(3): 313–349. DOI: 10.1177/0032329208320562.

Jensen, Jane. 1997. "Who Cares? Gender and Welfare Regimes." *Social Politics*, 4(2): 182–187. DOI: 10.1093/sp/4.2.182.

Lewis, Jane. 1992. "Gender and the Development of Welfare Regimes." *Journal of European Social Policy*, 2(3): 159–173. DOI: 10.1177/095892879200200301.

Orloff, Ann Schola. 1993. "Gender and the Social Rights of Citizenships: The Comparative Analysis of Gender Relations and Welfare States." *American Sociological Review*, 58(3): 303–328. DOI: 10.1146/annurev.soc.22.1.51.

Sainsbury, Diane. 1994. *Gendering Welfare States*. London: Sage.

Eating Disorders and Disordered Eating

CHRISTINA COTO
Argosy University, USA

Although the direct etiology of eating disorders is not entirely clear, it can be confirmed that gender role stereotypes do influence the problem, as is supported by the fact that 90 percent of eating disorder cases are found in women (Morris 1985). Martz-Ludwig (1995) found that women who identify with feminine gender roles are at a significantly higher risk for acquiring disordered eating habits and body image problems. This study also supports the evidence that women who strive to achieve the cultural ideals of feminine beauty are more susceptible to developing an eating disorder.

Women are bombarded with pressures from media to adhere to an unrealistic standard of beauty in which thinness is revered. Bonnie Morris (1985), a prominent second-wave feminist, offers an explanation of social status for the women who experience body dissatisfaction and eating disorders. In her article, she postulates that adhering to a strict eating regimen often escalates to the development of full-blown eating disorders because "that behavior pattern is regarded as an achievement, not only by the anorexic but by her peer group" (Morris 1985, 90). By associating a woman's status, character, and, ultimately, her worth, with low weight, the emaciated physique is set as an ideal and prompts unhealthy expectations for women (Morris 1985).

Some empirical studies look through a feminist lens at the origins of eating disorders. Snyder and Hasbrouk (1996) found that disordered eating habits were more widespread among college-aged women who identified with traditional sexist roles. Conversely, women who were connected to feminist tenets were less likely to develop eating disorders and body image issues. This finding supports the feminist assertion that sexist gender roles in patriarchal society contribute to many women's low self-esteem, distorted body issues, and disordered eating.

The media and fashion industry dictate the cultural ideal of the thin body with images of emaciated models displayed across the spectrum of media avenues. The fitness and diet industries generate millions of dollars annually by marketing the concept of the ideal body to women. There has been recent criticism of the media for portraying digitally enhanced images of unrealistically thin women as reasonable and achievable standards against which women should measure themselves (Grogan 2008). Critiques from feminists have suggested that a wide array of body types and sizes needs to be accepted.

Women in Western society are under great social pressure to be deemed "beautiful" by being thin (Grogan 2008). However, such beauty standards are often unrealistic for women to achieve (Tiggemann 2002). Furthermore, women's experiences of such pressure to attain the ideal body is correlated to dissatisfaction with their body and with eating disorders. It is, however, unclear why only some women who are exposed to these pressures and ideals develop eating disorders, while others do not. Given that women are particularly vulnerable to negative body image, comprehensive social change will be required to shift the relationship between a woman's inherent value and her physical appearance and weight (Paquette and Raine 2004).

According to objectification theory repetitive experiences of sexual objectification socialize women to treat themselves as objects to be seen and evaluated by outside critiques; in viewing their bodies as objects for others, they then adopt the objectification as valid (de Beauvoir 1949; Bartky, Diamond, and Quinby 1988). Self-objectification is cultivated in a culture where women experience persistent body surveillance. These chronic negative experiences lead to the sequelae of symptoms such as depression, low self-esteem, and disordered eating.

It is well documented that heterosexual women experience unhealthy body image and disordered eating due to high levels of social pressures to be thin. Moradi and colleagues' (2005) data posits that more than half of college women skip meals (59%); approximately one third restricted caloric consumption (37%), eliminated carbohydrates and fats (27% and 30%); and about one fourth fasted for more than 24 hours at a time (26%) in order to manipulate their body weight. There has been a paucity of research in examining the experience of non-heterosexual women in terms of body satisfaction and social pressures. However, some recent studies (Huxley 2010; Koff et al. 2010) have suggested that the pressure to be thin is ubiquitous, regardless of sexual orientation.

In one recent study, Koff and colleagues (2010) found that heterosexual and non-heterosexual women evidenced similar perceptions of their own bodies as well as that of the cultural ideal of the thin, feminine body. They also were found to have similar rates of body dissatisfaction, waist-to-hip ratio, breast size, and overall body fat. These results indicate that all women, regardless of sexual orientation and identity, are at risk of experiencing poor body image. While women are far more likely than men to develop eating disorders, due to the factors described above, men are not immune. Studies have found that gay and bisexual men in particular are prone to developing eating disorders as a result of the emphasis on physical attractiveness in gay male subcultures (Siever 1994).

In addition, athletes seem to be more susceptible to eating disorders than the general public (see Picard 1999). One study found that male athletes had higher rates of disordered eating than the general population, while female athletes experienced rates similar to those of general college populations (Stoutjesdyk and Jevne 1993). Stoutjesdyk and Jevne (1993) also found differences among different types of athletic groups, but only among females, with women in weight-restricted sports such as rowing, judo, diving, and gymnastics more likely to suffer eating disorders than other female athletes.

Picard (1999) found that, in general, athletes at higher levels of competition are more susceptible to eating disorders than lower-level athletes, and athletes in "lean sports" such as distance running were more prone to eating disorders than those in non-lean sports such as basketball and hockey. Differences between racial and ethnic groups have also been found, with Caucasian and Latina female high school athletes being at greater risk of developing eating disorders than their African American peers (Pernick et al. 2006).

Review of the literature on mass media, developmental psychology, and eating disorders suggests a profound need for additional etiological research based on an amalgamation of developmental social learning theory, social comparison theory, and vulnerability-stressor models of disordered eating (Grogan 2008). Further empirical testing needs to be done to explore possible ways to change the cultural ideal of the thin body and to minimize the stress related to binary gender role stereotypes.

SEE ALSO: Appearance Psychology; Athletics and Gender; Dieting; Gender Stereotypes; Images of Gender and Sexuality in Advertising; Psychology of Objectification; Self-Esteem; Sexual Objectification

REFERENCES

Bartky, S. L., Irene Diamond, and Lee Quinby, eds. 1988. *Feminism and Foucault: Reflections of Resistance*. Boston: Northeastern University Press.

Beauvoir, Simone de. (1949) 1997. *The Second Sex*. London: Vintage.

Grogan, Sarah. 2008. *Body Image: Understanding Body Dissatisfaction in Men, Women and Children*, 2nd ed. London: Routledge.

Huxley, Caroline J. 2010. "An Exploration of the Sociocultural Influences Affecting Lesbian and Bisexual Women's Body Image." Unpublished doctoral dissertation, University of the West of England, UK.

Koff, Elissa, Margery Lucas, Robyn Migliorini, and Samantha Grossmith. 2010. "Women and

Body Dissatisfaction: Does Sexual Orientation Make a Difference?" *Body Image*, 7(3): 255–258. DOI: http://dx.doi.org/10.1016/j.bodyim.2010.03.001.

Martz-Ludwig, Denise. 1995. *Evaluation of a Peer Leader Eating Disorders Prevention Program for College Sororities* (Order No. AAM9431472). Available from PsycINFO. (618740769; 1995-95003-066). Retrieved from http://search.proquest.com/docview/618740769?accountid=25260.

Moradi, Bonnie, Danielle Dirks, and Alicia V. Matteson. 2005. "Roles of Sexual Objectification Experiences and Internalization of Standards of Beauty in Eating Disorder Symptomatology: A Test and Extension of Objectification Theory." *Journal of Counseling Psychology*, 52(3): 420–428. DOI: http://dx.doi.org/10.1037/0022-0167.52.3.420.

Morris, Bonnie J. 1985. "The Phenomena of Anorexia Nervosa: A Feminist Perspective." *Feminist Issues*, 5(2): 89–99.

Paquette, Marie-Claude, and Kim Raine. 2004. "Sociocultural Context of Women's Body Image." *Social Science & Medicine*, 59: 1047–1058.

Pernick, Yael, Jeanne Nichols, Mitchell Rauh, Mark Kern, Ming Ji, Mandra Lawson, and Denise Wilfley. 2006. "Disordered Eating among a Multi-Racial/Ethnic Sample of Female High School Athletes." *Journal of Adolescent Health*, 38: 689–695.

Picard, Christy. 1999. "The Level of Competition as a Factor for the Development of Eating Disorders in Female Collegiate Athletes." *Journal of Youth and Adolescence*, 28(5): 583–594.

Siever, Michael D. 1994. "Sexual Orientation and Gender as Factors in Socioculturally Acquired Vulnerability to Body Dissatisfaction and Eating Disorders." *Journal of Consulting and Clinical Psychology*, 62: 252–260.

Snyder, Rita, and Lynn Hasbrouck. 1996. "Feminist Identity, Gender Traits, and Symptoms of Disturbed Eating among College Women." *Psychology of Women Quarterly*, 20(4): 593–598.

Stoutjesdyk, Dexa, and Ronna Jevne. 1993. "Eating Disorders among High Performance Athletes." *Journal of Youth and Adolescence*, 22(3): 271–282.

Tiggemann, Marika. 2002. "Media Influences of Body Image Development." In *Body Image: A Handbook of Theory, Research, and Clinical Practice*, edited by Thomas F. Cash and Thomas Pruzinsky, 91–98. New York: Guilford Press.

FURTHER READING

Pike, Kathleen M., Hans W. Hoek, and Patricia E. Dunne. 2014. "Cultural Trends and Eating Disorders." *Current Opinion in Psychiatry*, 27(6): 436–442.

Ecofeminism

SUSAN HAWTHORNE
James Cook University, Australia

Feminism has a wide-ranging remit and ecofeminism has broadened what many feminists thought of as feminism to include not only women's bodies, discrimination at work, and sexual violence but also the violence against the earth, peace, war, technology, international relations, as well as the spiritual dimension. The term was first used by Françoise d'Eaubonne (1974) in her book *Le féminisme ou la mort*.

Ecofeminism, from the beginning, recognized the connection between the treatment of women and of the earth. It was indeed the activism of women that gave us the most important early analyses of ecology – among them Rachel Carson's *Silent Spring* (Carson 1986/1962) and Judith Wright's *The Coral Battleground* (Wright 2014/1977). Anti-nuclear activist Helen Caldicott convinced the Australian government to sue France over atmospheric nuclear testing in 1971 and 1972. These battles continued with creative approaches to political protest: in 1980, women protesting at the Pentagon wove a web representing the interconnectedness of everything; at Greenham Common in 1983, women danced on the missile silos; 100 women arrested at the protest against Pine Gap in Central Australia all gave their names as Karen Silkwood; the Chipko women in India are remembered for protesting deforestation by hugging trees.

These actions have been accompanied by a burgeoning literature on militarism, environmental destruction, economics, globalization, colonization, and biodiversity as well as theoretical discussions on the nature of science, reductionism, the role of spirituality, the killing of the "goddess," women-centered knowledge, farming practices, seed saving, the relationship with land and water – just to name a few of the central themes of ecofeminism.

In *Feminism and Ecology* Mary Mellor (1997) acknowledges that while ecofeminism draws on both feminist and ecological philosophical traditions, it also challenges both strands. Indeed, Maria Mies and Vandana Shiva (1993) in *Ecofeminism* challenge the assumptions made by Marxists and scientists, thereby challenging major strands of male left and right ideologies. Furthermore, the connectedness between theory and practice reflects the radical feminist dictum that the personal is political. Ynestra King (1981) puts it this way:

> We are a woman-identified movement and we believe we have special work to do in these imperiled times. We see the devastation of the earth and her beings by the corporate warriors, and the threat of nuclear annihilation by the military warriors, as feminist concerns. It is the masculinist mentality which would deny us our right to our own bodies and our own sexuality, and which depends on multiple systems of dominance and state power to have its way.

These ideas are not new. Indigenous women and traditional farmers around the world have based their daily practice on such a philosophical stance. Australian Murri woman Lilla Watson said, "The future extends as far forward as the past, which means a 40,000 year plan" (Watson 1984). Such thinking goes well beyond the political conceptions of governments but is an idea that resonates for ecofeminists. Rokheya Hossain's 1905 science fiction novel *Sultana's Dream* concerns a country ruled by the Sultana which is organized around the principle of "horticulture" (Hossain 1988/1905). The term ecology was not yet invented but a social order arranged around ecological principles in a non-Western, mostly Muslim society, was.

The branches of ecofeminism spread around the world with activism by women from indigenous and traditional societies. Winona LaDuke documents the environmental destruction in the Attawapiskat First Nation in northern Ontario, Canada, where a process of "under-developing" is occurring. What she means is that formerly viable and sustainable communities are being mined, their social and environmental infrastructure destabilized with contaminated water and pollution, followed by stealing the wealth generated by the mines (LaDuke 2015, 221). The people of Kalimantan, Indonesia, suffer a similar fate. The forest peoples' impoverishment is an intentional part of government policy (Hawthorne 2002, 252–253).

In Germany (Gura 2015) and Bangladesh (Akhter 2015), seed savers are resisting governments and corporations by saving a wide variety of seeds that are generally not available. Seed savers have been prosecuted, while in Bangladesh Nayakrishi Andolon (New Agricultural Movement) small farmers have been saving seeds for many years, and Navdanya in India has pursued the same activities (Shiva 2015a). In Kenya, women farmers resisted the power of multinational corporations by growing beans (a crop important to women for nutritional and ritual reasons) between coffee trees (the cash crop planted by men). The intercropping practice improved soil fertility and reduced use of pesticides. Eventually, the women pulled out the cash crop coffee trees and burnt them. This resistance to export orientation allowed the women to re-establish locally controlled collective work practices. In the Pacific (and also in the Caribbean and other island nation tourist destinations) tourism, including ecotourism, has been criticized for destroying social cohesion and for making people landless in order to build hotels for tourists (Chailang Palacios, in dé Ishtar 1994, 85). In South America, the same process occurs, summarized nicely by Eduardo Galeano as the rich free trade purveyors who "turn everything they touch … into gold for themselves and rubbish for others" (Galeano 1973, 101).

Activists have also mounted legal resistance to destructive corporate behavior. Vandana Shiva and two co-respondents sued W. R. Grace in 2000 over the claim that the company held a patent on the neem plant. But such a course is not open to people whose knowledge is passed down orally, in contrast to the 2000-year-old written Sanskrit sources that Shiva was able to draw on. Marie-Monique Robin has investigated in a series of films and books the criminal activity of Monsanto. Scientists such as Mae-Wan Ho (1998, 2015), Floriane Koechlin (2015), and Maria Grazia Mammucini (2015) (in Shiva 2015b), among others, have pointed to the scientific flaws in so much of today's food production, while feminist economists such as Sabine O'Hara (1996), Marilyn Waring (1988), Maria Mies and Veronika Bennholdt-Thomsen (1999), and a host of others have challenged the underlying assumptions of neoclassical profit-driven economics.

Susan Griffin's *Woman and Nature* (Griffin 1978) and Mary Daly's *Gyn/Ecology* (Daly 1978) had a huge impact on ideas around ecofeminism. Both writers put radical feminist and ecological ideas at their center. Both played with language and with form and challenged the ways in which theoretical ideas can be presented. For Daly, the playfulness came through her use of neologisms and also creating new meanings for old words; Griffin used two contrasting voices: one was poetic and spare whereas the other cited the evidence factually.

Radical feminism has had a substantial influence on ecofeminist thinking, and not only the above writers but also others in books such as *Rape of the Wild* (Collard and Contrucci 1983) and *The Age of Sex Crime* (Caputi 1987), and *Wild Politics* (Hawthorne 2002) draw connections between violence against women and violence against the earth in a multiplicity of ways. Crossing cultural boundaries, books such as Diane Bell's hugely influential *Daughters of the Dreaming* (Bell 2002/1983) and Zohl dé Ishtar's *Holding Yawulyu* (dé Ishtar 2005) have enlarged the understanding of other knowledge systems, other ways of knowing about the world. A philosophy that is critical of the fundamental knowledge claims of patriarchy also needs alternative world views, that might support new approaches to living in the world. While horticulture enabled Rokheya Hossain (1988/1905) to imagine another world, radical feminists have creatively developed new systems of belief or built upon older systems. In a similar vein, the idea of *The Subsistence Perspective* as outlined by Maria Mies and Veronika Bennholdt-Thomsen (1999) builds on the idea of subsistence – low-consumption, highly productive ways of living – as an ecological and feminist practice. They also argue that it challenges the market-centric view of productivity. Marilyn Waring's analysis of the UN System of National Accounts in her book *Counting for Nothing* (Waring 1988) follows a similar thread, challenging the idea that domestic labor is unproductive or likewise that a living forest (as opposed to a clear-felled forest) has no value. These challenges to economics and militaristic thinking are important philosophical milestones for ecofeminism.

In *The Death of Nature*, Carolyn Merchant (1980) examines the way in which a scientific world view was generated during the enlightenment period. She argues that an increasing separation between nature and civilized "man" has led to objectification of nature as a "thing" to be used. She also argues that women too were objectified in comparable ways. This utilitarian view of the world enables technology, including destructive and out-of-control technologies. This is the grounding of critiques such as those in the anthology *Test Tube Women* (Arditti et al. 1984) around the new reproductive technologies or Rosalie Bertell's work on radioactivity (Bertell 1985) and the consequences of militarism (Bertell 2000). Maud Barlow's unpacking of the increasingly privatized ownership of water around the world continues the critique of market driven environmental destruction (Barlow 2007). The peak of this critique is that of the corporate seed giant, Monsanto, as seen in Marie-Monique Robin's book and film, *The World According to Monsanto* (Robin 2010). Robin accuses the corporation not just of uncontrolled pollution but also of willful criminality, documenting the connection between the military defoliant Agent Orange and the so-called "cure for world hunger," Genetically Modified Organisms.

Val Plumwood's *Feminism and the Mastery of Nature* (Plumwood 1993) takes the critique of knowledge further back to Plato, to his view of man as a master which has implications for women, enslaved peoples, domesticated animals, and plants which are made to serve humanity. She argues that rather than being the origins of civilization, it marks the point at which uncivil behavior toward women and nature became the norm. Vandana Shiva, in her classic book *Staying Alive* (Shiva 1989), picks up on Merchant's critique of science and takes it further, accusing scientists (Shiva trained as a physicist) of using violent reductionist thinking in an organic world. She argues that the natural and the supernatural should not be divided. Drawing on her Hindu tradition, she points out that Prakriti, associated with women, is both "activity and diversity" (Shiva 1989, 39); it is the source, the seed, the matrix. Shiva manages to breach the Western divide between science and spirit.

The anthology *Reweaving the World* (Diamond and Orenstein 1990) is a fine example of crossing this divide with contributions from well-known goddess scholars such as Starhawk (2003) and Charlene Spretnak (1991), Native American scholar Paula Gunn Allen (1986), and animal activist Mart Kheel (2007), as well as Shiva, Merchant, and King mentioned above. The links between the two, although not obvious to an outsider, become so when examining the history of patriarchy, the demise of women-centered religions, the persecution of witches, and the increasing separation of humanity from nature. Here too, ideas developed by groups such as the Chipko Women in their protests against the cutting of forests in India and the spiritual come together. It is what Vandana Shiva refers to as "the feminine principle." She also refers to the concept of *terra mater*, contrasting this with the colonizing concept of *terra nullius* used against indigenous peoples in Australia and Sub-Saharan Africa. A similar idea emerges from the worldview of the Ngarrindjeri people of South Australia, where the root forms of the words "land," *ruwi*, and "body," *ruwar*, are related (Bell 2014/1998, 622).

The analysis of colonization – of women and of the colonized peoples of the world – is something that Robin Morgan noticed in 1977 when she wrote (Morgan 1977, 161):

Women are a colonized people. Our history, values and (cross-cultural) culture have been taken from us – a gynocidal attempt to manifest most arrestingly in the patriarchal seizure of our basic and precious "land": our bodies.

Maria Mies's *Patriarchy and Accumulation on a World Scale* (Mies 1999/1986) might seem a long way from this spiritual take on ecofeminism, as it is a critique of Marxist theory and the way that women were eliminated from that analysis. She argues that abandoning violence is the first step in abandoning exploitation and she ties the exploitation of the earth to the exploitation of the poor including women and poverty-stricken workers (and there is a large overlap in these two groups). She argues for a reduction in export economies and an increase in self-sufficiency. Mies's analysis indicates that the interweaving forces of patriarchy and capitalism have the most impact on women and that structural change is required if women are to gain some semblance of equality. In this way, Mies directly connects the colonization of women and the earth. In turn, she is critical of the way in which nature is turned into an enemy and that "development" is something that poor countries need to "catch up" on. All this leads Mies in the end to turn to those who have maintained the traditions: the farmers of Bangladesh and Germany, including rituals around keeping the earth fruitful. Sinith Sittirak (1998) movingly shows the way in which development affects the real lives of people. Using her mother as an example, a woman who has never applied for a job but who is resourceful and skilled in many areas, shows her self-sufficiency within the Thai economy.

Ecological sufficiency is the focus of Ariel Salleh's anthology *Eco-sufficiency and Global Justice* (Salleh 2009). Contributors from every continent cover issues such as what counts as work, economics, sovereignty, complexity and relationship, and the material universes of fishing, nuclear testing, and water policies; there are particular essays on how the Kyoto Protocol is condemning women and children to destitution in Costa Rica. Ana Isla sums up the situation (Isla 2009, 213):

Ironically, Costa Rica as a country stands in much the same situation as its prostitutes – kept in financial debt by pimps, in this case, the World Bank and IMF, mining firms and environmental NGOs. But neither the nation nor its women can earn enough to pay off debts and regain autonomy.

Prostitution, debt, war, and farming make strange bedfellows, but the links are clear. Vandana Shiva, in her latest book *Seed Sovereignty, Food Security* (2015a), makes the point in her introduction that the industrial agricultural paradigm is no longer focused on life and food because its roots lie in war and militarism: explosives are re-purposed as fertilizers and chemicals used in war are now used to go to war against insects and plants. Killing, she says, has become more important than growing food (Shiva 2015a, 1–2).

Feminists from very different backgrounds, theoretical positions, and commitments for political change can be found united on ecofeminist issues. The reason for this is to be found in massive misuses of power by the military industrial complex, which includes government-sponsored war-mongering as well as corporate excesses resulting in pollution, environmental damage, and illness. Ecofeminism and the anti-globalization movement brought together many who were irate about these misuses. It drew in traditionally left-wing socialist Marxist feminists alongside those who were anti-war, against the nuclear industry, and peace activists of all hues; it brought in ecological economists alongside those who have spent years researching and uncovering pre-patriarchal civilizations and their accompanying goddesses; it brought in feminists from very different cultural backgrounds around the world because they recognized a possible precolonial knowledge system at its center; it brought in radical feminists with their holistic and complexity-based analysis of patriarchal violence and the various ways in which this is manifested; it brought in some liberal feminists and post-modern feminists because they believe in the need for change and the decisions we make affecting that change. This combination of feminist insight has made ecofeminism rich and complex.

SEE ALSO: Deep Ecology; Feminism, Multiracial; Feminisms, Marxist and Socialist; Indigenous Knowledges and Gender; Patriarchy; Pacifism, Peace Activism, and Gender

REFERENCES

Akhter, Farida. 2015. "Seed Freedom and Seed Sovereignty: Bangladesh Today." In *Seed Sovereignty, Food Security: Women in the Vanguard*, edited by Vandana Shiva, 235–253. New Delhi: Women Unlimited; Melbourne: Spinifex Press.

Allen, Paula Gunn. 1986. *The Sacred Hoop: Recovering the Feminine in American Indian Traditions*. Boston, MA: Beacon Press.

Arditti, Rita, Renate Duelli Klein, and Shelley Minden. 1984. *Test-tube Women: What Future for Motherhood?* London: Pandora.

Barlow, Maud. 2007. *Blue Covenant: The Global Water Crisis and the Fight for the Right to Water*. Toronto: McClelland & Stewart.

Bell, Diane. 2002. *Daughters of the Dreaming*. Melbourne: Spinifex Press. First published Sydney: Allen and Unwin, 1983.

Bell, Diane. 2014. *Ngarrindjeri Wurruwarrin: The World That Is, Was, and Will Be*. Melbourne: Spinifex Press. Originally published 1998.

Bertell, Rosalie. 1985. *No Immediate Danger: Prognosis for a Radioactive Earth*. London: The Women's Press.

Bertell, Rosalie. 2000. *Planet Earth: The Latest Weapon of War: A Critical Study into the Military and the Environment*. London: The Women's Press.

Caputi, Jane. 1987. *The Age of Sex Crime*. Bowling Green, OH: Bowling Green University Popular Press.

Carson, Rachel. 1986. *Silent Spring*. Harmondsworth: Penguin. Originally published 1962.

Collard, Andrée, and Joyce Contrucci. 1988. *Rape of the Wild*. Bloomington: Indiana University Press.

Daly, Mary. 1978. *Gyn/Ecology: The Metaethics of Radical Feminism*. Boston, MA: Beacon Press.

d'Eaubonne, Françoise. 1974. *Le féminisme ou la mort*. Paris: P. Horay.

Diamond, Irene, and Gloria Orenstein. 1990. *Reweaving the World: The Emergence of Ecofeminism*. San Francisco: Sierra Club Books.

Galeano, Eduardo. 1973. *Open Veins of Latin America: Five Centuries of the Pillage of a Continent*. New York: Monthly Review Press.

Griffin, Susan. 1978. *Woman and Nature: The Roaring Inside Her*. New York: Harper and Row.

Gura, Susanne. 2015. "Seed Emergency: Germany." In *Seed Sovereignty, Food Security: Women in the Vanguard*, edited by Vandana Shiva, 127–135. New Delhi: Women Unlimited; Melbourne: Spinifex Press.

Hawthorne, Susan. 2002. *Wild Politics: Feminism, Globalisation and Bio/diversity*. Melbourne: Spinifex Press.

Ho, Mae-Wan. 1998. *Genetic Engineering – Dream or Nightmare? The Brave New World of Bad Science and Big Business*. Bath: Gateway Books.

Ho, Mae-Wan. 2015. "The New Genetics and Dangers of GMOs." In *Seed Sovereignty, Food Security: Women in the Vanguard*, edited by Vandana Shiva, 113–124. New Delhi: Women Unlimited; Melbourne: Spinifex Press.

Hossain, Rokheya Sakhawat. 1988. *Sultana's Dream*. New York: The Feminist Press. Originally published Madras: The Indian Ladies Magazine, 1905.

Ishtar, Zohl dé. 1994. *Daughters of the Pacific*. Melbourne: Spinifex Press.

Ishtar, Zohl dé. 2005. *Holding Yawulyu: White Culture and Black Women's Law*. Melbourne: Spinifex Press.

Isla, Ana. 2009. "Who Pays for the Kyoto Protocol?" In *Eco-sufficiency and Global Justice: Women Write Political Economy*, edited by Ariel Salleh. 199–217. London: Pluto Press; Melbourne: Spinifex Press.

Kheel, Marti. 2007. *Nature Ethics: An Ecofeminist Perspective*. New York: Rowman and Littlefield.

King, Ynestra. 1981. "The Eco-feminist Imperative." In *Reclaim the Earth: Women Speak Out for Life on Earth*, edited by Leonie Caldicott and Leland Stephanie, 9–14. London: The Women's Press.

Koechlin, Floriane. 2015. "If People Are Asked, They Say No to GMOs." In *Seed Sovereignty,*

Food Security: Women in the Vanguard, edited by Vandana Shiva, 172–174. New Delhi: Women Unlimited; Melbourne: Spinifex Press.

LaDuke, Winona. 2015. "In Praise of the Leadership of Indigenous Women." In *Seed Sovereignty, Food Security: Women in the Vanguard*, edited by Vandana Shiva, 211–229. New Delhi: Women Unlimited; Melbourne: Spinifex Press.

Mammucini, Maria Grazia. 2015. "The Italian Context." In *Seed Sovereignty, Food Security: Women in the Vanguard*, edited by Vandana Shiva, 175–182. New Delhi: Women Unlimited; Melbourne: Spinifex Press.

Merchant, Carolyn. 1980. *The Death of Nature: Women, Nature and the Scientific Revolution*. San Francisco: Harper and Row.

Mellor, Mary. 1997. *Feminism and Ecology*. New York: New York University Press.

Mies, Maria. 1999. *Patriarchy and Accumulation on a World Scale: Women in the International Division of Labour*. London: Zed Books; Melbourne: Spinifex Press. Originally published 1986.

Mies, Maria, and Veronika Bennholdt-Thomsen. 1999. *The Subsistence Perspective: Beyond the Globalised Economy*. London: Zed Books; Melbourne: Spinifex Press.

Mies, Maria, and Vandana Shiva. 1993. *Ecofeminism*, 251–263. New Delhi: Kali for Women; London: Zed Books; Melbourne: Spinifex Press.

Morgan, Robin. 1977. *Going Too Far: The Personal Chronicle of a Feminist*. New York: Random House.

O'Hara, Sabine U. 1996. "Discursive Ethics in Ecosystems Valuation and Environmental Policy." *Ecological Economics Doublecheck*, 16(2): 95–107.

Plumwood, Val. 1993. *Feminism and the Mastery of Nature*. London: Routledge.

Robin, Marie-Monique. 2010. *The World According to Monsanto*. New York: The New Press; Melbourne: Spinifex Press; New Delhi: Tulika Books.

Salleh, Ariel. 2009. *Eco-sufficiency and Global Justice: Women Write Political Ecology*. London: Pluto Press; Melbourne: Spinifex Press.

Shiva, Vandana. 1989. *Staying Alive: Women, Ecology and Development*. New Delhi: Kali for Women; London: Zed Books.

Shiva, Vandana, ed. 2015a. *Seed Sovereignty, Food Security: Women in the Vanguard*. New Delhi: Women Unlimited; Melbourne: Spinifex Press.

Shiva, Vandana. 2015b "Sowing Seeds of Freedom." In *Seed Sovereignty, Food Security: Women in the Vanguard*, edited by Vandana Shiva, 265–273. New Delhi: Women Unlimited; Melbourne: Spinifex Press.

Sittirak, Sinith. 1998. *The Daughters of Development: Women in a Changing Environment*. London: Zed Books; Melbourne: Spinifex Press.

Spretnak, Charlene. 1991. *States of Grace: The Recovery of Meaning in the Postmodern Age*. San Francisco: HarperSanFrancisco.

Starhawk. 2003. *Webs of Power: Notes from the Global Uprising*. Gabriola Island, BC: New Catalyst Books.

Waring, Marilyn. 1988. *Counting for Nothing: What Men Value and What Women Are Worth*. Sydney: Allen and Unwin.

Watson, Lilla. 1984. "Aboriginal Women and Feminism." Keynote Speech presented at the Fourth Women and Labour Conference, Brisbane, July 1984.

Wright, Judith. 2014. *The Coral Battleground*. Melbourne: Spinifex Press. Originally published 1977.

FURTHER READING

Atkinson, Judy. 2002. *Trauma Trails, Recreating Songlines: The Transgenerational Effects of Trauma in Indigenous Australia*. Melbourne: Spinifex Press.

Caldicott, Helen. 2014. *Crisis Without End: The Medical and Ecological Consequences of the Fukushima Nuclear Catastrophe*. New York: The New Press.

Cuomo, Christine J. 1994. "Ecofeminism, Deep Ecology, and Human Population." In *Ecological Feminism*, edited by Karen J. Warren, 88–105. London: Routledge.

Langton, Marcia. 1998. *Burning Questions: Emerging Environmental Issues for Indigenous Peoples in Northern Australia*. Darwin: Centre for Indigenous and Cultural Resource Management, Northern Territory University.

Meadows, Donella H. 2008. *Thinking in Systems*. White River Junction: Chelsea Green Publishing.

Norberg-Hodge, Helena. 1991. *Ancient Futures: Learning from Ladakh*. San Francisco: Sierra Club Books.

Salleh, Ariel. 1997. *Ecofeminism as Politics: Nature, Marx and the Postmodern*. London: Zed Books.

Shiva, Vandana. 1993. *Monocultures of the Mind: Perspectives on Biodiversity and Biotechnology.* Penang: Third World Network.
Tuhiwai Smith, Linda. 1999. *Decolonizing Methodologies: Research and Indigenous Peoples.* Otago: Otago University Press; London: Zed Books.
Warren, Karen J., ed. 1994. *Ecological Feminism.* London: Routledge.

Economic Determinism

ULRIKA HOLGERSSON
University of Lund, Sweden

Economic determinism is a theoretical concept primarily associated with Karl Marx (1818–1883). Although the term economic determinism as such was not a part of original Marxist vocabulary, it has often been used when interpreting the intellectual world of Marx. The point of departure is thus his elaboration of a materialist conception of history. In a response to G. W. F. Hegel's (1770–1831) notion of history as governed by the fulfillment of ideas, Marx intended to put Hegel "on his feet." That is, instead of giving prominence to the world of ideas (symbolized by the head) as the constant source of world change, he pointed to the material aspects of human existence (the feet).

Fundamental to Marx's materialist conception of history is the notion of economic production transforming through history, following a certain set of phases, each characterizing different systems of society. During the course of history the productive forces (i.e., material, tools, labor) are refined due to technical development. As people find new ways of producing, social structures or relations of production (i.e., relations of ownership, power, and control of societal means) alter accordingly. Together the productive forces and relations of production form a historical mode of production, designating society at a specific point in time. Thus, history starts at a stage of primitive communism, succeeded by antique slave society, feudalism, capitalism, socialism, and – again – communism. In this chain, every stage comprises different structures of ruling and exploited classes, except for communism, the wholly equal society (Marx and Engels 1962/1848).

In this connection Marx uses the metaphor of base–superstructure, according to which, in every society, politics, religion, and spiritual life (the superstructure) are determined by the mode of production of material life (the base) (Marx 1962/1859). Hence, the class prevailing in the base establishes the overall world of ideas, as an ideological expression of its dominion (Marx 1970/1845).

Since the death of Marx the base–superstructure model has been subject to a wide and intense debate centered on the issue of economic determinism. Already in the 1890s the German social democrats Eduard Bernstein (1850–1932) and Karl Kautsky (1854–1938), inspired by Engels, established what they called orthodox Marxism. This theoretical system was characterized by a more scientific approach, stressing the unstoppable economic laws of historical development. Yet orthodox Marxism soon faced severe criticism. For instance, Italian politician Antonio Gramsci (1891–1937) emphasized the relative independence of the cultural sphere in relation to economy. Furthermore, the Praxis School, originating in Yugoslavia in the 1960s as an opponent of the economic determinism of communism, drew attention to the writings of the "young Marx." In parallel, the question of human ability to act as an independent subject was scrutinized in the West by, on the one side, cultural Marxists such as British historian E. P. Thompson (1924–1993) and, on the other, by advocates for a structural Marxism, like French philosopher Louis Althusser (1918–1990).

In an attempt to organize the commentators on economic determinism, we can reflect on their views of the relation between base and superstructure as positions on a sliding scale. At one end of the scale are proponents of an understanding of the relation between economy and culture as rather automatic, mechanical, and unilateral. At the other end, culture is understood as decidedly independent. In between, we find perspectives that imply some kind of interplay. Still, within the paradigm of Marxism, we cannot hold the opinion that culture determines economy, rather than the other way around.

However, political theorists Ernesto Laclau and Chantal Mouffe transgressed this border as they coined the concept of post-Marxism (Laclau and Mouffe 1985). Working their way through the history of Marxist philosophy they reached a point beyond Marxism, where the division of culture/language and the material no longer existed. This implies that no interests, class interests included, can be objectively derived from economy. Nor must a specific class interest determine a corresponding class identity. Rather, classes are discursive constructions constantly shaped in political struggle. Finally, there can be no last stage of history, as a communist society, where political conflict has come to an end.

Another important strand of criticism of economic determinism can be derived from feminism. Its starting point was the fact that the Marxist focus on production and economy ended in the exclusion of women. According to Marxism, only work conducted in the public sphere counted as productive, which in turn qualified a person as member of a class. Thus the women of the private sphere were members of a certain class only by association with their husbands or their male kin. Equally important was the presumption found with Engels (1940/1884) that the abolition of economic injustice between classes would automatically lead to gender equality. While still firmly situated within the paradigm, Marxist feminists of the 1970s argued that female labor should be defined as true labor, i.e., a crucial part of economic production. More far-reaching socialist feminists like Heidi Hartmann held that capitalism and patriarchy formed a dual system, closely connected, mutually dependent, none more important than the other, and thus equally essential to fight. Furthermore, Gayle Rubin called attention to the sexual reproduction of human beings, beside the production of goods, as determining historical development.

SEE ALSO: Capitalist Patriarchy; Division of Labor, Domestic; Feminism, Materialist; Feminisms, Marxist and Socialist; Feminist Economics; Patriarchy

REFERENCES

Engels, Friedrich. 1940. *The Origin of the Family, Private Property and the State*. London: Lawrence & Wishart. First published 1884.

Laclau, Ernesto, and Chantal Mouffe. 1985. *Hegemony and Socialist Strategy*. London: Verso.

Marx, Karl. 1962. Preface to A Contribution to the Critique of Political Economy. In Karl Marx and Friedrich Engels, *Selected Works*, vol. 1. Moscow: Foreign Languages Publishing House. First published 1859.

Marx, Karl. 1970. *The German Ideology*. London: Lawrence & Wishart. First published 1845.

Marx, Karl, and Friedrich Engels. 1962. *Manifesto of the Communist Party*. In Karl Marx and Friedrich Engels, *Selected Works*, vol. 1. Moscow: Foreign Languages Publishing House. First published 1848.

FURTHER READING

Dworkin, Dennis. 2007. *Class Struggles*. Harlow: Pearson Longman.

Holgersson, Ulrika. 2011. *Klass. Feministiska och kulturanalytiska perspektiv [Class: Feminist and Cultural Analytical Perspectives]*. Lund: Studentlitteratur.

McLellan, David. 2006. *Karl Marx: A Biography*, 4th ed. Basingstoke: Palgrave Macmillan.

Economic Globalization and Gender

VALENTINE M. MOGHADAM
Northeastern University, USA

Globalization is a multidimensional process of economic, political, and cultural change; its emergence in the 1980s and spread in the 1990s coincided with the weakening and eventual collapse of the communist bloc, the end of the Cold War, and the global expansion of capitalism. David Harvey defines contemporary economic globalization as characterized by a neoliberal model of capitalism based on the premise "that human well-being can best be advanced by liberating individual entrepreneurial freedoms and skills within an institutional framework characterized by strong private property rights, free markets, and free trade" (2005). Key ingredients of this model are private sector development, entrepreneurship, labor market "flexibility," and a reduction of the public sector wage bill. The role of the state is to facilitate conditions for capital accumulation, though it also may provide a "social safety net" for vulnerable social groups.

Neoliberal economic globalization and its political counterpart, liberal democracy, have been touted by its champions as the political–economic model best suited to promote growth, development, and citizen rights. Implementation of this model has had broad social ramifications, much of it messy and disruptive, although it has benefited some social strata in some countries. Studies by feminist social scientists as well as activists within transnational feminist networks have long been critical of economic globalization and its precursor, the structural adjustment policy package. Paradoxically, the era of economic globalization has coincided with the worldwide diffusion of norms of women's rights, wherein traditional gender relations have been contested, challenged, or renegotiated. Indeed, it is an irony of history that the women's human rights discourse and global women's rights agenda emerged parallel to the global spread of neoliberalism.

Research on women, gender, and economic globalization became prominent in the 1990s but originates in feminist studies of structural adjustments and the new international division of labor, starting in the early 1980s. A pioneering study by Diane Elson and Ruth Pearson (1981) framed the subject in terms of traditional gender ideology that facilitated the exploitation of female labor in the context of export-led manufacturing. Other studies on the maquiladoras along the US–Mexico border similarly examined the feminization of export manufacturing and the oppressive conditions under which women workers labored. Economist Guy Standing of the International Labor Organization (ILO) used cross-national data to show the correlation between increases in female economic activity and the growing "flexibilization" of labor markets and declines in male job opportunities (Standing 1989, 1999).

In a major contribution in 2003, Spike Peterson posited that the global political economy revolved around the triad of "productive, reproductive, and virtual economies." Integrating Marxist, feminist, world-systems, and postcolonialist analyses, she offered an alternative way "to see informal activities, flexibilization, global production, migration flows, capital movements, and virtual activities as inextricable and interacting dimensions of neoliberal globalization." Her feminist re-reading of neoliberal economic globalization also offered a systematic identification of the gendered ideologies, identities, and institutions that comprise each of the three interrelated economies.

Her book presaged the later emphasis on "financialization" – or growth and importance of the financial sector – within economic globalization (see also Peterson and Runyan 2009).

Another line of inquiry has emphasized the masculinities and femininities inscribed in globalization processes, institutions, and relations. For Gibson-Graham (1996), globalization could be seen as a "rape script" and a masculine project, and R. W. Connell referred to neoliberalism's "transnational business masculinity." Marchand and Runyan noted that "ministries that focus on domestic health, education, and social welfare are becoming increasingly disadvantaged or 'feminized' in relation to ministries of finance and economic affairs that are directly related to the global economy, and thus invested with masculine authority" (Marchand 2000; Marchand and Runyan 2000).

Because of the uneven nature of globalization's effects across the economic zones of the world-system and across social classes within nation-states, and also because of the effects of financialization on income inequality, mainstream economists and international organizations are divided as to the costs and benefits of globalization. Critics and champions will emphasize different aspects and consequences, and offer solutions ranging from "a fair globalization" (the ILO) to more free trade and deeper integration into global markets (the World Bank, the International Monetary Fund, and the World Trade Organization). Mainstream studies seek to show the positive or negative effects of trade and foreign direct investment on gender equality, or they present globalization as creating market opportunities for employment in less developed countries or as contributing to declines in gender inequality. For example, Chen et al. (2013) examine gender wage discrimination among exporting and non-exporting private enterprises and conclude that globalization encourages female employment and reduces gender discrimination; Dorius and Firebaugh (2010) find that gender inequality has been declining except in countries with rapid population growth; and Potrafke and Ursprung (2014) conclude that economic and social globalization exert a decidedly positive influence on the social institutions that reduce female subjugation and promote gender equality.

On the Left, detractors emphasize the following effects of economic globalization: social and income inequalities, new forms of poverty, and wealth concentrations; and the inordinate power wielded by the pro-market international financial institutions at the expense of both national sovereignty and the influence of non-governmental organizations. Among feminist scholars, there appears to be consensus that globalization has had varied meanings and consequences for women's human rights and gender equality, though neoliberal economic globalization is seen as having multiple negative consequences, especially on poor and working-class women.

For example, Carolyn Tuttle's study of the persistence of such consequences examines the effects of free trade on Mexican women's well-being (2012). Despite the promises of a thriving economy along the US–Mexico border made by the architects of the North America Free Trade Agreement (NAFTA), poverty remains widespread, unemployment high, and infrastructure poor. Working conditions remain poor, pregnant women workers may be fired, and unionization is blocked. While some of the women interviewed told Tuttle that a benefit of such employment was the camaraderie they shared with other women workers, the author found no evidence of overall empowerment. The study demonstrates that NAFTA failed to deliver on its promise to raise the living standards of *maquila* workers, most of whom are women, and helps to explain why illegal migration to the United States continues. Valeria Sodano (2011) argues that because women represent the poorest swathe of the world's population, they suffer the most from the growing wealth inequality and the concentration of power produced by economic globalization. Moreover, because of the traditional sexual division of labor and because of their low status in society, women are the most harshly exploited subjects in the system. Sodano's general conclusion is that the main means of resource allocation are not competitive markets, as often suggested in mainstream economics, but are instead power relations that ultimately stem from the patriarchal culture of violence and domination.

Although studies continue to focus on the adverse effects of economic globalization on women's well-being, scholars also study the ways that women navigate globalization's downside to provide for or empower themselves. As such, searching for women's agency is a key objective of many feminist studies of globalization. Some studies, for example, examine women's self-empowerment through various types of survival strategies in the informal sector, forms of materiality and mobilities such as cross-border trading or migration, and innovative ways of taking advantage of foreign direct investment across the various nodes of commodity chains. Everett and Charlton investigate women's struggles within and against globalization and development through case studies of sex trafficking, water, work, and health, exploring and assessing the individual and collective strategies women have used to improve their lives under globalization.

A burgeoning literature places the spotlight on female labor migration. In their paper on the connections between gender and international migration, Beneria, Deere, and Kabeer (2012) show how globalization, national economic development, and governance have contributed to the increasing commodification of care work on a global scale, to the feminization of migration, and to debates on citizenship and migrant workers' rights. This and many similar studies on female labor migration (see, for example, UN 2004) show the significance of remittances to economic development and to the value placed on migration and remittances in the globalization and development policy literatures. Other studies examine women's entrepreneurship and small business development; microlending as an instrument of poverty reduction and women's economic empowerment; reasons for the continued low labor force participation rates of women in the Middle East; and the presence or absence of women in the corporate sphere. The recent scholarship points to the variability in gendered labor regimes at the nexus of the global and the local nexus while not losing sight of the persistence of exploitation. The Rana Factory collapse in Bangladesh in 2013, when over 1,200 textile workers producing clothing for the world market perished, confirmed such exploitative conditions.

One may conclude that the diverse way in which women's labor and gender relations are inscribed along global commodity chains reflects and reinforces the social, income, and gender inequalities that are inherent across the capitalist world economy and within societies. Thus, while globalization has benefited women with certain skills, education, knowledge, mobility, and family backgrounds – which we might abbreviate to those with the requisite human and cultural capital – the vast majority of the world's women remain mired in poverty or in low-wage and insecure jobs. In the United States, the pioneer of neoliberal globalization, "social stratification" has worsened in recent decades; families lost jobs, medical insurance, and houses following the Great Recession; and women lag behind men in employment recovery. Rachel Dwyer's sociological study shows that in the United States, the demand for low-skilled jobs at the top of the income hierarchy and the supply of care workers at the bottom of the social hierarchy "contributed significantly and increasingly to job polarization from 1983 to 2007" (Dwyer 2013).

COLLECTIVE ACTION

As noted, economic globalization has generated strong critiques of the growing income inequalities, deteriorating public services, and rising costs of private services that accompanied neoliberalism. With the Great Recession that followed the US mortgage crisis of 2007, mass social protests erupted for civil, political, and economic rights. The Arab Spring of 2011 was one dramatic manifestation, resulting from the contradictions of the global economy, the possibilities for mobilization and cyberactivism in world society, and demands for inclusion, social justice, and dignity, including women's equality. Anti-austerity protests in Europe similarly put the spotlight on the devastating ramifications of neoliberal economic globalization and especially rampant financialization, with feminists pointing to its hyper-masculine features of reckless speculative activities, aggressive risk-taking, and excessively competitive behavior.

Since the mid-1980s, transnational feminist networks (TFNs) have drawn attention to the adverse consequences of a profit-driven model of global capitalism that "capitalizes" on women's subordination in various societies to drive wages down while hiring more women for world market production. Moghadam's (2005) analysis shows how the downside of economic globalization, coupled with the opportunities afforded by the global diffusion of the UN-promoted women's rights agenda and by the new information technologies, had generated new forms of transnational feminist activism. TFNs have focused on the realization of women's human rights; similarly, Moghadam, Franzway, and Fonow argue that economic globalization requires a focus on women's social and economic rights. Under economic globalization, "rights" and "profits" are often counter-posed to each other; non-state commercial actors do not align their conduct with respect for women's human rights; and not all governments are interested in ensuring labor rights or women's human rights when seeking private domestic or international investments. There is thus a role for feminist trade unionists in bridging the divide between the feminist and labor movements for a powerful coalition that could bring more effective pressure to bear on states and corporations for a more people-oriented globalization that is also women-friendly.

SEE ALSO: Feminism, Materialist; Feminisms, Marxist and Socialist; Feminist Economics; Feminization of Labor; Feminization of Poverty; Free Trade Zones; Gender and Development; Global Restructuring

REFERENCES

Beneria, Lourdes, Carmen Diana Deere, and Naila Kabeer. 2012. "Gender and International Migration: Globalization, Development, and Governance." *Feminist Economics*, 18(2): 1–33.

Chen, Zhihong, Ying Ge, Huiwen Lai, and Chi Wan. 2013. "Globalization and Gender Wage Inequality in China." *World Development*, 44: 256–266.

Dorius, Shawn, and Glenn Firebaugh. 2010. "Trends in Global Gender Inequality." *Social Forces*, 88(5): 1941–1968.

Dwyer, Rachel E. 2013. "The Care Economy? Gender, Economic Restructuring, and Job Polarization in the US Labor Market." *American Sociological Review*, 78(3): 390–416.

Elson, Diane, and Ruth Pearson. 1981. "Nimble Fingers Make Cheap Workers: An Analysis of

Women's Employment in Third World Export Manufacturing." *Feminist Review*, 7: 87–107.

Gibson-Graham, J. K. 1996. *The End of Capitalism (As We Knew It): A Feminist Critique of Political Economy*. Oxford: Blackwell.

Harvey, David. 2005. *A Brief History of Neoliberalism*. New York: Oxford University Press.

Marchand, Marianne. 2000. "Reconceptualizing 'Gender and Development' in an Era of 'Globalization.'" In *Poverty in World Politics: Whose Global Era?*, edited by Sarah Owen Vandersluis and Paris Yeros. Basingstoke: Macmillan.

Marchand, Marianne, and Anne Sisson Runyan, eds. 2000. *Gender and Global Restructuring: Sightings, Sites and Resistances*. London: Routledge.

Moghadam, Valentine M. 2005. *Globalizing Women: Transnational Feminist Networks*. Baltimore: Johns Hopkins University Press.

Peterson, V. Spike. 2003. *A Critical Rewriting of Global Political Economy: Integrating Productive, Reproductive, and Virtual Economies*. New York: Routledge.

Peterson, V. Spike, and Anne Sisson Runyan. 2009. *Global Gender Issues in the New Millennium*. Boulder: Westview Press.

Potrafke, Niklas, and Heinrich Ursprung. 2014. "Globalization and Gender Equality in the Course of Development." *European Journal of Political Economy*, 28(4): 399–413.

Sodano, Valeria. 2011. "The New Division of Labor in the Globalized Economy: Women's Challenges and Opportunities." *Forum for Social Economics*, 40(3): 281–298.

Standing, Guy. 1989. "Global Feminization through Flexible Labor." *World Development*, 17(7): 1077–1095.

Standing, Guy. 1999. "Global Feminization through Flexible Labor: A Theme Revisited." *World Development*, 27(3): 583–602.

Tuttle, Carolyn. 2012. *Mexican Women in American Factories: Free Trade and Exploitation on the Border*. Austin: University of Texas Press.

UN. 2004. 2004 World Survey on the Role of Women in Development: Women and International Migration. Accessed September 13, 2015, at www.unwomen.org/en/digital-library/publications/2005/1/2004-world-survey-on-the-role-of-women-in-development-women-and-international-migration#sthash.OT7Y2svT.dpuf.

FURTHER READING

Kalleberg, Arne. 2011. *Good Jobs, Bad Jobs: The Rise of Polarized and Precarious Employment Systems in the United States, 1970s–2000s*. New York: Russell Sage Foundation.

Moghadam, Valentine M. 2013. *Globalization and Social Movements: Islamism, Feminism, and the Global Justice Movement*, 2nd ed. Lanham: Rowman & Littlefield.

Naples, Nancy, and Manisha Desai, eds. 2002. *Women's Activism and Globalization*. London: Routledge.

Rees, Ray, and Ray Riezman. 2011. "Globalization, Gender and Growth." *Review of Income and Wealth*, 58(1): 107–117.

Salzinger, Leslie. 2003. *Genders in Production: Making Garment Workers in Mexico's Global Factories*. Berkeley: University of California Press.

World Bank. 2012. *World Development Report 2012: Gender Equality and Development*. Washington, DC: World Bank.

Educational Testing and Gender

THOMAS BREDA
Paris School of Economics, France

Educational tests are aimed at assessing academic achievement. In practice they take a variety of forms: paper and pencil or computer-based tests; externally graded tests (such as national exams) or tests graded directly by pupils' teachers. When students' genders are observed by the teachers, professors, or external evaluators grading the tests, the assessment may be biased because of gender discrimination. To measure pure gender differences in performance at school, it is necessary to rely on gender-blind tests (anonymous computerized or written tests). The comparison of gender-blind with non-gender-blind tests calling for the same skills can then provide a measure of gender bias in evaluation.

GENDER DIFFERENCES IN TEST SCORES

The most comprehensive source of information regarding educational skills around the world is the Programme for International Student Assessment (PISA), conducted by the Organization for Economic Cooperation and Development (OECD) every 3 years since 2000. PISA tests in mathematics, science, and reading are designed to assess to what extent students at the end of compulsory education can apply their knowledge to real-life situations and be equipped for full participation in society. In 2012, the fourth PISA assessment included the 34 OECD member countries, but also 31 other countries, most of them developing and emerging countries.

Based on blind standardized tests, PISA reveals that in the 2000s, at the age of 15 girls outperformed boys in reading in virtually all PISA countries. The average advantage of girls over boys in reading proficiency at that age is strikingly large; it amounts to about 1 year of schooling in 2012 (OECD 2014). The gender gap in reading has also been documented and is fully confirmed by other studies and national blind educational assessments (for a review see Buchmann, DiPrete, and McDaniel 2008). However, the gap has increased during the past decade, with the relative standing of boys deteriorating further.

In contrast, at the age of 15 boys tend to outperform girls in blind standardized math and science tests. However, the gender gaps observed in those topics are on average three or more times smaller than those observed in favor of girls in reading tests. Contrary to the stereotype, they are also much less widespread; in mathematics, boys outperform girls in only 38 of the 65 countries participating in PISA.

In all topics, there is also an increasing proportion of boys who do not reach the baseline level of proficiency expected at the age of 15. Overall, the now well-documented fact that boys are increasingly lagging behind girls by the age of 15 has led researchers to start focusing primarily on boys.

The differences in test scores at the age of 15 can be partly explained by gender differences in behavior within and outside the classroom during adolescence. Outside the classroom, girls spend on average 1 hour more on homework than boys (OECD 2015). They also spend more time reading and less time playing video games (OECD 2015). Within the classroom, boys display more disruptive conduct and less positive orientations to learning activities (Zill and West 2001).

The advantage of girls in reading and of boys in mathematics grows during the life-course and is rarely found in the early grades (Willingham and Cole 1997). At a given age, it also exhibits strong variations across countries and time periods. Altogether, this suggests that gender differences in test scores mostly result from cultural rather than biological factors.

The way tests are framed and presented can lead to significant gender differences. For example, girls seem to be less resilient to test pressure and perform relatively worse during high-stake tests (Azmat, Calsamiglia, and Iriberri 2014). Early in life, girls show more interest on average in social stimuli and communication, while boys are more interested in dynamic and mechanical stimuli. As a consequence, tests based on dynamic media such as videos may favor boys more than the standard paper and pencil tests usually based on the reading of linear texts (Martin and Binkley 2009). Research in cognitive psychology has established some small gender differences (either in favor of females or males) in some cognitive tasks. Typically, boys are consistently better on average at tasks of mental rotation while girls are consistently better on average at tasks of verbal fluency (Halpern 2000). However, cognitive differences are usually considered too small and too specific to induce real gender differences in aptitude in the different academic fields, including mathematics and science (Spelke 2005). However, they induce differences in the way females and males typically process information, implying that small differences in the way questions in tests are framed can induce relatively large gender differences in performance, even if males and females master equally well the core ability construct they are tested on.

GENDER DISCRIMINATION AT SCHOOL AND UNIVERSITY

In settings where blind and non-blind tests calling for the same skills are available, it is possible to study gender biases in evaluation. A series of recent empirical studies based on the comparison of blind with non-blind tests consistently show that girls are not systematically discriminated against at school or university (Lindahl 2007; Lavy 2008; Hinnerich, Höglin, and Johannesson 2011; Kiss 2013; Terrier 2014). If anything, the bias in evaluation is found to be against boys.

However, evaluation bias might vary across fields, depending on how much gender-stereotyped a field is. Of all the potential explanations for the gender gap in science majors, a popular idea is that teachers and professors in those fields may be biased against females. Recent research suggests that discrimination tends to counteract stereotypes; with females being relatively more favored than males in more male-dominated fields of study and vice versa (Breda and Ly 2014; Terrier 2014). Hence, discrimination is probably not a credible explanation for the strong persisting gender gap in science which remains the largest difference between females' and males' educational outcomes.

SEE ALSO: Gender Bias in Research; Gender Blind; Gender Difference Research; Gender Inequality in Education

REFERENCES

Azmat, G., C. Calsamiglia, and N. Iriberri. 2014. "Gender Differences in Response to Big Stakes." CEP Discussion Paper no. 1314.

Breda, Thomas, and Son Thierry Ly. 2014. "Professors in Core Science Fields Are Not Always Biased Against Women: Evidence From France." Accessed August 26, 2015, at http://www.parisschoolofeconomics.com/breda-thomas/working_papers/GenderGapUlm.pdf.

Buchmann, C., T.A. DiPrete, and A. McDaniel. 2008. "Gender Inequalities in Education." *Annual Review of Sociology*, 34: 319–337.

Halpern, D.F. 2000. *Sex Differences in Cognitive Abilities*, 3rd ed. Mahwah: L. Erlbaum Associates.

Hinnerich, Björn Tyrefors, Erik Höglin, and Magnus Johannesson. 2011. "Are Boys Discriminated in Swedish High Schools?" *Economics of Education Review*, 30(4): 682–690.

Kiss, David. 2013. "Are Immigrants and Girls Graded Worse? Results of a Matching Approach." *Education Economics*, 21(5): 447–463.

Lavy, Victor. 2008. "Do Gender Stereotypes Reduce Girls' or Boys' Human Capital Outcomes?" *Journal of Public Economics*, 92: 2083–2105.

Lindahl, Erica. 2007. "Does Gender and Ethnic Background Matter When Teachers Set School Grades? Evidence From Sweden." IFAU Working Paper no. 25.

Martin, R., and M. Binkley. 2009. "Gender Differences in Cognitive Tests: A Consequence of Gender-Dependent Preferences for Specific Information Presentation Formats?" In *The Transition to Computer-Based Assessment*, edited by Friedrich Scheuermann and Julius Björnsson, 75–82.

OECD. 2014. "PISA 2012 Results: What Students Know and Can Do." *Student Performance in Mathematics, Reading and Science*, vol. 1, revised ed. Paris: PISA, OECD Publishing.

OECD. 2015. *The ABC of Gender Equality in Education: Aptitude, Behaviour, Confidence.* Paris: PISA, OECD Publishing.

Spelke, E.S. 2005. "Sex Differences in Intrinsic Aptitude for Mathematics and Science? A Critical Review." *American Psychology*, 60(9): 950–958.

Terrier, Camille. 2014. "Giving a Little Help to Girls? Evidence on Grade Discrimination and its Effect on Students' Achievement." PSE Working Papers, 2014–2036.

Willingham, W.W., and S.E. Cole. 1997. *Gender and Fair Assessment*. Mahwah: Lawrence Erlbaum.

Zill, N., and J. West, 2001. *Entering Kindergarten: A Portrait of American Children When They Begin School: Findings from the Condition of Education 2000*. Washington DC: National Center Education Statistics.

Elder Abuse and Gender

MARY CAY SENGSTOCK
Wayne State University, USA

BRENDA I. GILL
Alabama State University, USA

Presently the "elderly" comprise 12 percent of the global population with women accounting for a significant number of that population. It is projected in the UN World Population Report of 2014 that by 2050 people aged 60 years will increase to represent 21 percent of the world's population – a total of 2 billion – with females being a large percent of that population (United Nations 2014). Fifty-eight percent of all women live in developing countries. This figure is expected to increase to 75 percent by 2025. This population increase in older women signals both challenges and opportunities. Nonetheless, focus is on the perceived challenges as related to elder abuse. One such challenge is that of gender disparity in experiences of elder abuse. While both men and women experience elder abuse, these experiences are oftentimes more prolonged and intense for older women who tend to outlive their male counterparts. Additionally, this growth of older women compounded by structural inequalities such as low incomes, poor health services, gender discrimination, lack of access to educational opportunities, urbanization, changes in family, and participation of more women in the paid work force, lack of or inadequate pension schemes, high unemployment rates, and, in developing nations, the risk of non-communicable diseases in old age, worsening poverty, and inequality, combined with some societies' mourning rite of passage for widows, sexual violence, forced marriages, evacuation from homes, accusations of witchcraft, and other acts of violence that are culturally embedded, all exasperate elderly women's experiences with elder abuse.

Several variations of elder abuse definitions exist globally. Definitions of elder abuse require a cultural context and the inclusion of several variables. The term "older age" or "elderly," for example, is a socially constructed concept that varies globally. In most societies though, the onset of older age usually corresponds with the age of retirement. Hence, for most developed nations this is somewhere around ages 60 and 65. Despite the age disparity, elder abuse is recognized as an act that affects people who are no longer expected to carry out their family and work roles. Elder abuse can be initiated by family members or others known to the elderly persons. This abuse can occur in the elders' homes, in residential or other institutional settings. Elder abuse could be a single or repeated unbecoming acts and deliberate or accidental neglect that occur in relationships of trust that result in hurt or suffering to an older person (World Health Organization, WHO). Research and policy literature tend to classify elder abuse into seven main types: physical abuse, sexual abuse or abusive sexual contact, emotional or psychological abuse, neglect, self-neglect, abandonment, and financial abuse or exploitation. These can be broken into three broad areas of abuse, reported by elders as: neglect (isolation, abandonment, and social exclusion), violation (of human, legal, and medical rights), and deprivation (of choices, decisions, status, finances, and respect) (WHO/INPEA 2002, V). The National Aging Resource Center on Elder Abuse's (NARCEA) definition seems quite thorough and includes physical, emotional, financial, neglect, self-neglect, sexual abuse, and miscellaneous. Miscellaneous is spelled out to include violations of rights, medical abuse, abandonment, denial of privacy, or participation in decision making about health, marriage, and other personal issues (Tatara 1990).

Elder abuse, especially abuse perpetuated by family members, dates back to ancient times. Abuse of the elderly remained for centuries mainly a private matter. It received significant attention relatively late compared to child abuse and domestic violence. Reports in the British Scientific Journal in 1975 of "Granny battering" raised awareness to the problem, and elder abuse became publicized and first described (Baker 1975). This recognition was initially considered a social welfare issue and later a problem of aging. By the 1980s, elder abuse became a topic of interest and concern to the public, media, and the medical community. Mounting evidence suggests that in most societies elder abuse is a growing public health and criminal justice issue. In the United States all states have statutes or adult protective service laws addressing elder abuse.

Risk factors for abuse are at four levels: the individual, relationship, community, and sociocultural levels. Risk factors generally include dementia, mental disorders, alcohol and substance abuse, gender, living situations, abusers' dependency on the older person, long history of poor family relationships, less spare time to offer caregiving services, social isolation, lack of or inadequate social support, perceptions of elderly, and distribution and maintenance of material goods such as houses, migration, lack of sufficient funds, standards of health care, level of staff training, inadequate policies, or implementation of existing policies (WHO 2002; Centers for Disease Control 2013).

Though several incidence and prevalence studies have been conducted, the need for more intervention studies is recognized. Elder abuse continues to affect women more. It receives scant recognition, it is underreported, underresearched, lacks extensive data, and is awarded insufficient financial and policy support in most nations globally. Systematic collection of prevalence statistics and studies on elder abuse remain non-existent in some societies. Some authorities suggest the need for more theory driven, empirical, cross-cultural, and international studies to provide data on the phenomenon of elder abuse.

SEE ALSO: Aging, Ageism, and Gender; Emotional Abuse of Women; Intimate Partner Abuse

REFERENCES

Baker, A. A. 1975. "Granny-battering." *Modern Geriatrics*, 5: 20–24.
Centers for Disease Control (CDC). 2013. Understanding Elder Abuse. Accessed September 4, 2015, at http://www.cdc.gov/violenceprevention/pdf/em-factsheet-a.pdf.
Tatara, T. 1990. *NARCEA's Suggested State Guidelines for Gathering and Reporting Domestic Elder Abuse Statistics for Compiling National Data*. Washington, DC: National Aging Resource Center on Elder Abuse.
United Nations. 2014. The World Population Situation in 2014: A Concise Report. United Nations, Department of Economic and Social Affairs, Population Division. Accessed September 4, 2015, at http://www.un.org/en/development/desa/population/publications/pdf/trends/Concise%20Report%20on%20the%20World%20Population%20Situation%202014/en.pdf.
WHO/INPEA. 2002. *Missing Voices: Views of Older Persons on Elder Abuse*. Geneva: World Health Organization.
World Health Organization (WHO). 2002. World Report on Violence and Health. Accessed

September 4, 2015, at http://www.who.int/violence_injury_prevention/violence/world_report/en/introduction.pdf.

FURTHER READING

Jackson, S. L., and T. L. Hafemeister. 2013. Understanding Elder Abuse: New Directions for Developing Theories of Elder Abuse Occurring in Domestic Settings. US Department of Justice, Office of Justice Programs, National Institute of Justice. Accessed September 4, 2015, at https://www.ncjrs.gov/pdffiles1/nij/241731.pdf.

Embodiment and the Phenomenological Tradition

DONGXIAO QIN

Western New England University, USA

One of the most influential contributions of phenomenology to contemporary phenomenological psychology and anthropology is evident in its tradition's focus on "embodiment." Embodiment is not a theory, or a group of theories, but a different way of thinking and knowing about human beings, one that is in contrast to the Western dualistic thinking of mind and body as separated entities. The embodiment in phenomenological tradition refers to the bodily aspects of human beings and subjectivity. The body is not only an object that is available for scrutiny but also a locus from which our experience of the world is arrayed. The body is not an entity that can be examined and interpreted in epistemological or aesthetic terms, it is a living entity by which, and through which, we actively experience the world (Csordas 1990). Embodiment can be defined in a way that reflects the phenomenological philosophy of Merleau-Ponty as how we live in and experience the world through our bodies, especially through perception, emotion, language, and movement in space, time, and sexuality. Embodied views of humans allow us access to what ordinarily is taken for granted in everyday living, including practical knowledge.

Embodiment also means being situated within the world, and being affected by social, cultural, political, and historical forces. From a phenomenological perspective, the living body is considered as the existential null point from which our various engagements with the world – whether social, eventful, or physical – are transacted. The literature on the embodiment in phenomenology is vast, following the works of Edmund Husserl, Maurice Merleau-Ponty, and Martin Heidegger. The phenomenological framework aims to understand precisely the world as a relation between the natural and the cultural, the objective and the subjective, the thinking and non-thinking beings. In Husserl's phenomenology (1989), the idea of embodiment coincides essentially with the identification of the *experienced body* itself as the central location of any *perceptual*, as well as *imaginative*, feeling. Therefore, any intentional function connecting a subjective experience to the domain of external objects can be conceived on a bodily related basis. In other words, the human being's total consciousness is in a certain sense, by means of its hyletic substrate, bound to the body (Husserl 1989). The consequences of embodiment for phenomenology are also emphasized in the last part of Husserl's works, where an important aspect of his genetic phenomenology concerns the relevance of the *life-world*. According to Husserl (1970), if the *self is originally embodied*, the relationships and the interaction with the surrounding environment assume the role of critical condition for the possibility of any subjective *lived* experience. Following this line of thought, the life-world, as it is defined by a subject's direct and pre-epistemic interaction with the system of objects within which every *life-praxis* is engaged, emerges as a basic priori according to which all knowledge finds its own root grounded in a universal a priori which is in itself prior, precisely that of the pure life-world (Husserl 1970). Accordingly, the role of the body for the phenomenon of perspectivity lies in the assumption that an *un-thematic* "being-in a life-world" functions as the condition of possibility for all phenomena; so that the presence of a system constituted by corporeal features and kinesthetic dynamics emerges as the *transcendental condition* of all lived experiences. Therefore it seems possible to hypothesize that, using the Husserlian terminology, the *transcendental subject* also is a function shaped by the nature of the human embodiment. In this manner Husserl attributes a critical importance to human embodiment, making *corporeality* a limiting constraint to a purely intellectual understanding of what he calls the life-world.

Within the early phenomenological tradition, Maurice Merleau-Ponty (2002/1945), more than Husserl, focused his attention on the body's role in the construction of subjective experience. Capturing the Husserlian idea of phenomenal body with the concept of *corps propre* (i.e., one's own body), with a radical difference in comparison to Husserl's kinesthetic view, Merleau-Ponty has introduced the active participation of many bodily functions in the constitution of the external world experience, emphasizing the role of the *agentive* character that accompanies the human embodied nature. Attending to the layer of living experience, the phenomenon of being-in-the world, a phenomenological framework recognizes that all contact with the world occurs through negotiations between the intentions of the subject and the givens of the world or rather that subjectivity and the world condition each other. This definition of phenomena operates on both the ontological and the epistemic levels. Merleau-Ponty never separates the ontological and epistemological aspects of the subject and being-in-the world. One's experience of the world phenomenally occurs through embodiment. Moreover, one experiences the body phenomenally. Merleau-Ponty does not naively situate the body in the world and assume that all bodies see and experience more or less the same thing. Instead, recognizing that all bodies are not exactly and entirely alike, he theorizes how each body's positioning in the world reflects the body's differences. In other words, Merleau-Ponty's attention to embodiment heeds not only the role of the body in general but its particularities. Because of the differences of the body, each individual's position within the world facilitates a unique perspective of the world. The uniqueness of each position does not derive solely from its spatial position; each body occupies a unique position in the world because each body builds up a horizon of immanent personal experiences. As such, each body's optimal distance for perception exhibits the subject's relation with the object of perception in the world. Because of the differences of the body, each subject has her own unique blind spot; the subject cannot possess full self-consciousness of the situations of his or her own body at any moment.

Within a dualistic metaphysics, philosophy had abstracted away the differences among subjects, depicting subjects as replaceable, because the only important aspect of human beings is the status of thinking beings. In highlighting the roles of the particularities of embodiment, Merleau-Ponty rescues each person for her unique perspective. Merleau-Ponty insists that because of the singular position of each body within the world each body can contribute uniquely to the knowledge of the world. In contrast to the dualistic metaphysical stance where only thinking beings can act, and where the body as a non-thinking being cannot act, Merleau-Ponty's phenomenology challenges this neat separation by insisting that only embodied subjects act in the world. Phenomenology, with Merleau-Ponty's appreciation for the particularities of embodiment, serves as an ideal framework for thinking about the meaning of the embodiment of subjectivity and selfhood. Embodied selfhood takes place within the contextual world into which each person is born and lives. In *Being and Time* we are told by Heidegger (1962) that being a self in an authentic way means *being-in-the-world*. World is the structure of meaningful relationships in which a person exists and in the design of which he participates. "Being-in-the-world" expresses that self and world are a unitary, structural whole. Self implies the world, and world self; there is not one without the other, and each is understandable only in terms of the other. The self is revealed when reflected in the worldly beings with which one constructs his/her self. The self is always one's openness and involvement with other beings in the world. One comes to know oneself not so much by abstract self-reflection as by interacting with others in social groups into which one was born. To be a human always means to be with other people. To be an authentic self is to be contextualized in the world. Based on Heidegger's claims about *being-in-the-world*, we perceive that authenticity of self as a continuum, an extension of the inner psyche composed by a bundle of traits to the embodiment of worldly beings contextualized in the meaningful relationships at large. The authentic self is one that is constantly aware of and interacting with others in changing sociocultural contexts. To be an authentic self is to be aware of the world in the form of "we." "We" awareness is accordingly an intersubjective self-awareness, it is an awareness of oneself as representative of a community.

Debate about embodiment is heated in some of the recent psychological literature. Overton (1994) called for an endorsement of a major paradigm shift in psychology by embracing embodiment as a way of overcoming subject/object dualism. Sampson (1993) proposed establishment of embodiment in psychology as a way of overcoming both the discourse of dominant Western medicine and recent social constructionism. He advocated for embodiment as a way to include voices of history, culture, and community that have been previously excluded. This world is shaped by culture, society, history, and personal relationships and it must be interpreted to be understood. As embodied beings, we know the world through shared understandings, making the world a social and intersubjective experience. What one person experiences in the world may be similar to that which others experience because all of us open into the same world and, thus, our experiences may be similar. Perception of others varies by race and gender, and it entails cultural understandings, meanings, and a general orientation. In order to affirm a self-celebratory cultural belief, Western psychology has participated and encouraged the belief in a negative relationship between self and other. The existing mainstream psychological theories concern the common notion that self-development evolves through stages of ever increasing levels of separation and spheres of mastery and personal independence. This theory emphasizes "the separate self," an autonomous, "self-contained entity" (Sampson 1993). According to this construal of self, the person is viewed as a "container" (Sampson 1993) and as a bounded, unique, more or less integrated motivational and cognitive universe, a dynamic center of awareness, emotion, judgment, and action organized into a distinctive whole and set contrastively both against other such wholes and against a social and natural background (Geertz 1975). The self characterized as such a self-contained entity exhibits a firm self–other boundary. The others are not an intrinsic part of the self. This exclusive conception of the individual defines the self as a separate entity whose essence can be meaningfully abstracted from the various relationships and in-group membership that he or she has (Sampson 1993).

Challenges to the modern Western view of self have also come from anthropologists and cultural psychologists who study how self and culture are co-constituting and co-constituted in cross-cultural contexts (Geertz 1975; Shweder 1991). They define "culture" as a symbolic and behavioral inheritance received from the historic and ancestral past that provides a community with a framework for other-directed and vicarious learning and for collective deliberations about what is true, beautiful, good, and normal. As noted above, the modern Western view is *peculiar* in its cultural emphasis on individualism. Many other cultures value collectivism and do not conceptualize the person apart from his or her relationships. They exhibit what Sampson (1988) called "ensembled individualism," in which the self versus the non-self boundary is less sharply drawn and others are included within the sense of self. For Markus and Kitayama (1991) the Japanese interdependent self is a "self-in-relation-to-other" so that, "the expression and the experience of emotions and motives may be significantly shaped and governed by a consideration of the reactions of others" (pp. 4–5). For Shweder and Bourne (1984), Indian self is "sociocentric" since individual interests are subordinated to the good of the collectivity. For Dio (1973), Ho (1993) and Kim and Berry (1993) the "self" in traditional Asian cultures cannot be defined outside of its relationships. For Howell (1981), the Chewong of Malaysia does not distinguish sharply between the individual and nature. For Brabeck (1996), Mayans' sense of self in Guatemala arises from and has meaning only within "circles of belonging" – the community. For Kirkpatrick and White (1985), a non-Western self-conception is one in which some collectivity – "the family, community, and even the land is a cultural unit with experiential capacities" (p. 11). For Tu (1985), a classic sense of Chinese self is embedded in "webs-of-relationships." In Chinese culture, self is very much influenced by traditional Confucianism, which has become a dominant philosophy and human ethics guiding the mind, thoughts, and behavior of Chinese people. Confucian teachings are not abstract, they are primarily concerned with human relationships and interactions. It is only through the *web of social relations* that the self can maintain a wholesome and personal identity. The social relations that define the self in terms of family, community, and society are the realms of selfhood (Tu 1985). The uniqueness of the self in Chinese perception is immanent within a ceaseless process of broadening and deepening relationships. The authenticity of Chinese self is perceived as "*being-in-webs-of social relations*" (Qin 2006, 2009).

The non-Western self emphasizes that "we"-awareness as a type of self-awareness. The self as an embodiment of social relations in the world echoes Husserl's argument that different types of "we-hood" designate different modes of I-subjectivity. Each we involves a centering in me who has this we-hood. These insights from phenomenology often informed critical reflections on the nature of subjectivity, self-experiences, and personhood in an attempt to demonstrate the limits of purely subjectivist approaches in psychology and anthropology. They have also inspired a growing number of psychologists and anthropologists to argue for the merits of approaching embodiment, inter-subjectivity, and self-in-relations as core theoretical constructs more broadly defined. Although phenomenology has contributed to the development of psychology and anthropology, one of the most pressing critiques holds that phenomenological approaches ignore the critical cultural contexts that constitute one's life and subjectivity. More recently critical cultural and feminist theorists (Gergen 2001; Lykes and Qin 2001; Qin 2004; Crawford 2006) called for a critical and local interpretation of culture and self. A critical perception notes that culture is not necessarily coherent and homogeneous: individuals participate in multiple cultures in various ways. In fact, the phenomenological perspective of embodiment and subjectivity ignores the interlocking systems of critical cultural elements as the determinants of selfhood. According to critical cultural and feminist perspectives, culture is composed of many critical elements, that is, social class, gender, power, race/ethnicity, sexuality, and many differing symbolic and behavioral inheritances of a community. Self is culturally situated and constrained by these critical cultural elements. Culture is also experienced locally: individuals appropriate complex interlocking system of race, class, gender, and power relations in their self constructions within their specific local and historical environment. Re-conceptualizing culture as critical and local has theoretical and practical implications for psychologists and cultural theorists to study various groups of people's lived experiences and to elaborate how they construct "selfhood" in creative and multiple ways.

In conclusion, in this entry I have discussed how "embodiment" was defined in phenomenological tradition and how Merleau-Ponty, Husserl, and Heidegger's thoroughgoing examination of the concept of "being-in-the world" gives rise to a form of existential analysis that allows for the development of cultural-existential approaches to understanding subjectivity/selfhood in psychology and anthropology. By engaging in thinking of culture and self from a local and critical perspective, or rather critical thinking which moves beyond Western individualism toward holistic and collectivist understanding of human experience, we are able to redefine the embodiment of subjectivity/selfhood in terms of lived human experiences embedded in the world. Moreover, it is in and through the cultural flesh of the world that human beings, as the embodiment of the existential null point from which our various engagements with the world – whether social, cultural, or historical – are constructed and transformed.

SEE ALSO: Feminism, Existential; Individualism and Collectivism, Critical Feminist Perspectives on

REFERENCES

Brabeck, Mary. 1996. "The Moral Self, Values, and Circles of Belongings." In *Women's Ethnicities: Journeys through Psychology*, edited by K. F. Wyche and F. J. Crosby, 145–165. Boulder: Westview Press.

Crawford, Mary. 2006. *Transformations: Women, Gender and Psychology*. New York: McGraw-Hill Higher Education.

Csordas, Thomas. 1990. "Embodiment as a Paradigm for Anthropology." *Ethos*, 18: 5–47.

Dio, Takeo. 1973. *Anatomy of Dependence*, trans. J. Bester. Tokyo. Kodansha International.

Geertz, Clifford. 1975. "On the Nature of Anthropological Understanding." *American Scientist*, 63: 48.

Gergen, Mary M. 2001. *Feminist Reconstructions in Psychology: Narrative, Gender, and Performance.* Thousand Oaks: Sage.

Heidegger, Martin. 1962. *Being and Time*, trans. J. Macquarrie and E. Robinson. London: SCM Press.

Ho, David F. 1993. "Relational Orientation in Asian Social Psychology." In *Indigenous Psychologies: Research and Experience in Cultural Context*, edited by U. Kim and J. W. Berry, 240–259. Newbury Park: Sage.

Howell, Samuel. 1981. "Rules Not Words." In *Indigenous Psychologies*, edited by P. Heelas and A. Lock, 133–142. London: Academic Press.

Husserl, Edmund. 1970. *Ideas Pertaining to a Pure Phenomenology and to a Phenomenological Philosophy*, trans R. Rojcewicz and A. Schuwer. Dordrecht: Kluwer Academic Publishers.

Husserl, Edmund. 1989. *The Crisis of European Sciences and Transcendental Phenomenology: An Introduction to Phenomenological Philosophy*, trans. David Carr. Northwestern University Press: Evanston.
Kim, U., and J. W. Berry. 1993. *Indigenous Psychologies: Research and Experience in Cultural Context*. Newbury Park: Sage.
Kirkpatrick, J., and G. M. White. 1985. "Exploring Ethnopsychologies." In *Person, Self, and Experience: Exploring Pacific Ethnopsychologies*, 3–32. Berkeley: University of California Press.
Lykes, Brinton M., and Dongxiao Qin. 2001. "Collectivism and Individualism." In *Encyclopedia of Women and Gender: Sex Similarities and Differences and the Impact of Society on Gender*, edited by Judith Worell, vol. 1, 625–631. San Diego: Academic Press.
Markus, Hazel, and Shinobu Kitayama. 1991. "Culture and the Self: Implications for Cognition, Emotion, and Motivation." *Psychological Review*, 98: 224–252.
Merleau-Ponty, Maurice. 2002. *Phenomenology of Perception*, trans. Colin Smith. London: Routledge. First published 1945.
Overton, Willis F. 1994. "The Arrow of Time and Cycles of Time: Concepts of Change, Cognition, and Embodiment." *Psychological Inquiry*, 5: 215–237.
Qin, Dongxiao. 2004. "Toward a Critical Feminist Perspective of Culture and Self." *Feminism & Psychology*, 14(2): 297–312.
Qin, Dongxiao. 2009. *Crossing Borders: International Women Students in American Higher Education*. Lanham: University Press of America.
Qin, Dongxiao, and Brinton M. Lykes. 2006. "Reweaving a Fragmented Web of Self: A Grounded Theory of Self-Understanding among Chinese Women Students in USA." *International Journal of Qualitative Studies in Education*, 19(2): 177–200.
Sampson, Edward. 1988. "The Debates on Individualism: Indigenous Psychology of the Self and Their Role in Personal and Societal Function." *American Psychologist*, 43, 15–22.
Sampson, Edward. 1993. *Celebrating the Other: A Dialogic Account of Human Nature*. Boulder: Westview Press.
Shweder, Richard A. 1991. *Thinking Through Cultures: Expeditions in Cultural Psychology*. Cambridge, MA: Harvard University Press.
Shweder, Richard A., and Edward J. Bourne. 1984. "Does the Concept of the Person Vary Cross-Culturally?" In *Culture Theory: Essays on Mind, Self, and Emotion*, edited by R. A. Shweder and R. A. Levine. Cambridge: Cambridge University Press.
Tu, Wei-Ming. 1985. *Confucian Thought: Selfhood as Creative Transformation*. New York: State University of New York Press.

FURTHER READING

Hegel, Georg. 1977. *Phenomenology of Spirit*, trans. A. V. Miller. Oxford: Oxford University Press.

Emotion Work

ANDRZEJ KLIMCZUK
Warsaw School of Economics, Poland

MAGDALENA KLIMCZUK-KOCHAŃSKA
University of Warsaw, Poland

Emotion work refers to the psychological processes necessary to regulate emotions that are desired in specific private life conditions. It includes controlling the intensity and quality of the individual's feelings that are not related to the public sphere and are not undertaken for reasons associated with paid work.

However, part of employment that involves work performed by using feelings is called emotional labor. Contemporary service economies are based on the growing number of domains in which jobs are related to the provision of services to individuals, such as an airline flight attendant, waitress, bartender, and so forth. Such jobs are characterized by "selling feelings," which then become a commodity, and by the domination of women's employment.

The concept of emotion work was introduced by American sociologist Arlie Hochschild (1979, 1983) in her study on flight attendants and bill collectors. She argues that such jobs are characterized by emotional and service aspects, and are done mainly by women. Other examples are a waitress, nurse, amusement park greeter, insurance agent, nail salon attendant, food handler, and emergency operators.

According to Hochschild, emotion work is the effort involved in manipulating the emotions of self and others and as generating feelings that are appropriate for a situation. Such work is the act of trying and may lead or not to the successful outcomes. It may also be called emotion "management" or "regulation" when it refers to efforts to maintain balance in a relationship using the creation, transformation, or inhibition of feelings. Emotion work includes both shaping and suppressing feeling. It also differs from "emotional intelligence" in that it includes the sensing of others' emotions and competencies such as self-awareness, self-control, empathy, active listening, and the skill to resolve conflicts and cooperate with others (Guy, Newman, and Mastracci 2008).

Hochschild distinguishes between emotion work and emotional labor. The first refers to the private context where feelings are valued in relationships with family and friends. The latter is a social and economic exchange value of work sold for a wage. Emotional labor takes place in a paid, public environment with customers or coworkers that demand displaying and expressing certain emotions which are desired and consistent with organizational aims.

Hochschild describes two broad types of emotion work and three techniques of emotion work. The first type is evocation focused on an initially absent desired feeling and the second is suppression focused on an initially present undesired feeling. The first technique is a cognitive attempt to change images, thoughts aimed at changing associated feelings. The second technique is a bodily attempt to change physical symptoms of emotions (for example, slow breathing). The third is an expressive attempt to change gestures (for example, trying to smile).

Emotional labor occurs in face-to-face or voice-to-voice interactions with clients (for example, patients, children, customers, passengers, or guests); includes behavioral expressions that aim to change others' emotions, attitudes, and behaviors; and contains displaying of emotions related to social expectations (Zapf 2002). It is also possible to distinguish emotional labor by the episodes (for example, dealing with an angry customer before or after dealing with an angry coworker), by the job (different professions, possibilities of controlling other employees), and by the person (various individual characteristics) (Ashkanasy and Cooper 2008).

Emotion work and emotional labor may be analyzed on the levels of working, the organizing of work, and the sociocultural embedding of organizations (Sieben and Wettergren 2010). In the first case, emotions are created as antecedent consequences of work tasks. For example, it is a motivating joy with the work, fear of a certain task, and the shame of a failure. Emotion may represent the object of work (influencing others' emotions), a means while working (usage of own emotions to fulfill tasks), and a condition of work (establishing or altering certain feelings). At the level of organizing, emotions are related to the work-setting influence, organization-specific emotion rules, and resources that are producing and reproducing emotions. The sociocultural embedding of the work refers to social structures like gender, class, or race that have an influence on emotion appearances. Examples include gendered expectations within organizations, emotion work in the household with a different standard of caring by women than men, and cultural beliefs in the service industry that women are more suited to emotional labor.

Emotion work was also expanded into the category of "intimate labor" (Parreñas and Boris 2010), which includes occupations primarily held by women related to care, domestic, and sex work that involve bodily and psychic intimacy (for example, manipulating genitalia, wiping noses, lifting torsos, feeding, listening, talking, holding). These labors are stigmatized by relation to dirt, bodies, and intimacy.

Related research fields include "aesthetic labor," which focus not only on how companies attempt to support emotional labor as it may have an influence on satisfaction of clients and service users, but also to stimulate the "right look" of employees and discriminate those who are perceived as less physically attractive (Warhurst and Nickson 2009). Another concept is "body labor" that refers to the provision of body-related services, managing the physical work of hands and the bodies they touch, particularly in the beauty industry (Kang 2010). Recent studies include "embodied labor" such as commercial surrogacy, which consists of a rental of one's body by somebody else, the use of the worker's body as a site, resource, requirement, and product, as well as fields of resistances and negotiations between the surrogate, the family, the clinic, and the state (Pande 2014).

SEE ALSO: Division of Labor, Gender; Feminist Theories of Organization; Leadership and Gender; Occupational Segregation; Self-Esteem

REFERENCES

Ashkanasy, Neal M., and Cary L. Cooper, eds. 2008. *Research Companion to Emotion in Organizations*. Northampton, MA: Edward Elgar.

Boris, Eileen, and Rhacel S. Parreñas, eds. 2010. *Intimate Labors: Cultures, Technologies, and the Politics of Care*. Stanford: Stanford Social Sciences.

Guy, Mary E., Meredith A. Newman, and Sharon H. Mastracci. 2008. *Emotional Labor: Putting the Service in Public Service*. Armonk: M. E. Sharpe.

Hochschild, Arlie R. 1979. "Emotion Work, Feeling Rules, and Social Structure." *American Journal of Sociology*, 85(3): 551–575.

Hochschild, Arlie R. 1983. *The Managed Heart: Commercialization of Human Feeling*. Berkeley: University of California Press.

Kang, Miliann. 2010. *The Managed Hand: Race, Gender, and the Body in Beauty Service Work*. Berkeley: University of California Press.

Pande, Amrita. 2014. *Wombs in Labor: Transnational Commercial Surrogacy in India*. New York: Columbia University Press.

Sieben, Barbara, and Åsa Wettergren. 2010. "Emotionalizing Organizations and Organizing Emotions: Our Research Agenda." In *Emotionalizing Organizations and Organizing Emotions*, edited by Barbara Sieben and Åsa Wettergren, 1–20. New York: Palgrave Macmillan.

Warhurst, Chris, and Dennis Nickson. 2009. "'Who's Got the Look?' Emotional, Aesthetic and Sexualized Labour in Interactive Services." *Gender, Work & Organization*, 16(3): 385–404.

Zapf, Dieter. 2002. "Emotion Work and Psychological Well-Being." *Human Resource Management Review*, 12(2): 237–268.

Emotional Abuse of Women

KEITH E. DAVIS
University of South Carolina, USA

CHRISTOPHER T. ALLEN
University of Massachusetts Lowell, USA

Emotional abuse can be conceptualized as any set of activities designed to humiliate or otherwise reduce the standing of another person. While research has typically focused on examining the activities in intimate relationships (such as with a partner, friend, or family member), these activities can also occur between people who are not intimately connected, such as in professional settings (commonly referred to as harassment). Garfinkel (1956) called such activities *status degradation ceremonies*, and described them as interactions that remove people from a place of value and restrict their freedom within a community. As a result of these activities, behaviors (and, in extreme cases, thoughts and feelings) a person could previously perform are now restricted or forbidden. Ossorio (2013) described how such activities look in dyadic interactions – in which one person denounces and degrades another – and also how these processes can be internalized and carried out against oneself (commonly referred to as negative self-talk in the clinical literature). Research shows that much emotional abuse is reciprocal, so that when P tries to degrade O, O often resists the degradation and attempts to do likewise to the original perpetrator of abuse.

Despite decades of research, the term *emotional abuse* is not one that has been used consistently in the literature. Some authors have referred to "emotional abuse" whereas others have used "controlling abuse," "psychological abuse," "psychological maltreatment," "psychological torture," "verbal aggression," "verbal abuse," or "verbal battering" (for a review, see Follingstad 2007). The range of terms used to describe these phenomena has reflected a lack of consensus regarding the definition of these terms. A growing consensus has developed among scholars who look at the issue in the United States and among the 28 European Union nations (examples are given below).

Better measures of emotional abuse have focused not merely on specific behavioral acts but on their perceived implications for recipients. For example, the following items were used to measure "expressive psychological aggression" by the 2010 National Intimate Partner and Sexual Violence Survey (Black et al. 2011): "Acted very angry in a way that seemed dangerous"; "Told me that I was a loser, a failure or not good enough"; "Called me names like ugly, fat, crazy, or stupid"; "Insulted, humiliated, or made fun of me"; and "Told me that no one else would want me." Four out of the five items used to measure such psychological aggression represent the victims' perception of being subjected to a form of degradation.

This national survey treated coercive control as the second aspect of psychological abuse and measured using 13 items, the five items most highly endorsed by victims being (1) "Tried to keep me from seeing or talking to family and friends"; (2) "Made decisions that should have been mine to make"; (3) "Kept track by demanding to know where I was and what I was doing"; (4) "Made threats to physically harm me"; and (5) "Destroyed something that was important to me." The first three of these behaviors reflect attempts to put the woman in a subordinate place in the relationship – as a lesser person who is not eligible to manage her own life. The impact of degradation and controlling behaviors is maintained through the threat of physical harm and destroying something of value. Research suggests that these three components – degradation, control, and credible threat – constitute the core components of emotional abuse in the sense that, together, they constitute the most extreme and detrimental cases of abuse.

MEASURES OF EMOTIONAL ABUSE

Most studies into these phenomena have relied on self-reported survey data from women who were asked about their experiences of emotional abuse victimization. Even if using our earlier conceptualization – "any set of activities designed to humiliate or otherwise reduce the standing of another person" – such an approach clearly has limits.

For example, measurement tools often do little to capture the context in which emotional abuse occurs. As we see with Garfinkel's description of emotional abuse as an *interaction*, the behavioral context simply cannot be ignored (Garfinkel 1956). For example, saying "I'm going to kill you" to someone means something very different when said during a heated argument than when said while playing video games. Whether or not such an utterance constitutes emotional abuse is a question of its impact. As noted by Follingstad and Rogers (2014), emotionally abusive behavior will likely have an emotional and/or behavioral impact on its target. However, it is important to note that some persons subjected to apparently abusive behavior do not seem to see their partner's behavior that way.

To address some of the conceptual and measurement limitations mentioned above, Follingstad and Rogers (2014) recently published a revision of the "Measure of Psychologically Abusive Behaviors" that assesses behavioral and emotional impact of behaviors across 14 categories.

PREVALENCE RATES FOR WOMEN AND MEN

Follingstad and Rogers (2014) reported no gender differences in the rates of severe psychological abuse among respondents describing their "worst relationship," although types of abuse experienced did differ by gender. Black et al. (2011) reported that slightly more than 40 percent of women in their national sample had experienced both expressive aggression and coercive control. In the case of men, 32 percent reported expressive aggression and 42.5 percent coercive control. There was no difference between men and women on coercive control, but fewer men reported being the targets of expressive aggression.

The European Union Agency for Human Rights conducted a survey entitled *Violence Against Women: an EU-Wide Survey* of 42,000 participants in 28 countries (European Union Agency for Human Rights 2014). Twenty-three items were used to assess psychological abuse, many of which overlapped with the CDC study reported above (Black et al. 2011), but new issues concerned economic violence (five items) and blackmail/abuse of children (two items). Forty-three percent of women reported some form of abuse in a previous or current relationship, with the most common forms being (emotionally) abusive behaviors (32 percent) and (coercively) controlling behaviors (35 percent). The specific items parallel those commonly occurring in the United States.

WHAT ARE THE CONSEQUENCES?

This is a difficult question to answer with any certainty. There are at least two problems in getting to the facts. First, the ideal study would follow individuals/families over time to determine what consequences occur to those who have been emotionally abused versus those who have not. Second, the ideal study would have measures of emotional abuse as distinct from physical and sexual abuse. As these often, but not always, occur together in the same relationships, it may be impossible to parse consequences by type of abuse. In other words, one needs to distinguish between consequences to those who have been either physically or sexually abused (or both) and those who have only been emotionally abused.

Demonstrating the greater negative consequences to the satisfaction of the scientific community has been harder to accomplish. However, recent work has provided a substantial amount of evidence supporting this point, especially in studies following children into adulthood. Keyes and colleagues (2012), in a nationally representative study of 34,653 US adults, found that emotional abuse (when carefully distinguished from other aspects of childhood maltreatment) associated with pathological adult behavior. For women, emotional abuse was correlated with externalizing disorders (e.g., substance use) – but not for men. Emotional abuse was strongly related to internalizing disorders (e.g., depression and anxiety disorders) for both men and women, but more strongly for women. Interestingly, emotional abuse has been more consistently related to depression than either physical abuse or sexual abuse (Alloy et al. 2006).

TREATMENT OF ABUSE VICTIMS

Few studies have specifically focused on victims of emotional abuse, but the clinical lore is that some abuse victims have patterns of emotional reactions similar to those of rape victims. However, in many cases, what one finds is evidence of enhanced depressive episodes, lower self esteem, and substance abuse, in addition to anxiety disorders.

Where evidence suggests post-traumatic stress disorder (PTSD) or serious trauma reactions, there is good evidence that two forms of treatment are effective in the treatment of rape survivors with PTSD. We do not claim that these are the only treatments that can be helpful for victims of prolonged, severe emotional abuse.

The two treatments are cognitive processing therapy (CPT) and exposure therapy. CPT is an adaptation of the evidence-based therapy known as cognitive behavioral therapy (CBT) used by clinicians to help clients explore recovery from PTSD and related conditions. The theory of CPT conceptualizes PTSD as a disorder of "non-recovery" in which erroneous beliefs about the causes and consequences of traumatic events produce strong negative emotions and prevent accurate processing of the trauma memory and natural emotions emanating from the event. It is a manualized therapy that includes common elements from general cognitive behavioral treatments. CPT is a manualized treatment typically administered over 12 sessions and has been shown to be effective in treating PTSD across a variety of populations, including combat veterans and sexual assault victims (Resick et al. 2008).

Exposure therapy, previously known as imaginal flooding therapy, involves carefully exposing the patient to prolonged and repeated imagined images of the trauma until the images no longer cause severe anxiety. Research by Foa et al. (1991) showed that exposure therapy was effective in reducing PTSD symptoms of rape victims, including persistent fear. The improvements were seen immediately after exposure therapy, and were shown to be sustained during a 3-month follow-up. Meta-analyses find that each of these approaches are effective and that the effects last over significant periods (3 months or more), but that no one treatment is superior to the others (Vickerman and Margolin 2009).

Given the conceptualization of emotional abuse offered in this entry, a key element is the loss of one's place in one's world. A particularly relevant book summarizing treatments of depression from a status dynamic formulation has recently appeared (Holmes 2013) and provides numerous examples of exactly how to help persons suffering from abusive relationships and other status losses to recover from depression. No single school of therapy has a monopoly on effectiveness in such treatments. We conclude with the observation that anti-depressive and anti-anxiety medications have *not* been shown to be more effective than the range of psychological interventions discussed above.

SEE ALSO: Intimate Partner Abuse; Sexual Coercion; Sexual Terrorism

REFERENCES

Alloy, Lauren B., Lyn Y. Abramson, Wayne G. Whitehouse, Michael E. Hogan, Catherine Panzarella, and Donna T. Rose. 2006. "Prospective Incidence of First Onsets and Recurrences of Depression in Individuals at High and Low Cognitive Risk for Depression." *Journal of Abnormal Psychology*, 115(1): 145–156. DOI: 10.1037/0021-843X.115.1.145.

Black, Michele C., Kathleen C. Basile, Matthew J. Breiding, Sharon G. Smith, Mikel L. Walters, Melissa T. Merrick, Jieru Chen, and Mark R. Stevens. 2011. *The National Intimate Partner and Sexual Violence Survey (NISVS): 2010 Summary Report*. Atlanta: National Center for Injury Prevention and Control, Centers for Disease Control and Prevention.

European Union Agency for Fundamental Rights. 2014. *Violence against Women: an EU-Wide Survey. Main Results*. Luxembourg: Publications Office of the European Union.

Foa, Edna B., Barbara Olasov Rothbaum, David S. Riggs, and Tamera B. Murdock. 1991. "Treatment of Posttraumatic Stress Disorder in Rape Victims: a Comparison between Cognitive-Behavioral Procedures and Counseling." *Journal of Consulting and Clinical Psychology*, 59(5): 715–723.

Follingstad, Diane R. 2007. "Rethinking Current Approaches to Psychological Abuse: Conceptual and Methodological Issues." *Aggression and Violent Behavior*, 12: 439–458. DOI: 10.1016/j.avb.2006.07.004.

Follingstad, Diane R., and M. Jill Rogers. 2014. "The Nature and Prevalence of Partner Psychological Abuse in a National Sample of Adults." *Violence and Victims*, 29(1): 3–23. DOI: 10.1891/0886-6708.09-160.

Garfinkel, Harold. 1956. "Some Conditions of Successful Degradation Ceremonies." *American Journal of Sociology*, 61: 20–24.

Holmes, James R. 2013. *Depression Doesn't Always Have to Be Depressing*. Pensacola: Pelican Press.

Keyes, Katherine M., Nicholas R. Eaton, Robert F. Krueger, Katie A. McLaughlin, Melanie M. Wall, Bridget F. Grant, and Deborah S. Hasin. 2012. "Childhood Maltreatment and the Structure of Common Psychiatric Disorders." *British Journal of Psychiatry*, 200: 107–115. DOI: 10.1192/bjp.bp.111.093062.

Ossorio, Peter G. 2013. *Seminar on Clinical Topics: the Collected Works of Peter G. Ossorio*, vol. VII. Ann Arbor: Descriptive Psychology Press (originally published as *LRI Report No. 11*. Whittier and Boulder: Linguistic Research Institute, 1976).

Resick, Patricia A., Tara E. Galovski, Mary O'Brien Uhlmansiek, Christine D. Scher, Gretchen A. Clum, and Yinong Young-Xu. 2008. "A Randomized Clinical Trial to Dismantle Components of Cognitive Processing Therapy for Posttraumatic Stress Disorder in Female Victims of Interpersonal Violence." *Journal of Consulting and Clinical Psychology*, 76(2): 243–258. DOI: 10.1037/0022-006X.76.2.243.

Vickerman, Katrina A., and Gayla Margolin. 2009. "Rape Treatment Outcome Research: Empirical Findings and State of the Literature." *Clinical Psychology Review*, 29(5): 431–448. DOI:10.1016/j.cpr.2009.04.004.

FURTHER READING

The best single book about recognizing and avoiding abusive relationships is

Fairweather, Lynn. 2012. *Stop Signs: Recognizing, Avoiding, and Escaping Abusive Relationships*. Berkeley: The Seal Press [a publisher of groundbreaking books by women for women].

A classic is

Stark, Evan. 2009. *Coercive Control: How Men Entrap Women in Personal Life*. New York: Oxford University Press.

In our experience, reading the autobiographical accounts of women who have broken free may be the best medicine of all.

Employment Discrimination

DORIS WEICHSELBAUMER
University of Linz, Austria

A standard economic definition of discrimination is that individual workers who have identical productive characteristics are treated differently because of the demographic groups to which they belong. Discriminatory treatment can concern wages, the likelihood of being hired or promoted, and even the assignment of tasks. In this entry discrimination based on the demographic characteristics of sex and sexual orientation will be discussed.

Historically, unequal treatment of men and women has been the norm in labor markets. The sexual division of labor held women responsible for the home, i.e., housework and care work, while the "male breadwinner" had to generate the household income. Women's secondary status in the labor market has also been established formally. For example, in the early twentieth century, "marriage bars" existed in countries like the United States that banned married women from employment in particular occupations, for example education and clerical jobs. Also minimum wages were set differently for men and women, granting women lower wages. Only from the mid-century on did legislators begin to introduce equal treatment laws with the aim of erasing sex discrimination. Laws that protect gays and lesbians from employment discrimination were introduced only in recent decades and cover only certain states and employment relations.

The most well-known economic theory on discrimination was provided by Becker (1971), who argued that it results from some "majority group" members' "taste" against working with members of a "minority group." For example, studies have illustrated heterosexuals' dislike of interacting with gays and lesbians. Such dislike may lead to workplace discrimination. But also men may have a dislike of working with women in positions they deem inappropriate for a woman. If women enter previously male-dominated spheres, men may fear for their male privileges. As a result, such women may be discriminated against even though men do not hold a dislike of women in general.

Another explanation for unequal treatment has been developed by Phelps (1972) and Arrow (1973), who argued that under conditions of incomplete information, individuals are judged on the basis of beliefs about group averages ("statistical discrimination"). Numerous reasons have been proposed why women on average, yet not individual women, may be less productive and therefore suffer from statistical discrimination. Most importantly, women of childbearing age may be expected to drop out of the labor market. As a result, employers may hesitate to hire them or may pay them lower wages. Because in Western societies women are still held responsible for household and care work, they are often also considered to lack the capacities and availabilities required for a high-flying career. Many also consider women to be more risk-averse, less competitive, and less successful negotiators. Most current economic research therefore examines whether these factors may be responsible for women's inferior labor market status. Interestingly, though, little research focuses on productive characteristics in which – according to existing stereotypes – women may have an advantage (e.g., accuracy, insusceptibility to corruption).

The most common way to analyze sex discrimination is to compare the wages of equally qualified men and women. Depending on the context, studies usually reveal that women earn 5–25 percent less than men with identical qualifications (Weichselbaumer and Winter-Ebmer 2005). Unfortunately there is little consensus on how to interpret these results. While some authors argue these findings document discrimination, others – particularly more mainstream economists – believe in a perfect functioning of markets that should reward workers of identical productivity with identical wages. Consequently, the latter insist that the lower wages of women must result from lower productivity that is simply unobservable in the data. For example, they point out that due to socialization women may be less focused on their careers, which reduces their productivity on average but is typically unobservable for the researcher.

Contrary to mainstream economists, feminist economists have argued that the gender wage gap obtained in these studies may actually *under*estimate sex discrimination in the labor market. This is because studies often control for factors that are affected by discrimination themselves. If studies control for the occupation a person works in, for example, they compare the wages of men and women who have managed to be hired in this occupational field. However, as experimental studies show, women are often also discriminated in their access to particular professions – particularly if these are well paid.

Most experiments that examine discrimination in hiring use a method called correspondence testing. Qualitatively identical applications, one with a woman's name and one with a man's name, are sent out in response to job advertisements. If one applicant receives significantly more invitations to an interview than the other, this, by definition, can be assigned to discrimination. Riach and Rich (2002) provide an overview of different experimental studies in different countries and find significant sex discrimination in many contexts. Discrimination is particularly pronounced against women in male-dominated occupations. There is also discrimination against men in female-dominated jobs which, however, typically receive lower pay.

Wage studies and experiments have also been conducted to examine discrimination based on same-sex sexual orientation. Wage studies indicate that gay men earn less than equally qualified heterosexual men; however, lesbians seem to earn similar or higher wages compared with heterosexual women. Besides other reasons, this may be because lesbians are not subjected to the heterosexual division of labor in the household and have fewer career interruptions due to maternity. That lesbians' higher wages do not imply freedom from discrimination has been illustrated in numerous correspondence tests. In many countries women, like men, are significantly less likely to be invited to an interview if they indicate voluntary engagement in a gay or lesbian organization in their résumé and thereby signal a same-sex sexual orientation (Weichselbaumer 2013). Labor market discrimination therefore remains a social ill that women and sexual minorities, besides other groups, still suffer from.

SEE ALSO: Division of Labor, Gender; Gender Wage Gap; Glass Ceiling and Glass Elevator

REFERENCES

Arrow, Kenneth. 1973. "The Theory of Discrimination." In *Discrimination in Labor Markets*, edited by Orley Ashenfelter and Albert Rees, 3–33. Princeton: Princeton University Press.

Becker, Gary. 1971. *The Economics of Discrimination*. Chicago: University of Chicago Press.

Phelps, Edmund. 1972. "The Statistical Theory of Racism and Sexism." *American Economic Review*, 52: 659–661.

Riach, Peter, and Judith Rich. 2002. "Field Experiments of Discrimination in the Market Place." *Economic Journal*, 112: 480–518.

Weichselbaumer, Doris. 2013. "Discrimination in Gay and Lesbian Lives." In *Handbook of Research on Gender and Economic Life*, edited by Deb Figart and Tonia Warnecke, 236–254. Northampton: Edward Elgar.

Weichselbaumer, Doris, and Rudolf Winter-Ebmer. 2005. "A Meta-Analysis on the International Gender Wage Gap." *Journal of Economic Surveys*, 19: 478–511.

Empowerment

SHARON LAMB and MADELINE BRODT
University of Massachusetts Boston, USA

The concept of empowerment was a part of nineteenth-century social reform movements to help those afflicted by poverty and what was considered in the day to be immorality. For example, habitual drunkenness was defined as "negative liberty," the problem described as an individual not working toward a common goal (Cruikshank 1999). The idea of empowering others to benefit them, as well as the greater social good, flourished in the fields of social work and community psychology. It found meaning outside of these fields with Paolo Freire's influential book, *Pedagogy of the Oppressed* (1970). According to Freire, powerlessness is systemically produced and maintained by social institutions and those with power. Those in poverty, oppressed by powerful institutions, needed not only to participate in group dialogue and activism, but also to come to understand their powerlessness differently. Freire described three concepts that underlie the pedagogy of the oppressed toward empowerment. The first concept, "conscientization," refers to the need for individuals to develop a critical awareness of sociopolitical and economic conditions in order to then take action against injustice. The second concept is "constructivism." Freire considered constructivism a type of learning that is not passive, but an act of active construction and meaning-making that contributes to conscientization. The third concept, "praxis," reflects Freire's idea that the oppressed must join together collectively and put theory into practice. Thus education for empowerment involves developing critical consciousness, self-motivated education as meaning-making, and collective action. One or all of these ideas is embedded in much of the work on empowerment that has followed.

More recently, scholars have also pointed to aspects of empowerment that are similar to Freire's: the intrapersonal or psychological (self-efficacy or a belief in one's self-efficacy), the interpersonal (people in similar positions vis-à-vis oppression can come together with more powerful institutions to identify sources of oppression and devise ways to change power relations), and the behavioral (the activism or joint action that would produce change and work toward an equalizing of power). Bay-Cheng (2012) asserts that all three components need to be present, and rarely does one find in the empowerment literature the idea of personal agency without critical consciousness, or critical consciousness with action toward social justice would be sufficient.

Within the study of empowerment, there has also been discussion about whether empowerment is a process or an end-state. Bay-Cheng (2012) notes that it is both, but conceptualizing it as an end-state serves as an ideal for social justice. In contrast, Rappaport (1987) specifically emphasizes that it is a process through which one gains the capability to control one's own affairs, and obtains the freedom to act individually rather than in a way prescribed by any group.

As a process, some scholars have theorized developmental stages for empowerment. Gutiérrez (1994) proposed that stressful life experiences begin the process, causing an individual to identify with others with regard to the social forces that shape them. Carr (2003) suggests that one simply needs to recognize one's position (or take a position) for the process of empowerment to begin. Other scholars see the journey toward empowerment less connected to any specific event, thus able to be regenerated when a new event comes along. Carr criticizes developmental models by pointing out that they are tied to a specific history and context and are not universal. The discourse around development can undermine the sociopolitical, contextual, and social nature of the process with language like "infancy stage," which positions those without power as infants in relation to those who would help them come to power. This is a demeaning way to understand those who live in poverty and/or are oppressed by their circumstances.

Some feminist scholars focus on the repressive and regressive nature of the use of the word empowerment. Empowerment can easily be turned into a self-help project (Becker 2005), or a project with regard to fixing oneself or fixing one's thinking rather than applying that power toward the social conditions that contribute to the formation of selves and ideologies. If empowerment is a self-help project, then, as Kitzinger (1991) points out, victims (she uses the example of female rape survivors) are themselves to blame for their rape and for their lack of recovery. Lack of empowerment thus becomes a personal failure. Riger (1993) has argued that if the focus is on the sense of empowerment rather than adequate access and control of resources, the status quo is supported. She notes that many intervention efforts enter at the level of increasing self-esteem but then do little to actually enhance a person's ability to act in a way that gives them more power in relation to resources and policies.

The framing of empowerment may reveal more about those with power and their ability to frame ideas over those with less power. For example, common notions about empowerment reflect individualistic and capitalist society with a focus on conflict and control, where cooperation and communion are undervalued. At times, the discourse around empowerment holds up individual men and women as ideals of empowerment – heroes, so to speak – and solidarity and group collaboration become invisible.

Within feminism, consciousness-raising in the 1960s and 1970s was viewed as a method of politicizing women to work together for equality and social justice, but also in collaboration with each other. It was believed at the time that those who had power benefited from women's competition with one another and lack of solidarity as women. Consciousness-raising was aimed at helping women to see "women's problems" as institutionally labeled and supported problems, rather than problems relating to inequality and oppression. For example, the sharing of rape stories was meant to help women see that rape was a social problem of patriarchy, that it occurred more than was previously believed, that institutions like the system of justice supported rape inadvertently, that women were not to blame for being raped, and that together they could fight against the social institutions that supported rape culture.

Feminists in the field of gender and development (GAD) define empowerment as a "counterhegemonic" political process by which "subaltern" women would come together to discuss their experiences and become aware of structural processes shaping their lives and those of their communities (Sharma 2008). With this awareness, they would be mobilized to fight against the different modes of oppression and transform power relationships in their homes, communities, and larger society. Feminist analysis of empowerment projects also reveals the depoliticizing effect of a government-sponsored "will to empower" (Cruikshank 1999). Calls for empowerment, once associated primarily with radical left and feminist movements, have been adopted by development and other government agencies in ways that often support neoliberal and anti-welfare goals (Sharma 2008; Naples 2013).

Feminist theory today has incorporated postmodern and poststructuralist thinking, including the idea of multiple, fluid, and intersecting identities, and the difficulty of changing power relations when ideologies and institutions that support change are also influenced by the status quo of power relationships. Debates about the sexualization of girls and female adolescent sexual development focus on girls' widespread adoption of a kind of sexuality that has been labeled as empowered by the media and by girls themselves (Gill 2008). Images of supposedly empowered, sexually objectified women in advertising, TV, and movies serve to contradict older stereotypes of women as passive and lacking in agency. Gill (2008) questions how progressive these images are. Lamb (2010) also questions the nature of this representation of empowerment, stating that it bases empowerment on an imitation of what the culture considers to be a stereotypical male sexuality. Lamb and Peterson (2012) debate whether interpreters of girls' behavior ought to consider that the girls "feel empowered" when enacting stereotypical and what has been called pornography-inspired acts. Many scholars argue that empowerment needs to be more than a psychological state of feeling powerful or efficacious; it also needs to be tied to a politics that fights oppression. To the extent that girls and women enact a porn-inspired sexuality to combat shame and passivity stereotypes of female sexuality, it could be argued that their consciousness contributes to a reading of their acts as empowered. But to the extent that these actions and thoughts are based on feeling empowered without any thought to the contribution of their acts to further oppression of women, or the buying into a system that contributes to structural inequalities of gender and race, these acts are not empowered. Such acts, then, are part of what sociologists call a "commodified reflexive project of the self which has intensified the pressures on and expectations of women's presentation, body management and sexuality" (Rahman and Jackson 2010, 209).

Empowerment thus is an elusive concept that can refer to the fight against oppressive forces that individuals, through group action, education, and critical consciousness, participate in. However, empowerment processes can also reinscribe paternalistic relationships between the oppressed and those who would rescue them, as well as mystify the way in which social institutions maintain an individualized notion of empowerment to guard against political action. Feminist scholars have pointed to the ways in which political aspects of empowerment can be reformed in a problematic way as personal and individual goals, thus separating individual change from the social institutions that oppress and that form individual thought and identity. Those who use such a term would wisely also examine the power relationships between helper and those deemed oppressed. In the end, scholars seem to agree that critical consciousness with regard to social institutions and solidarity with others toward group action are at the heart of an empowerment process that can mean something.

SEE ALSO: Consciousness-Raising; Feminism and Postmodernism; Feminism, Poststructural; Feminisms, Postmodern; Gender Oppression; Patriarchy; Rape Culture

REFERENCES

Bay-Cheng, Laina. 2012. "Recovering Empowerment: De-personalizing and Re-politicizing Adolescent Female Sexuality." *Sex Roles*, 66(11–12): 713–717.

Becker, Dana. 2005. *The Myth of Empowerment: Women and the Therapeutic Culture in America*. New York: NYU Press.

Carr, E. Summerson. 2003. "Rethinking Empowerment Theory Using a Feminist Lens: The Importance of Process." *Affilia*, 18(8): 8–20.

Cruikshank, Barbara. 1999. *The Will to Empower: Democratic Citizens and Other Subjects*. Ithaca: Cornell University Press.

Freire, Paulo. 1970. *Pedagogy of the Oppressed.* New York: Herder and Herder.

Gill, Rosalind. 2008. "Empowerment/Sexism: Figuring Female Sexual Agency in Contemporary Advertising." *Feminism & Psychology*, 18(1): 35–60.

Gutiérrez, Lorraine 1994. "Beyond Coping: An Empowerment Perspective on Stressful Life Events." *Journal of Sociology and Social Welfare*, 21: 201–219.

Kitzinger, Celia. 1991. "Feminism, Psychology and the Paradox of Power." *Feminism & Psychology*, 1(1): 111–129.

Lamb, Sharon. 2010. "Porn as a Pathway to Empowerment? A Response to Peterson's Commentary." *Sex Roles*, 62(5/6): 314–317.

Lamb, Sharon, and Zoe Peterson. 2012. "Adolescent Girls' Sexual Empowerment: Two Feminists Explore the Concept." *Sex Roles*, 66(11/12): 703–712.

Naples, Nancy. 2013. "'IT'S NOT FAIR!': Discursive Politics, Social Justice and Feminist Praxis. SWS Feminist Lecture." *Gender & Society*, 27(2): 133–157.

Rahman, Momin, and Stevi Jackson. 2010. *Gender and Sexuality: Sociological Approaches.* Cambridge: Polity.

Rappaport, Julian. 1987. "Terms of Empowerment/Exemplars of Prevention: Toward a Theory for Community Psychology." *American Journal of Community Psychology*, 15(2): 121–148.

Riger, Stephanie. 1993. "What's Wrong with Empowerment." *American Journal of Community Psychology*, 21(3): 279–292.

Sharma, Aradhana. 2008. *Logics of Empowerment: Development, Gender, and Governance in Neoliberal India.* Minneapolis: University of Minnesota Press.

Entrepreneurship

ATTILA BRUNI
University of Trento, Italy

Until the beginning of the 1980s entrepreneurship studies concerned themselves almost entirely with men, and gender was seen as an irrelevant issue. In fact, economics and social sciences always used "man" as an abstract concept to denote one sex as much as the other. Yet the symbols employed have constructed a social actor who obeys rationality rather than emotionality, who behaves selfishly rather than cooperatively, and who is oriented to the public rather than to the private, thereby invisibly assuming norms of masculinity (Bruni, Gherardi, and Poggio 2004). Not by chance, critical approaches to management and organization studies have shown how modern economic rhetoric often described entrepreneurship as an activity geared to the "discovery of new lands" and undertaken by "explorers," establishing an automatic relation between the qualities of an entrepreneur (leadership, risk-taking, rational planning) and a model of male rationality. Entrepreneurship is historically located in the symbolic universe of the male and its practices are strongly related to that of hegemonic masculinity: competitiveness, self-promotion, and authoritarianism. In this way, it has been argued, entrepreneurship turns into an entrepreneur-mentality (Bruni, Gherardi, and Poggio 2004), producing its own (gendered) subject: *entrepreneur* and not *entrepreneuse*. Entrepreneur-mentality – paying homage to Foucault's term "governmentality," which denotes the emergence of an entire system of thought about the practice of government – is constructed through the discursive practices of entrepreneurs, the media that represent their achievements, and the scientific texts that expound theories of entrepreneurship, and in its turn becomes the plot and constraint for entrepreneurial action and discourse.

As for gender studies, strands of research in gender and entrepreneurship can be divided into three main approaches:

1 *Essentialist.* Gender is equated with sex and men and women are treated on the

basis of different biological and psychological characteristics that can be identified and measured quantitatively. Research concentrates mainly on women entrepreneurs, seeking to evidence a purported model of female enterprise characterized by a greater capacity to manage within-firm relations, but also lesser competitiveness in the market (compared with male enterprises). Although this approach has been the first in posing at the center of the debate on the issue of female entrepreneurship, it is commonly criticized because of its perpetuating gender assumptions and stereotypes. Assuming theories about entrepreneurship and economic rationality to be gender neutral, in fact, this strand of studies tends to reproduce an abstract model of the firm, as well as of men and women.

2 *Feminist*. Gender is not simply sex-based, but it is constructed socially, on the basis of a gendered socialization process and an unequal distribution of power between men and women. Research concentrates on the experiences of women entrepreneurs in order to give voice to their needs, problems, and peculiarities. An achievement of this approach has been evidencing the differences among the experiences of female entrepreneurs, and therefore the limitations of the quantitative research that yields a one-dimensional image of the female entrepreneur. There is no single woman entrepreneur, no single "female enterprise," but rather women entrepreneurs with different histories, experiences, and problems. Not coincidentally, the pluralization of the experiences of women entrepreneurs is the result of an increasing use of qualitative methodologies attentive to differences among women and firms (Neergaard and Ulhøi 2007).

3 *Poststructuralist*. Gender is a doing, a collective performance enacted in appropriate situations and with regard to a symbolic universe (so that men and women can both perform male or female). Research focuses on how "doing entrepreneurship" often involves the mobilization of gendered and gendering practices, so that performing gender becomes one of the (hidden) competences to be activated while doing entrepreneurship. This approach wants to unveil the masculine discourse in which entrepreneurship is embedded and which positions men and maleness as "the standard," thereby constructing women as "the other" (Ahl 2004). Following this line of research, it has been shown how the image of the entrepreneur is also biased in racial and sexual terms, so that entrepreneurs are constructed not only as male, but also as white and heterosexual.

Although these approaches developed in different periods (the essentialist in the 1970s to 1980s, the feminist in the 1980s to 1990s, and the poststructuralist in the 1990s to 2000s), nowadays they proceed in parallel. Especially in mainstream economic journals, essentialist and feminist approaches continue to be the main reference frame, even if (as poststructuralists argue) no study has yet been able to demonstrate a significant correlation between the sex of the entrepreneur and business results. Lines of inquiry continue to be those typical of "standard" entrepreneurial literature (characteristics and motivations of women entrepreneurs; management of female-owned firms; finance and related issues; business networks, performance, and growth), although research has evidenced that male and female entrepreneurs often have the same needs (e.g., access to credit) and motivations (e.g., independence).

At the same time, research on gender and entrepreneurship has challenged the wider mainstream theory on entrepreneurship, emphasizing how entrepreneurial action stands in relation to a broader cultural and symbolic world; how it can result from necessity as well as opportunity; how it is often a shared activity, embedded in family dynamics; how entrepreneurs do not always pursue economic profit; how the meanings and practices of entrepreneurship can vary in different cultures and situated contexts. In other words, entrepreneurship can be a critical area of activity for fostering social change (Calás and Smircich 2009).

SEE ALSO: Feminisms, First, Second, and Third Wave; Gender as a Practice; Hegemonic Masculinity

REFERENCES

Ahl, Helene. 2004. *The Scientific Reproduction of Gender Inequality: A Discourse Analysis of Research Texts on Women's Entrepreneurship*. Stockholm: Liber.

Bruni, Attila, Silvia Gherardi, and Barbara Poggio. 2004. *Gender and Entrepreneurship: An Ethnographic Approach*. London: Blackwell.

Calás, Marta B., and Linda Smircich. 2009. "Extending the Boundaries. Reframing Entrepreneurship as Social Change through Feminist Perspectives." *The Academy of Management Review*, 34(3): 552–569. DOI: 10.5465/AMR.2009.40633597.

Neergaard, Helle, and John P. Ulhøi, eds. 2007. *Handbook of Qualitative Research Methods in Entrepreneurship*. Cheltenham, UK: Edward Elgar Publishing.

FURTHER READING

Calás, Marta B., Linda Smircich, and Kristina Bourne. 2007. "Knowing Lisa? Feminist Analyses of Gender and Entrepreneurship." In *Handbook of Women in Business and Management*, edited by Diana Bilimoria and Sandy K. Piderit, 78–105. Cheltenham, UK: Edward Elgar Publishing.

Jennings, Jennifer E., and Candida G. Brush. 2013. "Research on Women Entrepreneurs: Challenges to (and from) the Broader Entrepreneurship Literature?" *Academy of Management Annals*, 7: 661–713. DOI: 10.1080/19416520.2013.782190.

Environment and Gender

KEIKO HIRAO
Sophia University Graduate School of Environmental Studies, Japan

Gender is deeply connected in the way humans relate to and understand the natural environment. Access to and knowledge of natural resources, ownership, and resulting conflict are not only affected by social class, race, and ethnicity, but also by gender. The connection between gender and the environment was first brought up in developmental discourse along with the international women's movement. The "women's view" inspired by feminist scholarship has also provided critical reflections on Western philosophy and science and consequently has delivered important lines of environmental research and active movement. The accumulation of gender-disaggregated data revealed how men and women are affected differently by nature. Women are more vulnerable to the effects of natural disasters and climate change, primarily because women constitute the majority of the poor, and are more dependent on livelihoods that rely on natural resources. On the other hand, women are the ones who lead protests against environmental pollution. Women are also reported to hold stronger pro-environmental values, beliefs, and attitudes than do men. These gender differences are arguably due to gendered division of household labor that make women responsible for the health and maintenance of households, thus making them more alert to environmental dangers.

GENDER, DEVELOPMENT, AND ENVIRONMENTAL POLICIES

The gendered nature of the human–environment relation was first brought up in the context of developmental policies. In the 1970s, scholars and practitioners raised questions about women's unequal positions in development, and began questioning the assumption of gender neutrality in both the costs and the benefits of development. They also drew attention to the critical roles that women play on the ground in environmental management. One of the pioneering works in this field was Ester Boserup's *Women's Role in Economic Development*. It called for attention to the significance of women's contributions in agricultural economies and the lack of acknowledgment of their work in developmental projects. It showed, for example, that women often did more than half of the agricultural work, up to 80 percent in some cases.

The UN Decade for Women between 1975 and 1985 and the World Conferences on Women played an important role in connecting gender and environmental policies. In 1975, at the First World Conference on Women in Mexico City, Vandana Shiva, an Indian environmental activist, brought the issue of women and the environment into public awareness. She reported the Chipko movement in the Himalaya region, which later became an iconic example of a women-led environmental protection movement. The Chipko women tried to protect the trees in their community against commercialized deforestation by embracing the trees. They knew that the woods had more function and value than just providing lumber; they served as a reservoir of water and food. The case of the Chipko movement illustrates the vital connection between land rights and environmental justice.

In 1995, at the Fourth World Conference on Women in Beijing, special attention was paid to the interconnectedness between poverty, gender, and environmental justice. The Strategic Action and Objectives adopted at the conference dedicated a full section to women and the environment. They maintain that environmental protection and social justice require the involvement of women in economic and social development. They also call for full and equal participation of women and men as agents and beneficiaries of sustainable development.

While the women's movement began to incorporate environmental issues, international conferences on the environment and sustainable development began to take a gender perspective. The United Nations Conference on Environment and Development, known as the "Earth Summit," held in Rio de Janeiro in 1992, adopted an agreement, Agenda 21, which incorporated a chapter on women. Chapter 24 of the Agenda 21 document required the signing countries to bring women into environmental decision-making for two reasons. First, women are disproportionately affected by negative environmental impacts because of their social and domestic roles and greater likelihood of poverty. Second, because of the roles assigned to women, they have a closer relationship with and knowledge of the environment.

"WOMEN'S VIEW" AND CRITICAL APPRAISAL OF WESTERN PHILOSOPHY AND SCIENCE

As languages that have gender in their noun-class system usually assign the feminine to nature-related terms, nature has traditionally been associated with femaleness. The *closeness* of women to the natural environment has long been a basis for the inferior position of women vis-à-vis that of men. This idea can be traced to the Western tradition of philosophy and science, which assumed that the level of a society's civilization and the intellectual ability of an individual were to be measured by the distance from the natural world. Whereas modern empirical science claimed to be value free, scientific knowledge was in fact constructed in a gender-biased way from the standpoint of the "knower" being primarily dominated by men because women were excluded from formal intellectual training.

Since the 1980s, there has been an increasing amount of evidence to help unravel the gender bias that affects the metaframe, the methodology, and the quality of scientific research. One such example is Donna Haraway's work in primatology. While male researchers focused on the observation of male primates in an attempt to explain food provision and social order, they established that such provision and organization necessitated aggression and dominance. Conversely, where women researchers focused on female primates, to explain the same social processes, they found the primacy of the opposite skills, cooperation and communication. This simplified synopsis of Haraway's account of primate research illustrates how gender affects the framing of a scientific question and consequently the results of the research.

The "women's view" within natural sciences that has provided critical reflections on science and technology has led to important lines of environmental research. One such pioneer was Ellen H. Swallow Richard, who is known as the first female MIT graduate and the founder of home economics. Richard's interest in the sanitation of the home environment turned her attention to the quality of air and water. She conducted the first scientific study on water pollution by performing a series of water tests on samples collected from all over the state of Massachusetts. The result was the "Richards' Normal Chlorine Map," which predicted inland water pollution. Based on her work, the state of Massachusetts established the first water quality standards in the United States and built the first modern sewage treatment plant. Richard's work on sanitation in the home led to the development of a study she named Oekology, which later became ecology. In this regard, Richards is credited as the founder of ecology.

Rachel Carson's *Silent Spring* (1962) is another example of how a critical appraisal of science and technology develops environmental research and active movement. Carson was the first to describe and give warning of the catastrophic consequences of the use of pesticides on nature and humans. She showed how the pesticide DDT moves from sprayed plants to non-sprayed plants and into the food chain, unintentionally killing beneficial insects and also birds that eat those insects, and consequently poisoning larger animals and humans. In spite of a fierce attack from the chemical industry, her book gained public and political support that led to legislation banning the use of DDT, the enactment of the Environmental Protection Act, and the subsequent foundation of the Environmental Protection Agency in the United States.

As noted before, Western philosophy traditionally measured the maturity of a civilization by the distance between a society and the natural world. Such a view sought to impose a presumed masculine intellectual order on what was thought to be feminine chaotic nature. One of the theoretical arguments criticizing this Western worldview is ecofeminism. There are many theoretical lines within this approach, but the highest common factor would be that they emphasize and embrace women's privileged bond with nature and the environment. They also see a parallel connection between degradation of the natural environment and patriarchal society oppressing women. Vandana Shiva, mentioned above, and Maria Mies are the two leading figures who represent ecofeminist thought particularly from the Global South. They maintain that women have a special connection to the environment through their daily interactions. They also emphasize women's vital role in subsistence economies and their holistic and ecological knowledge of processes in nature.

The assumption of women's closeness to nature is widely discussed in gender studies, and at times it serves as a double-edged sword. Feminists and ecologists both criticized ecofeminism for focusing too much on a mystical connection between women and nature, claiming that these thinkers are essentialist. The theoretical debate among feminists on the relationship between women and nature continues today, playing an important role in advancing gender analyses in environmental research.

GENDERED NATURE OF HUMAN–ENVIRONMENT RELATIONS

Gender mainstreaming and feminist scholarship have encouraged international agencies to assimilate gender-disaggregated data that reveal how the human–nature relation is mediated through gender. This section discusses: (1) how the impact of the natural environment is mediated through gender; and (2) how gender affects the ways in which human society relates to the natural environment.

Natural disasters, such as earthquakes, epidemics, floods, and tsunamis, do not affect men and women equally. On average, women and girls are more adversely affected by natural disasters than are men and boys. In other words, natural disasters kill more women than men. The greater the disaster, as measured by the number of casualties, the stronger is the effect on the gender gap and the negative effect on women. However, the extent of the gendered effect depends on the socioeconomic status of women and how roles are assigned for men and women in the affected country (Neumayer and Plumper 2007).

For example, the tsunami of December 2004 that hit 13 countries in Asia and Africa killed more women than men. Although the exact toll is unknown, Oxfam International reported that in Indonesia, females accounted for 70–80 percent of deaths, and in India, almost three times as many women were killed as men. Social norms and roles and behaviors provide reasons for gendered vulnerability. The heavy clothing worn by Muslim women prevented them from running in an emergency. Self-rescue skills, such as swimming and climbing trees, were not taught to girls. More importantly, women's role in looking after children and the elderly hampered their efforts to put their own lives first.

In the Han-shin Awaji Earthquake that hit Japan in January 1995, 1.5 times as many women died as men, but in the Great East Japan Earthquake of March 2011, the gender difference among deaths was smaller with a ratio of only 1.1. In the Kobe Earthquake in 1995, many elderly single women died because they lived in poor residential areas, which were more heavily damaged and caught fire. On the other hand, in the case of the Great East Japan Earthquake, it was age rather than gender that affected the death toll. The elderly (age 60 years and over) made up 64.4 percent of the total deaths. Within the same age group, more women died than men because women live longer and are overrepresented among the elderly. When the demographic composition is taken into consideration, slightly more men than women are reported to have died from the disaster. This case illustrates the importance of the socioeconomic structure of gender in a given society when considering the gender effect of natural hazards. It also calls for attention to the necessity to have more nuanced data on women's position in a given society because in most indicators on gender equality, Japan usually ranks very low on the scale of gender equality.

The negative effects of climate change are being felt in many areas, especially in relation to agriculture and food security. Just like natural hazards, climate change does not affect people equally. Rather, it is the poor, the marginalized, and the oppressed who are most impacted. While data suggest an overall reduction of extreme poverty worldwide, women are overrepresented among the population living on or below $1.25 per day. This is particularly true in the least developed countries. Moreover, although the farming population has been declining worldwide, the proportion of women in agriculture has increased since the 1960s, especially in the developing countries. This feminization of agriculture has many roots: more women are working in the field, fewer men are working in agriculture, and the increased availability of gender-disaggregated data has only just begun to capture women already working in the field. In any case, it is evident that women are more vulnerable to the effects of climate change than men; primarily because women constitute the majority of the poor, and are more dependent on livelihoods that rely on natural resources, which are directly affected by climate change. In many cultures, women are responsible for food production, household water supply, and energy for heating and cooking. These tasks are becoming more difficult with the increasing impact of climate change. The increased difficulty of securing a basic livelihood prevents more girls than boys from receiving education, severely limiting the chance for their empowerment.

While more women than men are susceptible to changes in the natural environment, they are the ones who spearhead protests against environmental pollution. Women are reported to make up 60–80 percent of the membership of mainstream environmental organizations and even more in grassroots organizations. The anti-pollution movement and political actions of the past have been led by women, including Ellen Swallow Richards, Rachel Carson, as discussed above, Lois Gibbs of the Love Canal incident, and Erin Brockovich, who fought the Pacific Gas and Electric litigation, to name just a few.

The reason for women's substantial involvement in the environmental movement is arguably due to the gendered division of household labor. As women are traditionally responsible for the health and maintenance of households, they are the first to notice environmental dangers. Likewise, systematic studies on gender differences in environmental concerns find that women report stronger pro-environmental values, beliefs, and attitudes than do men. This gender difference is particularly notable in studies examining concerns about environmental problems that pose health and safety risks to participants and their families.

A series of international documents on the environment and gender stress that women suffer more from environmental change because they are more vulnerable to health impacts due to pregnancy and breastfeeding. They are also more seriously exposed to environmental hazards due to a lack of resources to ameliorate negative change. Likewise, gender-specific divisions of labor within the household and labor market can all be linked to the invisible workload that women bear for the environment. Findings from research suggest a necessity for environmental policies and for theoretical studies on sustainability research that factor in women's unpaid labor and time.

SEE ALSO: Androcentrism; Climate Change and Gender; Ecofeminism; Environmental Disasters and Gender; Environmental Justice;

Essentialism; Feminist Objectivity; Feminist Standpoint Theory; Feminization of Poverty; Gender and Development; Gender Bias in Research; Gender Blind; Gender Inequality and Gender Stratification; Gender Mainstreaming; Mother Nature; Patriarchy; Positionality; Postcolonialism, Theoretical and Critical Perspectives on; Poverty in Global Perspective; Sexual Subjectivity; Status of Women Reports; Sustainable Livelihoods; Third World Women; UN Decade for Women; Women in Development; Women in Science; Women's Worlds Conference

REFERENCE

Neumayer, Eric, and Thomas Plümper. 2007. "The Gendered Nature of Natural Disasters: The Impact of Catastrophic Events on the Gender Gap in Life Expectancy, 1981–2002." *Annals of the Association of American Geographers*, 97(3): 551–566.

FURTHER READING

Arora-Jonsson, Seema. 2011. "Virtue and Vulnerability: Discourses on Women, Gender and Climate Change." *Global Environmental Change*, 21(2): 744–751.

United Nations Environmental Programme. 2005. *Mainstreaming Gender in Environmental Assessment and Early Warning*. New York: United Nations Environmental Programme.

United Nations Population Fund. 2009. *The State of World Population 2009: Facing a Changing World: Women, Population and Climate*. New York: United Nations Population Fund.

Environmental Disasters and Gender

LENA DOMINELLI
Durham University, UK

CONTEXT

Social relations occur within a gendered world. The struggle for equality has been written about for many centuries (e.g., Wollstonecraft 1792) and in many cultures. However, men and women inhabit different social spheres and inequality persists at some level in all countries. Notions of equality rooted in universalism suggest a similarity of experiences and approaches which fail to respond to the specificities of men's and women's experiences in all aspects of life including among the diverse groups within the category of "woman." Consequently, many texts in the disaster literature do not distinguish between men's and women's experiences of them. For universalized conceptions of environmental risk, see Douglas and Wildavsky (1982) and Jaeger (2006). Regardless of whether disasters are considered "natural" – like earthquakes and volcanic eruptions – or (hu)man-made – like climate change, industrial pollution, and armed conflict – vulnerability to the risks that environmentally situated hazards and their ensuing disasters pose is exacerbated by social factors that impact upon everyday life practices such as gender, age, disability, ethnicity, class, and sexual orientation (Wisner et al. 2004; Dominelli 2012). Thus, differentiation is found in experiences of environmental disasters, with poor marginalized adult women, older women, and children being those most adversely affected.

Those subscribing to universalism contest the idea that unequal gender relations make women's experiences of thinking, being, and doing in the world different from men's and reject postmodern feminists' view of the uniqueness of individual and subgroup experiences. Although gender increases women's vulnerability during disasters, women are not only victims, they are also survivors with active agency. Moreover, women usually support the rest of their family when disaster strikes, providing the care, goods, and services they need for survival in precarious circumstances and developing community resilience (Cutter et al. 2008; Dominelli

2013c). Also, regardless of whether a disaster is a slow-onset one, like poverty or famine, or a rapid onset one, like an earthquake, women are always at the frontline as family members and workers including social workers and health workers. The United Nations and governments often draw upon women's informal care to develop sustainable responses during the recovery and reconstruction phases of disasters. Sustainability here means meeting people's needs today without jeopardizing the capacity of future generations to fulfill theirs. The capacity to mitigate vulnerability or prepare for disasters is affected by income levels, social support networks, resources, and geographic locale. People living in low-income countries are affected more than those living in high-income countries. They account for 76 percent of damages caused by disasters; 92 percent of those affected and 65 percent of economic losses (IFRC 2009).

METHOD

The literature contains ample evidence of women's differentiated experiences of natural and (hu)man-made disasters (Dominelli 1991; Enarson and Morrow 1998; Pyles 2007; Alston and Whittenbury 2013). Findings from ethnographic research of disasters over several years and continents by Dominelli (2012, 2013a,b,c) have also revealed women's experiences as gendered, and differentiated according to age, stage in the life cycle, ability, ethnicity, and culture.

RESULTS

Women's experiences of disasters are different from men's. Additionally, they vary among women according to age, ability, ethnicity, cultural traditions, social norms, and economic conditions. To begin with, women's condition is shaped by the socioeconomic status of the families into which they are born and marry, their expectations about gendered behavior at specific ages, the roles that adult men and women can hold, and the level of education that women can attain. Male violence against women and children – a disaster of social origins – is common globally. Environmental disasters, whether natural or (hu)man-made, exacerbate existing inequalities between men and women, especially in situations of armed conflict where men, the majority of arms-bearers, subject women and children to unprecedented levels of violence as occurred in Bosnia-Herzegovina and Rwanda. Women's bodies, as signifiers of the nation (Yuval-Davis, Anthias, and Kofman 2005; Yuval-Davis 2006), have been raped and murdered to heap humiliation on a country, especially the menfolk who are deemed as lesser men for being unable to "protect their women." The children resulting from such assaults are often unwanted by either their mothers or the ethnic group pertaining to her because of the shame heaped upon the family, not just the woman. Thus, women and children bear a double jeopardy that is often unacknowledged by their country.

Additionally, there are other sources of inequality and increased levels of vulnerability that women experience as a result of environmental degradation including industrial pollution of the air, water, and soil in their habitat and the processes of receiving aid. These are linked to: women's specific bodily needs; the receipt of aid at different stages in the disaster (immediate relief, recover, reconstruction, and prevention); women's involvement in decision-making processes; and exposure to risk as indicated below.

WOMEN'S SPECIFIC BODILY NEEDS AND ASSOCIATED RISKS

Refugee camps created for disaster migrants are poorly designed to meet women's bodily needs linked to cleanliness, menstruation, pregnancy, breastfeeding, and childrearing. These camps are often overcrowded and lacking in decent sanitation facilities including safe, clean places in which to bathe, change sanitary towels (which are usually not available), breastfeed, and care for children and older people, especially when ill. Facilities for tasks that involve the washing of clothing and cooking for their families are also inadequate. Camp conditions place women at greater risk of physical and sexual violence at the hands of men. Additionally, women carry an extra burden and associated risks when undertaking daily life activities like fetching water from places at some distance from where their family is based, standing in queues to receive food aid, bottled water, or medicines, and taking children and older people requiring medical attention to clinics. Yet, they are also expected to complete the usual daily tasks of feeding their family and keeping their temporary shelter clean.

Soils and waters that become heavily degraded through industrial pollution or sewage following a natural disaster such as flooding can increase the risk of ill health (Bullard 1994), miscarriage among pregnant women, as well as damage their own and their children's health. In other disasters, pregnant women may not receive the food, especially the vitamins and minerals, required by a growing fetus and so the child might acquire a disability, and/or compromise the health of both mother and child. Many women become anemic during long stays in refugee camps where food is scarce, and getting sufficient calories into their own mouths is a lesser priority than feeding the men and children.

Older, frail women with impaired mobility and other health issues often perish on route to the refugee camps, and once there, their specific needs are seldom recognized, including that of caring for older, more sensitive skin, and meeting daily nutritional requirements. Also, their reliance on other, usually younger, women, to provide for their daily needs ranging from receiving food rations to having company, exacerbates their vulnerability as dependent persons unable to meet these needs themselves independently (Oven et al. 2012; Dominelli 2013a,b,c). Climate change is likely to exacerbate these burdens, not least because extreme weather events such as droughts, heat waves, cold snaps, and wild fires are likely to increase in frequency and intensity (Field 2012; Oven et al. 2012) and welfare state provisions reduce through austerity measures (Sevä 2009). The complexities of daily life and retaining one's original identity within the confines of a disaster that obliterates any semblance of a place called "home," challenges the views of intersectionality as developed by Crenshaw (1989) because even one's geographic location has become fluid and uncertain.

Disabled women of all ages, including those disabled by the disaster, for example, by walking over an unexploded landmine while foraging for food or losing limbs in an earthquake, are discriminated against. Seldom do camp conditions include facilities that meet their specific mobility requirements or provide aid and adaptations to make living in temporary shelters more comfortable. Becoming disabled could also mean that women who had previously been eligible for marriage become less so, because men are less likely to want to marry disabled women and have children with them. Thus, disabled women may find that everyday life activities associated with womanhood will be denied them.

RECEIVING AID

Women are often the last to receive aid, especially as many donors assign this to households rather than individuals. In other situations, cultural norms, for example, women's exclusion from family decision-making structures and ownership of property are replicated by aid donors. In the 2004 tsunami in Sri Lanka, for example, unmarried women who had lost their fathers, brothers or, if married, husbands, could not get aid in their own right, leaving them without the support to which they were officially entitled because cultural norms got in the way. In observing these norms, donors reproduced patriarchal relations that disadvantaged women. Patriarchal relations are also reinforced through many income generation projects aimed at women because these are usually associated with activities that women normally do, for example, embroidering, cooking, washing clothes, looking after children. While this may be respecting local traditions, it does not help those women who wish to branch out into other economic areas. For example, in the Sri Lankan fishing villages affected by the 2004 tsunami, some women who had lost their husbands wanted to take up fishing to retain the family tradition of being a fishing family, but were not given boats by donors because in that part of the world women were forbidden from entering fishing boats because they would "pollute" these and render them useless (Dominelli 2013c). Women's desires for sexual expression, control over their bodily integrity, and economic self-sufficiency are ignored.

At the same time, men who became drunk and beat up women and children out of frustration at losing their livelihoods, often their fishing boats, were not helped to rebuild their lives and learn other skills when they were too frightened to go out to sea again (Dominelli 2013a,b). Thus, men's emotional needs relating to the trauma of their experiences and to reequipping themselves for a different kind of life was ignored by aid donors. By not considering the impact of patriarchy in holding back men and women, donors are depriving them of opportunities that could improve their life circumstances.

WOMEN'S ROLES IN DECISION-MAKING

Enarson and Morrow (1998) highlighted the lack of involvement of women in decision-making processes in humanitarian situations. Dominelli's (2013a,c) findings reaffirmed this exclusion and highlighted the dangers that women aid workers ran not only in increased physical and sexual assaults on them, but in everyday instances of sexual harassment when riding buses, for example. Foreign aid workers were at greater risk than local women. Moreover, those workers who formed relationships with local men could disgrace themselves and their projects when these broke down. Decision-makers seldom concerned themselves with such issues, and women aid workers often accepted this as the price they paid for wanting to help others in distress.

SEE ALSO: Climate Change and Gender; Domestic Violence in the United States; Environment and Gender

REFERENCES

Alston, M., and K. Whittenbury, eds. 2013. *Research, Action and Policy: Addressing the Gendered Impacts of Climate Change*. London: Springer.

Bullard, R. 1994. *Unequal Protection: Environmental Justice and Communities of Color*. San Francisco: Sierra Club Books.

Crenshaw, K. 1989. "Demarginalizing the Intersection of Race and Sex: A Black Feminist Critique of Antidiscrimination Doctrine, Feminist Theory, and Antiracist Politics." *University of Chicago Legal Forum*, 140: 138–167.

Cutter, Susan, et al. 2008. "A Place-Based Model for Understanding Community Resilience to Natural Disasters." *Global Environmental Change*, 18: 598–606.

Dominelli, L. 1991. *Women across Continents: Feminist Comparative Social Policy*. London: Harvester-Wheatsheaf.

Dominelli, L. 2012. *Green Social Work*. Cambridge: Polity Press.

Dominelli, L. 2013a. "Environmental Justice at the Heart of Social Work Practice: Greening the Profession." *International Journal of Social Welfare*, 22(4): 431–439. DOI: 10.1111/ijsw.12024.

Dominelli, L. 2013b. "Gendering Climate Change: Implications for Debates, Policies and Practices." In *Research, Action and Policy: Addressing the Gendered Impacts of Climate Change*, edited by M. Alston and K. Whittenbury, 77–94. London: Springer.

Dominelli, L. 2013c. "Mind the Gap: Built Infrastructures, Sustainable Caring Relations and Resilient Communities in Extreme Weather Events." *Australian Social Work*, 66(2): 204–217. DOI: 10.1080/0312407X.2012.708764.

Douglas, M., and A. B. Wildavsky. 1982. *Risk and Culture: An Essay on the Selection of Technical and Environmental Dangers*. Berkeley: University of California Press.

Enarson, E., and B. Morrow. 1998. *The Gendered Terrain of Disaster: Through Women's Eyes*. Miami: Florida International University.

Field, C., ed. 2012. *Managing the Risks of Extreme Events and Disasters to Advance Climate Change. Special Report of the Intergovernmental Panel on Climate Change, (IPCC)*. Cambridge: Cambridge University Press.

IFRC (International Federation of the Red Cross and Red Crescent Societies). 2009. *Global Disaster Report*. Geneva: IFRC.

Jaeger, M. M. 2006. "What Makes People Support Public Responsibility for Welfare Provision: Self-Interest or Political Ideology? A Longitudinal Approach." *Acta Sociologica*, 49(3): 321–338.

Oven, K., et al. 2012. "Climate Change and Health and Social Care: Defining Future Hazard, Vulnerability and Risk for Infrastructure Systems Supporting Older People's Health Care in England." *Journal of Applied Geography*, 33: 16–24.

Pyles, L. 2007. "Community Organizing for Post-Disaster Social Development: Locating Social Work." *International Social Work*, 50(3): 321–333.

Sevä, I. J. 2009. "Local Contexts, Social Risks and Social Spending Preferences: A Multi-Level Approach." *Acta Sociologica*, 52(3): 249–262.

Wisner, B., P. Blaikie, T. Cannon, and I. Davis. 2004. *At Risk: Natural Hazards, People's Vulnerability, and Disaster*. London: Routledge.

Wollstonecraft, M. 1792. *A Vindication of the Rights of Woman*. Boston: Peter Edes.

Yuval-Davis, N. 2006. "Intersectionality and Feminist Politics." *European Journal of Women's Studies*, 13(3): 193–209.

Yuval-Davis, N., Floya Anthias, and Eleonore Kofman. 2005. "Secure Borders and Safe Haven and the Gendered Politics of Belonging: Beyond Social Cohesion." *Ethnic and Racial Studies*, 28(3): 513–535.

FURTHER READING

Beck, U. 1992. *The Risk Society: Towards a New Modernity*. London: Sage.

Cheong, P. H., R. Edwards, H. Goulbourne, and J. Solomos. 2007. "Immigration, Social Cohesion and Social Capital: A Critical Review." *Critical Social Policy*, 27(1): 24–49.

Manyena, S. B. 2006. "The Concept of Resilience Revisited." *Disasters*, 30(4): 433–450.

Vertovec, S. 2010. "Towards Post-Multiculturalism? Changing Communities, Conditions and Contexts of Diversity." *International Social Science*, 61(199): 83–95.

Environmental Justice

JONI ADAMSON
Arizona State University, USA

The environmental justice (EJ) movement is generally recognized as having originated in the United States in the 1980s. Early organizers redefined the word "environment" to mean the places we "live, work, play, worship, and learn" (Adamson, Evans, and Stein 2002). This more inclusive view of human interaction with the biogeophysical world brought environmental issues "home" and made it clear that discussions of "nature" needed to go beyond common understandings of "wilderness" to address human activities that threaten natural habitats and non-human species.

Today, women around the world are playing a major role in the EJ movement as they work for an "intergenerational justice" that would ensure cleaner, safer homes, communities, playgrounds, gardens, rivers, forests and oceans for their own and succeeding generations (Di Chiro 2013). From Love Canal in New York, to the mouth of the Mississippi River in Louisiana to the Niger Delta in Africa (each places where multiple toxic spills have occurred), female organizers such as Lois Gibbs, Wangari Maathai, Dorceta Taylor, and Winona LaDuke have made it clear that environmental hazards have been inequitably distributed, with poor people and people of color bearing a greater share of the burden than richer people and white people (LaDuke 1999; Krauss 2009; Taylor 2009). Currently, women from around the world are making the often imperceptible, yet material impacts of catastrophic environmental change visible, by calling attention to the ways in which gender discrimination and violence, toxic spills, mountaintop coal removal, and sea level rise are connected to social and environmental inequities that are leading to growing numbers of displaced "environmental refugees" (Adamson 2012; Barry 2012; Di Chiro 2013).

Scholars have created a vast literature of case studies, demographies, and statistics proving that globalization and development are contributing to toxic dumps, abandoned city lots, infrastructure disinvestment, species extinctions, deforestation, erosion, and acidifying oceans (Adamson et al. 2002; Sze 2007; Di Chiro 2013). Engaging in intersectional analysis that focuses on these problems, and which borrows from women's studies, gender studies, ecofeminist studies, critical race studies, ecocriticism and ethnic studies, scholars who focus on environmental justice are concerned not only with public policy, but also with culture, ideology, and representation. They see the expressive arts – novels, films, community gardens, street theater – as effective means through which to offer individuals and communities creative ways to uncover problems that often are connected, such as sexual and gender discrimination, poverty, and environmental degradation in both urban and non-urban places (Stein 2004, 13; Adamson 2012).

The "deep history" of the movement has been traced back to the first indigenous uprising and slave revolts in the colonial world (LaDuke 1999; Adamson et al. 2002) while many of the most successful strategies for contemporary organizing have been borrowed from the abolition, women's suffrage and civil rights movements. A defining moment in movement organization took place in 1991, when over 300 community leaders from the United States, Canada, Central and South America, and the Marshall Islands convened the First National People of Color Environmental Leadership Summit in Washington, DC. Delegates drew up *The 17 Principles of Environmental Justice* which outlines fundamental values and actions that continue to provide a guiding vision for the movement today (Di Chiro 1996).

Both environmental justice analysis and women's and gender studies have revealed the ways that normative discourses surrounding what is "natural" or "unnatural" are written into policies and laws that often disadvantage women, people of color, or the poor. For example, debates about climate change that incorrectly link assumptions about overpopulation to the "fertility" of third world women rather than to overconsumption of resources in the developed world can function to expose certain groups and individuals to environmental injustices and to sexual and gender discrimination (Stein 2004, 6). This illuminates the reasons why discourses surrounding "nature" and what is "natural" must always be analyzed critically (Stein 2004, 6; World People's Conference 2010).

SEE ALSO: Anti-Globalization Movements; Anti-Racist and Civil Rights Movements; Ecofeminism; Environment and Gender; Environmental Disasters and Gender; Environmental Politics and Women's Activism

REFERENCES

Adamson, Joni. 2012. "'Spiky Green Life': Environmental, Food, and Sexual Justice Themes in Sapphire's *PUSH*." In *Sapphire's Literary Breakthrough: Feminist Pedagogies, Erotic Literacies, Environmental Justice Perspectives*, edited by Elizabeth McNeil, Neal Lester, DoVeanna Fulton Minor, and Lynette Myles, 69–88. New York: Palgrave Macmillan.

Adamson, Joni, Mei Mei Evans, and Rachel Stein, eds. 2002. *The Environmental Justice Reader: Politics, Poetics, Pedagogy*. Tucson: University of Arizona Press.

Barry, Joyce M. 2012. *Standing Our Ground: Women, Environmental Justice, and the Fight to End Mountaintop Removal*. Athens, OH: Ohio University Press.

Di Chiro, Giovanna. 1996. "Nature as Community: The Convergence of Environment and Social Justice." In *Uncommon Ground: Rethinking the Human Place in Nature*, edited by William Cronon, 298–320. New York: Norton.

Di Chiro, Giovanna. 2013. "Climate Justice Now! Imagining Grassroots EcoCosmopolitanism." In *American Studies, Ecocriticism, and Citizenship*, edited by Joni Adamson and Kimberly N. Ruffin. New York: Routledge.

Krauss, Celene. 2009. "Mothering at the Crossroads: African American Women and the Emergence of the Movement against Environmental Racism." In *Environmental Justice in the New Millennium: Global Perspectives on Race, Ethnicity, and Human Rights*, edited by Filomina Chioma Steady, 65–89. New York: Palgrave Macmillan.

LaDuke, Winona. 1999. *All Our Relations: Native Struggles for Land and Life*. Cambridge, MA: South End Press.

Stein, Rachel. ed. 2004. *New Perspectives on Environmental Justice: Gender, Sexuality and Activism*. New Brunswick: Rutgers University Press.

Sze, Julie. 2007. *Noxious New York: The Racial Politics of Urban Health and Environmental Justice*. Cambridge, MA: MIT Press.

Taylor, Dorceta. 2009. *The Environment and the People in American Cities, 1600s–1900s*. Durham, NC: Duke University Press.

World People's Conference on Climate Change and the Rights of Mother Earth, 2010. Accessed August 28, 2015, at: http://pwccc.wordpress.com/support/.

FURTHER READING

McGurty, Eileen. 2009. *Transforming Environmentalism: Warren County, PCBs, and the Origins of Environmental Justice*. New Brunswick: Rutgers University Press.

Morello-Frosch, Rachel, and Edmond D. Shenassa. 2006. "The Environmental 'Riskscape' and Social Inequality: Implications for Explaining Maternal and Child Health Disparities." *Environmental Health Perspectives*, 114(8): 1150–1153.

Pellow, David, and Robert Brulle, eds. 2005. *Power, Justice, and the Environment: A Critical Appraisal of the Environmental Justice Movement*. Cambridge, MA: MIT Press.

Environmental Politics and Women's Activism

EMILY HUDDART KENNEDY
Washington State University, USA

Women's role in politics and how this shapes environmental outcomes are a promising emergent area of scholarship. A small but empirically rigorous area of research demonstrates that the number of women who serve as elected representatives in national politics is positively associated with the number of pro-environmental policies put forward by a government. That is, countries with more equitable gender representation in parliament or congress have lower levels of environmental impact, per capita (Ergas and York 2012). Further evidence of this phenomenon includes the relationship between female political representation and the percentage of environmental treaties that are ratified (Norgaard and York 2005) and the extent to which protected ecosystems are safeguarded (Nugent and Shandra 2009). Explanations for the mechanisms that link gender, political representation, and environmental protection are in their infancy.

These initial observations, combined with evidence from the literature on gender and environmental justice, suggest that women play an important role in public-sphere efforts to protect human and non-human environments. However, a contradictory body of research and subsequent empirical study merits discussion.

Paul Mohai (1992) noted a surprising finding in his research on environmental concern and public-sphere environmentalism. To clarify, when scholars refer to public-sphere environmentalism, some of the activities they use to operationalize the term include writing to newspapers or public officials, donating money to an environmental organization, and being a member of an environmental organization. For decades, survey research has demonstrated that women show more environmental concern than men (Ozanne et al. 1999). Yet Mohai observed a paradox: although women show more environmental concern, they were less likely to be active members of environmental organizations or participants in environmental public discourse.

Thus a key question concerning women's involvement in the public dimensions of environmentalism is, "If women are more concerned about the environment, why don't they engage in more public-sphere activities?" Two points worthy of mention are that environmental organizations with the greatest membership are hunting and fishing groups (Bosso 2005). Given the gendered nature of these activities, it should come as little surprise that men are more likely to be members than women; women are more likely to be members of environmental justice organizations (discussed below). Second, measuring public-sphere involvement without making reference to efforts such as campaigning for a candidate based on his or her environmental platform and networking in support of environmental issues overlooks the work necessary to hold public-sphere events such as protests (O'Shaughnessy and Kennedy 2010).

A final emergent line of inquiry takes issue with the pressure placed on women to protect the environment in private and public spheres. As MacGregor (2007) points out, women already shoulder a much greater burden to adopt and sustain efforts in the household but are still taken to task for not being more active in the public sphere. Thus, as ecofeminists have long argued, scholars in this area argue for gender equity as a necessary prerequisite to sustainability, arguing that a society that has not negotiated a fair division of responsibility for work within and outside the workplace will be unable to achieve economic, social, or environmental sustainability (Plumwood 1993). Discrepancies between men and women often emerge in empirical research when the focus is on who is spearheading efforts to protect communities and resist polluters (Taylor 2002; Verchick 2004; Bell and Braun 2010; Perkins 2012). In fact, Di Chiro (1992, 109) estimates that women compose 90 percent of active environmental justice organizations in the United States. This gendered composition is unlike any other arm of the environmental movement (Taylor 2002). Thus a key question asked by scholars of environmental justice is, "Why do women become engaged in environmental justice at higher rates than men?"

Explanations for women's disproportionate participation in environmental justice movements enjoyed nearly a decade of consensus before empirical challenges opened up new lines of inquiry. Since the late 1990s, scholars tended to agree that women become involved as mothers concerned about the health of their families (Verchick 2004). Popularized in media stories and films describing the lives of prominent American women such as Erin Brockovich and Lois Gibbs, the irate mother fearlessly campaigning against corporate indifference to the health of low-income communities is a fashionable topos. However, recently evidence suggests that the "motherhood-as-gateway-to-activism" explanation fails to account for many women's pathways into environmental justice (Perkins 2012).

Certainly, being a mother has been demonstrated to be a powerful driver of engagement in environmental justice, a relationship explained by the historical delegation of the responsibility for childcare and family health to women (Krauss 1993; Sze 2004). Yet scholars warn us to avoid essentializing women's connection to the environment as mediated by motherhood: what about mothers motivated by other concerns? What about women without children who become involved in environmental justice? Would we explain male participation through the lens of fatherhood? Future research could engage questions that take a broader perspective of women's engagement in environmental justice and apply the same standard of inquiry to gender that has been developed to identify disproportionate toxic burdens by race and class.

Women are also more active in household pro-environmental behavior (PEB). PEB refers to behavior undertaken with the intention of maintaining or enhancing environmental health (Stern 2000) and scholars differentiate between private-sphere (or household) PEB and public-sphere PEB. Public-sphere PEB was described in the discussion of environmental justice and environmental politics; the focus here is on the household sphere.

Household PEB includes activities such as using environmentally friendly cleaning products, hanging laundry to dry, growing food, turning down the thermostat, taking shorter showers, and using public transit to avoid driving. Surveys from different national contexts affirm that women engage in these activities with greater frequency than do men (Hunter et al. 2004; Xiao and McCright 2015).

Within sociology and social psychology, scholars use survey data to theorize the relationship between values, attitudes, and household PEB while controlling on sociodemographic variables including gender (Zelezny et al. 2000). Key research questions include, "Who engages in household PEB?" and "What is the relationship among values, attitudes, and household PEB?" Thus, the gendered nature of participation in household PEB is not treated as the outcome of interest; rather, gender is treated as one of several other factors influencing whether or not one engages in household PEB.

In the environmental social science community, household PEB is seen as a category of behavior we ought to encourage as a society. For instance, Dietz (2015, 1) calls for research that seeks to understand why households are not adopting "simple and money-saving" activities that could protect the environment. However, from a gendered perspective, it is important to keep in mind the view that household PEB may add to the list of chores already shouldered by women. In the vast literature on the gendered nature of household labor, scholars note some promising trends in gender equity – women are increasingly likely to work outside the home and family decision-making is also shared more equitably (Belch and Willis 2002). However, the recent emphasis on protecting the environment through our household routines may be exacerbating the already inequitable division of domestic labor (Oates and McDonald 2006).

Investigation at the nexus of social research on the environment and gender studies is growing in importance and popularity. Simultaneous and converging socioecological trends are implicated in the much-warranted upsurge of interest in the relationship between gender and the environment – in particular between women and the environment. The threat of climate change and related impacts on fuel prices and food and water security is associated with increased pressure from grassroots organizations and community resistance efforts, and women have historically played an important role in voluntary and civic associations (Naples 1998; Taylor 2002). Moreover, as the state retreats from the work of upholding the "common good," more is expected from the private sphere to advance social and environmental justice. Again, women's participation in household efforts to reduce environmental impact tends to be greater than men's (Hunter et al. 2004). Emerging from these and related trends are potential concerns for gender equity and sustainability and the relationship between the two (MacGregor 2007).

SEE ALSO: Ecofeminism; Environment and Gender; Environmental Disasters and Gender; Environmental Justice; Women's Political Representation

REFERENCES

Belch, Michael A., and Laura A. Willis. 2002. "Family Decision at the Turn of the Century: Has the Changing Structure of Households Impacted the Family Decision-Making Process?" *Journal of Consumer Behavior*, 2(2): 111–124.

Bell, Shannon E., and Yvonne A. Braun. 2010. "Coal, Identity, and the Gendering of Environmental Justice Activism in Central Appalachia." *Gender & Society*, 24(6): 794–813.

Bosso, Christopher J. 2005. *Environment, Inc.: From Grassroots to Beltway*. Wichita: University of Kansas Press.

Di Chiro, Giovanna. 1992. "Defining Environmental Justice: Women's Voices and Grassroots Politics." *Socialist Review*, 22(4): 93–130.

Dietz, Thomas. 2015. "Altruism, Self-Interest, and Energy Consumption." *Proceedings of the National Academy of Sciences of the United States of America*, 112(6): 1654–1655.

Ergas, Christina, and Richard York. 2012. "Women's Status and Carbon Dioxide Emissions: A Quantitative Cross-national Analysis." *Social Science Research*, 41(4): 965–976.

Hunter, Lori M., Alison Hatch, and Aaron Johnson. 2004. "Cross-National Gender Variation in Environmental Behaviors." *Social Science Quarterly*, 85(3): 677–694.

Krauss, Celene. 1993. "Women and Toxic Waste Protests: Race, Class and Gender as Resources of Resistance." *Qualitative Sociology*, 16: 247–262.

MacGregor, Sherilyn. 2007. "No Sustainability Without Justice: A Feminist Critique of Environmental Citizenship." Presented at the PSA Conference, April 2007, Bath, UK.

Mohai, Paul. 1992. "Men, Women, and the Environment: An Examination of the Gender Gap in Environmental Concern and Activism." *Society and Natural Resources*, 5: 1–19.

Naples, Nancy. 1998. *Grassroots Warriors: Activist Mothering, Community Work, and the War on Poverty*. New York: Routledge.

Norgaard, Kari, and Richard York. 2005. "Gender Equality and State Environmentalism." *Gender & Society*, 19(4): 506–522.

Nugent, Colleen, and John M. Shandra. 2009. "State Environmental Protection Efforts, Women's Status, and World Polity: A Cross-national Analysis." *Organization & Environment*, 22(2): 208–229.

Oates, Caroline J., and Seanaidh McDonald. 2006. "Recycling and the Domestic Division of Labour: Is Green Pink or Blue?" *Sociology*, 40(3): 417–433.

O'Shaughnessy, Sara, and Emily H. Kennedy. 2010. "Relational Activism: Re-imagining Women's Environmental Work as Cultural Change." *Canadian Journal of Sociology*, 35(4): 551–572.

Ozanne, Lucie K., Craig R. Humphrey, and Paul M. Smith. 1999. "Gender, Environmentalism, and Interest in Forest Certification: Mohai's Paradox Revisited." *Society & Natural Resources*, 12(6): 613–622.

Perkins, Tracy E. 2012. "Women's Pathways into Activism: Rethinking the Women's Environmental Justice Narrative in California's San Joaquin Valley." *Organization & Environment*, 25(1): 76–94.

Plumwood, Val. 1993. *Feminism and the Mastery of Nature*. London: Routledge.

Stern, Paul C. 2000. "Toward a Coherent Theory of Environmentally Significant Behavior." *Journal of Social Issues*, 56(3): 407–424.

Sze, Julie. 2004. "Gender, Asthma Politics, and Urban Environmental Justice Activism." In *New Perspectives on Environmental Justice: Gender, Sexuality, and Activism*, edited by Rachel Stein, 177–190. New Brunswick: Rutgers University Press.

Taylor, Dorceta E. 2002. *Race, Class, Gender, and American Environmentalism*. General Technical Report PNW-GTR-534. Portland: United States Department of Agriculture, Forest Service, Pacific Northwest Research Station. Accessed September 13, 2015, at www.fs.fed.us/pnw/pubs/gtr534.pdf.

Verchick, Robert. 2004. "Feminist Theory and Environmental Justice." In *New Perspectives on Environmental Justice: Gender, Sexuality, and Activism*, edited by Rachel Stein, 63–77. New Brunswick: Rutgers University Press.

Xiao, Chenyang, and Aaron M. McCright. 2015. "Gender Differences in Environmental Concern: Revisiting the Institutional Trust Hypothesis in the USA." *Environment and Behavior*, 47(1): 17–37.

Zelezny, Lynnette C., Poh-Pheng Chua, and Christina Aldrich. 2000. "Elaborating on Gender Differences in Environmentalism." *Journal of Social Issues*, 56(3): 443–457.

Epistemology of the Closet

LUCY E. BAILEY
Oklahoma State University, USA

The concept, epistemology of the closet, is the focus of a text by the same name that English Professor Eve Kosofsky Sedgwick (1950–2009) published with the University of California Press in 1990 and updated in 2008. The text is a pioneering work in the development of queer theory as a field of analysis. Sedgwick's central argument is that contemporary systems of thought and knowledge are deeply and centrally structured – but often invisibly so – by particular and relational definitions of "homo/heterosexual." Sedgwick insisted that an anti-homophobic stance and theoretical lenses from contemporary gay male thought must inform any study of Western politics and culture. Sedgwick developed her ambitious analysis during the political and health crisis of the 1980s in which gay people faced significant social stigma, anti-sodomy laws, and the devastating effects of HIV/AIDS. While her arguments bear the imprint of that historical context, and the field of queer theory has expanded since that time, Sedgwick's critical tools have enduring salience for resisting forms of gay oppression and tracing relations between sexuality and knowledge.

Sedgwick's phrase, "the epistemology of the closet," refers to the centrality of the modern category of "homo/heterosexuality" to systems of Western thought and culture. She signals this (variously visible and invisible) structuring through the metaphor of "the closet," which has historically represented an oppressive space for gay subjects. The "closet" is a multidimensional concept that functions in particular ways. It is a metaphor for the oppressive ways in which gays have been forced to hide their sense of self and relationships – a site in which they are variously hidden and silenced – and it is also the place through which they come to be "known" and revealed. The closet reinforces concepts of insider/outsider and us/them and hides hybridity and nuance. Key to understanding Sedgwick's argument about the function of the closet is her premise, like Foucault's, that "knowledge" and "sexuality" are intertwined, and presumptions of ignorance tied to the closet regulate human relations in varied ways.

The modern definition of homo/heterosexual is foundational not only to understanding the daily oppression facing gay people but to structuring a range of other binary and relational elements of Western culture such as secrecy/disclosure, natural/artificial, and knowledge/ignorance that shape the very way we think about the world. The late nineteenth-century shift from understanding same-sex sexuality in terms of behavior, or acts, to conceptualizing it as a category of identity, even a species of people called the Homosexual (and significantly, by extension, the Heterosexual), has been central to the formulation of the epistemology of the closet. Sedgwick conceptualizes the categories of the "homosexual" and "heterosexual" as fundamentally related and argues that the "heterosexual" can only "know" and recognize her/himself through the "open secret" of the closet where the "homosexual" resides. The notion of the closet enables "heteronormativity," the set of structural practices that reflect the premise that "heterosexual" is a stable, unquestioned, and legitimate identity and that sexual relations between members of the opposite sex are the only normal and acceptable expression of sexuality.

The epistemology of the closet stretched theories of sexuality and gender at the time in multidimensional ways. Like the work of Judith Butler, and Gayle Rubin, Sedgwick's analysis advanced the productive uncoupling of sex, sexuality, and gender to serve anti-homophobic scholarship and politics. Turning away from feminist analyses common to studying sexuality, Sedgwick viewed their gendered focus and analytic tools inadequate to charting the nuances of sexuality that exceed gender. While the modern concept of homosexuality does rely on a concept of gender in that same-sex relations are a key difference that signals "homosexuality," Sedgwick insists that the concepts of gender and sexuality, like race and class, are intersecting but not "coextensive." Scholars cannot assume a priori how gender will factor in to analysis of sexuality or how the concerns of lesbians and gay subjects will intersect. Through her analysis of the closet, Sedgwick separates concepts that are often conflated, centers sexuality as a particular and imperative site of analysis, and considers the project of "anti-homophobic inquiry" as unique from other justice-oriented inquiries.

To trace how the epistemology of the closet is enacted, Sedgwick analyzes a variety of classic nineteenth- and twentieth-century texts by Herman Melville, Oscar Wilde, Henry James, and others, to demonstrate diverse male relationships and persistent investments in identifying a heterosexual or homosexual person at work in the texts, and, more broadly, the social and political relations of power they signal. Key to her work is that conceptions of homosexuality are historically constructed and situated and that political interventions must be particular and strategic.

FUTURE DIRECTIONS

The "epistemology of the closet" that Sedgwick detailed in 1990 synthesized complex strands of thought to conceptualize sexuality in new ways and to trace its presence in areas ostensibly unrelated to sexuality. Although Sedgwick herself refused to consider her work in terms of its longevity or generalizability (1990, 12), her analysis spurred a subsequent wave of anti-homophobic analyses in gay and lesbian studies and offered tools for rendering sexuality both visible and central in thought and constructions of knowledge. The concept of the closet reveals the ideological investments in constructing knowledge, the embodied effects of such constructions on real lives, as well as the importance of mobilizing a "*practical* politics" (Sedgwick 1990, 13, emphasis in original) to confront injustice. Sedgwick's concept remains foundational to the field of queer theory even as contemporary analyses of sexuality, transgender issues, and other LGBTQ issues follow new directions. New closets surface with new meanings and implications, and people still enter and exit them as circumstances demand.

Some scholars were critical of the broad sweep of Sedgwick's conceptual claims and postmodern investments rooted in literary analyses that did not attend to empirical studies of sexuality. Others were critical of her choice to exclude lesbians from initial conceptions of the closet, and to distance feminism and gender from an integral role in anti-homophobic projects and conceptions of sexuality. Because her analysis springs from the figure of the gay male, and she does not explore the ways other analytics such as race might be central to the closet, some have revisited these points as sites of departure for their own investigations, considering her arguments in racial, geographic, or feminist terms. Spatial and cross-cultural analyses of the concept of the closet point out its limits for capturing expressions of sexuality in different cultural contexts. The concept remains generative even as scholars point out its limitations.

SEE ALSO: Queer Theory; Sexual Minorities

REFERENCE

Sedgwick, Eve K. 1990. *Epistemology of the Closet*. Berkeley: University of California Press.

FURTHER READING

O'Rourke, Michael, ed. forthcoming. *Reading Eve Kosofsky Sedgwick: Gender, Sexuality, Embodiment*. London: Palgrave.

Essentialism

ALISON STONE
The University of Lancaster, UK

Essentialism was the subject of heated feminist debate from the 1970s into the 1990s, continuing today. Feminists have often criticized other feminists for being "essentialist"; those criticized have responded sometimes by denying that they are "essentialist" and sometimes by defending "essentialism." Identifying central themes in these debates is difficult because the notion of essentialism has taken on a plurality of meanings. But the main things for which feminists criticize one another under the heading of "essentialism" are: (1) making biological determinist claims, that is, claiming that women's (or men's) biology gives rise to their social positions, values, or ways of acting; (2) making universal claims about all women which actually only apply to some women; (3) making any claim that certain experiences, situations, or concerns are common to all women; and (4) assuming that the word "woman" has one single meaning.

These meanings have an underlying unity that lends coherence to these debates. The meanings of "essentialism" radiate out from traditional philosophical essentialism: the belief that things have "essential" as well as "accidental" properties. Essential properties are properties that objects must necessarily have in order to belong to a particular kind. For example, for metal to be gold it must have atomic number 79; without that it cannot belong to the kind gold.

Transposed into feminist contexts, essentialism becomes the view that there are properties that are essential to women, in that any woman must necessarily have those properties to be a woman at all. So defined, essentialism entails a closely related view, *universalism*: that there are some properties shared by, or common to, all women – since without those properties they could not be women in the first place. "Essentialism" as debated in feminist circles often embraces this composite view: that there are properties essential to women and which all women (therefore) share. This definition leaves open that one might be an essentialist *and* think that the properties essential to all women are socially constructed. Thus, although "essentialism" is often equated with "biological determinism," in fact biological essentialism is only one possible form of essentialism.

Before second-wave feminists disseminated the sex/gender distinction, a biological version of essentialism was part of common sense, according to which women are women in virtue of their biological features and capacity for bearing children. Some radical feminists have also claimed that women are constituted as women by their biological features and by distinctive values and attitudes that result from their biology, e.g., a tendency to create caring, non-hierarchical relationships. In that context, socialist feminists began to criticize radical feminists for being "essentialist," instead defending social constructionism: the view that feminine roles and identity are shaped by social structures and norms, not biology. Despite rejecting biological essentialism, many influential feminist theorists of the 1980s, such as Catharine MacKinnon, went on to endorse non-biological forms of essentialism: thus for MacKinnon, to be a woman is just to be socially constructed as a sexual object, subordinate to men as sexual subjects.

In the later 1980s, many feminist thinkers (and classically Spelman 1988) criticized the essentialism of MacKinnon and others. These critics, amongst them many black women and women of color, argued, first, that universal claims about women's social position or identity are invariably false. There are no common experiences, social positions, or sense of psychological identity that are common to all women, because norms of femininity are fundamentally different in different societies and groups.

Second, anti-essentialists argued that claims that women share common experiences or social positions are politically problematic. Since there is no real unity to women's situation, (falsely) universalist claims about women always position *specific* groups of women as the norm. The experiences of socially privileged groups of women – white, middle-class, heterosexual, able-bodied women – become normalized in this way. Because these women suffer only from their gender and not also from other intersecting forms of oppression, these women's experiences are taken to exemplify the oppression that women suffer *just as women*. Other women then become marginalized within feminist practice and theory.

The growing rejection of essentialism prompted a counter-tendency – "anti-anti-essentialism" – emphasizing the political need for essentialism. The problem was that anti-essentialism seemed to have "cast doubt on the project of conceptualizing women as a group" (Young 1994, 713). By denying that women have shared features, anti-essentialism seemed to make it impossible to say that women are a social group united by a distinctive form of oppression, gender oppression. This in turn seemed to undermine feminist politics: if women do not share any common form of social oppression, then they cannot be expected to mobilize around any shared opposition to a common plight or any shared political identity or allegiance. Thus anti-essentialism seemed to undermine feminism both as social critique and as a political movement for social change.

These considerations have led a range of further positions to emerge. One is "strategic essentialism," the defense of essentialism as a political strategy: women may not really share any common features, but we still need a politics that acts and speaks as if women had a unity, to make collective action possible. Another response, from Iris Marion Young (1994), is that women are not a unified group but a "series": their lives are structured by the same set of material objects and realities – a common set of gender rules and codes – but women take these up in vastly different contexts and experience the same material structures quite differently. Stone (2004) objects that Young's is still ultimately an essentialist position, arguing instead that women have a "genealogy." Debate continues, but the plurality of feminist approaches to essentialism is now widely accepted.

SEE ALSO: Biological Determinism; Gender, Definitions of; Strategic Essentialism

REFERENCES

Spelman, V. Elizabeth. 1988. *Inessential Woman: Problems of Exclusion in Feminist Theory*. London: The Women's Press.

Stone, Alison. 2004. "Essentialism and Anti-Essentialism in Feminist Philosophy." *Journal of Moral Philosophy*, 1(2): 135–153. DOI: 10.1177/174046810400100202.

Young, Iris Marion. 1994. "Gender as Seriality: Thinking about Women as a Social Collective." *Signs*, 19(3): 713–38. DOI: 10.1086/494918.

Ethic of Care

JO BRIDGEMAN
Sussex Law School, University of Sussex, UK

The ethic of care responds to dominant norms of the Western liberal tradition, challenging the construction of the subject as separate, individualistic, autonomous, and self-interested and the employment of abstract universal principles to resolve conflict, dilemmas, and problems. The ethic of care offers a theoretical framework, an analytical tool, and a focus upon caring practices.

Sometimes categorized as an example of cultural feminism, the origins of the ethic of care are located by some in male and female identity development or Sara Ruddick's *Maternal Thinking* (Ruddick 1983). Hugely influential to contemporary concepts of the ethic of care is Carol Gilligan's *In a Different Voice* (Gilligan 1982) in which she identified a different voice to that of studies of moral development carried out by her supervisor, Lawrence Kohlberg, in which women had been held to be less developed morally than were men. In Kohlberg's view, moral maturity involved the prioritization of competing, abstract, universal, principles through an adversarial battle. Gilligan's research identified three stages of moral development in which the activity of caring and maintenance of relationships were central and in which both responsibilities to others and individual rights were protected. Identification of this different voice – a voice of connection, care, and response – alongside that of equality, fairness, and rights – suggested the transformative potential of responsibility and care toward oneself and required the integration of care and justice. Importantly, this different voice is not an alternative to the ethic of justice; justice and care need to be integrated (Gilligan 1982, 100). There is no justice without care; no care without justice.

The key features of an ethic of care are as follows. First, rather than understanding persons to be primarily separate, self-interested, rational individuals whose principal concern is to protect themselves from invasion by others but who form relations by agreement and resolve conflict through the application of abstract, universal principles, feminist theories of care and responsibility understand individuals to be primarily connected through relationships and concerned with maintaining relationships with others. It conceives of the relational self whose interests are inevitably tied to those of others. Second, dependency and vulnerability are acknowledged as universal experiences from which arise needs that have to be met through dependency work (Kittay 1999). Third, the relational self takes responsibility for meeting the needs of others who are dependent upon them; responsibility for others arises out of relationships rather than being imposed by another's rights or by the state. Fourth, an ethic of care approach highlights the importance of emotion and context in working out what we ought to do, rather than the abstract implementation of universal rules.

From an appreciation that care is important in human life but often disguised, ignored, or unappreciated, feminists have explored different aspects of care. Joan Tronto identifies within the practice of caring the stages of caring about, taking care of, care giving, and receiving care (Tronto 1993, 105–107). Care has been identified as requiring an attitude, or mental disposition, accompanying the physical labor of care so that both "love and labor" are required. Feminists have emphasized that recognition of the importance of care in the lives of all is to acknowledge the practices, the resources, and the emotions in caring relationships challenging idealistic portrayals of caring as altruistic or selfless acts.

One critique of Gilligan's work is that her ethic of care perspective is essentialist, that the care perspective is aligned with a distinctly female voice arising from empirical studies with women, who had previously been excluded. The argument is that to focus upon a caring ethic or caring activity is to perpetuate and enhance a connection between women and care, valorizing women's caring role, further entrenching women in caring positions and reinforcing women's oppression and subordination to men. Catharine MacKinnon, for example, has argued that the ethic of care is the "articulat[ion] of the feminine" and may encourage "women [to] identify... with what is a positively valued feminine stereotype," in other words, that women use the language of care because that is the only activity for which they are valued within society. Although this criticism is valid for some accounts, such as the material connection employed by Robin West (West 1988), Carol Gilligan herself states that she was seeking to identify a contrasting approach and not to make an observation about the sexes (Gilligan 1982, 2), that the care perspective is not biologically determined nor unique to women, and that most people reason in both terms. And although it remains true that women perform more of the caring work, to recognize caring is not to perpetuate this but to demand recognition of care as an essential part of life and to secure value for caring and the providers of care.

The principles of care ethics have been employed, beyond psychology, in a wide range of disciplines, including sociology, philosophy, political theory, international relations, social policy, and law. Within this work, the principles have been applied to a wide range of subject matters, both private and public, from legal process, family law, and policy, the care of children post-separation, healthcare, care work, work and family life, social welfare, migration and care, to citizenship.

Others have sought to respond to critiques of individualism and abstraction inherent within liberal approaches through the development of the concepts of relational autonomy and relational rights, both of which recognize the situated nature of the self and the importance of context to the exercise of autonomy or fulfillment of rights; or they have argued for a focus upon vulnerability in order to challenge the dominant view of the autonomous, rational, legal, and economic actor, and a different perspective from which to develop responses to social and legal problems.

SEE ALSO: Biological Determinism; Emotion Work; Essentialism; Feminism, Cultural; Masculinity and Femininity, Theories of

REFERENCES

Gilligan, Carol. 1982. *In a Different Voice: Psychological Theory and Women's Development.* Cambridge, MA: Harvard University Press. Reprinted with new preface in 1993.

Kittay, Eva Feder. 1999. *Love's Labor: Essays on Women, Equality and Dependency.* New York: Routledge.

Ruddick, Sara. 1984. "Maternal Thinking." In *Mothering*, edited by Joyce Trebilcot, 213–230. Totowa: Rowman & Allanheld.

Tronto, Joan. 1993. *Moral Boundaries: The Political Argument for an Ethic of Care.* New York: Routledge.

West, Robin. 1988. "Jurisprudence and Gender." *University of Chicago Law Review*, 55(1): 1–72.

Ethics, Moral Development, and Gender

MARY BRABECK and SARA FRY
New York University, USA

Over the centuries moral philosophers, biologists, and social science researchers have focused on the concept of gender differences, and in particular gender differences in morality. From Plato and Aristotle, through Freud and Erikson, men have been characterized as having a rational, justice-based moral perspective, and women as possessing an emotional, intuitive morality. The latter has been considered inferior.

Recently feminist ethicists have identified five themes (Brabeck 2000) derived from feminist theory that form a corrective to the dominant male philosophical traditions. Furthermore, feminist social scientists have examined the empirical evidence for the claims that women are more intuitive, empathetic, and caring, and the assumption that men are more deliberate, judicial, and rational in their moral choices. This entry reviews the claims of feminist ethicists and the empirical findings of social science regarding gender differences in morality.

Ethics is the philosophical branch concerned with how people ought to act, what principles should guide behavior, and how people should live together. Ethical principles are used as professional guidelines to guide professionals and aid them in making ethical judgments. Most professional schools recognize the importance of ethics instruction in professional education and often training in ethics is an explicit requirement for program accreditation and professional licensure. Research on the development of professional ethics and the ethical practice of professionals is burgeoning.

The phrase "feminist ethics" was first used in the late 1970s. It is the effort to revise the dominant Western ethical theories that often devalue or ignore women's moral experiences and the ethical qualities associated with women. Feminist ethicists and social scientists use feminist ethical theory as a unique lens for determining what one ought to do and deciding a course of action in the face of competing ethical claims.

There are five overarching themes that form the basis for feminist ethics. First is the assumption that women and their experiences have moral significance. While that may seem self-evident, over the millennia philosophers and social scientists have labeled women's morality as immature and less rational than males'. Western philosophers and theologians (Plato, Aristotle, Augustine, through Descartes and Kant), psychologists (Freud, Erikson), and sociologists (Talcott Parsons) have deemed women morally inferior to men. The experience of the "weaker sex" throughout history has been ignored as not pertinent to moral questions, and traits culturally associated with men (e.g., independence, autonomy, individuality) and male experiences (e.g., war and work) have been privileged over female traits (e.g., empathy, sympathy, connection) and experiences (e.g., mothering and caregiving). However, feminists claim that what is called "women's work" is important in the moral formation of all people. Feminist theorists have redefined what it means to be human by drawing on the theory and research that indicates seeking and forming relationships, being empathic, connected to others, and forming communities are all essential aspects of what it means to be human for both men and women.

The second theme of feminist ethics is the assertion that subjective knowledge can illuminate moral issues. Most moral theory from Plato to Rawls has assumed that rational, objective thought is what elevates humans over all other forms of life. But feminists have argued that intuition, and ideas derived from feelings and subjectivity, are also legitimate ways of knowing.

The idea that feelings rather than rationality alone can lead to moral impulses was proposed by David Hume in the eighteenth century. Feminist theorists (e.g., Baier 1994) likewise claim that ethical responses are guided by subjectivity, not reason alone. The emphasis on sentiments and feelings reveals our existence as interdependent and embedded in particular relationships, cultures, and communities. Recognizing that this embodied state is an aspect of all human experience requires attentiveness to the particular, concrete, and unique experiences of persons, rather than universal ideal principles that are uniformly applied. Recognizing that each person's subjectivity is unique requires empathy along with reason, and caring relationships along with arguments for universal rights and justice. Moral adequacy reformulated by feminist ethics requires paying loving attention to the particularities of an individual's and community's concrete experiences.

The third theme of feminist ethics is that a critique of male distortions of women must be accompanied by a critique of all discriminatory distortions, including racism, homophobia, classism, and other dehumanizing misrepresentations. Social change must be an emancipatory movement not just for women, but for all people, especially the marginalized and disenfranchised. In this way, feminist ethics joins multicultural ethics and other efforts to achieve social justice. Both feminist and multicultural ethics subscribe to a liberational ethic, concerned with liberating all oppressed persons.

The fourth theme of feminist ethics is that people are morally compelled to engage in analysis of the context and attend to the power dynamics of that context. Feminist ethics require attending to the way that power distorts all human endeavors, including feminists'. Drawing from postmodernist theory, feminists interrogate the inherent power hierarchies that affect what we accept as "knowledge," especially gendered knowledge. For feminists, how power affects claims regarding ethics or truth includes interrogation of how one's own situation of power and privilege affect one's own ethical stance.

Finally, feminist ethics require feminists to engage in action directed at achieving social justice. This mandate makes feminist ethics both an explicitly political activity and a humanitarian one. While the well-being of women is the starting place, the good of all is the aim of feminist ethics. Building on the work of social psychologist Kurt Lewin and Brazilian educator Paulo Freire, feminists engage in reflection, knowledge generation, and community development efforts that strive to bring about more just and equitable life conditions in communities and achieve social justice for all. The five themes of feminist ethics describe a more complete view of human ethical capacity.

While ethical theory is the study of what "ought" to be, social science is the study of "what is." Kohlberg's developmental-cognitive approach to moral development has dominated the field of moral psychology. He researched moral reasoning, or the psychological process of deciding what is the right thing to do, using the Moral Judgment Interview (MJI). Kohlberg's theory of moral reasoning is comprised of six moral stages, beginning with the morality of obedience or fear of punishment (Stage 1), instrumental egoism or reciprocal thinking (Stage 2), interpersonal concordance or the desire to be approved as a moral person (Stage 3), conformance to law and order or duty to the societal rules (Stage 4), consensus building or social contract reasoning (Stage 5), and principled justice reasoning (Stage 6).

Some of Kohlberg's early work claimed that boys were more likely to be at Stage 4 and girls at Stage 3. And some research found men more likely to reach the highest stage than women. Since the stages are considered hierarchical, this is tantamount to claiming that boys and men are more moral than girls and women.

Carol Gilligan challenged Kohlberg's claims to gender differences. In interviews, she asked boys and girls, men and women, at different ages, to identify a moral dilemma they faced and describe what they decided to do and why. Through these interviews she identified the "feminine voice" as an alternative moral perspective. Gilligan and other feminist social scientists examined the experiences of girls and women caring for and protecting others. According to these relational feminists, women's "moral self" is based on human connections and relationships and a woman's moral voice reflects an "ethic of care."

Gilligan claimed women have a care orientation and men a justice orientation. However, the empirical evidence for differences in morality between boys and girls, men and women is complex. In part, this complexity results from the fact that morality is not a single dimension or unitary construct. Just as there are multiple principles in ethics, there are multiple psychological processes that are involved in morality.

In 1994, James Rest organized what was known about the psychology of morality into four separate components, each of which engage different psychological processes and together produce moral behavior. The four-component model (Rest and Narvaez 1994) reflects not only cognitive developmental models of morality, such as Kohlberg's, but also social learning theory, behavioral views, and psychodynamic approaches. Rest's four-component model is useful in examining the question of whether there are gender differences in morality. The components are: (1) Moral Sensitivity – interpreting the ethical factors of a situation; (2) Moral Judgment – reasoning about which action is morally right/wrong and justifying moral choices; (3) Moral Motivation – prioritizing moral values over other values such as personal gain; and (4) Moral Character – having moral character and the skills to implement a moral decision and behave morally.

Rest's first component, Moral Sensitivity, involves imagining potential scenarios regarding the consequences a course of action might have, empathy, and role-taking skills. Some psychologists have suggested that the care and justice orientations that Gilligan described are related to Rest's idea of ethical sensitivity. Researchers have found that the use of a care ethic versus the ethic of justice depends on the type of moral dilemma. When issues involve relationships or responsibilities to people, both boys and girls invoke a care orientation. For issues that involve adjudicating rights and conflicting claims, both invoke a justice orientation.

Bebeau (2014) has extensively studied the development of ethical sensitivity in dental students and dentists using the Dental Ethical Sensitivity Test (DEST). Research shows that ethical sensitivity is distinct from moral reasoning and it can be taught. Recent meta-analytic studies (Bebeau and Brabeck 1987; You, Maeda, and Bebeau 2011) have found small but significant gender differences with women scoring higher in ethical sensitivity. These findings could not be attributed to differences in measures of ethical sensitivity or education of participants. However, while women display greater sensitivity to ethical issues than their male colleagues, differences were not related to the proclivity for women to use a care ethic or men to use a justice orientation.

Moral Judgment is the second component in Rest's four-component model. Once a person is aware of the ethical issues in a situation, one must reason about what is morally justifiable. Moral reasoning is the ability to identify what one *should* do to act morally and how one can defend that choice of action. As noted above, the MJI measures moral reasoning. Hypothetical moral dilemmas are followed by a series of questions. For example, in the "Heinz Dilemma," Heinz has a sick wife who needs medicine for her to live. Heinz cannot buy the medicine so, should he steal it? Why or why not? Responses are coded based on the rationale given for a course of action.

James Rest used the same moral dilemmas but standardized the test, which was cost efficient and easier to score. The Defining Issues Test (DIT) is a multiple choice test; participants are presented with a moral dilemma and must evaluate items that describe the most essential considerations for deciding the case. Ratings of the 12 items indicate the level of Kohlberg's stages of moral judgment.

Ample research exists that indicates there is no gender bias in Kohlberg's MJI measure. Meta-analytic studies have found that girls are at no disadvantage when moral reasoning is measured by the MJI or the DIT. And age and experience are far better predictors of moral judgment than is gender. Research also reveals that both principles of justice and care are involved in moral reasoning and both are used by males and females to resolve an ethical dilemma.

Component 3, Moral Motivation, entails placing importance on moral values that are in direct competition with other values. For example, a person may want to be honest, but greed might be a more powerful motivation and lead to dishonesty. A person with moral motivation puts ethical values ahead of other values. Bebeau (2006) links professional identity to ethical professional decisions and argues that moral motivation comes from seeing oneself as morally responsible and acting in a way that is consistent with this self-definition.

Bebeau has examined data from practitioners disciplined by licensing boards. She has told life stories of moral exemplars, and has developed the Professional Role Orientation Inventory (Bebeau, Born, and Ozar 1993) to assess how professionals conceptualize their roles and responsibilities. While she has been able to distinguish different levels of professional identity formation, and identified strategies to facilitate identity development during professional education, gender differences appear small (You, Maeda, and Bebeau 2011) and favor females. You (2007) reported that women (from five cohorts of dental school graduates) made greater gains in formation of a moral identity than their male colleagues. However, much more research is needed on how men and women form a moral identity and to what degree they differ in this attribute.

Moral Character or moral action is the final component of Rest's four-component model. Moral character involves competence in problem-solving and interpersonal skills. Character combines both a person's behavior (competence) and individual qualities, traits, and virtues, such as moral strength, self-discipline, courage, and fortitude (Bebeau 2006). A person can be morally sensitive (component 1), make good moral judgments (component 2), and place a high priority on moral values (component 3), but if a person is lacking competence or character, moral failure will occur. Developing self-regulation, self-efficacy, grit, and implementation abilities are critical for moral action.

Personality theory and research indicate that a fully integrated moral identity and behavior consistent with that identity generally do not develop until midlife. Both men and women undergo the same character development process; identity and character development is a lifelong process for both men and women.

Moral action has been studied in a variety of ways, reflecting different understandings of the construct. Social-role theory suggests that male gender role socialization fosters helping that is chivalrous, while female gender role fosters nurturance and caring. However, meta-analytic studies indicate that while men help strangers more than women and women receive more help from strangers than men, findings are inconsistent. And various attributes of the studies (e.g., different risks in a situation for a man versus a woman) affect the findings. Using cases from dental practice, You, Maeda, and Bebeau (2011) found women were able to develop more adequate action plans to resolve ethical problems than their male counterparts, though it is unclear what explains this difference.

Several studies investigated trustworthiness in economic games or in evaluation of human faces. Results suggest that women are more trustworthy and tend to emphasize equality and harmony in interpersonal relationships more than men (e.g., Bereczkei, Birkás, and Kerekes 2007; Buchan, Croson, and Solnick 2008). These studies, however, are suggestive rather than conclusive and a good deal more research is needed to develop conclusions regarding gender differences in moral character or behavior.

SEE ALSO: Ethic of Care; Feminist Epistemology; Feminisms, Postmodern; Gender Difference Research

REFERENCES

Baier, Annette. 1994. *Moral Prejudices: Essays on Ethics*. Cambridge, MA: Harvard University Press.

Bebeau, Muriel J. 2006. "Evidence-Based Character Development." In *Lost Virtue: Professional Character Development and Modern Medical Education*, edited by Nuala Kenny and Wayne Shelton, 47–86. Amsterdam: Elsevier.

Bebeau, Muriel J. 2014. "An Evidence-Based Guide for Ethics Instruction." *Journal of Microbiology and Biology Education*, 15(2): 124–129. DOI: http://dx.doi.org/10.1128/jmbe.v15i2.872.

Bebeau, Muriel J., and Mary Brabeck. 1987. "Integrating Care and Justice in Professional Education: A Gender Perspective." *Journal of Moral Education*, 16: 189–203.

Bebeau, Muriel J., David Omar Born, and D. T. Ozar. 1993. "The Development of a Professional Role Orientation Inventory." *Journal of the American College of Dentists*, 60(2): 27–33.

Bereczkei, Tamás, B. Birkás, and Z. Kerekes. 2007. "Public Charity Offer as a Proximate Factor of Evolved Reputation-Building Strategy: An Experimental Analysis of a Real-Life Situation." *Evolution and Human Behavior*, 28(4): 277–284.

Brabeck, Mary M., ed. 2000. *Practicing Feminist Ethics in Psychology*. Washington, DC: American Psychological Association.

Buchan, Nancy R., Rachel T. A. Croson, and Sara Solnick. 2008. "Trust and Gender: An Examination of Behavior and Beliefs in the Investment Game." *Journal of Economic Behavior & Organization*, 68: 466–476.

Rest, James, and Darcia Narvaez, eds. 1994. *Moral Development in the Professions*. Hillside, NJ: Lawrence Erlbaum.
You, Di. 2007. *Interrelationships and Gender Differences among Components of Morality for Dental Students*. Ann Arbor: Proquet Information and Learning.
You, Di, Yukiko Maeda, and Muriel J. Bebeau. 2011. "Gender Difference in Moral Sensitivity: A Meta-Analysis." *Ethics & Behavior*, 21(4): 263–282. DOI: 10.1080/10508422.2011.585591.

FURTHER READING

Bebeau, Muriel J., and Mary Brabeck. 1994. "Ethical Sensitivity and Moral Reasoning among Men and Women in the Professions." In *Caring Voices and Women's Moral Frames: Gillian's View*, edited by Bill Puka, 240–259. New York: Garland.
Bebeau, Muriel J., Y. Maeda, and Di You. 2011b. "Gender Differences in Ethical Abilities of Dental Students." *Journal of Dental Education*, 76(9): 1137–1149.
Cross, Susan E., and Hazel Rose Markus. 1993. "Gender in Thought, Belief, and Action: A Cognitive Approach." In *The Psychology of Gender*, edited by Anne E. Beall and Robert J. Sternberg, 55–98. New York: Guilford Press.
Eagly, Alice H., and Maureen Crowley. 1986. "Gender Helping Behavior: A Meta-Analytic Review of the Social Psychological Literature." *Psychological Bulletin*, 100(3): 283–308.
Enns, Carolyn Zerbe 1997. *Feminist Theories and Feminist Psychotherapies: Origins, Themes and Variations*. Binghamton, NY: Haworth Press.
Jaggar, Alison M. 1991. "Feminist Ethics: Projects, Problems, Prospects." In *Feminist Ethics*, edited by Claudia Card, 78–106. Lawrence: University Press of Kansas.

Eugenics, Historical and Ethical Aspects of

KAREN WEINGARTEN
City University of New York, USA

Although the influence of eugenics can still be felt in the twenty-first century, it was an especially respected field of inquiry in the early to mid-twentieth century when the majority of physicians, biologists, and social scientists viewed eugenics as a legitimate scientific field for advancing the human race, primarily through controlling reproduction. The term comes from the Greek word *eugenes* and has been translated to mean good in stock or wellborn. It was first coined in 1883 by Francis Galton, who was interested in studying the inheritance of genius through generations. Galton, a cousin of Charles Darwin's, called his theory "practical Darwinism," and he hoped his ideas would influence the elite and educated to reproduce more in order to better society. The emergence of eugenics, however, can be traced even further back than Galton to at least Thomas Malthus who, writing in 1798 ("Essay on the Principle of Population"), argued that without population regulators human numbers would grow exponentially around the world. He asked whether this growth might lead to a degradation in the quality of human life, as the world contained more people than it could support. In 1852, Herbert Spencer reversed Malthus's argument by theorizing that the competition for resources advanced human civilization through competition, and to describe this phenomenon he coined the term "survival of the fittest," which became a catchphrase in support of eugenics. In the 1890s the German biologist August Weismann's theory of "germ plasm" reimagined how traits are transmitted from parents to offspring through inherited cellular matter, and his theory added one of the final building blocks in the establishment of eugenics. Weismann's conception of germ plasm overturned the French scientist Lamarck's theories that environmental effects could change physical characteristics in a parent, which were then passed on to the child. However, not all eugenicists would reject Lamarck's theories. In France and in several Latin American countries, including Brazil, Lamarck's theories were influential and led to forms of eugenics that encouraged improved social conditions for impoverished and disenfranchised citizens.

The earliest eugenic societies arose in response to Galton's imperative that those deemed "fit" should reproduce more to improve the population. Germany formed the first eugenic society in 1905 called the German Society for Race Hygiene. Britain followed in 1907–1908 with the Eugenics Education Society in England, the Eugenics Record Office in the United States opened in 1910, and the French Eugenics Society in 1912. Through the influences of these organizations, eugenics soon emerged as a worldwide philosophy, and even though its influences took different forms, eugenic policies impacted countries as far as Japan, Brazil, Argentina, Mexico, Australia, and Sweden.

Eugenics began, as Galton first envisioned it, as an argument to better the British national character by encouraging those seen as reproductively fit to breed more. By the turn of the century, however, in Germany, England, and the United States, arguments for sterilization, euthanasia, and the denial of public assistance to those deemed "unfit" or feebleminded were all justified by the same eugenic logic that claimed its mission was to better the human race.

In Europe, the first eugenic sterilization laws were introduced in Switzerland in 1928 and were followed soon after by laws in Denmark in 1929. While contemporary critics tend to view eugenics as a malicious practice developed by Nazi Germany, these early laws were justified as progressive and scientific methods for the public good. When viewed retrospectively, the impact of eugenic sterilization laws was enormous. In the United States, which implemented the first and most expansive sterilization laws, it is estimated that between 1907 and the end of World War II roughly 60,000 to 70,000 people were sterilized. These numbers do not even take into account the thousands of undocumented people who were forcibly sterilized in prisons. By 1933, following the example of the United States, Nazi Germany passed the most encompassing sterilization law yet, and marked people with many forms of physical and mental disability, as well as those considered to have aberrant sexualities, as candidates for sterilization.

Lamarckian-influenced eugenics, which emphasized improving environmental conditions, reigned in France and in Latin America for longer than in England, the United States, and Germany, and the effects of many of its policies are still seen today. In Brazil, for example, eugenic societies set up infant care clinics and educated the public about venereal disease, and in Mexico eugenics tended to focus on infant and maternal care, birth control, and disease prevention. Eugenics in Latin America, however, did not only have positive effects. Brazil used eugenics to justify racist immigration selection procedures that favored white Europeans, and they endorsed moralizing anti-alcohol campaigns. This form of eugenics, often called "preventative eugenics," was modeled after French eugenics, which encouraged pronatalism and obstetric care under the assumption that if women received better care during their pregnancies then they would give birth to healthier infants. While these forms of eugenics did have lasting effects, by the 1930s many Latin American countries also began implementing the more discriminating and racist eugenic practices developed by their northern neighbor, the United States.

The outcome of the 1927 US Supreme Court case *Buck v. Bell* resonated worldwide. Oliver Wendell Holmes, Jr., who was then Chief Justice of the court, upheld a Virginia law that mandated forced sterilization for anyone who was deemed "socially inadequate." As a result, Carrie Buck, who was born to an unmarried mother and was pregnant out of wedlock herself, was declared "unfit" and sterilized against her will. Holmes, in his decision, infamously declared that "Three generations of imbeciles are enough," and those disturbing words would haunt the court as an echo of one of its most troubling decisions. Buck, according to the court's decision, was labeled feebleminded because she had premarital sex and a child out of wedlock. The court decided that this behavior, and any other form of sexuality that was considered aberrant – including homosexuality – legitimized forced sterilization for the good of the human race and American citizenry. The case's outcome not only validated other sterilization laws in the United States, but also led to the passage of similar laws in Canada, Switzerland, Japan, and each of the Scandinavian countries. Shortly after, in Germany, Hitler passed the 1933 law "For the Prevention of Hereditarily Diseased Offspring" that led to the sterilization of more than 400,000 people, and later to similar operations in the death camps of the Holocaust.

While Germany's eugenic practices have left the most well-known and horrifying imprint, many of their policies were influenced by ideas that first emerged in the United States. The institutionalization of the American eugenic movement can be traced to Charles Benedict Davenport and his colleague at the Eugenics Record Office, Harry Hamilton Laughlin. Both adapted Galton's theories about heredity into a widely popular eugenics campaign that advocated sterilization. While in England eugenics was developing into a discourse about class difference, Davenport, Laughlin, and soon many of the scientists who followed their lead turned it into a discourse about race and sexuality that emphasized racial classifications and marked those with any form of aberrant sexuality – or even those perceived as *too* sexual – as feebleminded. They helped define the purpose of eugenics as that of racialized nation-building, a goal that would be embraced to its limit by the National Socialist Party in Germany.

Early twentieth-century British and American feminists and advocates for women's reproductive equality were also not only influenced by eugenics but wielded eugenic discourse to their benefit because they viewed it as a legitimate and powerful scientific discourse. In England, the 1880s saw not only the coining of the term eugenics but also the rise of the New Woman. These women, who were middle class and white, embraced feminism and women's independence, and often wielded the rhetoric of eugenics to gain support for their causes. Eugenic feminism, associated with some New Woman campaigns, sought to depict motherhood as a duty to the nation, and part of advancing that duty, they argued, was to allow women more control over choosing their partners so that they could better the race and contribute more fully to the British nation and empire. The Eugenics Education Society, for example, believed that heredity determined class, and with the help of New Women like Sarah Grand, they fought to create policies and practices that would curtail so-called excessive fertility and educate the public about what constitutes a healthy marriage. Similarly, Marie Stopes, a leading birth control activist in England, was initially attracted to the growing eugenics movement in 1930s Germany because of its strict new policies that sought to curb "racial degeneration" and the spread of venereal disease. Stopes's affinity for the National Socialist Party ended quickly, however, when Hitler shuttered every new birth control clinic in Germany, and the two countries went to war.

The United States also saw a strong link between eugenics, birth control activism, and feminism, particularly in the work of

Margaret Sanger. While the extent of Sanger's commitment to eugenic ideology has been controversial, more recent scholarship has demonstrated that she saw eugenics not only as a means to further her birth control agenda, but also as a coherent way of viewing reproductive politics. Critics like Nancy Ordover note that while Sanger did not embrace eugenics because of its racism – and Sanger did, in some cases, distance herself from eugenics' more explicit racist beliefs – she did argue that if birth control education was publicly supported and if better forms of birth control were found, then the race would be improved because "unfit" women could be encouraged to have smaller families – or no children at all. In her journal the *Birth Control Review* she regularly published articles by herself and by noted eugenicists that argued for the need to view birth control policy and eugenics as intertwined. Even more insidiously, she supported Clarence Gamble's experiments with poor, uneducated women to develop better forms of birth control. Beginning in the 1930s and through the 1950s, in rural Appalachia, with working-class Mexican American women in California, and in Puerto Rico, Gamble handed out experimental and untested forms of chemical jellies, foams, powders, sponges, and ultimately the early versions of birth control pills to see how successful his inventions were in preventing pregnancy and how severe the side effects were in response. Sanger worked closely with him on many of these projects, and was particularly supportive of his quest to develop a pill and test it on Puerto Rican women.

The widespread influence of eugenics can also be seen in the work of W. E. B. Du Bois, who rallied for the advancement of African Americans and often employed eugenic rhetoric toward that goal. In the early twentieth century, he was among those published in Sanger's journal to support birth control, which he also saw as a means to improve middle-class African Americans. Like Sanger, Du Bois sought to encourage the "fittest" blacks to reproduce more, and he hoped that birth control would limit the number of children had by impoverished and working-class blacks. Even as Du Bois fought American racism and worked hard to establish programs to uplift African Americans, many of his ideas about fitness were borrowed from eugenic ideals that privileged the middle class and shunned any form of perceived sexual deviance. And like those eugenicists, Du Bois also developed theories – like his concept of the Talented Tenth – that argued that the best black Americans had traits that were inherited and biologically imbued. Du Bois's support of eugenics – in a revised form – demonstrates the wide influence eugenics had, and its firm place in American science and social science as a legitimate field.

Unfortunately, eugenics did not die with the end of World War II and Hitler's implementation of its ideologies on a massive scale. In Puerto Rico, Gamble continued to employ eugenics as a means to justify his experiments on Puerto Rican women using the birth control pill. These women were never informed that the pill was still in its experimental stages, and in many cases they had severe and irreversible side effects. Sterilization laws were still enforced in many states until as late as 1979, when California overturned its laws, and disproportionately targeted African American, Mexican American, and Native American women, as well as women who were deemed to have low IQs. In England, through the 1970s, education policy – which influenced the funding of schools and the distribution of scholarships – and mental healthcare were shaped by a eugenic ideology that portrayed the lower classes as less intelligent and more susceptible to psychosis because of their genetic destinies.

While most historians argue that the 1980s saw the end of the eugenics movement in the United States with the overturning of the last sterilization laws, more recently eugenics – or as it is sometimes termed, neoeugenics – has resurfaced in discussions of prenatal testing, where the unlikely allies of disability rights activists and anti-abortion activists have accused doctors and parents-to-be of engaging in eugenic practices when they choose to abort fetuses with chromosomal abnormalities. Prenatal testing, which can include a series of procedures ranging from early ultrasound to amniocentesis to a new blood test that examines fetal cells in the pregnant woman's blood, can now identify a range of chromosomal abnormalities, such as Down Syndrome and the more devastating Tay Sachs. As these tests have become more accurate and available earlier in a woman's pregnancy, many women now choose to have them, and many also choose to abort the fetus if an abnormality is found. Disability rights activists have argued that this is a form of eugenics because it not only reduces natural human diversity, but it also creates a culture that devalues and marginalizes those living with disabilities. They also suggest that as fewer babies are born with Down Syndrome and other disabilities, fewer resources will be allotted to those who are alive and disabled because they form a smaller percentage of the population.

Experimental forms of birth control also continue to evoke controversy as many, like the 1990s contraceptive Norplant – a device that was implanted in women's arms – are targeted at working-class women, black women, and other women who have been historically disenfranchised. In the case of Norplant, which places six capsules in women's arms and protects them from pregnancy for five years, many women later admitted that they felt coerced by welfare programs to have the contraceptive implanted. And once on Norplant many also began experiencing a range of side effects such as headaches, depression, ovarian cysts, arm swelling and infection at the site of implantation, and increased cholesterol levels. More complicated, if women decided they wanted to have Norplant removed because of these side effects or because five years elapsed (leaving the device in for more than five years could lead to life-threatening ectopic pregnancies), the required surgery to remove the contraceptive often left women with even greater problems. Many doctors were inexperienced with removal procedures and left women with painful scar tissue and damaged nerves as they had to root around in women's arms to remove broken pieces of the Norplant rods. Later it was discovered that Norplant had been approved by the Federal Drugs Administration (FDA) with limited testing, primarily as a means to target welfare mothers and reduce the number of children they had.

Eugenics, or neoeugenics, continues to influence laws and social policies about immigration, reproduction, sexuality, and disability. Its legacy can be seen in sensationalized books like the 1994 *The Bell Curve* by Charles Murray and Richard Herrnstein, which justifies immigration quotas based on IQ and argues for the termination of welfare based on the misguided assumption that it encourages women with low IQs to reproduce. These arguments echo the eugenic rhetoric of the early twentieth century, and they seem to periodically resurface even as the scientific establishment, led by prominent thinkers such as the late Stephen Jay Gould, has convincingly quashed the scientific basis of biological determinism. Eugenics, however, continues to live on. Its appeal was once premised in its ability to tie together race and gender, human diversity and reproduction. Historically, women have felt the brunt of its policies, but at various times in history it focused on eliminating or containing anyone whose identity fell outside various racial, sexual, intellectual, or physical norms. As reproductive technologies advance and allow us to control components of procreation never imagined possible, the role of eugenics and its inheritors in shaping new policies is uncertain.

SEE ALSO: Abortion, Legal Status in Global Perspective; Assisted Reproduction; Birth Control, History and Politics of; Contraception and Contraceptives; Disability Rights Movement; Eugenics Movements; Family Planning; Genetics and Racial Minorities in the United States; Genetics Testing and Screening; Nazi Persecution of Homosexuals

FURTHER READING

Buck v. Bell, 247 U.S. 200, 47 S. Ct. 584, 71 L. Ed. 1000 (1927).
DiKötter, Frank. 1995. *Sex, Culture, and Modernity in China: Medical Science and the Construction of Sexual Identities*. Honolulu: University of Hawaii Press.
Hanson, Clare. 2013. *Eugenics, Literature, and Culture in Post-War Britain*. New York: Routledge.
Kevles, Daniel J. 1985. *In the Name of Eugenics*. New York: Knopf.
Kline, Wendy 2005. *Building a Better Race: Gender, Sexuality, and Eugenics from the Turn of the Century to the Baby Boom*. Berkeley: University of California Press.
Kluchin, Rebecca M. 2009. *Fit to Be Tied: Sterilization and Reproductive Rights in America, 1950–1980*. New Brunswick: Rutgers University Press.
Kühl, Stefan. 1994. *The Nazi Connection: Eugenics, American Racism, and German National Socialism*. Oxford: Oxford University Press.
Lombardo, Paul A., ed. 2011. *A Century of Eugenics in America: From the Indiana Experiment to the Human Genome Era*. Bloomington: Indiana University Press.
Ordover, Nancy. 2003. *American Eugenics: Race, Queer Anatomy, and the Science of Nationalism*. Minneapolis: University of Minnesota Press.
Rapp, Rayna. 1999. *Testing Women, Testing the Fetus: The Social Impact of Amniocentesis in America*. New York: Routledge.
Richardson, Angelique. 2003. Oxford: Oxford University Press.
Roberts, Dorothy. 1997. *Killing the Black Body: Race, Reproduction, and the Meaning of Liberty*. New York: Vintage Books.
Schoen, Johanna. 2005. *Choice and Coercion: Birth Control, Sterilization, and Abortion in Public Health and Welfare*. Chapel Hill: University of North Carolina Press.
Stepan, Nancy Leys. 1991. *"The Hour of Eugenics": Race, Gender, and Nation in Latin America*. Ithaca: Cornell University Press.

Eugenics Movements

MAYA SABATELLO
Columbia University, USA

The eugenics movement was consolidated around the world during the first three decades of the twentieth century. It was particularly strong in the United States and, after World War I, in Germany. Indeed, it is especially associated with the pervasive abuse by the Nazi regime during World War II, epitomized by the Aryan plan and the implementation of eugenic doctrines on a large scale. However, it is important to recognize that the eugenics movement reflected an international trend (e.g., Adams 1990; Kevles 1995): throughout the 1920s, the eugenics movement also existed in Canada, Britain, and Scandinavia, as well as elsewhere in Continental Europe and other parts of Latin America and Asia. Moreover, it had much more in common with valid and well-intentioned science and public health programs than had historically been thought (Kühl 2013). Eugenics is thus also reflective of the potential – and danger – of emerging sciences in the realm of reproduction and family planning.

The eugenics movement was led by mainstream scientists – with white, middle-class, professional backgrounds – who sought to solve anti-social behaviors such as crime, prostitution, poverty, and alcoholism by applying rational principles of science. Significantly, it was a point of convergence for both conservative and progressive social reform movements: both shared the belief that anti-social behaviors are grounded primarily in biology, and also that biology can be used to remedy these social ills. The evolving field of public health further bolstered the movement (Pernick 1997; Birn and Molina 2005). Notwithstanding eugenicists' criticism of public health initiatives to increase survival rates for the least competent through measures such as sanitation, hygiene, and state medicine, there was much commonality in the goals, methods, programs, and personnel that occupied both fields. Public health officials were increasingly dedicated to disease eradication (rather than just reduction of morbidity), adopted disease prevention methods of segregation and quarantine, and expanded the notion of heredity beyond genes to include germ transmission and social responsibility of parents to promote good health for future generations. Additionally, mixed teams of public health professionals and eugenicists provided public health services (Pernick 1997). Subsequently, the movement was in a strong position to sway policymakers and public opinion to create programs to inspect immigrants for both infectious and hereditary diseases, and to promote state-authorized sterilization as a measure to control undesired breeding.

Eugenicists – and subsequently state-sanctioned policies – focused efforts on two main programs related to family planning. *Positive eugenics* (originated by Galton) intended to encourage "superior" people to procreate. It was advocated by eugenicists, pediatrics, and other health reformers in the beginning of the twentieth century, when other initiatives such as backing family wages, universal preschools, and foster care were adopted to improve the conditions of childhood and of the human stock more generally (Birn and Molina 2005). In Britain, for instance, positive eugenics led to proposals of a family allowance that would be proportional to income: the better off a family was, the larger the allowance the family would receive (these proposals failed). In the United States, "Fitter Family" competitions were held at a number of state fairs. The winners received a trophy after taking an IQ test as well as the Wasserman test for syphilis (Kevles 2011).

Negative eugenics focused on "breeding out" certain "defective" human characteristics by limiting reproduction or altogether eliminating the unfit. Initially, the main targets were individuals with a variety of mental conditions and behaviors defined as criminal or immoral. However, the rubric later extended to ethnic and minority groups, and people belonging to low socioeconomic statuses. Methods to implement negative eugenics included segregating those deemed unfit and prohibiting them from having sexual relations; restricting the number of immigrants from Southern and Eastern Europe, the Balkans, Russia, and others who were considered to weaken the genetic pool (for instance, the Johnson-Reed Act (1924) in the United States; Wikler 1999; Allen 2001); and, notably, sterilization laws. Such laws allowed the forced sterilization of individuals who resided in state institutions and were determined to be genetically "defective."

Economic considerations further played a role in the adoption of sterilization laws in parts of Canada, the Deep South, North Carolina, and California in the United States, and throughout Scandinavia. Eugenicists emphasized the costs of funding institutional care and poor relief, especially given the worldwide economic depression in 1929. Economics was additionally an important factor in Germany during the 1930s when eugenicists advocated for euthanasia: supporting those who were sterilized was viewed as too expensive (Kevles 2011).

While eugenics movements across the world shared the goal of improving human heredity and social good, they differed in their focuses. For instance, whereas negative eugenics and sterilization laws were prevalent in Protestant settings, the Catholic Church endorsed positive eugenics but strongly opposed negative eugenics and sterilization laws. This latter position reflected the Catholic Church's religious doctrines about family planning: the first coincided with the church's ideology of enhancing prenatal and childraising circumstances, the latter contradicted with its positions on abortion and reproduction (Wikler 1999). Similarly, although race occupied a major role among American and Canadian eugenicists, it was only a minor issue in Scandinavian and British eugenics. The stream of immigrants reaching North America from Eastern and Southern Europe since the late nineteenth century and the evolution of public health institutions as key sites of racialization account for this difference. As these immigrants were disproportionately represented among the "deviants," it raised the concern that they might out-reproduce natives of Anglo stock, thus reducing the quality of the American population. Subsequently, sterilization laws were generally enforced on a racial and class basis, and immigrants of color were targeted (Kevles 2011; Kühl 2013).

Notwithstanding the significant support that the eugenics movements received throughout the mid-1930s, criticism was increasingly voiced beginning in the mid-1920s (Kühl 2013). Questions about the scientific validity of the eugenics doctrines and about the class, racial, and immigration basis thereof began to emerge. Consequently, many American states as well as British Columbia did not enforce their eugenic sterilization laws, and efforts to pass such a law in Britain (the Mental Deficiency Act in 1913) altogether failed (Kevles 2011). But it was only in the aftermath of World War II that the movement came to a halt. The discrediting of "Nazi science" (Kühl 2013) and the revelation of the horrific execution of eugenic policies by Nazi Germany – from the legislation of imposed sterilization to the anti-Semitic programs of euthanasia as well as the systematic murder of political prisoners, gypsies, and Jews in concentration camps – were major reasons for the emerging aversion to eugenics. The rising international agenda of human rights, including the movements for women's rights and reproductive freedom since the beginning of the 1960s, have further led to the demise of the historical eugenics movement (Kevles 2011).

Eugenics ideology and practice did not disappear, however. Sterilization of Roma women without their knowledge during cesarean sections or abortions was a widespread governmental policy in communist countries throughout the 1970s and 1980s. It remained a common practice in Eastern and Central Europe after the collapse of the Soviet Union in 1989 and well into the twenty-first century. The European Court of Human Rights issued a few judgments against Slovakia concerning such sterilizations, finding them to be in violation of the prohibition of inhumane or degrading treatment and of the right to respect for private and family life (*V.C. v. Slovakia* (2011); *N,B, v. Slovakia* (2012)). The denial of reproductive and sexual rights through forcible sterilization often further follows the historical class and socioeconomic minority divides. In California, in the period between 2006 and 2010, over 100 women in state prisons were reportedly pressured to consent while they were pregnant or during delivery for tubal ligation (sterilization). Poor inmates, especially those deemed likely to return to prison in the future, were especially targeted. Moreover, in many countries, including France, the United States, Australia, the United Kingdom, and India, girls with disabilities are at risk of being forcibly sterilized at the request of their guardians. Although this procedure is arguably performed in order to enable the guardians to better care for the girl or to protect the girl-child from sexual abuse, other children are not subjected to such invasive medical procedures for the convenience of their parents or caretakers, and the "protection argument" has repeatedly been proven wrong. Contemporary debate about whether newborns with disabilities will receive medical treatment or be left to die further illustrates the present application of old eugenics and the economic considerations involved in the determination of the unfit, whom eugenicists argue should be eliminated for the public good.

More recently, developments in the study of human genetics and biotechnology, especially in the realm of assisted reproductive technologies, have reignited old debates about eugenics. The completion of the Human Genome Project in 2003 was pivotal. It provided new knowledge about genetics, and created a revolution in the diagnosis of diseases and disorders, along with possible therapies, cures, and even possible enhancements of one's genetic endowment. Assisted reproductive technologies – especially techniques for genetic screening of embryos before implantation in the womb (preimplantation genetic diagnosis (PGD)) and of fetuses in utero – as well as gene therapy on germ line (which changes the sperm or egg of an individual in a way that is passed on to the offspring) are notable.

Seemingly, the use of such technologies differs from the historical eugenics movement. Whereas the latter was governmentally sanctioned and pursued (so-called "strong eugenics"; Hampton 2005), the former requires individual consent. But there is much commonality between them. Reproductive and screening technologies have been gradually incorporated into routine healthcare, and they are implemented on a large scale. They are increasingly paid for by both private and national healthcare systems, creating social and institutional pressure to conform and test for possible genetic abnormalities. In effect, they use genetic profiling to select for embryos deemed "most fit" and to "breed out" what are considered "undesirable genes" (Kevles 2011). As such, they may also reflect the extent of the societal (in)tolerance and (dis)respect of human difference: the screening out or abortion of embryos with the "wrong" sex (commonly sex selection for boys) and of embryos with genetic disorders (from mere propensity for disability to other conditions such as Down Syndrome). Such practices raise profound questions about the role of culture in family planning, the scope of one's autonomy and reproductive freedom in choosing what kind of children one will have, and importantly, as Hampton (2005) suggested, whether such technologies simply reflect a shift to a newer form of "family eugenics." Moreover, disability advocates raise the concern that these technologies lead to the endorsement of narrow notions of normality, whereby gender and disability are viewed merely as a biological and personal trait (and a problem), and subsequently, that they exacerbate the stigmatization, exclusion, and devaluation of such "different" individuals as persons. This is troubling, especially because the demarcation of normality is not absolute. For instance, deaf individuals who belong to the deaf community or individuals with dwarfism who associate with Little People of America may choose, as part of their sense of cultural identity, to utilize such technologies to have a child with the same genetic condition. Conversely, emerging technologies open the door for genetic engineering to create a child according to aesthetic standards, intellectual abilities, athletic talents, and so forth (so-called "utopian eugenics") (Reinda 2000). Human rights protections are thus cardinal so that developments in biotechnology and genetics do not turn into a reincarnation of the old eugenics.

SEE ALSO: Assisted Reproduction; Disability Rights Movement; Eugenics, Historical and Ethical Aspects of; Family Planning; Genetics and Racial Minorities in the United States; Genetics Testing and Screening; Nazi Persecution of Homosexuals; Normalization

REFERENCES

Adams, Mark B., ed. 1990. *The Well-Born Science: Eugenics in Germany, France, Brazil, and Russia*. New York: Oxford University Press.
Allen, Garland E. 2001. "Is a New Eugenics Afoot?" *Science*, 294: 59–61.
Birn, Anne-Emanuelle, and Natalia Molina. 2005. "In the Name of Public Health." *American Journal of Public Health*, 95(7): 1095–1097.
Hampton, Simon Jonathan. 2005. "Family Eugenics." *Disability & Society*, 20(5): 553–561.
Kevles, Daniel J. 1995. *In the Name of Eugenics: Genetics and the Uses of Human Heredity*. Cambridge, MA: Harvard University Press.
Kevles, Daniel J. 2011. "From Eugenics to Patents: Genetics, Law, and Human Rights." *Annals of Human Genetics*, 75: 326–333.
Kühl, Stefan. 2013. *For the Betterment of the Race: The Rise and Fall of the International Movement for Eugenics and Racial Hygiene*. New York: Palgrave Macmillan.
N.B. v. Slovakia, Application no. 29518/10, Judgment of the European Court of Human Rights, 12 June, 2012.
Pernick, Martin S. 1997. "Eugenics and Public Health in American History." *American Journal of Public Health*, 87(11): 1767–1772.
Reinda, Solveig Magnus. 2000. "Disability, Gene Therapy and Eugenics – A Challenge to John Harris." *Journal of Medical Ethics*, 26: 89–94.
V.C. v. Slovakia, Application no. 18968/07, Judgment of the European Court of Human Rights, 8 November, 2011.
Wikler, Daniel. 1999. "Can We Learn from Eugenics?" *Journal of Medical Ethics*, 25: 183–194.

Eurocentrism

AMA MAZAMA
Temple University, USA

Eurocentrism is a cultural, social, political, and economic system of domination that accompanied the expansion of Europe during its colonization of many parts of the world. It is fair to state that the rise of Eurocentrism coincided with an era of rare imperialism, exploitation, and promotion of greed. In addition to justifying European exploitation of foreign lands, Eurocentrism also condoned the oppression of women of all colors, given the prevalence and idealization of patriarchy in Western societies. Indeed, patriarchy, which is characterized by the disproportionate power of men in the economic, social, political, and religious spheres, has led to attempted male control over women's bodies, more particularly their reproductive capacity and sexuality.

While much attention has been given to Eurocentrism in recent years, the concept has received different treatments, depending on whether the emphasis is placed on the economic dimension of Eurocentrism or its cultural aspect.

The first trend is best represented by the Marxist economist Samir Amin, who undertook to scrutinize the concept in his book *Eurocentrism*, published in 1989. Operating within the paradigmatic confines of dependency theory and world-system theory spearheaded by Immanuel Wallerstein, Amin predictably argued that capitalism could no longer be regarded as a phenomenon occurring within particular national borders but as a worldwide and highly integrated system within which countries at the "center" (Europe) exploit countries at the "periphery" (the so-called third world). Eurocentrism, in Samir Amin's view, is one of the major tools used by the global capitalist system to reproduce itself and expand. In typical Marxist analysis, though, Amin gives the economy precedence over all else, and treats culture simply as superstructure, ultimately determined and shaped by the economic mode of production and stages of development. This leads Amin to greatly downplay the existence of European cultural characteristics, while insisting on the other hand on the cultural similarities displayed by societies at the same general stage of economic "development." As a result, and quite ironically, Samir Amin's analysis of Eurocentrism reads more like an analysis of "Capitalocentrism" than anything else. Thus, while useful, Amin's analysis suffers from its inability to account for the deep ethnocentrism that lies at the heart of Eurocentrism.

Indeed, one must remember that along with the imperialistic intrusion of Europe into Africa, Asia, America, and the Pacific regions after Christopher Columbus's voyages to the Americas came the often harsh imposition of European religion, language, customs, and symbol systems under the pretext of European cultural superiority. For instance, starting in the fifteenth century and drawing to a close with the independence of many African nations in the 1950s and 1960s, Europe sought to turn Africans into Europeans in names, desires, opinions, fashion, religion, and tastes. It is this often devastating infliction of European culture in the name of a so-called Greek miracle and European exceptionalism and under the guise of "progress" and "civilization" that led scholars like Molefi Kete Asante (1998) and others working within the Afrocentric paradigm to develop a cultural analysis and critique of Eurocentrism in the 1980s and 1990s.

Thus, from an Afrocentric standpoint, Eurocentrism must be understood first and foremost as a form of relentless ethnocentrism, informed by at least four assumptions that have played a major and negative role as far as people of color are concerned: (1) all human beings evolve along the same line; (2) the European experience is universal; (3) Europeans are superior; and (4) "others" are defined by their experiences with Europeans. In other words, the Eurocentric paradigm rests, among other things, on the belief in the superiority and universality of the European experience. Indeed, in that linear and evolutionary schema of thought, the West claims that when it talks about itself it is also ipso facto talking about all human beings. The history of all women, men, and children in the world supposedly naturally coincides with that of Europeans. The latter are thus implicitly or explicitly held to be the universal norm by which other people's intellectual, cultural, and social "progress" (or lack of it) will be evaluated. Indeed, if all human beings share a common essence, it is obvious that, within the Eurocentric paradigm, human beings have not all reached the same stage of development. It is rather clear, from reading Eurocentric writers, that Europe precedes the rest of humankind, and time after time it is suggested that people of color must emulate Europeans in order to put an end to their inferior condition.

Moreover, its ability to parade and hide its European specificity as "universal" and "objective" has rendered Europe's presence conspicuous – allowing the European cultural and historical experience to become invisible and infiltrate people of color's consciousness. The violence that this process of imposition entails can hardly be underestimated, nor can its psychological and mental ravages be ignored. What happens here is that Europe attempts to occupy all human space, at the very expense of those whose cultural worth and historical depth it denies. Thus, it must be recognized that, in the end, Eurocentrism and its attendant attempted suppression of indigenous cultural mores, and imposition of itself in the name of a self-proclaimed superiority, are part and parcel of a narrative of white superiority, indeed a devastating racial mythology for those subjected to it and falling for it.

SEE ALSO: Patriarchy; Universal Human Rights

REFERENCES

Amin, Samir. 1989. *Eurocentrism*. New York: Monthly Review Press.
Asante, Molefi Kete. 1998. *The Afrocentric Idea*. Philadelphia: Temple University Press.

FURTHER READING

Asante, Molefi Kete. 1980. *Afrocentricity: The Theory of Social Change*. Buffalo, NY: Amulefi.
Blaut, James M. 2000. *Eight Eurocentric Historians*. New York: Guilford Press.
Diop, Cheikh Anta. 1990. *Civilization or Barbarism: An Authentic Anthropology*. New York: Lawrence Hill.
Mazama, Ama. 1995. Review of *Eurocentrism*, by Samir Amin, New York: Monthly Review Press, 1989. *Journal of Black Studies*, 25(6): 760–764.

Extended Families

ROBERT TEIXEIRA
Ontario College of Art and Design University, Canada

An extended family is generally defined as two or more generations (by blood, adoption, or marriage/cohabitation) sharing one or more households connected by varying degrees of kinship. The term "extended family" has had a complex and ambiguous status in family studies. Uses of the term have harkened back to a largely mythological past where rural or pioneer families were often depicted in terms of several generations living under one roof, despite empirical evidence such as statistical studies and national censuses to the contrary. Such is the case with French sociologist Frédéric Le Play (1806–1882), a pioneer of empirical studies on the family who conducted extensive research on the European rural "stem family" or extended family. A proponent of traditional values, he vaunted their traditional hierarchy as he decried the rise of the nuclear family, considering it "unstable."

Despite these more recent studies, there is evidence of extended families forming the substrate of feudal economies in the Middle Ages. Corresponding changes to women's and children's social status and familial arrangements were brought by the advent of industrial capitalism which shifted production outside the household (Mandell 1988). As common life tended to be more public – with domestic privacy and a concept of individualism in this period reserved only for the aristocracy – extended family ties were necessary for subsistence and survival and tended to mitigate nuclear family relationships among the populace in the Middle Ages and early modern epochs (Duby 1988). Research on Aboriginal societies in North America and elsewhere have highlighted tightly knit communal organization in which extended families formed the basis for survival, social reproduction, and the transmission of culture within bands, clans, tribes, and nations (Ambert 2015).

While definitions and conceptual practices attendant on the "extended family" generally trend toward social science, ethnology and anthropological disciplines that privilege Western standards and perspectives, cross-cultural, post-colonial, and "third-wave" feminist perspectives point toward a restaging of family studies, research, and theories toward more critical paradigms for understanding a panoply of changes driven by economic, social, sexual, and religious factors (Hennon and Wilson 2008; Abela and Walker 2014). For instance, the role of consanguinity and traditional genealogical descent on lesbian, gay, bisexual, and transgender (LGBT) family formations has been analyzed as regulatory practices of the state that uphold traditional definitions of family (Weston 1997). In addition, recent studies on changing family forms have pointed to the negative pressure of globalization and neoliberal economic policies scaling back nuclear family formations. The ability for couples to set up separate households is deferred, and the consequent production of "velcro" or "boomerang" children is now a well-established fact. More recent work on queer kinship probes the "bodily" practices and meanings of "belonging," asking how dominant patterns are sutured through law and social practices that exclude "queer" and innovative household and family formations. These critical studies on kinship seek to expand notions of belonging based on the possibilities of the body, and practices of support, affect, and care not necessarily tied to blood relations and which signal forms of belonging that "both inhabit and exceed the matrix of couplehood and reproduction" (Freeman 2007, 295).

Inequalities are related in complex ways to the structure or forms that families take. In looking at how stratification affects family forms, there are a wealth of sociological studies that aim to understand a diverse set of factors that nudge individuals into family formations that we can call extended. Low incomes increase the likelihood that poor or working-class individuals will inhabit extended family forms even if they would perhaps prefer the greater privacy afforded by the nuclear family. Studies carried out on black inner-city families have shown that black women are less likely to meet what are considered eligible men for marriage and cohabitation than their white counterparts. The combined factors of racial prejudice and the effects of systemic class and racial oppression have produced a situation where black women and men have a greater degree of constrained choices about the kind of families they inhabit. Moreover, women providing support in inner cities for children from a variety of families may offer a way to envision family formations that are communal and community-based, often headed by women who are working as dual wage earners and providing care for children in the community.

SEE ALSO: Incest, Social Practices and Legal Policies on; Kinship; Patriarchy; Same-Sex Families

REFERENCES

Abela, Angela, and Janet Walker, eds. 2014. *Contemporary Issues in Family Studies: Global Perspectives on Partnerships, Parenting and Support in a Changing World*. Oxford: Wiley-Blackwell.

Ambert, Anne-Marie. 2015. *Changing Families: Relationships in Context*, 3rd ed. Toronto: Pearson.

Duby, Georges, ed. 1988. *A History of Private Life II: Revelations of the Medieval World*, translated by Arthur Goldhammer. Cambridge: Harvard University Press.

Freeman, E. 2007. "Queer Belongings: Kinship Theory and Queer Theory." In *A Companion to Lesbian, Gay, Bisexual, Transgender, and Queer Studies*, edited by George E. Heggerty and Molly McGarry, 295–314. Oxford: Blackwell.

Hennon, Charles B., and Stephan M. Wilson, eds. 2008. *Families in a Global Context*. New York: Routledge.

Mandell, Nancy. 1988. "The Child Question: Links Between Women and Children in the Family." In *Reconstructing the Canadian Family: Feminist Perspectives*, edited by Nancy Mandell and Ann Duffy, 49–81. Toronto and Vancouver: Butterworths.

Weston, Kath. 1997. *Families We Choose: Lesbians, Gays, Kinship*. New York: Columbia.

FURTHER READING

Adams, Bert N., and Jan Trost, eds. 2005. *Handbook of World Families*. London: Sage.

Ariès, Philippe. 1962. *Centuries of Childhood: A Social History of Family Life*, translated by Robert Baldick. New York: Vintage.

Baker, Maureen. 2001. *Families, Labour and Love: Family Diversity in a Changing World*. Vancouver: UBC Press.

Eichler, Margrit. 1997. *Family Shifts: Families, Policies, and Gender Equality*. Oxford: Oxford University Press.

Scott, Jacqueline, Judith Treas, and Martin Richards, eds. 2004. *The Blackwell Companion to the Sociology of Families*. Oxford: Blackwell.

Fairy Tales

PAULINE GREENHILL
University of Winnipeg, Canada

Fairy tales can be oral (told by people in different geographic locations and at various historical times up to the present) and/or literary (written by known authors). All concern the fantastic, the dark, the dreamy, the wishful, and the wonderful. They usually involve an unpromising hero or heroine who overcomes challenges using both magical and ordinary means. People of all genders and sexualities are fairy-tale tellers and audiences. Further, the genders and sexualities represented in these stories are more diverse than many people presume.

Historically, most folklorists (scholars of traditional cultural forms and their communication) understood fairy tales as traditional narratives of wonder and magic, transmitted orally, informally, locally, and face-to-face within communities and social groups. Oral fairy tales have no single textual form, but come in different versions, which reflect the time and place of their telling. Identifying recurring plot patterns in folktales internationally led folklorists to categorize them in numbered types, resulting in the Aarne–Thompson–Uther (ATU) classification system. Not all folktales are fairy tales, however; folklorists understand the latter as *Märchen*, the wonder tales or "tales of magic" numbered 300–749 in the ATU index (Uther 2004 I, 174–396).

Literary fairy tales concern wonderful and magical events and times and are written by authors such as Hans Christian Andersen, L. Frank Baum, Lewis Carroll, Mary Louisa (Stewart) Molesworth, Edith (Bland) Nesbit, and Oscar Wilde. Though based primarily in an individual writer's creativity, literary fairy tales may draw upon previously published or unpublished materials for their characters and plot. The oral–literary distinction may seem easy, but the actual differences are not always clear. Oral fairy tales are often collected and transcribed into written form (such as the works of the Grimm brothers) and most folks in the Global North now encounter all kinds of fairy tales mainly in books and on film. Some fairy tales come in both traditional and literary forms. Andersen's "The Princess and the Pea" is based on a traditional folktale type called "The Princess on the Pea" (ATU 704). And the two forms are rarely discrete in the popular imagination; Andersen's "The Little Mermaid" is generally seen as the same kind of story as the oral/traditional "Sleeping Beauty" (ATU 410). Thus, though literary tales may have an original text, many are intermediated into other forms, from film to television to graphic art to novels, just like oral tales.

To complicate the picture further, most twenty-first century folk from the Global North know oral tales primarily from written versions noted by scholars like the Brothers Grimm, whose anthology *Children's and Household Tales* is probably the best-known printed collection. Perhaps the most popular versions of oral and literary tales are the films by the Walt Disney Company. These two male-identified cultural gatekeepers, the Grimms and Disney, may be responsible for some feminists, beginning in the 1960s and 1970s, dismissing the fairy tale as a hopelessly and irredeemably heteropatriarchal and sexist genre. Both the Grimms and Disney heavily edited and expurgated the stories they retold. The Grimms foregrounded moral lessons and inserted Christianity into their tales. Often their stories punish women who fail to be appropriately submissive. In their version of "Snow White" (ATU 709), the evil stepmother must put on red-hot iron shoes and dance herself to death at the story's end. In their "Cinderella" (ATU 510A), pigeons peck out the eyes of the main character's wicked stepsisters. The Grimms also changed evil *mother* figures into evil *stepmothers*, being unable to conceive of biological mothers treating their children badly, as in "Hansel and Gretel" (ATU 327A) when she suggests abandoning the children in the woods. The best-known Grimm tales almost invariably pit a young, beautiful, passive, innocent maiden against an old, ugly, active, evil crone. Disney went even further than the Grimms, overdetermining the innocent persecuted heroine's role, and ensuring that she vanquishes her would-be nemesis, the old witch whose beauty has faded, through rescue by a handsome prince who represents hegemonic masculinity. No wonder feminists were unimpressed!

Yet many (male) collectors gathered fairy tales from women tellers, like the Grimms' Dorothea Viehmann, Jeanette Hassenpflug, and Dortchen Wild. And fairy tales have been rehabilitated from feminist perspectives through a variety of means. The best-known dozen or so traditional fairy tales do not in fact reflect the genre as a whole in their representation of gender roles. Storytellers and scholars alike have recovered and retold less familiar fairy tales that do not maintain white supremacist capitalist heteropatriarchy. Writer Angela Carter's *The Virago Book of Fairy Tales* (1990), for example, includes narratives under headings like "Brave, bold and wilful," "Clever women, resourceful girls and desperate stratagems," and "Good girls and where it gets them." Carter also reworked and retold fairy tales from feminist perspectives in *The Bloody Chamber and Other Stories* (1979). Both well-known and less familiar fairy tales have been approached by feminist and queer/LGBTQ writers, including Olga Broumas, Emma Donoghue, and Jeanette Winterson, teasing out their implications for non-normative sexualities (Turner and Greenhill 2012).

To give one example of just how weird and wonderful a well-known fairy tale can be when approached from feminist and queer perspectives, and the variety of genders and sexualities that it can represent, take the familiar "Little Red Riding Hood" (ATU 333). Most North Americans know the version published by the Grimms in which Little Red Cap, bringing a basket of food to her sick grandmother, meets a wolf in the forest who asks where she is going, and then precedes her to the house where he swallows the grandmother. When Red arrives, the wolf has installed himself in the grandmother's bed, in her clothes. Red comments, in a formulaic series, what big ears, hands, and mouth the grandmother/wolf has, and he eats her too. A passing woodsman shoots the wolf and rescues the grandmother and Red. They put stones in the wolf's belly. When he tries to escape he dies.

But there are at least two other European forms, distinguishable by their endings. In the French text published by Charles Perrault (1628–1703), no savior delivers Red and her grandmother, and the appended moral is thoroughly patriarchal:

> Children, especially attractive, well bred young ladies, should never talk to strangers, for if they should do so, they may well provide dinner for a wolf … [T]here are various kinds of wolves. There are also those who are charming, quiet, polite, unassuming, complacent, and sweet, who pursue young women at home and in the streets. And unfortunately, it is these gentle wolves who are the most dangerous ones of all. (Ashliman 2015)

A third ending, found in oral French versions, involves Red's self-rescue, sometimes aided by female helpers. She recognizes that the wolf is not her grandmother, but goes along with the plot, removing her clothes and getting into bed. Then she tells the wolf that she must relieve herself. Suspicious, he ties a string to her leg, but she undoes the knot. When he discovers her ruse, the wolf runs after her. At the river, washerwomen on the other bank throw sheets across and pull Red to safety. They make the same offer to the wolf, but let go when he is in the middle of the river and he drowns.

Often understood as a parable of rape (implicit in Perrault's moral), ATU 333 not only refers to threatened sexual violence, but also to sexual attraction (potentially mutual) between an adult male and a young girl. The adult male wolf is not only a cross-dresser, transgendering himself in the grandmother's clothing, but also a transbiological figure – a wolf representing himself as a human. Fairy tales are queer, then, not only in the nineteenth- and twentieth-century usage to mean odd, strange-making, eccentric, different, and yet attractive, but also because they implicate lives and theories relating to sexes and sexualities beyond the mainstream and deviating from an alleged norm. That is, binaries of female/male, homosexual/heterosexual, and transgender/cisgender (non-transgender) are not the only possibilities these narratives work with. Further, fairy tales' interpenetration of fantasy and reality allow for eccentricity and strange-making and invite ambiguity and ambivalence, which can spill into the domains of sex, gender, sexuality, and species.

Queer, transgender, and transbiology (humans transforming into or acting or dressing as animals, or animals as humans) appear, for example, in Marie-Catherine d'Aulnoy's (1650–1705) literary fairy tale, "Belle Belle or the Knight Fortuné." A noble but poor father sends his daughter, Belle Belle, off to war in his place. She receives a magical talking horse from a fairy in disguise whom she assists. Dressed as a man, Belle Belle becomes Fortuné (Lucky) and acquires seven miraculous helpers – Strong-Back, Fleet-Foot, Good-Shot, Quick-Ear, Impetuous, Drinker, and Glutton – on their way to join the king's army. The queen (the king's sister) falls in love with the disguised knight; Belle Belle is attracted to the king. The queen's feelings are unrequited, so she tricks her brother into sending Fortuné away to do impossible tasks which s/he completes with her/his helpers' aid. The queen becomes so jealous that she tells the king that Fortuné has attacked her, and s/he is sentenced to death. When her/his coat and vest are removed so s/he can be stabbed, her/his biological sex is revealed. The queen dies and the king marries Belle Belle.

The cross-dressed Belle Belle knows s/he is not Fortuné, but struggles with her/his unrequited (different sex, same gender) love for the king and lack of interest (same sex, different gender) in the queen. The latter's attraction to Fortuné could be termed lesbian – by a presumed cisgender woman toward a cross-dressed woman. In addition, a talking horse transbiologically traverses the boundary with humans, and the ostensibly human helpers with their magical gifts go well beyond conventional ideas of *Homo sapiens*. This fairy tale, like many others, represents a range of genders and sexualities.

SEE ALSO: Cross-Dressing; Queer Theory; Sexism; Sexual Assault/Sexual Violence; Third Genders; Witches

REFERENCES

Ashliman, D.L. 2015. Little Red Riding Hood. Accessed July 15, 2015, at http://www.pitt.edu/~dash/type0333.html.

Carter, Angela. 1979. *The Bloody Chamber and Other Stories*. London: Victor Gollancz.

Carter, Angela. 1990. *The Virago Book of Fairy Tales*. London: Virago.

Turner, Kay, and Pauline Greenhill, eds. 2012. *Transgressive Tales: Queering the Grimms*. Detroit: Wayne State University Press.

Uther, Hans-Jörg. 2004. *The Types of International Folktales: A Classification and Bibliography*, 3 vols. Helsinki: Academia Scientiarum Fennica.

FURTHER READING

Warner, Marina. 1994. *From the Beast to the Blonde: On Fairy Tales and Their Tellers*. London: Chatto & Windus.

Zipes, Jack. 2003. *The Complete Fairy Tales of the Brothers Grimm*, 3rd edn. New York: Bantam Books.

Families of Choice

ALEXIS DEWAELE
Ghent University, Belgium

The concept of families of choice refers to the commitment of chosen, rather than fixed, relationships and ties of intimacy, care, and support. It contains honorary relatives (friends of the family who are called uncle or aunt by children), workplace families (a group of intimately bonding people who share common work-related tasks), and friends as family (see, e.g., Stack 1974). The latter are not restricted to a sexual minority population. Members of an ethnic minority group often build strong emotional ties and share feelings of loyalty that originate in a common descent and life circumstances. In this case, belonging to the same ethnic group is experienced as belonging to the same family (Nardi 1999). Fictive kin can also refer to peer groups helping youth to attain access to college, a form of social capital for vulnerable or deprived groups in society (e.g., immigrants, homeless people), added family members within the context of non-biological parenthood (e.g., in the case of alternative insemination, surrogacy, fosterage, adoption), and supportive non-family ties in the case of aging adults (see, e.g., Tierney and Venegas 2006). From this perspective, "friends as family" seems to refer to a functional social network dynamic that starts to operate when more traditional family networks fail.

For lesbians, gay men, and bisexuals (LGBs) friends as family became a form of political affirmation toward rights for sexual minorities, particularly in the United States (Weston 1991) and to some extent in the United Kingdom (Giddens 1992). It also has its roots in a political project, as within the context of HIV/AIDS these chosen families became a necessary answer to the failure of families of origin and the state to respond adequately to what had become a life-threatening situation for many gay men. Those gay men who were sick and dying often did not have access to the support of their families of origin. Self-organization in the form of a strengthened gay and lesbian community was an appropriate answer to this lack of more traditional sources of support.

Studies show that LGBs more often rely on friends than on family for sexuality-related problems. These friends offer social support, a sense of unity, act as role models, and provide the recognition that is often lacking in their own family (Elizur and Ziv 2001). When family ties are disturbed, conflictual, or even completely severed because of a lack of understanding after an individual's coming out, friendship ties compensate for the loss of support. For LGBs, social support from peers is especially relevant during the development of their sexual identity, and even more so when family members do not accept their sexual orientation. A majority of the young LGB participants in research by Nesmith, Burton, and Cosgrove (1999) had either no or disturbed relationships with their parents. However, they escaped from minority stress (i.e., the psychosocial stress derived from minority status) by maintaining strong and close relationships with peers within the LGB community. For elderly LGBs, these ties with peers are particularly important as their family networks are often weak or nonexistent (Heaphy and Yip 2003).

Families of choice (also referred to as chosen families, extended family, or fictive kin; see, e.g., Weston 1991; Berger and Mallon 1993; Cody and Welch 1997) emphasize the importance of social support from sexual minority peers in cases where family ties are lacking. Research comparing the confident support networks of 1,199 heterosexuals with 2,754 LGBs has shown that the latter group primarily relies on friends for support while heterosexuals primarily rely on family. However, despite these chosen families, young LGBs (aged 28 years or younger) reported a significantly lower number of confidants than young heterosexuals. Therefore, young LGBs might be specifically vulnerable for absent social support in the case of a difficult sexual identity process (Dewaele et al. 2011). An ethic of friendship is especially important for LGBs as a heteronormative climate offers few opportunities to meet peers. Stretching the concept of family, and thus incorporating relationships that are not related to blood ties, also means challenging cultural norms. This could be seen as a claim by sexual minorities for recognition of a non-normative sexual orientation. The myth of a harmonious and warm family circle is a powerful and attractive symbol that is connected to the concept of sexual diversity.

Families of choice are characterized by continuity, a shared history, accessibility (e.g., in an emergency), stability, and commitment. In comparison with biological family ties, they are usually less diverse in age composition. Some LGBs replace their entire family with friends, others integrate friends into their family of origin, and a third group sees family and friends as two separate worlds while still considering family as primordial. There is some diversity in integrating friends within family networks depending on the extent of homonegative attitudes among family members. An evolution in the societal climate plays a central role in this dynamic as the former offers more opportunities to blend family and friends (Nardi 1999).

The concept of families of choice originates from Anglo-Saxon literature. Therefore, it is not culturally neutral and scholars should refrain from conceptualizing it as a universal phenomenon. Individuals from different cultures might differ in how friendship and family are experienced and identified. Giddens (1992) refers to families of choice as a phenomenon that is characteristic of a postmodern society in which individuals free themselves from traditional normative role patterns. Network analysis also shows that there seems to be a trade-off between the number of family and friendship ties in a personal social network. As these networks consist largely of family and friends, these two groups are proportionally divided in relation to each other: more friends means fewer family members, and vice versa (Wellman and Potter 1999). As opportunities to establish social networks and to choose our own social ties have increased, families of choice are a phenomenon that is not specific to sexual minorities.

SEE ALSO: Sexual Minorities

REFERENCES

Berger, Raymond M., and David Mallon. 1993. "Social Support Networks of Gay Men." *Journal of Sociology and Social Welfare*, 20: 155–169.

Cody, Paul J., and Peter L. Welch. 1997. "Rural Gay Men in Northern New England: Life Experiences and Coping Styles." *Journal of Homosexuality*, 33: 51–67.

Dewaele, Alexis, Nele Cox, Wim Van den Berghe, and John Vincke. 2011. "Families of Choice? Exploring the Supportive Networks of Lesbians, Gay Men and Bisexuals." *Journal of Applied Social Psychology*, 41: 338–357.

Elizur, Yoel, and Michael Ziv. 2001. "Family Support and Acceptance, Gay Male Identity Formation, and Psychological Adjustment: A Path Model." *Family Process*, 40: 125–144.

Giddens, Anthony. 1992. *The Transformation of Intimacy: Sexuality, Love and Eroticism in Modern Societies*. Cambridge. Polity.

Heaphy, Brian, and Andrew K. T. Yip. 2003. "Uneven Possibilities: Understanding Non-Heterosexual Ageing and the Implications of Social Change." *Sociological Research Online*, 8(4). Accessed June 10, 2015, at http://www.socresonline.org.uk/8/4/heaphy.html.

Nardi, Peter M. 1999. *Gay Men's Friendships: Invincible Communities*. Chicago: University of Chicago Press.

Nesmith, Andrea A., David L. Burton, and T. J. Cosgrove. 1999. "Gay, Lesbian, and Bisexual Youth and Young Adults: Social Support in Their Own Words." *Journal of Homosexuality*, 37: 95–108.

Stack, Carol B. 1974. *All Our Kin: Strategies for Survival in a Black Community*. New York: Basic Books.

Tierney, William G., and Kristan M. Venegas. 2006. "Fictive Kin and Social Capital: The Role of Peer Groups in Applying and Paying for College." *American Behavioral Scientist*, 49: 1687–1702.

Wellman, Barry, and Stephanie Potter. 1999. "The Elements of Personal Communities." In *Networks in the Global Village: Life in Contemporary Communities*, edited by Barry Wellman, 49–81. Boulder: Westview Press.

Weston, Kath. 1991. *Families We Choose: Lesbians, Gays, Kinship*. New York: Columbia University Press.

Family Planning

DANIELA STEHLIK
Australian National University, Australia

Family planning (FP) – an outcome of the Industrial Revolution and the growth of Western capitalism in the nineteenth century – stands at the convergence of several major current societal influences including population control, race, and the role of the family as well as technological changes such as public health improvements, mass education, and mass media. Globally, institutional "planning" for family size can be observed as either promoting or curtailing such growth.

Institutional control over women's bodies in general and their fertility in particular has a long and complex history, which continues to impact the way in which FP is currently discussed, and how decision-making by the state affects women in society today. This complex interrelationship between the state and FP policies is illustrated here through an Australian case example, which offers a perspective on the power of such policies and the increasingly subtle ways that they influence present-day society.

Terms such as "family planning," "birth control," and/or "contraception" are often used interchangeably. However, the first is understood to be institutionally controlled by the state as the "family" itself is seen as an institution that is controlled to restrict behavior, while "contraception" can best be considered as resting in the domain of more active and personal decision-making by individual women.

Prior to the nineteenth century, any contraception was formally rejected on religious grounds, despite being discreetly practiced by those who had either the education or the wealth to do so. With better public health infrastructure, infant mortality decreased and families became larger, resulting in dramatic urban population growth. Consequently, the question of just how societies could manage to feed, house, and educate this growing population became a critical one for governments.

The writings of Thomas Malthus (1766–1834) were a pivotal influence in early population discussions. His *Essay on the Principle of Population* (1798) argued that there was an inverse relationship between population growth and the ability of agricultural production to keep up with the demands resulting from such growth. In his lifetime, the transition from rural to urban society was completed and around 50 percent of the population of Britain were living in cities by 1850. Checks on such population growth, according to Malthus, could be large-scale events such as famine, disease, or wars, or more personal decision-making such as abstinence or later marriage. He did not support birth control, as at the time it was considered to lead to a decline in morality and a possible breakdown of monogamy and therefore the family unit. However, his polemic gave the state impetus to consider how it could better manage and control population growth, and his writings continue to influence discussion about global population growth. Interestingly, Grimshaw et al. (1994) suggest that the migration to the cities may also have had an influence on the "disappearance" of tried and tested contraceptive practices during the nineteenth century. Such "knowledge and means may have been lost when young people left home, for English cities or for the colonies," while the "non-use of withdrawal, probably the most significant contraceptive before the invention of the pill, must have been due to men's reluctance to limit their fertility and their pleasure, and to women's inability to deny them" (1994, 93).

Throughout the nineteenth century, consideration was focused, with some increasing anxiety, on just *which* population should be growing. In other words, those parts of the population who were educated, middle class, economically secure, and capable of self-control were to be encouraged; those parts of the population who were poor, idle, uneducated, and dependent, and, it was considered, were having far too many children, should be better controlled. By the end of the nineteenth century, education about birth control was well integrated within the middle classes, as the burgeoning mass media was disseminating such information more broadly. As a result, the intense focus of state-controlled "family planning" became largely associated with the working classes and also became intertwined with race. Malthus's arguments directly influenced others whose work became critical in shaping societal attitudes, including Charles Darwin (1809–1882) (natural selection/evolution) and Herbert Spencer (1820–1903). The writings of Spencer, particularly those concerned with population and what has come to be known as "Social Darwinism" (he coined the term "survival of the fittest"), were subsequently a direct influence on the policies associated with social determinism and eugenics. In this way they became linked with a powerful "white and male" worldview associated with the growth of empire and colonialism in the early twentieth century. Jill Julius Matthews argues that social determinism emerged as an ideology of population that had as its central focus "women's bodies; [while] its principal mode of control was women's work within their families; [and] its central icon was the 'Ideal Mother'" (1984, 75, cited in Howe and Swain 1992, 168).

Australia has always had, and continues to have, a concern about population. As a large continent, distant from major European population centers but closer to Asian ones, it became directly preoccupied with ensuring that any immigration should maintain, and grow, the dominant Anglocentric culture. There was a fear not only of white population decline, but also of a lack of future workforce – the so-called "race suicide." These imperatives can be seen to have directly influenced the new nation at its federation in 1901, where the continued declining birth rate became a major concern. Over a period of a generation, a reduction of an average seven children in 1881 to an average of four children in 1911 resulted in the establishment of a Royal Commission in 1903/1904 which reported that this decline could be directly attributed to "deliberate prevention of conception, and destruction of embryonic life" (Santow et al. 1988, 147, cited in Carmichael 1992, 128). This, combined with a growing national mood of "Australia for the white man," resulted in population policies that encouraged FP – i.e., growth of those families that were needed for the state, and a curbing of those families (lower socioeconomic status) that were not. To encourage growth of its Anglo population, the Australian government began to develop policies associated with maternal healthcare and maternity grants (1905), with a maternity allowance in 1912 as a cash bonus; while it had little effect on the birth rate itself at the time, it remains nevertheless an essential component of current family policy.

At the turn of the twentieth century, the first-wave feminist movement – particularly the suffragettes – took the lead in discussions about the role of women in public society. Their demand for political suffrage and for equality in marriage can be seen as a direct rejection of the dominant ideology of woman as the "Angel in the House" with the domestic sphere being her "natural" place. Aspects of this debate, which became known as the "Woman Question," divided the early feminists. Some argued that birth control would enable too much sexual freedom and would damage societal structures through rejection of marriage, increased prostitution, and unwanted children born to single mothers. Others promoted birth control as a fundamental aspect of a woman's right to have control over her own body. An issue common in this debate in Australia was that of public health control over venereal disease; some feminists supported legislation for its compulsory notification on the grounds of equal health, while others viewed it as a loss of civil liberties. The first-wave feminists were also conflicted about contraception, as on the one hand they wanted women to have access to planning technologies, and to curb venereal disease, while on the other hand any advertising of contraception was rejected because it was believed that it could enable sexual "adventures" for both women and men.

In the first two decades of the twentieth century, birth control and the increasing availability of interuterine contraceptive devices meant that any "planning" for family was, for the first time, a decision that women could take alone. This became very political, and was also fraught with ideologies of race. There were some key advocates such as Marie Stopes (1880–1958), who, in 1918, wrote the bestseller *Married Love* and was a champion for women's rights, but who remained a committed eugenicist with views that would today be considered racist. She argued that "through Science," birth control will "raise the race" (Briant 1962, 131). Nevertheless, her writings were very influential (even in the colonies), as were those of another advocate,

Margaret Sanger (1879–1966), who coined the term "birth control" and whose publications included *What Every Girl Should Know* (1912), *What Every Mother Should Know* (1921) (a "birds and bees" fable about sexual reproduction), and *Family Limitation* (1917). In the latter publication, which Sanger aims directly at working-class women, she argues that they "should not have more than two children at most. The average working man can support no more and the average working woman can take care of no more in decent fashion" (Sanger 1917, 1).

The direct relationship between class and FP firmed as it became taken for granted that working-class children were considered not to grow up in healthy environments and it was believed that they were often parented by mothers who were lacking in skill and education. This fundamental aspect of FP continues to the present, as discussed further below. It is interesting to note that, as a direct result of Stopes's and Sanger's advocacy, by the 1930s there were birth control clinics in the United Kingdom and United States, while Australia did not have any.

The eugenics aspect to family planning policy took a chilling turn during the years leading up to and including World War II. For the first-wave feminists, the state-controlled dictates to promote an Aryan race in Germany through the slaughter of many millions forced a serious reconsideration of the purpose and values that had previously underpinned the FP project.

This opportunity arose after the war as the foundations of reconstruction through capitalism and its welfare systems were developed. The family emerged postwar as fundamental to state systems, whether politically capitalist, socialist, or communist. We can see through the growth of the so-called nuclear family, the fashioning of the "teenage years," the ideology of home, and the role of men and women in this part-state, part-marketing world how marriage and the family became central to the reshaping of postwar Western society.

Global population grew in this period and FP became caught up in the politics of developing countries and in the aid responses from developed countries. Malthusian anxieties about population control began to emerge again in the 1960s as the developing world experienced rapid population growth, a trend that concerned those who supported the limitation of population through zero population growth (ZPG) (essentially a limit of two children). A subsequent report, *Limits to Growth* (1972) commissioned by the Club of Rome, which argued that population growth interacts negatively with finite resources, also had a great impact. Another influential text – *The Population Bomb* (1968) – predicted global starvation unless radical action was undertaken. These first world arguments can be seen to have had a direct impact on third world family planning policies. Examples include the Philippines, where national FP was implemented in the early 1970s (and where recent reproductive health legislation has been challenged in the Supreme Court by the Catholic Church), and China's "one child" policy implemented in 1979. The Chinese FP policy has given way to the increasing pressure exerted by the population's move to urban settings and into middle class, and a cancellation of the policy has been announced for the Spring of 2016. The inherent paradox within FP policy is that it is always focused on the most vulnerable in society, in China as elsewhere, and evidence is mounting that those with wealth and education in China are increasingly able to avoid such policies.

In Australia, there was an increase in population from 7.4 million in 1945 to 10.4 million in 1960, and then to 12.6 million by 1970. The majority of this growth (2.9 percent) was due to natural increase (the so-called Baby Boom), while the rest was due to immigration (1.9 percent) (Australian Bureau of

Statistics 1996). While promoting growth, this ideology of family conversely placed pressure on *unmarried* mothers, and during the period from 1930 to 1982 the institutionalized welfare state determined punitive responses to Australian single mothers by compelling them to give up their babies to "forced adoption" systems. In March 2013, the Australian government made a formal apology to these women, estimated to number over 250,000.

The introduction of mass birth control technologies in the early 1960s – specifically the contraceptive pill – gave the second-wave feminist movement a platform from which to argue that FP should be a woman's personal choice, and that the state – if it had to be involved – should assist and support such choice, but not determine it. The mass media, and especially women's magazines, ensured that personal contraception technologies became widely known. As a result, state-based FP became intertwined with the goals and aspirations of the women's movement, particularly women's health policies and programs. Since then, FP policies in Western democracies have become normalized and now appear well integrated into societal norms.

FP itself is no longer considered "radical" or a challenge to societal structures. It has become technologized, with information provided as to various alternative birth control methods. However, this institutionalized FP has its vocal critics. As the nuclear family ideals are challenged, and "families" are increasingly adopting alternative patterns, such as melded, cohabitation, single, and gay and lesbian parenting, these alternatives have undermined the fixed ideologies of "family" and "marriage" and have resulted in political backlashes, specifically regarding the declining birth rate.

There are some direct examples of how FP remains a central political platform for all sides of politics, and how the state continues to influence public attitudes toward the place of the family, of marriage, and of women in society. In Australia, for example, in the mid-1990s, the aid that it was preparing to give to developing nations became highly politicized as demands were made by conservatives that such aid be tied to a ban on any funds being spent on family planning and abortion. In the next decade, a socially conservative political party was established called Family First, and in 2004 the then-conservative treasurer stated that women should have "one [baby] for mum, one for dad, and one for your country" as he announced a "baby bonus" of AUS$3,000. It was subsequently estimated that this policy alone resulted in a population increase of 12,000 between 2004 and 2006, increasing the fertility rate by 3.2 percent. This program was changed in 2013, following the announcement of policies to adopt a paid parental leave scheme instead. However, since the reelection of a conservative federal government in September 2013, the politicization of FP has again emerged as an issue for the determination of Australian aid to developing countries.

Policies associated with FP and with women's rights are therefore deeply connected to the history and culture of each country. They continue to remain vulnerable to political and religious ideologies and will continue to surface as future challenges.

SEE ALSO: Abortion, Legal Status in Global Perspective on; Assisted Reproduction; Birth Control, History and Politics of; Contraception and Contraceptives; Eugenics, Historical and Ethical Aspects of; Eugenics Movements; Families of Choice; Pro-Choice Movement in the United States; Pro-Life Movement in the United States; Sterilization

REFERENCES

Australian Bureau of Statistics. 1996. ABS Australian Social Trends 1996 4102.0. Accessed October 30, 2013, at http://www.abs.gov.au/AUSSTATS/abs@.nsf/2f762f95845417aeca2570

6c00834efa/e2f62e625b7855bfca2570ec0073cdf6!OpenDocument.

Briant, Keith. 1962. *Passionate Paradox: The Life of Marie Stopes*. New York: Norton.

Carmichael, Gordon A. 1992. "So Many Children: Colonial and Post-Colonial Demographic Patterns." In *Gender Relations in Australia: Domination and Negotiation*, edited by Kay Saunders and Raymond Evans, 103–143. Sydney: Harcourt Brace Jovanovich.

Grimshaw, Pat, Marilyn Lake, Ann McGrath, and Marian Quartly. 1994. *Creating a Nation*. Ringwood, Victoria: McPhee Gribble Penguin Books.

Howe, Renate, and Shurlee Swain. 1992. "Fertile Grounds for Divorce: Sexuality and Reproductive Imperatives." In *Gender Relations in Australia: Domination and Negotiation*, edited by Kay Saunders and Raymond Evans, 158–174. Sydney: Harcourt Brace Jovanovich.

Malthus, Thomas. 1798. *An Essay on the Principle of Population*. London: J. Johnson.

Sanger, Margaret. 1917. *Family Limitation*, 6th ed. Accessed October 23, 2013, at http://www.gutenberg.org/catalog/world/readfile?fk_files=1641599&pageno=2.

Stopes, Marie. 1918. *Married Love or Love in Marriage*. New York: Critic and Guide.

FURTHER READING

Brown, Richard. 2002. *Society and Economy in Modern Britain (1700–1859)*. London: Routledge.

Damousi, Joy. 1992. "Marching to Different Drums: Women's Mobilisations, 1914–1939." In *Gender Relations in Australia: Domination and Negotiation*, edited by Kay Saunders and Raymond Evans, 350–375. Sydney: Harcourt Brace Jovanovich.

Gonzales, Iris. 2013. "Philippines: Right to Family Planning Compromised." *New Internationalist*, April 10. Accessed October 31, 2013, at http://newint.org/blog/2013/04/10/philippines-reproductive-health-law/.

Healy Fenton, Anna. 2013. "China's Billionaires Ignore One Child Rule." *South China Morning Post*, October 30. Accessed October 31, 2013, at http://www.scmp.com/comment/blogs/article/1343807/chinas-billionaires-ignore-one-child-rule.

Maiden, Samantha. 2013. "Julie Gillard's Cut-Price Abortion Drug as RU486 Slashed to $12." *Daily Telegraph News*, June 30. Accessed October 31, 2013, at http://www.dailytelegraph.com.au/news/nsw/julia-gillards-cut-price-abortion-drug-as-ru486--slashed-to-12/story-f.

Peatling, Stephanie. 2013. "Echoes of Harradine in Madigan's Meddling on Abortion." *Sydney Morning Herald* February 27. Accessed October 31, 2013, at http://www.smh.com.au/federal-politics/political-opinion/echoes-of-harradine-in-madigans-meddling-on-abortion-20130227--2f59t.html.

Saunders, Kay, and Geoffrey Bolton. 1992. "Girdled for War: Women's Mobilisations in World War Two." In *Gender Relations in Australia: Domination and Negotiation*, edited by Kay Saunders and Raymond Evans, 376–397. Sydney: Harcourt Brace Jovanovich.

Spearitt, Katie. 1992. "New Dawns: First Wave Feminism 1880–1914." In *Gender Relations in Australia: Domination and Negotiation*, edited by Kay Saunders and Raymond Evans, 325–349. Sydney: Harcourt Brace Jovanovich.

Wilkinson, M. N. 1986. "Good Mothers – Bad Mothers: State Substitute Care of Children in the 1960s." In *Gender Reclaimed: Women in Social Work*, edited by Marianne H. Marchant and B. Wearing, 93–103. Sydney: Hale Iremonger.

Family Wage

JULIA WARTENBERG
Independent scholar

The traditional notion of family wage refers to a nuclear family where the male (husband/father) is cast in the breadwinner role as a single-wage earner, while the female (wife/mother) is cast in the caregiving role responsible for domestic duties. Both the woman and the children are dependent upon the man for economic resources, thus a foundational premise of this model is that a man's wages are sufficient to meet family needs. This model has been falling out of date for a number of decades as a result of women entering the paid labor force, some becoming primary breadwinners; wage stagnation necessitating families to become dual-wage earner households; and the rise in number of homosexual couples, single-parent families, and multi-generational households. The initial critique for family wage originated from the feminist movement (Creighton 1996).

Two key standpoints have critiqued the family wage model and its depiction of the relationship between gender and work. The first stresses the role of patriarchy, arguing that men came to control women's paid labor and that women's fewer economic resources pushed them into a subordinate position in the public and family economy. The second underscores the role of working-class resistance and their effort to use the family structure to raise wages (May 1982).

The family wage model first gained attention in the early 1800s. The rise of the theory's influence corresponded with increased industrialization, labor activism, and trade unionist rhetoric of the working class which characterized that time (Fraser 1994). During the agrarian era, women, children, and men were employed and the idea that a male breadwinner could earn sufficient income to support a family was illogical to the working class. The creation of factories and their influence on labor practices helped drive the emergence of family wage (Land 1980). Indeed, the model's growth was influenced by trade unionists and the working class as they fought for increased workers' wages. Working-class advocates maintained that a family wage would provide a solution to the inadequate and decreasing wages that resulted in the poverty of workers and their families. Thus, one reason for demanding the family wage was to realize an increase in the amount that was earned under current wage rates and eliminate the need for children and women to supplement the male's wages. Initially, the belief that the male was the family breadwinner meant that only women had to leave the paid labor force. It was not until the second half of the nineteenth century that family wage added children. The purpose of the family wage came to mean that the adult male wage was to provide a decent standard of living for and support a family and their social and economic reproduction (Fraser 1994; Land 1980; May 1982).

During the early nineteenth century, gender ideology in the industrialized West increasingly focused on separate spheres for women and men; men were to hold public positions including wage-earning jobs, and women were to be responsible for caregiving and domestic duties. This ideological separation did more than idealize the female domestic caregiver role, it provided rationalization and validation for women to be treated as second-class earners in the paid labor force through three practices: (1) giving women lower wages, (2) denying women certain jobs and classifying others as female-work, and (3) denying married women employment all together. In so doing, the relationship of men, women, and children became one where men were viewed as a necessary financial resource for the survival of all. Furthermore, it cemented the notion that it was socially desirable for a woman to be financially dependent on the man. Domestic welfare was equated with neither women nor children working and signified a certain standard of living (May 1982; Carlson 1996).

But there was another underlying argument for keeping women out of the labor force. The family wage model was based on the premise that all women would eventually become wives and mothers and therefore would want and need to leave the paid labor force. The argument held that by entering the labor force, women diminished earnings and made it increasingly difficult for wages (of men) to ever reach a living standard. Proponents of family wage maintained that women and children had to be kept out of the labor force precisely so that they did not create competition for men, who were working to provide all the necessities for their families. In addition, for those women who did work, it was supposed that perhaps their earned income provided the family with some financial help, but it was done so to the detriment of the children's and family's overall well-being. This eventually led to the belief and practice that males' minimum wages needed to be based on the fact that the man would eventually be financially responsible for a dependent family, regardless of whether he currently had one. Conversely, a woman was believed to eventually marry and become dependent. Never was it supposed that a woman would be the financial head of household. The result was a heavy depression of female wages (May 1982; Fraser 1994; Carlson 1996).

The ideology of the male-earned family wage served as a powerful argument for women's domestic role and second-wage earner position. To this day, many maintain the ideal family construction is one of a male breadwinner and female caregiver. Despite its dominance, evidence indicates that the majority of workers never received a family wage nor do they today.

SEE ALSO: Feminisms, First, Second, and Third Wave; Gender Inequality and Gender Stratification; Gender Wage Gap

REFERENCES

Carlson, Allan C. 1996. "Gender, Children, and Social Labor: Transcending the 'Family Wage' Dilemma." *Journal of Social Issues*, 52(3): 137–161.
Creighton, Colin. 1996. "The 'Family Wage' as a Class-Rational Strategy." *Sociological Review*, 44(2): 204–224.
Fraser, Nancy. 1994. "After the Family Wage: Gender Equity and the Welfare State." *Political Theory*, 22(4): 591–618.
Land, Hilary. 1980. "The Family Wage." *Feminist Review*, 6: 55–77.
May, Martha. 1982. "The Historical Problem of the Family Wage: The Ford Motor Company and the Five Dollar Day." *Feminist Studies*, 8(2): 399–424.

FURTHER READING

Barrett, Michelle, and Mary McIntosh. 1980. "The Family Wage: Some Problems for Socialists and Feminists." *Capital & Class*, 4(2): 51–72.

Fashion

DENISHIA HARRIS
University of Connecticut, USA

Fashion (the term used to connote visible styles of clothing or types of material that are highly valued at a particular time) creates and attributes meaning and symbolic values to particular forms of material culture (Crane and Bovone 2006). The consumers of these goods for the purpose of body dressing take part in shaping the meanings of these material goods, which are the medium through which social life is experienced and expressed. The ability to self-fashion in ways that appeal to dominant ideas of taste is often indicative of social class, and can be used as a social, institutional, and cultural exclusionary practice. Clothing, in a sense, is embedded with a host of symbolic values, ideas centered on authenticity, legitimacy, and class preferences.

Knowledge of clothing appropriateness, especially in relation to the dominant ideas of body types, can work as a form of cultural capital in public spaces. Cultural capital is often used as a conceptual tool to understand or decode fine art, music, fashion, and a host of leisure activities that the dominant classes value (Bourdieu 1987). The capacity to understand these forms of culture, according to Bourdieu, is often unequally distributed across social classes since the mode of transmission is primarily within the family. Long-term exposure to atmospheres that enhance cultural capital allows for the development of taste in "legitimate culture," which contemporarily can be read as popular culture.

Cultural capital, understood in this way, links consumer goods to social norms that govern ideas related to legitimacy, which in turn mediate ideas relating to taste, status, and distinction. Taken together, taste, status, and distinction function as markers of social status, which facilitates the unequal participation of certain groups in status-producing activities, while providing opportunities for social advancement among groups that possess status by virtue of their race and/or class position, or have access to cultural knowledge through outside means (Bourdieu 1987; Halle 1992).

When conceptualized as a form of cultural capital, clothing can be seen as providing individuals with opportunities for social advancement depending on the importance of self-presentation within a given social setting. One such example is ideas related to "dressing for success" when working in corporate environments or dressing for religious services. Being appropriately dressed in these spaces could provide individuals with a degree of acceptance and belonging that is not extended to those who do not follow dress code expectations. Self-fashioning as a form of cultural capital also intersects with gender in a myriad of ways since women typically are expected to be fashionable socially, adorned with various accessories, and properly groomed according to dominant standards, which are not expectations of their male counterparts. Media cultures also work to forward ideas about the importance of self-fashioning and style as a way of securing a romantic partner, career advancement, and self-esteem development.

Processes of self-fashioning, such as body dressing and hairstyling, often mediate the types of experiences that individuals have with their physical bodies, especially in the public realm (Merleau-Ponty 1976). When coupled with gender, class, sexuality, and race, these experiences become both heightened and complex; as such, body dressing and self-fashioning take on a number of forms and functions in the public lives of individuals. Although body dressing is a significant practice in the everyday lives of all individuals, these practices can often be taken for granted or imagined as frivolous endeavors if an individual is overly concerned with his or her outward appearance. However, these practices (which can be read as performative in nature) are essential elements of socialization in public life, bearing more importance in some spaces than others (such as the workplace). A variety of cultural values that are associated with different styles and dress preferences become attached to individual race, class, gender, and sexual identities. As a result, different types of dress and style preferences are often read as visible representations of identity and are presumed to communicate signals about morality, dignity, and deviance. This is especially true for both women and people of color (Collins 2005).

Like many social behaviors, rules regulating dress expectations are often taken for granted and routinely enforced, although many individuals seek to be innovative and defy popular notions of dress and style. The physical body, once dressed, provides the material for the performance of identity and the showcasing of social belonging. According to Entwistle and Wilson (2001) body dressing not only makes visible the intentions of individuals on a daily basis but is also the medium through which individuals are read by strangers. All cultures participate in the process of body dressing and adornment, to some extent, through avenues such as tattooing, clothing, hairstyles, and piercings (Douglas 1973). Clothing and the "self" are closely intertwined, especially when one considers the location of clothing in relation to the body and its ability to act as a filter between our private and social worlds (Crane and Bovone 2006).

Social worlds are shaped by a plethora of bodily practices and interactions, as individuals negotiate, conform to, or reject social norms, of which dress and style are a part. For instance, the unclothed or improperly clothed body is often subjected to social stigma in public spaces as a result of both social norms and political legislature that govern the degree to which a body should be covered or uncovered in public and in private (Entwistle and Wilson 2001). These ideas related to the properly clothed (and unclothed) body are typically structured around beliefs about gender norms, religion, race, class, and sexuality. Scholars have shown that the way in which a woman's body is clothed (or unclothed) is often considered to be an indicator of a variety of personal attributes such as sexual availability, values, morals, and self-esteem (Collins 2005). On the other hand, most clothing styles for men, especially styles that are associated with white middle-class males, are typically not subjected to the same types of social stigmas and ideas related to morality and values as those of women. However, it is important to note that styles that are favored by subcultures or men of color (such as urban wear that stems from hip-hop culture) are often associated with social deviance and, in some cases, delinquency (May and Chaplin 2008).

In many ways, body dressing functions as an avenue of self-expression that is rooted in aesthetic sensibilities and dominant notions of style and culture. As such, body dressing should be viewed neither as simply applying accessories and materials that serve only as a source of protection from the forces of nature nor as mere outer decoration to conceal one's naked body. It is important to consider the ways that individuals express facets of identity through modes of dress, such as morality, which can be read, understood, and interpreted by strangers in both private and public spaces. The social body, which is the body that enters the public domain, plays an expansive role in determining how the boundaries of dress are enforced and structured depending on the social locations. Mechanisms for ensuring that dress code standards are followed and adhered to can often vary from time to place (Entwistle and Wilson 2001).

Self-fashioning and body dressing also allow individuals to characterize facets of their identities through visual representations. Individuals shape their appearances through a variety of situated bodily practices. Through these processes, body dressing and style act as mechanisms for managing individual appearance in daily life while also helping to situate one's visual identity as it relates to social expectations. Through body dressing, individuals are able to construct "appearances" as well as an understanding of their relationship to others, the consumer market, and media cultures (Entwistle and Wilson 2001). These entities become especially important in the creation of boundaries of social life, market participation, and citizenship. Styles of dress that are seen as aesthetically displeasing or gender inappropriate become socially stigmatized and can affect individuals who opt, through choice or circumstance, not to stay within the dominant perimeters of style and clothing boundaries.

Pervasive images related to style and beauty can also shape the ways in which both women and people of color conform to, reject, or transform cultural standards and expectations related to self-fashioning. Previous research has shown that popular ideas (often disseminated through channels such as print media and television) about "normal" bodies, standards of beauty, and the importance of hyperconsumption of clothing and personal care products disproportionately affect the two aforementioned groups. However, in view of their low-ranking status positions in many of the racial hierarchies present in, but not limited to, the West, women of color often rely on self-fashioning and consumption to do identity work as well (Lamont and Molnar 2001). According to Lamont and Molnar (2001), black women spend more on personal care products and luxury consumer goods than their white counterparts, despite a lower median household income. Also, black women are often subjected to popular beauty ideas and standards that are premised on European features such as straight hair and lighter skin tones (Collins 2005). Scholars have also shown how, both historically and contemporarily, the physical features, hairstyles, and dress preferences that are associated with women of color are seen as undesirable since they are typically marginalized within the realm of popular culture. As a result, the lack of diverse representation in popular culture, specifically as it relates to beauty standards, styles of dress, and bodily adornment, can lead to discrimination, negative mental health outcomes, and harmful beauty rituals that put women of color at risk for physical disfigurement and extreme bodily pain.

For instance, many African-descent women often have hair textures that are curlier than their white counterparts and often choose to chemically alter their hair texture for the purposes of creating a texture that is more straight than frizzy. For some women, the decision to alter their hair texture is conceptualized as a personal choice for the purposes of having a style that is "easier to manage" and provides versatility; however, it should be noted that straight hair is also associated with European hair textures, which are predominant in popular culture. Women of African descent who choose not to alter their hair with chemicals, and thus do not fit easily into dominant notions of beauty and style, could hinder the degree to which they are socially accepted and even achieve career advancement. Employers have previously prohibited certain hairstyles that African-descent women typically prefer, such as braids, under doctrines of professionalization within their work environments (Bird and Tharps 2002). Thus, chemically altered hair can be used as a form of cultural capital by African-descent women in order to achieve both social and institutional gains. Taken together, the choice to adhere to, or reject, dominant standards of beauty by women of color, and women in general, goes beyond stagnant ideas of hyperindividualism and conforming to social norms. Additionally, women are often concentrated in white-collar careers that tend to conceptualize women as key representatives of the company image since they are often the first people outsiders meet in an organization (such as administrative assistants). As such, women in general within the labor force frequently have heightened concerns and expectations related to dress and self-presentation (Lamont and Fournier 1992).

Bodies navigate through space and time with knowledge of themselves as gendered, with women being more body conscious than men because of their identity being so closely tied with their body type and mechanics (Mauss 1973). Bodily practices, such as self-fashioning and dress, are a part of the operations of power that work to render bodies docile and obedient (Foucault 1977). As such, the process of dressing often codes bodies as being both meaningful and productive within public and private spaces (Entwistle and Wilson 2001). The body can be understood as the property of the individual and of the social world; as a result of this dual ownership, the body is both subjected to, and managed by, social forces that impose ways of being and that shape ideas of social appropriateness (Goffman 1971). According to Douglas (1973), the social body works to constrain the ways in which the physical body is both seen and experienced. As such, social, political, and cultural doctrines and expectations provide guidelines about how bodies should be dressed and maintained; these ideas are also shaped and governed by popular media cultures, the labor force, religion, and families. The social relationship that exists between dress, the body, individuals, and society is one of co-dependency, as they each rely on one another for varying forms of social meanings and validation. These relationships of power often structure meanings of dress and style, which act upon physical bodies in ways that are celebratory, discriminatory, and liberating.

SEE ALSO: Body Politics; Class, Caste, and Gender; Skin Lightening/Bleaching

REFERENCES

Bird, Ayana, and Lorie Tharps. 2002. *Hair Story: Untangling the Roots of Black Hair in America*. New York: St. Martin's Press.
Bourdieu, Pierre. 1987. *Distinction: A Social Critique of the Judgement of Taste*. Cambridge, MA: Harvard University Press.
Collins, Patricia Hill. 2005. *Black Sexual Politics: African Americans, Gender, and the New Racism*. New York: Routledge.
Crane, Diana, and Laura Bovone. 2006. "Approaches to Material Culture: The Sociology of Fashion and Clothing." *Poetics*, 34: 319–333.
Douglas, Mary. 1973. *Rules and Meanings: The Anthropology of Everyday Knowledge*. New York: Penguin.
Entwistle, JoAnne, and Elizabeth B. Wilson. 2001. *Body Dressing*. New York: Berg.
Foucault, Michel. 1977. *Discipline and Punish: The Birth of the Prison*. New York: Pantheon.
Goffman, Erving. 1971. *Relations in Public*. New York: Harper Perennial.
Halle, Dave. 1992. "The Audience for Abstract Art: Class, Culture, and Power." In *Cultivating Differences: Symbolic Boundaries and the Making of Inequality*, edited by Michèle Lamont and Marcel Fournier, 131–151. Chicago: University of Chicago Press.
Lamont, Michèle, and Marcel Fournier, eds. 1992. *Cultivating Differences: Symbolic Boundaries and the Making of Inequality*. Chicago: University of Chicago.
Lamont, Michèle, and V. Molnar. 2001. "How Blacks Use Consumption to Shape Their Collective Identity: Evidence from Marketing Specialists." *Journal of Consumer Culture*, 1(1): 31–45.
Mauss, Marcel. 1973. "Technologies of the Body." *Economy and Society*, 2(1): 70–88.
May, Reuben A. Buford, and Kenneth Sean Chaplin. 2008. "Cracking the Code: Race, Class, and Access to Nightclubs in Urban America." *Qualitative Sociology*, 31: 57–72.
Merleau-Ponty, Maurice. 1976. *The Primacy of Perception*. Evanston, IL: Northwestern University Press.

Fatherhood Movements

NANCY SANTUCCI and JOCELYN CROWLEY
Rutgers University, USA

Fatherhood movements are broad-based forms of collective action that focus on more clearly defining the role of fathers in modern families. These movements are concentrated in industrialized nations including the United States, Canada, Sweden, England, and Australia. Fatherhood movements are composed of two types of organizations: those that concentrate on advocacy and policy research and those that are membership based with actual fathers as participants. Fathers are attracted to all of these organizations in order to redefine their roles in the changing nature of families.

Various factors have contributed to the development of fatherhood movements including shifting demographics, fluctuating gender roles, and women's increased participation in the labor market. For the past 30 years, household demographics have changed throughout the world. These demographics include the increase of children living with single parents, the decline of marriage, the increase of divorce, and the rise of nonmarital births, all of which lead to more children living away from their fathers (Collier and Sheldon 2006). When these trends began, child custody and child support laws became essential. Decisions needed to be made about where a child would reside and who would assume responsibility for the costs of raising that child. Formula-based custody decisions generally favored mothers based on a variety of factors. Fathers commonly provided payments to mothers for child support.

Gender roles are also changing from the traditional roles of the father as breadwinner and the mother as housewife. Women are employed in paid work and are more likely than ever to be breadwinners in their families. Therefore, in contrast to women of previous eras, many more women today view paid work as part of a fulfilled life.

Despite the increase of women's participation in the labor market and paid work, men's participation in unpaid care work has not increased at the same rate. Women generally spend more than twice the amount of time as men on care work. Fathers' time with children is often filled with more playtime and leisure, while mothers' time is consumed with caretaking tasks. Consequently, while the roles outside of home have changed significantly, the duties of women as primary caregivers have not; this contributes to the disproportionate number of custody cases that favor women.

However, since the 1980s, the perception of a "good father" has also changed. Good fathers are considered involved fathers. They are also more emotionally invested and spend more time with their children as compared with fathers from earlier decades. For some, the breadwinner role is not sufficient and men are expected to be nurturing and hands-on with their children. With this emerging idea of what constitutes a good father, men are increasingly expected to fight for a strong relationship with their children (Collier and Sheldon 2006).

The groups that have emerged out of the fatherhood movement vary in their missions. Pro-marriage groups, for example, are dominant in the United States and stress that marriage and parenthood should be sequential; they tend to be oriented toward advocacy rather than membership based. Pro-marriage groups promote marriage as necessary for positive relationships between fathers and children. These groups also argue that motherhood is more biologically instinctive than fatherhood. Therefore, in order for fathers to contribute their time, money, and energy into a family, marriage should be encouraged (Gavanas 2004). Another critical belief of pro-marriage groups is that the roles of men and women in a family are complementary. While they can be loving, men should be focused more on financially providing for the family and women should be more responsible for caregiving needs. In this way, a perfectly functioning family unit can be formed.

The National Fatherhood Initiative (NFI) is one example of an influential, pro-marriage group. The NFI was founded in 1994 and focuses on media campaigns and training on fatherhood skills in community-based organizations. It also produces research on the importance of fathers in children's lives. Fathers can donate to NFI or sign up to receive advice from the NFI's Dads Club, an Internet-based source of informational exchange. Other pro-marriage groups include the Institute for American Values, a research organization that was formed in 1987 and publishes articles on American culture and the importance of marriage, among other topics.

Like the pro-marriage groups, responsible fatherhood groups promote the presence of fathers in children's lives. Responsible fatherhood groups focus on the role of fathers in a family and their necessity for social order and the well-being of children (Gavanas 2004). Responsible fatherhood groups believe that the absence of fathers is at the root of many social problems. Some groups promote the traditional, less-engaged type of fatherhood, while others advocate on behalf of a more modern fatherhood that places less significance on gender in regard to caretaking tasks. Much of the emphasis of responsible fatherhood groups has been on reviving the importance of male parenting in low-income neighborhoods. These are places where single parents – primarily women – are often left to parent on their own. According to responsible fathers' groups, fathers in these communities need to assume greater control over their own educational investments, employment trajectories, and citizenship duties in order to be the best parents possible to their children. Similar to pro-marriage groups, many of these responsible fatherhood groups are not membership groups, but rather focus on research and advocacy.

For instance, the United Kingdom's Fatherhood Institute, a think tank, focuses on supporting both mothers and fathers in their dual roles as caretakers and wage earners. The Institute also aims to prepare boys and girls for a future of caretaking. Another example of a responsible fatherhood group is Men Care. Men Care is a global campaign that promotes men as non-violent caregivers through the media and advocacy. Men Care partners with other organizations to provide education on their common ideas of responsible fatherhood.

Spiritual groups are another type of fatherhood movement. These groups see the social progress of the 1960s as a hindrance to the natural order of a household. Religious groups use biblical imagery to carve out a particularly male position in the family (Gavanas 2004). Placing God at the center of this order, these groups believe that men must reassert their natural, authoritative positions in their families. Like the pro-marriage groups, spiritual groups see men's and women's roles as well defined. Stressing biological differences between men and women, the groups maintain that men and women occupy separate roles in the social structure, with men as heads of households and women taking on secondary, supportive roles (Crowley 2006).

Spiritual groups are mostly dominant in the United States and are membership based. Promise Keepers is one of the most influential of these groups. Promise Keepers groups exist in Canada and New Zealand in addition to the United States. The group follows a set of seven promises that center on obedience to God's word. Its main web site encourages men to lead their families to church by referencing "collapsing" marriages and a "crumbling" society. The Promise Keepers hold conference events that frequently fill arenas. Attendees generally pay an admission price to participate.

Lastly, fathers' rights groups (FRGs) are another fatherhood movement; they focus on individual fathers' rights in the context of separation and divorce. These groups exist in many countries. The differences among the groups depend upon various characteristics of a country, including its religious composition, accepted gender roles, and formal legal systems (Collier and Sheldon 2006). FRGs are membership based and, unlike many of the other types of movements, meet in person regularly (Crowley 2006). These groups operate on the premise that they do not have equal rights with mothers in the family law courtroom.

FRGs generally have in-person meetings that attract both men and women. Women often attend as new wives, girlfriends, or relatives of men in order to provide support. Members of FRGs see case management as a main motivation of attending meetings. Members will ask each other for advice about their court cases during their meetings. Many have questions about how the case will proceed and are looking to receive guidance from the group (Crowley 2008). This free advice reduces the need to hire a lawyer. In addition, the meetings proceed in a way that allows any member to have an opportunity to speak. Other members will offer information on legal tactics and stories of their own experiences in dealing with similar problems (Crowley 2006). At times, local attorneys attend the meetings in the hope of obtaining new clients, but also to offer free counsel about the court system.

Emotional assistance is another part of the foundation of many FRGs. After divorce or separation, men may seek a way to express their emotions, but ultimately find few outlets (Crowley 2008). While many women have developed support systems necessary to cope with the ending of their relationships and marriages, men do not necessarily have this same built-up network of friends and close familial associates. The FRGs provide a safe space for men to discuss their feelings. Just as FRGs reduce the need for lawyers, these networks of fathers serve as substitute therapists for members (Crowley 2006). Members have a common bond and feel more equipped to face their cases with the support of their fellow members.

Lastly, a large part of the meeting time is devoted to strategies to affect public policy. The fathers in these groups believe they can influence public policy through their strength in numbers. A group of fathers with the same complaints is more seriously considered by policymakers than just one father speaking out on his own.

First, one of the most important public policy issues that members wish to reform in the United States is the country's child support laws. The penalties for non-compliance with child support laws have increasingly strengthened since the mid-1970s (Collier and Sheldon 2006). Many group members argue that men and women now have equal opportunities at home and in the workforce. Therefore, child support laws are outdated and unnecessary. Those who wish to change the laws believe the mathematical formula used to determine child support, as well as the tax codes, discriminate against them. In many cases, they also believe that women will use the child support money on themselves, not their children (Collier and Sheldon 2006).

Second, FRG members who wish to influence public policy also focus on child custody reform. Joint legal and joint physical custody are the two types of custody in the United States. Joint legal custody refers to the shared parental influence over decisions made that affect the child's life. Joint physical custody occurs when a child spends equal time in each parent's household. While mothers were favored overwhelmingly for custody at the beginning of the twentieth century, the "best interests of the child" became the basis of decisions in later years (Collier and Sheldon 2006). Yet children are still overwhelmingly placed in their mother's custody according to this standard. FRGs believe this is because judges treat fathers unequally. Members maintain that men and women are equally skilled in the caretaking sphere, and therefore they should be treated equally in custody decisions. Ultimately, if FRGs were to be successful, achieving joint child custody would lead to the elimination of child support.

Fatherhood movements overall have not been without their detractors. In the case of pro-marriage campaigns, responsible fatherhood initiatives, and spiritual fatherhood movements, some scholars have questioned these groups' common claims. Prominent among these principles is a moral philosophy that argues that all families should be organized around a strong male leader/father figure. This assertion not only serves to reinforce rigid sex roles within the family, but also casts other family types, such as those headed by women, as deficient. In addition, these fatherhood movements often suggest that traditional, father-headed families are the only way to cure a variety of social ills such as crime, adolescent pregnancy, and even poverty. Critics argue that the origins of these social problems are extremely complex and not necessarily solved by the institution of father-headed families.

Fathers' rights movements in particular have received additional scrutiny. Feminists have asserted that FRGs have argued for increased custodial rights not as a way to spend more time raising their children, but rather to exert additional control over their former partners. In this way, feminists have maintained that these groups want more rights regarding their children, but not more responsibilities.

Domestic violence groups have also criticized FRGs for minimizing the seriousness of violence in families. On this point, many FRGs complain that domestic violence groups demonize all men as potential abusers and thus intimidate men from seeking increased custodial time with their children. In addition, FRGs frequently suggest that women are as violent as men along such metrics as the severity and frequency of abuse wielded, a claim that domestic violence groups dispute.

Finally, scholars have pointed out that FRGs can potentially do serious harm to their own members (Flood 2012). FRGs spend significant time providing case management and emotional assistance to their members. However, in the process of offering men advice on these issues in a meeting setting, leaders (as well as other members) can perpetuate feelings of hate toward female ex-partners and overall frustration with the court system. Rather than provide fathers with useful information about how to heal from their familial break-ups, these groups then may simply reinforce negative views about women overall and discourage men from taking an active role in doing the difficult daily work of providing care for their children.

SEE ALSO: Child Custody and the Father Right Principle; Division of Labor, Domestic; Domestic Violence in the United States; Fathers and Parenting Interventions; Head of Household and Supplementary Earner

REFERENCES

Collier, Richard, and Sally Sheldon. 2006. *Fathers' Rights Activism and Law Reform in Comparative Perspective*. Oxford: Hart Publishing.

Crowley, Jocelyn E. 2006. "Organization Responses to the Fatherhood Crisis: The Case of Fathers' Rights Groups in the United States." *Marriage and Family Review*, 39: 99–120. DOI: 10.1300/J002v39n01_06.

Crowley, Jocelyn E. 2008. *Defiant Dads: Fathers' Rights Activists in America*. Ithaca, NY: Cornell University Press.

Flood, Michael. 2012. "Separated Fathers and the 'Fathers' Rights' Movement." *Journal of Family Studies*, 18: 235–245.

Gavanas, Anna. 2004. *Fatherhood Politics in the United States: Masculinity Sexuality, Race, and Marriage*. Chicago: University of Illinois Press.

FURTHER READING

Boyd, Susan B. 2003. *Child Custody, Law, and Women's Work*. Toronto: Oxford University Press.

Dragiewicz, Molly. 2011. *Equality with a Vengeance: Men's Rights Groups, Battered Women, and Antifeminist Backlash*. Boston: Northeastern University Press.

Fineman, Martha A., and Michael Thomson. 2013. *Exploring Masculinities: Feminist Legal Theory Reflections (Gender in Law, Culture, and Society)*. Farnham, UK: Ashgate Publishing.

Heath, Melanie. 2012. *One Marriage Under God: The Campaign to Promote Marriage in America (Intersections)*. New York: New York University Press.

Fathers and Parenting Interventions

ADRIENNE BURGESS
Fatherhood Institute, UK

Family scholars, policymakers, and practitioners increasingly recognize the theoretical and practical importance of carrying out research on men and fathers and engaging them in interventions with families (O'Brien 2011). Interventions can have a meaningful positive impact on mothers' parenting, especially when they are substantial and delivered by well-trained professionals. It is likely that fathers' parenting can also be positively supported through such means. However, in this field, preoccupation with women's experiences has led to biases, oversights, and gaps in knowledge, such that the evidence base relating to fathers' participation in interventions that address parents' knowledge, attitudes, skills, and self-efficacy in parenting is small, methodologically weak, and overwhelmingly from the global north (Western contexts) (McAllister et al. 2012).

Thousands of such interventions that have engaged mothers have been reported in the international literature. However, a systematic review of the international evidence in English-language publications (Panter-Brick et al. 2014) identified only 92 that addressed fathers or couples or, when engaging with "parents," disaggregated participation and findings by sex-of-parent. Most were in the global north, with 57 from the United States and Canada. Only 12 were found in non-Western contexts (the global south) in Turkey, Ukraine, Israel, Jordan, Iran, Mexico, Brazil, Peru, China, Niger, and Pakistan. In both Western and non-Western contexts, sample sizes of fathers were usually small, the impact of engaging with both parents (as opposed to just one) was almost never measured, and outcomes were generally recorded only in the very short term and mainly relied on parent report. Only 11 of 34 programs identified as "exemplars" by Panter-Brick and colleagues benefited from randomized controlled trial (RCT) evaluation (eight of these were in the United States). Only 11 reported impacts on children (none in the global south).

Failure by practitioners, policymakers, and program evaluators to address men's parenting and other relevant behaviors makes mothers unfairly responsible for implementing and maintaining change in families (Zanoni et al. 2013). In addition to greater sharing of responsibilities, benefits for mothers when fathers are also engaged include more sensitive interactions with (and attachment to) their children. Specific positive changes recorded in fathers' parenting include sensitivity to infant cues, improved communication with children and mothers, more positive parenting attitudes, and more time spent with their child, as well as reduced intrusiveness and harsh parenting, particularly where their participation in the program is substantial (Burgess 2009; Panter-Brick et al. 2014).

Practitioners often seek to engage fathers in men-only groups. While positive changes can be achieved, men-only groups are unacceptable to many fathers and when both parents are engaged, changes at home are introduced more quickly and gains are maintained for longer (Cowan et al. 2009). Home-visiting can be a productive arena for engaging fathers, and activity-based rather than discussion-based interventions may have greater appeal for fathers (these may also appeal to mothers). Use of video (self-recorded, perhaps on a phone, with playback and discussion with a trained professional) has been well received by parents of both sexes (Lawrence et al. 2013).

Since parenting interventions are often designed with mothers in mind, and do not address either gender or co-parenting issues, content, style, methods, goals, and facilitator training may need to be modified to include fathers and couples successfully (Lundahl et al. 2008). And to ensure that sufficient fathers will attend, health, education, and family service providers must operate from a "father-inclusive" perspective. This means that, family-by-family, they proactively seek to engage the fathers and father figures, record their details and build relationships with them, as they do with mothers.

Understanding and addressing the fundamental dimension of gender in parenting programs is as significant as current efforts to target different subgroups of mothers (single mothers, teen mothers, minority-group mothers, etc.) The gendered and social nature of parenting means that fathers and mothers arrive with distinct expectations, assets, constraints, and experiences. These cannot be homogenized or overlooked.

SEE ALSO: Child Sexual Abuse and Trauma; Gender Identities and Socialization; Gender Stereotypes; Parenting in Prison

REFERENCES

Burgess, Adrienne. 2009. Fathers and Parenting Interventions: What Works? Abergavenny: Fatherhood Institute. Accessed July 15, 2014, at: http://www.fatherhoodinstitute.org/shop/fathers-and-parenting-interventions-what-works/.

Cowan, P. A., C. P. Cowan, M. K. Pruett, K. Pruett, and J. J. Wong. 2009. "Promoting Fathers' Engagement With Children: Preventive Interventions for Low-Income Families." *Journal of Marriage and Family*, 713: 663–679.

Lawrence, P. J., B. Davies, and P. G. Ramchandani. 2013. "Using Video Feedback to Improve Early Father–Infant Interaction: A Pilot Study." *Clinical Child Psychology and Psychiatry*, 18(1): 61–71.

Lundahl, B.W., D. Tollefson, H. Risser, and M. C. Lovejoy. 2008. "A Meta-Analysis of Father Involvement in Parent Training." *Research on Social Work Practice*, 18: 97–106.

McAllister, Fiona, Adrienne Burgess, Jane Kato, and Gary Barker. 2012. *Fatherhood: Parenting Programs and Policy – A Critical Review of Best Practice.* London/Washington, DC: The Fatherhood Institute/Promundo/MenCare. Accessed July 15, 2014, at: http://www.fatherhoodinstitute.org/2012/fatherhood-parenting-programmes-and-policy-a-critical-review-of-best-practice/.

O'Brien, Margaret. 2011. "Fathers in Challenging Family Contexts: A Need for Engagement." In *Men in Families and Family Policy in a Changing World*. New York: United Nations Department of Economic and Social Affairs. Accessed July 15, 2014, at: http://www.un.org/esa/socdev/family/docs/men-in-families.pdf.

Panter-Brick, Catherine, et al. 2014. "Engaging Fathers: Recommendations for a Game Change in Parenting Interventions Based on a Systematic Review of the Global Evidence." *Journal of Child Psychology and Psychiatry*. Published online July 1, 2014. Accessed July 15, 2014, at: http://onlinelibrary.wiley.com/doi/10.1111/jcpp.12280/pdf

Zanoni, L., W. Warburton, K. Bussey, and A. McMaugh. 2013. "Fathers as 'Core Business' in Child Welfare Practice and Research: An Interdisciplinary Review." *Children and Youth Services Review*, 35(7): 1055–1070.

FURTHER READING

Brandon, Marian, Peter Sidebotham, Sue Bailey, and Pippa Belderson. 2011. A Study of Recommendations Arising from Serious Case Reviews 2009–2010. London: Department for Education. Accessed July 15, 2014, at: https://www.education.gov.uk/publications/eOrderingDownload/DFE-RR157.pdf.

Featherstone, Brid, Mark Rivett, and Jonathan Scourfield. 2007. *Working with Men in Health and Social Care*. London: Sage.

Female Criminality

ALLISON K. ARNEKRANS
Central Michigan University, USA

BRIEF HISTORY

Throughout the past century, writings on female criminal behaviors have been few in number and biologically deterministic in their approach. The topic has not been treated as a particularly important or pressing social problem, not only because of its comparative infrequency with male criminality, but also because of the nature of the offenses committed by women. For example, early studies found that females gained attention for crime due to misconduct, ungovernability, or running away from home, while current studies reveal that females generally tend to commit non-violent or petty offenses. From an international perspective, male criminality and masculinity have been more clearly researched and focused on how male issues are affecting society as a whole (e.g., crime, sex roles, employment, etc.) (Owen 2012). More specifically, men involved in crime and violence have been targeted as an issue of concern, as opposed to discussing the female perspective on this issue.

Early descriptions claimed that women's criminal behavior was largely ignored, and still others dismissed early attempts to explain the behavior since they stem from purely sexist and biological-related thinking. Furthermore, some criminologists defend the lack of attention given to women and crime because they do not comprise a large percentage of criminals in addition to the general effect of the crime on others. Regardless of the stance, the female prison population was relatively small and received little attention before the 1980s.

Since that time, there has been a surge in women entering the justice system. The United States, for example, imprisoned 11,212 women in 1977, and by 2004 this number had increased by 757 percent (Frost, Greene, and Pranis 2006). To provide a gender comparison, according to the Bureau of Justice Statistics (BJS) (US Department of Justice 2006), at year-end 2003, there were 6.9 million people on probation, in prison or jail, or on parole in the United States. Of the individuals who were under the jurisdiction of a state or federal prison in 2003, 1,368,866 were men, and 101,179 were women. According to the BJS, men are almost 15 times more likely to be incarcerated than women.

There have been many reasons given for the drastic increase in the number of women prisoners, including the closing of psychiatric hospitals that lead jails and prisons to become alternative housing options for those affected by mental illness, and the harsher government policies and enactment procedures, such as the "War on Drugs," mandatory minimum sentencing laws, and the three strikes legislation. All of these events have increased the entire prison population, particularly the female population. Jails and prisons have been unable to keep up with this increase, resulting in women becoming a "population ignored" by the justice system. Psychiatric disorders are disproportionately higher among women prisoners, and women are often housed far from their places of residence, leaving them lonely and unable to access supports (e.g., lawyers, family) (Braithwaite, Treadwell, and Arriola 2008). Additionally, men's incomes worldwide are about 180 percent of women's, indicating that men have more access to power, control, and resources than women do in terms of both entering and exiting the justice system (Connell 2000).

Despite some of these factors, official statistics, specifically in the United States, for female criminality are sometimes a problematic source of information on this topic given the gender biases and variation in how many people are at various stages throughout the justice system (i.e., arrested, probation, sentencing, in jail or prison, on parole, etc.). Internationally, some crimes never come to the point of entering the justice system due to violence/death handled outside the system, escaping consequence, and/or judicial manipulation that overlooks crime in some countries (Owen 2012).

SEX ROLES AND CRIMINALITY

Some contemporary criminologists argue that male/female differences in arrest rates can be attributed to the fact that there are protective and caring attitudes toward women in society. Females are said to be shown favorable treatment at every stage of the judicial process, from arrest, through prosecution and conviction, and into sentencing. Societal attitudes aimed at the protection of women result in increased leniency toward them (Moulds 1980). Despite this, the system is eager to enact harsher penalties when women violate traditionally feminine roles (e.g., homicide as a result of perpetrating intimate partner violence toward a male). As a result, some believe that crime rates are not a true representation of criminal behavior because bias is built into the justice system.

Subsequently, a patriarchical society and upbringing have also been studied as having an effect on female criminality. Those in support of this notion hypothesize that patriarchical cultures promote criminal behavior since the pressures of fulfilling the female role and being subject to victimization at the hands of males push many women into crime. In other words, for decades, women have been devalued in the workplace, community, and home in some form or another. Due to this lack of acknowledgment, some women resort to crime or violence to receive notoriety, regardless of the type of attention. This is especially an issue from a global perspective, where there are clear disparities among the sexes. For example, women represent approximately 70 percent of the 1.3 billion poor people of the world. Compared with men, girls and women are most likely to be undernourished and receive fewer healthcare opportunities. Out of approximately 900 million illiterate adults in the world, 66 percent are female (Powell 2006). Overall, women have acted with criminal intentions to seek respect, out of necessity, or even to fight against the notion of inequality.

In addition to the biases and types of relationships, researchers have often found that of those adult female inmates in the penal institution, women typically played supporting roles to men. Women rarely assaulted healthy and alert males by themselves, rather women would attack males who were drunk, asleep, or caught off-guard, or completed their attacks with the assistance of another person. Furthermore, women most often attacked persons with whom they had an affectionate relationship, making their victims different from crimes usually committed by males. Therefore, if a female acts alone, the crime will likely involve a less violent crime (i.e., prostitution, petty theft, drug trafficking) than their male counterparts.

DRUG USE/ABUSE

While several researchers better understood female criminality from sex roles perspectives, still others have begun to understand the phenomenon by assessing female drug use/abuse. In the early 1990s, researchers suggested that women were beginning to show patterns of addiction and criminality similar to those of men. Taylor (1993) carried out an ethnographic study of drug-abusing women, which rejected the view often portrayed in the literature that women are passive, socially outcast, and not in control of their own lives. In contrast, she stated that women were active in their own lives, making choices during each stage of development, and had not been forced into a life of addiction by a man. Despite this, female criminality consisted mainly of theft and selling drugs, as opposed to drug use. So while her study supports the idea that drug-abusing women show certain similarities to men, their crime patterns and motivations toward deviance were shown to be different.

It was also noted in the literature that although women tend to have later crime debuts, they hold a longer career in crime. They commit more "victimless" crimes and have more drug-related offenses then men. Drug-related offenses are those committed to obtain the means to buy drugs (e.g., shoplifting, fraud, drug peddling) as opposed to narcotic crimes like smuggling and dealing. Some have described female abusers as "weak" and "ineffectual," in addition to needing more support and having a higher incidence of illness. Lack of self-confidence and loss of relationships during periods of abuse were also mentioned.

ROMANTIC PARTNER VIOLENCE

In recent years, there has been much research conducted to assess the influence of romantic partners on the development and continuity of delinquency and anti-social behavior beginning in adolescence and the progression into adulthood. Several researchers have identified intimate partner relationships during early adulthood as playing a key role in determining the likelihood of continuity and change in an individual's offending future.

A connection has also been made that men, not women, are clearly connected to violence and crime. Throughout the United States and Europe, for example, though both men and women can be involved in domestic violence, men are far more likely than women to be the perpetrators of serious injury against their partners. In many Middle Eastern countries violence toward women is socially accepted and sometimes an expected societal norm.

There is a clear agreement in recent research that people tend to choose environments that are compatible with their own dispositions and prefer to affiliate with others similar to themselves (e.g., Capaldi, Kim, and Owen 2008). As a result, individuals with anti-social tendencies who form relationships with similar partners are less likely to change because the similarities between the partners create an environment that reinforces, facilitates, and sustains initial tendencies. Such a claim may help account for the stability of anti-social behavior across the lifespan.

Despite this, there is some debate as to whether males and females are differentially influenced by their partners' anti-social behavior. Some studies have suggested that romantically linked males often initiate females into delinquency and crime (e.g., Chesney-Lind and Shelden 2003). Results also showed that being involved in a relationship with a criminal partner increased the risk of criminal involvement for both young adult males and young adult females, providing support for a social influence for both sexes. This social influence carries on through adulthood and has been shown to affect adult criminality rates.

SEE ALSO: Domestic Violence in the United States; Gender Stereotypes; Intimate Partner Abuse

REFERENCES

Braithwaite, R. L., H. M. Treadwell, and K. R. J. Arriola. 2008. "Health Disparities and Incarcerated Women: A Population Ignored." *American Journal of Public Health*, 98: S173–S175. DOI: 10.2105/AJPH.98.Supplement_1.S173.

Capaldi, D. M., H. K. Kim, and L. D. Owen. 2008. "Romantic Partners' Influence on Men's Likelihood of Arrest in Early Adulthood." *Criminology*, 46: 267–299. DOI: 10.1111/j.1745-9125.2008.00110.x.

Chesney-Lind, M., and R. G. Shelden. 2003. *Girls, Delinquency, and Juvenile Justice*, 3rd ed. Belmont, CA: Wadsworth Publishing.

Connell, R. W. 2000. *The Men and the Boys*. Berkeley: University of California Press.

Frost, N., J. Greene, and K. Pranis. 2006. *Hard Hit: The Growth in the Imprisonment of Women*,

1977–2004. New York: Women's Prison Association and Institute on Women and Criminal Justice.

Moulds, E. 1980. "Chivalry and Paternalism: Disparities of Treatment in the Criminal Justice System." In *Women, Crime, and Justice*, edited by Susan K. Datesman and Frank R. Scarpitti. New York: Oxford University.

Owen, T. 2012. "Theorising Masculinities and Crime: A Genetic-Social Approach." *International Journal of Criminology and Sociological Theory*, 5(3): 972–984.

Powell, J. L. 2006. *Rethinking Social Theory and Later Life*. New York: Nova Science Publishers.

Taylor, A. 1993. *Women Drug Users: An Ethnography of a Female Injecting Community*. Oxford: Clarendon Press.

US Department of Justice. 2006. Bureau of Justice Statistics: Prisoners in 2005. Accessed August 1, 2014, at http://www.bjs.gov/content/pub/pdf/p05.pdf.

Female Farming Systems

ELIZABETH RANSOM
University of Richmond, USA

WYNNE WRIGHT
Michigan State University, USA

CARMEN BAIN
Iowa State University, USA

Female farming systems is a concept that draws attention to women's (re)productive roles in agriculture with particular attention to questions of power, equity, inclusion, and empowerment. As a concept, female farming systems were originally linked with women in low-income countries (Boserup 1970) and focused solely on women's contributions at the farm-level. More recent scholarship has shifted to the broader concepts of gender and agriculture. Gender, rather than simply women, provides a space for interrogating the ways in which relationships are socially constructed through gender meanings and practices between men and women in diverse locations (Bock 2006). Moreover, more recent gender and agriculture scholarship focuses not only on farm women in both high and low-income countries, but also recognizes women's contributions as extending beyond the agricultural production sphere (e.g., processing, retail, consumption). Nonetheless, female farming systems as an organizing concept highlights what was a surprisingly neglected field of study until the 1970s and provides insights into the gendered nature of agriculture. Historically, the term "farmer," like so many other occupations, presumed a male identity. Yet, from the 1970s to the present, studies reveal the vast and varied activities of female food producers.

From the late 1970s to the early 1980s studies highlighting the overlooked and undervalued contributions of women in agriculture in both low- and high-income countries proliferated. Scholars began to raise questions regarding power and inequality within farm households, thereby emphasizing that "women enter and engage in farming through specific kinship relations, as wives, daughters, mothers and widows" (Shortall 2006, 20). From this research there has been growing emphasis on choice, agency, resistance, and the altering of gender identities over time (Shortall 2006, 21), although the degree to which each of these topics is emphasized in low-income countries differs from high-income countries. For example, many recent studies focus on the role of women in high-income countries in alternative agricultural movements (e.g., sustainability initiatives), which is much less the case in low-income countries. Despite the shift in the literature to emphasizing agency and resistance among female farmers, the persistence of paternalistic farming structures cross-culturally has been documented, raising further questions about power and equity for female farmers.

In her now classic study, Boserup's (1970) *Women's Role in Economic Development* was the first to draw attention to the invisibility of women in agriculture in low-income countries. Boserup challenged the prevailing assumption that while women helped to produce subsistence crops for household consumption they were not involved in agriculture as a productive economic activity. In fact, women make essential economic and non-economic contributions to agricultural economies and rural livelihoods across low-income countries. Nevertheless, many national accounts fail to capture the contributions of women due to the persistent bias of counting work as economically productive only when money is exchanged.

Based on the aggregate data, the FAO (2011) estimates that women in low-income countries comprise approximately 43 percent of the agricultural labor force, and approximately 400 million producers, or two thirds of the world's poorest livestock keepers, are women. However, this figure hides the enormous variation in women's participation across and within countries. For example, the aggregate data suggests that women comprise 20 percent of the agricultural labor force in Latin America and the Caribbean, rising to almost 50 percent in Africa. Quantifying women's contribution to agricultural activities is problematic. In most farm households both men and women are engaged in crop and livestock production, however, the specific roles of women and types of activities in which they engage vary by age, social class, country, and region. Analysts often attempt to calculate output by assuming that women grow specific crops or raise certain kinds of livestock and men others, and then aggregate these values by gender to determine how much is produced by women. Many gender analysts expect that such calculations underestimate the specific roles of women and types of activities in which they are engaged.

While women dominate smallholder and subsistence agricultural production systems and as non-wage farm laborers, especially in Africa, Asia, and the Caribbean, women also engage as commercial farmers, wage farm workers, traders, and rural entrepreneurs in low-income countries. In fact, women farmers in low-income countries are typically involved in a range of livelihood strategies, including producing crops, caring for livestock, growing, processing, and preparing food, collecting fuel and water, and trading and marketing agricultural products (SOFA Team and Doss 2011). These roles are also changing as social and economic forces transform the agricultural sector in many places. Agriculture is becoming increasingly feminized, especially in sub-Saharan Africa, where women are more and more responsible for the farm as men exit from the sector to migrate to urban areas in search of paid work, or as a result of involvement in civil wars and conflicts, or deaths and illnesses from HIV/AIDS. The feminization of agriculture is also occurring due to women being integrated as low-cost, "unskilled," labor into export value chains, such as specialty fruits and vegetables, and cut-flowers (SOFA Team and Doss 2011).

Despite the significant participation of women in agriculture in low-income countries, women's contribution could be even greater. Research shows that farm production levels by women are significantly lower than those of men. These differences are not because women are less skilled, but the result of gender-based inequalities and discrimination that limit women's access to, or control over, key agricultural resources and inputs such as land, labor, credit, seeds, fertilizer, equipment, education, training, and extension services. Women and female-headed households are also disadvantaged due to lower levels of wealth and education compared with their male counterparts. These disadvantages are even more problematic for the significant share of households headed by women, which, for example, is around 30 percent in Eastern Africa. The FAO (2011) estimates that crop yields could increase by 20–30 percent if women had the same access to resources and inputs that men do and that this increase in agricultural output could reduce the number of undernourished people in the world by 12–17 percent.

Ownership and access to land is a major constraint for women farmers, especially female-headed households. Rates of land ownership by women are much lower than for men. For example, women own only 5 percent of land in Northern Africa and only 15 percent in sub-Saharan Africa (FAO 2011). In many societies, women are discriminated against in both legal and customary land tenure systems where laws and tradition bar women from owning and inheriting land. Over the past decade, many countries in Africa have instituted new laws to strengthen the rights of women to own and inherit land. Nevertheless, even in these countries, the ability of women to exercise their legal rights to land is limited by their lack of knowledge about the laws and the failure of the state to implement and enforce the law. Without the ability to use land as collateral, women are severely disadvantaged in accessing credit, which limits their ability to purchase essential inputs, such as seeds, tools, and fertilizers, or invest in irrigation and land improvements. Such constraints limit female producers' abilities to enhance their incomes and improve household food security.

The roles of women in agriculture in high-income countries may differ from that of women in low-income countries, but the constraints that have limited the opportunities of female producers have many similarities. Not unlike women in low-income countries, women in the Antipodes, European, and North American farming systems have also historically been marginalized from farming by denying them access to the material resources needed for success such as land, labor, and capital. Land transfer/inheritance practices have historically favored men. For example, until the 1990s, the French legal system conferred rights of ownership, control, and decision-making to male farmers alone, denying women rights to the legal occupational status of farmer and the material resources to engage in farming. The French government considered farm women as *sans profession* (without a profession), and maintained this practice through legal codes. Similarly, the formal and informal transfer of farming knowledge in high-income countries has favored men. While young boys were socialized on the farm by their farmer fathers and taught agricultural science in public schools, young girls were directed to home economics education to prepare them to take roles as wives and mothers. Lastly, access to capital has eluded many women as financial institutions and government programs fail to recognize women as "real farmers" and systemically discriminate in favor of men.

A number of rural sociological studies undertaken since the 1980s have shown that women make a sizable economic contribution to the farm household and rural economy in high-income countries (Sachs 1983; Alston 1995). Like their non-farm peers, they also carry a disproportionate share of the household and childcare burden, and often provide invaluable off-farm income that is responsible for subsidizing the farm operation. In the past three decades, the changing structure of rural economies forced many women into the paid labor force for the first time. Economic decline, coupled with agricultural specialization and technological advancement, often furthered women's marginalization from farming. As a result of the structural transformations, many women turned to off-farm work, which provided access to new streams of income and other resources. As such, some scholars concluded that women's off-farm work is empowering and facilitates women's decision-making on farm matters. Other scholars have challenged this notion, contending that the jobs available to farm women are limited in rural economies, forcing women into unfulfilling and poorly paid employment. Moreover, time spent off the farm diminishes the importance of the type of farm work they are able to accomplish within time constraints and further reduces women's authority in a family farm setting. Shortall (2002, 171) argues that it is "women's off farm work that keeps farming male." Similar to non-farm women who experience the so-called second shift of household and childcare in addition to their formal employment, farm women experience the so-called third shift, in which they maintain off-farm employment, household and childcare, and on-farm tasks.

Regardless of these challenges, women in high-income countries are increasingly establishing themselves as farmers either independently of males or as equal partners. As of 2012, women made up 30 percent of the farm population in the United States, 28 percent in Australia, and over 25 percent in France. This trend is part of a growing feminization of agriculture that typifies many high-income countries as new opportunities emerge for female farmers. Women farmers differ from men in a number of ways. Women farmers are more likely to have attained a higher level of education than male farmers. They are also likely to be older than male farmers. The average age of US women farmers is 59 years versus 57 years for men. This is, in part, explained by the fact that farming is a second career that many women turn to later in life.

Women in high-income countries often organize their farming activities differently from men. Women are more likely to engage in production practices that are smaller in scale, more labor intensive, and generate smaller agricultural sales. Women are more likely to embrace a wider variety of value orientations in their work beyond the pursuit of economic growth. They tend to be more reliant on local or regional markets than national or global markets, some research suggests that they tend to be oriented to more sustainable production practices, and they frequently espouse the integration of values such as education, conservation, and aesthetics in their operation. These differences are believed to be due, in part, to the legal and socio-technical barriers women have faced in accessing technology, knowledge, markets, land, labor, and capital. It is also due to inroads from the feminist movement that opened new doors to women that were closed only two or three decades ago. In part because of the obstacles women have faced, they are now emerging as agricultural leaders in advancing new production models that are intended to further sustainable agrifood production. Women are increasingly seen as the mobilizing force helping to shape a new type of farming system that prioritizes community and economic embeddedness, environmental integrity, and spirituality.

A unifying issue across high- and low-income countries is the role that women play in the social reproduction of the household, which includes feeding their families. This means women across the globe continue to be disproportionately responsible for food production for home consumption in low-income countries, food shopping in high-income countries, and food preparation in the home. Because of this gendered division of labor, women often shape the diet and nutrition of a family. For these reasons, female farming systems, especially in low-income countries, have gained renewed attention from governments and development agencies, who understand that empowering women in production contributes to improved household food access and well-being, especially for children. Despite significant strides made, it is clear that both laws and other social institutions will need to change to secure women's rights to land and other valuable resources needed for creating sustainable farming systems. In addition, there is still an overwhelming bias toward assuming women are not farmers, despite abundant evidence that women are engaged in a wide range of agricultural activities. This bias has ripple effects for female farming systems in terms of women's ability to access resources to improve production techniques, such as extension services and farmer-to-farmer training, as well as in terms of women's representation in the leadership structure of agricultural organizations (see Meinzen-Dick et al. 2011). While these concerns disproportionately impact women in low-income countries, often with more dire consequences, such biases also continue to constrain women engaged in farming systems in high-income countries.

SEE ALSO: Division of Labor, Gender; Feminization of Labor; Gender and Development

REFERENCES

Alston, Margaret. 1995. *Women on the Land: The Hidden Heart of Rural Australia*. Kensington: UNSW Press.

Bock, Bettina. 2006. "Introduction: Rural Gender Studies in North and South." In *Rural Gender Relations: Issues and Case Studies*, edited by Bettina B. Bock and Sally Shortall, 1–18. Cambridge, MA: CABI Publishing.

Boserup, Ester. 1970. *Women's Role in Economic Development*. London: Earthscan.

FAO. 2011. The State of Food and Agriculture. *Women in Agriculture: Closing the Gender Gap for Development*. Rome: Food and Agriculture Organization of the United Nations.

Meinzen-Dick, Ruth, et al. 2011. *Engendering Agricultural Research, Development, and Extension*. Washington, DC: International Food Policy Research Institute.

Sachs, Carolyn. 1983. *The Invisible Farmers: Women in Agricultural Production*. Totowa: Rowman & Allenheld.

Shortall, Sally. 2002. "Gendered Agricultural and Rural Restructuring: A Case Study of Northern Ireland." *Sociologia Ruralis*, 42(2): 160–175.

Shortall, Sally. 2006. "Gender and Farming: An Overview." In *Rural Gender Relations: Issues and Case Studies*, edited by Bettina B. Bock and Sally Shortall, 19–26. Cambridge, MA: CABI Publishing.

SOFA Team, and Cheryl Doss. 2011. "The Role of Women in Agriculture," ESA Working Paper No. 11-02, March. Rome Agricultural Development Economics Division, FAO.

Female Genital Cutting

LAUREN M. SARDI and PRISCILLA MARIE MALDONADO
Quinnipiac University, USA

Female genital cutting (FGC) is a term that encompasses a variety of procedures performed on female genitalia. FGC has been categorized by various governmental agencies and non-governmental organizations (NGOs), many of whom are concerned specifically with the ways in which these procedures violate Western notions of human rights. Female genital cutting is also referred to as female genital mutilation (FGM) by some groups in order to demonstrate the ways in which many of these procedures permanently alter and damage both the internal and external female genital anatomy. Such procedures may interfere with activities such as urination, menstruation, sexual intercourse, and childbirth. Scholars also note that FGC is responsible for short- and long-term negative health outcomes including pain, hemorrhage, infection, scars, cysts, maternal and infant mortality, and prolonged labor or infertility.

According to the World Health Organization (WHO), female genital mutilation/cutting (FGM/C), as it is referred to in its definition, involves the "total or partial removal of the external female genitalia or other injury to the female genital organs for non-medical reasons" (2008, 4). There are currently over 91 million girls and women in Africa alone who have been genitally cut or mutilated, and over 3 million girls are at risk of being cut or mutilated each year.

Four main types of FGM/C are: (1) *clitoridectomy*, or the partial or total removal of the clitoris and/or prepuce (foreskin); (2) *excision*, or the partial or total removal of the clitoris and labia minora, with or without excision of the labia majora; (3) *infibulation*, or the narrowing of the vaginal orifice with the creation of a covering seal by cutting and repositioning the labia minora and/or the labia majora, with or without excision of the clitoris; and (4) all other harmful procedures to the female genitalia for non-medical purposes, including pricking, piercing, stretching, or incision of the clitoris and/or labia; cauterization by burning of the clitoris and surrounding tissues or scraping of the vaginal orifice, and/or the introduction of corrosive substances or herbs into the vagina to tighten it or to cause bleeding (Chalmers and Hashi 2000; WHO 2008).

In its various forms, FGC is mainly practiced among 28 different countries in Africa, some countries in Asia, including India, Malaysia, and Indonesia, and other countries in the Middle East, including Yemen, Oman, the United Arab Emirates, Bahrain, and Northern Iraq (Kaplan et al. 2013). Although even rough estimates are difficult to obtain, the WHO draws upon work by Yoder and Khan (2008) who note that infibulation, the type of FGM/C that people most commonly associate with mutilation, accounts for a very small percentage of the total number of procedures performed. Such current estimates note that Types I and II account for approximately 85–90 percent of all cases of FGC (WHO 2008) and that Type III accounts for approximately 10 percent of all cases (Yoder and Khan 2008).

Female genital cutting in all of its forms is currently illegal in the United States as well as in many other countries. In 1996, the United States Congress enacted a number of provisions as part of the Illegal Immigration Reform and Immigrant Responsibility Act, which criminalizes the practice of FGC on a person under 18 years of age for non-medical reasons. Since 1998, several states have also enacted similar laws that institute criminal sanctions against the practice of FGC, including California, Colorado, Delaware, Illinois, Maryland, Minnesota, Missouri, Nevada, New York, North Dakota, Oregon, Rhode Island, Tennessee, Texas, West Virginia, and Wisconsin (Center for Reproductive Rights 2004).

Activists and scholars who are against the practice of FGC commonly cite cultural and social reasons for its perpetuation, including cleanliness and appearance, but they usually stress the issue of patriarchal control of female sexuality (Chalmers and Hashi 2000; Dustin and Davies 2007). As Rahman and Toubia (2000) note, there are a number of differing reasons behind FGC; in some countries, such as Egypt, Sudan, or Somalia, FGC is practiced ostensibly in order to preserve girls' virginity. In other countries, such as Kenya or Uganda, FGC is often performed to reduce a woman's sexual desire, which would then allow husbands to have several wives.

Thus, female genital cutting serves to reduce women's sexual desire on a number of levels, depending upon the ways in which a woman's sexuality has been socially constructed in any given society. By "maintaining" a woman's virginity or marital fidelity, these social controls are instituted to protect male sexuality at the expense of women's sexual fulfillment. Another type of vaginal modification or mutilation, although not specifically described as cutting, includes labial elongation, in which the labia minora are pulled and lengthened, often in communal settings for the purposes of obtaining social capital and building networks. Until 2008, labial elongation was included as a WHO Type IV form of female genital mutilation, although that label has since been removed. Reasons for this practice include "hiding" or covering the vaginal opening or to increase sexual pleasure for males during heterosexual intercourse (Larsen 2010).

Female genital cutting is also practiced for religious purposes within various Muslim communities. Although there is no religious mandate for the procedure, it is commonly viewed as a cultural imperative for girls to be formally recognized and accepted into the Islamic faith. *Sunna*, which falls under the WHO's Type I classification of FGM/C and which is the most common type of cutting performed for religious purposes, is usually done during infancy or childhood before a girl is 10 years old (Hayford and Trinitapoli 2011).

However, several forms of FGC have been practiced in the United States; in the Victorian era, circumcisions and chemical removal of the clitoral hood, clitoris, and/or other erogenous tissue were performed on females to prevent practices that were deemed socially unacceptable, such as masturbation or premarital sex (Bell 2005). As Green (2005) also notes, other common and current forms of FGC actually include various forms of plastic surgery including vaginoplasty, labiaplasty, and other procedures that women consent to as part of the "designer vagina" phenomenon in many Western countries, including the United States, in which vaginas and labia should appear a certain way to match hegemonic cultural norms.

SEE ALSO: Chastity; Child Sexual Abuse and Trauma; Clitoridectomy, Female Genital Cutting Practices, and Law; Cosmetic Surgery in the United States; Gender-Based Violence; Sexual Regulation and Social Control

REFERENCES

Bell, Kirsten. 2005. "Genital Cutting and Western Discourses on Sexuality." *Medical Anthropology Quarterly*, 19: 125–148.

Center for Reproductive Rights. 2004. "Legislation on Female Genital Mutilation in the United States." Accessed August 10, 2015, at http://reproductiverights.org/sites/default/files/documents/pub_bp_fgmlawsusa.pdf.

Chalmers, Beverley, and Kowser Omer Hashi. 2000. "432 Somali Women's Birth Experiences in Canada and Earlier Female Genital Mutilation." *Birth: Issues in Perinatal Care*, 27: 227–234.

Dustin, Donna, and Liz Davies. 2007. "Female Genital Cutting and Children's Rights: Implications for Social Work Practice." *Child Care in Practice*, 13: 3–16.

Green, Fiona J. 2005. "From Clitoridectomies to 'Designer Vaginas': The Medical Construction of Heteronormative Female Bodies and Sexuality through Female Genital Cutting." *Sexualities, Evolution & Gender*, 7: 153–187.

Hayford, Sarah R., and Jenny Trinitapoli. 2011. "Religious Differences in Female Genital Cutting: A Case Study from Burkina Faso." *Journal for the Scientific Study of Religion*, 50: 252–271.

Kaplan, Adriana, et al. 2013. "Female Genital Mutilation/Cutting: The Secret World of Women as Seen by Men." *Obstetrics and Gynecology International*, 2013: 1–11. DOI: 10.1155/2013/643780.

Larsen, Josefine. 2010. "The Social Vagina: Labia Elongation and Social Capital Among Women in Rwanda." *Culture, Health & Sexuality*, 12: 813–826.

Rahman, Anika, and Nahid Toubia, eds. 2000. *Female Genital Mutilation: A Guide to Laws and Policies Worldwide*. New York: Zed Books.

World Health Organization (WHO). 2008. "Eliminating Female Genital Mutilation: An Interagency Statement." Accessed August 10, 2015, at http://www.who.int/reproductivehealth/topics/fgm/prevalence/en/.

Yoder, P. Stanley, and Shane Khan. 2008. "Numbers of Women Circumcised in Africa: The Production of a Total." *Demographic and Health Research*, 39: 1–19.

Female Orgasm

ROY J. LEVIN

Porterbrook Clinic, UK

The human female orgasm, despite years of scientific study, is still a "riddle, wrapped in a mystery inside an enigma" (to quote a Churchillian remark). Why is this so? It is because we are not clear about its induction, its neurophysiology, its pharmacology, and its biological function(s). This entry will detail some of these problems.

How is the female orgasm defined? Many definitions have been proposed, but because we are unsure of its neural mechanisms we can only attempt an operational definition based on observable and reported characteristics. The most comprehensive is that of Meston and colleagues (2004), namely "a variable, transient peak sensation of intense pleasure, creating an altered state of consciousness, usually accompanied by involuntary, rhythmic contractions of the pelvic striated circumvaginal musculature, with concomitant uterine and anal contractions and myotonia that resolves the sexually induced vasocongestion (sometimes only partially), usually with an induction of well-being and contentment." Thus the female orgasm, like that of the male, exhibits both physical and subjective mental activity. In both sexes the increases induced by sexual arousal in blood pressure and heart and respiratory rate are at their peak, with concomitant facial grimacing and often verbal and non-verbal vocalizations (Masters and Johnson 1966). It is thought that the mental experience is the same because when descriptions of their orgasms are written by men and women with references to genitalia or sex removed, it is impossible to judge whether these have been written by men or women. Despite the obvious similarities, there are differences between the orgasms of the sexes, namely:

1. females can have repeated or multiple orgasms separated by a very short interval;
2. females can have orgasms of extended duration (status orgasmus) that last for a considerable time;
3. the recorded contractions of the pelvic musculature in males have a divided pattern not seen in females;
4. in males when orgasm is initiated its activity continues automatically even if the stimulus that activated it ends; with females it is claimed that if the stimulus is stopped the orgasm also ends;
5. in males the first orgasm is the most satisfying, but in females subsequent orgasms can be even more so.

Ever since Sigmund Freud opined in 1905 that the induction of the female orgasm by stimulation of the clitoris was of an immature origin and nature and that it needed to be replaced for full mature femininity by the induction of orgasms from penile vaginal intercourse (PVI) alone, the question of the dual orgasm typology (vaginal orgasms and clitoral orgasms) for females has been highly contentious. Some practitioners of the psychoanalytical movement went so far as to claim that the clitoris undermined healthy femininity, but with the rise of biological psychiatry together with feminist criticisms such concepts became outmoded. However, controversial studies have been reported resurrecting the concept that orgasms induced by PVI alone are superior in beneficial effects to their induction by clitoral stimulation, but these have been criticized by others (see for full references Levin 2011a, 2012, 2014; Prause 2012). Many women need clitoral stimulation to obtain their orgasm even during coitus, but there is no absolute certainty for figures representing how women globally obtain their orgasms; estimates suggest approximately 30 percent never achieve orgasm from PVI alone, although some estimates are much higher, while 10 percent do not achieve orgasm from any stimulation (anorgasmia).

The induction of orgasm in the female can occur from stimulating non-genital sites (e.g., nipples, breasts, anus, perineum – the area between the anus and the vaginal introitus, urethra), hypnosis, and even from exercise, but the stimulation of the genitalia and their surrounds is normally the best facilitator (see Levin 2011a, 2015). These structures include the external clitoris (hood, shaft, and glans) and the internal clitoral crus and clitoral bulbs, labia minora, periurethral glans (vestibule area around the urinary meatus), the anterior vaginal wall including Halban's fascia (in the space between its anterior wall and the bladder), and the "G-spot."

Surprisingly, yet another contentious feature of the female orgasm is its possible function(s). There is no disagreement that it gives the greatest pleasure without recourse to drugs and that as its pleasure can never be recalled exactly, it creates the desire for repetition. However, there are two major groups attributing its functionality. One regards it as an evolutionary adaptation involved in reproduction via sperm transport, while the other regards it as a by-product of mammalian bisexual potential, and it occurs because it is adaptive for males (see Lloyd 2005 for critical discussion). Most now accept that it is not essential for reproduction as the uterine contractions induced at orgasm do not mediate or facilitate sperm transport, despite many speculative claims in the literature (see Levin 2011b for references). Some suggest that it is involved in mate selection, arguing that those males of high genetic quality who can induce orgasm by coitus in the female are more likely to be chosen subsequently as mating partners. In fact there are many other speculative functional claims, but, as has been stated, an evolutionary interpretation that they are adaptive is untestable because there is no crucial test that can falsify the hypothesis (Levin 2012).

Since the advent of brain imaging to measure regional cerebral blood flows using functional magnetic resonance imaging (fMRI) or positron emission tomography (PET) a few studies have tried to examine what areas of the female brain are either activated, inhibited, or unaffected during orgasm. Unfortunately there is no consensus between these studies, one study claiming that only a few areas are activated with many deactivated, while a second study describes the involvement of many activated areas. The reasons for this dichotomy are multiple and involve differences in the ways fMRI and PET imaging data are statistically computed, in the corrections applied for head movements that can cause serious errors, in the methods of activating the orgasm, and in type of control used for assessing the "basal" brain activity that has to be subtracted from the aroused state to delineate the activity specific to the orgasm. It is clear from the studies, however, that there is no single site for orgasm in the brain; rather, there is a common multiple site coactivation. While specific areas appear to be switched on or off or remain unchanged, we do not know how these are coordinated and thus we cannot reverse engineer an orgasm from the knowledge we have so far.

SEE ALSO: Neuroscience, Brain Research, and Sexuality; Sexualities

REFERENCES

Freud, Sigmund. 1905. *Three Essays of the Theory of Sexuality*. London: Hogarth.

Levin, Roy J., ed. 2011a. Special Issue: "The Human Orgasm." *Sexual and Relationship Therapy*, 26: 299–341.

Levin, Roy J. 2011b. "Can the Controversy about the Putative Role of the Human Female Orgasm in Sperm Transport be Settled with our Current Physiological Knowledge of Coitus?" *Journal of Sexual Medicine*, 8: 1566–1578.

Levin, Roy J. 2012. "The Deadly Pleasures of the Clitoris and the Condom – A Rebuttal of Brody, Costa and Hess." *Sexual and Relationship Therapy*, 27: 273–295.

Levin, Roy J. 2014. "Should the Clitoris become a Vestigial Organ by Personal 'Psychological Clitoridectomy'? A Critical Examination of the Literature. *Journal of Woman's Health Issues and Care*, 3: 4–14.

Levin, Roy J. 2015. "Recreation and Procreation: A Critical View of Sex in the Human Female." *Clinical Anatomy*, 28: 339–354.

Lloyd, Elisabeth A. 2005. *The Case of the Female Orgasm: Bias in the Science of Evolution*. Cambridge, MA: Harvard University Press.

Masters, William H., and Virginia E. Johnson. 1966. *Human Sexual Response*. Boston: Little, Brown.

Meston, Cindy M., Elaine Hull, Roy J. Levin, and Marca Sipski. 2004. "Disorders of Orgasm in Women." *Journal of Sexual Medicine*, 1: 40–48.

Prause, Nicole. 2012. "A Response to Brody, Costa and Hess (2012): Theoretical Statistical and Construct Problems Perpetuated in the Study of Female Orgasm." *Sexual and Relationship Therapy*, 27: 260–271.

Femicide

NEHA KHETRAPAL
Macquarie University, Australia

Femicide (sometimes called feminicide) as a term was first used in England to explain killings of women in 1801. The modern day explanation was developed in the 1970s by Diana Russell at the first International Tribunal on Crimes Against Women held in Brussels, Belgium. It falls under the rubric of gender-related killing, involves the killing of a woman or girl, and is an extreme example of violence against women. When the gender of the victim is irrelevant to the killing then the crime is considered non-femicidal in nature (Russell and Harmes 2001). The term was proposed as an alternative to homicide which is more gender neutral in nature (Radford and Russell 1992). Femicide is usually perpetrated by men but in some cases even female family or group members may also be involved.

There are different contexts that may give rise to femicide. Common ones are murder due to intimate violence, infanticide and gendered sex selection, torture and slaying of women, dowry related killings, honor killings, purposeful targeting of women during armed conflicts, genital mutilation, witchcraft, deliberate targeting of aboriginal or indigenous women, and human trafficking. Common reasoning might suggest that gendered murders are associated with poverty and lack of education but data shows that urban middle classes contribute heavily. For instance in India, 8 million female fetuses have been aborted over the past decade as these people had better access to prenatal screenings.

For the 2004–2009 period, the global estimate for femicide was calculated to be about 66,000 victims per year. Jaurez, Mexico has witnessed the highest number of femicide cases in 2005. But getting an exact global estimate for the crime is difficult given the fact that it is sometimes sanctioned religiously or by society. Still, there are many sources of information that can be used to gather data for the purpose of compiling the statistics, for instance, cases registered with local police, cases filed with local courts, media coverage, and reports from medical examiners or the mortuary or in some cases national databases. However, a growing body of evidence suggests that the majority of the victims are targets of intimate relations, hence this will be discussed in some detail here.

South Africa experiences femicide resulting from intimate relations every six hours. In India, approximately 5,000 deaths a year are attributed to this cause although the number is said to be much higher because of hundreds of unreported cases. Statistics from Europe show that there are 3,500 deaths each year with higher risk for women aged between 35 and 44 years. Roughly two women are killed in a week in the United Kingdom. In Ontario, killings by intimate partners accounted for 63 percent to 76 percent of all women killed between 1974 and 1994. Preliminary findings of a recent study by the World Health Organization reveal that 35 percent of murders reported across the world are committed by intimate partners. The main reason behind these murders is jealousy on the part of the males (Polk 1994) arising from sexual rivalry or a woman's intention to terminate the relationship. The intention to kill is basically intertwined with efforts to reinforce patriarchy and control. Studies also show that separation triggers a sixfold increase of violence that ultimately results in murder. These killers are not just husbands or boyfriends but also include rejected or past lovers, spouses, and perpetrators of incestuous relations. Stalking is shown to be highly prevalent before the murder as stalking partners are prone to be controlling and physically and sexually violent. For instance, a study conducted in the 1990s found that approximately 23.4 percent femicide victims were stalked prior to their deaths in North Carolina.

There could be many ways in which a woman is killed, such as beating, setting on fire, and poisoning. Reports from the Department of Justice in the United States show that men commonly use firearms. There have been different characteristics associated with the offenders and victims (Taylor and Jasinski 2011). Perpetrators are likely to be older than the victims and have been found to have *not* finished high school, suffer from poor mental health, and have a history of drug and alcohol abuse or even pet abuse. Often the victims have been identified as pregnant, submissive, and spending more time in the domestic household. On the other hand, less is known about attempted femicide although it is established that many victims report a high level of violence against them. An evaluation of the hospital emergency services in Santiago, Chile showed that 73 percent of women who presented for injuries in 1986 were the target of violence perpetuated at home.

Many people do not recognize violence against women as a crime as many times this violence is institutionalized through family and social frameworks, and even religious traditions. Often intimate killings are also viewed sympathetically particularly in patriarchal societies. Therefore putting an end to it is extremely difficult although decreasing the numbers will require multifaceted efforts like implementing strong legislation for crime against women, promoting awareness at all levels including education of boys and girls on gender sensitive issues, empowering women socially, politically, and economically, encouraging women to report episodes of violence and minor issues of domestic violence against them, and providing a supportive network for affected families. To quote an example, women's participation in Indian governance has increased due to the reservation of 33 percent of seats for women in India.

SEE ALSO: Matrix of Domination; Sex Discrimination

REFERENCES

Polk, Kenneth. 1994. *When Men Kill: Scenarios of Masculine Violence*. Cambridge: Cambridge University Press.

Radford, Jill, and Diana E. H. Russell. 1992. *Femicide: The Politics of Woman Killing*. New York: Twayne Publishers.

Russell, Diana E. H., and Roberta A. Harmes. 2001. *Femicide in Global Perspective*. New York: Teachers College Press.

Taylor, Rae, and Jana L. Jasinski. 2011. "Femicide and the Feminist Perspective." *Homicide Studies*, 15(4): 341–362. DOI: 10.1177/1088767911424541.

FURTHER READING

Caputi, Jane. 1987. *The Age of Sex Crime*. London: Women's Press.

Dobash, Rebecca E., and Russell P. Dobash. 1998. *Rethinking Violence Against Women*. Thousand Oaks: Sage.

Feminine and Masculine Elements

JOSEPH MOLLEUR

Cornell College, USA

In many religious, spiritual, and mystical traditions, feminine and masculine elements (also commonly known as feminine principle and masculine principle, respectively) signify properties, traits, concerns, or values that are traditionally understood especially to pertain to feminine and masculine gender, and to female or male divine and human beings. The notion of "element" is taken largely in a literal sense in Daoism and in many contemporary neo-pagan movements such as Wicca, as signifying one of the several components or constituents that underlie and account for the make-up of all things occurring in the cosmos, including human beings. While the ancient Greco-Roman world did not necessarily understand the four classical elements of earth, air, fire, and water in gender-specific terms, they are commonly held to be gender-specific in neo-pagan circles today, where earth and water are identified as feminine whereas air and fire are seen as masculine. Earth's fecundity, stability, and ability to nurture life and water's health-restoring and purificatory properties are among the attributes that qualify these elements as feminine. Air's associations with mental and communicative abilities and fire's relation to strength and tenacity, are among the traits that qualify these elements as masculine. Habashi (2000) has shown that these same four elements are identified in Zoroastrian sources that actually predate the corresponding Greek sources, and furthermore that in Zoroastrianism the elements are specifically understood as having religious or spiritual associations. A prominent feature of Zoroastrian faith is that the most appropriate symbol for the supreme God, Ahura Mazda, is fire – an undying flame. In the Daoist tradition there are actually five elements, of which three are considered to be primarily feminine or *yin* in nature (water, earth, and metal), and two mainly masculine or *yang* (fire and wood). Receptivity, creativity, persistence, stability, and strength are among the properties associated with water, earth, and metal that give rise to their characterization as feminine, and passion, aggression, initiative, and a penchant for dynamic and bold activity are the properties associated with fire and wood that give rise to their characterization as masculine (Levitt 1998).

Religion scholars have often categorized the Eastern traditions of Hinduism and Buddhism together with the Western Abrahamic faiths of Judaism, Christianity, and Islam as the five major world religions. In these religions, unlike Daoism and neo-paganism, the feminine element is understood in a more symbolic or metaphorical sense as a constellation of personality attributes that are viewed as archetypically feminine, and masculine element as attributes that are archetypically masculine. It is in this sense that the phenomenon is sometimes designated "feminine/masculine principle" as an alternative to "feminine/masculine element." In Hinduism, the archetypical feminine is identified in three primary ways: as *Prakriti* (power inherent in material nature), as *Shakti* (supreme female power or energy), and as *Maya* (illusoriness or power to delude). These qualities are viewed as pertaining to both goddesses and female human beings, and they traditionally provoke two contrasting reactions: wonder and awe, on the one hand, and suspicion and mistrust, on the other. From the perspective of patriarchy, such awesome and potentially dangerous female powers need to be kept under careful guard (Pintchman 1994). The archetypical masculine is defined by such attributes as immutability, self-sufficiency, pure being, and pure consciousness, and is variously named *Ishvara* (controlling lord), *Purusha* (primordial male person), Shiva (the deity whose primary task is the periodic destruction of the universe), and Vishnu, the deity who preserves the universe and saves it from catastrophes until it is time for Shiva to perform his characteristic task. In Indian Buddhist traditions (both Theravada and Mahayana), because of his bodily strength, physical attractiveness, unsurpassed virility, martial skills, and personal charisma, the Buddha is viewed as the perfection of masculinity (Powers 2009), whereas in Buddhist traditions associated with Tibet, the masculine element or principle is conceived more esoterically in terms of the attributes of form, effective intentional action, blissful joy, and compassion (Gross 1984). Apart from a few texts comparing the Buddha to a mother, there is not a significant notion of feminine element or principle in Theravada traditions. However, in the Tibetan expression of the religion, the idea of a feminine principle figures prominently, conceived somewhat esoterically in terms of the attributes of space, accommodation, void or emptiness, and discriminative wisdom (Gross 1984).

Turning to the Abrahamic faiths, in both Judaism and Christianity the feminine element centers on the notion of mercy, and incorporates such attributes as compassion, forgiveness, magnanimity, and love. The masculine element centers on the notion of justice, and incorporates such attributes as power, sovereignty, vengeance, and the exercise of reason. These attributes, applied to God, give rise to the shared Jewish and Christian image of God as a father, king of kings, ultimate judge, and leader of armies (Schoenfeld and Mestrovic 1991). In Judaism, these attributes are especially reflected in the notion of *Shekhinah*, which designates the indwelling presence of God on Earth understood in overtly feminine terms. In Christianity, the feminine element has most often been associated with Roman Catholic and Eastern Orthodox devotion to the Blessed Virgin Mary, and also the notion of the Church "herself" as a mother figure (Schoenfeld and Mestrovic 1991). Finally, in Islam, the feminine element focuses on the attributes of mercy, compassion, love, gentleness, creativity, infinity, and beauty – all of which are understood to pertain directly to God (Dakake 2006). The masculine element as it relates to God focuses on God's majesty, invincibility, transcendence, and unlimitedness, accounting for such divine titles as Lord, Judge, and King. When applied to the human practice of the spiritual life, the masculine element in Islam refers to an active, rather than passive, orientation, and emphasizes the importance of intellect in one's religious life (Dakake 2006).

Concerning the future of the notion of the feminine/masculine element, a recurring theme in many contemporary religious, spiritual, and mystical movements is a critical attitude toward women being limited by traditional, stereotypical notions of what constitutes quintessentially feminine traits, concerns, or activities; the same goes for men and traditionally masculine stereotypes. These contemporary movements commonly suggest one of two alternatives to the inherited views and practices. First, some continue to find considerable meaning in their tradition's notions regarding the feminine/masculine element or principle, but insist that, in order for a person to be a fully integrated and well-balanced human being, both women and men should, as best they can, develop, utilize, harmonize, and synthesize both feminine and masculine elements within themselves. The second, more radical, alternative challenges and rejects the very notion that some traits and values are essentially feminine or essentially masculine, preferring instead to speak simply of non-gendered "human traits" that all people, both women and men, can and should share in equally.

SEE ALSO: Feminist Christology; Feminist Theology; Masculinism; Masculinities; Mysticism; Women-Church; Yin-Yang

REFERENCES

Dakake, Maria Massi. 2006. "'Walking upon the Path of God Like Men?': Women and the Feminine in the Islamic Mystical Tradition." In *Sufism: Love & Wisdom*, edited by Jean-Louis Michon and Roger Gaetani, 131–151. Bloomington: World Wisdom.
Gross, Rita M. 1984. "The Feminine Principle in Tibetan Vajrayana Buddhism: Reflections of a Buddhist Feminist." *Journal of Transpersonal Psychology*, 16(2): 179–192.
Habashi, Fathi. 2000. "Zoroaster and the Theory of Four Elements." *Bulletin for the History of Chemistry*, 25(2): 109–115.
Levitt, Susan. 1998. "The Five Taoist Elements: Fire, Earth, Metal, Water and Wood." *Feng Shui Journal*, 4(1): 22–25.
Pintchman, Tracy. 1994. *The Rise of the Goddess in the Hindu Tradition*. Albany: State University of New York Press.
Powers, John. 2009. *A Bull of a Man: Images of Masculinity, Sex, and the Body in Indian Buddhism*. Cambridge, MA: Harvard University Press.
Schoenfeld, Eugen, and Stjepan G. Mestrovic. 1991. "With Justice and Mercy: Instrumental-Masculine and Expressive-Feminine Elements in Religion." *Journal for the Scientific Study of Religion*, 30(4): 363–380. DOI: 10.2307/1387274.

FURTHER READING

Chaudhuri, Haridas. 1954. "The Concept of Brahman in Hindu Philosophy." *Philosophy East and West*, 4(1): 47–66.
Gombrich, Richard. 1972. "Feminine Elements in Sinhalese Buddhism." *Wiener Zeitschrift für die Kunde Südasiens*, 16: 67–93.
Nasr, Seyyed Hossein. 1980. "The Male and Female in the Islamic Perspective." *Studies in Comparative Religion*, 14(1–2). Accessed October 28, 2014, at www.studiesincomparativereligion.com.
Schimmel, Annemarie. 1975. *Mystical Dimensions of Islam*. Chapel Hill: University of North Carolina Press.
Scholem, Gershom. 1991. *On the Mystical Shape of the Godhead: Basic Concepts in the Kabbalah*, trans. Joachim Neugroschel, edited and revised by Jonathan Chipman. New York: Schocken Books.

Feminism, Aboriginal Australia and Torres Strait Islands

CAROLYN SCHWARZ
Goucher College, USA

Since the emergence of the feminist movement in the early twentieth century, there has been a diversity of feminisms that have taken shape in Indigenous Australia. One form is that of first-wave white Australian feminists in campaigns for Aboriginal rights. Recent scholarship on Australian feminism by historians Fiona Paisley, Marilyn Lake, and Allison Holland has shown that during the 1920s and 1930s a number of feminist organizations were involved in Aboriginal reform politics that were part of the wider humanitarian movement. Governmental policies concerning Aboriginal people during this era were based on a eugenicist project of "biological absorption." Central to this project was the removal of so called "half-caste" or "mixed-race" children from their Aboriginal mothers and placement usually in government or mission-run institutions with the aim of eventually breeding out the Aboriginal race. Feminists of the time, such as Mary Bennett, Ada Bromham, Bessie Rischbieth, Jessie Street, and Constance Cook, campaigned in women's journals and at national and international forums for the just treatment of Aboriginal women who were denied their rights as mothers under the biological absorption policy. They adopted a protectionist approach that envisaged the formation of the welfare state as a way to ensure the rights of Aboriginal women and children. This approach also called for the return of land to Aboriginal people so that Aboriginal women could be free from the sexually exploitative conditions of the frontier that feminists equated with slavery and to protect the integrity of Aboriginal family and community life. Arguably, of the feminist writing about Aboriginal issues during this period, Mary Bennett's book *The Australian Aboriginal as a Human Being* (1930) was the most influential and became the "bible of the Aboriginal rights movement" (Holland 1995, 54) after World War II. While interwar feminists were progressives of their time, the historical scholarship has shown that their feminism had maternal, racist, and even eugenicist underpinnings that were prevalent in the feminisms of colonialism. This was especially evident in the claims of interwar feminists to speak "on behalf" of Aboriginal women and in their calls for white women to be appointed and paid as their professional protectors in order to "uplift" the Aboriginal race.

The work of Lake indicates that the postwar period ushered in a feminism that replaced an emphasis on maternalism and protectionism with one that drew from the labor movement and the anti-discrimination politics that began to take hold among leftist activists in Australia during that time. From the 1940s through to the 1960s, the Australian feminists of the interwar period continued to campaign for Aboriginal rights but the campaigns of this later period focused on equal pay and legal rights for Aboriginal people, as exclusionary clauses of the Australian Constitution had denied them access to the benefits of citizenship enjoyed by white Australians. Some of the first-wave feminists formed coalitions with trade unions, left-wing politicians, and indigenous men and women activists, such as Pearl Gibbs, Kath Walker, Doug Nicholls, and Faith Bandler, to promote equal citizenship.

Although this movement for inclusion eventually led to the passage of the 1967 Federal Referendum, which removed the exclusionary clauses from the Constitution, it came to be criticized for its assimilationist orientation. The 1970s thus saw the rise of a politics of self-determination led by indigenous activists and based on the rights of indigenous people to land as the original inhabitants of Australia. Some four decades after the pro-Aboriginal, first-wave feminism campaign began, white Australian feminists were no longer at the forefront of Aboriginal causes.

Another form of feminism that emerged in Indigenous Australia is that of feminist ethnography or feminist anthropology. Anchored to the second-wave feminist concerns about reproductive issues, childcare, and work and to debates in anthropology about the universalism of gender inequality, the status of Aboriginal women was a main theme of the feminist scholarship on Aboriginal society in the 1970s and 1980s. The book *Women's Role in Aboriginal Society* (Gale 1974) set the tone for the discussion with descriptions of Aboriginal women's autonomy, agency, and independence despite the presence of what many researchers saw as sexual asymmetry in Aboriginal social life. Two influential anthropologists writing during this period were Gillian Cowlishaw and Annette Hamilton. Cowlishaw's work addressed marriage, reproduction, and socialization among the Rembarrnga in Northern Australia and showcased women's control over their pregnancies and challenges to male dominance. Hamilton looked at women's rituals – a subject that had been explored by Phyllis Kaberry in her seminal work on Aboriginal women nearly three decades earlier – as well as reproduction and labor relations. For the Pitjantjatjara in Central Australia, one of the groups with whom Hamilton worked, men experienced some degree of control over women's productive labor. Hamilton argued that reproductive matters were, however, overseen in the women's realm. Pitjantjatjara women had an active and secret ritual life – one that stressed female solidarity, societal roles, and sexuality – carried out separately from the ritual life of men.

Arguably, the most well-known ethnography of Aboriginal society born from the second-wave feminist movement is Diane Bell's *Daughters of the Dreaming* (1983). The argument of Eleanor Leacock that gender asymmetry was not a universal phenomenon but the historical product of state formation and the capitalist mode of production had a strong influence on Bell's work. Based on research with Kaytej and Warlpiri women in Central Australia, Bell argued that with the advent of colonialism and sedentary life, Aboriginal women's status had been considerably weakened. However, while male dominance marked the politico-economic realm in contemporary life, women could separate from the larger community by living in the single women's camp where they were free to express their independence and autonomy in the rituals that were the focus of the camp. Bell's work in the single women's camp led her to conclude that men and women had separate ritual lives but that both were equally sacred and equally important to the reproduction of societal values. While men's rituals focused on creative powers, the rituals of women, which were no less important than those of their male counterparts, focused on emotional management and social harmony. Although Bell's book helped to correct some of the androcentric biases found in earlier ethnographies of Aboriginal ceremonial life, it has been criticized on methodological grounds and for its overtly dichotomous representation of Aboriginal ritual life, the second of which could equally apply to Hamilton's work.

The legacy of feminist anthropology can be seen in some of the scholarship on indigenous Australia that was produced in the 1990s and 2000s. Instead of focusing on women's status, ethnographers turned to study how persons were constituted as gendered subjects and embedded in indigenous forms of sociality and value systems. Victoria Burbank took up the topic of female-initiated aggression in her book *Fighting Women: Anger and Aggression in Aboriginal Australia* (1994). In it she challenged assumptions about the supposed unnaturalness of female aggression to show that it was culturally appropriate for Aboriginal women to initiate aggression against men or other women in response to aggression or to express anger. Aggression, she suggested, could be a "positive, enhancing act" that afforded women some measure of self-protection and that contributed to self-worth. Revisiting the theme of women's rituals, Françoise Dussart argued in her work that kin relatedness played a far more prominent and pervasive role in ritual than gender among Warlpiri living in Central Australia. Within the kin group, men and women often performed together in rituals and also shared ritual knowledge. Even gender-specific rituals, she argued, were based on ritual knowledge held jointly by men and women or involved both men and women in their preparations. Moreover, the authority of female ritual leaders rested not on their marital status, as Bell had maintained earlier, but on affiliation with the kin group and its strength in the community. The subject of masculinity also came into view in contemporary ethnography, primarily in the writings of Richard Davis. In his work on the Torres Strait Islands, Davis argued that Islander men engaged in a kind of political project as they reshaped globally available ideas of masculine power – ones from which they were often excluded – to construct their own versions of identity and masculinity.

Another key development concerning feminism in Indigenous Australia is the critique offered by indigenous activists and academics of second-wave feminism and some of the feminist anthropologists who took up its charge. Since the 1970s, indigenous writers have criticized the feminist movement as a movement of white, upper- and middle-class Australian women from which Aboriginal women were alienated. Jackie Huggins, Pat O'Shane, Bobbi Sykes, and Meredith Burgmann argued that racism, and the poverty that came with it, not sexism was the greatest oppressor of Aboriginal women. This was a fact that white feminists had failed to understand and even recognize. A call was put out for white feminists to acknowledge their racism and contributions to the oppression of Aboriginal women and the ways that sexism was shaped by racism. Moreover, these writers argued that the interests of white feminists and the conditions they faced were very different from those of Aboriginal women. Feminist campaigns for abortion rights, childcare, work equality, and sexual liberation did not really resonate with the experiences of Aboriginal women. Aboriginal women did seek the right to control their own fertility, but having been subjected to unwanted sterilization, this included the "right to have as many children as they wanted" (Huggins 1994, 71). Access to childcare was not as difficult for Aboriginal women as it was for white women since they were embedded in networks of extended kin. Aboriginal women sought to fight against discrimination in the workplace and in the educational system but this was more about racism than sexism since Aboriginal women had better educational levels than Aboriginal men and, when employed, had higher status jobs than Aboriginal men. Moreover, in matters of sexuality, Bobbi Sykes argued that, unlike white women, Aboriginal women had to confront racist myths of "the over-sexed black woman" (1975, 319). They sought the "right to say 'no'" more often than they sought the "right to say 'yes'" (Sykes 1975, 319). A "Black Women's Movement" – as many female indigenous writers have referred to it – was thus forged apart from the feminist movement to articulate the concerns of Indigenous women. Anthropologist and Aboriginal activist Marcia Langton has argued that central to this movement, and the organizational bodies and conferences that were born from it, were land rights, self-determination, and the right to sovereignty. Other key issues were access to healthcare and housing, freedom from discrimination in the welfare and educational systems, substance abuse, and the development of community services. Lawyer Larissa Behrendt has maintained that although the African American critique of American feminism and the one put forward by herself and other Aboriginal women have some parallels, different histories have given rise to divergent concerns between the two groups. Foremost among these divergences are those illuminated by Langton and others – land and sovereignty rights.

A well-known and widely publicized moment in the history of the Indigenous critique of the feminist movement is the so-called Bell-Huggins debate. In a 1989 issue of *Women's Studies International Forum*, Diane Bell claimed to "break the silence" about intraracial rape in Aboriginal communities. The central position of Bell's article was that intraracial rape was "everyone's business" and thus a matter to be dealt with by the Australian legal system. In a letter to the editors after the article's publication, historian Jackie Huggins, and 11 other Aboriginal women, challenged Bell's position on a number of grounds and also her right to speak for Indigenous women. Intraracial rape was the business of Aboriginal people, they wrote, and it had not been marked by silence in the first place – there were long-held mechanisms for talking about and dealing with rape in Aboriginal communities. The Australian legal system was not equipped to address intraracial rape, and could even lead to further burden, because it failed to take into account racial oppression as a contributing factor to sexual violence. Another point of contention raised in the letter was that Bell had listed Topsy Napurrula Nelson as the article's co-author. Bell, they charged, had merely positioned her key informant, Nelson, in this way to support her claim to have the authority to speak on the subject of intraracial rape. The context within which the Bell-Huggins debate unfolded revealed the "profoundly unequal" (Stringer 2012, 24) position that Aboriginal women held in Australian feminist discussions. The editors of the journal took two years to publish the letter, which they claimed was a personal attack on Bell, and did so only alongside an updated article from Bell and letters from both Nelson and Bell. Moreover, as gender studies scholar Rebecca Stringer has argued, the stance of "everyone's business" taken by Bell in the debate has been revived in current policy discussions to bolster support for the government takeover of the lands and resources of some 70 Northern Territory Aboriginal communities. These policy developments undermine the efforts of the earlier self-determination era and have attracted the criticisms of many feminists and Aboriginal activists.

The most comprehensive and recent account of Australian feminism from an Indigenous writer is Aileen Moreton-Robinson's *Talkin' Up to the White Women: Indigenous Women and Feminism* (2000). The book is a critical examination of feminist representations of Indigenous women, and in particular, the ways that white feminists have been positioned as the "invisible, natural, normal" and "all-knowing subject" and Indigenous women as the racialized "Other." The central argument of the book is that it is the invisibility of whiteness as ideology and practice that gives whiteness its power. This race dominance that is enjoyed by white feminists is predicated on colonialism and the dispossession of Indigenous people, although white feminists have failed to interrogate the effects of their dominance in any thoroughgoing and complex way. To make whiteness visible and to unmask the power relations that it has entailed, Moreton-Robinson looks at Indigenous women's self-representations in life writings and in their fraught encounters with the white feminist movement. Her conclusion is that if feminism is to contribute to a transformation of the racial order, there must be full involvement of Indigenous women in Australian feminism. This can only happen, however, when white feminists concede to "relinquish some power" – as well as theorize that relinquishment – and prioritize Indigenous concerns.

SEE ALSO: Feminisms, First, Second, and Third Wave; Feminist Activism; Feminist Ethnography; Gender, Politics, and the State in Aboriginal Australia and Torres Strait Islands

REFERENCES

Bell, Diane. 1983. *Daughters of the Dreaming*. Sydney: George Allen Unwin.
Bennett, Mary. 1930. *The Australian Aboriginal as a Human Being*. London: Alston Rivers.
Burbank, Victoria. 1994. *Fighting Women: Anger and Aggression in Aboriginal Australia*. Berkeley: University of California Press.
Gale, Fay, ed. 1970. *Woman's Role in Aboriginal Society*. Canberra: Australian Institute of Aboriginal Studies.
Holland, Allison. 1995. "Feminism, Colonialism and Aboriginal Workers: An Anti-Slavery Crusade." In *Aboriginal Workers*, edited by Ann McGrath and Kay Saunders with Jackie Huggins. Special issue of *Labour History*, 69: 52–64.
Huggins, Jackie. 1994. "A Contemporary View of Aboriginal Women's Relationship to the White Women's Movement." In *Australian Women: Contemporary Feminist Thought*, edited by Norma Grieve and Ailsa Burns, 70–79. Melbourne: Oxford University Press.
Moreton-Robinson, Aileen. 2000. *Talkin' Up to the White Woman: Aboriginal Women and Feminism*. St. Lucia: University of Queensland Press.
Stringer, Rebecca. 2012. "Impractical Reconciliation: Reading the Intervention through the Huggins-Bell Debate." *Australian Feminist Studies*, 27(71): 19–36.
Sykes, Bobbi. 1975. "Black Women in Australia: A History." In *The Other Half: Women in Australian Society*, edited by Jan Mercer, 313–321. Ringwood: Penguin Books.

FURTHER READING

Lake, Marilyn. 1998. "Feminism and the Gendered Politics of Antiracism, Australia 1927–1957: From Maternal Protectionism to Leftist Assimilationism." *Australian Historical Studies*, 29(110): 91–108.
Paisley, Fiona. 2000. *Loving Protection? Australian Feminism and Aboriginal Women's Rights 1919–1939*. Melbourne: Melbourne University Press.

Feminisms, Anarchist

ABBEY WILLIS
University of Connecticut, Storrs, USA

Anarchist feminism (sometimes referred to as anarcha-feminism or anarchafeminism) does not have one sole definition or interpretation since both feminism and anarchism vary in their theoretical positions. As with different types of feminism (liberal, radical, Marxist, socialist, etc.), anarchism also has differing interpretations and practices (individualist, syndicalist, communist, etc.). The broadest definition of the term would be that anarchist feminism is an anti-state, anti-capitalist, and anti-hierarchical form of feminism based on the negation of class society and structured domination, coercion, and control. At the same time, one could say that anarchist feminism is also a type of anarchism that figures in analyses of gender, sex, and sexuality as salient for liberatory praxis as any other axis of power in society.

Anarchist feminists often deem the goals of feminist struggle as unrealizable and unattainable without the co-struggle for anarchism, and vice versa. Anarchism (sometimes referred to as libertarian socialism) is often poorly described as simply a struggle against the state (see, e.g., Eltzbacher 2004). More accurately defined, anarchism is a historically specific political philosophy, process, and method based on the struggle against hierarchical society (Schmidt and van der Walt 2009). Not simply against the state, anarchism is against all forms of structured domination, exploitation, and oppression, and in favor of creating social relationships based on free association and mutual aid. Anarchism stands out not only as a vision of a free society, but also as a theory of how to struggle *toward* that society. Most importantly in this regard, anarchism argues for a consistency of means and ends – emphasizing what some feminists call *prefigurative politics*. Thus, to achieve a non-hierarchical society, the *struggle* for that society must be modeled non-hierarchically within our movements and our daily lives. Anarchism, then, would most likely be considered feminist (or, at the least, include aspects of feminism) if we understood feminism, broadly, as the struggle for gender and sexual equality. Although noting this connection, history has demonstrated that, oftentimes, anarchist struggles (like many political struggles) have relegated issues of gender and sexuality to the backburner (Ackelsberg 2005). However, throughout its history and contemporarily, there have been numerous accounts of anarchist struggles that utilize a feminist analysis, though not all its theorists/practitioners would necessarily use the term "feminist" in describing their political positions (e.g., during the Spanish Civil War, the Mujeres Libres did not identify as "feminist" – see the entry on anarchism and gender in this encyclopedia).

Anarchist feminism might be understood in relation to other types of feminism. The focus of liberal feminism is equal political and economic inclusion within already existing social institutions vis-à-vis gender. This means that liberal feminism does not necessarily problematize or critique societal institutions as they are; rather, the goal is to make these institutions equally accessible to both men and women. Radical feminism, a very broad tradition within feminism, acknowledges and criticizes patriarchy as a system of power in which male supremacy oppresses women as a group. Unlike liberal feminism, however, radical feminism *does* seek to create an entirely new, non-patriarchal society. In many facets, radical feminism understands patriarchy to be the central structure by which women are oppressed (see especially Firestone 1970). The goal for radical feminism, broadly, is to overthrow patriarchy and eliminate male supremacy and sexist gender roles. Marxist feminism, also a broad tradition within feminism, centers capitalism as the mode of production that structures the rest of society – more generally, this is a feminist extension of Marxist theory. Issues of gender oppression are often tied back to capitalism and its ability to saturate the rest of society. Private property and the invisibilization of reproductive labor are central critiques of Marxist feminism. Goals for Marxist feminism include working toward communist social relations that do not exclude women from productive labor and end the economizing relations that arise from capitalism, private property, and wage labor. Socialist feminism might be understood as a critique of Marxist feminism as too economistic, theorizing that both patriarchy and capitalism, *together*, are the root of women's oppression – this view is known as "dual systems theory." Socialist feminism can be viewed as a synthesis of Marxist and radical feminism since it focuses on economic and cultural oppression of women.

Anarchist feminism can be understood as differing from these other forms of feminism in that it critiques institutionalized and coercive hierarchy *writ large*. This means that anarchist feminism – according to its proponents – critiques institutions that are largely left unanalyzed by other forms of feminism. Most notably, anarchist feminism is critical of the state as an authoritarian and violent structure *in and of itself* (i.e., not just the "patriarchal" or "capitalist" state), as well as holding critiques of cultural and economic forms of gendered and sexualized oppression for all people.

Louise Michel, Emma Goldman, and Voltairine de Cleyre were well-known anarchists and feminists living from the mid- and later nineteenth century into the early and mid-twentieth century. They were prolific writers, orators, agitators, and organizers, often speaking against capitalism, the state, militarism, and marriage, and in favor of free association and a society based on mutual aid, free from exploitation and oppression. While writing and speaking out against forced sterilizations and the institution of marriage, Goldman also seemed to have anticipated queer understandings of gender and sexuality, writing that "[i]t is a tragedy, I feel, that people of a different sexual type are caught in a world which shows so little understanding for homosexuals, is so crassly indifferent to the various gradations and variations of gender and their great significance in life" (quoted in Katz 1976, 378–379). Voltairine de Cleyre wrote and spoke about social issues including sex trafficking, prostitution, and marriage, which helped to extend and apply anarchist critiques of society to women and women's issues more specifically. Louise Michel was a central organizer of the Paris Commune in 1871 and a powerful orator thereafter until her death.

Anarcha-feminism is found throughout the world contemporarily as well, both in the practice of social antagonists and in scholarship. Since anarchism was a central component of Occupy Wall Street (Bray 2013) and was present in the uprisings in Tunisia, Egypt, and Greece and the student movements in Chile, Quebec, and the United Kingdom, one can find anarcha-feminist theories and practices within each of these struggles. To name one example, in Tunisia, the organization Feminism Attack! was formed due to other Tunisian feminist organizations being "pseudo-bourgeois" and "serv[ing] the system" (Le Monde Libertaire 2013). This tendency has also been reflected in scholarship, such as the participatory action research done by the anarcha-feminist CRAC Collective in Montreal. Much of this anarcha-feminist scholarship and organizing has taken on queer theoretical calls to "trouble" categories of gender and sexuality (see, e.g., the edited collection *Queering Anarchism*, edited by Daring et al. 2012) and develop an intersectional understanding of oppression and exploitation (Rogue and Volcano 2012). Thus, anarcha-feminism, while firmly rooted historically, has taken on contemporary developments in movement practice and theory to evolve into a strong feminist current in existing struggles and academic work.

SEE ALSO: Anarchism and Gender; Capitalist Patriarchy; Feminism, Radical; Feminisms, Marxist and Socialist

REFERENCES

Ackelsberg, Martha A. 2005. *Free Women of Spain: Anarchism and the Struggle for the Emancipation of Women*. Oakland: AK Press.

Bray, Mark. 2013. *Translating Anarchy: The Anarchism of Occupy Wall Street*. Winchester: Zero Books.

Daring, C. B., J. Rogue, Deric Shannon, and Abbey Volcano, eds. 2012. *Queering Anarchism: Addressing and Undressing Power and Desire*. Oakland: AK Press.

Eltzbacher, Paul. 2004. *The Great Anarchists: Ideas and Teachings of Seven Major Thinkers*. Mineola: Dover Publications.

Firestone, Shulamith. 1970. *The Dialectic of Sex: The Case for Feminist Revolution*. New York: William Morrow.

Katz, Jonathan. 1976. *Gay American History: Lesbians and Gay Men in the U.S.A.* New York: Thomas Y. Crowell.

Le Monde Libertaire. 2013. "Feminism Attack! Anarchist Feminism in Tunisia." Accessed December 15, 2013, at http://www.monde-libertaire.fr/antisexisme/16593-feminism-attack-le-feminisme-anarchiste-en-tunisie.

Rogue, J., and Abbey Volcano. 2012. "Insurrection at the Intersections: Feminism, Intersectionality, and Anarchism." In *Quiet Rumors: An Anarcha-Feminist Reader*, edited by the Dark Star Collective, 43–46. Oakland: AK Press.

Schmidt, Michael, and Lucien van der Walt. 2009. *Black Flame: The Revolutionary Class Politics of Anarchism and Syndicalism (CounterPower*, vol. 1). Oakland: AK Press.

FURTHER READING

The Anarcha Project. Accessed December 15, 2013, at http://www.anarcha.org/.

Brigati, A. J., ed. 2004. *The Voltairine de Cleyre Reader*. Oakland: AK Press.

Dark Star, ed. 2012. *Quiet Rumors: An Anarcha-Feminist Reader*, 3rd ed. Oakland: AK Press.

Goldman, Emma. 1910. *Anarchism and Other Essays*. New York: Mother Earth Publishing Association.

Shannon, Deric. 2009. "Articulating a Contemporary Anarcha-Feminism." *Theory in Action*, 2(3).

Feminism, Black

ROSE M. BREWER
University of Minnesota Twin Cities, USA

The roots of black feminism are radical. This locates its theory and practice in the liberation of all people, which is not surprising given that black feminism in its contemporary and historical face(s) was born in struggle. The much cited "Combahee River Collective Statement" is one of the finest examples of this radical tradition. The women of Combahee asserted that the collective's black lesbian feminism is located in solidarity with progressive black men while "being fully cognizant of the negatives of male socialization in this society" (Combahee River Collective 1977). The Collective supported the "struggle alongside black men to fight racism, but against black men to fight sexism."

Furthermore, the Combahee River Collective developed one of the earliest articulations of black feminist intersectional thinking, delineating the deep interrelationality of racism, sexism, heterosexism, and classism. They argued that the struggle against patriarchy must occur simultaneously with the struggles against imperialism, racism/white supremacy, and capitalism. Even in the nineteenth century the advocate for black women's rights Anna Julia Cooper understood the deep connection between race and gender and the imperative to fight for justice on both fronts (Cooper 2000).

Once black feminism's genealogy is located in its radical groundings, there are, in fact, black feminism(s). While the roots are oppositional, not all black feminists articulate a radical social transformational theorization. Nonetheless, there are some general principles, as noted by Arkadie (2008), Collins (1990), and others who capture the core ideas of black feminism. Arkadie points out that in black feminist thinking, gender is deeply intertwined in race and class, but a distinctive attention to gender informs black feminist thought. In other words, gender matters. In this same vein, black feminists Johnnetta Cole and Beverly Guy-Sheftall contend that black society (in the United States) is formed by normative gender roles (i.e. men should be dominant and women subservient) that too often goes unchallenged (Cole and Guy-Sheftall 2003). They further argue that definitions of black manhood often depends in part on the subjugation of black women.

Nonetheless, black feminist struggles have never been strictly about dismantling patriarchy. Robert and Pam Allen note in their analysis of black social movements in twentieth-century United States that by 1920, when women's suffrage was finally enacted, white women forsake anti-lynching as a platform, acquiescing to racism (Allen and Allen 1983). Given white supremacy, it was not in the interests of white women to raise a voice for black women's rights (Dill 1979).

By the mid-twentieth century, the Civil Rights movement was embroiled in the struggle against racial inequality, and the Black Power movement emphasized national self-determination in the late 1960s into the 1970s. It is frequently assumed that the majority of black women in these movements put race first. However, this is too simple a reading of the times. White (2001) points out that by the 1970s black lesbian feminists had organized, and a group of black women came together to form the National Black Feminist Organization.

Nonetheless, contestation around the meaning of black feminism is evident. Much of this discussion is US centered, but black feminisms have emerged throughout Africa and the African diaspora. The philosophical splintering on conceptualization runs the gamut from a mild form of feminism that weakly chastises men for sexism, placing a strong emphasis on the significance of complementarity in African life, to womanism in its various expressions that articulates a specific black woman cultural sensibility. Some versions of womanism locate it deeply in African principles rather than white European women's culturally saturated feminism (Hudson-Weems 1998). The broader history of gender and black nationalism in the 1960s and 1970s is more complex and oppositional to male chauvinism and sexism within black communities. Reproductive rights would square off with nationalist thinking about the gender responsibilities of black women (Allen and Allen 1983). Nonetheless, black women's feminisms across the ideological spectrum have been defined in joint struggle with black men against racism.

Certainly the signature contribution of late twentieth- and twenty-first-century black feminism is the articulation of an intersectional analysis. Intersectionality has been accepted across a range of fields to represent the analytical approach to understanding how multiple categories of difference can and do overlap and intersect in the lives of black and non-black men and women. The result is unique social positions of marginalization and oppression that have been historically ignored by not only scholars and academics, but also society at large. Simply put, this mode of analysis represents the race, class, and gender paradigm that has been designed to address the multiplicity of these systems of inequality. They exist *in relation to* one another, and not as separate, exclusive entities (Arkadie 2008). This approach strongly rejects the additive approaches to systems of oppression, which means adding on a so-called "secondary" category of oppression such as class to a central or "main" category of oppression such as race. The life experiences of people socially positioned to experience the intersections of categories of discrimination represent a knowledge base that has long been ignored, and which, under the intersectionality approach, creates unexplored areas of analysis that can shed further light into the process and ramifications of the social construction of difference and inequality. Black feminism lifts up the experiences of women who have heretofore been silenced by their marginal positions in multiple categories of difference. Black feminists have consistently articulated this frame (James 1997).

The intersectional frame is built on simultaneity, multiplicity, and relationality. This theoretical grounding is being developed in academia, but during the mid-1960s in the United States it emerged in on-the-ground survival struggles, in reaction to the narrowness of white feminism (Hull, Bell-Scott, and Smith 1982). It developed in response to the black male politics of the day, which were aligned with much narrower notions of male/female relations.

The work of black feminist E. Frances White makes this point quite clearly (White 2001). For example, she points out that in the race-centered political stances found in traditional analyses of black men, a gender-centered analysis is often not visible. However, this erasure of gender among black "race" men and women is matched by the erasure of race in white feminism. Neither of these approaches is analytically robust and they need to be re-theorized. Given this, intersectional theorizing is core to a black feminist approach (Collins 1990).

The theorization of intersectionality yokes race, class, and gender relationally and interrelationally (Dill 1979; hooks 1984; King, 1988; Collins 1990; White 2001; Cole and Guy-Sheftall 2003; Oyewumi 2005; Reddock 2007). This means that the systems are deeply shaping of one another. It can be thought about in the context of the gendered, racialized, and class histories of African peoples. These interrelated histories cannot be written strictly as comparative narratives; the issue is how deeply dependent and interconnected these systems are. Indeed, running through this thought is the idea of the traditions of the African world, deconstructing either/or thinking which underpins Western epistemology.

Masculinity, too, is gendered, raced, and classed. Indeed, racialized, capitalist patriarchy profoundly shapes male/female, LGBT, and queer realities. Thus, the significance of the everyday, the local, and grounded is central. Grounded situational analysis is the starting point for understanding black women's lives. Also, black women are placed at the center of racialized/gendered analyses. This requires explicating the interplay between agency and social structure as central to black feminist theory and practice. The simultaneity of oppressions means that these inequalities are in play at the same time, not decontextualized but placed in historical context.

Neocolonialism, imperialism, and racism/white supremacy operate as hegemonic signifiers of black feminisms across the African diaspora. The race fiction, for example, was called into being simultaneously around the making of whiteness, maleness, and femaleness. In the nineteenth-century European imperial order, this thinking saturated the African continent and nearly all of what became known as the Third World.

Moreover, new analyses about the meaning of women, feminism, and the bio-logic of Western thinking are being theorized in a growing body of work on African feminisms. The analysis of sociologist Oyeronke Oyewumi is a case in point. The ideological rationalization for colonialism and exploitation takes on a number of dimensions, including language distortions and inaccuracies. Certainly the so-called "absolute inferiority" of Africans was called into being in deep relationality with the expropriation of labor, enslavement, land theft, and the making of empire. Fundamentally, a Western body logic was imposed on the African world, with destructive consequences for female power (Oyewumi 2005).

Ferguson (2003) draws deeply upon black feminist thinking while simultaneously challenging the heteronormative in theorizing. He points out that even before black feminism's visibility in the halls of academia, there was a long history of black women acting on both gender and race lines. By articulating a queer of color critique, Ferguson lifts up the scholarship of black Lesbian feminists such as Barbara Smith and Audre Lorde (Lorde 2007). Also, he centers black trans women of color in his articulation of a queer of color critique.

Black lesbian feminist theorist Cathy Cohen in *Boundaries of Blackness*, while deploying intersectional thinking, develops a theory of marginalization in her work (Cohen 1999). She articulates a theory of inequality in which a marginalized group internalizes and replicates forms of marginalization found in the dominant group. This conceptualization, of course, has profound implications for understanding the black LGBT population. Cohen takes on the thorny issue of AIDS in black life given this marginalization theory. Her work is intersectional and black feminist while not explicitly utilizing the trilogy of race, class, and gender.

Relatedly, black trans women have increasingly intervened in queer and radical black feminist theorizing. They are making visible challenges to some of the core concepts regarding representation and self-definition. Transgender interventions disrupt the narrow notions of gender, complicating black feminist thinking regarding gender binaries. For example, one term to describe those who do not identify as completely male or female is genderqueer. This does not apply to all transgender people, but it gives greater complexity to the deep relationality of gender and race (Terrell 2011).

These interventions are especially relevant in the arena of popular culture. How African American women are represented emerges out of the distortion of the black cultural experience in the United States. Collins, for example, traces the underpinnings of the negative images such as Jezebel and Welfare Queen attached to black women. These images get rearticulated over historical time, continuing to reappear in new guise (Collins 1990). Indeed, the caricatures that are deeply embedded in popular imagery reflect a simultaneous racial, gender, and class logic of distorted black womanhood. These issues go to the heart of black feminism. Yet, the difficulties of understanding complexity within black communities, complicated by age, region, ethnicity, class, and sexualities, are not easily resolved. The difficulties of theorizing the multiplicity across the African world, cross cut by nation, age, sexualities, region, ethnicity, and class, are daunting. Nonetheless, black feminists have placed gender at the center of race and class analyses. Clearly, black life and thought are being rearticulated through the complex and intersectional.

Black feminist thinking is being deployed across the African world. A good deal of the work considers the social, economic, and political status of African and African diasporic women in the global economy today. New analyses about the meaning of women, feminism, and the bio-logic of Western thinking are being theorized in a growing body of work on African feminism. The analysis of sociologist Oyeronke Oyewumi (2005) is a case in point. The past 500 plus years of the interrelated histories of white supremacy, enslavement, colonialism, imperialism, neocolonialism, and neoliberalism articulate this dynamic. Black feminist analysis across the Anglo-Caribbean world is intersectional, placing emphasis on colonialism as well as racism and sexism. And clearly, as Reddock (2007) contends, racism, gender, and nation are deeply intertwined in Afro-Caribbean lives. Women bear the brunt of transnational neoliberal capitalist exploitation in the black Caribbean. Their productive and reproductive labor are highly exploited. Very low pay and disruption of women's informal economic networks are part of the liberalization of trade confronting the black Caribbean.

Moving across the African diaspora to a black British context, in a classic piece by Hazel Carby (1982), "White Woman Listen! Black Women and the Boundaries of Sisterhood," expressed are some of the core ideas found in transnational black feminisms. Carby engages in a stirring critique of a white feminism unmediated by attention to race. Thus the black British context exemplifies how a generic sisterhood inattentive to racism and white supremacy must be contested. Entering black feminist theory and practice through the black British lens, Carby articulates the black feminist imperative of centering racism while simultaneously challenging patriarchy and class exploitation. This is the radical point of departure for black feminisms across the African diaspora.

SEE ALSO: Intersectionality; Womanism

REFERENCES

Allen, Robert, and Pam Allen. 1983. *Reluctant Reformers: The Impact of Racism on American Social Movements*. Washington, DC: Howard University Press.

Arkadie, Devon. 2008. "Race, Class, Gender and Black Feminism." Unpublished lecture, University of Minnesota, Minneapolis.

Cole, Johnnetta B., and Beverly Guy-Sheftall. 2003. *Gender Talk: The Struggle for Women's Equality in African American Communities*. New York: One World.

Carby, Hazel V. 1982. "White Woman Listen! Black Feminism and the Boundaries of Sisterhood." In *The Empire Strikes Back: Race and Racism in 70s Britain*, edited by The Centre for Contemporary Cultural Studies, 212–235. London: Hutchinson.

Cohen, Cathy. 1999. *Boundaries of Blackness*. Chicago: University of Chicago Press.

Collins, Patricia Hill. 1990. *Black Feminist Thought*. Boston: Unwin Hyman.

Combahee River Collective. 1977. "Combahee River Collective Statement." Accessed February 18, 2012, at http://historyisaweapon.com/defcon1/combrivercoll.html.

Cooper, Anna Julia. 2000. *A Voice from the South*. Chapel Hill: University of North Carolina Press. First published 1892.

Dill, Bonnie. 1979. "The Dialectics of Black Womanhood." *Signs*, 4: 553–555.

Ferguson, Roderick. 2003. *Aberrations in Black: Toward a Queer of Color Critique*. Minneapolis: University of Minnesota Press.

hooks, bell. 1984. *Feminist Theory: From Margin to Center*. Boston: South End Press.

Hudson-Weems, Clenora. 1998. "Africana Womanism." In *Sisterhood, Feminism, and Power: From Africa to the Diaspora*, edited by Obioma Nnaemeka, 170–182. Trenton: Africa World Press.

Hull, Gloria T., Patricia Bell-Scott, and Barbara Smith, eds. 1982. *All the Women are White, All the Blacks are Men, But Some of Us are Brave: Black Women's Studies*. New York: Feminist Press.

James, Joy. 1997. *Transcending the Talented*. New York: Routledge.

King, Deborah. K. 1988. "Multiple Jeopardy, Multiple Consciousness: The Context of a Black Feminist Ideology." *Signs*, 14: 42–72.

Lorde, Audre. 2007. *Sister Outsider*. New York Crossing Press. First published 1984.

Oyewumi, Oyeronke. 2005. *African Gender Studies*. New York: Palgrave Macmillan.

Reddock, Rhoda. 2007. "Diversity, Difference and Caribbean Feminism: The Challenge of Anti-Racism." *Caribbean Review of Gender Studies*, 1: 1–24.

Terrell, Kellee. 2011. "Black and Transgender: A Double Burden." Accessed June 16, 2014, at http://www.theroot.com/articles/culture/2011/10/black_and_transgender_a_double_burden.html.

White, E. Frances. 2001. *Dark Continent of Our Bodies: Black Feminism and the Politics of Respectability*. Philadelphia: Temple University Press.

Feminism, Chicana

JESSICA VELASQUEZ, ALEJANDRA PÉREZ, and ELIZABETH HUFFAKER
University of Washington Bothell, USA

Chicana feminism takes into account the experiences of Mexican American women, including attention to the intersection of gender, sexuality, religion, nationality, race, and ethnicity. In its early years, the Chicana feminist movement found itself in a double bind, caught between the Chicano movement, which rebelled against assimilation into the dominant US culture, and their feminist aspirations.

The term Chicano/a originated at the beginning of the 1920s as pejorative slang to describe people of Mexican descent living in the United States. In the 1960s, as mixed blood people of white and indigenous ancestry, many Mexican Americans realized that they were facing similar equity issues to black people in the United States. Inspired by the black civil rights movement, many Mexican Americans dropped their white identity and identified as persons of color by embracing and reclaiming the formerly derogatory term, Chicano/a.

Beginning in the 1960s, the Chicano movement concentrated on issues of justice, equality, and economic rights. Dominant US society expects all immigrants to assimilate and abandon their ethnic cultures. Yet people of color are prevented from blending into the hegemonic society, because of institutions, laws, and ideologies that are prejudiced against "mixed blood" people. Although the United States identified Mexican Americans as white, Chicanos demanded to be recognized as a separate race and have distinct civil rights.

Chicanas were involved in the Chicano movement, yet the movement proved antithetical to women's liberation. Women activists were placed in supporting roles, excluded from traditional politics, decision-making, and leadership positions (Blackwell 2011, 65). Despite this, Chicana feminists continued to participate in the Chicano movement while advancing their own feminist agenda. Chicana activist writer Mirta Vidal reported that women warned Chicanos that sexism and opposition to women's rights could divide the movement (Vidal 1971, 4).

Within the Chicano movement, Chicanas experienced marginalization. Maintaining cultural nationalism, and its attendant machismo, was considered important to the Chicano movement. Additionally, some Chicano men maintained that feminism and nationalism are contradictory. Chicana feminists, on the other hand, believed that machismo was a continuation of the colonization and repression of both men and women in early Mexican history. Chicana activists fought a multi-front battle against machismo within the Chicano community and racism in the general society (García 1989, 221–223).

Chicana feminists argued that Chicano men were aligning with white males in their own discrimination through denying half of La Raza population civil rights (Vidal 1971, 6). Responding to accusations of Chicana feminists assimilating into the white culture, Francisca Flores argued that birth control, abortion, and sex education were not only white issues. She referred to the Chicano culture as "our culture hell", which became a slogan of the Chicana movement, identifying that their repression came from within (García 1989, 227–228).

The first national Chicana Conference was held in 1971 in Houston, Texas, attended by 600 women. Chicana feminists sought to promote a positive attitude toward sexuality without the restraints of culture and religion. As with other feminist movements in the United States, Chicana feminists openly discussed legal abortions, birth control, and autonomy over their own bodies. They identified the Catholic Church as repressive toward women. The conference attendees acknowledged the La Raza concept of a unified family, but recognized that Chicanas are often single parents, unsupported by Chicano fathers. The activists argued that "Chicana motherhood should not preclude educational, political, social, and economic advancement" (Alexander 2008).

As Chicanas became self-reliant, they were conflicted by the belief that a "good woman" meant "mother" (Castillo 1994, 117). The cultural traditions from the Church gave women two possible identities: Mary, who was a pure virgin mother; and Eve, who was sinful – the "virgin–whore dichotomy" (Castillo 1994, 66). Chicanas argued women's submission to the patriarchal church was brought to Mexico by European colonialism, therefore another "Anglo thing" (Vidal 1971, 6). The pull of their cultural traditions were in constant conflict with the feminists' efforts toward self-determination.

While both male and female Chicano/as are subjected to US racial economic exploitation, Chicana feminists saw a double exploitation due to their race and gender. The feminists claimed that the Chicano movement addressed the issue of economic racial oppression, yet did not address economic sexism within the workforce. Challenging the intersection of economic racism and sexism became critical to the Chicana feminist movement (García 1989, 223–224).

Chicanas acknowledged the need to rewrite their group identity, thereby paradoxically repressing their own cultural identity (Alarcón 1990, 252). Chicana feminists maintained that their oppression was perpetuated by three systems: racism, sexism, and classism. They believed the sexism Chicanas experienced was distinct from women of other races because their cultural heritage differed (Vidal 1971). Chicanas recognized that their intersectional oppression was in the home and in society. This generated direction and energy for the Chicana feminist movement.

In the 1960s and 1970s, Chicana feminists maintained a constant flow of writings in the alternative press. Their contributions were unacknowledged due to the omission of women from machista Chicano culture (Alarcón 1990, 249). However, the tradition continued, and in 1981 Gloria Anzaldúa and Cherríe Moraga edited *This Bridge Called My Back: Writings by Radical Women of Color*, which continues to influence feminist knowledge production and activism. Chicana feminists today are active in politics, education, access to healthcare, and environmental justice, due to their understanding of the intersectionality of all civil rights.

SEE ALSO: Borderlands; Community and Grassroots Activism; Feminism, Black; Feminism, Latina; Feminism, Lesbian; Intersectionality

REFERENCES

Alarcón, N. 1990. "Chicana Feminism: In the Tracks of 'the' Native Woman." *Cultural Studies*, 4(3): 248–256.

Alexander Street Project. 2008. "The Sixties: Primary Documents and Personal Narratives, 1960 to 1974." Accessed August 20, 2015, at http://alexanderstreet.com/products/sixties-primary-documents-and-personal-narratives-1960-1974.

Blackwell, Maylei. 2011. *Chicana Power: Contested Histories of Feminism in the Chicano Movement*. Austin: University of Texas Press.

Castillo, Ana. 1994. *Massacre of the Dreamers: Essays on Xicanisma*. Albuquerque: University of New Mexico Press.

García, A.M. 1989. "The Development of Chicana Feminist Discourse, 1970–1980." *Gender and Society*, 3(2): 217–238.

Vidal, Mirta. 1971. "Chicanas Speak Out – Women: New Voice of La Raza." Women's Liberation Movement. Accessed August 20, 2015, at http://library.duke.edu/rubenstein/scriptorium/wlm/chicana.

FURTHER READING

Acevedo, Luz del Alba. 2001. *Telling to Live: Latina Feminist Testimonios*. Durham: Duke University Press.

Anzaldúa, Gloria. 1987. *Borderlands/La Frontera: The New Mestiza*. San Francisco: Spinsters/Aunt Lute.

Martínez, Elizabeth. 2008. *500 Years of Chicana Women's History/500 Años de Historia de las Chicanas*, bilingual edition. New Brunswick: Rutgers University Press.

Moraga, Cherríe. 1983. *This Bridge Called my Back: Writings by Radical Women of Color*, 2nd ed. New York: Kitchen Table, Women of Color Press.

Trujillo, Carla. 1991. *Chicana Lesbians: The Girls our Mothers Warned us About*. Berkeley: Third Woman Press.

Feminism, Chinese

LETA HONG FINCHER
Tsinghua University, China

Since the founding of the People's Republic of China in 1949, various forms of authoritarianism have prevented the rise of an independent, large-scale Chinese feminist movement and Chinese feminism has been overwhelmingly dominated by the Communist Party-backed official state agency representing women, the All-China Women's Federation (Quanguo Fulian). Small groups of feminist activists in recent years have staged innovative acts of "performance art" to raise awareness about women's rights abuses. Nonetheless, they are severely constrained by the Chinese state's elaborate "stability maintenance" system set up to absorb all expressions of political opposition. Very few Chinese women identify themselves as feminist in spite of the significant increase in gender inequalities in recent years of market reforms and rapid economic growth. Still, some women resist patriarchal norms and intense marriage pressure through individual life choices, such as choosing to stay single rather than get married.

This entry focuses on feminist political activism in the People's Republic of China in the context of rising gender inequalities during the most recent stage of postsocialist market reforms since the beginning of the twenty-first century. Due to space limitations, it does not examine the vibrant feminist movements in Taiwan, Hong Kong, or the Chinese diaspora in other countries (Chen 2011), nor does it provide a literature review of semantic interpretations of the term "feminism" (*nüquan zhuyi* or *nüxing zhuyi*) within China. As Tani Barlow (2004, 3) documents in her historical genealogy of the category of "woman" (*funü*), feminism in modern Chinese history has been "an integral part of contemporary deliberations about the nation and its development."

The emancipation of women was a key goal of both China's Communist Revolution, which culminated in the founding of the People's Republic of China in 1949, and, decades before that, the Republican Revolution, which toppled the country's last dynasty, the Qing (1644–1911) (Liu, Karl, and Ko 2013). The Communist Party publicly celebrated gender equality and sought to harness women's labor in boosting the nation's productivity with expansive initiatives such as assigning urban women jobs in the planned economy and mobilizing hundreds of millions of rural women to work in the fields. The Marriage Law of 1950, a cornerstone of the Communist Revolution, abolished arranged marriages, polygamy, and prostitution, granting women more financial independence and expanded freedoms in the public arena.

There is extensive debate over the degree to which women's gains during the early Communist era were real or merely rhetorical. For example, anthropologist Guo Yuhua's study of women's memories of 1950s agricultural collectivization in a northern Chinese village documents tremendous suffering as women were required to assume a double burden of performing all domestic chores – sometimes having to let children go hungry during the day in the absence of help – while also having to go out into the fields to perform agricultural work alongside the men (Guo 2003).

Yet even though gender equality was never truly realized during the Mao era in spite of the rhetoric of "women's liberation" (*funü jiefang*), a large body of evidence indicates that economic inequality in gender has increased substantially in China's postsocialist era. In China today, gender discriminatory norms are exacerbated by breakneck economic growth and market reforms dismantling the public sector, a massive propaganda infrastructure that maintains a tight grip on information, and a well-financed "stability maintenance" (*weiwen*) system set up to strictly limit freedom of association (Lee and Zhang 2013). "The fragility of state feminism can be seen in the rapidity and ease with which a more overt patriarchal culture has reasserted itself with the return to a privatized economy and transnational capital in the post-Mao era," writes Mayfair Mei-hui Yang (1999, 39).

Feminist groups advocating for greater women's rights protections in China are required to comply with onerous regulations to gain registration as formal non-government organizations (NGOs or *feizhengzhi zuzhi*) if they wish to operate legally. When feminist groups are not officially registered as a legal entity, the activists must use their personal bank accounts to pay bills such as rent for office space, making it extremely difficult to operate. Leading activists with officially registered women's NGOs state that there is virtually no room for an independent women's movement outside of the government's top-down mobilization of women in service to the nation. Moreover, women's rights NGOs constantly risk closure by the authorities if they become too influential and are seen as posing a threat to Communist Party rule. For example, the founder of the Weizhiming Women's Center in Hangzhou, Wu Rongrong, announced that she had to shut down the group in May 2015 after most of its members came under police investigation.

Since the early twenty-first century, mostly anonymous feminist volunteers (*zhiyuanzhe*) in grassroots groups (*caogen zuzhi*) have staged innovative acts of performance art (*xingwei yishu*) to protest about abuses of women's rights in China. For example, in August 2014, four young women in Guangzhou posted pictures of themselves on Sina Weibo, China's version of Twitter, dressed only in T-shirts and underpants beside a message written in red saying "my vagina does not come free with my labor" to protest rampant sexual harassment in the workplace. The photo was quickly retweeted hundreds of times on Weibo and other social media platforms. Other acts of feminist performance art included young women dressing in white wedding gowns smeared with red paint to protest domestic violence and women shaving their heads in public to protest against gender-based quotas favoring the admission of men over women to university programs. Yet even these very small-scale forms of performance-art-as-protest can incite police harassment.

The most highly publicized women's rights action (*xingdong*) occurred in February 2012, when a group of feminist activists occupied a men's public lavatory in Guangzhou, southern China, and invited women into the vacated men's stalls to shorten their typically long wait. The lesbian activist who helped organize the Occupy Men's Toilets (*zhanling nan cesuo*) demonstration, Li Maizi, said in an interview with the author that her group deliberately chose a cause that was not too politically "sensitive" (*mingan*), in an effort to avoid police interference.

Yet despite choosing a politically innocuous cause, when she and several other activists began to expand the Occupy Men's Toilets campaign to Beijing, they were obstructed by the Chinese security apparatus, with a group of police officers telling the activists that they were assembling in public without permission and detaining Li and another activist for the day. Police also showed up on Li's doorstep on the morning of another planned protest against mandatory gynecological exams for women seeking civil service jobs. The police interrogated her, then ordered her to stay home that day and the next. The harassment of Li and fellow feminists illustrates the effectiveness of the stability maintenance system set up by the Chinese government to control all forms of political opposition. Sociologists Lee and Zhang (2013) detail how the Chinese "grassroots state" penetrates into local communities to gather information on citizens and defuse conflict that might threaten social stability. In such a politically repressive environment, feminist activists must constantly second-guess the government in order to avoid potentially harsh penalties such as police harassment or arrest.

In addition, lesbian organizations are marginalized by officially registered Chinese women's rights groups. Author interviews indicate that the Women's Federation rarely included work on lesbians because they are considered too politically "sensitive." Chinese society has become more accepting of the lesbian, gay, bisexual, transgender, and queer (LGBTQ) community over the past decade and a half, after the government took homosexuality off its list of "mental diseases" in 2001 (Engebretsen 2014). But changing conservative attitudes toward women and families will likely take many decades, as various waves of the "Women Return to the Home" (nüren huijia) movement have recurred ever since the onset of economic reforms in 1980 (Li Yinhe 1994; Tong 2008).

China still had no specific law in 2014 to prevent or punish domestic violence in spite of many years of efforts by feminist activists. As a result, even if a woman has carefully documented abuse at the hands of her intimate partner through police and medical reports, it is extremely difficult for her to secure a protection order from a Chinese court. While women's rights NGOs were lobbying for passage of intimate partner violence legislation, lesbian groups tried to push for an acknowledgment that same-sex couples should also be protected from violence. Yet members of registered women's rights organizations said that without the imprimatur of the Women's Federation, they did not dare raise issues related to lesbians, according to Xu Bin, the founder of Tongyu, an unofficial group for lesbian, bisexual, and transgender women.

Continuing restrictions on feminist advocacy take place against a backdrop of rising gender inequalities. Over the past two decades, a combination of factors – the dismantling of the planned economy, the privatization of housing and subsequent skyrocketing of home prices, sharp setbacks to married women's property rights through a new judicial interpretation of the Marriage Law in 2011 (Li Ying 2011), and a state media campaign to stigmatize single educated women as "leftover" women (shengnü) – has contributed to a new backlash against the gains of educated women in particular (Fincher 2014). Studies find that China's gender income gap (Cohen and Wang 2008) and gender gap in labor force participation rates have increased substantially since the 1990s (Jiang 2004).

Moreover, since the privatization of formerly public housing in 1998, the subsequent real estate boom has created a stark new gender wealth gap. Property is the biggest source of wealth in cities such as Shanghai and Beijing, but in a deeply patriarchal society, Chinese women have largely missed out on arguably the greatest accumulation of residential property wealth in history (Fincher 2014). Studies indicate that China's market reforms overall have substantially increased the gender asset gap (Li et al. 2008). According to the nationwide Third Sample Survey on the Social Status of Women in 2010, conducted by the Women's Federation and the National Bureau of Statistics, only 13.2 percent of married women in China own property in their own right, as compared to 51.7 percent of married men with sole ownership of residential property (All-China Women's Federation 2011).

The Women's Federation has pushed for the adoption of useful legislation, such as the "Law on Protecting Women's Rights and Interests" in 1992, which was revised in 2005. Yet the Women's Federation role is largely to serve the Communist Party in carrying out state policies rather than to protect women's rights. For example, the Women's Federation took a leading role in a state media campaign to pressure urban educated women in their mid- to late twenties to stop pursuing their career ambitions and get married.

In 2007, the Women's Federation defined the term "leftover" women (*shengnü*) as single women older than 27, and China's Ministry of Education added the term to its official lexicon, according to the state-run Xinhua News Agency. Since then, the Chinese state media has aggressively promoted the term through articles, surveys, cartoons, and editorials stigmatizing educated women who are single, often referring to a "crisis" in growing numbers of educated women who "cannot find a husband" (Fincher 2014).

The political space for feminist activism – or any form of rights activism – had contracted at the end of 2014. Dozens of activists had been detained or arrested that year on charges of "illegal assembly" or, in some cases, "inciting subversion," according to human rights groups. Feminist activists interviewed by the author said that the government crackdown had had a chilling effect on their advocacy: many did not dare organize any public demonstrations, and they expected a long period of "struggle." As one activist said: "I think that in about 30 years, we should be able to see some real change."

Given the difficulties of organized feminist advocacy, many women resist patriarchal norms and intense marriage pressure through individual life choices, such as making a deliberate choice to reject marriage; using homonyms for the term "leftover" (*sheng*) to describe themselves on Weibo as "victorious" (another word with the same sound as *sheng* but a different character); or saving up money to purchase a home in their own name to strive for economic independence. One self-identified Beijing feminist said in an interview that "the government has inserted itself into the tiniest, most minute details of an individual's life." She added that the institution of marriage in China "basically benefits men … [so] the most rational choice is to stay single."

SEE ALSO: Feminism in Northeast Asia; Feminism in Southeast Asia; Gender and History of Revolutions in East Asia; Gender, Politics, and the State in East Asia; Lesbian and Gay Movements; Women's and Feminist Activism in East Asia

REFERENCES

All-China Women's Federation (ACWF). 2011. "Third Sample Survey on the Social Status of Women in 2010." *Executive Report in Funü yanjiu lun cong [Women's Research Collection]*, 6 (108): 5–15. Summary accessed January 6, 2014, at http://www.wsic.ac.cn/academicnews/78621.htm.

Barlow, Tani. 2004. *The Question of Women in Chinese Feminism*. Durham, NC: Duke University Press.

Chen, Ya-chen. 2011. *The Many Dimensions of Chinese Feminism*. New York: Palgrave Macmillan.

Cohen, Philip, and Wang Feng. 2008. "The Market and Gender Pay Equity: Have Chinese Reforms Narrowed the Gap?" In *Creating Wealth and Poverty in Postsocialist China*, edited by Deborah Davis and Wang Feng, 35–51. Stanford: Stanford University Press.

Engebretsen, Elisabeth. 2014. *Queer Women in Urban China: An Ethnography*. New York: Routledge.

Fincher, Leta Hong. 2014. *Leftover Women: The Resurgence of Gender Inequality in China*. London: Zed Books.

Guo, Yuhua. 2003. "Psychological Collectivization: The Cooperatives and Transformation of Agriculture as in the Memory of the Women" [Xinling de jitihua: Shanbei Jicun nongye hezuohua de nüxing jiyi]. *Social Sciences in China*, 4: 48–61. Accessed August 25, 2014, at http://mjlsh.usc.cuhk.edu.hk/Book.aspx?cid=4&tid=367.

Jiang, Yongping. 2004. "Employment and Chinese Urban Women Under Two Systems." In *Holding Up Half the Sky*, edited by Tao Jie, Zheng Bijun, and Shirley Mow, 207–220. New York: The Feminist Press at the City University of New York.

Lee, Ching Kwan, and Yonghong Zhang. 2013. "The Power of Instability: Unraveling the Microfoundations of Bargained Authoritarianism in

China." *American Journal of Sociology*, 118(6): 1475–1508. DOI: 10.1086/670802.

Li, Ying. *Netease* [Wangyi] 2011. "Wo kan hunyinfa sifa jieshi san" [My view of Judicial Interpretation Three of the Marriage Law]. Accessed January 4, 2014, at http://lady.163.com/11/0815/02/7BFDPCRB00262613.html.

Li, Yinhe. 1994. "'Nüren huijia' wenti zhi wo jian" [The "Women Return to the Home" question from my perspective]. *Shehuixue Yanjiu*, 1994 (6).

Li, Xiaoyun, Dong Qiang, Liu Xiaoqian, and Wu Jie. 2008. "Gender Inequality and Poverty in Asset Ownership." *Chinese Sociology and Anthropology*, 40(4): 49–63. DOI: 10.2753/CSA0009-4625400404.

Liu, Lydia, Rebecca Karl, and Dorothy Ko, eds. 2013. *The Birth of Chinese Feminism: Essential Texts in Transnational Theory*. New York: Columbia University Press.

Tong, Xin. 2008. "Sanshi nian Zhongguo nüxing/xingbie shehuixue yanjiu" [Thirty years of sociology of women's/gender studies in China]. *Funü yanjiu luncong* 2008 (3). Accessed January 6, 2014, at http://wen.org.cn/modules/article/view.article.php/597.

Yang, Mayfair Mei-hui. 1999. "From Gender Erasure to Gender Difference: State Feminism, Consumer Sexuality, and Women's Public Sphere in China." In *Spaces of Their Own: Women's Public Sphere in Transnational China*, edited by Mayfair Mei-hui Yang, 35–67. Minneapolis: University of Minnesota Press.

FURTHER READING

Davis, Deborah, and Sara Friedman, eds. 2014. *Wives, Husbands, and Lovers: Marriage and Sexuality in Hong Kong, Taiwan, and Urban China*. Stanford: Stanford University Press.

Evans, Harriet. 2007. *The Subject of Gender: Daughters and Mothers in Urban China (Asian Voices)*. Lanham, MD: Rowman & Littlefield.

Hershatter, Gail. 2011. *The Gender of Memory: Rural Women and China's Collective Past*. Berkeley: University of California Press.

Zhou, Songqing. 2010. "*Shengnü*" yu xingbie tongzhi ["Leftover" women and gender domination]. *Zhongguo qingnian yanjiu* (China Youth Studies) 5.

Feminism, Cultural

KRISTINA B. WOLFF
Gender Research Institute at Dartmouth College, USA

Cultural feminism seeks to understand women's social locations in society by concentrating on gender differences between women and men. This type of feminism focuses on the liberation of women through individual change, the recognition and creation of "women-centered" culture, and the redefinition of femininity and masculinity. Cultural feminism utilizes essentialist understandings of male and female differences as the foundation of women's subordination in society.

Early cultural feminists sought to reclaim and redefine definitions of femininity and masculinity through recognizing and celebrating women's unique characteristics. Cultural feminists believe that women are inherently nurturing, kind, gentle, egalitarian, and non-violent. These tenets can be traced back to the *first wave* of feminism. During this time, scholars such as Jane Addams and Charlotte Perkins Gilman stressed the superiority of women's values, particularly compassion and pacifism, believing that these would conquer masculine qualities of selfishness, violence, and lack of self-control in relation to sexual behavior. This was also a means to challenge the dominant cultural discourse that women were inferior and subservient to men. Efforts at fighting women's subordination included working for women's suffrage, women's right to free expression, and women's culture as well as outreach to poor and working-class women. The decline of this early stage of cultural feminism has been attributed to World War I and societal reaction to these early feminists' opposition to the war.

Cultural feminism returned during the *second wave* of feminism in the early 1970s, when it reemerged out of the radical feminist movement. *Radical feminism* directly challenges biological definitions of male and female while actively working toward eliminating women's oppression. One aspect of this type of feminism was the minimization of gender differences and advocation of androgyny. Within the movement, lesbians seeking to achieve recognition for their efforts, as well as visibility, created another body of feminism, *lesbian feminism*. Lesbian feminism focuses on unique issues that homosexual women face within feminism and throughout society, as well as examining the ways in which sexuality is socially constructed. Included in both lesbian and cultural feminism is the practice of separatism, the creation of spaces, groups, and communities that are separate from men. Cultural feminists employed some of the practices of both radical and lesbian feminism but diverged from them due to its central focus. Cultural feminism emphasizes a need to highlight women's uniqueness and feminine qualities as positive attributes rather than erasing the differences between men and women, as stressed in radical feminism. It also modified lesbian feminism to create a feminism that appealed to a wider audience, while retaining a women-centered focus. Cultural feminism is bounded by the practice of concentrating on the differences between genders as its foundation, while placing "woman" at the center. While there is great variety within this body of feminism, the main areas of scholarship focus on individual change, the development of women's culture, the redefinition of femininity and masculinity, and examinations of sexuality.

Foundationally, cultural feminism is the reclaiming and redefinition of female identity. Women's liberation occurs through the rejection of society's conception of "woman" since this is based on a male model of understanding. During a time period when some other branches of feminism were rejecting traditional values of womanhood, challenging and/or erasing what was understood as inherently female, cultural feminists sought to revalidate the essence of what it means to be "female" by embracing and reappropriating female attributes. This practice focuses on honoring one's femaleness through challenging traditional definitions of "woman" as well as the expected gender roles as defined by men. At the same time, traits that are attributed to women, such as the natural ability to nurture, are viewed as positive attributes that should be honored.

The early process of redefining and reclaiming femaleness took shape in a variety of forms and largely concentrated on changing personal behavior and attitudes and on creating a cultural transformation. This included the recognition and development of women's culture to counter women's invisibility, subordination, and often isolation from one another. Women's experience is the foundation of a "sisterhood," based on the belief that all women share a commonality due to gender. Women sought to establish "safe" places, free from male dominance, where they could build community. Often these events or spaces did not allow men to participate, thus giving women freedom from men and men's subordination. Some defined this process of creating strong relationships and women-centered spaces as "female bonding." This label sought to capture the inherent essence in women, one that naturally ties them together. Its purpose is to demonstrate the importance of placing "woman" at the center of their lives. The term also clashes with lesbians, as cultural feminists primarily defined "female bonding" as a non-sexual, emotional connection. The result was that lesbianism quickly became subsumed under the label and, once again, left on the margins. Culturally, there was a surge in women's scholarship, art, and literature which focused on issues specifically related to and about women. Throughout the United States, women-centered events and spaces were established. This included, but was not limited to, music festivals, businesses and organizations, women's centers, domestic violence shelters and rape crisis centers, and numerous community groups. Additionally, Take Back the Night marches were established to draw attention to rape, domestic violence, and abuse of women.

Central to this cultural shift is the development of an alternative consciousness, one that rejects what is "male" and how society is defined through a male lens. Cultural feminists view essentialist definitions of female and the qualities attached to understandings of femininity as powerful assets for women. Socially conditioned aspects of femininity, which include characteristics such as passivity and submissiveness, are redefined and revalidated as exemplifying women's innate ability to be nurturing, loving, non-violent, cooperative, and egalitarian in nature. Men and masculinity are viewed as inherently violent, aggressive, and competitive. Men are seen as the "enemy" by virtue of their biological maleness. Women are subordinated due to men's nature. Women are also secondary because contemporary Western society and Western thought do not value women's virtues. Instead, male thought and ideas of hierarchy, domination, and independence are held in the highest esteem. Cultural feminism challenges these male values, seeking to change society and methods of governing through emphasizing women's natural ability to solve conflict through cooperation, pacifism, and non-violence.

These changes in viewpoint, in placing women at the center, created a shift and dramatic growth in feminist scholarship. Cultural institutions that were often viewed as secondary in importance in society, such as women's roles, primary modes of employment, and motherhood, were now examined through a female lens. For example, Adrienne Rich and Nancy Chodorow examined the richness of women's experiences and roles as mothers, and Carol Gilligan joined Chodorow in utilizing psychological theories to further understand gender differences, thus helping to establish *psychoanalytic feminism*. Deborah Tannen's scholarship explores gender differences in the way men and women communicate with one another. Mary Daly, who also is influential in radical feminism, critiques and creates new languages as well as a feminist theology, both of which place women as central to her development of these new meanings. Ingrained in all of these "new" forms of scholarship is the inherent belief that women have certain innate qualities that should finally be recognized and honored by society, rather than remaining invisible or denigrated.

Included in these critiques and new scholarship was the development of standpoint theory and feminist epistemology. Both recognize that women have a unique perspective based on their experiences as women and that this should be valued, explored, and learned from. Both directly challenge traditional approaches to knowledge and understanding, recognizing these as grounded in and stemming from elite males in society. *Standpoint theory* posits that women's understanding of the world is different from men's, even if it is shaped by men's definitions. This difference is based on women's experiences and knowledge, both formal and informal. Women's perspectives vary in ways that are visible and invisible and affect the ways in which people understand and also approach the social world. Sandra Harding's development of a *feminist epistemology* centers on critiquing society's understanding and creation of knowledge, thus shaping the ways in which science and the quest for knowledge occur. Harding analyzes traditional approaches to expanding knowledge in society from a woman's standpoint to illustrate how women's "ways of knowing" differ from men's. This ever expanding scholarship assisted in providing a foundation for the establishment of women's studies as a discipline, as well as in the development of many other concentrations and changes in focus of numerous disciplines. In sociology, for example, it provides a foundation for the sociology of sex and gender, feminist sociology, and feminist methods within sociology.

Inherent in the focus on differences between genders is the issue of sexuality and sexual practices. Approaches to sexuality vary. Some cultural feminists embrace women's ability to reproduce and promote it as "the" source of female power. They believe that men are afraid and/or jealous of women and their ability to reproduce and thus they try to control reproduction through a variety of means, including policy and technology. One direct result of this belief was the development of women's resources for healthcare and reproduction, including the publication in 1970 of *Our Bodies, Ourselves* by the Boston Women's Health Book Collective, which was the first publication dedicated to women's health written by and for women. Other cultural feminists seek to reclaim the power of positive sexual practices and desires through exploring women's fantasies, desires around intimacy, and ability to be open to and want emotional experiences. Addressing the focus of sexual behavior on the pleasures of women links directly back into radical feminism, which sought to highlight the importance of women enjoying sex. This included a reformulation of heterosexual practices that sought to concentrate on women's satisfaction instead of men's.

Some also focus on men's sexual behavior as a specific practice of male domination over women. Female sexuality is believed to naturally concentrate on relationships and intimacy. The focus is on reciprocity and caring rather than solely engaged on physical ecstasy. Sexuality for men is believed to be primarily focused on the merger of power and orgasm. Men naturally concentrate on their own physical desire, seeking to maintain power over women. Men want to be intimate with women in order to satisfy their own needs. In this respect, men and women are viewed as complete opposites.

Some cultural feminists advocate that women embrace their femininity as well as their sexuality by rejecting sexual activity with men, viewing male penetration as domination. Many of these early feminists were also part of the radical feminism movement. Some of these women also apply the term "female bonding" here to illustrate the conscious focus on surrounding oneself with other women and having them fulfill every need, including as sexual partners. This approach to sexuality led to the creation of the anti-pornography movement and also created a split among cultural feminists, particularly those who do not view sexual behavior as a source of men's domination.

One of the accomplishments of cultural feminism was the emergence of the anti-pornography movement. This movement materialized out of the establishment of women's groups and organizations, particularly those that focused on issues of domestic violence, abuse, and rape. One of the beliefs of the movement is that men are unable to control themselves, that their desire to dominate women is due to their biological makeup. Women are then responsible for curtailing and controlling their behavior. This approach is very similar to the first wave of feminism, including those women involved in the temperance movement. Pornography is believed to perpetuate our culture's misogyny and also causes violence against women, often because it depicts women being subjected to acts of violence. Some claimed that rape was simply due to men's male essence, and others proclaimed that "porn is the theory, rape is the practice" (see, e.g., Brownmiller 1975; Dworkin 1979). It is believed that pornography also affects women negatively, compelling them to accept the negative images of women. The movement has had a varied history of success, resulting in the creation of anti-pornography legislation and increased regulation, particularly around issues of age of participants and the elimination of highly violent images. It also continues to critique the role of pornography in society and has developed another area of feminist scholarship surrounding law, media, and sexuality studies. While many communities adopted strict anti-pornography laws, many of these have been overturned on constitutional grounds.

Cultural feminism continues to influence current feminisms as well as other disciplines, including sociology, in particular concerning issues of women and work, mothering, sexuality, and women's role as "caretaker." Cultural feminism is one of the most successful and influential types of feminism. However, it is not without critics. One of the most common critiques concerns its reliance on applying biological definitions of "woman." The use of essentialist conceptions of "woman" reifies the societal beliefs it seeks to redefine. This key premise tends to invoke a universal conception of what "woman" is, failing to offer a response to traditional patriarchal beliefs of women and men. By embracing socially constructed ideas of femininity and masculinity, there is an implication that women cannot escape their destinies as females. Also embedded within these biological assumptions is the premise that women's duty is to control men because they cannot control themselves due to their inherent essence. By relying on women to change their behaviors and seek to control men, cultural feminism leaves unchallenged the overarching system of patriarchy, which shapes societal understandings and practices of gender. Some early cultural feminists such as Adrienne Rich, Andrea Dworkin, and Susan Brownmiller have also offered critiques, but these are largely based on the application of essentialist definitions of "woman" rather than the belief itself. For some, the application is not complete without female scientists researching women's natural traits from their own perspective, thus countering male biases.

By seeking to unite all women under a banner of a "global sisterhood," many argue that differences based on race, class, nation, status, age, and other complexities in women's lives are erased. In many ways, cultural feminists have broadened their focus and depth of analysis to include other elements of culture. This includes the unique history and practices of women of color in the United States as well as women's experiences in other nations. However, the criticism remains that through maintaining a singular focus on "woman," even with this expansion, these other factors remain in a secondary position. Additionally, many of the feminists who do utilize a wider definition of cultural feminism, one that includes race, class, age, and so on, resist using an essentialist foundation of gender and instead focus on the complexities of all of these differences.

Another strong critique of cultural feminism is that it resulted in establishing "rules" as to "who" could be a feminist. Women were expected to embrace the concept of being "woman-centered" or "woman-identified." This often resulted in an expectation that women would decrease their involvement with and reliance on men. This practice did not last long, nor was it widely embraced by all cultural feminists. Additionally, men were discouraged from being part of this type of feminism no matter how "liberated" they might have been. Women were expected to change their ideas and behaviors in order to liberate themselves, yet many women felt judged as not being "feminist enough" or "women-centered enough," and that only true feminists were in a position to determine who or what "woman" meant. This created and encouraged an elitist attitude within cultural feminism. Additionally, by not challenging patriarchal systems that create and perpetuate the ideology that women are inferior to men, this type of feminism fails to address larger systemic issues and relies on meeting needs within the status quo rather than critiquing the status quo.

ACKNOWLEDGMENT

This entry is based in part on a previously published entry by Kristina Wolff: K. Wolff, "Cultural Feminisms," in G. Ritzer (ed.), *Blackwell Encyclopedia of Sociology*, Blackwell Publishing, UK, 2007. Reproduced with permission.

SEE ALSO: Essentialism; Feminism, Lesbian; Feminism, Liberal; Feminism, Materialist; Feminism, Multiracial; Feminism, Postcolonial; Feminism, Radical; Feminisms, First, Second, and Third Wave; Feminisms, Postmodern; Feminist Activism; Feminist Epistemology; Feminist Methodology; Feminist Standpoint Theory; Feminist Studies of Science; Gender Belief System/Gender Ideology; Gender Development, Feminist Psychoanalytic Perspectives on; Patriarchy; Subaltern; Women's Ways of Knowing

REFERENCES

Brownmiller, Susan. 1975. *Against Our Will: Men, Women, and Rape*. New York: Simon and Schuster.
Dworkin, Andrea. 1979. *Pornography: Men Possessing Women*. New York: E. P. Dutton.

FURTHER READING

Addams, Jane. 1960. *Jane Addams: A Centennial Reader*. New York: Macmillan.
Alcoff, L. 1988. "Cultural Feminism Versus Post-Structuralism: The Identity Crisis in Feminist Theory." *Signs: A Journal of Women in Culture and Society*, (13): 405–436.
Daly, Mary. 1978. *Gyn/Ecology: The Metaethics of Radical Feminism*. Boston: Beacon Press.
Daly, Mary. 1985. *Beyond God the Father: Toward a Philosophy of Women's Liberation*. Boston: Beacon Press.
Donovan, Josephine. 1985. *Feminist Theory: The Intellectual Traditions of American Feminism*. New York: F. Ungar.
Echols, Alice. 1983. "The New Feminism of Yin and Yang." In *Powers of Desire: The Politics of Sexuality*, edited by Ann Snitow, Christine Stansell, and Sharon Thompson, 439–459. New York: Monthly Review Press.
Griffin, Susan. 1981. *Pornography and Silence: Culture's Revenge Against Nature*. New York: Harper & Row.
Irigaray, Luce. 1994. "Equal to Whom?" In *The Essential Difference*, edited by Naomi Schor and Elizabeth Weed, 63–81. Bloomington: Indiana University Press.
Morgan, Robin. 1977. *Going Too Far: The Personal Chronicle of a Feminist*. New York: Random House.
Rich, Adrienne. 1977. *Of Woman Born*. New York: Bantam.
Tannen, Deborah. 1990. *You Just Don't Understand: Women and Men in Conversation*. New York: William Morrow.

Feminism, Eighteenth-Century Britain

LISA MARUCA
Wayne State University, USA

The term "feminism" is a problematic one when discussing eighteenth-century Britain. Since the word did not come into being until the late nineteenth century, it was not available as a concept that could connect women with shared philosophical and political ideals. Yet in many ways, the eighteenth century, with its increasing discourse of individualism, emphasis on education, and creation of the public sphere, was a period in line with feminist values. And indeed, women did contribute to the Enlightenment projects of expanding rights, increasing literacy, and creating spaces for discussing the issues of the day. Despite the reification of sexual difference in this period that essentialized feminine behaviors and placed real limitations on what women were authorized to do or say in polite society, women in eighteenth-century Britain contributed actively and publicly to improve their plight and the oppression of others. A few of these women even began to self-consciously identify themselves as part of a group defined by gender and a gendered hierarchy, arguing for a loosening of some of the restrictions placed on all of them. We can retrospectively identify a constellation of women who purposefully and publically pushed back against the cultural norms that confined them, added to the world of ideas despite strictures against female learning, or explicitly advocated for changes in women's legal or social positions. For some, these ideals were realized in their writing; for others, in the ways in which they lived their lives, especially women who found themselves in the glare of public scrutiny. It is important to point out, though, that women in this period could only go so far in promoting women's issues; they did not advocate for legal equality, domestic parity, or the right to vote. Their lives are marked by contradiction, and when compared to later feminists, they may seem conservative. However, the work they did laid an essential foundation. Common themes in eighteenth-century women-centered writing in Britain include women's essential rationality; women's need for a better education; the freedom to marry a partner of one's choice or indeed freedom from marriage; the appropriateness of publication in an age that still celebrated modesty as an essential feminine virtue; and the ability of a woman to earn a living from her pen when necessary. Interestingly, though, none of these areas is truly distinct from the others.

PHILOSOPHY AND RELIGION

Despite the secularization of everyday life in Britain during this period, religion remained a powerful force in the lives of most women. Indeed, some of the most influential women of the eighteenth century used religious ideals to advocate for women. Mary Astell (1666–1731) was the first woman to lay down the philosophical tenets of what we now call feminism in a systematic way. She wrote specifically for a female audience, calling herself a "Lover of her Sex" on the title page of her first book. She often lamented her and other women's lack of formal education, but emphasized that women were created by God as rational beings whose immaterial and therefore genderless intellect gave them the capacity to puzzle through any logical conundrum. Indeed, she thought that women who did not exercise their innate intellectual capacities, whether through social pressure or family prohibitions, exhibited a lack of gratefulness for God's gifts.

Astell detailed these ideas in *A Serious Proposal to the Ladies, for the Advancement of Their True and Greatest Interest* (1694). This treatise advocated for a "Protestant convent" or women's college, a refuge away from worldly distractions as well as a place for quiet reading and reflection. She envisioned a community fueled by female fellowship, devoted to rational pleasures and religious contemplation. In Astell's mind, this was a haven of chastity: no sexuality was permitted in this scheme. (In correspondence, Astell explained that her primary earthly "desire" – her term – and emotional attachments were only toward her female friends.) Astell followed up her first book with a second volume, *Serious Proposal, Part II* (1697), a "how to" text laying down her "System of Principles" that taught women how to think rigorously about rational and spiritual matters, which she saw as intrinsically linked. This work was immediately popular, appearing in five editions by 1701, and read by generations of women.

In *Some Reflections upon Marriage* (1700), Astell disparaged most conjugal unions, which she saw as inherently economic, not a result of romantic love or sexual attraction. Analyzing the problem of a sensible woman's vulnerable, submissive position in relation to an authoritative but not always rational husband, she did not advocate for equality within marriage but for a woman's right to *abstain from* matrimony. She believed that most men did not respect women, but used them as housekeepers and breeders of children. Given the domestic duties assigned to women, Astell saw even happy marriages as a waste of their higher rational talents.

EDUCATION AND SCHOLARSHIP

At mid-century, the Bluestockings gave women a new public role. Elizabeth Montagu (1718–1800), known as the "Queen of the Blues," was an early, unofficial leader; important members included Sarah Scott, Elizabeth Carter, Elizabeth Vesey, Frances Boscawen, Hester Chapone, and Catherine Talbot. A circle of men and women of the middle and upper classes who united to discuss intellectual issues and support the arts, the group was named for the everyday legwear that symbolized the group's ethos of informality and (relative) class leveling. Active in the 1750s and 1760s, the Bluestockings espoused a belief in the equality of the sexes in rational discussion and a limited social mobility based on intellectual merit and morality. They were famously memorialized in Richard Samuel's painting, *The Nine Living Muses of Great Britain* (1778), and their own scholarly works were read widely and respected. One of these scholar muses, Catherine Macaulay (1731–1791), lauded as the first female historian, wrote an eight-volume *History of England*, a 20-year project. Macaulay was influenced by her participation in Nonconformist religious groups (though she never left the Anglican Church), and the *History* reflects her politics in its emphasis on English struggles for natural rights. She went on to write more explicitly political tracts espousing her radical republican ideals. Overall, while the Bluestockings encouraged women's education, avidly reading and promoting the scholarly work of women writers, their view on women's sexual conduct was quite conservative. While in the latter decades of the eighteenth century the word "bluestocking" began to be used derogatorily to chastise women for being unattractive, strident pendants, their existence did pave the way for more radical forms of feminism.

A second generation influenced by and sometimes identifying as Bluestockings included political radical Anna Seward, literary historian Clara Reeve, learned writer Hester Thrale, and religious educator Hannah More. The morally conservative, zealously religious More (1745–1833) expanded literacy to the working classes through her Sunday School movement and the publication of her entertaining yet morally didactic pamphlet series, *The Cheap Repository Tracts*. Her wildly popular *Strictures on the Modern System of Female Education* (1799) sold seven editions during its first year in print. Although her linking of female morality with the moral state of the nation would come to be seen as retrograde, her own achievements as a pedagogue helped expand roles for women. A friend of William Wilberforce, she was also an abolitionist who published the poem *Slavery* in 1788 in time for the first parliamentary debate on the slave trade. Other female educators who wrote for children include Anna Laetitia Barbauld (also a respected poet), Maria Edgeworth (also a popular novelist), Sarah Trimmer, and Eleanor Fenn.

DOMESTIC POLITICS

Like Macaulay, inspired by the Dissenting movement's daring new ideas of liberty, Mary Wollstonecraft (1759–1797) also used Christian values to argue against women's subjugation, though, unlike Astell, she publicly embraced women's role in marriage. It is no accident that her seminal and beloved work, *A Vindication of the Rights of Woman* (1792), was preceded by *A Vindication of the Rights of Man* (1790), for Wollstonecraft saw women's freedom in the context of the breakdown of other social hierarchies. The *Rights of Woman* was written in reply to Rousseau's *Émile*, an educational treatise that, although influencing Wollstonecraft's notions of the innate rationality of children, positioned women as subservient and passive. She argued instead that women should rise above petty competition for men, cast aside a focus on superficial achievements and niceties, and work to improve their character and intellect through rational education. Although she put this in a religious, socially traditional context – women empowered to become more virtuous became better Christians and mothers – she also dared to argue that women's self-improvement was an important end in and of itself. Although her use of the term "rights" in her title has led some to call her the first feminist, she actually discusses women's domestic duties and the state of their souls more than their legal status.

WOMEN'S LITERATURE

Contrary to early twentieth-century canons that dismissed all early women writers save Jane Austen, famously sending Virginia Woolf to look for "Shakespeare's sister" in *A Room of One's Own*, eighteenth-century women writers were quite popular and respected in their own time. Feminist literary historical work in the 1980s recovered a long list of women novelists – indeed, women were among the most published writers and most dedicated readers of this genre. However, work over the last 20 years has uncovered an even more voluminous output in poetry, religious writing, and even politics.

Novels by both sexes have been key texts for feminist analysis given that in this period the protagonist was almost always a young woman of marriageable age. Women writers were thought to be perfectly suited for this burgeoning genre, with its emphasis on domestic themes, courtship plots, narrative sincerity, and epistolary techniques. Delriviere Manley was an early experimenter with the genre, writing scandalous *romans-à-clef* about court life. Eliza Haywood was one of the century's most prolific writers, bridging the gap from early amatory fiction to mid-century novels of conduct. She also worked as a publisher and editor of the periodical *The Female Spectator*. Other women novelists who focused on the social and moral development of central female characters include Sarah Fielding, Charlotte Lennox, and Frances Burney.

Poets include Anne Finch, Elizabeth Singer Rowe, and Katherine Philips. Eighteenth-century women poets focused on art, education, and religion, but also on female friendships, as well as social and political issues. These were not just well-educated women of the upper classes: working-class women such as Ann Yearsley, Mary Collier, and Mary Leapor published poetry as well.

TRAVEL

Lady Mary Wortley Montagu (1689–1762) could also be included in the category of literature, although, born into a noble family, she had an aristocrat's disdain for the impropriety of publication. Nonetheless, in manuscript verses circulated within her mostly aristocratic coterie she corrected male-authored misogynistic poems, parried published personal attacks by fellow Augustans Pope and Swift, and bemoaned women's oppression in marriage. Occasionally these made their way to print, though never with her permission.

Lady Mary Wortley Montagu is most famous, however, for being the first Western woman to travel to Turkey, writing about the harems there from an insider's perspective. Her major work, *The Turkish Embassy Letters* (1763), was originally a bound manuscript for close friends, though she did arrange for its posthumous print publication. These letters are notable for the respect she shows for a very different culture and religion, especially for women's roles within it. She reflected on the cross-cultural commonality of women's confined position in society, famously describing a scene in which the undressed women in a bath, which she described approvingly as a "Women's coffee house," exclaim over the tyranny of her corset. She wrote self-consciously about how her unique position allowed her to view an aspect of life that had been purely fictionalized by male explorers, though she mostly only consorted with women of the highest classes. It was also in Turkey that she encountered the inoculation against smallpox, a disease that had almost killed her and did prove fatal to her brother. Lady Mary Wortley Montagu became a stalwart promoter of the controversial practice, mostly through her network of acquaintances, but also, anonymously, in print.

WORK

A study of feminism in eighteenth-century Britain would be incomplete without recognizing the unsung women who did not write literature or philosophy, but showed through their daily work that women were as capable as men. Women were active in a number of trades, with widows often taking over on the death of their husbands. Indeed, Daniel Defoe advised tradesmen to marry women who could be a helpmeet in business. They worked as servants, artisans, agricultural laborers, midwives, unpaid married business partners, but also business owners. Of course, we must be wary of calling these working women "feminists," since they identified more through their trade or family connections than by gender. Unfortunately, as the century progressed, however, sexual divisions reified, and women became more and more relegated to the domestic sphere. The Industrial Revolution's curtailment of cottage industries and family businesses further limited concepts of "women's work." Moreover, throughout the century, the laws of coverture still held sway, preventing women with male family members from acting as economic actors in their own right.

CONCLUSION

A brief overview of eighteenth-century feminist thought and activity in Britain leaves out more than it can cover. The burgeoning discourse of individualism within a still hierarchical society meant that women seldom sought to forge bonds of "sisterhood" across social rank, and even more rarely reflected on women of color. Nonetheless, this period saw a rapid rise in literacy for all women, but especially in the middle classes, as well as a dramatic increase in the number of women authors in all genres. These women in print not only often supported themselves economically, but gave women a public, and often explicitly political, voice. The traces they have left us allow us to imagine a feminist Enlightenment.

SEE ALSO: Cult of Domesticity; Feminist Consciousness in Historical Perspective; Private/Public Spheres

FURTHER READING

Gordon, Lyndall. 2005. *Vindication: A Life of Mary Wollstonecraft*. New York: HarperCollins.
Grundy, Isabel. 1999. *Lady Mary Wortley Montagu*. Oxford: Oxford University Press.
Hill, Bridget. 1989. *Women, Work and Sexual Politics in Eighteenth-Century England*. Oxford: Basil Blackwell.
Perry, Ruth. 1986. *The Celebrated Mary Astell: An Early English Feminist*. Chicago: University of Chicago Press.
Pohl, Nicole, and Betty A. Schellenberg, eds. 2005. *Reconsidering the Bluestockings*. Oakland, CA: University of California Press.
Taylor, Barbara. 2003. *Mary Wollstonecraft and the Feminist Imagination*. Cambridge: Cambridge University Press.
Todd, Janet. 1989. *The Sign of Angellica: Women, Writing and Fiction, 1660–1800*. New York: Columbia University Press.

Feminism, Existential

CHRISTINE L. QUINAN
Utrecht University, The Netherlands

Feminist philosopher Simone de Beauvoir's pronouncement "One is not born, but rather becomes, woman" (de Beauvoir 2009, 283) could rightfully mark the birth of an existential feminism. Indeed, de Beauvoir's *Second Sex*, originally published in 1949 in French and first translated into English in 1953 and again in 2009, remains the founding work for an existential philosophical approach to examining the condition of women. In *The Second Sex*, de Beauvoir set out to understand woman's inferior status, turning first to disciplines such as biology, psychoanalysis, and historical materialism and then to lived experience to attempt to uncover why woman is relegated to the status of Other and why this then becomes internalized.

Existential feminism, which could also be substituted with "feminist existentialism," takes as its point of departure the notions that (1) woman is the product of social and cultural construction and (2) woman is Other. One of de Beauvoir's primary arguments is that nature does not define woman; her body is not enough to place her in an inferior societal position. For de Beauvoir, the body imposes limits on us, but it is society that constructs the two genders of man and woman and the roles that accompany them. To a certain extent, we are free to choose our gender, but de Beauvoir recognizes the influence of environment and society. Situation plays an important role in one's formation, a point on which existentialists have differing opinions with some, like Sartre, giving more weight to choice than situation. (See Kruks 1998 for more on this question.)

Based on the tenets of existentialism, existential feminism subscribes to notions of engagement and responsibility, both of which play a role in overcoming artificial inferiority and liberating all human beings. Jean-Paul Sartre's famous "existence precedes essence" (Sartre 2007, 26) pithily summarizes existential philosophy: human beings have no inherent or predetermined identity; instead, they create their own realities through their choices and actions. A corollary becomes that humans are then condemned to freedom because they cannot escape the fact that they must constantly make choices and, more importantly, that they are responsible for their corresponding actions. They cannot fall back onto "bad faith" but instead must transcend their situations.

According to de Beauvoir and other existentialists, liberation is only found in transcendence (the opposite of which is immanence and alienation). In the case of women, they must, then, perpetually surpass the limits of their material situation to achieve new freedoms. The existence of others in this process (and the bearing of this recognition on individual reality) is elaborated throughout de Beauvoir's body of philosophical and literary work. Our relationship with and connection to others gives value to our lives. The existence of others is a pathway to self-knowledge, but freedom can only be achieved through the freedom of all human beings. In short, others are a necessary – even if both beneficial and troublesome – aspect of human existence.

However, existential feminism presents a number of "catch-22s," including the problem of economic independence. De Beauvoir scholar Toril Moi elaborates: "As long as women are prevented from earning their own living, they will always be dependent on others. Women actually seeking paid work, however, are confronted with class exploitation and sexist oppression at every turn … A painful paradox thus emerges: only work can emancipate women, yet nothing enslaves them more completely" (Moi 1998, 74).

Existential feminism has not been immune from other criticism. Its philosophical jargon has been accused of being inaccessible to the layperson and not offering a solution to women's oppression. De Beauvoir in particular has been heavily criticized for her takes on motherhood, most specifically her rejection of maternity because she believed it to limit women's ability to transcend their material situations. More generally, this signaled an ambivalent position taken by existential feminism towards the body, which would later be taken up by feminists who reevaluated and revalued the place of embodiment in feminist theory and activism and in individual experience.

Nevertheless, the legacies of Beauvoirian existential feminism are wide-ranging. As Rosemarie Tong details, postmodern feminism, for example, is indebted to de Beauvoir's brand of existential feminism, even as it takes it in new directions: "Woman is still the other, but rather than interpreting this condition as something to be transcended, postmodern feminists proclaim its advantages" (Tong 2014, 192).

Judith Butler would draw upon de Beauvoir's notion of becoming, stating "if gender is something that one becomes – but can never be – then gender is itself a kind of becoming or activity, and that gender ought not to be conceived as a noun or as a substantial thing or a static cultural marker, but rather as an incessant and repeated action of some sort" (Butler 1999, 143). In line with existential feminism, this formulation uncovers how gender itself can become an act of transcendence, a formulation that allowed Butler to make larger theoretical arguments on the performative aspects of gender.

Existential explorations of the status of women also left their mark on writers and theorists often grouped under the label "French feminism," including Hélène Cixous, Luce Irigaray, Julia Kristeva, and Monique Wittig. Particularly in their exploration of phallogocentrism, they each took up the idea of "woman as other" but brought it in radically new directions that signaled the birth of sexual difference theory.

Finally, it is important to note that de Beauvoir distanced herself from the label "feminist" well after the publication of *The Second Sex*, only embracing it in 1972, after diving into feminist work with France's Mouvement de Libération des Femmes. Therefore, in some ways, "existential feminism" did not appear until nearly two decades after its founding document, even as there surely existed individuals who may have identified in this way.

SEE ALSO: Androcentrism; Biological Determinism; Feminism and Postmodernism; Feminism, French; Feminism, Poststructural; Feminist Theories of Experience; Phallocentrism and Phallogocentrism

REFERENCES

Beauvoir, Simone de. 2009. *The Second Sex*, trans. Constance Borde and Sheila Malovany-Chevallier. New York: Vintage Books. First published in French in 1949.
Butler, Judith. 1999. *Gender Trouble: Feminism and the Subversion of Identity*. New York: Routledge. First published 1990.
Kruks, Sonia. 1998. "Beauvoir: The Weight of Situation." In *Simone de Beauvoir: A Critical Reader*, edited by Elizabeth Fallaize, 43–71. New York: Routledge.
Moi, Toril. 1998. "'Independent Women' and 'Narratives of Liberation'." In *Simone de Beauvoir: A Critical Reader*, edited by Elizabeth Fallaize, 72–92. New York: Routledge.
Sartre, Jean-Paul. 2007. *Existentialism is a Humanism*, trans. Carol Maccomber. New Haven: Yale University Press. First published 1946.
Tong, Rosemarie. 2014. *Feminist Thought: A More Comprehensive Introduction*, 4th ed. Boulder: Westview Press.

FURTHER READING

Bauer, Nancy. 2001. *Simone de Beauvoir, Philosophy, and Feminism*. New York: Columbia University Press.
Beauvoir, Simone de. 1970. *The Ethics of Ambiguity*, trans. Bernard Frechtman. New York: Citadel Press.
Kruks, Sonia. 2001. *Retrieving Experience: Subjectivity and Recognition in Feminist Politics*. Ithaca: Cornell University Press.

Feminism, French

BRONWYN WINTER
The University of Sydney, Australia

This entry covers primarily so-called "second-wave" feminism, but it should be noted that French proto-feminism dates back at least to the seventeenth century if not before, and feminist activism (self-named as such or not) grew following the French revolution, with women such as Olympe de Gouges, Flora Tristan, Jeanne Deroin, Marguerite Durand, and Hubertine Auclert, among many others, forming part of the French feminist historical canon. There exist a number of studies in English, with Moses (1985) and Foley (2004) providing a good overview, especially of the nineteenth century.

As concerns the "second wave" of French feminism, the topic has been subject to different interpretations in the Western English-speaking world and indeed beyond. Its early scholarly treatment by scholars such as Duchen (1986, 1987) and Marks and Courtivron (1987) focused on the feminist movement and feminist theoretical debates between the May 1968 worker and student uprisings and the early to mid-1980s. The subsequent "postmodern turn" in feminist scholarship, starting in North America, brought in a new interpretation of "French feminist theory," resulting in somewhat of a "theory war" among Anglo-world scholars on what, exactly, French feminism was. There has also been a plethora of literature in English on the protracted French debate on the Islamic headscarf, which erupted in 1989 and has continued more or less to the present day, although this entry will not cover this issue directly. More recently, Anglo-world scholarship has taken on board insights from the late 1980s to 1990s "theory war" to reflect the diversity of feminist thinking, scholarship, and activism in France.

THE IMPACT OF SIMONE DE BEAUVOIR

Although, as elsewhere in the Western world and indeed beyond, the "second-wave" French feminist movement grew out of late-1960s activism on issues such as workers' rights, the Vietnam war, and civil rights, the French and international second-wave movements and theories drew enormous inspiration from the groundbreaking and quasi-encyclopedic work of Simone de Beauvoir, *The Second Sex* (1949, with new – and first complete – translation by Borde and Malovany-Chevallier in 2009) (Beauvoir 2009). Any analysis of second-wave French feminism must therefore necessarily include consideration of Beauvoir, and of subsequent discussion of her work.

Beauvoir opened *The Second Sex* by stating that she "hesitated a long time before writing a book about women" because "the subject [was] irritating, especially for women, and it [was] not new," yet "the volumes of idiocies churned out over this past century do not seem to have clarified the problem" (Beauvoir 2009, 3). So Beauvoir set to work, producing a treatise of roughly 1000 pages in which she explored history, anthropology, politics, cultural and literary production, and women's day-to-day experience and came up with her famous sentence, "One is not born, but rather becomes, woman" (Beauvoir 2009, 293), along with her analysis of men's construction of "woman" as the Other to their One. *The Second Sex* was read throughout France by women of all walks of life and social classes, and subsequently around the world. Her analysis was to inspire second-wave activism and theory in France and elsewhere, and soon became the subject of ongoing feminist theoretical debate (see, for example, Simons 1995; Fallaize 1998) and international celebration as scholars and activists from around the world discussed the impact of Beauvoir in a variety of national, theoretical, and activist contexts (Delphy and Chaperon 2002).

Beauvoir's impact in second-wave French feminism extended beyond her writing. She was involved in feminist activism, becoming president of the Committee for Djamila Boupacha, an Algerian independence activist tortured by French authorities, and signing on, as a gesture of solidarity, as co-author to feminist lawyer Gisèle Halimi's banned 1962 book on Boupacha, for which Halimi risked both disbarment and prison. Beauvoir was also one of the signatories, in 1971, of the "Manifeste des 343," in which 343 women stated that they had had abortions, as a political statement in favor of the legalization of abortion.

Beauvoir was thus an exemplary figure both in the French tradition of "public intellectuals" and in establishing, well before the emergence of the "second wave," a pattern of feminist theory grounded in experience and feminist activism grounded in analysis. She was, notably, the Editor-in-Chief of the journal *Nouvelles Questions Féministes* and wrote the preface to *Chroniques d'une Imposture*, a collection of work opposing the politics of the group Psychanalyse and Politique (see below). In 2008, the year of the centenary of Beauvoir's birth, the Prix Simone de Beauvoir was set up at the initiative of Julia Kristeva, to "reward the exceptional works and actions of women and men who, in the spirit of Simone de Beauvoir, contribute to promoting women's freedom in the world".

THE PSYKÉPO DEBATE

Early French "second-wave" theory and activism were marked by three main currents (although not all feminist writing from the period falls neatly within one or other of them): Marxist feminism (often called "Lutte des classes" feminism in France), grouping tendencies from socialist to Trotskyist, and of which a primary focus, alongside the public-sphere campaigns typically waged by Marxist or socialist feminists, was the long campaign for abortion rights; materialist feminism (cf. radical feminism elsewhere), from which radical lesbian analysis also grew; and so-called "difference feminism," largely influenced by psychoanalytic, particularly Lacanian, theory, of which one of the main proponents was the group Psychanalyse et Politique (also known by the abbreviated nickname "Psyképo").

Psyképo, grouped around the controversial figure of Antoinette Fouque, was an important presence in the early movement, running the publishing house and bookshop Des Femmes, which produced a great number and diversity of early feminist writings. The group became both divisive and, paradoxically, a unifying force within the feminist movement when in 1979 it registered a new NGO under the name "Women's Liberation Movement" and the women's liberation symbol (women's symbol with a clenched fist inside the circle) as the association's logo. Fouque also formally registered both the name and the logo with the National Institute for Intellectual Property. In protest, other currents within the Women's Liberation Movement, as well as Beauvoir and scholars such as well-known historian Michelle Perrot, publicly denounced this move, and the "Lutte des classes" and "radicales" came together in a rare unanimity, in their publication titled *Chroniques d'une Imposture* (Association du Mouvement pour les luttes féministes 1981), opposing Psyképo's unilateral appropriation of the name and one of the symbols used by a large and internally diverse political movement.

The Psyképo women did not embrace the term "feminism" which they saw as negating liberation. The rest of the movement disagreed.

THE "FRENCH FEMINISM" THEORY WAR

Notwithstanding the French controversy, scholars across the Atlantic, especially feminist philosophy scholars, became interested in "difference feminism" in the 1980s, alongside an interest in Lacanian psychoanalysis and Derridean deconstruction. These scholars widely took up the use of the word "feminine," calqued on French *féminin*, which means both "feminine" and "female," mostly without drawing attention to the ambiguity or intended meaning in French. *Écriture féminine,* as discussed by Cixous in particular, also became a popular topic in US literary criticism focusing on "French feminism." These characterizations of "difference feminism" became the dominant representation of "French feminism" in Anglo-world scholarly discussions by the end of the decade. Works such as those by Moi (1985), Whitford (1991), and Oliver (1993) painted a picture of this "French feminism" as represented by and largely by the work of theorists such as Luce Irigaray, Julia Kristeva, and, occasionally, Hélène Cixous. These three writers were all very different from each other, however, and only Irigaray clearly identified as feminist. Cixous was associated with the Psyképo group whereas Kristeva, although not overtly hostile to feminism, did not identify explicitly as feminist. Grosz's 1989 study of Kristeva, Irigaray, and Michelle Le Doeuff (the last of whom, although a philosopher, is very far from being a "difference feminist"), while pointing out that all three are quite different, nonetheless reinforced the association between French thinkers who were quite different and may or may not have identified as feminist at that time (Grosz 1989).

In response, Delphy (1995), Moses (1996), and Winter (1997) criticized this Anglo-world representation of "French feminism" as both narrow, inadequately representing the diversity of French feminist thought, and in some cases, as indicated above, erroneous as two of the key thinkers discussed did not identify as feminist. Delphy proposed that a lower-case "f" be used when discussing french feminism made-in-USA, and that upper case be used when discussing feminist activism and theories emanating from France. Some studies published in the United Kingdom at that time also rekindled an interest in French materialist feminism and theorization of gender, (hetero)sexuality, and violence (e.g., Jackson 1996; Leonard and Adkins 1996; Allwood 1998).

As a result of these varied representations and debates, understandings within international scholarly communities of "French feminism" now vary widely, depending on the politics, level of expertise (including knowledge of French language), and geographical and disciplinary locations of those conducting the studies and discussions.

FRENCH FEMINISM IN THE THIRD MILLENNIUM

One of the problems with presenting a body of feminist work produced in a language other than English to an English-speaking readership is the lack of available translations. As we have seen above, translation also concerns the passage of ideas from one context to another and impacts on how those ideas are represented. A great deal of work by French feminists, including some less recent work and a huge body of scholarly and journalistic writing in French on the "hijab debates" produced since the early 1990s, has not been translated into English. For example, outside specialist circles, the work of a number of French feminist historians such as Christine Bard, Christelle Taraud, and Sylvie Chaperon is little known in the English-speaking world. One notable exception is Michelle Perrot, whose international co-edited work *History of Women in the West* has been published in several languages. Yet feminist writing, publishing, and bookselling are healthy in France, as demonstrated by the activities of the Parisian feminist bookshop Violette and Co, and by the visible presence of feminist books on the shelves of large commercial bookshops such as La FNAC.

The second-wave movement celebrated its fortieth anniversary in 2010 (the beginning of the movement was symbolically marked on August 26, 1970, by a small group of women who placed a wreath at the tomb of the unknown soldier at the Arc de Triomphe in Paris with the slogan "There is someone more unknown than the unknown soldier: his wife"). The fortieth anniversary celebrations were accompanied by public rallies, debates, exhibitions, press coverage, and a number of new publications reflecting on 40 years of feminism in France. Around the time of this anniversary, a number of new feminist initiatives became highly visible, some with accompanying publications. Whether one can call these initiatives "third" or "fourth" wave is debatable, but they have responded to a need for renewed activism, and new forms of feminist expression, in the third millennium. One such initiative that has particularly captured feminist imagination, and recalls the symbolic actions of the heyday of the "second wave," is the group La Barbe, which means, literally, beard, and figuratively, "how boring"! Women wearing fake beards congregate to demonstrate wherever they see sexism at work and are now a regular feature of feminist gatherings and demonstrations. Another group, Osez le féminisme!, attracts younger women and some men and publishes an online newsletter. New magazines such as *Causette* ("chat," also a homophone of the first name Cosette), and *Clara* aim to reach a wider and younger readership with feminist messages.

A recurrent theme among French feminists since the 1980s (even before the first Islamic headscarf affair of 1989) has been the politics of race, gender, migration, religion (not only Islam), and the state in France. Unfortunately, most of the large number of works written in French, including several by women of Muslim/immigrant background and, as mentioned above, several works on the Islamic headscarf issue, have not been translated, despite extensive discussion of these issues in the English-speaking world (e.g., Scott 2007; Winter 2008; Raissiguier 2010). One work, written by an activist, that has been translated is Fadela Amara's *Ni Putes Ni Soumises* (translated as *Breaking the Silence*) (Amara and Zappi 2006). Ni Putes Ni Soumises (neither whores nor doormats) is an organization co-founded by Amara in 2003 to defend the voices of (primarily North African) immigrant-background women who combated sexism and male violence in their own communities and were staunch defenders of secularism. The organization has been controversial because of its closeness in style to SOS-Racisme, the association from which it largely emerged, and because of its apparently cosy relationship with the political class on both sides. Amara in particular was criticized for accepting a junior ministry offered by newly elected President Sarkozy in 2007 (a ministry she subsequently lost in a 2010 reshuffle). At the same time, the organization, and Amara personally, have mobilized large numbers of North African-background women around male violence and sexism more generally, and freedom of and from religion.

As concerns the development of women's studies in France, the climate for feminists in the academy is still relatively chilly, notwithstanding some progress in recent years. Such marginalization does not bode well for increases in translation of the work of important French feminist thinkers, including younger academics such as Natacha Chetcuti and Jules Falquet. As for feminists who write from outside the university system, such as Caroline Fourest and Fiammetta Venner, who have written a number of books on gender, religious conservatism, and the state and edit the well-respected feminist journal *Prochoix*, the English-speaking world may yet have to wait many years to read the bulk of their work.

SEE ALSO: Feminism and Psychoanalysis; Feminism, Radical; Feminisms, Marxist and Socialist; Feminist Literary Criticism; Radical Lesbianism

REFERENCES

Allwood, Gill. 1998. *French Feminisms: Gender and Violence in Contemporary Theory*. London: Routledge.

Amara, Fadela, with Sylvia Zappi. 2006. *Breaking the Silence: French Women's Voices from the Ghetto*, trans. Helen Harden Henut. Berkeley: University of California Press.

Association du Mouvement pour les luttes féministes. 1981. *Chroniques d'une imposture: du mouvement de libération des femmes à une marque commerciale*. Paris: Association du Mouvement pour les luttes féministes.

Beauvoir, Simone de. 2009. *The Second Sex*, trans. Constance Borde and Sheila Malovany-Chevallier. New York: Jonathan Cape.

Delphy, Christine. 1995. "The Invention of French Feminism: An Essential Move." *Yale French Studies*, 87: 190–221.

Delphy, Christine, and Sylvie Chaperon, eds. 2002. *Cinquantenaire du Deuxième sexe*. Paris: Editions Syllepse.

Duchen, Claire. 1986. *Feminism in France: From May '68 to Mitterrand*. London: Routledge.

Duchen, Claire. 1987. *French Connections: Voices from the Women's Movement in France*. Amherst: University of Massachusetts Press.

Fallaize, Elizabeth. 1998. *Simone de Beauvoir: A Critical Reader*. London: Routledge.

Foley, Susan K. 2004. *Women in France since 1989: The Meaning of Difference*. Basingstoke: Palgrave Macmillan.

Grosz, Elizabeth. 1989. *Sexual Subversions: Three French Feminists*. Sydney: Allen and Unwin.

Jackson, Stevi. 1996. *Christine Delphy*. London: Sage.

Leonard, Diana, and Lisa Adkins. 1996. *Sex in Question: French Materialist Feminism*. London: Taylor and Francis.

Marks, Elaine, and Isabelle de Courtivron, eds. 1987. *New French Feminisms: An Anthology*. New York: Pantheon Books.

Moi, Toril. 1985. *Sexual/Textual Politics: Feminist Literary Theory*. London: Routledge.

Moses, Claire. 1985. *French Feminism in the 19th Century*. New York: State University of New York Press.
Moses, Claire. 1996. "Made in America: 'French Feminism' in United States Academic Discourse." *Australian Feminist Studies*, 11(23): 17–31.
Oliver, Kelly. 1993. *Reading Kristeva: Unraveling the Double-bind*. Bloomington: Indiana University Press.
Raissiguier, Catherine. 2010. *Reinventing the Republic: Gender, Migration, and Citizenship in France*. Stanford: Stanford University Press.
Scott, Joan Wallach. 2007. *The Politics of the Veil*. Princeton: Princeton University Press.
Simons, Margaret A., ed. 1995. *Feminist Interpretations of Simone de Beauvoir*. University Park: Penn State University Press.
Whitford, Margaret. 1991. *Luce Irigaray: Philosophy in the Feminine*. New York: Routledge.
Winter, Bronwyn. 1997. "(Mis)representations: What French Feminism Isn't." *Women's Studies International Forum*, 20(2): 211–224.
Winter, Bronwyn. 2008. *Hijab and the Republic: Uncovering the French Headscarf Debate*. Syracuse: Syracuse University Press.

FURTHER READING

Célestin, Roger, Eliane DalMolin, and Isabelle de Courtivron. 2003, *Beyond French Feminisms: Debates on Women, Politics, and Culture in France, 1981–2001*. Basingstoke: Palgrave Macmillan.
Moi, Toril. 1991. *French Feminist Thought*. Oxford: Wiley-Blackwell.
Oliver, Kelly, ed. 2000. *French Feminism Reader*. Lanham: Rowman and Littlefield.

Feminism, Indo-Caribbean

BRINDA J. MEHTA
Mills College, USA

Indo-Caribbean feminism has its roots in the history of Indian indenture, in the capitalist pre- and post-plantation economy of the Caribbean islands, and in patterns of resistance to colonial and patriarchal subjugation. Indian history in the Caribbean begins with the official "abolition" of African slavery in 1838 when a second wave of so-called "voluntary migration" was mobilized from India by the British in 1838 and by the French in 1848 in the form of the indentured labor trade. European sugar plantation owners still needed a cheap and industrious agricultural workforce that was familiar with the particularities of tropical plantation culture (Mehta 2004). Thousands of rural Indians destined for the Caribbean were recruited to work in the British colonies, primarily from the northern Indian states of Bihar and Uttar Pradesh, while the French recruiting strategies focused on the southern state of Tamil Nadu. The majority of the Indians were taken to the British colonies of Trinidad and Guyana, where they are still an ethnic majority even today, while smaller numbers arrived in Jamaica, Grenada, Surinam, Barbados, and St. Lucia. The major French migrations targeted Martinique, Guadeloupe, and French Guiana.

According to Hindu belief (one of the principal religions of Indian indentured laborers), the traversing of large expanses of water, such as the kala pani or black waters of the Atlantic, was associated with contamination and cultural defilement as it led to the dispersal of tradition, family, class, and caste stratifications, and to the general loss of a "purified" Hindu essence. Kala pani crossings were initially identified with the expatriation of convicts, "low" castes, social pariahs, and other "undesirable" elements of society: those who braved the kala pani were automatically compromising their Hindu-ness. Although a minority, Indian women were also an integral part of this migrating labor diaspora. These women felt they had the most to gain by crossing over to distant lands because their working-class and poor status often confined them to rigid Hindu patriarchal structures in India, making them victims of abusive familial and communal traditions. Enduring the hardships of the overseas crossings was a worthwhile risk to take because it offered the potential for renegotiations of gender identity within the structural dissolutions of caste and class categorizations that occurred during the transatlantic displacements. The women therefore seized the opportunity to transcend their marginality within the nuclear Hindu family by embracing a more expansive Indian diasporic community of Hindus and Muslims, even though Hindu men dominated recruitment figures.

Many of the kala pani women traveled alone, thereby dispelling myths about their satellite status as wives and daughters. These women included widows, sex workers, single women, young girls resisting an arranged marriage with older men, married women anxious to leave abusive relationships, and others who saw themselves as non-conforming Indian women and girls. Their very decision to leave rather than accept a disenfranchising social and sexual status quo can be considered their first feminist act. Individual acts of subjectivity were later consolidated into communal bonds of sisterhood during the long and arduous ocean journeys as the women created their own solidarity networks as *jahaji-bahin* or ship-sisters and, later, on the plantation estates. The ship-sisters adopted a communal identification as part of their new diasporic "dis-location," while providing each other with the necessary protection and support systems against their social and sexual exploitation on the boats of indenture and, once on land, under the Caribbean plantation system.

During the crossings, the women had to protect themselves from the sexual violations of crew members and migrating Indian men. In the Caribbean, they confronted a hydra-headed patriarchy of colonial, Afro-Caribbean, and Indian men that had been conditioned by class-based, racialized, and sexualized myths of Indian women's moral lasciviousness (Shepherd 2002). These myths contributed to some of the worst social and sexual excesses against Indian women in the form of "sexploitation" (Shepherd 2002), domestic violence, and labor disparities found in unequal wages, inhuman working conditions, and the risk of sexual aggression in the workforce. It is therefore appropriate to state that Indo-Caribbean feminism emerges from four important circumstances: the process of displacement, the violence of gender relations, a resistance to Hindu and Muslim cultural and gender dictates, and a tradition of hard work (Haniff 1999). These factors dispel misconceptions about Indian women's social dependence on men and their secondary contributions to Caribbean society. As estate workers, women played a very important part in labor production and revised their marginal social status as income earners.

Misogyny, racism, and class barriers have played a major role in the marginalization of Indo-Caribbean feminism in the region, in the ambivalent position of Indian women within their Hindu, Muslim, and Christian communities, and in this feminism's liminal status within dominant Afro-centered feminist and literary discourses despite the important theoretical and literary contributions of Indo-Caribbean women. Still considered an "emerging" field, Indo-Caribbean feminism bears the burden of historical, gender, and cultural stereotyping. This marginalization has been further impacted by the imposition of cultural normativity and gender role conformity within Indo-Caribbean communities. These refracted ideologies are inscribed within communal identity politics on the one hand, and cultural insularity on the other (Hosein and Outar 2012).

Nevertheless, the *jahaji-bahin* ethos has proved to be of particular importance to Indo-Caribbean women as it provides the necessary framework for Indo-Caribbean feminism linking the women's history of indenture with their postcolonial Caribbean identity. This trope maps a particular Indo-Caribbean feminist cartography of gendered and social relations that includes negotiations of dominant paradigms of Afro-centeredness, shifting gender roles within public and private space, a call to creativity, revisions in traditional prescriptions of heteronormative sexuality, mediations in inter- and intra-group relationships, feminist reinterpretations of religion, and the affirmation of women's political agency, as demonstrated by the 2010 victory of the Indian-anchored People's Partnership party led by an Indo-Trinidadian woman, Kamla Persad-Bissessar.

Indo-Caribbean feminist thought thereby situates itself within the broader perspectives of postcolonialism and transnational feminism on the one hand, and regional and culture-specific forms of gendered resistance on the other hand. Embracing an intersectional positionality, Indo-Caribbean feminism celebrates the distinctiveness and heterogeneity of Indian women's experiences in the Caribbean. These experiences are highlighted in influential discourses, such as dougla poetics (Puri 1999), dougla feminism (Kanhai 1999), kala pani textuality (Mehta 2004), matikor sexuality (Kanhai 1999; Mohammed 2012), and, as mentioned earlier, the *jahaji-bahin* principle (Mahabir and Pirbhai 2013). Puri's dougla poetics opens an important physical and metaphoric space for Indo-Caribbean/Afro-Caribbean relational dialogues that permit the legitimacy and visibility of disallowed identities. The term dougla refers to a mixed-race African and Indian identity considered a taboo in conservative Hindu communities due to associations of racial impurity and bastardization. By reclaiming the term as a more affirming locus of postcolonial identity, dougla poetics subverts purist framings of identity through multicultural, intra-ethnic, and cross-political affiliations. The idea of inclusiveness and plurality is further discussed in Kanhai's formulation of dougla feminism, a cross-cultural gendered poetics of solidarity and cooperation among Indian and African women in the Caribbean. However, both theories have been critiqued for their exclusion of other Caribbean ethnicities, including Chinese, Arab, and indigenous.

Mehta's kala pani textuality is an interdisciplinary discourse of rupture that initiates transgressive boundary crossings in literature, culture, and feminist thought. As a form of border textuality, this theory creates the space for multiple female positionalities by contesting the patriarchal stranglehold of coloniality, nationalism, and postcoloniality in Indo-Caribbean communities. An important factor in these transgressions is the affirmation of woman-centered cultural spaces such as matikor, a ceremony of sexual initiation for a new bride on the eve of her wedding. In this woman-dominated space, the bride-to-be receives her sexual education through sexual ribaldry, a parody of sex roles, transvestism, erotic role-play, storytelling, and jokes. Expressing themselves through their sexuality and sensuality, these women subvert patriarchal impositions on the female body through uncensored speech, female intimacy, and uninhibited physical expression as a form of matikor queer politics (Pragg 2012). Chutney music and dance are also examples of woman-centered spaces of resistance, sexual agency, and cultural reclaiming. Chutney refers to a vernacular form of Indo-Caribbean music and dance that has its roots in non-Brahmanic Indian folk traditions. The political dimensions of chutney are located in women's contestations of class distinctions and patriarchal Hindu notions of female propriety. Chutney dancing celebrates female sexuality in the open forum of chutney festivals and matikor ceremonies. These dances involve pelvic gyrations locally called "wining" and other uninhibited body movements to the accompaniment of equally provocative lyrics and rhythms. These songs call for the emancipation of Indo-Caribbean women from the power structures of Caribbean patriarchy and they engender new definitions of femininity from a more affirming feminist perspective. Chutney has also fused with the Afro-Caribbean-derived soca music in bonds of cultural syncretism. Chutney artiste Droopatee Ramgoolan was the first Indo-Caribbean woman to cross the lines of gender and race by entering the male-dominated Afro-Caribbean realm of calypso. This disruption of heteronormative patriarchal and cultural spaces by "queer desire" and feminist cultural assertions permits the articulation of alternate sexualities and modes of cultural collaboration denied by traditional morality and social codes. Norms of acceptable female decorum are prescribed by organizations such as Trinidad's male-governed Hindu Sanatan Dharma Maha Sabha and others like them.

Indo-Caribbean feminism finds its most articulate expression in women's literature written from anti-patriarchal, anti-racist, queer-centered, and social justice perspectives. Writers as diverse as Ramabai Espinet, Shani Mooto, Lakshmi Persaud (Trinidad), Narmala Shewcharan, Ryhaan Shah, Mahadai Das, Gauitra Bahadur (Guyana), Laure Moutoussamy (Martinique), Arlette Minatchy-Bogat (Guadeloupe), Asha "Cádani" Radjkoemar (Suriname), among a host of others, have used literature in the form of novels, short stories, plays, poetry, and memoirs to create discursive spaces that redefine Indo-Caribbean women's sexual, social, ethnic, and cultural identities from a decolonial gendered perspective. These writings unravel the complex and multifaceted aspects of Indo-Caribbean women's lives that seek more wholesome representations against the grain of traditionalism, racialism, and parochialism. These women's kala pani crossings in text are feminist acts of subjectivity that find their source and inspiration in the brave transoceanic crossings of their feminist foremothers.

SEE ALSO: Patriarchy; Sexual Citizenship in the Caribbean; Sexualities; Third World Women; Victimization; Women's and Feminist Activism in the Caribbean; Women's Writing

REFERENCES

Haniff, Nesha. 1999. "My Grandmother Worked in the Field: Honorable Mention. Stereotypes Regarding East Indian Women in the Caribbean." In *Matikor: The Politics of Identity for Indo-Caribbean Women*, edited by Rosanne Kanhai, 18–31. St. Augustine, Trinidad and Tobago: University of the West Indies Press.

Hosein, Gabrielle, and Lisa Outar, eds. 2012. "Indo-Caribbean Feminisms: Charting Crossings to Geography, Discourse and Politics." *Caribbean Review of Gender Studies*, 6: i–x. Online version.

Kanhai, Rosanne, ed. 1999. *Matikor: The Politics of Identity for Indo-Caribbean Women*. St. Augustine, Trinidad and Tobago: University of the West Indies Press.

Mahabir, Joy, and Mariam Pirbhai. 2013. *Critical Perspectives on Indo-Caribbean Women's Literature*. New York: Routledge.

Mehta, Brinda. 2004. *Diasporic (Dis)locations: Indo-Caribbean Women Writers Negotiate the Kala Pani*. Kingston, Jamaica: University of the West Indies Press.

Mohammed, Patricia. 2012. "Changing Symbols of Indo-Caribbean Femininity." *Caribbean Review of Gender Studies*, 6, edited by Gabrielle Hosein and Lisa Outar, 1–16. Online version.

Pragg, Lauren. 2012. "The Queer Potential: (Indo-)Caribbean Feminisms and Heteronormativity." *Caribbean Review of Gender Studies*, 6, edited by Gabrielle Hosein and Lisa Outar, 1–14. Online version.

Puri, Shalini. 1999. "Canonized Hybridities, Resistant Hybridities: Chutney Soca, Carnival and the Politics of Nationalism." In *Caribbean Romances: The Politics of Regional Representation*, edited by Belinda Edmondson, 12–38. Charlottesville: University of Virginia Press.

Shepherd, Verene. 2002. *Maharani's Misery: Narratives of a Passage from India to the Caribbean*. Kingston, Jamaica: University of the West Indies Press.

FURTHER READING

Pirbhai, Mariam. 2009. *Mythologies of Migration, Vocabularies of Indenture*. Toronto: University of Toronto Press.

Feminism, Islamic

HAIDEH MOGHISSI
York University, Canada

There is no coherent, self-identified, and easily identifiable "Islamic feminist" ideology and movement that operates within the boundaries of Muslim-majority societies. Islamic feminism, as a concept, found currency mostly in the mid-1990s, to distinguish a brand of feminism or the activities of Muslim women who seek to reform, in women's favor, gendered social and legal provisions in Muslim-majority societies. If feminism is understood, simply, as an intellectual and political campaign to change legal and cultural constraints and gender practices in favor of women, then it has a long history in the Middle East, North Africa, and South Asia. The publication of a rapidly expanding literature on gender and Islam since the 1980s has amply demonstrated the fact that at least since the mid-nineteenth century, Muslim women have protested about the rigid religious and cultural practices and discriminating traditions in their societies and have demanded reforms.

The protesting women, believers or non-believers, practicing or non-practicing alike, often argued that if the Qur'an and the Prophet's teachings were understood accurately and followed thoroughly and thoughtfully, women would not be denied their just and proper rights. Instead, they targeted misogynistic interpretations of the Qur'an and the male-serving fabrications of *hadith* (the sayings on religion and daily life attributed to the Prophet) as the reasons for social and economic retardation of their societies and deprivation of the female citizens. With rare exceptions, the compatibility or incompatibility of Islam with women's rights at no point was an issue for these reformers. A goal of the women's rights campaign at the time was to persuade the Islamic jurists (*ulama*) and the ruling elites to venture modification of certain rulings taken from Shari'a (Islamic legal practices) in favor of women in order for them to fit the changing conditions of their societies and women's role in them.

The reemergence of concerns and ensuing tensions over Islam and women's rights must be understood in the context of the intensified social and political turmoil in the region since the late 1970s. This might be seen as a retreat from the optimism or the less religious rigidity of earlier periods, when varying degrees of economic modernization and efforts at social engineering also assisted women's growing access to education and paid work, their unhindered visibility in public life, and freer interactions between the sexes. In this period certain social reforms in favor of women seem to have relaxed deeply engrained social attitudes and gender biases, as well as Muslim male anxieties regarding changing gender roles.

Favorable external factors also positively affected the campaigns for women's rights in the region. One important factor was liberal feminists' successful use of global institutions and international meetings (such as the United Nations specific meetings in Mexico City, 1975; Copenhagen, 1980; and Nairobi, 1985) for promoting women's concerns and rights. The injection of the idea or the rhetoric of gender equality into governments' official policies and the advent of state-sponsored women's organizations in Muslim-majority countries, except in Saudi Arabia and the neighboring Gulf states, must be seen in this light. All these developments seemed to have pushed back orthodox readings of Islamic prescriptions and the influence of religious rules regarding women's social roles. The continued resistance against these developments by Islamist groups such as the Muslim Brotherhood in Egypt, Jama't Islami in Pakistan, and Khomeinists in Iran did not seem to have the power to halt the social transformations in favor of women. Over a century of Muslim women's struggle for legal and social rights seemed close to fruition everywhere.

This was, however, a temporary episode in the life of Middle Eastern, North African, and South Asian societies and in the existence of their female populations. The 1979 revolution in Iran and the subsequent establishment of the first Islamist state in the region was a defining point in that it prompted greater Islamic militancy and instigated more active and sometimes violent opposition to the idea of gender equity as un-Islamic and a Western ploy. Attempts at reversing the previous decades' developments with regard to women's rights also revitalized debates and disputes over the question of Islam and women's rights.

However, the heightened anti-women's rights regulations and policies that followed particularly the rise to power of Islamists in Iran, and in Pakistan under General Zia ul Haq, alarmed practicing Muslim women and secular activists throughout the region. Fearful of losing even the modest opportunities of the previous decades, women's movements gained momentum against re-Islamization policies and practices. From Sudan to Iran, Pakistan, and elsewhere, individual activists and loosely organized women's groups rose to the challenges posed by the Islamists, using the limited political and cultural spaces available to them to reawaken the female population to the idea that they are entitled to a just and dignified life and equal rights with men.

Women's resistance and their quiet and resolute campaign for rights in all known Muslim-majority countries on behalf of women included attempts at challenging the interpretations and prescribed understandings of the Muslim male elite and jurists regarding the Qur'anic legal and moral principles that define and determine the extent and limits of women's rights within the family and beyond. Many women among this group are believing Muslims. However, their ranks also include individuals without religion who, in the absence of available secular spaces, have once more resorted to the strategy used by the pioneers of women's rights decades earlier, arguing that women's degraded conditions are the result of gender-biased misreadings of the Qur'an, not the text itself.

The strategy of drawing upon an alternative reading of the Qur'an and other sacred texts to articulate women's rights within the Islamic context is carried on by women who, with some exceptions, do not choose or feel the need to identify themselves necessarily as feminists. But their activities have inspired and enthused some West-based feminist scholars in the field of Middle East and Islam studies, and reinvigorated the debate over whether Islam – a religion and a worldview that centers on the hierarchy of rights and justifies men's and women's differential rights based on the idea of men's superiority in intellect, cognitive capacity, and faculty of judgment – can be squared with feminist ideology that holds patriarchy, men's power, and sexism, not biology, as the causes of women's restricted life options and opportunities. It then followed whether or not Muslim women activists who campaign for women's rights within an Islamic framework can be identified as Islamic feminists. A main area of contestation is the potential and limitations of this brand of feminism. This question has impelled two opposing tendencies, one embracing Islamic feminism as the only banner under which the region's women can or should fight for justice and equality, the other dismissing it as the tendency that reduces women's identity and experiences to their actual or nominal affiliation with Islam, erasing their profound distinctions across class, racial, ethnic, and geographical location.

The debates over Islamic feminism as a concept and a strategy were initially more passionately and persistently followed by Iranian feminists in the diaspora. But the relevance of the question has extended beyond Iran and has encouraged contributions from other scholars in the field.

The argument of the supporters of Islamic feminism (Najmabadi 1997, 1998; Majid 1998; Badran 2001; Cooke 2001, to name a few) is that secular discourses and attempts at promoting gender equality have been discredited as "elitist," modernist, or "white" and "West-oriented." Islamic feminism is an effective strategy developed by Muslim women to speak for themselves and articulate their own priorities and demands for improving women's lot. Moreover, Islamic feminism challenges and reforms the Islamic doctrine from within rather than advocating a Western model of gender relations; it has opened up a much needed space for dialogue between secular and religious women, bridging the ideological and practical gap between them.

The enthusiasts among the proponents of the notion of Islamic feminism argue that it is "a feminism true to its society's traditions" and "a resistance to cultural conversion," endeavoring "to release western women's claim on feminism" (El Guindi 1996, 159–161). They also argue rhapsodically that Islamic feminism is the "revolutionary paradigm" of our time, its scope so large and so "thoroughly revolutionary" that "it may well be one of the best platforms from which to resist the effects of global capitalism" and thus to contribute to a "rich, egalitarian, polycentric world" (Majid 1998, 355). The celebration of Islamic feminists goes so far as to suggest that even though Islamist movements are patriarchal and oppressive to women, women can find room to maneuver within the less extremist Islamist mainstream, as Islamist feminists are doing (Badran 2001).

Challengers of the concept (Mojab 1995; Moghissi 1999; Al-Ali 2000; Mirza 2002; Shahidian 2002) focus on its nuances and the implications for women's rights activism in the region. They argue that the manipulation of gender issues and feminist concepts by Islamists, and the very fact that, in the absence of secular spaces in the region, some secular women's rights activists also make use of the Islamic framework in demanding change, have confused the first group of scholars who embrace "Islamic feminism" with undue enthusiasm. They express concerns that overexcitement about Muslim women's campaigns for their rights has the potential of diverting attention from the fact that women are daily brutalized by legal and extra-legal oppressive Islamist practices and traditions. The heady enthusiasm of proponents of Islamic feminism in its extreme manifestations, it is suggested, means that these scholars "have been actively, if unwittingly, engaged in muting those groups and individuals who have opposed or reacted against Islamism" (Al-Ali 2000, 25). Others are critical of Islamic feminists for not "recognizing the heterogeneity of Muslim societies," for not "interrogating their own frame of reference," and for finding "irrelevant" concerns of women who are at the political margin of these societies (Mirza 2002, 13). Some among this group argue that it is true that the local traditions, ethnic composition of a society, and the level of its economic development determine how rigidly Islamic teachings and traditions regarding women's rights and relations between the sexes are imposed and followed. But in the end, if the Qur'anic instructions are taken literally, Islamic individuals or societies cannot favor equal rights for women in the family or in certain areas of social life. Consequently, Islam is reconcilable with feminism only when Islamic or Muslim identity is reduced to a matter of mere spiritual and cultural affiliation.

Islamic feminism undoubtedly is a contested and tangled subject. But throughout the Middle East, North Africa, South Asia, and the Pacific region, women are actively engaged, in many different ways, in the struggle for gender democracy and equal rights. Some of these women identify themselves as Muslims or have adopted Islam as their cultural identity. To identify them from outside as "Islamic feminists" or "Muslim feminists," or to use any other identifier to label their activities, does not change the reality that they are simply women who have a vision of another world in which women can live with dignity, equality, and justice and that they work under difficult conditions to make such a world possible.

SEE ALSO: Islam and Gender; Islam and Homosexuality; Patriarchy

REFERENCES

Al-Ali, Nadje. 2000. *Secularism, Gender and the State in the Middle East: The Egyptian Women's Movement*. Cambridge: Cambridge University Press.

Badran, Margot. 2001. "Understanding Islam, Islamism, and Islamic Feminism." *Journal of Women's History*, 13(1): 47–52.

Cooke, Miriam. 2001. *Women Claim Islam: Creating Islamic Feminism Through Literature*. New York: Routledge.

El Guindi, Fadwa. 1996. "Feminism Comes of Age in Islam." In *Arab Women: Between Defiance and Restraint*, edited by Suha Sabbagh. New York: Olive Branch Press.

Majid, Anouar. 1998. "Politics of Feminism in Islam." *Signs*, 23(2): 321–361.

Mirza, Qudsia. 2002. "Islamic Feminism, Possibilities and Limitations." In *Law After Ground Zero*, edited by John Strawson. Sydney: Glasshouse Press.

Moghissi, Haideh. 1999. *Feminism and Islamic Fundamentalism: The Limits of Postmodern Analysis*. London: Zed Books.

Mojab, Shahrzad. 1995. "Islamic Feminism: Alternative or Contradiction?" *Fireweed*, 47 (Winter): 18–25.

Najmabadi, Afsaneh. 1997. "Feminism in an Islamic Republic." In *Transition, Environment, Translation: Feminisms in International Politics*, edited by Joan Scott, Cora Kaplan, and Debra Keates. London: Routledge.

Najmabadi, Afsaneh. 1998. "Feminism in an Islamic Republic: Years of Hardship, Years of Growth." In *Islam, Gender, and Social Change in the Muslim World*, edited by Yvonne Y. Haddad and John Esposito. New York: Oxford University Press.

Shahidian, Hammed. 2002. *Women in Iran: Emerging Voices in the Women's Movement*. London: Greenwood Press.

Feminism, Latina

KATIE L. ACOSTA
Georgia State University, USA

In one of her final essays, Gloria Anzaldúa (2002) describes a moment of crisis at a feminist academic conference. A rift occurred between the white feminists and the feminists of color based on women of color's desires to have their experiences of oppression as racialized others validated and acknowledged as a legitimate and distinct form of oppression from which others can learn. The tension that Anzaldúa recounts conveys the sentiment felt by many feminists of color who question their belonging in middle-class white feminist circles. From these tensions Chicana feminism and later Latina feminism emerged in the academy. Chicana feminists have created theory that privileges lived experience as a site for knowledge and have challenged dominant paradigms of theory in the abstraction. Their goal has been to unite not based on consensus but rather to find one's voice from within *sitios y lenguas* (spaces and discourses). Emma Pérez (1998, 88) challenges feminists of color to create *sitios y lenguas* (our own spaces and discourses) within which there is no need to resolve difference. *Sitios y lenguas* allow marginalized feminists to find empowerment and validation in creating their own discourses in a space separate and apart from the Eurocentric and patriarchal academy. By starting from *sitios y lenguas*, Chicana feminists have been successful in building coalitions with other feminisms in the United States as well as in Latin America.

Inspired by many Chicana feminists with whom they share a marginality in the academy, Latina feminists have questioned their own sense of belonging. Within ethnic studies programs and political movements, Latina feminists have struggled to carve a space to do gender and sexuality work. In gender studies programs and within feminist movements, Latina feminists resist having the plurality among them ignored (Latina Feminist Group 2001). In one effort, the Latina Feminist Group forged a community for the purpose of creating a nuanced understanding of their differences and connections through testimonies. These feminists became the subjects of their writing and used *testimonios* as a tool to theorize their oppression, resistance, and subjectivity (2001, 19). *Testimonios*, or bearing witness to lived realities, has enabled Latina feminists to build what Cherríe Moraga calls "theory in the flesh" (Moraga and Anzaldúa 1981). Along with many feminists of color before them, Latina feminists privilege the lived experience in their writings and have resisted creating hierarchies of oppression.

While Latina and Chicana feminisms complement one another within the academy, they do have distinct roots. Chicana feminism originates from grassroots activism in the Chicano movement. Its goals in part originate from a desire to preserve the role of women in the historical narrative of precolonial Mexico. Rising to Emma Pérez's challenge, Latina feminism has carved out its own spaces within the academy and successfully created its own discourses. Latina feminists' efforts have facilitated alliances between Latino and gender studies programs, resulting in Latino studies programs becoming more cognizant of gender issues and gender studies programs paying more attention to gender inequalities globally (Acosta-Belén and Bose 2000). With these newly emerging interdisciplinary alliances, Latina feminists have successfully expanded discourses in various areas of study. Some of these intellectual expansions are synthesized below.

LATINA/O SEXUALITY

One of the most popular areas of research within Latina feminism has been Latina sexualities. Since Cherríe Moraga and Gloria Anzaldúa's (1981) seminal anthology, *This Bridge Called My Back*, there have been advancements in the area of Latina sexualities within both the humanities and the social sciences. Much of this work has fallen into several key sub-areas: adolescent sexual activity, women's reproductive rights, and gay and lesbian immigrant experiences.

Adolescent sexual activity

Research on adolescent Latina sexual behavior has explored the tensions that arise between parents and their daughters around dating, sex, and sexual communication. Asencio (2002) notes that the social construction of sexuality among Puerto Rican adolescent youth is based on gendered double standards and power differentials. However, Asencio notes, young Puerto Rican women are critical of these double standards, arguing that they inhibit open sexual communication. Like Asencio (2002), the majority of research on Latina adolescent sexual activity has approached this topic from the perspective of sexual health and familial tension. To expand upon these ideas, Lorena Garcia (2013) explores the ways that Mexican and Puerto Rican young girls negotiate sexual safety, sexual pleasure, and respectable femininity. With this work, Garcia sets out to shift the focus of youth sexuality scholarship away from its disproportionate emphasis on sexual risk and on to individual agency and control. To the previous research on mother–daughter sexual socialization, Garcia provides an in-depth analysis of Mexican and Puerto Rican adolescents as sexual subjects despite their mothers' tendencies to present them as victims. Garcia's work is helping to shift the direction of Latina adolescent sexuality research toward an exploration of young women's power in their relationships and their sexual desires.

Reproductive rights

Latina women have a complex history with reproductive rights in the United States and in their countries of origin. Their bodies have often been used as a site for procreation control. Iris Lopez's work focuses on Puerto Rican women's experiences with sterilization (Lopez 1997). In it, Lopez expands and contests what it means for Puerto Rican women in New York City to choose to be sterilized by accounting for their financial constraints and lack of access to quality healthcare. In the same vein, in her work on Mexican-origin women's reproductive freedoms, Elena Gutiérrez (2008) analyzes controlling images depicting these women as hypersexual baby breeders and traces the consequences of these images and racist stereotypes for policy reform. She notes that these socially constructed images have been manipulated to fuel anti-immigrant movements and have left Mexican-origin women the targets of coerced sterilization in Los Angeles. Ironically in an era where pro-choice movements are experiencing increased attacks on a woman's right to have an abortion, Latina feminists are finding themselves fighting for the right to procreate.

Gay and lesbian immigrant experiences

Scholars interested in the immigrant experiences of Latina lesbians have predominantly addressed issues of identity and family negotiations (Espín 1997; Acosta 2013). Espín notes that coming out for Latina lesbians can mean jeopardizing one's strong familial ties and connection to the larger Latino community. For this reason, she argues, Latina lesbians tend to only come out within a Western context and thus increase their invisibility within their communities. Consistent with Espín's work, Acosta (2013) finds that immigrant lesbian, bisexual, and queer (LBQ) Latinas have an easier time negotiating families of origin and choice if their origin families remain in their countries of origin. The distance created by immigration allows LBQ Latinas to spare their origin families the stigmatization that can come from gender and sexual transgressions. However, Acosta's work complicates Espín's use of "coming out to family," noting that LBQ Latinas find strategic ways to integrate their families of origin and choice in a cohesive support network regardless of whether or not they have ever verbally disclosed their sexualities to their families of origin. While Acosta notes that LBQ Latinas do experience resistance from origin families, these concerns are shaped not only by their sexual preferences but more so by their level of gender transgression.

Gender presentation as a constraint to sexuality has also been explored in research on Latino gay men. Peña (2013) explores the tensions between visibility and silencing strategies by tracing the negative historical images of the gay, flamboyant, undesirable *marielitos* alongside the Cuban American gay men in Miami in the 1990s. Peña finds Cuban gay men position themselves in relation to multiple racialized discourses of masculinity and distance themselves from effeminacy in part because of the correlations they draw between gender transgression and lower-class immigrant status. Decena (2011) echoes many of these ideas in his work, adding that while Dominican gay men associate masculine deportment with legitimacy and survival in public, among close friends some enjoy a playful suspension of this masculine code in order to enact intimacy with one another through effeminate physical and communicative language.

Collectively this young but expanding body of research on Latina/o sexualities brings up issues of visibility, social constraints via immigration, race, and class, and sexual desire, all of which will certainly continue to form the debates in future research.

LATINAS AND WORK

Another popular area of research within Latina feminism has focused on Latinas' work experiences. Hondagenu-Sotelo (2001) explores the working conditions of Latina immigrant domestic workers, noting that the informal and deregulated nature of domestic work creates an environment ripe for these women's exploitation. Since their employment as nannies and housecleaners transgresses the boundaries of work and family, Latina immigrants are susceptible to never being off the clock and must accept poor wages sometimes well below minimum wage. Another employment option available to immigrant Latinas that is less often explored in the scholarship is the garment industry. Puerto Rican migrants and Dominican immigrants in particular have historically had a strong presence working in the garment industry in the United States. Whalen (2002) offers a historical account on how the globalization of the garment industry first created opportunities for Puerto Rican and later Dominican women, thus shaping the migratory patterns in both countries. However, Whalen notes that the globalization of the garment industry results in economic displacement for Puerto Rican and Dominican women as factories consistently relocate (often overseas) in search of cheaper wages.

There has also been a growing body of research on educated Latinas in professional jobs (Segura 1997; Flores 2011). This research addresses the obstacles that Latinas face in predominantly white professional jobs. Segura (1997) finds that Chicanas working in clerical positions at a public university feel that their opportunities in the workplace are shaped by their skin tone, accents, and cultural mannerisms. The Chicanas in her study report constantly having to prove their competency at work and feeling as though their accomplishments are measured against the racist stereotypes that Mexicans are uneducated and always pregnant (1997, 301). However, Segura also notes that these Chicanas' experiences with discrimination at work ultimately reinforce their gender/race-ethnic identities. Flores (2011) finds that Latina teachers working among majority white co-workers are more isolated, report strained social relationships with their colleagues, and experience subtle forms of racism. Flores refers to Latina teachers in these work settings as *racialized tokens*, noting that these women often self-segregate in order to avoid dealing with the many obstacles that come with racial integration.

BUILDING BRIDGES, CREATING SOLIDARITY

Latina feminists have often concentrated their efforts on building bridges and solidarity through both scholarship and activism with other ethnic groups nationally and internationally (Acosta-Belén and Bose 2000). At times these efforts have been unsuccessful, as Elena Gutiérrez (2008) notes was the case when Chicana feminists fought for Mexican-origin women's reproductive rights. Their attempts to join the National Organization for Women were unsuccessful due to their emphasis on distinct kinds of reproductive freedoms. In this instance, distinct racialized experiences resulted in an inability to build coalitions. Instead, Latina feminist activists have focused on building Latina Advocacy Networks (LANs) that provide health workshops, hold marches, and are lobbying for reproductive justice. LANs' efforts on the ground are instrumental at a time when women's clinics throughout the country are being forced to shut down.

Latina feminist activists have made considerable gains in other areas as well. For instance, activists have focused on improving the working conditions of domestic workers, applying pressure for lobbyists to pass legislation guaranteeing fair wages and overtime pay for these workers. Activists have also mobilized heavily around immigration reform, fighting against the deportations of their family members and for the dreamers' right to a college education. These movements have been successful in uniting Latina/os across differences for a common cause. Their efforts have kept the marginalities of Latina/os in the United States in the public eye.

There are also times when efforts at coalition building have succeeded. Shapiro (2005) recounts her efforts alongside other US Latina feminists to serve as intermediaries between Latin American feminists and second-wave feminists in the United States. In her description of the many obstacles they encountered, Shapiro notes that Puerto Rican feminists held a rather unique position to serve as a bridge between US Latinas and Latin American/Caribbean feminists. The marginality that Latina feminists have experienced and their unique social positions within the borderlands have made them well equipped to take on the task of building bridges. It was after all a desire to build bridges that united feminists of color in creating *This Bridge Called My Back* (1981). Latina feminists can offer these experiences to others within the academy and activists working for social justice.

SEE ALSO: Borderlands; Feminism, Chicana; Feminism, Indo-Caribbean

REFERENCES

Acosta, Katie L. 2013. *Amigas y Amantes: Sexually Nonconforming Latinas Negotiate Family*. New Brunswick: Rutgers University Press.

Acosta-Belén, Edna, and Christine Bose E. 2000. "U.S. Latina and Latin American Feminisms: Hemispheric Encounters." *Signs*, 25(4): 1113–1119.

Anzaldúa, Gloria. 2002. "now let us shift … the path of conocimiento … inner work, public acts." In *this bridge we call home: radical visions for transformation*, edited by Gloria Anzaldúa and Analouise Keating, 540–578. New York: Routledge.

Asencio, Marysol. 2002. *Sex and Sexuality among New York's Puerto Rican Youth*. Boulder: Lynne Rienner.

Decena, Carlos Ulises. 2011. *Tacit Subjects: Belonging and Same-Sex Desire among Dominican Immigrant Men*. Durham, NC: Duke University Press.

Espín, Oliva M. 1997. *Latina Realities: Essays on Healing, Migration and Sexuality.* Boulder: Westview Press.

Flores, Glenda Marisol. 2011. "Racialized Tokens: Latina Teachers Negotiating Surviving and Thriving in a White Woman's Profession." *Qualitative Sociology,* 34: 313–335.

Garcia, Lorena. 2013. *Respect Yourself, Protect Yourself: Latina Girls and Sexual Identity.* New York: NYU Press.

Gutiérrez, Elena R. 2008. *Fertile Matters: The Politics of Mexican-Origin Women's Reproduction.* Austin: University of Texas Press.

Hondagenu-Sotelo, Pierrette. 2001. *Doméstica: Immigrant Workers Cleaning and Caring in the Shadows of Affluence.* Berkeley: University of California Press.

Latina Feminist Group, eds. 2001. *Telling to Live: Latina Feminist Testimonios.* Durham, NC: Duke University Press.

Lopez, Iris. 1997. "Agency and Constraint: Sterilization and Reproductive Freedom Among Puerto Rican Women in New York City." In *Situated Lives: Gender and Culture in Everyday Life,* edited by Louise Lamphere, Helena Ragoné, and Patricia Zavella, 157–171. New York: Routledge.

Moraga, Cherríe, and Gloria Anzaldúa, eds. 1981. *This Bridge Called My Back: Writings By Radical Women of Color.* New York: Kitchen Table: Women of Color Press

Peña, Susana. 2013. *Oye Loca: From Mariel Boatlift to Gay Cuban Miami.* Minneapolis: University of Minnesota Press.

Pérez, Emma. 1998. "Irigaray's Female Symbolic in the Making of Chicana Lesbian *Sitios y Lenguas* (Sites and Discourses)." In *Living Chicana Theory,* edited by Carla Trujillo, 87–101. Berkeley: Third Woman Press.

Segura, Denise. 1997. "Chicanas in White-Collar Jobs: You Have to Prove Yourself More." In *Situated Lives: Gender and Culture in Everyday Life,* edited by Louise Lamphere, Helena Ragoné, and Patricia Zavella, 292–310. New York: Routledge.

Shapiro, Ester R. 2005. "Because Words Are Not Enough: Latina Re-Visionings of Transnational Collaborations Using Health Promotion for Gender Justice and Social Change." *NWSA Journal,* 17(1): 141–172.

Whalen, Carmen Teresa. 2002. "Sweatshops Here and There: The Garment Industry, Latinas and Labor Migrations." *International Labor and Working-Class History,* 61: 45–68.

Feminism, Lesbian

KATH BROWNE
University of Brighton, UK

MARTA OLASIK
University of Warsaw, Poland

Lesbian feminism emerged in the United States of the 1970s to counter the heterosexism and lesbophobia in mainstream feminism on the one hand, and the ways in which sexual identities/lives/politics can be dominated by gay men on the other. Women in question were driven by anger regarding decades of obvious lack of representation and support from male gay movements and (heterosexual) feminism as a whole. There are different forms of lesbian feminisms. As a strand of radical feminism, some lesbian feminists have taken staunch positions in relation to trans women and bisexualities. These are not inherent to the positioning of lesbian feminisms, but this is often how they are presented. The very phrase "lesbian feminism" marks a certain point in history and the separatist tendency described below, and it is important to emphasize the existence of multiple lesbian feminisms.

In the 1970s some feminists attempted to distance their association with, and contest the visibility of, lesbians within the general feminist movement. They argued that overt connections with lesbians might weaken the feminist position and political chances; sexuality was not considered serious enough. As early as 1969, lesbians were called the "lavender menace" by Betty Friedan, the leading figure of early second-wave feminism. Consequently, lesbians within feminism have often been invisibilized and marginalized. It has been argued that in the 1980s and early 1990s "lesbian" continually disappeared from the feminist appropriation of the term "woman"; "women's" problems too often exclude those who are not heterosexual. This can be seen in the number of feminist books that ignore the contribution of diverse forms of lesbian feminisms to feminist theories and herstories.

Adrienne Rich, one of the key figures of lesbian separatism, explicitly showed feminists' ignorance in her highly influential 1980 essay offering an in-depth analysis of heterosexuality as an oppressive, and yet compulsory, institution (Rich 1993). Patriarchy, as well as the very category/institution of "woman" (Wittig 1992), was taken under scrutiny within sexual politics. Lesbian feminisms have resulted in an abundance of powerful academic works, political manifestos, fiction and non-fiction literature, and poetry. Because of the comprehensive and subversive character of these lesbian initiatives and texts of culture, the original lesbian separatism may have been the greatest time of lesbian existence and visibility to date.

In the main, lesbian feminisms argue that mainstream feminism is to a large extent heterosexist and ignores issues of sexuality, thereby rendering the institutional barrier of heterosexism invisible. "Lesbian feminist politics is a critique of the institution and ideology of heterosexuality as a cornerstone of male supremacy" (Bunch 1991, 320). Radical lesbians encouraged treating lesbian identity as an act of resistance, a political choice. They argued that women who function within the man–woman economy contribute to, and confirm, their own subjugation. Thus, a free woman should exist entirely apart from men, and contribute to the formation of lesbian and women's separatist communities. In this way, womanhood could be reinvented. Alongside Adrienne Rich and Monique Wittig, some of the most influential thinkers within lesbian feminism/separatism include Marilyn Frye, Rita Mae Brown, and Audre Lorde.

Similar to intersectional critiques of feminist thinking, sexuality cannot be "added" onto a list of differences between women, never to be addressed again. Instead, as with black feminism, heterosexism and homophobia alter the terms of oppression, illustrating that one form of feminism is not sufficient in addressing the diverse and multiple oppressions that coexist. Lesbian feminism acknowledges the overlapping of networks of power and is therefore able to challenge patriarchal society, heterosexism, homophobia, and hegemonic forms of feminisms. These feminisms are built on intersectionalities and are developed through lesbian black feminisms and Latina feminisms such as those of Gloria Anzaldúa and the Combahee Collective, as well as explorations of differences such as disability or poverty. However, the literature, more often than not, treats lesbian feminism and women of color feminisms as separate formulations.

Lesbian feminist perspectives have addressed the assumption that lesbianism is purely individual and/or biologically based deviance. What could be termed the social-constructionist viewpoint sees lesbianism as socially produced. This means that same-sex, different-sex, polyamorous, and heterosexualities are all cultural phenomena rather than something innate. They can therefore, above all, be related to questioning and challenging social and political hegemonies and norms – masculinities and heterosexualities.

Challenges to heterosexual norms can be used to broaden and diversify the term "lesbian." This category could include anyone who chooses to identify with the lesbian label regardless of their sexual preferences/activities or gendered *her*stories. In other words, this can be a political category that seeks to undermine the very basis of heterosexist and patriarchal society. Such an understanding of lesbianism is continuous with arguments regarding the historically and culturally contingent formation of labels. "Lesbian" for some became a fluid and encompassing category that did not lend itself to simple biological definitions or explanations, and in this way could be used for political ends.

Whilst lesbian feminisms came into existence by expanding the category of lesbian, some of its later forms asserted that lesbianism must be announced and performed in particular ways. In what is known as the sex wars, the politics of sexual practices was debated. Some authors, such as Jeffreys (2003), asserted that different forms of sexuality, including sadomasochistic practices, result in a mirroring of patriarchal oppression. Similarly, because patriarchy and compulsory heterosexuality are believed to be irrevocably intertwined, some lesbian feminists assert that feminism is only "true" when it is lesbian, or in any respect separate from men. Heterosexual feminists, then, are "conspiring with the enemy."

Others, such as Raymond (1979), have contended that trans women form a "menace." These lesbian feminists have taken essentialist views on embodiment and birth genders, contending that trans women are men seeking access to women's spaces, lives, and bodies. As such, trans women are seen as enacting patriarchal privileges and, thus, "deceiving" women.

However, there is much unease and critique of these forms of essentialist lesbian feminisms. There can be little doubt that some lesbian feminisms today are portrayed and performed in ways that can be seen as transphobic, and rally against heterosexualities in exclusionary ways. Still, lesbian separatism as a framework does have the potential to move beyond these forms of critiques and politics, embracing broader conceptualizations of both lesbians and feminists in ways that will work toward undermining the intersections of patriarchies and heterosexisms. Finally, though lesbian feminisms and separatisms emerged in places such as North America, the United Kingdom, and France, their geographical reach has spread throughout the last few decades. It is, however, worth noting that there are places all over the world where lesbian, as a separate discourse, has not come into existence.

SEE ALSO: Biological Determinism; Bisexuality; Feminism, Radical; Feminist Sex Wars; Heterosexism and Homophobia; Intersectionality; Lesbian and Womyn's Separatism; Patriarchy; Polyamory; Sadomasochism, Domination, and Submission; Social Constructionist Theory; Trans Identities, Psychological Perspectives; Transphobia

REFERENCES

Bunch, Charlotte. 1991. "Not for Lesbians Only." In *A Reader in Feminist Knowledge*, edited by S. Gunew, 319–325. London: Routledge.

Jeffreys, Sheila. 2003. *Unpacking Queer Politics: A Lesbian Feminist Perspective*. Cambridge: Polity.

Raymond, Janice. 1979. *The Transsexual Empire: The Making of the She-Male*. Boston: Beacon Press.

Rich, Adrienne. 1993, "Compulsory Heterosexuality and Lesbian Existence." In *The Lesbian and Gay Studies Reader*, edited by Henry Abelove, Michele Aina Barale, and David M. Halperin, 227–254. New York: Routledge.

Wittig, Monique. 1992. *The Straight Mind and Other Essays*. Boston: Beacon Press.

FURTHER READING

Calhoun, Cheshire. 1995. "The Gender Closet: Lesbian Disappearance under the Sign 'Women'." *Feminist Studies*, 21: 7–34.

Combahee River Collective. 1979. "A Black Feminist Statement." In *Capitalist Patriarchy and the Case for Socialist Feminism*, edited by Zillah R. Eisenstein. New York: Monthly Review Press.

Cruikshank, Margaret. 1992. "Lesbian Feminism." In *The Gay and Lesbian Liberation Movement*, 114–165. London: Routledge.

De Lauretis, Teresa. 1993. "Sexual Indifference and Lesbian Representation." In *The Lesbian and Gay Studies Reader*, edited by Henry Abelove,

Michele Aina Barale, and David M. Halperin, 141–158. New York: Routledge.
Frye, Marilyn. 1993. "Some Reflections on Separatism and Power." In *The Lesbian and Gay Studies Reader*, edited by Henry Abelove, Michele Aina Barale, and David M. Halperin, 91–98. New York: Routledge.
Garber, Linda. 2001. "The Social Construction of Lesbian Feminism." In *Identity Poetics: Race, Class, and the Lesbian–Feminist Roots of Queer Theory*, 10–30. New York: Columbia University Press.
hooks, bell. 2000. *Feminism is for Everybody: Passionate Politics*. Cambridge, MA: South End Press.
Lorde, Audre. 1993. "The Uses of the Erotic: The Erotic as Power." In *The Lesbian and Gay Studies Reader*, edited by Henry Abelove, Michele Aina Barale, and David M. Halperin, 339–343. New York: Routledge.
Lorde, Audre. 2007. "The Master's Tools Will Never Dismantle the Master's House." In *The Essential Feminist Reader*, edited by E. B. Freedman, 331–335. New York: Modern Library. First published 1984.
Rubin, Gayle. 1993. "Thinking Sex: Notes for a Radical Theory of the Politics of Sexuality." In *The Lesbian and Gay Studies Reader*, edited by Henry Abelove, Michele Aina Barale, and David M. Halperin, 3–44. New York: Routledge.
Vicinus, Martha. 1993. "'They Wonder to Which Sex I Belong': The Historical Roots of the Modern Lesbian Identity." In *The Lesbian and Gay Studies Reader*, edited by Henry Abelove, Michele Aina Barale, and David M. Halperin, 432–452. New York: Routledge.
Wilton Tamsin. 1995. *Lesbian Studies: Setting an Agenda*. New York: Routledge.

Feminism, Liberal

LUCY E. BAILEY
Oklahoma State University, USA

Liberal feminism is a form of feminist theory that has been instrumental in fueling women's rights movements and the significant legal, educational, and policy initiatives that have increased women's rights in diverse contexts grounded in political traditions of liberalism. Liberal feminism emerged from the political philosophy of liberalism centered on human beings' capacity for rationality and reason and their "natural" right to liberty. The world view of liberalism emerged as a distinct political tradition during the Enlightenment (seventeenth and eighteenth centuries), yet its empowering vision of freedom and equality primarily applied to men. The tenets of liberal feminist theory are perhaps the most familiar and widespread forms of feminism given its emphasis on individual rights, its influence in advancing equity initiatives in legal, political, and social spheres, and its visibility as a guiding philosophy in well-known women's organizations, such as, in the United States, the National Organization for Women. Each body of feminist thought conceptualizes different causes of and remedies for gender inequities. Liberal feminism includes diverse approaches focused on, variously, removing legal and social constraints or advancing conditions that support women's equality.

Liberal thought preceded the Enlightenment age but flourished as a cohesive school of thought during this active intellectual period when people began questioning long-revered traditions of religious and hereditary authority. Liberalism is a political philosophy with diverse and competing strands that is grounded in human beings' natural rights to liberty and the basis of numerous governments oriented to advancing, or limiting restrictions to, individual freedoms. Liberal traditions vary in their conceptions of "freedom" and their theory of the role the state should play in facilitating individual freedom. The seventeenth-century English philosopher, John Locke, is often referred to as the "father" of liberalism because his conception of man's natural rights, his advocacy for the separation of church and state, and his belief in the right for men to consent to the governance constituted a new and distinctive worldview.

Liberal feminist thought emerged from these strong philosophical traditions invested in liberty and extended these conceptions to women. While classic liberalism is invested in a vision of non-intrusive government that enables individual rights and freedoms, such as the right to property, to free speech, and to voting as fundamental expressions of liberty, liberal feminists have detailed the deeply gendered nature of these conceptions of rights that fail to uphold women's rights to actualize their individual freedoms. For example, women in diverse contexts have been systematically excluded from a vision of liberty that includes owning property, participating in the political process, or consenting to the governance that shapes the personal, social, and political conditions of their lives. Liberal feminists argue that patriarchal structures intrude on women's personal and political choices.

Key early figures influential in the efforts to extend important components of liberal political thought specifically to women included Mary Wollstonecraft (1759–1797), John Stuart Mill (1806–1873), and Harriet Taylor Mill (1806–1858). Wollstonecraft's classic text, *A Vindication of the Rights of Woman* (1998), remains a resource for tracing the tenets of what we now term liberal feminist thought. Wollstonecraft was an affluent English woman troubled by social forces that limited women's opportunities to hold meaningful roles. In *Vindication*, she advocated for education that would allow women to develop reason, key to self-control and self-governance. Cultivating reason through education would allow women to fulfill their family roles, to contribute to the overall good of society, and to develop their full human potential. These significant arguments are grounded in the belief that women, like men, are inherently capable of reason and it is social constraints, rather than biology, that limit their rights and ability to develop those capacities to achieve self-governance.

These important liberal feminist tenets – a belief in women's capacity for reason; a belief that social and political constraints interfere with women actualizing their full personhood; a vision of social reform to foster women's autonomy and gender equity – remain salient in contemporary expressions of liberal feminist thought. Yet liberal feminism, like liberalism more broadly, includes diverse strands and conceptions of liberty, autonomy, rights, property, economics, social justice, and morality, all of which shape its contours and implications.

One core difference among strands of liberal feminist theory concerns how the role of the state relates to women's freedoms. For example, classic liberal feminism seeks a state that is free of coercion limiting to women's individual rights and diligent in removing legal and political barriers that interfere with women's autonomy and liberties. Such conditions might include policies that protect against sex discrimination (e.g., the Equal Rights Amendment or Title IX of the United States Educational Amendment Acts of 1972 focused on educational institutions that receive federal funding). They might also include disrupting social conditions that normalize male power, violence against women, or restrictive gender roles. In this perspective, feminists seek a non-intrusive state.

In contrast, welfare liberal feminists conceive of a state that provides diverse resources that will enable differently positioned women to actualize freedom and equity. In this view, pervasive social and economic inequities shape women's lives and the state remains an important vehicle for advancing just and equitable conditions for women. Such state-sponsored programs might include Social Security and Medicaid or initiatives such as

Affirmative Action. These versions of feminism, both characterized as "liberal," are at odds in how to remedy women's access to their natural rights to liberty and autonomy, however conceived.

Other expressions of liberal feminism view women's autonomy as just one important aspect of seeking the "good life." Martha Nussbaum, for instance, envisions health, dignity, and participation in governance as necessary for full "functioning" and human "flourishing" (Nussbaum 1999). While such expressions of liberal feminism work to protect rather than evaluate women's choices – such as protecting women's right to participate in the pornography industry and keeping working conditions safe – others argue that some state restrictions in certain circumstances is warranted because women's participation could potentially contribute to oppressing others. These complex circumstances necessitate grappling with at times conflicting views of freedom and autonomy.

Varied critiques of liberal feminism have emerged from within fields of feminist thought, such as, for example, differences among classic and welfare feminists about how best to advance women's condition. Welfare feminists, for example, argue that the laws that treat women and men the same, aimed at protecting individual rights, are not enough to interrupt and alter the profound structural inequities that shape women's lives. Active intervention into structural oppression and structural remedies through healthcare, affordable housing, and educational resources are imperative.

Feminists aligned with other theoretical traditions, such as radical feminism, are concerned with liberal feminists' reliance on seeking equity and reform in existing political and social institutions rather than critiquing and striving for liberation from such institutions utterly seeped in heteronormative and patriarchal systems of thought. In this view, the state is always a source of systemic patriarchal oppression that perpetuates women's oppression. Other critics underscore that liberal feminism's origins in European, middle-class women's world views make it irrelevant to the lives and concerns of women of color, working-class women, lesbians, and women around the globe. In addition, community orientations and justice-based concerns are profoundly different, for example, from the conception of individual autonomy that concerns privileged Westerners. Recent critiques have turned to neoliberal expressions of feminism that root traditional liberal feminist claims for gender equity in market ideology.

SEE ALSO: Feminism, Eighteenth-Century Britain; Feminism, Radical; Patriarchy

REFERENCES

Nussbaum, Martha. 1999. *Sex and Social Justice*. New York: Oxford University Press.
Wollstonecraft, Mary. 1998. *A Vindication of the Rights of Woman*. New York: Norton. First published 1792.

FURTHER READING

Abbey, R. 2011. *The Return of Feminist Liberalism*. Montreal & Kingston: McGill Queens University Press.
Rhode, Deborah. 1997. *Speaking of Sex: The Denial of Gender Inequality*. Cambridge: Harvard University Press.

Feminism, Material

SUSAN HEKMAN
The University of Texas at Arlington, USA

Material feminism has its roots in feminists' discontent with the radical social constructionist approach that characterizes postmodernism. Material feminism is distinct from the earlier materialist feminism that had its roots in Marxism. This discontent was particularly acute in feminist critiques of science. Feminists such as Donna Haraway, Sandra Harding, and Helen Longino transformed science studies, challenging the sexist bias of scientific investigations. But with the advent of postmodernism, the objectivity of scientific knowledge came to be questioned, challenging the possibility of knowledge claims about the material world. Some feminists began to question this approach, arguing that the social constructionist position had gone too far. If we replace Truth with truths we lose any grounding in the real. No statement, scientific or otherwise, has any priority over any other statement: all are equally vulnerable to critique because all are social constructions.

By the end of the twentieth century feminists had begun to formulate an approach to overcome these obstacles. The theoretical basis for this approach lies in the work of several feminist critics of science. Donna Haraway (1997), whose work has been iconic in the evolution of feminist critiques of science, provides the impetus for the new generation of critiques in her recent work. The key to the new direction these critiques are taking is a movement anticipated by Haraway (1997): the movement from epistemology to ontology. Epistemology is the focus of social constructionism. Critiques emphasized the production of knowledge from an exclusively discursive perspective. The new generation of feminist theorists is arguing that the obsession with epistemology that characterized social constructionism is a dead end. Epistemology is of necessity about representation, and representation is necessarily about dichotomies. Representation gives us two choices: knowledge is either objective or subjective. As long as we remain within the purview of epistemology this dichotomy is inescapable.

There are two feminist theorists working today who bring theory and practice together in their discussions and thus reveal the full dimensions of the approach that will come to be called material feminism. Nancy Tuana and Karen Barad offer clear and compelling theoretical arguments, but they also show how these arguments play out in the real world of the political, economic, material, and scientific.

The work of Nancy Tuana has been at the forefront of defining a new approach for feminist theory and practice for several decades. Tuana is very clear about the necessity of transcending the dualisms that structure philosophical discussions. Since her pathbreaking article in *Hypatia* (1983), Tuana has made these dualisms the focus of her attention. This early article assessed the nature/culture dualism. In subsequent work one of her favorite targets has been the sterility of the realism/anti-realism debate. Feminist work in epistemology and science studies, Tuana argues, has begun to identify the need for a close and nuanced examination of the complexities of materiality, specifically the cognitive impact of embodiment and the relationship between human materiality and the more-than human world (2001, 221). The alternative that Tuana suggests is "interactionism," a position that describes the emergent interplay of materiality.

Tuana takes on the central issue of epistemology and ontology directly. She is dissatisfied with the correspondence/coherence option, arguing that we need a theory that posits the "coherence of interpretation, practice, phenomena, and materials" (2001, 228). The means of accomplishing this, Tuana argues, is to change our focus from epistemology to ontology. Against the social constructionist account she argues for a "new metaphysic" that grounds human ways of knowing in patterns of bodily being. Tuana's approach constitutes a bold philosophical move. She not only clearly defines the problem facing feminism and critical thought more generally, but she lays out a carefully defined alternative. Her "new metaphysic" addresses the key issues facing both philosophy and feminist theory. At the center of this metaphysics is her emphasis on embodiment. For Tuana, we always know as embodied human beings. This allows her to overcome the dualisms that plagued modernity: nature and culture, human and non-human, the discursive and the material. For Tuana, everything is always in flux; the human, more-than-human, material and discursive are interacting in a complex mix. The result is a transformation of our understanding of knowledge and the world that is revolutionary.

Karen Barad, like Tuana, offers an array of concepts to describe her approach. These include "intra-action," "agential realism," "performativity," and "onto-epistem-ology." Beginning in the mid-1990s, Barad published a series of articles that outlined the parameters of her approach. Then, in 2007, she published *Meeting the Universe Halfway: Quantum Physics and the Entanglement of Matter and Meaning*. This book provides the definitive statement of her theory. Her approach offers feminists and science critics a wholly new way to address questions of truth and knowledge. Her theory breaks new ground not only for feminists but for all theorists concerned with the future direction of knowledge.

The impetus for Barad's theory is her conviction that language has become the exclusive focus of contemporary thought to the exclusion of all other elements: "Language has been granted too much power. The linguistic turn, the semiotic turn, the interpretive turn, the cultural turn: it seems that at every turn lately every 'thing' – even materiality – is turned into a matter of language or some other form of cultural representation" (Barad 2007, 132). In this and other passages Barad has, in a sense, thrown down the gauntlet against the current orthodoxy, particularly in feminist theory. The "turns" she cites here – linguistic, semiotic, interpretive – have dominated feminist and critical thought for the last several decades. Taking on this orthodoxy, as Barad is all too aware, will not be easy. It will also not be popular. A whole generation of feminist scholars has been taught to put "matter" in scare quotes. Removing those scare quotes, making matter matter as Barad puts it, will be no mean feat.

This daunting task, however, is precisely the goal of *Meeting the Universe Halfway*. Barad begins the book by declaring: "Matter and meaning are not separate elements" (2007, 3). The subject of her book, thus, is "entanglements": to be entangled is not simply to be intertwined with another, but "to lack an independent, self-contained existence … individuals emerge through and as a part of their entangled intra-relating" (2007, ix). The thesis that Barad develops throughout her book is that quantum physics can show us how entanglement works, it can lead us out of the morass that takes absolutism and relativism as the only two possibilities (2007, 18).

What Barad offers in this course of her impressive book is what she claims is a deeper understanding of the ontological dimension of scientific practice. This entails, most centrally, a redefinition of realism. Realism, she asserts, "can offer a possible ballast against the persistent positivist scientific and postmodernist cultures that too easily confuse theory with play" (Barad 2007, 43). The notion of constructing a "ballast" gets to the heart of Barad's project: resisting the trend of contemporary theorizing not to take matter seriously. Her reference to "play" is also significant. It is a thinly veiled reference to the work of Derrida whose influence in feminist thought has been pervasive, and,

Barad would argue, pernicious. What Barad wants to do is to provide a counter to these tendencies, to resist the move to play that she sees as taking feminism away from its serious subject matter: matter. Barad realizes the difficulty of the task of challenging an established orthodoxy. But she is convinced that her goal, giving an account of materiality as an active and productive factor in its own right, is essential to the future of feminism.

Barad's most succinct statement of her position comes at the end of *Meeting the Universe Halfway*:

> On my agential realist account, scientific practices do not reveal what is already there; rather, what is "disclosed" is the effect of the intra-active engagements of our participation within and as a part of the world's differential becoming. (Barad 2007, 361)

And, finally: "We need to meet the universe halfway, to take responsibility for the role that we play in the world's differential becoming" (2007, 396).

The insights of Tuana and Barad have coalesced in what is now identified as the "new materialism." Myra Hird defines the new materialism as marking "a momentous shift in the natural sciences in the past few decades to suggest an openness and play within the living *and* non-living world, contesting previous paradigms which posited a changeable culture against a stable and inert nature" (2004, 2). Like Tuana and Barad the new materialists want to demonstrate how the new approach works in practice, how it makes a difference. Together the work of the new materialists demonstrates the differences entailed by defining materiality as both active and positive.

Tuana's "interaction" and "viscous porosity," Barad's "intra-action" and "agential realism," the "new materialism" of feminist science studies are, indeed, beginning to transform feminist approaches to knowledge. This transformation is evident in the feminist science studies cited above, but it has also made deep inroads into an area that has always been central to feminist analysis: the body. For feminism, the body is unavoidable, but it is also problematic. Women's bodies are the point of intersection between patriarchal structures and women's lives. It is women's bodies that feel the pain those structures create and it is also women's bodies that have been constructed as the cause of women's inferiority. Dealing with women's bodies has thus always been a necessary aspect of feminist analysis but also one of the most difficult.

In recent years the attempt to find an alternative to linguistic constructionism, an attempt that picks up many of the themes of Susan Bordo's work, has fueled a new approach to the body that radically alters the terms of the debate. Many feminists are now arguing that we should not be forced to choose between discourse and materiality, culture and nature. Rather we should devise an approach to the body that overcomes these dualisms, that defines the body as a "complex and dynamic configuration of events that includes the material and the corporeal" (Bray and Colebrook 1998, 44). Proponents of this approach to the body define the body as a "transformer," a complex interlay of highly constructed social and symbolic forces (Braidotti 2002, 20–22). This approach, they argue, constitutes a "healthy and exciting new era in feminist philosophy" (Kukla 2006, vii).

The feminist theorist who is most closely associated with this new approach to the body is Elizabeth Grosz. Her 1994 book, *Volatile Bodies*, stakes out what is at issue very clearly. At the outset Grosz states that we need to think about bodies in a non-dualistic way, to displace the centrality of mind in discussions of the subject and make the subject a corporeal being. But it is not enough only to avoid the dualisms that have defined the body in Western thought; we also need to avoid essentialism. Grosz argues that the means to accomplish this is to rethink one of the pillars of feminist thought: the sex/gender distinction: "Gender is not an ideological superstructure added to a biological base" (Grosz 1994, 58). Grosz's argument is that unless we can transcend this dichotomy that has grounded so much feminist thought, we will not be able to transform our approach to the body.

Like Grosz, Moira Gatens emphasizes sexual difference, challenging the neutrality of the body implicit in much gender theory. The connection between femininity and the female body, masculinity and the male body, she asserts, is not arbitrary (1996, 4). There are two kinds of bodies: male and female. Her thesis is that the same behavior will have different significance when acted out by male or female bodies (1996, 8–9). In order to formulate her alternative approach to the body, Gatens turns to the work of Spinoza. Unlike other theorists in the Western tradition, Spinoza presents a non-dualistic philosophy in which the body is the ground of human action. Building on Spinoza's work, Gatens develops a conception of the body that focuses on what Barad would call the intra-action of bodies and culture. For Gatens, bodies exist, but what they are at any given time is always historical and cultural: "Past contingencies become the material of present necessities" (1996, 103). Bodies are always in interconnection with other body complexes. Gatens concludes that it is only within these complex assemblages that sexed bodies are produced as socially and politically meaningful bodies (1996, 149).

Another theorist who begins with a consideration of feminist approaches to the body and moves on to an exploration of the broader framework of such analyses is Elizabeth Wilson. Wilson's premise is that despite intensive scrutiny of the body in recent feminist literature, certain fundamental aspects of the body, specifically biology and materiality, have been foreclosed (1999, 16). Like Grosz, Wilson believes that this foreclosure has both theoretical and political consequences.

The works of Grosz, Gatens, and many others indicate that feminists in many different fields are seeking an alternative to social constructionism. A sea change in feminism and critical theory is underway that is in the process of altering our fundamental understandings of the relationship between knowledge and the world. But much work remains to be done. The parameters of the new materialism, despite the careful work of the theorists described here, are still vague. Some aspects of the settlement, furthermore, most notably the analysis of science, are more developed than others. Finally, there is a glaring omission in these accounts that should be especially significant for feminists: few theorists discuss the implications of this approach for the social world. Although Tuana, Barad, and some of the other theorists discussed here have begun the difficult work of extending the approach to the social realm, the task is far from complete. But if this approach is to fulfill its potential to offer a transformed view of knowledge and the world, it must move beyond the confines of science. Most particularly, because it is a feminist approach, it must encompass the social as well as the scientific.

SEE ALSO: Feminism and Postmodernism; Feminist Studies of Science; Feminist Theories of the Body; Social Constructionist Theory

REFERENCES

Barad, Karen. 2007. *Meeting the Universe Halfway: Quantum Physics and the Entanglement of Matter and Meaning*. Durham, NC: Duke University Press.

Braidotti, Rosi, 2002. *Metamorphoses: Toward a Materialist Theory of Becoming.* Cambridge: Polity Press.

Bray, Elizabeth, and Claire Colebrook. 1998. "The Haunted Flesh: Corporeal Feminism and the Politics of (Dis)embodiment." *Signs*, 24(1): 35–67.

Gatens, Moira. 1996. *Imaginary Bodies: Ethics, Power, and Corporeality.* New York: Routledge.

Grosz, Elizabeth. 1994. *Volatile Bodies: Toward a Corporeal Feminism.* Bloomington: Indiana University Press.

Haraway, Donna. 1997. *Modest-Witness@Second Millenium – Female Man-Meets-Onco-Mouse: Feminism and Technoscience.* New York: Routledge.

Hird, Myra. 2004. *Sex, Gender, and Science.* New York: Palgrave.

Kukla, Rebecca. 2006. "Introduction: Material Bodies." *Hypatia*, 21(1): vii–ix.

Tuana, Nancy. 1983. "Refusing Nature/Nurture." *Hypatia*, special issue of *Women's Studies International Forum*, 6(6): 45–56.

Tuana, Nancy. 2001. "Material Locations." In *Engendering Rationalities*, edited by Nancy Tuana and Sandi Morgen, 221–243. Bloomington: Indiana University Press.

Wilson, Elizabeth. 1999. "Introduction: Somatic Compliance – Feminism, Biology, and Science." *Australian Feminist Studies*, 14(29): 7–18.

FURTHER READING

Alaimo, Stacy, and Susan Hekman. 2008. *Material Feminisms.* Bloomington: Indiana University Press.

Hekman, Susan. 2010. *The Material of Knowledge.* Bloomington: Indiana University Press.

Mol, Annette. 2001. *The Body Multiple: Ontology in Medical Practice.* Durham, NC: Duke University Press.

Feminism, Materialist

BRONWYN WINTER
The University of Sydney, Australia

The term "materialist feminism" has been interpreted in various ways, but its common element is a feminist analysis of patriarchal power, and of gender, as the product of social relations (rather than primarily or solely economic, cultural, or discursive). It origins lie in Christine Delphy's 1970s reclaiming and reconfiguration of historical materialism to analyze patriarchal power relations. In this way, materialist feminism both derives from and departs from Marxism. The term was subsequently "revived or perhaps reinvented" (Jackson 2001, 283) in the United States, notably through the work of Hennessy (1993) and Hennessy and Ingraham (1997). Materialist feminism is thus distinct from both Marxist or socialist feminism, and the more recent "material feminism," with which it bears no specific genealogical relation.

In 1970, Christine Delphy published an article titled "L'ennemi principal" ("The Main Enemy") in the French journal *Partisans* (Delphy 1977). In that article, she applied historical materialism – that is, the idea that social relations of domination develop historically through the material process of appropriation by the dominant class of the labor of the dominated class – to the analysis of the appropriation of women by men. She argued that all contemporary societies, including "socialist" ones, depended on the appropriation by men of women's domestic and caring labor, and the "upkeep" provided to women in exchange for this labor is not considered a wage but simply a necessary responsibility in order to ensure that her labor power is maintained. Women's domestic and caring labor is "naturalized" and considered to exist outside the socioeconomic relations of production. Delphy argued that on the contrary, gendered relations are not presocial, nor are they simply a by-product of capitalism, but develop out of social relations in which one class (men) appropriates the lives and labor of another class (women). These relations, being social and produced historically in material conditions, can be changed. Following the publication of *The Main Enemy* in translation in 1977, Delphy was much criticized across the English Channel for adulterating Marxism (Barrett and McIntosh 1979), whereas in fact she was developing a new feminist theory using Marxist methods, providing an analysis of gendered relations as economic, certainly, and cultural, certainly, but above all social.

This analysis was subsequently extended by Colette Guillaumin, who, in a two-part essay published in Issues 2 and 3 of the materialist feminist journal *Questions Féministes* in 1978 and titled "Pratique du pouvoir et idée de Nature" ("Practice of Power and Idea of Nature"), used the term "sexage" (an adaptation of the French term for slavery, "esclavage"), to describe the material relations of the appropriation of women by men. She identified five ways in which this appropriation occurs: appropriation of time; appropriation of the products of women's bodies (childbearing); sexual obligation; and "the physical charge of disabled members of the group (disabled by age – babies, children, old people – or illness and infirmity), as well as the health members of the group of the male sex" (Guillaumin 1995, 181). She further spelled out the means through which this appropriation occurs: the labor market; spatial confinement; show of force; sexual constraint; and "the arsenal of the law and customary rights" (Guillaumin 1995, 196).

Across the Atlantic, the move away from Marxism and modernism by feminist theorists, many of whom had themselves started as Marxist, into postmodernist thinking that privileged the cultural and the contingent over the material and structural, was met by the "reinventing" of materialist feminism. Hennessy (1993) rearticulated materialist feminism as an analysis of gendered social relations as constituted historically by a multiplicity of factors such that the category "woman" is "traversed by more than one differential axis" (p. xii). It continues to differ from Marxist or socialist feminism in that it does not privilege economic relations and from poststructuralist or postmodern feminism in that it does not privilege discourse or cultural construction. At the same time, both Hennessy in her 1993 work and Hennessy and Ingraham in their subsequent work (1997) sought to stress the material foundations of culture and discourse as ideology (cf., Marx's idea of "superstructure"), arguing for a move away from the postmodern preoccupation with representation. The production of the subject and agency, they argued, needed to be linked to the material conditions of the formation of that subject, and not simply considered as the product, and in turn creator, of discourse.

It has also been suggested that radical feminist analyses of the state and critiques of Marxist analyses thereof, such as MacKinnon (1982, 1989), are expressions of materialist feminism in that their core argument is that "sexuality is to feminism what work is to Marxism: that which is most one's own, yet is most taken away" (MacKinnon 1982, 515). This appropriation is institutionalized, culturally, politically, and legally.

More recently, Karen Barad (2007) and others have developed another response to the "cultural turn" in feminist theory through the idea of "material feminism" as related to Barad's concept of "agential realism." Although it does contain an element of analysis of the materiality of women's experience, material feminism does not have any specific genealogical or historical relationship with materialist feminism. The emergence of this later theory and the nomenclature used do, however, add to the confusion that has surrounded the term "materialist feminism." The common denominator of this last, however, is the insistence on the idea that both gender itself and male domination of women – and indeed, the "identities" that result from these processes – are socially and historically constituted, and that the cultural and discursive cannot be separated from the material and from (historical/geographical) context.

There has recently been a resurgence of interest in French materialist feminism, through, for example, a symposium held at Princeton University in November 2014 and a series of panels at the international Francophone feminist research conference at the Université du Québec à Montreal in August 2015. US understandings of materialist feminism are also finding new applications in ethnographic research (e.g., Naples 2007).

SEE ALSO: Feminism, French; Feminism, Material; Feminism, Radical; Feminisms, Marxist and Socialist; Radical Lesbianism

REFERENCES

Barad, Karen. 2007. *Meeting the Universe Halfway: Quantum Physics and the Entanglement of Matter and Meaning*. Durham, NC: Duke University Press.

Barrett, Michèle, and Mary McIntosh. 1979. "Christine Delphy: Towards a Materialist Feminism?" *Feminist Review*, 1: 95–106.

Delphy, Christine. 1977. *The Main Enemy*. London: Women's Research and Resources Centre.

Guillaumin, Colette. 1995. "The Practice of Power and Belief in Nature: Part I: The Appropriation of Women." *Racism, Sexism, Power and Ideology*, 176–207. London: Routledge.

Hennessy, Rosemary. 1993. *Materialist Feminism and the Politics of Discourse*. New York: Routledge.

Hennessy, Rosemary, and Chrys Ingraham, eds. 1997. *Materialist Feminism: A Reader in Class, Difference, and Women's Lives*. New York: Routledge.

Jackson, Stevi. 2001. "Why a Materialist Feminism is (Still) Possible – and Necessary." *Women's Studies International Forum*, 24(3–4): 283–293.

MacKinnon, Catharine A. 1982. "Feminism, Marxism, Method, and the State: An Agenda for Theory." *Signs*, 7(3): 515–544.

MacKinnon, Catharine A. 1989. *Toward a Feminist Theory of the State*. Cambridge, MA: Harvard University Press.

Naples, Nancy A. 2007. "The Social Regulation of Community: an Intersectional Analysis of Migration and Incorporation in the Heartland." *The Journal of Latino-Latin American Studies*, 2(3): 16–23.

FURTHER READING

Jackson, Stevi. 1996. *Christine Delphy*. London: Sage.

Leonard, Diana, and Lisa Adkins. 1996. *Sex in Question: French Materialist Feminism*. London: Taylor and Francis.

Feminism, Multiracial

MICHELE TRACY BERGER
University of North Carolina at Chapel Hill, USA

SILVIA BETTEZ
University of North Carolina at Greensboro, USA

Women of color have always taken active interest in women's issues. However, their experience with feminist work has often been overlooked and is largely undocumented (Hurtado 1996). Multiracial feminism refers to the activist and scholarly work conducted by women of color and anti-racist white allies to promote race, class, and gender equality. In comparison to the highly documented second-wave white, middle-class feminism, which centered on abolishing patriarchy and privileged patriarchy as an oppression over all others, women of color feminism resists separating oppression and insists on recognizing the intersectionality of race, class, and gender oppression.

A metaphor increasingly used to identify the various stages of feminism in the United States has been that of "waves." The first wave denotes the period when white abolitionist women and free black women organized for the right to vote and won passage of the Nineteenth Amendment. The second wave is identified as 1970s feminism, which challenged women's exclusion from the public sphere of employment and politics. The third wave is ongoing and marks the ways in which young women manage some of the social and political freedoms gained from the previous generations. Multiracial feminist organizing and theory building can be identified throughout every historical period of these waves.

Multiracial feminism refers most often to the feminisms of Black/African American, Latina/Chicana, Native American, and Asian American women; however, it includes the voices of anti-racist white women and of all women of color including East Indian women, Arab women, mixed-race women, and women of color not from the United States. Multiracial feminists have often identified themselves under the rubric of "women of color." The identification of women of color as a political, strategic, and subjective identity category is a relatively recent phenomenon. The term "women of color" connotes both affinity and similarity of experience.

To demonstrate an alliance with women of color across the globe and a commitment to postcolonial struggles, in the early 1970s some feminist women of color in the United States began claiming the term "third world women" (Sandoval 1990; Mohanty, Russo, and Torres 1991). Third world feminists used the term to deliberately mark a connection with global women's issues foregrounding colonization, immigration, racism, and imperialism – concerns that many white feminists did not address.

This identification with other women across the globe also encouraged US women of color to acknowledge long traditions of anti-racist collective organizing that was often ignored, suppressed, or obscured during second-wave feminist activism. These conditions helped to solidify the strategic use of the term "women of color" and have supported over the last two decades global organizing in Brazil, England, Africa, Australia, and New Zealand. Aída Hurtado (1996) argues that there are four overarching principles that connect almost all feminists of color: (1) an insistence on recognizing the simultaneity of race, class, and gender oppressions; (2) a claim to their racial group's history as part of their activist legacy, including struggles in their native lands; (3) an understanding that theorizing can emerge from political organizing, everyday interactions, and artistic production as well as the academy; and (4) an opposition to heterosexism in their communities.

Although there are commonalities between multiracial feminists, there are also concentrations on specific topics that distinguish over 30 years of scholarship and activism. Asian American women have documented pervasive and debilitating stereotypes that promote passivity and exoticization, domestic violence, and the US military's role in sex tourism. African American multiracial feminists have consistently called attention to "controlling images" of black female bodies (especially regarding sexuality) that seek to justify disenfranchisement through law, ideology, and social policy. Chicanas and Latinas have often concentrated on immigration, challenging patriarchal definitions of family, the sexual double standard, and critiquing the black/white conceptualization of US racial politics. Sovereignty and land rights, environmental justice, spirituality, and experiences of cultural appropriation and genocide have been primary concerns of Native women who espouse multiracial feminism.

Multiracial feminism is often viewed in contrast and reaction to white, middle-class feminism; however, it is important to recognize that there have often been women of color working within white-dominated feminist groups pushing for a multiracial feminist politic. For example, two African American women, Margaret Sloan and Pauli Murray, helped found the National Organization for Women (NOW) in 1966, and black feminist Doris Wright was a founding member of *Ms. Magazine* in 1972 (Thompson 2001).

Women of color feminists organized around a wide range of public issues historically ignored by white, middle-class feminists. Multiracial feminism addressed reproductive rights, sterilization abuse, welfare rights, police brutality, labor organizing, environmental justice issues, rape, domestic violence, childcare access, school desegregation, prison reform, and affirmative action. To address these public issues, in addition to working in white-dominated groups, women of color also developed their own autonomous feminist organizations and caucuses. These organizations grew out of both civil rights groups and white women's groups. Black women organized in 1973 to create the New York-based National Black Feminist Organization (NBFO) and launched a conference attended by 400 women representing a variety of class backgrounds (Thompson 2001). Additionally, the NBFO inspired the formation of another black feminist group in 1974, the Combahee River Collective, who wrote a now famous statement describing the genesis and politics of black feminism. Other women of color groups that grew out of race-based political organizations include the Third World Women's Alliance, which emerged from the Student Non-Violent Coordinating Committee, the Chicana group Hijas de Cuauhtemoc, founded as an offshoot of the United Mexican American Student Organization, Asian Sisters, which grew out of the Asian American Political Alliance, and Women of All Red Nations (WARN), initiated by members of the American Indian Movement (Thompson 2001). These feminist multiracial groups addressed a multitude of issues related to racism, classism, and sexism that were affecting women of color.

Multiracial feminism came to the fore with the 1981 publication of *This Bridge Called My Back: Writings by Radical Women of Color*, an anthology representing black, Latina/Chicana, Native American, and Asian American women grappling with issues of racism, sexism, homophobia, and classism. The writings reflect women of color activism in previous years. Although there were activist women of color texts preceding *Bridge*, such as the anthology *The Black Woman* by Toni Cade Bambara (1970), the 1980s marked a burgeoning of feminist texts by women of color. In 1983, Barbara Smith published *Home Girls: A Black Feminist Anthology* featuring writings by black feminist activists, and in 1984, Beth Brant published *A Gathering of Spirit: A Collection by North American Indian Women*. All of these texts included the voices of lesbian and feminist women of color, and the second edition of *Bridge*, printed in 1983, provided a largely international perspective expanding the concept of intersectionality from race, class, and gender oppressions to include sexuality and nation.

Simultaneously, there was an explosion of creative work by multiracial feminists that contributed to the vibrancy of the activism of the late 1970s and early 1980s and that expanded the theory building that was taking place in multiple locations (e.g., community centers, conferences, women's centers, educational institutions). Writers of both fiction and non-fiction created academic and popular interest in exploring the multidimensional lives of women of color in ways that had not been previously attempted.

Alice Walker advanced the articulation of multiracial feminism as distinctive, culturally specific, and part of a legacy of social justice. Her groundbreaking book *In Search of My Mother's Gardens* (1983), a collection of essays, introduced the term "womanism." Walker does not reject the term "feminism" but offers a parallel affirmative expression for the multiple and complex ways that women of color view their communities and commitments in those communities. It also explores many facets of life important to women of color that a radical strand of 1970s feminism often eschewed, including spirituality, the suffering of men of color due to racist oppression, and the relationship between art and activism.

Multiracial feminism has been critical in identifying new metaphorical spaces for theory, praxis, healing, and organizing, highlighting the intersection of experience including the concept of "borderlands," "sister outsiders," "new mestizas," and "Woman Warriors" (Sandoval 2000). Transformation of the self is considered important to counteract the reductive and homogenizing tendencies of the uncritical idea of "sisterhood" espoused by white feminists; it can include renaming, recasting, and reclaiming buried components of one's identity. Women of color feminists organizing in early second-wave feminism, whose needs were often marginalized or ignored in both white women organizations and race-based organizations led by men, also emphasized the importance of creating exclusive women of color spaces, as evidenced by *This Bridge Called My Back* and the various women of color caucuses.

Women of color entered into the academy in greater numbers during the 1980s. Many were from activist backgrounds and espoused multiracial feminist viewpoints; they began documenting their experiences challenging prevailing theoretical frameworks. Some scholars revisited the historic tensions of the mainstream feminist movement, arguing for a more relevant analysis applicable to diverse communities. Beginning with her landmark book *Ain't I a Woman? Black Women and Feminism* (1981), bell hooks blended personal narrative, theory, and praxis in a distinctive style. hooks is one of the most prolific and widely read multiracial feminists. Multiracial feminism has changed the landscape of both theory and methods in the social sciences and humanities.

Multiracial feminists have argued that multiple oppressions can combine and create new and often unrecognized forms of encounters in daily life. The concept of "multiple oppressions" and the "intersection of experience" approach have been primarily used to help understand non-dominant groups' experiences navigating the social world. In the last 20 years, activists and theorists located outside the United States have developed these insights to support a global analysis of power and difference.

The call to redefine work through a race, gender, and class analysis has had a significant impact, beginning in women's studies and spiraling out across other fields and disciplines, especially in the field of sociology. Patricia Hill Collins introduced the concept of the "matrix of domination." She argues for viewing race, class, and gender as a central organizing principle that allows scholars to investigate how individuals and groups can simultaneously occupy areas of privilege and domination. Sarah Mann and Michael Grimes note the influence of "intersectional work" in the academy and suggest that its scope is pandisciplinary. Scholars have used the concept of "race, class, and gender" as an interlocking site of oppression, in multiple ways, to create theory as an analytical tool or as a methodological practice (Berger 2004). Research explicitly utilizing intersectional analysis tends to cluster in pockets in a few traditional social science disciplines (sociology, psychology, education) and in multidisciplinary programs including women's studies, ethnic studies, criminology, and environmental studies. Several sociologists have compiled anthologies that examine the intersections of race, class, and gender. Two key texts that provide a conceptual framework for understanding the complex intersections of oppressions have been written by sociologists: *Privilege, Power, and Difference* (2001) by Allan Johnson and *Understanding Race, Class, Gender, and Sexuality: A Conceptual Framework* (2001) by Lynd Weber.

Multiracial feminism is a burgeoning field that centers on the voices of women of color but includes writings by anti-racist white women, women outside the United States, and feminist men of color. Comprehending the intersections of oppressions in order to promote equity across lines of race, class, and gender and nation differences is a key component of multiracial feminism.

Sociologists have contributed greatly to this endeavor. Multiracial feminism offers new formulations about organizing, coalition building, and critical theory production. The field has reached a maturity and sophistication in both activist and scholarly communities, enriching the conceptualization of power, identity, and inequality.

ACKNOWLEDGMENTS

This entry is based in part on a previously published entry by Michele Berger: M. Berger, "Multiracial Feminisms," in G. Ritzer (ed.), *Blackwell Encyclopedia of Sociology*, Blackwell Publishing, UK, 2007. Reproduced with permission.

SEE ALSO: Black Feminist Thought; Feminism, Postcolonial; Feminisms, First, Second, and Third Wave; Feminist Activism; Intersectionality; Matrix of Domination; Subaltern; Third World Women

REFERENCES

Bambara, Toni C., ed. 1970. *The Black Woman: An Anthology*. New York: Washington Square Press.

Berger, Michele. 2004. *Workable Sisterhood: The Political Journey of Stigmatized Women with HIV/AIDS*. Princeton, NJ: Princeton University Press.

Brant, Beth, ed. 1984. *A Gathering of Spirit: A Collection by North American Indian Women*. Ithaca, NY: Firebrand Books.

Hurtado, Aída. 1996. *The Color of Privilege: Three Blasphemies on Race and Feminism*. Ann Arbor: University of Michigan Press.

Mohanty, Chandra T., Ann Russo, and Lourdes Torres, eds. 1991. *Third World Women and the Politics of Feminism*. Bloomington: Indiana University Press.

Sandoval, Chela. 1990. "Feminism and Racism: A Report on the 1981 National Women's Studies Association Conference." In *Making Face, Making Soul/Haciendo Caras: Creative and Critical Perspectives by Feminists of Color*, edited by Gloria Anzaldúa, 55–71. San Francisco: Aunt Lute Foundation Books.

Sandoval, Chela. 2000. *Methodology of the Oppressed*. Minneapolis: University of Minnesota Press.

Smith, Barbara, ed. 1983. *Home Girls: A Black Feminist Anthology*. New York: Kitchen Table Women of Color Press.

Thompson, Becky. 2001. *A Promise and a Way of Life: White Antiracist Activism*. Minneapolis: University of Minnesota Press.

FURTHER READING

Anzaldúa, Gloria. 1987. *Borderlands/La Frontera: The New Mestiza*. San Francisco: Aunt Lute Foundation Books.

Anzaldúa, Gloria, ed. 1990. *Making Face, Making Soul/Haciendo Caras: Creative and Critical Perspectives by Feminists of Color*. San Francisco: Aunt Lute Foundation Books.

Hull, Gloria T., Patricia Bell Scott, and Barbara Smith, eds. 1982. *All the Women Are White, All the Blacks Are Men, But Some of Us Are Brave: Black Women's Studies*. New York: The Feminist Press at the City University of New York.

Moraga, Cherríe, and Gloria Anzaldúa, eds. 1983. *This Bridge Called My Back: Writings by Radical Women of Color*, 2nd ed. New York: Kitchen Table Women of Color Press.

Wong, Diane, and Emilya Cachapero, eds. 1989. *Making Waves: An Anthology of Writings By and About Asian American Women*. Boston: Beacon Press.

Feminism, Nineteenth-Century United States

MICHELE A. ADAMS
Tulane University, USA

The historiography of nineteenth-century US feminism begins necessarily in the contemporary era when the long-term political quest for women's rights gained academic legitimacy. From the vantage point of the second-wave women's movement in the United States, which developed momentum in the 1970s, women's history and concomitant struggle for rights had been essentially invisible (Lerner 1979). Making that history visible and giving a voice to nineteenth-century feminism fell largely to second-wave academic feminists, who did so by defining distinctively women-oriented ways of "seeing" and "knowing." Women's Studies courses blossomed in colleges and universities in the 1970s, and it was within this context that feminist theory, feminist historical methodology, and standpoint epistemology flourished, enabling the "herstory" of movements for women's rights to emerge.

What is history like from women's perspective? Generally speaking, it is broader and more encompassing than its androcentric roots suggest. Wars, conflicts, (male) generals, and (overwhelmingly male) political leaders who masterminded and fought in these conflicts were the primary centerpieces of this earlier history. According to academic feminist theorists like Dorothy Smith (1987), Nancy Hartsock (1983), and Sandra Harding (1986), women's lives are instead grounded in the concrete, local, everyday world, where they were systematically omitted from history. Women's relationships to family and the labor force, their routinized tasks such as childcare, kin-keeping, and housework, have gone unnoticed, unrewarded, and unwritten in the annals of time *because* they circumscribe women's everyday lives. From the standpoint of women, these issues are crucial to an understanding of history – and this recognition encouraged academics to delve into nineteenth-century feminism, grounded as it was in women's everyday relation to family. With this in mind, twentieth-century feminists, particularly those in the academy, began to explore nineteenth-century feminism, intent on "bringing women back in" (DeVault 1999).

The nineteenth-century women's rights movement is considered to be the first wave of feminism in the United States. The movement's beginnings are generally traced to the Seneca Falls Woman's Rights Convention in 1848, with roots extending backward nearly three quarters of a century. Setting the tone for the movement's later emergence, Abigail Adams admonished her husband, John, to "Remember the Ladies" as he helped lay the basic ground rules for the new nation during the 1776 Continental Congress. Noting that "all Men would be tyrants if they could," she suggested that women would "not hold [themselves] bound by any Laws" in which they had no voice (PBS 2005). Nevertheless, in spite of this early support, it would be nearly 150 years before women would be allowed to vote in national elections.

"Feminism" was not a term used by early American pioneers of women's rights. In the United States, the term only came into common usage between the years of 1910 and 1914, tending at first to be deployed largely for its shock value. By about 1913, however, the term had become more widely claimed by women's advocates, male and female alike, who began to see it as epitomizing the modern struggle for women's rights (Cott 1987). In spite of feminism's late entry into the lexicon of the women's rights movement, early advocates shared with later feminists some common grounding beliefs, including equality between women and men.

SOCIAL AND DEMOGRAPHIC CONTEXT: DISORDER REIGNS

The nineteenth century was a time of change in the United States. The transition from rural agrarianism to an increasingly complex urban society with an industrializing "boom-and-bust" economy brought tension and anxiety as well as opportunity. Men and single women sought work in city factories, while married (white, middle-class) women were left to tend the home and children. Associated demographic changes included decreasing marriages and rapidly decreasing marital birthrate, and increased separation and divorce. Juxtaposed with these changes was a rapid acceleration in immigration over the course of the century, which brought new cultural mores to the United States. Nativism tinged with xenophobia linked patriotism with maintenance of the white, middle-class family, culminating in Theodore Roosevelt's expressed fear, in 1907, of the possibility of "race suicide" (Roosevelt 1907) in America, and a eugenics discourse began to suggest that higher class, "native" women were unpatriotic for refusing to have more children (Lindsay 1998). Alongside these demographic changes, increased opportunities for transportation and communication brought people into closer contact with each other and allowed rapid and far-spread dissemination of political, social, and cultural ideas.

DISCURSIVE AND LEGAL CONTEXT

Coverture

The doctrine of coverture, institutionalized in law and grounded in practice, was a vestige of early English common law that survived in the United States into the twentieth century, although its practical force began to diminish with the introduction of women's property laws in the mid-1800s. Pursuant to this doctrine, a woman became a "feme covert" at marriage, essentially assuming the public persona of her husband, who solely represented the family in civil society. In accordance with this doctrine, married women suffered a "civil death" relative to "feme sole," or single women, and could not sue or be sued; nor could they sign contracts, or own, will away, or transfer property in their own names. In effect, the doctrine of coverture rendered a married woman invisible in the public sphere.

Separate spheres and true womanhood

Two distinct, but related, discourses that shaped how women were perceived emerged in the nineteenth century: ideologies of "separate spheres" and "true womanhood." The notion of separate gendered spheres developed in concert with the changes associated with transition to an industrial economy, which ostensibly displaced men from the home into urban factories, making the former the domain of women. Rather than reflecting reality, however, which it did not for many people other than middle-class whites, separate spheres became an ideal around which gender was spatially organized. Men's work in the public sphere became associated with value, importance, and pay, while women's work in the domestic sphere was devalued, ostensibly unimportant, and unpaid. Moreover, the public sphere was identified with the exigencies and problems of the unstable economy, and the private sphere with escape from these problems (Bose 1987). Accordingly, women became responsible for providing men with a haven away from the dysfunction of the public sphere. And as a proscriptive ideology where women were concerned, crossing the boundary into the public sphere meant condemnation and loss of femininity for women.

At the same time, a parallel cultural discourse arose to articulate the characteristics and values delineating what it meant to be a "real" woman. Labeled "true womanhood," this ideology was instrumental in both shaping and controlling nineteenth-century American women by insisting on the immutability of their allegedly intrinsic virtues of religious piety, purity, submissiveness, and domesticity. A true woman, as identified by these virtues, was the one unchanging and stable element in a virtual sea of social instability, and anyone attempting to challenge or alter the ideal of true womanhood was perceived to be an enemy of women, the family, and the state (Welter 1966).

These two discourses, situated in a legal and practical context of coverture, comprised the superstructure on which the representation of women in the nineteenth century was constructed. Moreover, to the extent that this superstructure remained stable, it was seen as the epitome of order during this socially tumultuous century. The nineteenth-century women's rights movement was born and matured in the context of these discourses and learned to first use, then bend, and finally discard them as it sought to gain economic, political, and social rights for women in the public sphere and in the home.

ROOTS OF NINETEENTH-CENTURY FEMINISM

John Adams reportedly dismissed his wife's admonition to "remember the ladies," failing to take her seriously (Evans 1989). Even though the American Declaration of Independence encouraged many women to begin seeing themselves as autonomous and equal citizens, female autonomy was not a widely held belief or value. Women were perceived as second-class citizens, whose citizenship status was tied to their relationship to the home and family. The perception that "true" women belonged in the domestic sphere generally precluded them from using public lectures, the pulpit, or other such venues that might allow them to spread their argument for equal citizenship.

One way that even "true women" could enter the public sphere, however, involved simultaneously solidifying and blurring the boundaries between public and private spheres. The concept of republican motherhood incorporated the attitude that the duty of nineteenth-century mothers was to raise good moral (male) citizens, and that, in fact, mothers' domestic roles could and should be exploited to promote these public values (Kerber 1980). As the eighteenth century transitioned to the nineteenth, and demographic, cultural, and economic changes increased the perception of social disorder, republican motherhood took on increased significance and mothers began to take to the public sphere in the name of their families. Essentially, in their role as republican mothers, by re-envisioning the domestic sphere to incorporate the public realm, women began to gain a tentative foothold in the political domain of nineteenth-century America.

Republican motherhood took different forms during the first half of the century, encouraging women, doing their civic duty on behalf of their families, to move into teaching, religion, and religiously oriented benevolence causes such as those dealing with temperance, prostitution, and abolitionism. Nevertheless, public approbation of women's move into the public sphere, even in the name of motherhood and domesticity, was far from complete, with many seeing it as another intrusion on the social order. Initially acceptable for women to preach or give public lectures to other women, it was still a breach of womanly virtue for women to speak publicly to a mixed audience. Thus, when women such as Southern sisters Sarah and Angelina Grimké, as the first women to serve as agents for the American Anti-Slavery Society, spoke to mixed public crowds in New York and Boston for the abolitionist cause, they were continually forced to defend their right, as women, to speak in public (McGlen and O'Connor 1995).

Nevertheless, the abolitionist movement, in particular, provided a solid training ground and a point of comparison for those interested in promoting women's full political citizenship. Early feminists such as Angelina and Sarah Grimké, Lucretia Mott, Elizabeth Cady Stanton, Susan B. Anthony, and Lucy Stone, among many others, cut their teeth as anti-slavery proponents and were welcomed as active participants to the abolitionist cause. Thus, in 1840, when Elizabeth Cady Stanton and Lucretia Mott traveled to London with their husbands as delegates to the World Anti-Slavery Convention, they were stunned to be rejected as speakers because of their sex and forced to sit with other women, their seats demurely tucked behind a curtain. Once again, they were reminded that "true women" abstained from public participation. Angered, Stanton and Mott vowed to assemble a congress of women to address these inequities. Eight years later, in July of 1848, that congress was convened in Stanton's home town of Seneca Falls, New York.

SENECA FALLS AND BEYOND

In 1848, the "First Woman's Rights Convention" met in Seneca Falls, New York. Although hastily convened and poorly advertised, the conference brought together over 200 women and 40 men to consider the radical proposition that "all men and women are created equal" (Evans 1989, 95). In deference to the mixed crowd, James Mott, Lucretia's husband, led the assemblage. One of the centerpieces of the conference was the "Declaration of Sentiments and Grievances," written by Elizabeth Cady Stanton to enumerate a series of injustices that had been historically inflicted on women. The Declaration ended with a call to action, asking women to organize and petition for their rights. Included was a series of 11 propositions itemizing the various rights for which women might aim. The Declaration of Sentiments was signed by 68 of the women and 32 of the men present, and 10 of the 11 proposed statements of rights passed the assembled group with little opposition.

The only proposition that met with significant opposition was proposition nine, which called for women's enfranchisement. Opposed by Lucretia Mott, this proposition was seen as too radical. Ultimately, after Frederick Douglass, the only African American in attendance, voiced his support for the proposition, it, too, passed. Thus, the convention provided the initial volley in the women's suffrage movement, which ended 72 years later with ratification of the Nineteenth Amendment to the Constitution enfranchising women.

In 1848, the New York Married Women's Property Act, another event of significance for women's rights, was passed. Married women's property laws, although generally unrelated to petitioning by feminists, were largely intended to protect families from profligate men, and, by extension, the state from having to care for indigent families. Because coverture deemed that property brought to marriage by a woman became the husband's property, when he became indebted the property was subject to confiscation by debtors. Married women's property laws provided a partial corrective to this problem by preserving wives' prior-owned property outside of the husband's control. While not the first of its kind, the New York state law was one of the most comprehensive of the early married women's property acts passed, taking account of both real and personal property brought to the marriage by the wife. Importantly, this law served as a model for other states. While this law gave married women sole ownership of their separate property, it did not yet give them control over it, which was to come in a separate married women's property act passed by the New York legislature in 1860. Married women's property acts created a chink in the armor of the doctrine of coverture but much work remained for organized women's rights groups.

The Seneca Falls Woman's Rights Convention was the first organized meeting of advocates for women's rights, but other meetings quickly followed. Two weeks after Seneca Falls, a regional meeting was held in Rochester, New York, where it was decided that yearly conferences would be held around the country to continue discussions on women's rights and enfranchisement. Starting in 1850 and continuing through 1860, annual meetings of the National Women's Rights Convention were held in various locations. Nevertheless, no national associations of women's rights advocates were created prior to the Civil War, when annual meetings were halted for the war's duration.

In 1869, two rival national groups formed to address the issue of women's suffrage, with differences between the two focused on strategy and tone. One group, the National Woman Suffrage Association (NWSA) was founded by Elizabeth Cady Stanton and Susan B. Anthony, who were intent on pursuing a national constitutional amendment to enfranchise women. NWSA, however, saw the vote as only one aspect of its work. Following in the footsteps of the Seneca Falls Woman's Rights Convention of 1848, NWSA also advocated for women's rights in the workplace and the home, as well as education for women. Over the next several years, NWSA's reputation as a radical group increased, as it became associated with Victoria Woodhull and the "free love" movement, as well as litigation on behalf of the franchise. Losing members as a result, the group toned down some of its rhetoric on controversial issues such as divorce, all the while continuing to advocate for a constitutional amendment to enfranchise women. In 1877, Elizabeth Cady Stanton drafted a constitutional amendment to give women the vote. Every year, until its passage in 1919, this amendment was presented to the national legislature.

The second group, founded in 1869 by Lucy Stone, was the American Woman Suffrage Association (AWSA). Taking a more conservative approach than NWSA, this group's sole focus was the franchise, which it felt could best be accomplished by a state-to-state approach rather than a national constitutional amendment. NWSA and AWSA worked largely at odds over the years, as AWSA attempted to distance itself from what it considered the radical nature of NWSA's strategies and issues. Eventually, however, the two groups negotiated to work out common ground, merging to form the National American Woman Suffrage Association in 1890 (McGlen and O'Connor 1995).

Because women's enfranchisement was not immediately forthcoming, nineteenth-century feminism is often considered to have been a failure. Nevertheless, the movement alleviated a number of grievances exposed during the Seneca Falls Convention of 1848. Over the course of the last half of the nineteenth century, coverture was disrupted, grounds for divorce were expanded, women's property laws were passed, previously closed occupations were opened to women, and more women than ever before were becoming educated. Importantly, the women's movement had unsettled the ideologies of separate spheres and true womanhood, such that by the end of the nineteenth century, American women's participation in the public sphere was seen as normal and not intrinsically detrimental to their womanhood. Notably, however, nineteenth-century feminism was a movement of white, middle-, and upper-class women for white, middle-, and upper-class women. Crossing lines of race and class, as well as gender, remained for twentieth-century feminists to pursue.

SEE ALSO: Cult of Domesticity; Declaration of Sentiments; Feminisms, First, Second, and Third Wave; Feminist Consciousness in Historical Perspective; Private/Public Spheres

REFERENCES

Bose, Christine. 1987. "Dual Spheres." In *Analyzing Gender: A Handbook of Social Science Research*, edited by Beth B. Hess and Myra Marx Ferree, 267–285. Newbury Park, CA: Sage.

Cott, Nancy F. 1987. *The Grounding of Modern Feminism*. New Haven, CT: Yale University Press.

DeVault, Marjorie. 1999. *Liberating Method: Feminism and Social Research*. Philadelphia: Temple University Press.

Evans, Sara M. 1989. *Born for Liberty: A History of Women in America*. New York: Free Press.

Harding, Sandra. 1986. *The Science Question in Feminism*. Ithaca, NY: Cornell University Press.

Hartsock, Nancy. 1983. "The Feminist Standpoint: Developing the Ground for a Specifically Feminist Historical Materialism." In *Discovering Reality: Feminist Perspectives on Epistemology, Metaphysics, Methodology and Philosophy of Science*, edited by Sandra Harding and Merrill B. Hintikka, 283–310. Dordrecht, The Netherlands: Kluwer.

Kerber, Linda. 1980. *Women of the Republic: Intellect and Ideology in Revolutionary America*. Chapel Hill: University of North Carolina Press.

Lerner, Gerda. 1979. *The Majority Finds its Past: Placing Women in History*. New York: Oxford University Press.

Lindsay, Matthew J. 1998. "Reproducing a Fit Citizenry: Dependency, Eugenics, and the Law of Marriage in the United States, 1860–1920." *Law and Social Inquiry*, 23: 541–583.

McGlen, Nancy E., and Karen O'Connor. 1995. *Women, Politics, and American Society*. Englewood Cliffs, NJ: Prentice Hall.

PBS. 2005. "Abigail Adams' 'Remember the Ladies' Letter." Accessed April 14, 2014, at http://www.pbs.org/wgbh/amex/adams/filmmore/ps_ladies.html.

Roosevelt, Theodore. 1907. "A Letter from President Roosevelt on Race Suicide." *The American Monthly Review of Reviews*, 35: 550–551.

Smith, Dorothy. 1987. *The Everyday World as Problematic: A Feminist Sociology*. Boston: Northeastern University Press.

Welter, Barbara. 1966. "The Cult of True Womanhood: 1820–1860." *American Quarterly*, 18(2, part 1): 151–174.

FURTHER READING

DuBois, Ellen Carol. 1998. *Woman Suffrage and Women's Rights*. New York: New York University.

Kraus, Natasha Kirsten. 2008. *A New Type of Womanhood: Discursive Politics and Social Change in Antebellum America*. Durham, NC: Duke University Press.

National Park Service. 2014. "Women's Rights: Signers of the Declaration of Sentiments." Accessed April 20, 2014, at http://www.nps.gov/wori/historyculture/signers-of-the-declaration-of-sentiments.htm.

Feminism in North Africa

NADA MUSTAFA ALI
University of Massachusetts Boston, USA

"Feminism" is a contested term in the diverse countries of North Africa (Algeria, Egypt, Libya, Mauritania, Morocco, Sudan, Somalia, and Tunisia). While one of the oldest women's organizations in the subregion is the Egyptian Feminist Union, founded by Huda Shaarawi in 1923, and some of the organizations and activists in the region increasingly identify as feminists, others avoid the term, which is associated with negative stereotypes about Western feminisms. This tendency, which is also rooted in histories of British, French, and Italian colonialism, anti-colonial struggles, and anxieties arising from the region's precarious position globally, started to change gradually in the late 1980s and especially in the 1990s, when women's organizations and activists in the region strengthened their links with other feminist organizations worldwide. This impacted women's activism, and gender, feminist, and women's studies and pedagogies.

There is no consensus on the translation of "feminism" into Arabic, the official language in countries of North Africa. Feminist scholars and activists from across the Middle East and North Africa (MENA) spent hours discussing possible translations for "feminism" and "gender" in meetings organized in Cairo, Egypt by the Aisha regional network in the run-up to the United Nations Fourth Conference on Women. A common translation is *Niswya*, a word derived from *Niswa* (women), but some activists and scholars prefer to use the term "feminist" to avoid confusion. Others define themselves as *Genderyat* (gender*ists*) to emphasize their commitment to gender equality while also endorsing aspects of cultures that do not discriminate against women. Nonetheless, it is possible to describe many forms of intellectual and literary production and mobilization around women's human rights and gender equality in the region as feminist, if one defines feminism as the recognition that women face oppression and discrimination, and a determination to challenge oppression and transform gender relations (preferably through collective action).

Feminisms in North Africa are diverse, but it is possible to identify similarities that often shape the priorities and the dynamics of interaction within and between feminist and women's mobilizations in the subregion.

There is a tradition of women's direct or indirect leadership in some of the subregion's ancient civilizations, such as the Nubian civilization in Egypt and Sudan, where the *Kandace* queens assumed high leadership positions. Countries also share a history of British, French, or Italian colonialism, and a significant but often underdocumented role for women in anti-colonial struggles. While the role of *Mujahidat* (women fighters) in Algeria's anti-colonial armed struggle is well documented, for example, Somali women's roles (along with their resistance poetry) in mobilizing people and resources for the Somali Youth League, founded in 1943, is absent from the historical record.

Feminisms in the subregion operate in the context of what Sharabi (1992) called neopatriarchal states (regardless of the ideology of the regime in power), societies, and cultures: the result of the encounter between modernity and traditionalism in the context of dependent development.

Modern women's organizing in most North African countries emerged alongside anti-colonial national liberation struggles in the 1920s in Egypt, and in the 1950s in countries such as Sudan and Algeria. Generally, women activists and organizations prioritized national liberation and development, or approached women's human rights in light of broader socioeconomic and political questions. An example of the former approach is Algeria, where veteran Djamila Bouhired said at independence: "The young women of Algeria do not have time to discuss the problems of sex right now. We are still in a struggle to make our new country work, to rebuild the destroyed family, to preserve our identity as a nation" (quoted in Charrad 2001, 188). Algeria did not have an independent women's movement demanding women's human rights until the 1980s. In Egypt, Nabawiyya Musa published *Al-Mar'awa al-Amal* (Woman and Labor) in 1920, in which she contested views that objected to women's work in Egypt, and also challenged Western stereotypes about Arab women (Shaaban 2003, 13). Male feminist scholars such as Qasim Amin (1863–1908), who wrote *Tahrir al-Mar'ah* (Women's Liberation) in 1899 and *The New Woman* in 1900/1, discussed women's liberation.

At independence, feminist and women's movements in the subregion prioritized family law reform. Women's organizations also campaigned for suffrage and equal labor rights, and against harmful cultural practices such as female genital cutting and early marriage. Egypt has a long tradition of women's and feminist activism. Nasser's regime expanded education and employment for women. The country elected its first woman member of parliament (MP) in 1952. In Sudan, educated women formed several associations in the run-up to independence. In 1952, the Sudanese Women's Union (SWU) was established. The Union became increasingly associated with the Communist Party of the Sudan. With other women activists, it pressured successive postcolonial governments to secure women's right to vote (which women in Sudan won in 1965, after the overthrow of Sudan's first military rule through a popular uprising in 1964). Sudan elected its first woman MP, Fatima Ahmed Ibrahim, in the same year. The SWU demanded equal pay for equal work and favorable work conditions, including an hour's break during the day for lactating mothers.

In Libya, women gained suffrage in 1964. In 1969, a military coup replaced the ruling feudal monarchy with an authoritarian state that emphasized women's education and public roles. The country became a signatory to the Convention on the Elimination of All Forms of Discrimination against Women (CEDAW) in 1989 (Skaine 2008, 69). In Mauritania, although women won the right to vote in 1961, the first woman MP was elected in 1975 (Skaine 2008, 70). Historically, women's rights activism in the country lacked exposure. Despite a more visible role for women in government, the military coup of 2008 has restricted women's activism in a country where women face challenges of poverty, early and forced marriage, lack of access to education, and slavery. The Association des Femmes Chefs de Famille (AFCF) advocates for women's human rights and works to empower divorced women and widows. The organization also campaigns for higher participation for women. It runs literacy classes for girls, and supports cooperatives. AFCF formed a network of Mauritanian women's rights organizations to campaign for changing family law and to effect other policy changes. The Advocacy Initiatives Group for Women's Political Participation (G13PF) also advocates for women's participation in politics.

Morocco, Algeria, and Tunisia followed different paths regarding commitment to women's human rights, expressed, for example, in personal status laws after independence. Because Morocco's postcolonial government was allied with tribal kin groups, it adopted a conservative family law. Feminist activism by organizations such as l'Union d'action feminine and the Democratic Association of Moroccan Women (ADFM) resulted in a more progressive family law in 2004 (Moghadam 2015, 4). A coalition sought to implement Morocco's labor law. A network of feminist and human rights organizations has campaigned for a law to criminalize gender-based and sexual violence. The country elected its first female MP in 1993. However, following strong mobilization on women's participation in 2002, the country adopted a national list of 30 women for the legislative elections. Moroccan feminists such as Fatema Mernissi have produced sophisticated feminist literature that impacted the Maghreb region and beyond. Ethnic difference has marked feminist struggles. Berber women's organizations have developed a unique voice and organization (Sayigh 2003, 5).

In Algeria, a weak alliance between the ruling National Liberation Front (FLN) and tribal kin groups at independence resulted in a conservative family law despite the FLN paying lip service to women's liberation. Algeria elected its first woman MP in 1964. In 2012, after the introduction of a quota system, women won 31 percent of parliamentary seats, the highest in the region. Political liberalization in the 1980s and elections in 1991 brought the Islamic Salvation Front (FIS) to power. A 7-year insurgency resulted in over 100,000 deaths. In recognition of the role of feminist organizations in fighting Islamism, Algerian president Bouteflika appointed five well-known feminists to his cabinet.

Tunisia's postcolonial state, which developed in relative autonomy from tribal kin groups, recognized women's citizenship rights and developed a family law that expanded women's rights. Tunisia elected its first woman MP in 1959 and has historically had high participation of women in parliament and in government positions. Tunisia is home to pioneering activism on lesbian, gay, bisexual, and transsexual (LGBT) rights. Chouf, a coalition of multimedia activists, fights discrimination against women who have sex with women, and aims to ensure the safety of LGBT communities. Along with organizations in Egypt, Sudan, and elsewhere in the region, Chouf seeks to decriminalize LGBT activities, and to change negative perceptions about LGBTs.

In Somalia, Siyad Barre's military socialist rule introduced laws and policies that safeguarded women's rights, but did not undertake groundwork to change norms that sanctioned discrimination against women. In addition, the regime established its own Somali Women's Democratic Organization, but banned independent organizing. After the overthrow of Barre and the start of the civil war in the early 1990s, a vibrant women's movement emerged in the country and in exile.

Women's organizations working in the area of development proliferated in the 1980s. The United Nations Decade for Women and successive UN conferences offered networking and other opportunities for movement-building. Much of this activism, however, was depoliticized. It sought to insert women into development programs that were not gender-sensitive. A focus on project-based donor support deprived organizations of setting independent agendas and developing long-term visions and programs.

Politicized feminist mobilizations emerged out of discontent with the gendered politics of postcolonial regimes. Many initiatives started as study groups that developed into organizations committed to changing gender relations, and focused on taboo issues such as sexuality, honor, and religion. Egyptian Nawal El-Saadawi, and Moroccan Fatema Mernissi, who authored influential books, both formed organizations. El-Saadawi's Arab Women Solidarity Association (AWSA) was banned for several years. Egyptian left-leaning women university graduates founded the New Woman Research Center. The Egyptian Center for Women's Rights provides services that are linked to law reform and efforts to end gender-based violence, such as providing legal counseling for women. The same organization conducts research on sexual harassment. Tunisian feminists formed Women for Research and Development and the Association of Democratic Tunisian Women in the 1980s. Left-leaning activists in Sudan founded Al-Manar in the early 1990s, to address the impact of Islamism on women, campaign for legal reform, and provide paralegal and other support for women. The Gender Center addresses women's participation and human rights, and the former Salmma Women's Center and Ru'ya worked on sexuality and gender-based violence, among other issues. Organizations in exile worked to influence the agenda of Sudan's opposition from a women's rights perspective.

While most of the predominantly male ruling elites in the subregion identify as Arab and Muslim, the region hosts diverse ethnic, religious, and cultural groups. This, and sexuality, social class, and regional location (rural/urban), also form bases for inequality. Suppression of difference has resulted in protracted conflicts in countries such as Sudan and Morocco. These have affected women and men in distinct ways, and have given rise to strong women's peace movements, committed to social change. Based in Puntland, the Somali We Are Women Activists campaigns for women's human rights and participation at all levels, including in peace negotiations. Community Organization for Relief and Development, also in Puntland, aims to eliminate female genital cutting and to promote girls' education. The Somali Women Development Center empowers women and girls. In South Sudan, the Sudanese Women's Voice for Peace highlighted the plight of women affected by war, and campaigned for meaningful women's participation in peace negotiations.

Organizations and movements in the region face numerous challenges. *Al-Raida*, journal of the Institute for Women's Studies in the Arab World, devoted its 2003 centenary issue to Arab Women's Movements. Feminist scholars and activists argued that key challenges included the women's movement's failure to become an effective political force, the "NGOization" of the women's movement, a tendency of some women's organizations to reproduce hierarchies in their societies, and the lack of opportunities for collective action between feminist movements in the Arab Mashreq and the Maghreb (although the Aisha network, and Mashreq/Maghreb, offered a common platform for feminists and women's movements from across the MENA region). Another challenge has been the focus on policy and development research at the expense of politicized feminist intellectual and theoretical production, a shortcoming that journals such as *Feminist Africa* and the *Journal of Middle East Women's Studies* (JMEWS) have sought to address. Both offer fora for publishing research on and by feminist scholars and activists from across North Africa, but especially Egypt, Morocco, and Sudan. Women's studies or research centers at the University of Khartoum and Ahfad University for Women (Sudan), the American University in Cairo (Egypt), the University of Fes (Morocco), and the African Gender Institute (South Africa) offer pedagogies that draw upon different feminist theories and methodologies, taking into account the specificity of the region. These pedagogies often inform feminist activisms.

Feminists and women's rights activists played important roles in mobilizing for the popular protests that expanded from Tunisia to Egypt, Libya, other countries in the MENA region and globally in 2010 and 2011. The overthrow of long-standing dictatorships in Tunisia, Egypt, and Libya not only opened up spaces for activism in these and other countries, they also instigated constitutional and legal reform in countries such as Morocco, where the Association of Democratic Moroccan Women launched initiatives to discuss ways to ensure the changes also result in gender equality.

The euphoria of the Arab Spring has given way to general violence and a backlash against women's rights in parts of the subregion. Elections brought to power politicized Islamist movements that have utilized the atmosphere of dictatorship, economic crises, youth unemployment and inequalities, and corruption, to expand, especially among the urban poor since the early 1980s. The ideologies of these movements often undermined women's human rights and gender equality. In most countries, women's rights were "the first concessions Arab regimes [made] to fundamentalist pressures" (Traboulsi 2003, 19). Nonetheless, although Islamist movements and regimes have enjoyed the support of women (including educated, middle-class women), women's organizations in Algeria, Sudan, Egypt, and Somalia were key to opposing extremism.

Women's collective resistance to extremism is a cause for optimism, and so is the collective strategizing to ensure changes in the region do not reproduce gender inequalities. Tunisian feminists organized a protest upon the return of the leader of *Annahda* Islamic party from exile in January 2011; they also protested the party's attempts to change the gender equality clause in the Tunisian constitution. The Women and Memory Forum, the New Woman Foundation, and Nazra for Feminist Studies in Egypt have been documenting the gender-specific impact of change on women and girls. In Sudan, the former Salmma Women's Centre, and Ahfad University for Women, challenged gender-based violence and restrictions on women's dress and movement by dancing collectively in a vast but contained space as part of the One Million Rise global movement. Al-Karama, a regional movement, continues to strengthen the capacities of women and men from across the subregion to support peace-building and transformation in women's human rights.

SEE ALSO: Arab Spring Movements; Convention on the Elimination of All Forms of Discrimination against Women (CEDAW); Female Genital Cutting; Feminism, Islamic; Gender, Politics, and the State in Northern Africa; LGBT Activism in Northern Africa; Nationalism and Gender; Pacifism, Peace Activism, and Gender; Women's and Feminist Activism in Northern Africa

REFERENCES

Al-Raida. 2003. "Interviews: Current Challenges Facing the Arab Women's Movement." *Al-Raida*, special issue on Arab Women's Movements, 20(100).

Charrad, Mounira. 2001. *Women's Rights and the Making of Postcolonial Tunisia, Algeria, and Morocco*. Berkeley: University of California Press.

Moghadam, Valentine. 2015. "Women's/Feminist Activism in North Africa." Accessed March 10, 2015, at http://nuweb.neu.edu/cssh/wp-content/uploads/2013/08/Moghadam-Feminist-Activism-in-North-Africa-final-May-2014-2.pdf.

Sayigh, Rosemary. 2003. "Arab Women's Movements: Late Subjects of History." *Al-Raida*, 20(100): 4–9.

Shaaban, Bouthaina. 2003. "Preparing the Way: Early Arab Women Feminist Writers." *Al-Raida*, 20(100): 10–14.

Sharabi, Hisham. 1992. *Neopatriarchy: A Theory of Distorted Change in Arab Society*. Oxford: Oxford University Press.

Skaine, Rosemarie. 2008. *Women Political Leaders in Africa*. Jefferson: McFarland & Co.

Traboulsi, Fawwaz. 2003. "An Intelligent Man's Guide to Modern Arab Feminism." *Al-Raida*, 20(100): 15–19.

FURTHER READING

Al-Ali, N. 2002. *Secularism, Gender and the State in the Middle East: The Egyptian Women's Movement*. Cambridge: Cambridge University Press.

Ali, Nada M. 2015. *Gender, Race, and Sudan's Exile Politics: Do We All Belong to This Country?* Lanham: Lexington Books.

Cheref, Abdelkader. 2010. *Gender and Identity in North Africa: Postcolonialism and Feminism in Maghrebi Women's Literature*. London: I. B. Tauris.

Gray, Doris. 2012. *Beyond Feminism and Islamism: Gender and Equality in North Africa*. London: I. B. Tauris.

Mahmoud, Maimuna. 2014. *Women's Movements in Somalia*. Mogadishu, Somalia: The Heritage Institution for Policy Studies.

Moghadam, Valentine. 1993. *Modernizing Women: Gender and Social Change in the Middle East*. Boulder, CO: Lynne Rienner.
Sadiqi, Fatima. 2010. "Domestic Violence in the African North." *Feminist Africa*, 14: 49–62.
Sadiqi, Fatima. 2014. *Moroccan Feminist Discourses*. New York: Palgrave Macmillan.
Warsame, Fatima. 2015. "May 15, 1943: History Was Made in Somalia and Somali Women Were at the Heart of It." Accessed May 29, 2015, at http://fatimawarsame.tumblr.com/post/50561588854/may-15-1943-history-was-made-in-somalia-somali.

Feminism in Northeast Asia

BARBARA MOLONY
Santa Clara University, USA

Feminism in Northeast Asia has been intertwined with nationalism and the construction of gender by both the state and activists seeking a role in the modern state since the late nineteenth century. At the same time, Asian feminists were also closely tied to transnational feminist organizations such as the Woman's Christian Temperance Union (WCTU), Women's International League for Peace and Freedom (WILPF), and the Young Women's Christian Association (YWCA) before World War II. Those groups offered inspiration to Asian women's rights advocates and, in some cases, gave them a platform to influence ideas and discourses when it was difficult to do so in their home countries.

JAPAN

While Japan was not colonized in the late nineteenth century, it was subjected to unequal treaties and discriminatory treatment by Western powers. In response, the government and ordinary Japanese proposed a wide variety of legal, social, political, and economic changes to improve Japan's status in Western eyes. At times, the government's goals paralleled those of Japan's early feminists; for instance, both recognized the importance of education for women. But the national education system, which segregated boys and girls after sixth grade, educated girls as "good wives and wise mothers" who would, as productive wives, serve their families and the state and, as wise mothers, educate the next generation of boys to serve the nation. Feminists, on the other hand, saw women's education as advancing women's rights and permitting women themselves to serve the nation.

Japan's first movement for constitutional and civil rights emerged in the 1870s (Molony 2005). Its predominantly male activists were joined by a few women. In 1878, when prefectural assemblies were first elected, taxpaying widow Kusunose Kita (1836–1920) was lauded for her (unfortunately unsuccessful) effort to gain the vote. In the early 1880s, Kishida Toshiko (1861?–1901) inspired a generation of women with her speeches calling for equal rights, especially in marriage, to liberate women and strengthen Japan as a nation. Women's legal status was significantly inferior to men's in the pre-World War II era, and feminists struggled to improve it. Men were permitted to have concubines, and they enjoyed absolute priority in inheritance. Wives had no legal right of contract. The Public Peace Police Laws of 1890 and 1900 prohibited women from speaking at political rallies and joining political parties. This impeded feminists' organizing to improve women's status.

But even without an actual voice, women could use the printed word and they could join organizations that were reformist or religious rather than overtly political. The Women's Reform Society (WRS; Japan's branch of the transnational WCTU) was founded in 1886 (Lublin 2010). The WRS worked to end international sex trafficking, licensed prostitution within Japan, and marital inequality, contending that these practices damaged Japan's international reputation. The government viewed the WRS actions as reformist rather than political, and thus permitted them. (After World War I, the WRS became more overtly feminist-suffragist.) Socialist feminists had to maintain a lower profile than the middle-class Christian women of the WRS, but they, too, found ways to influence opinion. In the first decade of the twentieth century, socialist Fukuda Hideko (1865–1927) published a feminist newspaper, and other socialists appealed to the Japanese Diet to revise the Public Peace Police Laws to allow women to organize (Mackie 2003).

The Japanese cultural world took a feminist turn in the second decade of the twentieth century. Women entered the classroom as teachers, nurses served on the battlefield and in hospitals, actresses performed shocking plays like *A Doll's House*, and women poets and prose writers found wide audiences for their works. Though most girls were not educated beyond the sixth grade, literacy rates were high. Bicycles and trains gave both men and women mobility. Most Japanese women, unlike many Chinese and Korean women, had not been limited to the home and its environs in the premodern period, but modern forms of transportation brought many women and men together for the first time.

In 1911, Hiratsuka Raichō (1886–1972) founded the feminist Bluestocking Society. In the first issue of its journal, *Bluestocking*, Hiratsuka published an essay dubbed "the Feminist Manifesto," calling on women to reclaim their former status and brilliance through the written word. Soon, other magazines joined *Bluestocking* in appealing to women. In the mid-1910s, four feminist women, one of them Hiratsuka, engaged in a lively debate in the pages of these journals over "motherhood protection" (Rodd 1991). The debaters contested whether mothers should be financially independent before having children or be supported by their husbands or the state for their service through producing children. One debater, a socialist, claimed those positions were all "bourgeois" and that mothers could not be "protected" in the absence of a socialist revolution. By World War I, then, Japanese feminisms were nuanced and varied, but two results emerged from the debate: mothers came to be privileged over fathers (previously, fathers had often been viewed as superior at childrearing); and motherhood came to be seen as a justification for women's civil rights.

Many of these women in the public sphere were called "New Women," so it is no surprise that an explicitly feminist/women's rights organization, founded in 1919 by Hiratsuka, Oku Mumeo (1895–1997), and Ichikawa Fusae (1893–1981), called itself the New Women's Association (NWA; Molony 2004). The NWA fought for a repeal of the ban on women's participation in public political rallies (they won this in 1922) and for a woman's right to leave a marriage or engagement if her husband or fiancé had syphilis (they failed to achieve this). When the Tokyo-area earthquake killed 100,000 people and destroyed millions of homes and businesses in 1923, women's organizations of all types – Christian, Buddhist, alumnae organizations, housewives, and socialists – coalesced to carry out earthquake relief. The following year, several of those groups decided to address women's political rights. The Women's Suffrage League (WSL), which grew from this collaboration in 1924 and was led by Ichikawa Fusae, was the leading suffrage organization in the prewar period. Additional women's organizations supported votes for women; some of them criticized Ichikawa and the WSL for campaigning for supporters of women's rights, regardless of their positions on other issues. Ichikawa, influenced by America's Alice Paul, whom she met while in Washington, DC, stressed the importance of full civil rights over other issues.

While Japanese militarism at home and abroad repressed freedom of expression, feminist groups continued to meet throughout the 1930s. Annual All-Japan Women's Suffrage Conferences brought together women of diverse organizations from 1930 to 1937. The 1930 Conference persuaded the House of Representatives to pass a limited suffrage bill, although the more conservative House of Peers rejected it. The rise of militarism after the Manchurian Incident (1931), however, stifled the quest for the vote. The annual Conferences protested Japanese expansionism until 1934, when doing so became risky. In the 1920s and early 1930s, Japanese feminists had also made their voices heard through transnational organizations in which they played a significant role, including WILPF, YWCA, WCTU, and the Pan-Pacific Women's Association. For example, they delivered petitions for peace with 750,000 women's signatures to the male government delegates at the London Conference of 1930 (Molony 2010). In the late 1930s, feminists turned to community activism (like improving municipal utilities) and non-threatening feminist legislation (the Mother–Child Protection Law in 1937 that supported single mothers with children under 13). But seen as too Western and individualistic, suffrage was not granted until 1945.

During World War II, many feminists accepted government advisory positions to improve the lives of women and families, viewing this as a step toward greater political integration. By the 1980s, historians and feminists strongly critiqued Japanese feminists for collaboration with the wartime government; this has continued to be a major issue in the history of Japanese feminisms.

Within days of the end of World War II, Ichikawa reestablished the WSL. She visited Prime Minister Shidehara in October 1945, and he agreed to grant women the vote. The US military occupation forces concurred; women voted for the first time in 1946. In 1947, the new Constitution stipulated equal rights, the new Civil Code eradicated most – though not all – of the patriarchal provisions of the 1898 Civil Code, and the Labor Standards Law called for equal pay for equal work. Despite these laws, women continued to face discrimination, and feminist groups continued their struggles. They succeeded in ending licensed prostitution (1956), persuaded the government to allow Japanese mothers not married to Japanese nationals to pass their nationality on to their children (only fathers could do so before 1984) and to change education policy that required only girls to take home economics (1993), and forced the ending of "sex tours" to other countries in East Asia (1980s). Feminists supported the UN's International Women's Year (1975) with vigor and tried to force the government to pass a more rigorous employment law than the 1986 Equal Employment Opportunity Law (Molony 1995). Since then, strengthened employment and childcare leave laws have been passed. Gender-neutral education strategies are hotly contested. Academic feminism has taken off in every discipline (some academic feminists, like Ueno Chizuko, are also activists). Women play a significant role in the arts and culture. But Japan still lags behind most advanced industrial countries in pay equality and the percentage of public offices filled by women.

KOREA

A decade of international pressure in the 1860s and 1870s forced the Korean monarchy to open the country to trade and cross-cultural contact. Beginning with a treaty with Japan (1876), Korea signed a series of unequal treaties with Western powers. Korean reformers, mostly young men who had studied in Japan in the 1870s, called on the monarchy to face imperialist challenges by modernizing schools, international relations, national defense, hygiene, and government and attempted a coup (Kapsin Incident of 1884) to force the government to make those changes. When they failed, some activists were executed and others went into temporary exile in Japan or the United States. While in Japan, Pak Yŏng-hyŏ (1861–1939) became a strong advocate for equal rights for women and, linking feminism and nationalism, petitioned Korea's King Kojong to eliminate gender and class hierarchy to save Korea's sovereignty (Choi 2009).

Missionaries, many of them American Protestant women who enthusiastically promoted female education, entered the country after Korea's opening. One such missionary was Mary Scranton, whose Korean language instructor was Pak Yŏng-hyŏ. In 1886, Scranton founded Ehwa School, Korea's first girls' school. Over the next century, Ewha graduates became leading artists, writers, feminist and nationalist activists, and educators.

In addition to the elite, educated men of the Enlightenment Party, marginalized men and women were drawn to the Tonghak (Eastern Learning) movement in the 1860s. This religious movement blended Confucianism, Daoism, Buddhism, and shamanism, and called for more egalitarian relations between husbands and wives. Suppressed by the Korean government, Tonghak went underground until the 1890s, when a Tonghak uprising was the immediate cause for Chinese and Japanese intervention in Korean affairs in the Sino-Japanese War (1894–1895).

During that war, the Japanese government pressed the Korean government to implement the Kabo Reforms (1894–1896). These included a call for a constitutional monarchy, abolition of slavery, prohibition of early marriage, permission for widows to remarry, universal education, and the end of the hierarchical class system. Equally important, the reforms allowed activists in exile to return home. Sŏ Chae-p'il (1866–1951) returned from the United States in 1895 and founded the Independence Club, whose newspaper, *The Independent* (founded 1896), criticized Confucian-based gender inequality and called for women to be educated as "wise mothers and good wives" to serve the nation. *The Independent* sponsored lectures and public meetings in support of women's rights, and in 1898, Korea's first organization of feminist women, the Ch'anyang-hoe (Praise and Encouragement Association), came together. The upper- and middle-class women of this organization focused, unsuccessfully, on persuading the government to establish a secular girls' school. They also demonstrated for civil rights, outside the home and together with the Independence Club – a novel action for elite women who had generally been sequestered in previous centuries. Both groups were disbanded in 1898, but in the next decade a number of girls' schools were established, and by 1910, there were at least 28 feminist groups in Korea (Kim 1995). In 1907, women's organizations began to collect money to encourage Japan to disengage from Korea (unsuccessfully, as Korea became a Japanese colony in 1910), thereby linking feminism and nationalism. In 1908, Korea's first women's journal began publication.

Women's groups arose alongside men's national organizations in the colonial years. Women, especially Ewha graduates, played a major role in the anti-colonial March 1st (1919) movement. In April, the Korean Patriotic Women's Association was founded; it had 2,000 members by 1920. Although it focused more on national liberation than on women's issues, its positioning of women in the public arena modified notions of gender-appropriate behavior. By the mid-1920s, two main streams of women's nationalist feminism emerged: non-socialist transnational Christian groups like the YWCA and socialist organizations. In 1927, these two streams came together in the Kŭn-u-hoe (Association of the Rose of Sharon), but internal ideological divisions and external repression by the Japanese colonial authorities led to the Kŭn-u-hoe's demise (Wells 2004). That there were sufficient feminists in Korea to create such an organization attests to the growth of feminism. In addition, as in Japan in the early twentieth century, Korean New Women, many of them educated in schools like Ewha, appeared in the literary and artistic fields. New Women, who asserted the importance of "self-realization," came to be seen as promiscuous, however, and educated Korean women took to calling themselves "inteli" instead. In the 1930s, colonial oppression intensified, making feminist activism linked to nationalism impossible (Kim and Kim 2010).

Immediately after independence in 1945, socialist and conservative women's organizations emerged, but the Korean War (1950–1953) left Korea divided and devastated. Before the end of that war, several South Korean feminists formed the Institute for Women's Issues. Together with the YWCA, the Korean Women's Association, and several women's professional organizations, they created the Korean National Council of Women (KNCW) in 1959. When Park Chung-hee (1917–1979) seized power in a military coup in 1961, he outlawed most organizations, but allowed the KNCW, the Christian Academy, and Korea Church Women United to exist; Park believed they did not threaten his regime. During the 1970s, anti-government activism exploded, and Christian women's organizations were involved in aiding women workers and quietly supporting the pro-democracy movement. But their focus on women's issues was later criticized as being too conservative in the face of a repressive government.

Park's assassination in 1979 was followed by an even more repressive military regime under Chun Doo-hwan (1931–). Women's organizations became outspoken advocates for social change; women workers were joined by college students, professors, and professional women in the Association for Women's Equality and Friendship in 1983. But as with the earlier Kŭn-u-hoe, ideological differences contributed to the association's demise in 1986. The following year, the Korean Women's Associations United (KWAU) brought together pro-democracy feminists. For several years, the KNCW and KWAU worked at somewhat cross-purposes, but following South Korea's first democratic election of a civilian president in 1992, both umbrella associations tackled similar problems. These included workplace equality, elimination of sexual violence, inheritance equality, restitution from Japan for Korean sexual slavery in World War II, and greater female representation in government. In 2001, President Kim Dae-jung (1925–2009) created a cabinet-level Ministry of Gender Equality and placed KWAU members in government offices. His successor Roh Moo-hyun (1946–2009) went even further, passing laws to prevent prostitution and terminate the patriarchal family-headship system. Roh's conservative successor slowed the government's movement toward gender equality, but South Korean feminists continue to actively demand reforms. Park Geun-hye (1952–) was inaugurated in 2013 as South Korea's first woman president.

CHINA

Modern Chinese feminism emerged in the late nineteenth century and was grounded in nationalism. Throughout that century, the Qing dynasty (1644–1911) had been weakened by humiliating wars with England, France, and Japan and by even more destructive civil wars. Poverty and famine wracked the country, and economic development was hindered by the absence of a strong centralized state. Chinese reformers sought ways to overcome these challenges. Intellectuals in the governing elite, such as Kang Youwei (1858–1927), claimed that one major cause of China's weakness was its women. They asserted that women were insufficiently educated (a particularly damning characteristic in a culture that revered education and made it the basis for governing authority) and crippled by the practice of footbinding (Edwards 2010). Together with Chinese women – including pioneering feminists Hu Binxia (1887–1920s) and anti-Qing martyr Qiu Jin (1875?–1907) – and foreign Christian missionaries, reformers associated footbinding with cultural backwardness, replacing the notion that it was a refined practice. Within a single generation, the practice radically declined, and feminists highlighted natural feet as symbolic of women's and therefore China's strengthening.

Education was a second pillar of early feminism. Political activists Qiu Jin, Tang Qunying (1871–1937, a prominent suffragist of the 1910s), and He Xiangning (1879–1972, a leading Communist Party feminist), studied in Japan. In addition, a wave of medical students earned degrees in the United States. Women returned from both countries to serve as educators and feminist activists (Edwards 2010).

Suffragist feminists had collaborated with Sun Yat-sen's (1866–1925) Revolutionary Alliance to overturn the monarchy and found the Republic of China in 1912. Anticipating political equality, a number of suffragist groups sprang up in 1911. Five of them merged to form the Women's Suffrage Alliance (WSA) in February 1912. They were understandably furious when the first Constitution (March 1912), claiming to be based on Chinese ethnic principles, denied rights to women. Following the example of Britain's suffragettes, Tang Qunying's WSA smashed the parliament's windows (Edwards 2004). In September, American feminist Carrie Chapman Catt, in China for a speaking tour on behalf of the International Women's Suffrage Alliance, observed 10 women in a provincial assembly and assumed that China had granted women's rights. Catt reported this to shame Americans for dragging their feet on women's rights. Those women were removed by the following year. The WSA and other feminist groups were forced underground in 1913, reemerging, reinvigorated, in 1919.

Domestic struggles between military strongmen soon destroyed the fledgling Republic, and pressures from Japan exacerbated China's problems. Against that backdrop, ideas of how to create a new China that could stand up in the world gained traction. The "New Culture" movement of the 1910s particularly encouraged improving the status of women. Artists, intellectuals, and writers, men and women, published popular works that attacked women's lowly status under Confucianism as a metaphor for China's sorry plight. "New Women" created feminist organizations in Beijing and elsewhere, some with ties to international feminist groups like the WCTU and YWCA. After the May Fourth (1919) demonstrations, the Nationalist Party (GMD) and the Communist Party (CCP, founded 1921) called for women's rights (Wang 1999). Women gained the vote for provincial parliamentary elections in several provinces in the early 1920s.

The CCP worked under the umbrella of the GMD until forced out in 1927. This fractured the women's rights movement. The

GMD executed a number of leftist feminists, but others continued to work to persuade the GMD of the need for women's rights. Women gained parliamentary suffrage rights in GMD-controlled areas of China in 1936 (Edwards 2004). Although gender equality was a fundamental tenet of the CCP, it often conflicted with the conservative views of male peasants the CCP was trying to recruit. Moreover, feminism was viewed as divisive and "bourgeois." Political rights were thus delayed in CCP-controlled areas.

Following a brutal civil war, the CCP came to power in 1949 as the People's Republic of China (PRC). Women active in the CCP during the war years insisted that women's equality be written into the early PRC documents. Women obtained the vote in 1949, but it was fairly meaningless in the PRC's one-party system. The Marriage Law of 1950 allowed women to choose their husbands without parental pressure and to obtain divorces, but the law was often circumvented. Feminists helped create the All-China Women's Federation (ACWF) to serve the needs of women, but its existence allowed the CCP to claim that the women's organizations of the 1940s were now unnecessary and, in many cases, connected to transnational "bourgeois" feminism that highlighted gender struggles over class struggle (Edwards 2010).

The ACWF set up branches in cities and villages throughout the PRC and informed women about their rights. But some of its leaders ran afoul of Mao Zedong's "Anti-Rightists Campaign" in 1957, accused of suggesting that Chinese women still confronted problems, despite the PRC's socialism. The ACWF narrowly avoided being disbanded for those "bourgeois feminist errors" by creating a new historical narrative: that feudalism had oppressed women and there had been no feminist movement in China before the PRC elevated women to equality in 1949. Chinese feminism, which had been part of transnational feminism, withered away; like others in the PRC, women were isolated from most global contacts between the late 1950s and late 1970s. Feminism was a corrupt Western idea.

Much changed in the late 1970s. The death of Mao led to new opportunities for the ACWF, some desirable, some less so. They were charged with administering the unpopular population control program, which made them seem an arm of the state, and they tried to keep young women from taking part in activities like beauty pageants, which made them seem old-fashioned in a modernizing society. But eventually, the ACWF found its purpose in enforcing new laws to outlaw discrimination (1992 Women's Law), alerting the public to the kidnapping and sale of women as prostitutes or wives, combatting domestic violence, and improving childcare.

The 1995 UN Conference on Women in Beijing, which required that non-governmental organizations (NGOs) be allowed to meet in addition to official delegations, forced the PRC to accept the concept of independent women's organizations. But the government was nervous. A number of Western journalists and academics, as well as First Lady Hillary Clinton, requested data collected by the NGO Women's Research Institute (WRI; established in 1988) for their studies. This raised the PRC's suspicions, and the WRI was forced to restructure itself to survive. But many new NGOs emerged, and the ACWF restructured itself as well. Reluctant to call its activities "feminist," the ACWF used accepted PRC jargon to describe its international feminism as "joining tracks" with "the international women's movement" (Wang 2010, 107). The ACWF has also forged links with Chinese NGOs like the nationwide Stop DV (domestic violence) Network. Stop DV accepts contributions from global funding sources and makes grants itself to both government and private projects in China. Modern Chinese feminism has made significant gains since the Maoist years, and it continues to evolve.

SEE ALSO: Feminism, Chinese; Footbinding; Gender, Politics, and the State in East Asia; Nationalism and Gender; Sexual Citizenship in East Asia; UN Decade for Women; Women's Movements: Modern International Movements; Women's and Feminist Activism in East Asia

REFERENCES

Choi, Hyaeweol. 2009. *Gender and Mission Encounters in Colonial Korea: New Women, Old Ways*. Berkeley: University of California Press.
Edwards, Louise. 2004. "Chinese Women's Campaigns for Suffrage: Nationalism, Confucianism, and Public Agency." In *Women's Suffrage in Asia: Gender, Nationalism and Democracy*, edited by Louise Edwards and Mina Roces. London: RoutledgeCurzon.
Edwards, Louise. 2010. "Chinese Feminism in a Transnational Frame: Between Internationalism and Xenophobia." In *Women's Movements in Asia: Feminisms and Transnational Activism*, edited by Mina Roces and Louise Edwards. London: Routledge.
Kim, Seung-kyung, and Kyonghee Kim. 2010. "Mapping a Hundred Years of Activism: Women's Movements in Korea." In *Women's Movements in Asia: Feminisms and Transnational Activism*, edited by Mina Roces and Louise Edwards. London: Routledge.
Kim, Yung-Hee. 1995. "Under the Mandate of Nationalism: Development of Feminist Enterprises in Modern Korea, 1860–1910." *Journal of Women's History*, 7(4): 120–146.
Lublin, Elizabeth Dorn. 2010. *Reforming Japan: The Women's Christian Temperance Union in the Meiji Period*. Vancouver: University of British Columbia Press.
Mackie, Vera. 2003. *Feminism in Modern Japan: Citizenship, Embodiment, and Sexuality*. Cambridge: Cambridge University Press.
Molony, Barbara. 1995. "Japan's 1986 Equal Employment Opportunity Law and the Changing Discourse on Gender." *Signs*, 20(2): 268–302.
Molony, Barbara. 2004. "Citizenship and Suffrage in Interwar Japan." In *Women's Suffrage in Asia: Gender, Nationalism and Democracy*, edited by Louise Edwards and Mina Roces. London: RoutledgeCurzon.
Molony, Barbara. 2005. "The Quest for Women's Rights in Turn-of-the-Century Japan." In *Gendering Modern Japanese History*, edited by Barbara Molony and Kathleen Uno. Cambridge, MA: Harvard University Asia Center.
Molony, Barbara. 2010. "Crossing Boundaries: Transnational Feminisms in Twentieth-Century Japan." In *Women's Movements in Asia: Feminisms and Transnational Activism*, edited by Mina Roces and Louise Edwards. London: Routledge.
Rodd, Laurel Rasplica. 1991. "Yosano Akiko and the Taisho Debate Over the 'New Woman'." In *Recreating Japanese Women, 1600–1945*, edited by Gail Lee Bernstein. Berkeley: University of California Press.
Wang, Zheng. 1999. *Women in the Chinese Enlightenment: Oral and Textual Histories*. Berkeley: University of California Press.
Wang, Zheng. 2010. "Feminist Networks." In *Reclaiming Chinese Society: The New Social Activism*, edited by You-tien Hsing and Ching Kwan Lee. London: Routledge.
Wells, Ken. 2004. "Expanding their Realm: Women and Public Agency in Colonial Korea." In *Women's Suffrage in Asia: Gender, Nationalism and Democracy*, edited by Louise Edwards and Mina Roces. London: RoutledgeCurzon.

FURTHER READING

Anderson, Marnie S. 2010. *A Place in Public: Women's Rights in Meiji Japan*. Cambridge, MA: Harvard University Asia Center.
Edwards, Louise. 2008. *Gender, Politics and Democracy: Women's Suffrage in China*. Stanford: Stanford University Press.
Mann, Susan L. 2011. *Gender and Sexuality in Modern Chinese History*. Cambridge: Cambridge University Press.
Yoo, Theodore Jun. 2008. *The Politics of Gender in Colonial Korea: Education, Labor, and Health, 1910–1945*. Berkeley: University of California Press.

Feminism, Postcolonial

TARA HARNEY-MAHAJAN
University of Connecticut, USA

"Post-colonialism" refers broadly to nations or regions once dominated by the realities, processes, and power dynamics of imperialism and colonialism as well as the cultural phenomena – culture, art, literature, and politics – produced in or about places informed by the conditions of postcoloniality. "Postcolonialism," in contrast, is a critical framework employed to interpret these cultural phenomena, and it is also a methodology used to deconstruct superficial understandings of colonialism, the relationship between colonizer and colonized, decolonization, nationalism, post-colonialism, and, more recently, neocolonialism and globalization. Postcolonialism was inaugurated within the field of literary studies in the 1970s and 1980s, most notably with the now-canonical text *Orientalism* by Edward Said (1978), but it now comprises complex theoretical frameworks infiltrating most scholarly disciplines in the wide-ranging field of cultural studies. Early postcolonial theoretical texts, however, did not engage with the concept of gender within the histories and legacies of colonialism and post-colonialism in a sustained manner. In addition, as feminist theory and feminism(s) developed in the mid-to-late twentieth century, now-foundational scholarship radically intervened into how "third world women" were being constructed by "first world women" in the West: in Chandra Talpade Mohanty's essay entitled "Under Western Eyes" (Mohanty 1984), she uncovers "a latent ethnocentrism in particular feminist writings on women in the third world" and exposes how Western feminists objectify and victimize the third world woman, turning the third world woman into a cohesive, unified object, and victim, of study; Gayatri Chakravorty Spivak's essay entitled "Three Women's Texts and a Critique of Imperialism" (Spivak 1985) "firmly situates" *Jane Eyre*, a "cult text of Western feminism" within "the great age of European imperialism" (Gandhi 1998, 91). Given the sociocultural context of imperialism, largely ignored by Western feminist critics who instead consider the main protagonist's development at the expense of Bertha Mason, often simply read as Jane's "other," Spivak insists that Western feminism "reconsider its historical complicity with imperialist discourses" (Gandhi 1998, 91). Moreover, Spivak's contemplations on the female or gendered subaltern, which began with her 1988 essay "Can the Subaltern Speak?," intervened into the field of Subaltern Studies and have "spawned a series of critiques and responses that raise certain central questions in any discussion of feminism in/and postcolonialism: 'Who can speak and for whom?' 'Who listens?' 'How does one represent the self and others?'" (Bahri 2004, 199). Postcolonial feminists in the 1980s and 1990s were also interacting, influencing, and influenced by other social, intellectual, and theoretical movements – "nationalist struggles in the third world" as well as the "US-based 'women of color'" movement – which emerged "alongside the feminist and civil rights movements of the 1960s–1970s" and whose aim, among others, was to interrogate the Anglo-American women's movements of the 1960s and 1970s, which, in their call for women's solidarity, often conveniently ignored class and race (George 2006, 220).

To write about "feminisms, postcolonial," therefore, is to consider a complex terrain of theoretical interventions into the fields of postcolonial studies and Western feminist studies, and although the directions that postcolonial studies has taken since the 1970s have been diverse, they have been made all the more rich by the scholarship of postcolonial feminists and, more recently, queer postcolonial feminist scholarship (see the work of Ahmed, Gopinath, and Halberstam, for example). Put succinctly, the project of postcolonial feminism is one "of interrupting the discourses of postcolonial theory and of liberal Western feminism, while simultaneously refusing the singular 'Third World Woman' as the object of study" (George 2006, 211).

Given the diversity of voices in the field(s) of postcolonial feminism, it is instructive to survey scholarship that attempts to delimit the field of postcolonial feminism(s), starting in the late 1990s. In 1998, Leela Gandhi foregrounds the scholarship of Trinh T. Minh-ha, Mohanty, and Spivak, who collectively note that "liberal academic feminism" "silences the 'native woman' in its pious attempt to represent or speak for her" (Gandhi 1998, 89). But Gandhi wonders then if the "figure of 'feminist imperialist' – much like that of 'third-world woman' – fractures the potential unity between postcolonial and feminist scholarship" (Gandhi 1998, 91). Attempting to find some common ground between postcolonialism and feminism, Gandhi suggests a "combined offensive against the aggressive myth of imperial and nationalist masculinity," an area of analysis already under way with the scholarship of Anne McClintock, Jenny Sharpe, Frantz Fanon, and Ashis Nandy, for example. Noting how Nandy seizes on figures such as Gandhi and Oscar Wilde in order to "complicate the authoritative signature of colonial masculinity" and "protest the dubious worth of manly British robustness," Gandhi concludes with Virginia Woolf's "denunciation of aggressive masculinity," which "supplies the basis of a shared critique of chauvinist national and colonial culture," and invites more sustained theoretical interventions into these areas of inquiry (Gandhi 1998, 101).

In 2000, Rajeswari Sunder Rajan and You-me Park summarize the concerns of "metropolitan postcolonial feminism:" "issues of representation and questions of location," or, more broadly, "theory," and the "newly-motivated study of Third World women's writing in the classroom," about which they express serious concerns (Sunder Rajan and Park 2000, 54). They also want to reorient the field of postcolonial feminism and broaden the scope of the field(s) to include the "significant women's movement and gender issues in many postcolonial nations which are linked with feminist studies in the academy there" (Sunder Rajan and Park 2000, 53, 60). Glossing the field of transnational feminism, and citing the work of Inderpal Grewal and Caren Kaplan, Chandra Mohanty and M. Jacqui Alexander, Cherríe Moraga and Gloria Anzaldúa, Swasti Mitter, Cyntia Enloe, Maria Mies, and Sheila Rowbotham, Sunder Rajan and Park note that while transnational feminists are not necessarily preoccupied with questions about colonialism, they are deeply invested in interrogating the impact of neocolonialism, or colonialism's "successor" (Sunder Rajan and Park 2000, 57). As such, and given that many of the theorists cited above consider postcolonial and neocolonial issues, Sunder Rajan and Park maintain that these scholars might aid in "redefining and reconfiguring the discipline of postcolonial feminism" (Sunder Rajan and Park 2000, 57). Beyond transnational feminists, Sunder Rajan and Park point to postcolonial feminists located specifically in the "Third World," and despite differences in location, as well as serious differences in focus, such as the impact of religion on nationalism(s), postcolonial feminists are united in a shared project, one which insists "on understanding colonialism (and its legacy) and neocolonialism as one of the most important obstacles for the attainment of the more egalitarian and just world, and in its emphasis on women as the group who will not only benefit most from the changed world but also lead this particular historical transformation of humanity in the future" (Sunder Rajan and Park 2000, 67).

One of the first readers in the field of postcolonial feminism is the collection edited by Lewis and Mills (2003) (see also Narayan and Harding 2000), which aims "to resituate postcolonial theory in relation to feminism," particularly given the tendency to invoke the postcolonial "male greats" (Fanon, Said, and Homi Bhabha, for example) at the expense of ignoring contributions made by women scholars and activists, such as Angela Davis, Adrienne Lorde, and bell hooks (although Spivak is carved out as the "exceptionally cited female voice"). The six sections of the reader address the continuities and discontinuities in the field of feminist postcolonial theory, including concerns with "gender, economics, sexuality, representation and the development of political activism." Although not an exhaustive account, the reader speaks to the vibrancy of issues and voices within the field of postcolonial feminism, contextualizing complex issues such as the "Third-World" subject, feminist anti-racist politics, the veil, diaspora, and sexuality and sexual rights. In the early 2000s, perhaps as the field of postcolonial feminism becomes as institutionalized as postcolonialism within the university – the developments of which have their own historiography and repercussions – the tensions and commonalities between feminism(s) and postcolonialism(s) begin to coalesce, the implications of which Deepika Bahri begins to tease out: "A feminist position *within* postcolonialism must confront the dilemma of seeming divisive while the projects of decolonization and nation-building are still under way. Outside postcolonial studies, within the broader framework of mainstream feminism, postcolonial perspectives that focus on race and ethnicity may be perceived as forces that fragment the global feminist alliance" (Bahri 2004, 202). Moreover, "[d]ifferences between postcolonial feminist theorists surface repeatedly as the category of 'women of color' is fractured by the politics of location, strife between minority communities in the First World, women in diasporic communities, and women in the Third World" (Bahri 2004, 202). Yet the strength of postcolonial feminism, Bahri contends, is that it is a "dynamic discursive field," one that "consistently calls for sustained and instructive examination of its major premises, methods, and tensions" (Bahri 2004, 202, 203). Some of these key concepts, as Bahri elaborates, are "'Representation,' 'Third-World woman,' 'essentialism,' and 'identity,'" and the persistent efforts of postcolonial feminists, on the one hand, "to establish identity as relational and historical rather than essential or fixed," and, on the other, "to retain gender as a meaningful category of analysis" (Bahri 2004, 203).

Rosemary Marangoly George, in 2006, traces the development of postcolonial feminist scholarship, starting in the 1980s, beginning with what can now be called its "characteristic markings:" "the fashioning of cautionary signposts, the disclosure of absences, an insistence on what cannot be represented in elite texts, an emphasis on the more than 'purely literary,' and the persistent embedding of gendered difference in a larger understanding of race, nationality, class, and caste" (George 2006, 211–212). In the late 1980s and 1990s, postcolonial theorists disrupted and redefined the "role of literary texts" and also the "type" of texts historically understood as canonical: the idea that certain texts were deemed "worthy of scholarly attention" because they transcended politics and possessed "universally acknowledged" "pearls" of "wisdom" was thoroughly debunked (George 2006,

213). As postcolonial feminists contributed to this project of canon re-formation by uncovering the voices of women writers and re-reading canonical and non-canonical texts through the lens of gender, George echoes Bahri's understanding of one of the key tensions that postcolonial feminists foreground, writing that while postcolonial feminists intervened into postcolonial studies in order to "insist that men and women experience aspects of colonialism and post-colonialism differently," they also "vigorously maintained that gender was not *invariably* a fundamental marker of difference" (George 2006, 213).

Beyond challenging the foundations on which the standard European and British literary canons rested, postcolonial feminists powerfully addressed the "exalted yet largely symbolic status allotted to women in many nationalist struggles" and the consequences of this symbolic status for women in postin-dependence periods, which is that "gender symbolism in colonial and postindependence periods remains essentially unchanged" (George 2006, 221–222). During most independence struggles, and also after independence, George notes that "most nations were figured as female, and women were the ground on which national identity was erected" (George 2006, 222). Ania Loomba "succinct[ly] reformulates" Benedict Anderson's famous argument from *Imagined Communities* when she argues: "'If the nation is an imagined community, that imagining is profoundly gendered'" (George 2006, 222). George also issues a corrective to this generalizing statement, however: if women are relatively restricted by the limiting roles defined for them, George cites Lila Abu-Lughod's insistence that women in the Middle East, for example, can be "empowered" as well as "undercut" "by the weight of their symbolic place" in the home and in the nation.

While the conditions of postcoloniality led to a proliferation of national and diasporic literature (for example, Salman Rushdie's 1981 novel *Midnight's Children*), women's writing in the 1960s, 1970s, and 1980s confronted the contested place of "woman" in the postinde-pendence nation, typically written by the elite women of these national spaces: *The Country Girls Trilogy* by Irish writer Edna O'Brien, *Nervous Conditions* by Zimbabwean writer Tsitsi Dangarembga, and *That Long Silence* by Indian writer Shashi Deshpande, to name just a few, are representative of this genre. Postcolonial feminist literary critics analyzed these writers' representations of women confined and controlled within the boundaries of their domestic and national spheres: some critics read these novels as "representative" of women's experiences whereas others underscore the class positions of these writers and turn our attention, instead, to the myriad voices not accounted for within domestic literature written mostly by middle- and upper-class and caste women. Still, in much of domestic literature, it becomes apparent that postindependence, state-sponsored reproductive heteronormativity demands the heteronormative family mode – and the gendered hierarchy typically concomitant with such a structure – a structure to which novelists, in addition to postcolonial feminists, and increasingly queer studies scholars, begin to apply a tremendous amount of pressure. George concludes with the challenge that faces postcolonial feminist scholars within the Western academy in this era of "'global literary studies:'" " … to look beyond this location and engage with literary texts and literary criticism produced elsewhere, but always with a clear understanding of the pitfalls of apprehending the world with the aid of the old imperial analytical tools supplied by our common history of colonialism" (George 2006, 228). George also notes, however, that literature is only one mode of expression for artists, and perhaps, until recently, academics have privileged this genre – and within literature, anglophone texts – to the neglect of other mediums: "Some might argue that in many countries in the developing world, where illiteracy is widespread, film, storytelling, music, or drama may be the cultural forms to study" (George 2006, 224).

Although George writes that Mohanty's criticisms of Western feminism in her essay "Under Western Eyes" are "now part of the 'common sense' of the field," she also acknowledges that "imperialist first world reading[s] of third world women" particularly in "the mainstream US media" persist (George 2006, 221). It would seem that Mohanty herself would agree with this perpetual trend and questions the degree to which her concerns in 1984 have become "'common sense' in the field" (George 2006, 221). In 2003, Mohanty revisits her historic essay in her book-length study *Feminism Without Borders*, where she writes that many of the questions she initially posed in 1984 remain strikingly relevant, because "in spite of the occasional exception" "present-day scholarship tends to produce particular 'globalized' representations of women" (Mohanty 2003, 247). Mohanty continues: "Although representations of women [such as, for example, the ubiquitous global teenage factory worker, the refugee, the victim of war crimes] correspond to real people, they often stand in for the contradictions and complexities of women's lives and roles… The concern here is with whose agency is being colonized and who is privileged in these pedagogies and scholarship" (Mohanty 2003, 248). Put another way, both despite and because of the radical and innovative scholarship within the field of postcolonial feminism(s) over the last few decades, the project of postcolonial feminism remains as urgent as ever, particularly in the globalized world in which we all live.

SEE ALSO: Black Feminist Thought; Colonialism and Gender; Feminism and Postmodernism; Feminism and Psychoanalysis; Nationalism and Gender; Postcolonialism, Theoretical and Critical Perspectives on; Third World Women

REFERENCES

Bahri, Deepika. 2004. "Feminism in/and Postcolonialism." In *The Cambridge Companion to Postcolonial Literary Studies*, edited by Neil Lazarus, 199–220. Cambridge: Cambridge University Press.

Gandhi, Leela. 1998. *Postcolonial Theory: A Critical Introduction*. New York: Columbia University Press.

George, Rosemary Marangoly. 2006. "Feminists Theorize Colonial/Postcolonial." In *Cambridge Companion to Feminist Literary Theory*, edited by Ellen Rooney, 211–231. Cambridge: Cambridge University Press.

Lewis, Reina, and Sara Mills, eds. 2003. *Feminist Postcolonial Theory: A Reader*. New York: Routledge.

Mohanty, Chandra Talpade. 1984. "Under Western Eyes: Feminist Scholarship and Colonial Discourses." *Boundary 2*, 12(3): 333–358.

Mohanty, Chandra Talpade. 2003. *Feminism Without Borders: Decolonizing Theory, Practicing Solidarity*. Durham, NC: Duke University Press.

Narayan, Uma, and Sandra Harding, eds. 2000. *Decentering the Center: Philosophy for a Multicultural, Postcolonial, and Feminist World*. Bloomington: Indiana University Press.

Said, Edward. 1978. *Orientalism*. New York: Pantheon Books.

Spivak, Gayatri Chakravorty. 1985. "Three Women's Texts and a Critique of Imperialism." *Critical Inquiry*, 12(1): 243–261.

Sunder Rajan, Rajeswari, and You-me Park. 2000. "Postcolonial Feminism/Postcolonialism and Feminism." In *A Companion to Postcolonial Studies*, edited by Henry Schwarz and Sangeeta Ray, 53–71. Malden: Blackwell.

Feminism and Postmodernism

KRISTINA B. WOLFF
Gender Research Institute at Dartmouth College, USA

Postmodern feminism is a body of scholarship that questions and rejects traditional essentialist practices, as established in and by modernity. The general premise of postmodern social theory is a rejection of the Western ideal of establishing universal grand narratives as a means of understanding and explaining society. Postmodern theory directly challenges claims of a unified subject, which is then presented as representing an objective point of view – in essence, a "view from nowhere." Postmodern theory and practices recognize differences, making room for all to contribute and thus having a "view from everywhere" and eliminating the practice of positing one way or one understanding as representing or being "truth." The combination of postmodernist theory and feminism allows for a questioning of essentialist approaches within and outside of feminism, an expansion of feminist scholarship as well as contributing the lens of "gender" and other issues inherent to feminism to the body of postmodern scholarship.

Postmodern thought follows early feminist challenges to dualistic concepts, such as modernist practices of objectivity being favored over subjectivity, belief in rational thought over emotion, and the strength of nature over cultural constructions. Generally, this body of scholarship can be divided into three areas, *postmodernity*, *postmodernism*, and *postmodern social theory*. Postmodernity represents a specific political or social time period that follows the modern era. Some theorists believe that modernity shifted into postmodernity in the late twentieth century. Postmodernity stresses the importance of recognizing specific cultural, political, and historical moments connected to "who" or "what" is being studied. Postmodernism represents the cultural products that differ from modern products. These consist of a variety of things including architecture, movies, art, poetry, music, and literature. Lastly, postmodern social theory is a distinct way of thinking which is open to a range of possibilities, consisting of different approaches that move away from the constraints of modern thinking.

Early postmodern studies focus on language and discourse as sites of analysis. This practice emerges out of *poststructuralism*. While there is debate as to whether or not poststructuralism is a postmodernist project, it is recognized as the precursor of postmodernism. Poststructuralism seeks to uncover and understand general structures guiding all forms of social life. Early scholarship primarily emerged out of France with the work of Derrida, Foucault, Irigaray, and Kristeva. It focused on the areas of language, particularly linguistics and semiotics. Similar to postmodernism, it posits that subjectivity is not something that is fixed or variable; simply, it is socially constructed, therefore creating social reality. This field quickly expanded to include literary studies, philosophy, history, and the social sciences. Both poststructuralism and postmodernist approaches work to bring the margins into the mainstream as well as to deconstruct and decenter society, as a means to discover where and how power operates. *Deconstruction* posits that language is itself a social construction, therefore to understand its meaning we need to examine language in relationship to culture and society, in relationship to language itself. This process provides a means to uncover and understand the power connected to language, the ways in which language is used as a means of oppression. The concept and practice of deconstruction has been expanded beyond language, to understanding various complexities of human society as a means to uncover inequality. Postmodern feminism also examines the same academic areas and "traditional" feminist subjects including gender and sexuality, as well as the development of science and our conceptions of knowledge.

Gender is the core foundational piece of feminism. Recognizing the various roles of gender within society is also one of many strong contributions and accomplishments of feminism. Postmodern feminist theory challenges the very notion of gender, recognizing that it is socially constructed, fluid, and conceptualized within a specific historical, political, and cultural context. One of the critiques of feminism and feminist thought is the reliance upon essentialist beliefs of gender, the assumption that all "women" are the same based on biological as well as cultural understandings of what is defined as "female." Women of color, women from non-industrialized nations as well as lesbian and socialist feminists often challenge the assumption that "woman" alone is a unifying category, and its usage often excludes the complexities and differences of race, ethnicity, nationality, social class, and sexuality. Theorists such as Susan Bordo, Judith Butler, and Jane Flax criticize the traditionally fixed binary structure of gender. Their early work within postmodern feminism called for new narrative approaches to gender, ones that recognize the multiplicity of gender. Using postmodernist approaches, constructions of "women" (as well as "men") were now viewed through a variety of lenses at the same time, thus widening the scope to include issues of race, ethnicity, class, sexual orientation, and other differences that women face (Butler, Nicholson). Included within this analytical shift is the acknowledgment that the category of gender is simultaneously used as a means of oppression as well as a source of liberation.

Entangled with conceptions of gender is an assumption of heterosexuality. The combination of gender and sex is also intertwined with personal and public identities. Butler theorizes the interplay of these things as *performativity*, that gender and sexuality exist as a performance. Gender and sexual identities are layered, emerging in manifest and latent ways based on the individual as well as the cultural moment that she or he is in. For example, the manner in which a woman presents herself in public as well as the ways in which "she" is conceptualized in society is reliant upon cultural assumptions as well as her actual gender performance. There are layers of illusion in and on her exterior as well as interior levels of her body and soul. The repercussion of this is that societal norms are reified while other parts of us, our gender and sexual identities, remain hidden. The aspects that remain out of view as well as what is performed illustrate what is "right" or "true," thus reinforcing essentialist ideologies of gender and sexuality (Butler, Nicholson).

Therefore reality is a fabrication: what is seen on the exterior satisfies societal expectations, what resides on the inside remains hidden. Yet, our understandings and conceptions of sex, gender, and identity are social constructions. This then raises the question of what is real, demonstrating that the boundaries between what "is" and what is expected become blurred. Our concepts of what gender and sexuality are, are based on these constructions; therefore, there is no true meaning. Critics argue that this results in fragmentation between one's consciousness and idea of self. If people keep changing from moment to moment and our understandings of components of our identity continually are in flux, then how do we determine a sense of self? This split challenges not only understandings of male and female but also the distinction between public and private lives and identities. The combination of postmodernist theory with feminism expands the investigation and analysis of gender, looking at the relationships with other characteristics, differences, and identities, and thus the scholarship is reflective of the complexities of identity.

The shift from dualistic approaches to multifaceted examinations directly challenges the subject/object split existing in essentialism. The postmodern project of deconstructing and decentering understandings of "subject," in essence, creates the "death of man" as "man" ceases to be the center subject and therefore "woman" is no longer the object. Some feminists are opposed to this, fearful that women will lose their sense of agency in the process and that the foundation of "woman" will be erased. However, women have rarely been recognized or held in the subject position. One of the overarching tasks for postmodern feminists is to reconstruct conceptualizations of the subject/object split, recognizing it as a recreation of self, as a constituted self that has endless revolutionary potential. This shift is representative of one of the core purposes of feminism, to combine theory with practice.

One result of the challenge to and change in defining the relationship of subject and object is the reconception of understandings and practices of science. Certainly, the structures of Western science consist of dualistic approaches, theories that are used to explore and explain the complexities of human life, our physical and social worlds. The emergence of postmodernist thought pushes science to move beyond a singular, individual focus to an all-inclusive one, recognizing and containing multiple voices and viewpoints. Feminist theory recognizes the foundations of science as inherently masculine in structure, and while it includes essentialist, dualistic approaches to understanding the complexities of gender, feminism also inherently contains postmodernist practices as well. Feminist scholars such as Sandra Harding, Seyla Benhabib, Nancy Fraser, and Linda Nicholson explore philosophy, science, and Western understandings of knowledge. While some scholars argue that science cannot exist without its grounding in essentialism, without "objectivity," these feminist theorists directly challenge this belief. They call for feminist approaches that remove women and other marginalized groups from the position of subject, that which is being studied, to more central positions, where they are advancing knowledge in a variety of ways.

Sandra Harding's argument for the establishment of feminist epistemologies is one example of postmodernist feminist thought. Early approaches to questioning Western science and scholarship focused on bringing women to the center of analysis and calling for the establishment of feminist science. This is grounded in cultural feminist approaches, which focus on the differences between women and men. Therefore, by shifting the lens of inquiry away from a male viewpoint and instead stemming from and onto a female viewpoint, we can gain new insights, develop new bodies of knowledge, and use this as a means of eliminating gender inequality. Postmodern feminists directly challenge this approach due to its singular focus on understanding gender from a biological essentialist position. Simply changing the center does little to challenge the masculine, patriarchal structures used in Western scholarship. Harding argues for feminist science through the development of new feminist theories, methods, and epistemologies. She continues to utilize *feminist standpoint* as the cornerstone of developing new scholarship. Feminist standpoint recognizes that women's understanding of the world is different from that of men due to their experiences and knowledge (Hartsock, Smith). Postmodernist, postcolonial, and feminist scholars expand this concept to an inclusive standpoint, one recognizing the multiplicity of difference. This change becomes the foundation of developing feminist epistemologies, bodies of knowledge that do not reinforce existing hierarchical structures, that seek to expand scholarship, moving away from essentialist approaches.

Harding conceptualizes feminist epistemologies as justificatory strategies, challenging dominant understandings of knowledge, science, and scholarship, providing an alternative to traditional procedures grounded in hollow claims of objective, value-free research. These various "ways of knowing" add a richness, an opportunity to expand and enhance bodies of knowledge rather than focusing on the "self" of a particular powerful group or speaker. Feminist scholarship produces a diversity of women's work, which recognizes the complexities of difference and the ways in which these differences contribute to the quest for knowledge without privileging one type, approach, understanding, or interest(s) over another. The development of these strategies also provides methods, specific procedures that guide feminist research, theories, practices, and policies that advance knowledge and work to eliminate oppression and domination.

Inherent to feminism is the analysis of and challenges to existing power structures as well as how power and resistance operate. Postmodernist thought and practice ushers in new understandings of the ways in which social structures, boundaries, and power itself have changed. Donna Haraway's work illustrates these shifts in viewpoints. Utilizing the metaphor of a cyborg, she explores the complexities between modern and postmodern worlds, noting that women are no longer dominated by traditional means such as through the control of male expectations of mothering to beliefs of the purity and submission of all women. Haraway also uses discursive examples of the emergence of a postmodern world, noting that the term "women of color" represents an identity constructed out of difference and otherness (Nicholson).

The focus on the role(s) and impact of discourse, particularly as a site of power, is another common theme in postmodernist feminist scholarship (Butler, Fraser, Hartsock, Nicholson). The idea of a "female subject" is constituted in and by discourse. Resistance to this concept also exists within discourse; as Foucault theorizes, where there is power there is also resistance. Postmodern approaches disrupt discourse, particularly in relation to what the state produces and transmits to the whole of society. Traditionally, marginalized groups have created counter-discourses as a means of resisting power and as an attempt to enter into mainstream discourse, but these directly fought against dominance in modernist ways that kept them on the outer boundaries. With the shift and widening of focus that postmodernism brings, boundaries are blurred between public and private spaces, discourse and critiques of dominant discourses stemming from marginalized groups become part of the larger public debate. Therefore the complexities of gender, the inclusion of difference across race, ethnicity, nation, sexuality, age, and so on, become part of the conversations. Discourse is a site of power as well as a tool for social change. The creation of postmodern feminist methodologies allows for a deconstruction of texts, of discourse, which provides means to follow and understand the ways in which power flows through discourse and also creates vehicles for revolutionary change through the use of discourse.

There are critiques of postmodern feminism, which include the lack of the development of a critical political agenda, of a realistic means of social change beyond theorizing. Concerns center on the issue of social location, identity, and difference. Postmodernist approaches need to be mindful of recognizing and celebrating difference simply because it exists. Social location, particularly based on difference, is a site of negotiation and conflict. Some theorists define differences merely as illusion, disregarding real-life experiences due to difference. By universalizing all differences as inherent to all women, in turn women become marginal and united due to the status of "difference." This concentration on difference reproduces the "all or nothing" situation that is being critiqued with essentialist approaches. Cultural feminism unites women due to sameness of gender, whereas postmodern feminism unites women due to their differences. Both are viewed as extreme positions.

Scholars such as Paula M. L. Moya explain that categories such as race and nation status invoke specific experiences and identities that are often deconstructed or displaced within postmodernist scholarship. The result of this is a dismissal of women's identity and experiences as well as an erasure of characteristics inherent to their sense of identity, of self, and of commonalities that bind people together. Theorizing changes in identity is important, but there must be some integration with the realities of the real world, with actual experiences. Connections need to be made between conceptualization and feelings. The concern over the outright rejection of essentialist understandings of gender also results in the concern felt by many feminists about the erasure of woman as well as conceptions about gender overall. Can there be feminism, feminist thought, without the concept(s) of "woman," without a feminist standpoint? This also brings in concerns about the elite nature of postmodernist thought, particularly in relation to rejecting modern understandings of race, gender, class, and so on, as it has a different impact on white women with privilege than on women of color, women from non-Western nations, women who do not fall into the same categories as the elites.

One answer to the apparent limits of postmodernist feminism is the need to clearly situate it within specific historical, cultural, and political frameworks. This helps to avoid false generalizations and the development of similar situations that are being critiqued in essentialism. As Harding noted through defining feminist epistemologies as strategies, postmodernist practices can be strategically used. Linda Alcoff points out that women's position in society is continually changing; it is not static. Postmodern feminism can be successful through shifting approaches to combating oppression and domination, as women's statuses change. This includes working on collaborations and building coalitions across differences while also recognizing these differences.

ACKNOWLEDGMENT

This entry is based in part on a previously published entry by Kristina Wolff K. Wolff, "Postmodern Feminism," in G. Ritzer (ed.), *Blackwell Encyclopedia of Sociology*, Blackwell Publishing, UK, 2007. Reproduced with permission.

SEE ALSO: Feminism, Cultural; Feminisms, Postmodern; Feminist Standpoint Theory; Postmodern Feminist Psychology

FURTHER READING

Alcoff, Linda. 1988. "Cultural Feminism Versus Post-Structuralism: The Identity Crisis in Feminist Theory." *Signs: A Journal of Women in Culture and Society*, (13): 405–436.

Benhabib, Seyla, Judith Butler, Drucilla Cornell, and Nancy Fraser. 1995. *Feminist Contentions: A Philosophical Exchange*. New York: Routledge.

Bordo, Susan. 1990. "Feminism, Postmodernism, and Gender-Skepticism." In *Feminism/Postmodernism*, edited by Linda Nicholson. New York: Routledge.
Butler, Judith. 1999. *Gender Trouble: Feminism and the Subversion of Identity*. New York: Routledge. First published 1990.
Cixous, Helene. 1981. "The Laugh of the Medusa." In *New French Feminisms*, edited by Elaine Marks and Isabelle de Courtivron, translated by K. Cohen and P. Cohen, 245–261. New York: Schocken Books.
Flax, Jane. 1990. *Thinking Fragments: Psychoanalysis, Feminism, and Postmodernism in the Contemporary West*. Berkeley: University of California Press.
Foucault, Michel. 1980. *Power/Knowledge: Selected Interviews and Other Writings, 1972–1997*, edited by C. Gordeon. New York: Pantheon.
Fraser, Nancy. 1995. "Politics, Culture, and the Public Sphere: Toward a Postmodern Conception." In *Social Postmodernism: Beyond Identity Politics*, edited by Linda Nicholson and Steven Seidman, 287–312. New York: Cambridge University Press.
Haraway, Donna. 1991. *Simians, Cyborgs, and Women: The Reinvention of Nature*. New York: Routledge.
Hartsock, Nancy. 1997. "The Feminist Standpoint: Developing the Ground for Specifically Feminist Historical Materialism." In *The Second Wave: A Reader in Feminist Theory*, edited by Linda Nicholson, 216–240. New York: Routledge.
Hekman, Susan. 1990. *Gender and Knowledge: Elements of a Postmodern Feminism*. Boston, MA: Northeastern University Press.
Kipnis, Laura. 1989. "Feminism: The Political Conscience of Postmodernism?" *Social Text*, 21: 149–166.
Longino, Helen. 1993. "Feminist Standpoint Theory and the Problems of Knowledge." *Signs*, 19(1): 201–212.
Nicholson, Linda, ed. 1990. *Feminism/Postmodernism*. New York: Routledge.
Smith, Dorothy. 1987. *The Everyday World as Problematic: A Feminist Sociology*. Boston, MA: Northeastern University Press.
Yeatman, Anna. 1994. *Postmodern Revisionings of the Political*. New York: Routledge.

Feminism, Poststructural

HOLLY GIBLIN
Flinders University of South Australia, Australia

Poststructuralist feminisms refer to feminist critical engagements with questions of knowledge, language, power, identity, and difference. They are commonly associated with a shift in feminist praxis during the 1980s and early 1990s away from viewing women as a homogeneous group, and towards acknowledging the plurality of gendered identities and subjectivities. The development of poststructuralist feminisms is heavily indebted to feminist critical engagement with postmodernist, structuralist, and psychoanalytic frameworks. In deconstructing and reworking these frameworks, a particular target for poststructuralist feminist critique has been "traditional" disciplines and theories regarding knowledge creation, gender and sexuality, and identity formation.

The terms postmodern and poststructuralist feminisms are often used interchangeably within feminist scholarship as development in these fields often overlaps and is co-constitutive. They are similar in their aim to deconstruct dominant understandings of the self as "whole and coherent subjects with a unified sense of identity" (Weedon 1997, 173). However, unlike broader *postmodern feminisms* such as *postcolonial feminism* or *psychoanalytical feminisms* who are reluctant to do away with the idea that there might be essences to individual people's identities, poststructuralist feminisms seek to critique, deconstruct, and remake social categories and identities entirely. Poststructuralist feminisms focus on deconstructing how social categories and gendered identities such as "man" and "woman" are products of power, socially constructed *entirely through discourse*.

Importantly, poststructuralism refers to critical theoretical responses to theories of linguistic *structuralism*. Both structuralist and poststructuralist scholars are heavily indebted to Ferdinand de Saussure's views on how language influences our ability to know the world. Instrumental for structuralists and poststructuralists is Saussure's theory of the "sign" and development of the linguistics constructs known as the "signifier" and the "signified." Saussure referred to the spoken sound or symbol as the signifier, and the object or meaning which it meant to produce, the signified. Signs have no concrete meaning on their own and each derives its meaning from its relationship to other signs.

Structuralists and poststructuralists agree that language consists of coded systems of meaning that are developed in relation to each other rather than symbols used to directly translate real-world information. Language therefore, does not reflect a pre-given social reality but rather constitutes social reality for us (Weedon 1997, 22). At the same time, however, structuralism and poststructuralism depart in multiple ways. Structuralists such as Claude Lévi-Strauss argue that language structures all members of a given society in ways that can be reduced to essential characteristics such as gender and sexuality. Poststructuralists on the other hand, are not interested in finding universal truths, instead preferring to focus on pluralities, contradictions and subversions so as to not commit the structural violence of erasing difference. Structuralism is thus viewed by poststructuralists as deterministic, focusing more on language systems rather than individuals' abilities to subvert them. Poststructuralists are concerned with how power produces meaning through discourse, particularly in relation to how power is reproduced in the construction of difference.

Pertinent to poststructuralist theories of gender and sexuality identities is the appropriation of linguistic structuralism by Jacques Lacan, in his reworking of Sigmund Freud's theory of psychoanalysis. Lacan, inspired by Lévi-Strauss's structuralist approach to linguistics, posited that a child comes to know their world in relation to symbols and language, and that language is organized around a supposedly universal principle referred to as the phallus. Lacan did not believe that the unconscious was free from the structuring forces of language, indeed he thought it was structured like a language. Rather than women suffering from penis envy, as Freud determined, Lacan asserted that social systems were organized by language that centered on the phallus, an organizing principle that privileges masculinity, thus rendering the feminine lacking and wanting.

Post-Lacanian, structuralist and psychoanalytical feminist theorists such as Luce Irigaray, Julia Kristeva, and Elizabeth Grosz, however, critiqued the marginalizing effects of the assumptions of structuralism and psychoanalysis and forwarded their own critical reworkings to either center the feminine subject or deconstruct the naturalness of the masculine norm. Luce Irigaray (1974), for example, a student of Lacan's prestigious Freudian School of Paris, argued that much of Western philosophy and psychoanalytic theory only really served the interests of men, while women were relegated as "other," "nature," or "commodity." She argued that the preoccupation with the phallus was actually the symbol of a patriarchal culture, rather than a fact of language. On the topic of sexuality, she argued that heterosexuality – to which gender categories are normatively linked – was male-centered. In response, she developed a theory for bringing the female sexed subject into discourse.

Poststructural feminisms also stress the importance of locating claims to truths within their relative historical and disciplinary contexts so that these can be further interrogated. One of the ways in which hegemonic claims to knowledge and power are thought to develop is through the deployment of the logic of binary oppositions. Jacques Derrida posited that meaning was constructed through difference, rather than in relation to the phallus as in Lacanian theory. He agreed that how a person comes to knowledge is relative, temporary, and bound up in language (Weedon 1997). He also rejected the idea that signs were fixed, and that there was a stable distinction between signifiers and the signified. Signifiers do not always signify the same thing; furthermore, the signified cannot be fully defined and any attempt to do so results in more signifiers (Sarup 1988, 35). Sarup uses the analogy of a dictionary to explain this. The words you look up in a dictionary are signifiers, and the signified is what that word intends to describe. The paradox is that there is no single word to describe anything in full, as all words are relational. Instead you keep finding more signifiers that in turn result in more signifieds. Linguistic signs, therefore, are always changing, can have multiple meanings, and are always defined in relation to other words.

Derrida observed that much of Western thought is organized not just into contrasts but that these "binary opposites" were also hierarchical, privileging one term over the other. These binary opposites are not exclusive categories at far extremes of a naturally occurring dichotomy, but rather social constructs crucially dependent on each other and concerned with power. The privileged term would not exist without the marginalized term in which it leverages its power. Therefore, privileged social constructs and subjectivities such as masculinity or whiteness have no claim to power without having first marginalized those who have been marked as different.

Another way in which poststructuralist feminists analyze the power implicit in dominant social constructs is to look at how they are constituted through *discourse*.

The term discourse refers not to a specific language but to the historically situated, socially constructed, and institutionally specific meanings and structures that make up all speech and texts (Scott 1994, 284). That is, discourse refers to the meaning, and claims to power produced through everyday negotiations in language in particular times and places. "Truths" as they are expressed in language are seen as politically active, historically situated, and negotiated, rather than a mode by which people communicate "rational" conclusions to a universal and finite world. Claims to truth are always subjective and are also claims to power. Discourses on any given topic are also multiple, fluid, and contradictory especially when they intersect with people from different subject positions. Michel Foucault introduced the concept of discourse to describe the ways in which productive forces aid in the construction of knowledge and therefore claims to truth. In his book *The History of Sexuality*, Foucault (1990) claims that the Western world has pathologized sex and sexuality, making it a scientific object to which claims to essential truths about sexuality have been used to regulate social behavior. This was a very radical proposition to make, that sexuality, particularly heterosexuality, was a social construct, an institution, bound up in claims to knowledge and power.

One of the more eminent contributors to poststructuralist feminisms is Judith Butler. Heavily influenced by Foucault, Butler reached critical acclaim by challenging existing feminist theorizations about the sex/gender distinction and also for her theory of gender identity called *performativity*. Butler (1990) critiqued the distinction that had been drawn by feminists between sex, gender, and sexuality. Previously, second-wave feminists had drawn a line between sex and gender, arguing that your biological sex does not determine gender, and that the masculine and feminine attributes of gender are socially constructed. This approach was a direct attempt at combating "biological determinism," namely structuralist, essentialist, and often "scientifically proven" assumptions about gender that actively relegated women to multiple fixed and oppressed social positions. Butler argued that sexed bodies cannot be recognized, signified, without gender and that the ability to recognize "biological sex" is in itself socially constructed. Butler's approach fundamentally challenges the idea that biological sex is pre-discursive, and has opened up the possibility of considering the idea that both sex and gender are social constructs. Gender and sexuality, Butler argues, are also mutually reinforcing terms. Heterosexuality relies on the assumption that there are only two sexes, male and female. If sex and gender are shown to be social constructs then the whole notion of normative heterosexuality is also destabilized.

Also of credit to Butler, and of considerable contribution to poststructuralist feminist theorizing, is the leap she made from gender as a discourse to gender as *performative*. Drawing on Foucault's (1972, 49) assertion that "practices are the systematic formation of the objects in which they speak," she constructs sex and gender identities as the product of discursive practices. Discursive practices are culturally and historically specific sets of rules in language that organize and produce different forms of knowledge. According to Butler (1990, 1993), the process of becoming gendered is never complete, and we must continuously do gender through repeated displays of what is considered "natural." This is achieved through the repeated stylization of the body in ways that are recognizable, intelligible, to existing discursive practices or ideas about gender. For Butler, there is no "real" gender, only performances of discursive practices. Butler calls for people to make "gender trouble," to play with gender and expose the limits of the discursive practices that seek to limit the ways in which we know our bodies and construct our gendered and sexualized identities. Butler suggests one of the ways people do this is by deliberately violating the boundaries of gender through performances such as drag.

The appeal to poststructuralist feminists to establish gender as socially constructed is in its promise to undermine essentialist heteronormative ideas about sex, gender, and sexuality. It is also useful because if gender norms and ways of performing them are constantly being reproduced, then they should, and are, constantly changing, albeit in small moments in different times and places. The task at hand is ensuring that newly repeated discourses and performances change in ways that are beneficial to the feminist cause.

Poststructuralist feminist theory can also be a way of conducting social research as an approach to epistemological and methodological process that seeks to avoid the universalist and structuralist imperatives of "scientific" research. Challenging the ways in which dominant research methodologies reinforce systemic power relations has been a key agenda for feminist researchers for some time. Hesse-Biber, Leavy, and Yaiser (2004, 3) describe the poststructuralist feminist research process as a commitment to conducting research that is "attentive to issues of difference, the questioning of social power, resistance to scientific oppression, and a commitment to political activism and social justice." Poststructuralist feminist methodologies can do this. Irigaray, for example, has refrained from defining a feminine sexuality, and has instead focused on the patriarchal and phallocentric constructions of sexuality in psychoanalysis (Burke, Schor, and Whitford 1994). This approach shifts the focus away from limiting women to fixed and essential definitions while critiquing the naturalness of a phallocentric culture and way of knowing.

Weedon provides a rich and optimistic argument for how poststructuralism could effectively be used in feminist practice. She proposes that poststructuralism can be used not as an answer to solving feminist issues alone, but "as a way of conceptualizing the relationship between language, social institutions and individual consciousness, which focuses on how power is exercised and on the possibilities of change" (Weedon 1997, 19). The role of poststructuralist feminisms is therefore to address the inherent calls to power and claims of ultimate truth hidden in everyday language, to make them visible, and hopefully to encourage new conversations and discourses that can effect positive change for a broad range of different women and marginalized groups.

SEE ALSO: Discursive Theories of Gender; Feminism and Postmodernism; Feminism, French; Feminist Epistemology; Feminist Methodology; Gender Development, Feminist Psychoanalytic Perspectives on; Gender Identity, Theories of; Queer Theory

REFERENCES

Burke, Carolyn, Naomi Schor, and Margaret Whitford, eds. 1994. *Engaging with Irigaray*. New York: Columbia University Press.

Butler, Judith. 1990. *Gender Trouble: Feminism and the Subversion of Identity*. New York: Routledge.

Butler, Judith. 1993. *Bodies that Matter: On the Discursive Limits of Sex*. New York: Routledge.

Foucault, Michel. 1972. *The Archaeology of Knowledge*. London: Routledge.

Foucault, Michel. 1990. *The History of Sexuality: Volume 1. An Introduction*. London: Penguin. First published 1976.

Hesse-Biber, Sharlene, Patricia Leavy, and Michelle Yaiser. 2004. "Feminist Approaches to Research as a Process: Reconceptualizing Epistemology, Methodology, and Method." In *Feminist Perspectives on Social Research*, edited by Sharlene Hesse-Biber, and Michelle Yaiser. New York: Oxford University Press.

Irigaray, L. 1974. *Speculum of the Other Woman*. New York: Cornell University Press.

Sarup, Madan. 1988. *An Introductory Guide to Poststructuralism and Postmodernism*. New York: Harvester Wheatsheaf.

Scott, Joan W. 1994. "Deconstructing Equality-versus-difference: Or, the Uses of Poststructuralist Theory for Feminism." In *The Postmodern Turn: New Perspectives in Social Theory*, edited by Steven Seidman, 282–299. Cambridge: Cambridge University Press.

Weedon, Chris. 1997. *Feminist Practice and Poststructuralist Theory*. Cambridge, MA: Blackwell Publishers.

FURTHER READING

Beasley, Chris. 2005. *Gender & Sexuality: Critical Theories, Critical Thinkers*. London: Sage Publications.

Mann, Susan A. 2013. "Third Wave Feminism's Unhappy Marriage of Poststructuralism and Intersectionality Theory." *Journal of Feminist Scholarship*, 4: 54–73.

Waitt, Gordon. 2010. "Doing Foucauldean Discourse Analysis – Revealing Social Realities." In *Qualitative Research Methods in Human Geography*, edited by Ian Hay, 216–240. South Melbourne: Oxford University Press.

Feminism and Psychoanalysis

NATALIE KATE KAMBER
Deakin University, Australia

Freudian psychoanalysis develops a theory of the unconscious that ineluctably links sexuality and subjectivity together. In doing so, it reveals the ways in which our sense of self – as well as our political loyalties and attachments – are influenced by unconscious drives and ordered by symbolic structures that are beyond the field of individual agency. It is commonly assumed that any relationship between feminism and psychoanalysis would have to be founded on perfidious ground.

For example, in Sigmund Freud's lecture on "Femininity," while discussing the "riddle of femininity" (Freud 1968 [1933], 116) or of sexual differentiation, Freud impeaches women as "the problem" (Freud 1968 [1933], 113), all the while exculpating his female audience from this indictment by offering the hope that they are "more masculine than feminine" (Freud 1968 [1933], 117). We can see why many feminists have been wary both of the gendered biases contained in Freud's theories and of the overt content of his claims. This entry explains how and why feminist theory has, nonetheless, undertaken a serious re-reading of Freud and developed careful analyses of his fundamental concepts, working out their limits, impasses, and possibilities. It can be seen through the writings of such feminist writers as Simone de Beauvoir, Karen Horney, Juliet Mitchell, Hélène Cixous, Julia Kristeva, and Jessica Benjamin; Sigmund Freud's work on psychoanalysis has offered feminists challenges, revolutionized theories, and patriarchal targets.

In the same essay cited above, Freud writes that "psychoanalysis does not try to describe what a woman is – that would be a task it could scarcely perform – but sets about enquiring how she comes into being, how a woman develops out of a child with a bisexual disposition" (Freud 1968 [1933], 116). In employing the term "bisexual," Freud refers to the structure of the sexual instinct, not a relation to a sexual object; thus, the bisexual child is one who psychically is not yet either a man or a woman, whose instinctual life functions prior to sexual difference. Freud here portrays femininity as one trajectory of the Oedipal complex and indicates that sexed identity is a fragile achievement rather than a natural given or essence. By circumscribing the terrain on which the psychoanalytic account of sexual difference moves, and by seeing unresolved, even unresolvable, riddles where others might see the work of nature or culture, Freud problematizes any causal, seamless, or direct tie between sex, sexuality, and sexual difference. Psychoanalytic inquiry does not fit comfortably with, and even unsettles, biological theories of sex and sociological theories of gender, thus also complicating the sex–gender distinction as it has often been formulated in feminist debates. While sex and gender are sometimes construed in feminist theory in terms of the contrast between biology and culture – or nature and nurture – Freud's theory, as discussed below, challenges these dualisms, developing an account of the sexual drive that traverses the mental and the physical, and undergoes idiosyncratic vicissitudes rather than assuming a uniform anatomical or social shape. Whatever the hazards of Freud's writings on women, then, his work explores in new ways the meaning and possibilities of sexed identity.

Freudian psychoanalysis demonstrates the open-endedness of the body since, according to Freud, male and female children have little differentiation at birth. Rather, it is the Oedipal complex that separates them into their socially respective roles, with the position of the girl/woman falling below that of the boy/man. While it is not the mission of feminism to campaign for the return of equivalence to the sexes as alluded to by Freud, the body is no longer a natural entity as dominantly assumed. The Oedipal complex largely demonstrates the psychical differences that exist between the sexes and, interestingly, Freud did not affiliate his theories with biology. In this sense, it was through the body that Freud demonstrated the ways that phallocentrism fixes and writes upon bodies. Therefore, it is necessary to rethink and reconfigure the oedipalized body, seeing as it is a body that is fixed in patriarchy. This was one of the main feminist critiques of Freud and it is what this entry will focus upon. Specifically, the Oedipal complex locates the very psychical reproduction of patriarchy and explains the structure of sexual roles in Western society. Although Freud had no feminist intent in his writings, feminists have managed to find his work useful. The dilemma facing contemporary feminism, which is identified as post-1995 feminism committed to corporeality and difference, is that psychoanalysis proposes explanations for the reproduction of patriarchy and its rigid sexual roles. The goal of contemporary feminism is to break away from the circularity of the Oedipal complex and into new ways of thinking. The writings of these feminist authors, and the incorporation of Luce Irigaray's work on sexual difference, have helped to dismantle the circularity and dominance of the Oedipal complex by introducing a struggle for new ideas related to thinking of difference and becoming as ways of thinking and living. Feminism has in turn critiqued Freudian psychoanalysis while at the same time addressing whether it is feasible to move beyond its dominance, or if it is necessary to work within its framework with its given theories regarding the two sexes. The works of past and contemporary feminists offer ways of theorizing the problem that is encountered by the Oedipal complex: the reproduction of patriarchy. Feminism is a broad term and there are many different kinds of feminism. The feminism referred to in this entry is a contemporary feminism that is committed to difference, particularly sexual difference as well as corporeality.

While there is a vast body of work comprised of many disparate positions that might fall within the framework of psychoanalytic feminism, what can be seen as mutual is a descent from, respect for, and some minimal borrowing of Freudian accounts of the unconscious. Any legitimate psychoanalytic theory must in the very least provide an account of the unconscious and its bond with sexuality. However, it is precisely this descent that has also provided a barrier to feminist deployment, seeing as Freud is sometimes superficially read as proffering misogynist explanations of psychic structure, which is understood to reduce and diminish the diversity of individual women's experiences into a prescribed and predictable formula that will fit within its own theoretical parameters. Nonetheless, Freud's discussion – and hypotheses concerning hysteria, the Oedipal complex, female sexuality and femininity, and women's role in civilization – have provided the volatile grounds for contention and, in turn, for feminist re-articulation. Before any of the multiple articulations of psychoanalytic feminism can be discussed in more detail, we must first establish the historical and conceptual roots from which they arise. Since a great deal of psychoanalytic feminist theory is specifically concerned with revising the Oedipal narrative of Freud, this entry devotes particular attention to Freud's theories of the Oedipal complex and how they pertain to feminist theory and criticism.

FREUD AND THE PROBLEM OF FEMININITY

Freud recognized that he spoke about femininity in ways that did not always sound friendly to women. The most obvious reason for his animosity is his failure to grasp the cultural and historical specificity of his own insights. Freud writes as if the women in analysis with him embodied eternal femininity. Yet any clearheaded reading of his descriptions of women will find massive evidence of the time-bound nature of his views. The Oedipal complex is central to Freud's writings with regard to familial relations and also sexuality and sexual difference. It is through his writings on the Oedipal complex that the differences between boys and girls become clear, and sometimes not so clear.

What Freud does maintain is that femininity cannot be grasped from a biological or conventional perspective (Freud 1968 [1933], 114). Another way of putting this is that sexual difference is centrally concerned with psychical reality rather than material reality, with the realm of fantasy rather than nature or culture. The Oedipal story is the story of psychic development, the story of how we become subjects and in becoming subjects, how we become sexually differentiated.

According to Freud, both boy and girl begin in the same pre-Oedipal place, that is, emotionally attached to the mother. It is because of this initially shared position that Freud declares that the little girl is a little man, meaning that the infant is not yet sexually differentiated. It is for this reason also that Freud upholds the idea of a single, "masculine" libido. In Freud's view, the libido is not neutral because its original object of desire is the mother and this desire for the mother is connected to masculinity. However, Freud does acknowledge that in the libido's most primordial stages, there can be no sexual distinction. It is not until children pass through the Oedipal complex that they can be said to have a genital organization, one that is acquired through a relation to castration, the last stage in sexual development (following oral, anal, and phallic stages). Thus, during infancy, both children are seen as "little men," their desire defined by the terms of a single masculine libido.

Freud is confused by the way that femininity comes about, hence he referred to it as "the riddle of femininity." By referring to the riddle of femininity, this also suggests that Freud understands sexual identity not as a natural pre-given anatomical essence, but rather as a form of individuation and differentiation achieved through the complex interaction between the bodily drives and one's parents/family. However, the story of the boy follows a logical and steady trajectory since he retains his phallic pleasure and, although he must displace the immediate object of his desire, he can nonetheless look forward to substitute objects. The boy's Oedipal attachment to the mother follows unremittingly from a pre-Oedipal attachment until it is brought to an end by the threat of castration from the father. At the conclusion of the Oedipal complex, the boy identifies with the father, establishes a super-ego, and abandons the immediate object of desire with the promise that he will one day possess a similar object modeled on the mother. Yet the girl's Oedipal complex is necessarily more complicated as it is a secondary formation instigated by a break from the pre-Oedipal relation to the mother. Freud theorized that it is the understanding that the beloved mother is castrated that incites the little girl to redirect her love toward her father. Which is to say that, for the girl, castration does not resolve the Oedipal complex but instead causes her to enter it, and for this reason Freud claims that it is never wholly brought to a conclusion or demolished, thus – in his view – accounting for girls' weaker super-egos and lesser capacity for sublimation. The girl rejects her mother not in fear but in disdain and envy for what the mother does not possess. On the other hand, the father does not represent a threat (she finds herself already castrated) or the prospect of a fulfilled desire in the future (the only replacement for the missing penis is a child of her own), in the same way as he does for the boy who can identify with him and hope eventually to possess what he does. In turn, the only promise the father offers is as a shelter from loss, a loss that is represented by the mother who bears this loss and who is consequently responsible for the girl's own. In the girl's Oedipal scenario, the father stands for the virility of desire itself, which she herself lacks but might reclaim through another man's offer to have a child. In the trajectory of the girl's Oedipal complex, femininity is realized as the desire to be the object of masculine desire itself.

Sexual difference is important both socially and politically and in turn Freud's theories of sexuality and the unconscious involve not only individual psychology but also the constitution of social life. Sexuality and sexual identity are formed in ambivalent relation to others and pervade the bonds of civilization and throughout all social relations. In turning his attention to broader cultural questions, Freud proposed a story of the origin of political structures that correlates with his understanding of the individual psyche. To appreciate the political significance of the Oedipal complex, it is useful to locate it more broadly within the scope of Freud's understanding of group psychology. In *Group Psychology and the Analysis of the Ego*, Freud challenges any clear-cut opposition between group and individual psychology and claims that from the beginning human infancy is completely immersed in a world of others (Freud 1968). Identification and love shape the core of identity and are "social phenomena"; therefore, social relations are themselves premised on developments that occur within the family. It is thus important not to separate individual from group psychology or to assume that there is some kind of social instinct independent of the drives that motivate the individual.

FEMINIST CRITICISM OF PSYCHOANALYSIS

Even in Freud's own circle, not all analysts agreed with his evaluation and, in turn, women's sexuality and the roles of castration and penis envy were debated, notably among Karl Abraham, Ernest Jones, Helene Deutsch, and Karen Horney. Horney (1924, 25–60), in particular, argued for an intrinsic feminine disposition that is not simply a secondary formation premised on castration and also took issue with the alleged effects of penis envy and women's assumed feelings of inferiority. She said that women's feelings of inferiority originated not in their recognition of their own "castration" but rather in the realization of their social subordination. Thus, Horney proposes that women believe the lie ingrained in them by men that they like being exclusively feminine. The "healthy" woman, then, is one who will move beyond her absolute femininity to embrace an ideal self that will include both masculine and feminine traits. Horney posited that as soon as women learn to view themselves as men's equals, society would have little if any power over them. For Horney, the theory of penis envy will be refined by an enquiry of the symbolic and psychological meaning of body and its origin. In addition to this refinement, another insight in Freud's theory that is further developed in Horney's reading is that the formation of the gendered ego is always to be contextualized in the early development within family and parental relations. In addition to Freud's explanation of the desire for the father, Horney points out that the fathers' observable authority and superior status in the family also play a part in the early ego formation of the child. As with many later feminist criticisms of Freud, Horney attempted to reclaim female sexuality, and in turn an authentic form of the "feminine" itself, by imploring a genuinely independent nature and instead holding "culture" accountable for the subordinate status of women. However, by advocating the primacy of biological and social forces, Horney denies the idea that is central to Freud's hypothesis, the psychical realm of representation that is the "unconscious."

Later, Simone de Beauvoir addressed the discourse of psychoanalysis in *The Second Sex* (Beauvoir 1989 [1949]), dedicating an early chapter to her distrust of "The Psychoanalytic Point of View" (Beauvoir 1989 [1949], 38–52). She argues that Freud has not thought through the social origins of masculine and paternal power and privilege and in turn considers his theory to be an insufficient elucidation of woman's otherness. She claims that if women envy men, it is simply because of their social power and privilege, and not because of anatomical superiority. In the opening of the chapter, Beauvoir states that "psychoanalysis offers a perspective which she does 'not intend to criticize as a whole'" (Beauvoir 1989 [1949], 38), especially since it does accept that "no factor becomes involved in the psychic life without having taken on human significance" (Beauvoir 1989 [1949], 38); however, she questions both its dogmatic reliance on definite elements of development and its "embarrassing flexibility on a basis of rigid concepts" (Beauvoir 1989 [1949], 38). Like Horney, Beauvoir renounces Freud's idea that there is only one, masculine, libido and no feminine libido. Beauvoir reads Freud's account of penis envy critically and implores that the causality be turned around.

Beauvoir argues that "the little girls' covetousness, when it exists, results from a previous evaluation of virility" (Beauvoir 1989 [1949], 41). The penis does not enjoy a mysterious significance; it is rather the symbolizing object of the social situations that are faced by many individuals. For the little girl, "the place the father holds in the family, the universal predominance of males, her own education – everything confirms her in her belief in masculine superiority," and it is this social disadvantage that reminds her of her comparative biological deficit – that of castration – and in turn takes the biological to be the cause of the psychical and the social (Beauvoir 1989 [1949], 43). On the contrary, "it is not the lack of the penis that causes this complex, but rather the total situation; if the little girl feels penis envy it is only as the symbol of privileges enjoyed by boys" (Beauvoir 1989 [1949], 43). If the girl feels incomplete compared with a boy with a penis, it is not because the penis is in itself significant, but that the girl is mapping her sense of inferiority onto the sheer difference between penis and castration.

In a way, both Horney and Beauvoir make efforts to refine – or perhaps reclaim – Freud's theory, by introducing psychical and social dimensions to the theory of penis envy, and providing different possible explanations for the envy that Freud observes. The penis, for them, carries more psychical, symbolic, and social significance within a patriarchal society and family, and the inferiority felt by women is due to the social and historical symbolic meaning of the penis, namely the social superiority of men. In this way, Freudian theory is opened up to other possibilities than biological determinism, and serves as a resource for reflecting upon the connection between the individual psyche and one's social positioning. In other words, psychoanalysis assigns to women the same destiny of self-division and conflict between subjectivity and femininity that adheres to social precepts and biological norms. Psychoanalysis renders the characteristics of femininity and subjectivity as incompatible and disparate paths. Women might be able to be full subjects with agency, but only at the expense of their femininity. Or they can commence a life of femininity, but only by sacrificing their independence and agency.

"French feminist" critiques of Freudian psychoanalysis is in many ways an inaccurate term since the authors thus characterized are rarely of French origin or nationality (although French is the predominant language of their writing) and not necessarily overtly self-identified as feminist. The writers affiliated with what will be more accurately termed postmodern feminism, including (but certainly not limited to) Julia Kristeva,

Luce Irigaray, and Hélène Cixous, seek to get away from any absolute assertions of what a feminist should be, since they try to avoid phallocentric thought, or thought that centers around an absolute word. They write about both feminist theory and practice. Three of the main postmodern feminists, Hélène Cixous, Luce Irigaray, and Julia Kristeva, base their thought on Simone de Beauvoir's existentialism, Jacques Derrida's deconstructionism, and Jacques Lacan's interpretation of psychoanalysis. Each of them questions the relation between the maternal and the feminine, doubt that we can say what a woman is, worry about Freud's lack of attention to mothers, play with writing style, wonder about feminine subjectivity, ask if women can be subjects or citizens without adapting to masculine norms, impeach Lacan's phallocentrism, and suspect that access to language assimilates women into neutralized brothers. Thus, psychoanalytic feminists in the Lacanian mode privileged the analysis of self-construction through discourse over the biological and psychosocial implications of parenting, arguing that, in order to alter gender relations, we need to change language. In Lacanian psychoanalysis, the phallus is symbolic of the child's entry into language and culture under The Law of the Father, and Lacanian feminists wanted to interrogate and resist oppressive constructions of gender and sexuality encoded in language.

Irigaray and Cixous are known for their project *Écriture féminine*, an attempt to write from – or to discursively embody – the position of woman in order to challenge women's positioning in phallocentric culture. These writers argued that women needed to forego neutral, scientific masculine language and embrace a rebellious creativity based in subjective experience of the body and the feminine. In this they attempted to realize a female/feminine sex/subject outside of patriarchal definitions of woman. For Irigaray and Cixous, this involved celebrating women's diffuse and autoerotic sensuality, in contrast to the linear, focused dynamic of "phallic" sex, as well as critiquing the symbolic order through parody. Luce Irigaray is a psychoanalyst who believes that currently the feminine is defined by the patriarchy. More specifically, Irigaray searches for ways to find the "feminine feminine," or woman the way women see her. She encourages women to use a more active voice, to create a female sexuality, and to undo the effects of men's views of women by exaggerating those images. Although Irigaray is often self-contradictory, she relishes that fact because it means that she is not being tied down by phallocentric thought. However, Julia Kristeva's position is that there is a need to break down identity, especially sexual identity, to make it ambiguous, rather than specifically masculine and feminine. Her rejection of the Oedipal complex allows for a liberated person to switch between different stages of development as well as masculine, feminine, and many other concepts.

Unlike Beauvoir, these women are philosophically and temperamentally more sympathetic to the split of subjectivity detailed by psychoanalysis, the idea that I am not I, that self-division rather than self-identity is the fundamental feature of human existence, and therefore that the subject is not a unitary point of origin for choice. Like Beauvoir, they ask whether the structures of femininity and the structures of subjectivity are compatible and reconcilable, and are vexed by the apprehension that they are fundamentally at odds. While they aim to disentangle femininity from maternity, and provide a critique of their conflation, they also take seriously the significance of maternity for women and for children of both sexes. Because they concede the limits of sociocultural explanations for women's lack of standing in the social contract, and take femininity and the feminine body as points of departure for speech or writing, they have often been accused of essentialism. The work of Irigaray, Cixous, and Kristeva engages with and transforms the ideas of Freud and Lacan, and how they articulate sexual difference as integrally connected to the foundation, and ultimately disruption, of a symbolic order.

There are a number of Anglo-American (and Australian) feminist theorists and scholars who read Lacan and laid the groundwork for the passage from French to English and from France to the United States, Britain, and Australia in the 1970s, 1980s, and early 1990s. Prominent among these is Juliet Mitchell, but of course there are many more. While these theorists write in English, they still take their application from the French Lacanian approach to psychoanalysis and are generally classified in the field of "continental feminism." Responsible for resuscitating psychoanalysis within feminist discourse and responding to earlier feminist dismissals, their aim is to recover Freud's theories for feminist purposes. A strong example of this is seen in Juliet Mitchell's insight that "psychoanalysis is not a recommendation for a patriarchal society, but an analysis of one" (Mitchell 1973, xiii).

Juliet Mitchell wrote *Psychoanalysis and Feminism*, and her reading and understanding of Freud suggest how feminists should use his work as a "description" of patriarchy (Mitchell 1973, 337). Mitchell does not believe that Freud is contributing to the problem of patriarchy in his writings on both the Oedipal and castration complexes. This is not to say that she would believe Freud to be a feminist, she is simply more sympathetic to Freud and she does not believe he is "prescribing" his discoveries onto society (Mitchell 1973, 337). Mitchell finds Freud useful in the sense that he does explain the reproduction of patriarchy as well as gendered roles through his writings on each of the complexes. Mitchell goes on to write,

"[p]sychoanalysis does not describe what woman is – far less what she should be; it can only try to comprehend how psychological femininity comes about" (Mitchell 1973, 338). Freud made keen observations and yet was quick to admit when he was less enlightened on a topic such as femininity (see earlier). Of course, Mitchell is not the only feminist to see beyond the flaws of Freudian psychoanalysis, a theory that described femininity as the "dark continent." In *Sexuality in the Field of Vision*, Jacqueline Rose writes on this very same topic (Rose 1986). She argues that the problem is that if psychoanalysis is descriptive, it leaves no room to change the path of patriarchy, yet, if it is prescriptive, it is obviously equally problematic. Rose finds that judging Freud within this dichotomy is limiting. She feels that Freud cannot be placed only within these two possibilities of either being descriptive or prescriptive "to the extent that it is locked in this model" (Rose 1986, 92). While the point of so much feminist work was to critique Freud, there can be no denying that psychoanalysis has been and – will continue to be – useful; and to agree with Rose, seeing Freud on the end of a descriptive/prescriptive binary does not do justice to why psychoanalysis mattered so much for feminism in the 1970s, and why it is still so important to contemporary feminism.

Rather than focusing on the Lacanian-inspired feminist reinterpretation of psychoanalysis in the English-speaking world, the Anglo-American development of feminist psychoanalysis arose from British object relations theory, the most exemplary of which has been the work of Jessica Benjamin. What distinguishes this Anglo-American tradition from the aforementioned so-called French one is the importance it places on "intersubjectivity" (or pre-Oedipal sociality) along with its focus on the values of integration and wholeness, rather than those of self-division.

Benjamin is just as troubled by the psychoanalytic rendering of social life as synonymous with the world of men, one that is advanced purely on the basis of the father–son relation. She regards what she calls a "struggle for power" with contempt (Benjamin 1988, 6). She argues that it is a world in which women are merely the objects of desire, and believes that in forming their identity, subjects are reduced and bound by love to oppressive social relations. For this reason, she fears that "domination is anchored in the hearts of the dominated" (Benjamin 1988, 5), meaning that women are erotically attached to patriarchal power, and that psychoanalysis can help explain how and why this happens. Therefore, psychoanalysis supplies Benjamin with insights not only into the individual psyche but also into the organization, structure, and dissemination of political power. She builds on the foundation of Freud's Oedipal complex, and provides a critical revision of it to include the female's fight for independence. She argues that traditional Freudian theories doubtlessly reproduce patriarchal gender relationships, which are defined by domination and submission.

Benjamin understands the infant to be a fundamentally social creature, one that engages in the world with a desire for recognition. As a result, the child's identity is formed through the interplay between this desire and the response of another who either affirms or denies the child. Here Benjamin puts her emphasis on sociality and what she terms "intersubjectivity," and claims that it is not her intention to disregard the intrapsychic elements of subject formation; rather, she argues for "the interaction between the psyche and social life" (Benjamin 1988, 5). She maintains that the inner and the outer are not competing but complementary theoretical perspectives. However, she does situate identity generally, and gendered identity more specifically, within the range of the subject's manifold and ambiguous social identifications. Benjamin argues that domination occurs because of the failures of recognition manufactured within the political and social order.

Benjamin deconstructs Freud's reading of the Oedipal myth to show how it is predicated on binary oppositions that preclude the recognition of difference: if we do not acknowledge the mother as a separate subject on a theoretical and a practical level, Benjamin argues, then we cannot come into being as separate subjects either; for the self is dependent on the mother for the recognition she seeks, and if that mother does not survive, the self does not survive either. The repudiation of femininity that is written into the Oedipal complex by Freud as the incest taboo – the Oedipal injunction that one must not be like the mother in order to possess her, or the splitting off of identificatory love from object love, the latter of which reduces the other's subjectivity to a thing – has disastrous consequences for the boy's development of selfhood and agency.

In *The Bonds of Love* (Benjamin 1988), she puts forward a theory of sadomasochism that departs both from a drive-oriented Freudian account of masochism as aggression turned inward and from feminist accounts of women as unwilling victims of male domination. Instead, she insists that women are complicit with their own subordination and views sadomasochism through the lens of intersubjectivity (which asks us to think in terms of simultaneity rather than linearly, to see the self-other dyad from two different perspectives at the same time), as rooted in an imbalance between assertion of self and recognition of otherness. Our paradoxical dependence on others for our own sense of self is the core of the problem: if we destroy the other, there is no one left to recognize us but there is no way of avoiding the danger that the other can destroy us. For Benjamin, the solution to the paradox of recognition is for it to continue as a constant tension.

Freudian psychoanalysis presents a critical project, not necessarily a normative one. In developing a theory of the drives and the non-rational forces that move and impel us, the idea that we are incapable of complete self-knowledge or self-mastery, psychoanalytic theory also suggests that our individual characters and political communities are in fact precariousness in the sense of both our psychic and political identities. We cannot assume that the unconscious is either an innately transgressive or a moderate force. Rather, the unconscious is more likely an unreliable one, promoting dissent sometimes, obstinacy and self-preservation at other times. Although feminist theorists are in an uncomfortable alliance, the Freudian account of the unconscious provides feminist theory with resources for investigating both political and ontological matters. Ontologically, Freudian psychoanalysis offers a distinctively psychical understanding of sexual difference, providing inquiries into how we come to (mis)inhabit our bodies and our identities, an inquiry that is reducible to neither social nor biological classifications. Politically, Freudian psychoanalysis offers a rendering of the forces that impel us to make, break, and mend the bonds that hold us together. By offering an awareness of the formation of subjectivity and the fantasies of social life, Freudian psychoanalysis in turn enables a feminist critique of patriarchal social relations, including the symbolic bonds and subjective forces that reinforce identity and bind sexed subjects to relations of dominance and subordination. From Freudian psychoanalysis comes the concept of what it means to enter the social realm as a gendered subject. When historically situated, Freudian psychoanalysis makes it possible to become explicit about the political implications of each stage of the process of becoming a human subject and, above all, makes it clear that there are no unified, transcendental subjects. Rather, what we have is the subject-in-process, constantly being reproduced and repositioned through discursive networks and frameworks. What feminist critiques of Freudian psychoanalysis reiterate is the diversity of women rather than any notional woman. This includes the diversity among feminist theorists themselves who do not all speak from the same position.

SEE ALSO: Feminism, French; Feminist Literary Criticism; Patriarchy; Postmodern Feminist Psychology; Sexual Subjectivity

REFERENCES

Beauvoir, Simone de. 1989. *The Second Sex*, trans. H. M. Parshley. New York: Vintage Books. First published 1949.
Benjamin, Jessica. 1988. *The Bonds of Love*. New York: Pantheon Books.
Freud, Sigmund. 1968. "Group Psychology and the Analysis of the Ego." In *The Standard Edition of the Complete Psychological Works of Sigmund Freud*, ed. and trans. James Strachey, vol. XVIII. London: Hogarth Press. First published 1921.
Freud, Sigmund. 1968. "Femininity." In *The Standard Edition of the Complete Psychological Works of Sigmund Freud*, ed. and trans. James Strachey, vol. XXII. London: Hogarth Press. First published 1933.
Horney, Karen. 1924. "On the Genesis of Castration Complex in Women." *International Journal of Psychoanalysis*, 5: 50–65.
Mitchell, Juliet. 1973. *Psychoanalysis and Feminism*. New York: Vintage Books.

FURTHER READING

Benjamin, Jessica. 1998. *Like Subjects, Love Objects*. New Haven: Yale University Press.
Cixous, Hélène, and Catherine Clement. 1986. *The Newly Born Woman*, trans. Betsy Wing. Minneapolis: University of Minnesota Press. First published 1975.
Freud, Sigmund. 1968. *The Standard Edition of the Complete Psychological Works of Sigmund Freud*, ed. and trans. James Strachey. London: Hogarth Press.

Freud, Sigmund. 1968. "Three Essays on the Theory of Sexuality." In *The Standard Edition of the Complete Psychological Works of Sigmund Freud*, ed. and trans. James Strachey, vol. VII. London: Hogarth Press. First published 1905.

Freud, Sigmund. 1968. "Some Psychical Consequences of the Anatomical Distinction Between the Sexes." In *The Standard Edition of the Complete Psychological Works of Sigmund Freud*, ed. and trans. James Strachey, vol. XIX. London: Hogarth Press. First published 1925.

Freud, Sigmund. 1968. "Female Sexuality." In *The Standard Edition of the Complete Psychological Works of Sigmund Freud*, ed. and trans. James Strachey, vol. XXI. London: Hogarth Press. First published 1931.

Grosz, Elizabeth. 1990. *Jacques Lacan: A Feminist Introduction*. New York: Routledge.

Kristeva, Julia. 1984. *Revolution in Poetic Language*, trans. Margaret Waller. New York: Columbia University Press. First published 1974.

Mitchell, Juliet. 1982. "Introduction – I." In *Feminine Sexuality*, edited by Juliet Mitchell and Jacqueline Rose, 1–26. New York: Norton.

Rose, Jacqueline, 1982, "Introduction – II." In *Feminine Sexuality*, edited by Juliet Mitchell and Jacqueline Rose, 27–58. New York: Norton.

Rose, Jacqueline, 1986. *Sexuality in the Field of Vision*. London: Verso.

Feminism, Radical

BRONWYN WINTER
The University of Sydney, Australia

Radical feminism, sometimes called revolutionary feminism, or, in France, materialist feminism, is associated with so-called "second-wave" feminism, the Women's Liberation Movement, that emerged in the late 1960s and early 1970s. As the name implies, radical feminism sought to address the roots of women's oppression, positing that women and men constitute classes in a system of domination that had at its base the category of sex. In this sense, it drew on both Marxian analysis of an antagonistic, material, and sociohistorically constructed relationship between dominant and oppressed class and a Beauvoirian analysis of women as a caste (Beauvoir 1949).

IDEAS, PRACTICES, AND IMPACTS

Radical feminism is largely associated with the United States and, in that context, benefited from the experience and activism of the civil rights movement. Versions of radical feminism, however, existed in other Western English-speaking countries and also throughout Europe and beyond, where it had a different legacy, often related to extreme-left student activism around May 1968 or anti-war movements. It was highly influential in advancing feminist analyses of patriarchy as ideological, structural, and systemic in its operation and impacts. It also foregrounded marriage and the family as key sites of women's oppression and challenged the division between the private and the public. Radical feminists have historically been active in campaigns against violence against women, including, but not limited to, domestic violence, incest and pedophilia, rape, sexual harassment, and prostitution.

In keeping with the radical feminist core principle that ending women's oppression would necessitate a revolutionary overthrow of existing systems and the creation of new ways of functioning, radical feminists prioritized the creation of alternative structures. Central to these structures were women-only spaces, meetings, and activities, along with collective and consensual, thus non-hierarchical, forms of functioning. Not only were radical feminists centrally involved in setting up a range of autonomous women's services, including illegal ones (abortion clinics, rape crisis centers, women's shelters, women's health centers), they also worked to set up autonomous women's spaces such as women's centers, cafes, bookshops and libraries (and later, archives), art spaces, and so on. Although many of those feminist initiatives now benefit from government funding (and in some cases have been institutionalized in ways that are not always beneficial to women), or have been forced into closure, the importance of women's spaces and women's services informed by feminist, woman-centered approaches soon became a given in many feminist circles.

Autonomous voice was also important, and radical feminists produced a range of pamphlets, newsletters, magazines, creative writing, singers and bands, and theater groups. Part of this autonomous voice were consciousness-raising (CR) groups that were often associated with the idea that "the personal is political." In a 1969 essay popularizing this last term, Carol Hanisch distinguished CR groups from "therapy," in that CR groups enabled the discovery of the political and collective dimensions to the everyday personal experiences of women and the need for collective action to challenge these politics (Hanisch 1969). Radical feminist initiatives in the areas of political analysis, cultural expressions, and provision of women's services have significantly contributed to transforming mainstream approaches in these areas, in addition to informing research on women and feminism.

Although there was often crossover in forms of action between radical feminists and other feminists, and in many cases radical feminists worked alongside socialist, liberal, and Marxist feminists to achieve common goals, these latter groups tended to be more involved in reformist campaigns aimed at the state or at the traditional left (trade unions, political parties, and so on), focusing on capitalism or sex inequality in the public sphere as priority issues. Radical feminists, on the other hand, placed far less faith in the capacity of these institutions and organizations to change and considered socialist or liberal feminist analyses of patriarchy to be insufficient. Socialist and liberal feminists were similarly often hostile to radical feminism as "bourgeois" or too separatist. Radical feminists also privileged imaginative direct actions, such as spray-painting sexist advertising or "Take Back the Night" marches against male violence, now an annual event in many parts of the world. Even if many radical feminists now work in institutional structures such as universities or various branches of public services, or institutionally funded women's services, most retain a high level of distrust of institutional and hierarchical forms of organizing.

KEY TEXTS AND SUBSEQUENT SCHOLARSHIP

Two key texts and names in the formation of what Denise Thompson has called the (radical) feminist "system of values and meanings" (as opposed to ideology, which is developed to justify relationships of domination) (Thompson 2001) are Kate Millet's *Sexual Politics* (Millett 1969) and Shulamith Firestone's *The Dialectic of Sex* (Firestone 1970). Millett located women's oppression in both the family and religion, stressing "the overwhelmingly *cultural* character of gender" (Millett 1969, 39), and Firestone opened her book with the sentence "sex class is so deep as to be invisible" (Firestone 1970, 1). Their discussion of the *culturally constructed* category of sex as so ingrained that it appears natural (although Firestone has been criticized for an overly biologically determinist approach to the history of patriarchy) owes a great deal to Beauvoir. The idea was later developed further by radical lesbian theorist Monique Wittig in her assertion that lesbians refute this cultural construction of "woman." Radical feminists have also critiqued heterosexuality as part of the ideology of male domination, although not all are themselves lesbian (e.g., Jackson 1999).

Many radical feminist scholars assert that because it analyzes the fundamental ideology and structures of male domination as a political system, radical feminism is in fact "feminism unmodified" (MacKinnon 1988; Bell and Klein 1996; Thompson 2001). They thus reiterate the origins of the idea of *radical* feminism, which investigates and acts on the roots of women's oppression. They reject the socialist feminist idea of "dual systems" – capitalism and patriarchy – arguing that sex is the fundamental principle of social organization and patriarchy is thus the core political system of domination. They similarly reject liberal feminist approaches to sex equality, arguing that such approaches, although often strategically important, cannot be the end goal of feminism because they simply align women with men in the public sphere within the existing patriarchal system.

CRITICISMS

Radical feminism has been criticized by other feminists or by women's studies scholars for a variety of reasons. First, because of its early focus on the cultural dimensions of patriarchy and on the creation of women's alternatives, it has been critiqued or even dismissed as "cultural feminism" and thus somehow lightweight, as failing to grapple with fundamental socioeconomic issues (Echols 1989). The subsequent interest of some radical feminists in women's spirituality, notwithstanding early and ongoing trenchant radical feminist critiques of religion as patriarchal, has fed this impression. Second, it has been dismissed as a "white" movement (as if major early theorists in many other branches of US feminism were not also white). In fact, much radical feminist work explicitly discusses race and class and some women of color such as Barbara Christian identified as radical feminist. The charge of "whiteness" also comes about in response to radical feminists' focus on commonalities of women's experience of male domination across cultures, and their opposition to cultural relativism. Third, the focus of many radical feminists on violence against women has led to the charge of "victim feminism," because their focus tends to be more on the situation and structures of oppression than on individual women's agency within them.

The most controversial aspects are no doubt the focus of many radical feminists on pornography and prostitution (e.g., Dworkin 1981; Jeffreys 1998; Whisnant and Stark 2004), along with their critiques of sadomasochistic sexual practices among lesbians (Linden et al. 1982) and transgender politics (Raymond 1979). Radical feminist analyses of pornography and prostitution consider them as part of a continuum within a culture of misogynist objectification of women and male violence; distinctions between "forced" and "free" prostitution are rejected. As concerns sadomasochism, the radical feminist argument is that sadomasochistic sexual practices reproduce abusive sexualities based on unequal power relationships. Those defending sadomasochism have argued that the practices explore these power relationships in consensual ways.

Radical feminist critiques of transgender politics are often assumed to be based on biological determinism, and radical feminists are often labeled "transphobic." Although some radical feminists privilege arguments about biology and bodily integrity, the main radical feminist argument has to do with analysis of the politics of male and female socialization and ongoing exercise of male power. If the process of gendered acculturation and political power begins at birth, then, they argue, an acculturated male cannot "become" a constructed female and vice versa. Moreover, for radical feminists, the idea of gender reassignment reinforces the very gender binaries that serve male domination. The transgender debates have typically played out in practice around admission or otherwise of male-to-female trans people into women-only services, spaces, and cultural events; these debates have extended to legal battles in some instances (e.g., *Nixon v. Vancouver Rape Relief* 1995).

Debates around radical feminist ideas and practices thus continue both inside and outside the academy. They often produce more heat than light, which is unfortunate, given radical feminism's historical and ongoing contribution to feminist reflection about the nature of patriarchy and women's situation and experience within it.

SEE ALSO: Feminism, Cultural; Feminism, French; Feminism, Lesbian; Feminisms, First, Second, and Third Wave; Feminist Activism; Feminist Publishing; Personal is Political; Radical Lesbianism

REFERENCES

Beauvoir, Simone de. 1949. *Le Deuxième sexe*. Paris: Gallimard.
Bell, Diane, and Renate Klein, eds. 1996. *Radically Speaking: Feminism Reclaimed*. North Melbourne: Spinifex Press.
Dworkin, Andrea. 1981. *Pornography: Men Possessing Women*. Boston: Dutton.
Echols, Alice. 1989. *Daring to Be Bad: Radical Feminism in America 1967–1975*. Minneapolis: University of Minnesota Press.
Firestone, Shulamith. 1970. *The Dialectic of Sex: The Case for Feminist Revolution*. New York: William Morrow.
Hanisch, Carol. 1969. "The Personal is Political." Accessed June 15, 2015, at http://www.carolhanisch.org/CHwritings/PIP.html.
Jackson, Stevi. 1999. *Heterosexuality in Question*. London: Sage.
Jeffreys, Sheila. 1998. *The Idea of Prostitution*. Melbourne: Spinifex Press.
Linden, Robin Ruth, Darlene R. Pagano, Diana E. H. Russell, and Susan Leigh Star, eds. 1982. *Against Sadomasochism: A Radical Feminist Analysis*. East Palo Alto: Frog in the Well Press.
MacKinnon, Catharine A. 1988. *Feminism Unmodified: Discourses on Life and Law*. Cambridge, MA: Harvard University Press.
Millett, Kate. 1969. *Sexual Politics*. New York: Doubleday.
Raymond, Janice. 1979. *The Transsexual Empire*. Boston: Beacon Press.
Thompson, Denise. 2001. *Radical Feminism Today*. London: Sage.
Whisnant, Rebecca, and Christine Stark, eds. 2004. *Not for Sale: Feminists Resisting Prostitution and Pornography*. North Melbourne: Spinifex Press.

FURTHER READING

Douglas, Carol Anne. 1990. *Love & Politics: Radical Feminist & Lesbian Theories*. San Francisco: ism press.
Morgan, Robin, ed. 1970. *Sisterhood is Powerful: an Anthology of Writings from the Women's Liberation Movement*. New York: Random House.

Feminism in South Africa

DENISE BUITEN
University of Notre Dame Australia, Australia

In addition to national and transnational struggles for gender equality, South African feminisms have been strongly shaped by struggles for political and racial equality. From the turn of the twentieth century through to the decades following apartheid, South African feminist activism and scholarship have engaged deeply with questions of racial and class difference and nationalism. To the extent that women's activism, both feminist and non-feminist, has been profoundly embedded in the anti-apartheid movement, scholars have shifted from regarding as separate women's organizing against national oppression and their organizing against gender oppression, instead considering the complex ways in which these nationalist and feminist movements have been closely intertwined (Hassim 2006).

UNEQUAL GENDERED EXPERIENCES

During apartheid rule, and preceding this during unequal racialized British colonial rule, women's experiences of gender oppression in South Africa were characterized by marked differences along racial and class lines (Walker 1991; Moolman 2009). Whereas white women experienced the weight of male-dominated political institutions and the constraints of expectations of middle-class female domesticity, black women's experiences were significantly shaped by racial and political disenfranchisement and the oppressive class conditions that stemmed from these inequalities. Black women were subject to racist misogyny at the hands of white men, and also racial and class oppression at the hands of white women. At the same time, black women experienced relative exclusion and limiting discourses around women's roles from within black nationalist movements. As such, while women's activism in South Africa was vibrantly represented and pursued, feminist concerns over gender equality had to be tackled along with nationalist concerns for racial and political equality.

EMERGING WOMEN'S MOVEMENTS

From the early twentieth century, prior to the birth of formal apartheid, black women struggled against low wages, poor working conditions, and various state attempts to regulate their movements and economic activities (Hassim 2006). Pass laws introduced to segregate racial populations while exploiting black labor were initially applied primarily to men, who were required to carry pass books with them when traveling outside racially and ethnically assigned homelands and designated areas. However, attempts in the 1910s and 1950s to extend pass laws to women were met with fierce protests and other forms of action, including the famous Women's March of 1956, which saw 20,000 women from the far ends of the country march upon the Union Buildings in Pretoria to protest against the pass laws.

Economic changes occurring in South Africa impacted significantly on women (Walker 1991), and many struggles against economic inequality at this time saw the significant involvement of women's movements, which understood and tackled their oppression as women as tied in with class oppression. This strand of feminist organizing took a "workerist" position drawing on Marxist feminism, whereby women's interests were not regarded as general but as determined by their class position. As such, many black women's organizations worked in close connection with unions and it was argued that women's interests would only be met through the overthrowing of racialized capitalist exploitation, which should take primacy in activist struggles against oppression. This position also sought to highlight the mismatch between the concerns of white middle-class and black working-class women, which formed part of the destabilization of the category "women" within feminist movements. Radical feminist movements in South Africa at the time, which often focused on women-specific issues such as gender-based violence and tended to distance themselves from male-dominated institutions and organizations such as trade unions, were relatively marginal at the time and had a higher membership of white feminists (Hassim 2006).

NATIONALISM AND WOMEN'S MOBILIZATION

During the concerted liberation struggles of the 1940s onwards, nationalist concerns subsumed those of feminists (McClintock 1991; Hassim 2006; Britton and Fish 2009). Nationalisms in South Africa, both Afrikaner and African, were highly gendered, assigning women and men unequal access to the privileges of nationhood and perpetuating unequal gendered roles within the movement (McClintock 1991). Although women were highly active in nationalist struggles, and indeed mobilized for such movements, this was done in a way that marginalized women's gendered interests, and relied on limiting gender constructs to forward the nationalist agenda (Hassim 1991; McClintock 1991; Hassim 2006; Britton and Fish 2009). Women were framed as "mothers of the nation," and many women's movements aligned themselves with a "motherist" approach, advocating for nationalist interests from within their roles as mothers.

Within African nationalist struggles, black women's protests against pass laws included objections on the basis of their interference with domestic roles, both within their own families and within white families as domestic workers (Britton and Fish 2009). Although this shed light on the connection between private spaces and nationalist interests, and created a platform for change, it also tended to re-enforce limiting gender constructs and hierarchies within the nationalist movement (Britton and Fish 2009). Women's politicization was largely framed as auxiliary within the African nationalist movement, as volunteers and supporters of the nation (McClintock 1991). "Feminism" was often regarded within the liberation movement as a form of cultural imperialism, and as a divisive force in competition with the objectives of national liberation (Britton and Fish 2009). Although this highlighted important questions about difference and the hegemony of white, middle-class forms of feminism, it also limited a more rigorous engagement with questions of gender difference within the nationalist movement.

Despite "attempts to delegitimize feminism as a political discourse, undercurrents of feminism seethed beneath the surface of women's political activities," and the roots of an indigenous feminism were taking hold (Hassim 2006, 34–35). Women also fought for gender recognition within the African nationalist movement, including full membership and voting rights within the African National Congress (ANC), which was achieved after 31 years in 1943 (McClintock 1991). The ANC Women's League was very active, particularly during the 1950s, and the Women's Charter calling for land redistribution, workers' rights, education, and other economic, social, and cultural rights did, in fact, precede and in many senses inspire the better known Freedom Charter of the ANC. At the same time, images of women as mothers of the nation, appealing to white women for solidarity, as mothers, with black women, continued to play a powerful and strategic role. In this way, women's concerns and interests were both subsumed by and tackled strategically within African nationalist movements.

Within Afrikaner nationalist movements at the turn of the twentieth century, at a time when Afrikaners were striving for independence from the British, ideologies of motherhood were harnessed in the service of gendered, economic, and racial motives (McClintock 1991; Vincent 1999). The icon and idealization of the *volksmoeder* (Afrikaans for "mother of the nation") within the Afrikaner nationalist movement at this time was, as McClintock (1991) pointed out, paradoxical. On the one hand, it inscribed (white) motherhood with a certain power and authority, and powerful images of motherhood were employed towards the achievement of women's suffrage; on the other hand, this image of motherhood was yoked to the role of domestic service, which was emphasized while women's extensive – and at times militant – participation in the nationalist movement was minimized in cultural and political representations (McClintock 1991; Vincent 1999). The image of the weeping mother during war overtook images of women as fighters and farmers. After the Anglo-Boer War (1899–1902), as South Africa became rapidly industrialized, drawing white working-class women increasingly into paid work in factories, revamped images of the *volksmoeder* were used to reinstate and attract women back into principally domestic unpaid roles. Later, during the rule of the apartheid government, images of women as mothers, bearers, and reproducers of the nation (McClintock 1991) were employed again within Afrikaner nationalist movements to argue for white women's right to vote in preservation of the white nation (Britton and Fish 2009). At the same time, however, the icon of the *volksmoeder* of Afrikaner nationalist movements, largely stripped of political agency and militancy in cultural and political representation, served to expunge white women's historical complicity in apartheid and racial oppression (McClintock 1991).

Across both African and Afrikaner streams of nationalism, the ways in which notions of motherhood were used in nationalist struggles demonstrate not only how male-dominated nationalist movements mobilized women through the use of existing – and limiting – gender identities and constructs, but also how they were implicated in re-enforcing racial and class divisions among South African women. At the same time, these historical trajectories of women's activism within nationalist movements demonstrate the complex ways in which racial, class, and gendered interests were intertwined, and the strategic deployment of gender constructs, particularly around motherhood, to improve women's positions.

FEMINISMS AT THE DAWN OF DEMOCRACY

As the country transitioned from apartheid to the new democratic dispensation in the early 1990s, women's movements mobilized to secure women's position within the post-apartheid state. Recognizing the unique opportunities for advancing women's interests inherent in such a transitional period, but skeptical of the capacity for true change for women through racial–political change alone, activists began to center more acutely on women's interests. The internationalization of feminist communication meant that women's movements were well aware of the poor outcomes that had been produced for women within other post-transition contexts. As such, women within the movement recognized that the emancipation of women could not be assumed a by-product of the achievement of democracy, and that the period of transition represented a critical strategic juncture for the establishment of women's rights (McEwan 2000). Women's movements joined to put immense pressure on the creation of constitutional mandates for gender equality, to assure gender representation in government, and to make formal legislative and policy changes guaranteeing women's rights (Hassim 2006; Britton and Fish 2009).

This led to an initial "intense focus on numbers" (Hassim 2006, 173) with regard to women's participation. The notion of equal representation of women in South Africa depended on the notion of "women" as a distinct constituency, and although this category continued to be particularly contentious due to significant racial and class inequalities existing between women in South Africa, strategically it was considered important to promote "women's interests" around certain key rights to participation, to ensure that gender concerns were not sidelined within national discourse. These interests acted as a central point of common agreement among diverse women who in many other respects shared very different experiences of patriarchy (Hassim, 2005, 2006).

In addition to getting women into government, a focal point for the 1990s was setting up a robust "national gender machinery" that would institutionalize gender equality through the creation of entities such as the *Commission on Gender Equality* and the *Office on the Status of Women* (Gouws 2010). A focus on liberal, individual rights and law reform for women was successfully pursued, and terms such as "gender equality," "women's empowerment," and "gender transformation" became embedded within South African political institutions and pursued through the National Gender Machinery. At the 1994 democratic elections, women secured one third of the seats in parliament (increased to a 50 percent parliamentary quota for women in 2007), Constitutional protections were put in place and legal reform in relation to a range of gender issues began (Britton and Fish 2009). There was huge hope and optimism among feminist advocates, as South Africa's institutions were rebuilt "by centralizing gender rights in order to improve the quality of life and status for all women in the country" (Britton and Fish 2009, 1).

However, although these feminist advances have been widely lauded as some of the most progressive in the world, this approach has also been variously critiqued by African feminist scholars as a form of "state feminism" that dilutes and sanitizes feminism in South Africa (Gouws 2010). The critique stems from two interrelated concerns: first, that state feminism has fostered apathy within the women's movement in a way that discourages robust, radical activism and praxis, and second, that it has contributed to an apparent fissure between formal legal and public rights for women, on the one hand, and lived experiences of severe gender inequality supported by deep, unchallenged ideas about gender on the other (Hassim 2006; Britton and Fish 2009; Gouws 2010).

State feminism is characterized by a top-down, institutional orientation towards gender equality. Gender is largely mainstreamed through the use of a gender "toolkit" to assess the differential impacts of policy on men and women, and a set of checklists that are applied within institutions in a way that resonates with other technocratic forms of governance and regulation (Gouws 2010). For feminist scholars, this can be problematic in terms of its compatibility with resistance to genuine, radical feminist change in institutions, and weaknesses in challenging established power (Bhana and Mthethwa-Sommers 2010; Gouws 2010). Further, for some it represents a sanitized, less vibrant feminist politics, discouraging civil society engagement and activism around gender, with the assumption that gender equality is taken care of by the state. As such, South African feminist scholars such as Hassim (2005) have argued that it represents an "inclusionary" gender politics preoccupied with formal gender equity over a "transformational" gender politics engaging more deeply and radically with gender constructs with the goal of comprehensive change. Inclusionary and transformational gender politics in post-apartheid South Africa need not always be seen as in opposition to one another, however, and these forms of feminism may be working side-by-side, employed strategically by the women's movement to achieve the best outcomes for women within the constraints of institutional and cultural context.

CHALLENGES

Post-apartheid gender analyses have variously pointed to the contradiction between the extensive formal rights and wins for women in South Africa's public sphere, and evidence of significant gender inequality related particularly to the "private" sphere

(Walsh 2006; Gqola 2007; Britton and Fish 2009). The unequal burden, particularly on black women, of the HIV pandemic and pervasive poverty, and having among the highest rates of gender-based violence in the world (Britton and Fish 2009), are issues that have pointed to the limitations of representational achievements for women. The 2006 rape trial of the later president of South Africa, Jacob Zuma, sharply highlighted the division between public rights and everyday discourses of gender. Both Zuma and his supporters (men and women) invoked a range of victim-blaming rape myths, with the alleged victim forced into hiding at the end of the trial, in which Zuma was acquitted (Motsei 2007). Subsequent high-profile cases of rape have also seen renewed debate about the nature of women's liberation in South Africa. It has been argued that changes to social relations and attitudes that underpin the gender inequality that persists in the face of comparative public empowerment remains the challenge for South African feminisms (Britton and Fish 2009).

One of the key challenges for South African feminists post-apartheid has been to contest "cultural" justifications used to legitimate inequalities between women and men, and to address the cultural imperialism represented by hegemonic white Western feminisms while carving out a rigorous intellectual and activist space for engaging with feminist politics and defining an indigenous feminism (Hassim 1991). Feminist scholars and activists have pointed to the tendency for white women to speak on behalf of black women, regarding them as objects of feminist knowledge rather than critical subjects, and to assume a universal feminist ideal that fails to address intersectional experiences of race, class, and gender inequality in South Africa (Lewis 1996; Ryan 1996; Hassim 2006). Elitism and classism within academic feminist circles, to the exclusion of working-class women and grassroots women's organizations, have been a particular point of discussion (Lewis 1996) with Marxist, postcolonial, and third world feminisms contributing significantly to debates over the shape of feminisms in South Africa, in which questions of difference remain paramount. As Hassim (1991) has argued, the pressing question post-apartheid is less whether feminism is relevant to South African women, and more what an indigenous feminism might look like.

SEE ALSO: Democracy and Democratization; Feminism, Black; Feminism, Postcolonial; Gender, Politics, and the State in Southern Africa; Intersectionality; Third World Women; White Supremacy and Gender; Women's and Feminist Activism in Southern Africa

REFERENCES

Bhana, Deevia, and Shirley Mthethwa-Sommers. 2010. "Feminisms Today: Still Fighting." *Agenda: Empowering Women for Gender Equity*, 24(83): 2–7.

Britton, Hannah, and Jennifer Fish. 2009. "Engendering Civil Society in Democratic South Africa." In *Women's Activism in South Africa: Working Across Divides*, edited by Hannah Britton, Jennifer Fish, and Sheila Meintjes, 1–42. Scottsville, South Africa: University of KwaZulu Natal Press.

Gouws, Amanda. 2010. "Feminism in South Africa Today: Have w-We Lost the Praxis?" *Agenda: Empowering Women for Gender Equity*, 24(83): 13–23.

Gqola, Pumla D. 2007. "How the 'Cult of Femininity' and Violent Masculinities Support Endemic Gender Based Violence in Contemporary South Africa." *African Identities*, 5(1): 111–124.

Hassim, Shireen. 1991. "Gender, Social Location and Feminist Politics in South Africa." *Transformation*, 15: 65–82.

Hassim, Shireen. 2005. "Terms of Engagement: South African Challenges." *Feminist Africa*, (4); http://www.feministafrica.org/04-2005/hassim.html.

Hassim, Shireen. 2006. *Women's Organizations and Democracy in South Africa: Contesting Authority*. Madison: University of Wisconsin Press.

Lewis, Desiree. 1996. "The Politics of Feminism in South Africa." In *South African Feminisms: Writing, Theory and Criticism 1990–1994*, edited by Margaret J. Daymond, 91–104. New York: Garland Publishing.

McClintock, Anne. 1991. "No Longer in a Future Heaven: Women and Nationalism in South Africa." *Transition*, 51: 104–123.

McEwan, Cheryl. 2000. "Engendering Citizenship: Gendered Spaces of Democracy in South Africa." *Political Geography*, 19(5): 627–651.

Moolman, Benita. 2009. "Race, Gender and Feminist Practice: Lessons from Rape Crisis Cape Town." In *Women's Activism in South Africa: Working Across Divides*, edited by Hannah Britton, Jennifer Fish, and Sheila Meintjes, 185–210. Scottsville, South Africa: University of KwaZulu Natal Press.

Motsei, Mmatshilo. 2007. *The Kanga and the Kangaroo Court: Reflections on the Rape Trial of Jacob Zuma*. Aukland Park: Jacana Press.

Ryan, Pamela. 1996. "The Future of South African Feminism." In *South African Feminisms: Writing, Theory and Criticism 1990–1994*, edited by Margaret J. Daymond, 31–36. New York: Garland Publishing.

Vincent, Louise. 1999. "A Cake of Soap: The *Volksmoeder* Ideology and Afrikaner Women's Campaign for the Vote." *The International Journal of African Historical Studies*, 32(1): 1–17.

Walker, Cheryl. 1991. *Women and Resistance in South Africa*. Claremont, South Africa: David Phillips Publishers.

Walsh, Denise. 2006. "The Liberal Moment: Women and Just Debate in South Africa, 1994–1996." *Journal of Southern African Studies*, 32(1): 85–105.

Feminism in Southeast Asia

BARBARA MOLONY
Santa Clara University, USA

European visitors to Southeast Asia in the eighteenth and nineteenth centuries frequently commented on the status of women, noting that throughout the region women appeared to play important roles in commerce, had some rights in marriage and inheritance, and participated in religious rituals, practices that eluded most European women at the time. However, these views obscured the great variety in cultures and religions among the region's people. Recent scholarship has called into question the notion that Southeast Asian women's status was universally high (Andaya 2007).

Southeast Asian societies did, however, have a significant common experience: from the late nineteenth to the mid-twentieth century, all but Thailand were subject to colonialism, a status that produced a variety of nationalist struggles. Most feminisms in Southeast Asia initially developed in the context of nationalism. The roles of women in feminist nationalism were both symbolic – women were constructed as representing the imagined community of the longed-for independent nation – and active – real women played roles in feminist and nationalist movements.

INDONESIA

Feminism in the predominantly Muslim Dutch East Indies emerged both as a struggle for gender equality – at first by Dutch women and later by anti-colonial Indonesian women – and as a way of framing a gendered concept of the nation.

The idealized image of womanhood, initially constructed by Dutch colonial authorities and later reclaimed and remolded by Indonesian nationalists, was based on the life of Raden Ajeng Kartini (1879–1904). Daughter of an elite Indonesian family, Kartini received a European-style education until the age of 12, when she was taken from school to prepare for marriage. She remained at home for another decade, reading works by Indian and European feminists and writing letters, some of which were later made public. (Some historians have questioned some of these letters' authenticity.) Many called for women's education to improve women's status and produce better mothers. After resisting marriage for a decade, Kartini married an elderly man with several wives, dying less than a year later following childbirth. Her death made her the symbol of feminine nobility. The Dutch promoted Kartini as the exemplar of genteel Javanese womanhood whose education blended the best of Dutch and Indonesian cultures. However, Kartini's letters were also laced with criticisms of colonial rule, a viewpoint the Dutch suppressed. Several decades later, Kartini was recast as a different type of national symbol by Indonesian nationalists. Long after independence, during the last decades of the twentieth century, Indonesian schoolgirls honored her as the mother of the nation on "Mother Kartini Day."

Until the late 1930s, Dutch colonial feminists were more likely to seek political equality with Dutch men, whereas Indonesian feminists focused on social reforms such as girls' education, improving conditions of work, and opposition to child marriage. Dutch women founded a branch of Holland's Women's Suffrage Association (WSA) in 1908. The colonial branch was integrated into transnational feminism and was visited in 1912 by Carrie Chapman Catt, the American who was president of the International Woman Suffrage Alliance. But of the hundreds of members of that branch, only one woman was ethnically Indonesian. When Dutch women in the metropole gained the vote in 1919, the WSA branch demanded the vote for colonial women and representation on the People's Council, a newly created colonial political advisory congress. The Dutch authorities turned them down for contradictory reasons: (1) the authorities claimed that because Indonesian women viewed suffrage as something that divided women from their husbands and families, giving Indonesian women the vote could be resisted as too Western; and (2) the Dutch were concerned about rising Indonesian nationalism in the 1920s, leading them to fear that giving political rights to Dutch women and not to Indonesian women would exacerbate anti-colonial tensions (Blackburn 2004, 81–83). Indonesian feminists also had some differences with one another, mainly over the role of religion in a future state. Many of the early twentieth-century reformist groups discussed the need for secular marriage laws at the first Indonesian Women's Congress in 1928; in 1930, a nationalist organization, Isteri Sedar (Aware Women) was founded to advance marriage reform and national independence. Some Muslim members of these groups rejected the groups' opposition to polygyny, however (Ramusack and Sievers 1999).

The colonial authorities finally appointed a woman to the People's Council in 1935. However, she was ethnically European, and Indonesian women reacted by embracing political rights. Several became members of municipal councils. In 1939, 45 women's groups demanded Indonesian women's representation on the People's Council, and the male-led Indonesian nationalist movement, which had ignored women's rights earlier, now called for universal suffrage. In response, the colonial authorities granted women limited rights, but they were not able to exercise these rights before Japan invaded the colony in February 1942.

After the War, Indonesian women and men worked together for independence from The Netherlands, gaining it in 1949. The patriarchal family was made a central component of social control for the next half century. National elections were inaugurated in 1955, but few women were elected and none served in the cabinet before the 1990s.

Reforms came slowly: wives gained some rights under the 1974 marriage law, which raised the age of marriage, required women's consent to marriage, and granted women the right of divorce. (Muslim families were partially exempt from this law, since their divorces could be handled in Islamic courts.)

At the same time, women were valorized as mothers. Activist women took this notion of women, which could have limited their options, and turned it to challenge the state. They demanded basic commodities as mothers who supported their families. They played a role in occupying parliament in 1998, protesting the rapes of ethnically Chinese women. Muslim women's groups repudiated men's characterization of those rapes as part of *jihad*, viewing them instead as male violence against women. Activists have used the UN Convention on the Elimination of All Forms of Discrimination against Women (CEDAW) to demand improvements in women's labor conditions. Muslim and secular feminists have drawn closer in recent decades, as the former have worked to redefine Islam to be more supportive of women's rights (Blackburn 2010; Rinaldo 2010). By the late 1990s, several women served in important cabinet positions, and Megawati Sukarnoputri, a Muslim, served as president from 2001 to 2004. In the last decade, however, more conservative Islamic governments challenged women's rights. Feminists have continued to struggle against unequal conditions of work, violence against women, and patriarchal treatment of women in law and the family.

VIETNAM

Feminism in predominantly Buddhist, Confucian, and, later, Catholic Vietnam has long been connected to the nation. The heroism of women warriors – notably the Trung sisters in the first century and Triêu Thi Trinh in the third century, who committed suicide rather than surrender as they led struggles to resist Chinese domination – helped construct the notion of Vietnam as an independent country (Lessard 2004). Until the early nineteenth century, Vietnamese women had some rights unheard of in most other societies before the modern period. For example, a woman's consent was necessary for marriage, women had the right to divorce, wives and daughters were entitled to inheritance, the eldest daughter carried out ancestor rituals in the absence of a son, and at least during the thirteenth century, women could take examinations to enter the scholarly ruling class (Chiricosta 2010). The reign of the Gia-long Emperor in the early nineteenth century, however, took away most of these rights, placing women under the control of their fathers, husbands, and sons, and requiring them to adhere to the Four Virtues of housewifery, appearance, speech, and conduct.

Following several decades of French incursion, Vietnam was divided into three French colonies in the 1880s. The French were both a source of nationalist and feminist ideology and an inspiration for feminist anti-colonialism. As in other colonies, nationalist resistance movements initially called on women to assist in the larger anti-colonial campaign rather than focusing on women's specific concerns under colonialism. Early on, French policies disrupted the handicraft production women had engaged in, leaving few employment options other than domestic service and prostitution.

The anti-colonial Association of the People Devoted to the Just Cause (founded 1883) included women members and was at one time led by a woman (Lessard 2004). Women's assistance in armed resistance groups led to a debate among anti-colonialists about the role of women in the nationalist movement. One of Vietnam's pre-eminent male nationalists, Phan Boi Chau (1867–1940), called on

Vietnamese women to be both activists and symbols (that is, as mothers of the nation). Phan and other male leaders stressed education to increase women's participation in national affairs. Vietnam's French authorities also stressed women's education, but they saw it as enhancing women's ability to promote French culture in their families. The French opened several schools for girls in the first decade of the twentieth century, and the Vietnamese added additional schools in the next few decades.

Greater educational opportunities for girls produced a growing number of young women who sought to abandon Confucian limitations on women's behavior, adopted Western-style clothing, asked for new opportunities in the colonial government and society, and, in some cases, joined women's and nationalist organizations. These demands for women's equality and rights challenged the French in ways they had not anticipated. In the 1920s and 1930s, journals and newspapers edited by and for women emerged, covering the political spectrum from advocacy of equal political rights (considered a bourgeois or elitist notion by those on the left) to a Marxist position that considered feminism divisive.

The Vietnamese Youth League (founded 1925) and the Vietnamese Nationalist Party (founded 1927), both prominent anti-colonial movements, were compelled to address women's issues because many of their women members demanded equality. The Youth League, led by Marxist nationalist Ho Chi Minh (1880–1969), declared that national liberation must precede women's liberation. The group's journal, *Youth*, criticized women for attending to family matters rather than dedicating themselves to revolutionary activism; the journal failed to consider, however, who would take care of the family (Tai 1992). Feminist ideas were widely disseminated through a popular journal, *Ladies' News*, published from 1929 to 1934. *Ladies' News* covered worldwide feminism, attacked Confucianism, and advocated women's education and rights. Its ideology borrowed from both liberal and Marxist ideas.

Both the Youth League and Vietnamese Nationalist Party were suppressed by the French in the late 1920s, leading to the demise of the latter and the transformation of the former into the Indochinese Communist Party in 1930. The same year, the communists formed a separate women's organization, the Vietnam Women's Union (VWU); by the end of World War II, about one quarter of all Vietnamese women were members. Despite the group's call for gender equality, however, its primary goal was national independence and class struggle.

Vietnam declared independence in 1945, but the French returned. After the French defeat in 1954, the country was then divided in two, engendering a long-term war for reunification (1975). While the men were away at war, women in the Democratic Republic of Vietnam (DRV; North Vietnam) took positions in local administration and played increased roles in agriculture and production. Women's social participation peaked in the early 1970s, dropping after 1975, when the men returned from the battlefield. The DRV constitution in theory granted gender equality in all aspects of life, but in 1975 even the VWU criticized women's emancipated behavior as too westernized, individualistic, and disruptive of social harmony (Chiricosta 2010). A decade later, the VWU, responding to the liberalization of the economy in 1986 and the government's designation of the family as the basic unit of production, began to take on a role of feminist advocacy, pushing for the Law on Gender Equality (implemented in 2007). Nevertheless, the VWU is primarily viewed as an organ of state, rather than independent, feminism. More independent feminism is advocated by NGOs, some of which have joined the National Committee for the Advancement of Women (founded 1993) in fighting violence against women, advocating greater awareness of HIV/AIDS, and offering low-cost loans to women.

CAMBODIA

Cambodia, like Vietnam, was part of the French Indochinese Union before gaining independence in 1953. As in other colonies, feminism was initially tainted by its connection to colonial rule. Although some women called for equal rights, the Cambodian nationalist movement of the 1940s and 1950s, when attempting to mobilize women, stressed women's roles as helpers, especially as housewives to activist men.

After World War II, elites in this Buddhist society sought to recreate pre-colonial Cambodian "tradition." They looked to the Cambodian royal family for models of this tradition, a choice that emphasized societal hierarchy and male leadership. In the Cambodian-style feminism that emerged from this focus, women were constructed as supporters of men. In 1949, the newly established Women's Association (WA) framed women's roles as domestic and supportive, and other newly created women's groups followed suit. In the early 1970s, as civil war raged in Cambodia, young women were expected to be both mothers and fighters. During the genocidal Khmer Rouge era (1975–1979), the wife of the regime's dictator took over the presidency of the WA (Jacobsen 2010). Pro-women policies reemerged after 1979, when the WA shifted its focus to improving women's education, health, and livelihoods. The WA lost government support in 1992, and numerous NGOs sprang up to address a wide variety of feminist issues, especially violence against women. Many of these new feminist groups' activities were coordinated through the Amara Women's Network, founded in 1995. Women's groups played an active role in elections in the early 2000s, but their involvement was not rewarded with government positions. Feminist groups continue to tread carefully, stressing the complementarity of women and men and downplaying the concept of "feminism," which is seen by many Cambodians as destructive to their "traditional" culture and for which there is no direct translation in the Cambodian language (Jacobsen 2010).

MALAYSIA

Malaysian women were granted voting rights with independence from Britain in 1957. Earlier movements on behalf of women emerged in the interwar period: for example, the Malay Women Teachers' Union was founded in 1929; in the 1930s, women protested against sexual molestation and exploitation of female laborers; and Muslim intellectuals demanded Muslim women's right to education (Ng, Mohamad, and Tan 2006). As in other colonial societies, nationalist movements recruited women in the 1940s and 1950s, and the desire for independence was more critical to women in the nationalist struggle than women's rights. Islamic fundamentalism began to grow in the 1970s, adversely affecting women. Reform has been slow in Malaysia – it took more than 10 years to get a Violence Against Women Act passed (1995), for instance – but today over 250 NGOs cut across religious and ethnic lines, bringing together consumer, environmental, and religious reformers. Few women, even activists, call themselves "feminists," however, as the term is perceived as too Western. Most take care to be perceived as moderate in this conservative society (Ariffin 1999).

THAILAND

Predominately Buddhist, Thailand escaped colonial status, and therefore did not have a feminist movement inspired by nationalism. Historians have attributed Thailand's independent status to a monarchy whose interest in reform beginning in the mid-nineteenth century persuaded possible colonizers to leave them alone. The national story of women's rights is connected to the historical narrative of the monarchy's modernization. Like Indonesia, Thailand had a pioneering "feminist," Amdaeng Muan, a commoner who successfully petitioned King Mongkut in 1865 for the right to choose her own husband. In 1868, Mongkut extended that right to all commoners – although not to the elite, who could still be forced into marriage by their families – for which he earned recognition in the eyes of the West as a progressive monarch and in the eyes of later Thais as a proto-feminist. Later monarchs enhanced the image of the monarchy as progressive by requiring both boys and girls to attend school in 1921 and improving the status of women in marriage (Loos 2004).

When a military coup replaced Thailand's absolute monarchy with a constitutional monarchy in 1932, the new government granted women and men equal voting rights. Although allowed to run for parliament (the first woman elected to parliament, in 1957, was a Prime Minister's wife), women were not allowed to run for many local offices until 1984. Never having struggled against patriarchy for national voting rights or against a colonial power for independence, Thai feminism took a different path from other Southeast Asian feminisms.

The Women's Association of Siam (founded 1932) stressed women's education, particularly as a way to create better mothers, supported women laborers, and accepted sex workers as members. During the 1930s, elite women participated in charitable organizations under royal sponsorship, and women's magazines published articles that attacked polygyny and patriarchy (Falk 2010). Despite the existence of the monarchy, military dictatorships effectively ruled Thailand until 1973. Student activists, both men and women, joined others in overthrowing the military and ushering in democracy in 1973. This government survived until 1976, when another military coup took over. Democracy returned in 1981, with a few short-term military coups in the years since. In 2014, Thailand's first woman prime minister, Yingluck Shinawatra, was ousted by a military coup.

Between 1973 and 1976, numerous women's organizations emerged, including the Association for the Promotion of the Status of Women, Women Lawyers' Association of Thailand, Association for Civil Liberty, Christian Women's Association, and feminist organizations at universities. An Equal Rights Protection Law was passed in 1974. Anti-democratic forces took over in 1976. Progressive feminist organizations reemerged in the 1980s, focusing on civil rights, ending violence against women, improving conditions of sex work (the leading organization in this area is EMPOWER), labor reform, and establishing emergency homes for women and children. Thai women have also played an important role in regional and transnational feminist organizations. Feminist Buddhist nuns also contribute to women's rights movements (Falk 2010).

PHILIPPINES

Predominantly Catholic, the Philippines had the distinction of being twice colonized – by Spain from 1565 to 1898 and by the United States from 1902 to 1946. Femininities and feminisms developed in both colonial eras and have continued to change in the seven decades since the Philippines gained independence. Feminist ideas and movements were engendered both through nationalist anti-colonialism and through exposure to the colonists' attitudes toward gender.

Spanish colonization curtailed women's previous marital and inheritance rights. Accustomed to playing a role in their communities, some women, such as Gabriela Silang (1731–1763), joined men in the struggle against colonialism. At the end of the nineteenth century, elite Filipinas demanded education to improve the status of women. Ironically, the great independence fighter and novelist, José Rizal, created an enduring female character, Maria Clara, whose obedience and passivity came to be idealized by early nationalists although, by the 1920s, attacked by feminists (Roces 2010). Nationalism and feminism had a rocky relationship. This did not keep some women from contributing to the armed struggle against Spain, where they served as medics, spies, and soldiers (Roces 2004).

Feminism under American colonialism took different approaches. Planning to "modernize" the Philippines, the Americans promoted education for women and permitted men to run for elective office (although Americans ruled at the top). Some Americans in the colonial government supported women's suffrage. Filipina women took the opportunity to organize. The Asociación Feminista Filipina (founded 1905) sought to end early marriage, improve working conditions for women and children, and serve on boards of education (this last demand was explicitly political). The Asociación Feminista Ilonga (founded 1906) called for women's suffrage (Roces 2004). Elite Filipina women established the journal *Filipinas* in 1909 to encourage women's participation in nation-building. At the same time, the Americans encouraged Filipinas to create women's clubs to undertake civic charity, such as supplying milk for children and running nursery schools.

In 1912, Carrie Chapman Catt visited the Philippines on her worldwide suffrage tour. The National Federation of Women's Clubs (NFWC), until 1921 a civic organization, jumped onto the suffrage bandwagon that year. Most Filipina men other than Senator Rafael Palma, who strongly advocated women's rights in 1919, were uninterested in women's suffrage. Feminist nationalists faced a dilemma: while most nationalist men either ignored the woman question or considered women's rights a colonialist transgression of the "traditional" Maria Clara role for women, most Americans in the Philippines supported women's rights. What should feminist nationalists do?

Their solution was to work for voting rights. The Americans began to plan for an independent state and called for a Filipino Constitutional Convention in 1934. The Convention rejected women's suffrage, but provided that women would be enfranchised if a women's plebiscite within 2 years of ratification of the constitution gained 300,000 votes for suffrage. In 1935, men (and women!) were allowed to vote for the constitution; the document denied women the vote, but its passage allowed the Philippines greater independence as a commonwealth. Women's next vote was in 1937 – the women's plebiscite. The NFWC organized tirelessly; 447,725 women voted for women's suffrage and 44,307 voted against (Roces 2004). In succeeding decades, women worked alongside men for national independence and, after independence, for social improvement and other broad goals rather than feminist goals. Many women's organizations were run by politicians' wives.

Student activism injected the feminist movement with renewed energy in the 1960s, and in 1970, the Free Movement of

New Women (MAKIBARA) was founded to protest social injustice, beauty pageants, and the increasing repression of the Ferdinand Marcos regime. In 1972, Marcos declared martial law, and MAKIBARA was silenced. Leftist activists went underground for the remainder of the decade; women in these movements felt that their concerns were marginalized by the men (Roces 2010). Following the Marcos government's 1983 assassination of the popular opposition politician Benigno Aquino, Jr, activists' attention was focused on ridding the country of Marcos and his cronies. GABRIELA (General Assembly Binding Women for Reforms, Integrity, Equality, Leadership, and Action), founded in 1984 with an acronym honoring Gabriela Silang, moved decisively to feminist actions after "People Power" brought Cory Aquino, Benigno's widow, to the presidency in 1986. Thousands of NGOs joined GABRIELA in the following decades, working on such issues as violence, marriage rights, sex trafficking, political and legal rights, religious feminism, and the feminization of global poverty. Catholic nuns have been some of the most effective and outspoken feminists in the Philippines in recent years. There have been several women's political parties, and Filipina women have exported Filipina-style feminism through their leadership roles in United Nations organizations.

Throughout Southeast Asia, with the exception of Thailand, which avoided being colonized, feminism developed alongside anti-colonialist nationalism. And yet, despite the important roles of women in liberation movements, feminism took a back seat to struggles for national independence. In recent decades, women's movements have reemerged, defining themselves as indigenous to avoid being labeled as Western and, therefore, foreign.

SEE ALSO: Convention on the Elimination of All Forms of Discrimination against Women (CEDAW); Feminist Movements in Historical and Comparative Perspective; Nationalism and Gender; Women's and Feminist Activism in Southeast Asia

REFERENCES

Andaya, Barbara Watson. 2007. "Studying Women and Gender in Southeast Asia." *International Journal of Asian Studies*, 12: 113–136.

Ariffin, Rohana. 1999. "Feminism in Malaysia: A Historical and Present Perspective of Women's Struggles in Malaysia." *Women's Studies International Forum*, 22(4): 417–423.

Blackburn, Susan. 2004. "Women's Suffrage and Democracy in Indonesia." In *Women's Suffrage in Asia: Gender, Nationalism and Democracy*, edited by Louise Edwards and Mina Roces, 79–105. London: RoutledgeCurzon.

Blackburn, Susan. 2010. "Feminism and the Women's Movement in the World's Largest Islamic Nation." In *Women's Movements in Asia: Feminisms and Transnational Activism*, edited by Mina Roces and Louise Edwards, 21–33. London: Routledge.

Chiricosta, Alessandra. 2010. "Following the Trail of the Fairy-Bird: The Search for a Uniquely Vietnamese Women's Movement." In *Women's Movements in Asia: Feminisms and Transnational Activism*, edited by Mina Roces and Louise Edwards, 124–143. London: Routledge.

Falk, Monica Lindberg. 2010. "Feminism, Buddhism and Transnational Women's Movements in Thailand." In *Women's Movements in Asia: Feminisms and Transnational Activism*, edited by Mina Roces and Louise Edwards, 110–123. London: Routledge.

Jacobsen, Trudy. 2010. "'Riding a Buffalo to Cross a Muddy Field': Heuristic Approaches to Feminism in Cambodia." In *Women's Movements in Asia: Feminisms and Transnational Activism*, edited by Mina Roces and Louise Edwards, 207–223. London: Routledge.

Lessard, Micheline R. 2004. "Women's Suffrage in Viêt Nam." In *Women's Suffrage in Asia: Gender, Nationalism and Democracy*, edited by Louise Edwards and Mina Roces, 106–126. London: RoutledgeCurzon.

Loos, Tamara. 2004. "The Politics of Women's Suffrage in Thailand." In *Women's Suffrage in Asia: Gender, Nationalism and Democracy*, edited by

Louise Edwards and Mina Roces, 170–194. London: RoutledgeCurzon.

Ng, Cecilia, Maznah Mohamad, and Tan Beng Hui. 2006. *Feminism and the Women's Movement in Malaysia: An Unsung (R)evolution*. London: Routledge.

Ramusack, Barbara N., and Sharon Sievers. 1999. *Women in Asia: Restoring Women to History*. Bloomington: Indiana University Press.

Rinaldo, Rachel. 2010. "The Islamic Revival and Women's Political Subjectivity in Indonesia." *Women's Studies International Forum*, 33: 422–431.

Roces, Mina. 2004. "Is the Suffragist an American Colonial Construct? Defining 'the Filipino Woman' in Colonial Philippines." In *Women's Suffrage in Asia: Gender, Nationalism and Democracy*, edited by Louise Edwards and Mina Roces, 24–58. London: RoutledgeCurzon.

Roces, Mina. 2010. "Rethinking the 'Filipino Woman': A Century of Women's Activism in the Philippines, 1905–2006." In *Women's Movements in Asia: Feminisms and Transnational Activism*, edited by Mina Roces and Louise Edwards, 34–52. London: Routledge.

Tai, Hue-Tam Ho. 1992. *Radicalism and the Origins of the Vietnamese Revolution*. Cambridge, MA: Harvard University Press.

Feminisms and Argumentation

CATHERINE HELEN PALCZEWSKI
University of Northern Iowa, USA

Feminisms intersect with argumentation in all its forms: as a particular type of speech act, as a process of decision-making, and as an epistemological process. An argument is a particular type of statement: a claim supported by reasons and evidence (e.g., all people, regardless of sex, are equal because they share in the immanent value of humanity). Argument also can refer to an interactional process where two or more interlocutors exchange ideas and reasons, either privately or publicly, in a single moment in time (e.g., a particular discussion about the allocation of housework) or across time (e.g., the extended controversy over woman suffrage). Arguments also carry with them epistemological issues: what counts as evidence, who counts as an authority, and what conclusions are warranted? Most argumentation scholars distinguish argument, as a form of interaction that includes reason-giving, from verbal altercations.

Feminists disagree about whether argumentation's form and its intent to persuade are inherently and irredeemably patriarchal or masculinist as well as whether argument is necessary and productive for feminist advocacy. Feminist scholars from composition, communication studies, philosophy, and political science have argued about whether argumentation can serve feminisms' liberatory goals. Three questions guide the scholarship.

First, is argument inherently patriarchal? Scholars informed by cultural or difference feminisms propose that argumentation, particularly the adversarial method as an ideal that informs philosophical method (Moulton 1983), has been so structured by war and aggression metaphors that it is unavoidably patriarchal and epistemologically suspect (Ayim 1988). In communication studies, Foss and Griffin (1995) propose that traditional rhetoric, premised on argument and persuasion, necessarily contains "efforts to dominate another"; in contrast, their alternative of *invitational rhetoric* has as its "goal … the understanding and appreciation of another's perspective rather than the denigration of it" (1995, 6). Adversariality is eschewed because "in invitational rhetoric … resistance is not anticipated" (1995, 6).

Calls to reject argument as inherently masculinist often fall into the trap of essentialism. Many who critique argument do so from the assumption that men and women argue differently. However, that is not necessarily borne out by research and ignores the other differences that exist between women and between men (Rooney 2010). Elshtain (1982) urges scholars to "move beyond a view of language as simply or inexorably 'power over,' discourse as domination, or discourse as unavoidably masked, and toward speech as part of an emancipatory effort, a movement toward social clarity and self-comprehension" (1982, 605). In many ways, one can substitute *argument* for *language* in Elshtain's passage, where the challenge for feminists becomes finding emancipatory forms of argument, dispute resolution, reason-giving, discovery, and persuasion. bell hooks (1989) defends the necessity of taking an adversarial position, particularly for the marginalized, as politically productive when she describes "talking back" (defined as "speaking as an equal to an authority figure ... daring to disagree and sometimes ... just ... having an opinion") as an "act of resistance, a political gesture that challenges politics of domination that would render us nameless and voiceless" (1989, 5, 8).

Second, what models of feminist argumentation exist? If argumentation's masculinist bias is not inherent, then feminist interventions should be able to correct the masculinist effects of the argument-as-war metaphor. The feminist models of argument described call for a reorientation of argumentation away from winning, and toward understanding and a privileging of consensus, while not losing the critical analytics associated with engaged argument.

Informal logicians in philosophy have offered *coalescent argument*, which also reminds arguers of the situatedness of communication. The goal of coalescent argument "is not to determine how to eliminate or criticize or defeat the presented view, but how to understand, incorporate, respect and move toward consensus" (Gilbert 1994, 109). Communication studies scholars have developed *cooperative argument*, a process that retains an emphasis on "reasoned interaction" and seeks to help people make the "best decisions in any given situation" (Makau and Marty 2001, 87). Political scientist Jane Mansbridge (1983) contrasts adversarial and consensual forms of democracy. Adversarial democracy assumes conflicting interests and hence requires equal protection of interests and near-anonymous interchanges, with majority rule ultimately determining decisions. Consensual democracy assumes common interests and requires equal respect and face-to-face interaction, with consensus operating as the decision rule (1983, 5). Mansbridge explains: "[T]he central assumption of unitary democracy is that, while its members may initially have conflicting preferences about a given issue, goodwill, mutual understanding, and rational discussion can lead to the emergence of a common enlightened preference that is good for everyone" (1983, 25).

Central to these alternative models is recognition of the need for deliberative argumentative exchanges. Even if the content and form of argumentation remains largely the same, the orientation of the arguers to the exchange is radically transformed away from the adversarial paradigm. However, even alternate models deserve careful feminist critique. Even if women and men do not possess distinct argumentative styles, people perceive women's arguments through a gendered lens that expects women to perform feminine style. Thus, women may exist in a double bind: those who engage in adversarial argument face censure for failure to perform their gender in a socially approved way while those who engage in cooperative forms of argument may be dismissed as simply engaging in feminine (and, thus, less rigorous) forms of exchange.

Third, in what ways do feminist theories inform argumentation analyses? Feminist studies of argumentation have expanded what counts as an argument and what counts as evidence in argument. Feminist scholars have identified the non-linguistic or extradiscursive components of rhetoric and argumentation (Palczewski 2002). Validating the connection between the personal and political, feminist scholars have studied the role of personal testimony in public policy argument. Feminist epistemology has challenged the distinction between knowledge and experience and how it works to devalue what women say by relegating them to the world of experience and declaring them incapable of producing knowledge (Code 1991).

Across these three questions, feminist scholars agree that not only is argument contingent and provisional, but that knowledge and reason are situated and contextual. In order to fully conceptualize argumentation, scholars must recognize that particular human bodies, socially inscribed in distinct ways, proffer arguments within particular analytic frameworks, inflected by intersecting social locations, dependent upon socially validated warrants. Argumentation takes place within a conceptual framework infused by sex, race, class, sexuality, gender, and other intersecting axes of power. Thus, the feminist contribution to argumentation is the way it makes visible how patriarchal frameworks are part and parcel of argument unless those frameworks are challenged.

SEE ALSO: Essentialism; Feminism, Cultural; Feminist Epistemology; Feminist Methodology

REFERENCES

Ayim, Maryann. 1988. "Violence and Domination as Metaphors in Academic Discourse." In *Selected Issues in Logic and Communication*, edited by Trudy Govier, 184–195. Belmont, CA: Wadsworth Publishing Co.

Code, Lorraine. 1991. *What Can She Know?* Ithaca, NY: Cornell University Press.

Elshtain, Jean Bethke. 1982. "Feminism Discourse and Its Discontents: Language, Power, and Meaning." *Signs*, 7: 603–621.

Foss, Sonja, and Cindy Griffin. 1995. "Beyond Persuasion: A Proposal for an Invitational Rhetoric." *Communication Monographs*, 62: 2–18.

Gilbert, Michael A. 1994. "Feminism, Argumentation and Coalescence." *Informal Logic*, 16: 95–113.

hooks, bell. 1989. *Talking Back: Thinking Feminist, Thinking Black*. Boston: South End Press.

Makau, Josina M., and Debian L. Marty. 2001. *Cooperative Argumentation: A Model for Deliberative Community*. Prospect Heights, IL: Waveland.

Mansbridge, Jane. 1983. *Beyond Adversary Democracy*. Chicago: University of Chicago Press.

Moulton, Janice. 1983. "A Paradigm of Philosophy: The Adversary Method." In *Discovering Reality*, edited by Sandra Harding and Merrill B. Hintikka, 149–164. Boston: D. Reidel.

Palczewski, Catherine Helen. 2002. "Keynote Address: Argument in an Off Key." *Communicative Reason and Communication Communities*, edited by G. Thomas Goodnight, et al., 1–23. Washington, DC: National Communication Association.

Rooney, Phyllis. 2010. "Philosophy, Adversarial Argumentation, and Embattled Reason." *Informal Logic*, 30: 203–234.

Feminisms, First, Second, and Third Wave

IRIS VAN DER TUIN
Utrecht University, The Netherlands

A logic of "feminist waves" structures the ways in which Western academic and non-academic feminists tell stories about their past and present. The notions of "first-wave," "second-wave," and "third-wave feminism" are common currency in feminist discourse. In spite of this, waves are generally reckoned to constrain how we plot and plan feminism. The wave-logic is argued to be a source of processes of inclusion and exclusion within feminism.

Developments in feminism are generally narrated according to a model of three waves – occasionally more. The first feminist wave crested around 1900 and concerned the struggle for the North American and northern and western European women's right to vote, for women's access to education, and for changing matrimonial law. Famous first-wave feminists include Elizabeth Cady Stanton and Susan B. Anthony from the United States, suffragettes Millicent Fawcett and Emmeline Pankhurst from the United Kingdom, and medical doctor Aletta Jacobs from the Netherlands.

The second wave of feminism is generally dated between 1968 and 1980. The movement is represented by feminists such as Kate Millet and Jill Johnston from the United States, Germaine Greer from Australia (working from the United Kingdom), and Alice Schwarzer from Germany. Geographically, the second wave remains similarly situated, but the second wave includes the work of feminists such as Egyptian Nawal El Saadawi and events around the Iranian revolution. Second-wave feminists objected to the strategy of the first feminist wave ("equality feminism" was exchanged for feminisms of "difference") and the results of equality feminism were questioned. This is because the rights gained had not changed the minds and practices of men and women. During the second feminist wave of the late 1960s and entire 1970s, theories of the body, sexuality, and relationships were revolutionized. "The personal is political" became the quintessential feminist slogan (Hanisch 1970).

Third-wave feminism started in the United States in the 1980s and has a popular culture component. In several Eastern European countries, "state feminism" was exchanged for activist, DIY feminism in the 1980s as well. Music and English language zines capture the first feminist outbursts of the daughters of second-wave feminists. The wave is distinguished by its online presence as well as a curious split between "slutwalks" on the one hand, and "ladyfests" on the other. The emergence of Web 2.0 allowed third-wave feminism to travel to regions other than North America, Australia, and Europe. The "Arab Spring," for example, can be seen as an outbreak of a third-wave feminism, induced by social media, in North Africa and the Middle East. Reflecting upon the current "tech-savvy and gender-sophisticated" generation, Jennifer Baumgardner (2011, 250) affirms the existence of a "fourth feminist wave."

First-wave and second-wave feminisms are both well-established categories. Third-wave feminism is their less established counterpart. On the one hand, the term "third-wave feminism" has to compete with "postfeminism." On the other, third-wave feminism does not have the benefit of hindsight although this is changing with the affirmation of fourth-wave feminism. Rebecca Walker, daughter of the famous second-wave black feminist Alice Walker, declared "I am not a postfeminism feminist. I am the Third Wave" (1992). This statement captures the paradoxical state of third-wave feminism. First, a new feminist wave is inaugurated. This is done in an individualist manner: "*I am* the Third Wave." Second, continuity is sought with the work of feminist foremothers by declaring that third-wave feminism is *not* a postfeminism. The characterization of third-wave feminism is still in the making. An encyclopedia of third-wave feminism has been published (Heywood 2005) and the New York-based Third Wave Foundation of Walker and Amy Richards, among others, has a history that goes back to the beginning of the 1990s. But Anglo-American and continental European feminists under 40 struggle to (re-)claim the term "feminism" for their activities. The reason for this is that we are said to exist in a postfeminist age (see Bolotin 1982).

Postfeminism signifies at least two positions: the first is that feminism is no longer necessary. This postfeminist stance is founded in the idea of a postpatriarchal society; the negation of feminism is based on an embracing of postpatriarchy. Second is the embracing of postfeminism as such, which implies that one's *feminism* is a *post*-feminism. The latter presupposes a specific (pejorative) definition: feminism is a theoretical, political, and artistic stance that forecloses a playful approach towards sex, gender, and sexuality, desire, bodies, and representation. Because of the alleged foreclosure, feminism is seen as antagonistic to a critical and creative consciousness. Hence, feminism has to be left behind in order to respond effectively to women's oppression.

Postfeminists do not battle against the model of feminist waves. This would require postfeminism to become an oppositional collective and thus reinsert it within the wave-logic. This is not to the taste of postfeminist individualism. A "postfeminist wave" is a contradiction in terms. Hence, the critique of the model of feminist waves is part of the second feminist wave within which the wave metaphor was coined (Lear 1968).

Black and lesbian feminisms are sometimes talked about in terms of waves. The first wave of black feminism has close ties with the abolitionist movement against slavery. Sojourner Truth is a prominent example of anti-slavery activism within and outside of the North American women's movement. The Civil Rights movement forms the context of second-wave black feminism in the United States. Black women were experiencing the sexism of black men and racism in the women's liberation movement of the 1960s. Frances Beale, Angela Davis, and Michele Wallace are well-known second-wave black feminists. However, they have often asked how the non-adjectified wave-model ("the" first and second waves) could possibly represent their work, the work of the abolitionist movement, and the black liberation movement. Alternative terminologies such as Alice Walker's "womanism" and Cherríe Moraga's and Gloria Anzaldúa's "Chicana feminism" signify the writing and activism on the intersection of race/ethnicity and sex/gender.

Lesbian feminists and separatists such as Adrienne Rich, Rita Mae Brown, and Sheila Jeffreys have asked questions structurally identical to those of black feminists. The struggle of lesbians during the second feminist wave took place on two fronts also. An anti-heterosexist battle was fought within the women's liberation movement and anti-sexism was fought within the gay movement. Lesbian feminists, who had gathered in groups such as Radicalesbians, asked their sisters: what is the feminist movement up to in terms of sexuality? Does feminism imply a radicalization of heterosexuality or a political choice for lesbianism? Does the model of waves allow for the inclusion of lesbian women who lived their lives around 1900? And before that? Or is feminism an imperialism that repeats certain characteristics of patriarchal history writing?

Many second-wave feminists have applied more than one identity category to themselves. Audre Lorde, for example, used her lesbian sexuality, Caribbean-Americanism, motherhood, profession (poetry writing), and activism in order to define her identity. This "diversity thinking" or "intersectionality" has been named the defining characteristic of third-wave feminism (Zack 2005). This gesture of claiming space for hyphenated identities has a downside to it because in becoming part of the third-wave feminists like Lorde and the Combahee River Collective are erased from the second wave. The gesture whitewashes the second wave and does not do justice to the intrafeminist struggle of complexly located feminists. White heterosexual feminists had to be made aware of their privileged hyphenated identities. Black (and) lesbian feminists initiated this consciousness raising.

The feminist wave-model is itself based on a model of kinship relations that does not do justice to the experiences of black and lesbian women. The relation between mothers and daughters has differing features in black communities. Kinship relations among African Americans or in the Caribbean are often relations between women and upbringing does not necessarily involve a blood tie in this context. The relations between these women are often less rooted in conflict, whereas the metaphorical mother–daughter relation between first-wave and second-wave feminists, and the literal mother–daughter relation between second-wave and third-wave feminists *is* conflict-based (Rich 1976; Henry 2004). The kinship model has a white bias. In the case of lesbian women, reproduction does not (only) designate biological and social divisions of labor between men and women. Hence, the wave model suffers from heterosexism and biologism as well.

Women's history must not repeat the parameters of malestream history writing. How is it possible to ensure that feminists living before 1900 remain on the map of feminist story telling? How to do this both inside and outside contemporary gender studies classrooms? Where to place the ones who worked prior to the first wave; women like Christine de Pisan and Mary Wollstonecraft? How to accommodate the influential works of Virginia Woolf and Simone de Beauvoir, who completed their masterpieces of feminist philosophy and creative writing in between the first and second feminist waves? How to work with the feminisms of women who made alternative choices, such as Emma Goldman who opted for anarchism? In the light of all these eruptions of feminism, a model of *six* feminist waves, spanning European history from the fifteenth century until the beginning of the twenty-first, becomes an option (Akkerman and Stuurman 1998). But then again: how to develop transnational feminist stories featuring Asian feminists, Latin American feminists, or feminists from former communist countries?

It is questionable to what extent feminists *practice* the wave-logic since such a logic is only applicable after the fact. When the journalist Martha Weinman Lear coined the term "the second feminist wave" in 1968, the first wave came into being retroactively. In other words, in spite of the active and inspiring content of the diverse feminist waves, the fundamental problem of the wave model pertains to the impossibility of demarcating space-time. Talking about feminist waves involves a repetition of narrow national and generational borders. Thought and activism are nationally indexed and glued to a specific time of age cohorts. In spite of the inspirational contents of fifteenth-century feminism, the aforementioned six waves project has not been able to tackle these fundamental matters. Nevertheless, we find feminist wave-talk in pop and countercultural feminism, and in academic feminism alike.

False space–time linearities are being undone by queer and quantum feminists. Elizabeth Freeman (2010) has coined the term "temporal drag" in order to do justice to the anachronism that is inherent to feminist activism, research, and identification. Scholars like Vicki Kirby and Karen Barad attempt to formulate how "inheritance" – communication across generations – is plural and excessive. The reconfiguration of the concept of the feminist wave takes place in the wake of these attempts at telling truly differing feminist stories. The question is what the *ontology* of a feminist wave looks like (Aikau 2007; van der Tuin 2011). Waves function as metaphors for feminist movement in which crests and undercurrents alternate. Feminist waves are successive, since they presume a progress narrative, and they are supposed to respond to one another in a dualist way since they imply a pattern of sequential negation. Describing the history of feminism according to a model of waves, scholars assign individual feminists and feminist groups to certain waves, and vice versa. The waves then become denominators. Despite the cyclical movement of the physical phenomenon of perpetual curling, cresting, and breaking, waves become locatable in time and space. Doing research with waves has paralyzing effects. The question after the ontology of waves asks: does water – the physical H_2O cycle – ever sit still?

SEE ALSO: Feminist Activism; Feminist Movements in Historical and Comparative Perspective; Personal is Political; Postfeminism

REFERENCES

Aikau, Hokulani K. 2007. "Between Wind and Water: Thinking About the Third Wave as Metaphor and Materiality." In *Feminist Waves, Feminist Generations: Life Stories from the Academy*, edited by Hokulani K. Aikau, Karla A. Erickson, and Jennifer L. Pierce, 232–249. Minneapolis and London: University of Minnesota Press.

Akkerman, Tjitske and Siep Stuurman, eds. 1998. *Perspectives on Feminist Political Thought: From the Middle Ages to the Present*. London and New York: Routledge.

Baumgardner, Jennifer. 2011. *F'em!: Goo Goo, Gaga, and Some Thoughts on Balls*. Berkeley: Seal Press.

Bolotin, Susan. 1982. "Views from the Post-Feminist Generation." *New York Times Magazine*, 29–31, 103–116. 17 October.

Freeman, Elizabeth. 2010. *Time Binds: Queer Temporalities, Queer Histories*. Durham: Duke University Press.

Hanisch, Carol. 1970. "The Personal is Political." In *Notes from the Second Year: Women's Liberation*, edited by Shulamith Firestone and Anne Koedt, 76–78. New York: Radical Feminists.

Henry, Astrid. 2004. *Not My Mother's Sister: Generational Conflict and Third-Wave Feminism*. Bloomington: Indiana University Press.

Heywood, Leslie L., ed. 2005. *The Women's Movement Today: An Encyclopedia of Third-Wave Feminism*, vols 1 and 2. Westport: Greenwood Press.

Lear, Martha Weinman. 1968. "What Do These Women Want? The Second Feminist Wave." *New York Times Magazine*, 24–33. March 10.

Rich, Adrienne. 1976. *Of Woman Born: Motherhood as Experience and Institution*. New York: W.W. Norton.

van der Tuin, Iris. 2011. "Gender Research with 'Waves': On Repositioning a Neodisciplinary Apparatus." In *Theories and Methodologies in Postgraduate Feminist Research: Researching Differently*, edited by Rosemarie Buikema, Gabrielle Griffin, and Nina Lykke, 15–28. London and New York: Routledge.

Walker, Rebecca. 1992. "Becoming the Third Wave." *Ms*, January/February: 39–41.

Zack, Naomi. 2005. *Inclusive Feminism: A Third Wave Theory of Women's Commonality*. Lanham: Rowman & Littlefield.

FURTHER READING

Hemmings, Clare. 2011. *Why Stories Matter: The Political Grammar of Feminist Theory*. Durham: Duke UP.

Hesford, Victoria. 2013. *Feeling Women's Liberation*. Durham: Duke University Press.

Hewitt, Nancy A., ed. 2010. *No Permanent Waves: Recasting Histories of U.S. Feminism*. New Brunswick: Rutgers University Press.

Feminisms, Marxist and Socialist

NAZNEEN KANE
Mount St. Joseph University, USA

Marxist and socialist feminisms are branches of feminist theory and practice that integrate the theoretical assumptions of both feminism and Marxism. They rose in popularity in the 1960s and 1970s as a response to the perceived limitations of liberalism and Marxism. Also sometimes referred to as materialist feminism among Anglo-world feminists (French materialism shared more similarities with US and UK radical feminisms), these branches of feminism share a focus on investigating the intersection of gender and class and aim to liberate women from the economic and material sources of women's oppression. Specifically, they are concerned with the ways in which women are oppressed through capitalism and the accumulation of private property. Marxist and socialist feminisms have made remarkable contributions to both Marxist theories and feminist theories. In sociology, Marxist and socialist feminist theories have profoundly impacted scholarship in a variety of fields, including gender, wage labor, family, development, and social class.

Feminism(s) have a conflicted, but well-established, history of engagement with Marxism. Scholars most commonly locate the emergence of Marxist and socialist feminist thinking in the early years of the second wave of feminist organizing (Nicholson 1997). While Marxist and socialist feminist practice and thinking emerged before the political and social movements of the second wave, it is during this historical moment that they rose in popularity. Attempts to merge systematically Marxism and feminism are most commonly linked to women's liberation movements, the rise of the New Left, and the return to Marxist social thought in academia that occurred in the 1960s and 1970s. These historical events led many feminists to turn to Marxist conceptions of society to understand the contours of women's oppression. However, this convergence of Marx's social thought and feminist thought was not seamless or without virulent criticism. Numerous debates and points of contention arose from this union. For example, in her landmark essay, "The Unhappy Marriage of Marxism and Feminism," Heidi Hartmann (1979) argues that the integration of the two schools of thought and practice are problematic owing to the way in which the struggle against patriarchy too often is subsumed by the focus on social class. On the other hand, she argues, feminism alone too often ignores the historical and material conditions that are highlighted in Marxist analyses.

While Marxist and socialist feminisms espouse some notable points of divergence, they generally share several theoretical assumptions and arguments. First, both take a revolutionary orientation toward social change. Critical of "liberal feminisms" that sought reforms in various social domains, Marxist and socialist feminists commonly argue that women cannot be freed from patriarchy without a dramatic transformation of the capitalist social order. The accumulation of profits, they argue, primarily benefits men and relies upon women's unpaid domestic labor to reproduce the status quo. Because women's unpaid labor at home and their underpaid labor in the labor market are viewed as a source of oppression and exploitation, they argue that equality cannot be achieved without an overthrow of the capitalist system.

Second, Marxist and socialist feminisms share a common theoretical foundation. Both are rooted in the social thought of Karl Marx and Friedrich Engels. Although Marx and Engels did not systematically investigate gender inequality, in *The Origins of the Family, Private Property, and the State*, Engels (1884) argued that the subordination of women is the result of social relations and processes. Contrary to the popular view that gender differences are essential and rooted in women's biology, Engels linked gender relations to a society's mode of production. Engels argued that the evolution of human societies (from hunting-gathering to agricultural to capitalist) led to the gendered division of labor and the devaluation of women's labor. The division of labor in this emergent economy led to the view of women as property of their fathers and husbands. Engels argued that a revolution, involving the overthrowing of capitalism, would also free women from the bonds of patriarchy. This rooting of gender oppression in the material conditions of society is an important theoretical tenet of Marxist and socialist feminisms and is often referred to as historical materialism.

Third, Marxist and socialist feminisms generally engage with historical materialism, a theoretical and methodological approach articulated by Marx in his critique of capitalism. According to Marx, changes in the political and social organization of human societies emerge from changes in the mode of production. Historical materialism seeks to investigate and identify the material conditions from which dominant ideologies and culture emerge. Although not all Marxist and socialist feminist thinkers are historical materialists, historical materialism is commonly engaged to understand how the dynamics of the sex–gender system are related to changes in the economic sphere of society.

Fourth, Marxist and socialist feminists generally share the assumption that epistemology and social action are inextricable. Consequently, both focus on producing knowledge for the purpose of social transformation. According to Hennessy and Ingraham (1997), the knowledge claims emerging from Marxist and socialist feminisms are emancipatory and seek social change that eliminates the exploitation of women. Knowledge, they argue, is contested terrain because dominant beliefs and ideologies support the ruling class. Producing "emancipatory knowledge" is key to the overthrow of the capitalist system of power. The vitality of numerous feminist socialist activist organizations reflects this historical and modern focus on social action.

Marxist and socialist feminist thought has also diverged from Marxism, moving beyond some of its purported theoretical and methodological limitations. A key criticism is that Marxism has insufficiently theorized and analyzed the ways in which gender and sex weave into the politics and processes of social class. Indeed, throughout the feminist movements of the 1960s and 1970s in the United States, a common theme in Marxist and socialist feminist thought was the argument that Marxism was androcentric. Thus, while Marxism was viewed as a useful entry point for analyzing the exploitation of women's labor, a number of criticisms were launched against Marxist thought. A key argument was that Marxist intellectuals and political organizations failed to take women's oppression seriously in both scholarship and practice (Hennessy and Ingraham 1997). For example, in Heidi Hartmann's landmark essay, "The Unhappy Marriage of Marxism and Feminism" (Hartmann 1979), she argues that the categories of Marxism are "sex-blind." She extends Marx's ideas of reproduction, exploitation, labor, and private property to incorporate the dimension of patriarchy. Second, Marxism was routinely criticized for being ahistorical. Marxist feminists sought a deeper understanding of the historical variations within and across societies and felt that the "grand theory" offered in Marx's writings was inadequate. Alternatively, they called for a deeper understanding of the social relations between men and women that reproduced patriarchy in everyday life. Although they agreed that oppression was rooted in structure, many Marxist and socialist feminists sought for a deeper understanding of the individual behaviors, practices, and ideologies carried out by men and women that maintained patriarchy. They wanted to explain why capitalism produced a social order in which women were subordinate to men and not vice versa (Hennessy and Ingraham 1997; Ritzer and Stepnisky 2013).

According to Ritzer and Stepnisky (2013), Marxist feminism is a largely dormant theory, although it laid the foundation for an active and growing body of contemporary socialist feminist thought. Socialist and Marxist feminisms share an emphasis on materialism, but socialist feminisms seek to extend and move beyond the conceptual framework of Marxist feminism in several notable ways. First, socialist feminists have argued that Marxist feminist analyses are too reductive. Hartmann (1979), for example, argued that Marxist feminism often subsumes the feminist struggle into the struggle against capitalism. Although socialist feminists largely agree that capitalism is a source of gender oppression, they also view gender as a constitutive feature of social life that is independent of, not only a by-product of, social class relations. Whereas in traditional Marxist analysis the economic base is conceptualized as determining the superstructures of society (i.e., politics, culture, religion, ideology, etc.), in socialist feminism, gender is also viewed as being constitutive of social life.

Second, socialist feminisms extend the definition and methodology of historical materialism beyond an investigation of a society's economic base. Socialist feminist thought generally argues that patriarchy operates in many, if not all, social spheres. Whereas Marxist feminisms most often interrogate the economy and material conditions of a society, socialist feminisms have been interested in investigating patriarchy in multiple spheres of social life, including politics, education, religion, and culture. This broadened focus is due in part to the influence of radical feminists who were critical of economic determinism and drew attention to the multiple forms of violence being waged against women, including sexual and symbolic violence. Socialist feminisms generally focus on liberation in all domains of the social world. In this way, they apply the methodology of historical materialism to all spheres of social life.

Third, socialist feminisms have been more attentive to the intersections of multiple systems of power as they intersect with social class and capitalist relations. This line of scholarship explores how race, sexuality and sexual orientation, and other dimensions of power constitute differential experiences for women under monopoly capitalism.

Fourth, socialist feminists have argued that Marxist feminists operate through a reductive framework, often ignoring the role of agency and individual social action (Ritzer and Stepnisky 2013). This criticism focuses on articulating the ways in which individuals both contest and collude with capitalist and patriarchal relations in everyday life. These criticisms take many forms but often argue that Marxist feminists depict women as falsely conscious, or unaware of the systems of oppression in which they live. Socialist feminisms generally seek to avoid a deterministic approach to women's oppression by examining how women contest social power through micro-political acts of agency and resistance.

Whereas some argue that socialist feminist theorizing is a remnant of the past, others argue that it is a flourishing and timely school of thought (Holmstrom 2002). Practitioners of socialist feminism often describe it as an ongoing epistemic and political project. Relevant sites of analysis include the global expansion and economic power of monopoly capitalism, the gendered formations of global economic inequality, and the economic and sexual exploitation of poor women of color under global capitalism. New directions in Marxist and socialist feminisms also seek to understand how the intersections of multiple systems of power shape the lives of women under monopoly capitalism in variable ways. This research interrogates sexuality, race, ability, and the politics of identity as they converge in class-specific ways. Intersectional approaches attend to differences across groups of women and do not assume that all women have a universal experience. These approaches often highlight and examine hierarchies among women and the ways in which some women are privileged by social class. Finally, a prolific body of feminist scholarship, often identified as post-Marxist, applies an anti-capitalist perspective to cultural domains. Feminist scholars such as Donna Haraway, Judith Butler, and Michele Barrett exemplify attempts to work with, but also beyond, materialism and the limitations of Marxist feminism. Indeed, contemporary socialist feminism is a wide-ranging project that addresses numerous topics and extends beyond the original preoccupations of Karl Marx.

SEE ALSO: Cyborg Manifesto; Division of Labor, Gender; Economic Determinism; Feminism, Cultural; Feminism, French; Feminism, Liberal; Feminism, Materialist

REFERENCES

Engels, Friedrich. 1884. *The Origins of the Family, Private Property, and the State.* Hottingen-Zürich: Verlag der Schweizerischen Volksbuchhandlung (in German).
Hartmann, Heidi. 1979. "The Unhappy Marriage of Marxism and Feminism: Towards a More Progressive Union." *Capital & Class*, 3(2): 1–33. DOI: 10.1177/030981687900800102.
Hennessy, Rosemary, and Chrys Ingraham, eds. 1997. *Materialist Feminism: A Reader in Class, Difference, and Women's Lives.* New York: Routledge.
Holmstrom, Nancy, ed. 2002. *The Socialist Feminist Project: A Contemporary Reader in Theory and Politics.* New York: Monthly Review Press.
Nicholson, Linda. 1997. "Introduction." In *The Second Wave: A Reader in Feminist Theory*, edited by Linda Nicholson, 1–5. New York: Routledge.
Ritzer, George, and Jeffrey Stepnisky. 2013. *Sociological Theory.* New York: McGraw-Hill.

FURTHER READING

Eisenstein, Zillah, ed. 1978. *Capitalist Patriarchy and the Case for Socialist Feminism.* New York: Monthly Review Press.

Haraway, Donna. 1985. "Manifesto for Cyborgs: Science, Technology, and Socialist Feminism in the 1980s." *Socialist Review*, 80: 65–108.

Feminisms, Postmodern

CLARE BARTHOLOMAEUS
Flinders University of South Australia, Australia

INTRODUCTION

Postmodern feminisms cover a range of positions and, when considered as a group, have perhaps been the most widespread academic feminist perspective since the 1990s. Postmodern feminisms move on from but are still inspired by Simone de Beauvoir's *The Second Sex* (1972, published in French in 1949), which most notably argued that "[o]ne is not born, but rather becomes, a woman." This position that becoming a woman is a process, and that "woman" is culturally and socially constructed, is shared by many feminists, and the strongest versions of this can be found in postmodern feminisms. Many postmodern feminisms share some common features, often drawing from broader versions of postmodernism/poststructuralist theories, such as critiquing grand narratives and universal theories, critiquing the concept of a universal woman, critiquing the idea that there is a "truth" waiting to be uncovered, viewing language as constructing reality rather than representing it, and focusing on an understanding of power as productive. Postmodern feminisms are characterized by fluidity, instability, and fragmentation, and are a strong version of social constructionism.

Feminist theories broadly and postmodern theories are both distinct from Enlightenment thinking, and challenge ideas such as universal theories, objectivity, rationality, and rigid concepts of identity. Postmodern feminisms have been influenced by a number of broader postmodern thinkers (who do not always identify with the concept of "postmodern"), particularly Foucault, Derrida, and Lyotard, as well as reworkings of Freud and Lacan. Key postmodern feminist perspectives are diverse, ranging from post-Lacanian psychoanalytic "French feminism" (Irigaray, Cixous, Kristeva) to feminism influenced by Freud and psychoanalytic theories (Flax) to corporeal feminism (Grosz) to postcolonial feminist work using deconstruction (Spivak) to strong versions of social constructionism theorizing the performativity of gender (Butler).

CENTRAL THEMES OF POSTMODERN FEMINISMS

Many postmodern feminisms share several key themes, which draw on different ideas and are influenced by broader postmodern thinkers. Postmodern feminisms question many of the premises of feminism that were dominant in the 1970s (particularly liberal, Marxist/socialist, and radical feminisms), such as a shared cause of oppression among women, the idea that there is a universal "woman," the goal of emancipation from patriarchy, and the view that power is inherently repressive and can be thrown off. Where previously *the* cause of gender inequality was sought out (for example, socialist feminists viewed gender inequality as tied to the sexual division of labor), postmodern feminists critique the very idea of "truths."

Postmodern feminisms critique grand narratives and universal theories. Broad explanatory theories or accounts of knowledge, history, and social organization are questioned as being able to account for diversity. This position has been influenced by Jean-François Lyotard's (1984) suspicion of metanarratives (such as Marxism or Christianity), which he viewed as key to the meaning of postmodern. From this perspective, metanarratives are only one narrative/discourse. Lyotard prefers the use of "little narratives" or local theories which are multiple and diverse and do not attempt to universalize. Postmodern feminists also draw on Michel Foucault's critique of the idea of history as linear or progressive. Such an understanding challenges an Enlightenment vision of history as always progressive. Postmodern feminists critique first- and second-wave feminisms for their focus on building toward end goals, particularly equality with men, the emancipation of women, and the end of patriarchy.

The theorizing of power within postmodern feminisms is particularly important. Much of this thinking draws on and extends the work of Foucault who, while being a key influence on postmodern feminist thinkers, accounted little for gender. Foucault's framing challenges traditional views of power as repressive and "top-down" (e.g., 1980). Power is theorized as being everywhere – power is productive, is not necessarily negative, and cannot be "overthrown." Foucault's conception of power operating through discourse has been particularly important to postmodern feminisms. Knowledge and perceptions of what is "true" are constructed via discourse, where certain discourses gain influence and legitimation. Foucault also views subjects as produced in discourse. Because power is productive, discourse produces and genders subjects, as particular discourses which elaborate patriarchal ideology are legitimated more than others.

Postmodernism critiques the idea of unitary subjects. In particular, postmodern feminisms critique the idea of a universal "woman" which does not account for differences between women, such as ethnicity or class. The idea of a shared "sisterhood" (largely among white, middle-class, Western women), which was previously viewed as a strength of feminism, is challenged and such a framing is critiqued for leaving out many women. Rather, postmodern feminisms favor viewing *women* as historically and locationally specific, with some postmodern feminist theories extending this by only using "woman/women" for strategic political purposes, or by doing away with the concept altogether.

A key concept utilized by several postmodern feminist thinkers is Jacques Derrida's version of deconstruction (e.g., 1976). Deconstruction is a critique of the hierarchical oppositions that have structured Western thought, for example, inside/outside, mind/body, natural/cultural, form/meaning, and attempts to show that such oppositions are neither natural or given, but are, in fact, constructed. Derrida stresses that there is no specific method to do this, because doing so would fix its meaning. Derrida's related concept of *différance*, which plays on the similarity between "differ" and "defer," means that words suggest other meanings than the contexts they were used in. Postmodern feminists have used versions of deconstruction to denaturalize language and knowledge systems that privilege masculine over feminine.

Finally, many postmodern feminisms have been inspired by psychoanalytic theories and reworkings of Sigmund Freud (e.g., 1965) and Jacques Lacan (e.g., 1977). In particular, some feminists have found Lacan's view of the subject as constituted by language rather than biology to be useful for reimagining female subjectivity. While Lacan's interpretation of Freud has been taken up by some postmodern feminists, it has also been critiqued and reworked, particularly the idea that women represent lack.

KEY EXAMPLES OF POSTMODERN FEMINISMS

While postmodern feminisms share similarities, there is great diversity among them, and there are specificities relating to different approaches and thinkers. The thinkers most influential to postmodern feminisms (although not necessarily viewing themselves in this way) are Irigaray, Cixous, Kristeva, Flax, Grosz, Spivak, and Butler.

In the 1970s, postmodern feminisms were associated specifically with "French feminism." Broadly, "French feminists" are concerned with exploring the relationships between language, sexuality, and power. Some "French feminist" work utilizes postmodernist and modernist concepts, where modernist thinking is apparent in discussions of clear gender distinctions (which sometimes appear to be biologically essentialist) and the presumed universality of their ideas. Examining three key "French feminists" (Irigaray, Cixous, and Kristeva) shows the differences (and similarities) between them.

Luce Irigaray argues that men and women are fundamentally different (difference feminism), and therefore believes that achieving equality is impossible (e.g., Irigaray 1985). She views female and male libidos as distinct, as well as female and male sexuality. Her work challenges Lacan's focus on what female sexuality lacks. For Irigaray, female sexuality is diffuse and constant (females have genitals which are "two lips" touching), whereas male sexuality is related only to the penis. The joining of females and males can only be done by repressing the female. Therefore, female sexuality and bodies should be celebrated in separation from men (implying separatism), and only by being separate from men can women be removed from patriarchy. Alongside paying attention to female sexuality, Irigaray suggests women create a female/gender-neutral language and mimic the "feminine role." While Irigaray can be viewed as fitting with difference feminism, she believes that what being female is cannot be reduced to something in particular and is always multiple, thus rejecting the idea of unitary subjects.

Another key "French feminist" is Hélène Cixous, who advocates for women to write *as* a woman and for women, and believes feminine writing can enable change and challenge patriarchy (e.g., "Sorties" in 1986). Like Irigaray, Cixous engages in difference feminism because she emphasizes differences between the sexes. She critiques Lacan for positioning woman as representing lack and she views the feminine libido as beginning in the pre-Oedipal stage, before the feminine is later repressed. Influenced by Derrida, she critiques binaries, and argues that all binaries are related to the man/woman binary, where the second word relates to and is lesser than the first. All Western philosophies place woman with passivity and position woman as secondary and marginal. She discusses *écriture féminine* (feminine writing) as different from *littérature* (masculine writing), viewing connections between female sexuality and feminine writing and between male sexuality and masculine writing. She draws on Derrida's deconstruction where she regards *écriture féminine* as being able to change the dominance of men's writing and provide other ways of thinking.

Differing from Irigaray and Cixous, Julia Kristeva rejects the linking of biological man and "the masculine," and biological woman and "the feminine" (e.g., 1986). Kristeva uses deconstruction to argue that there is no essential womanhood and, indeed, "woman" can only be used as a political strategy, as it does not actually mean anything. Employing and extending Lacan, Kristeva theorizes subjectivity and language as coexisting. She views language as producing speaking beings, and theorizes the subject as in process and unstable. She differentiates between "semiotic" language (poetic, maternal, linked to femininity) and "symbolic" language (rational, paternal, linked to masculinity), arguing that these can be drawn on regardless of sex.

These three "French feminists" share many similarities in their thinking, especially their focus on language, sexuality, and power, and engagement with psychoanalysis. However, there are variations in their theorizing, such as their view of the subject. While Irigaray argues that there are significant distinctions between male and female, she rejects the idea of unitary subjects. Kristeva offers a more thoroughly postmodern account, viewing the subject as in process, unstable, and produced in language, a framing which is also evident in her use of femininity and masculinity rather than female and male. Cixous focuses her analysis on feminine writing rather than subjectivity, and her work offers little in the way of theorizing the subject. In addition, the ways in which these thinkers advocate for women to act politically relate broadly to language for Irigaray and Cixous, but differ between them. Irigaray suggests the creation of a female/gender-neutral language, along with implying the need for separatism because equality between women and men is impossible. Cixous, drawing on ideas of deconstruction, advocates for women to write. Finally, Kristeva is wary of the centrality of politics in feminism, and thus is less specific with calls for action.

Like "French feminists," Jane Flax also uses psychoanalysis, but her work is influenced more by Freud than Lacan. She returns to Freud's psychoanalytic writing about the self, arguing that it is important to critically engage with his work. She discusses psychoanalysis, feminist theory, and postmodernism in relation to each other, arguing that these are the most useful ways of thinking to understand current society (see Flax 1987). Her more recent work (since the late 1980s) is a departure from her early 1980s writing which was more modernist in approach. She notes similarities between feminist and postmodern theorizing, including a move away from Enlightenment ideas, critiques of the idea of a universal woman (instead advocating for attention to differences between women), and emphasis that there is no one cause of (unequal) gender arrangements. Flax argues that analyzing gender relations is key to feminist theory, and views postmodern ideas as useful to examine "ambivalence, ambiguity, and multiplicity," as well as to denaturalize taken-for-granted ideas. The way in which she does this allows room to discuss language and social practices together.

Elizabeth Grosz (previously writing as Elizabeth Gross) also draws on psychoanalysis, but uses a post-Lacanian perspective. Grosz argues for a "corporeal feminism," where analysis is focused on bodies in order to show that they are produced in certain ways rather than being ahistorical and natural (see 1994). By paying attention to bodies, subjects can no longer be viewed as neutral, and assumptions such as universality – which have worked to position women as subordinate to men – can be problematized. Grosz argues that other thinkers, including Foucault, have discussed the body as unitary, without taking into account that there are two or more kinds of bodies, and that *bodies* should be thought about, rather than the "body." These ideas are similar to those of Irigaray and some other "French feminists" who view embodiment as necessarily involving two or more kinds of bodies. Grosz writes from a different feminism position, although she advocates for using "woman" only as a political strategy. Grosz draws on Lacan's idea of a Möbius strip as useful to discuss the subject. She modifies Lacan's thinking to show the links between mind and body and how they turn into one another, and to break down ideas of an interior/inside (psychical) and exterior/outside (corporeal). For Grosz, bodies are both social and material but she argues that gender is sometimes discussed only in terms of the social.

Some postcolonial perspectives also draw on feminisms and postmodernism, such as the work of Gayatri Chakravorty Spivak (e.g., 1988). Like many other feminists, she rejects the idea of a universal "woman," all of whom experience the same forms of oppression. Spivak uses deconstruction to critique, appropriate, and strategically use what can be called Western male theories rather than ignoring them. She critiques concepts of separate West and non-West worlds (and of non-West worlds as singular), including the tendency of some feminists (such as "French feminists") to speak in this way. She is also critical of postmodern thinkers, particularly Foucault and Deleuze, for making generalizations based on their writing in the West and for framing some of their concepts as universal. Spivak writes about the "subaltern" (developed further in relation to postcolonialism from Gramsci's usage) to refer to a subordinate position in relation to ruling authority, such as in colonialism. She writes specifically of the "female subaltern" to refer to both patriarchal and colonial power. Spivak differs from strongly postmodern feminist perspectives because she considers "strategic essentialism," in terms of drawing on identity categories such as "women," useful for political reasons and so that particular groups of people are not ignored.

Judith Butler is arguably the most prominent postmodern feminist thinker today. Her work can be viewed as strongly postmodernist because she discusses the possibility of a society not organized in terms of male/female. *Gender Trouble* (1990) was one of Butler's early books, and remains her most influential work. Butler strongly critiques the idea of "women" as being able to stand for a collective identity. Relatedly, she is against separatism, as implicitly advocated for by writers like Irigaray. Butler views gender as performative, as repeated performances of normative gender signifiers. There is no "real," "true," or "original" gender identity to uncover behind the performance. Gender is a discourse, linked with power and constituted by language. Butler argues that gender and sex should not be necessarily connected, and that both are constructions (rather than just gender, which is more typical in feminist thinking). When they are thought of separately, gender is free from being limited to particular bodies (male/female) and, instead, "man" and "masculine" may "signify" a female body (or a male body), and "woman" and "feminine" may "signify" a male body (or a female body). Butler uses the example of drag to highlight how the signifiers of gender are free-floating, and to emphasize the constructed nature of gender. Butler's work is prominent in feminist studies, and is particularly influential in sexuality and Queer studies.

CRITIQUES OF POSTMODERN FEMINISMS

While it is a key broad perspective in current academic feminist theorizing, postmodern feminisms have been critiqued for a range of reasons, particularly from other feminists. These critiques relate to specific forms of postmodern feminisms, postmodern feminisms generally, and postmodernism more broadly.

Key critiques focus on the question of whether feminism can still be political and/or "emancipatory" if it is postmodern in form; or, from the other direction, whether postmodernism itself is compatible with feminism if feminism is centered on the idea of emancipation. Critics argue that postmodern feminisms are at risk of relativism, where no beliefs, interpretations, or ideas are considered better than others because there is no larger truth or moral order to arbitrate. This is a crucial flaw because it would mean postmodern feminisms do not indicate clear pathways to change. Postmodern feminists would respond that strategies such as deconstruction are a pathway for change (e.g., see discussions of "French feminists" and Spivak, above), and others would argue that in discussing the operations of power through discourse there arise possibilities for disrupting existent power structures (such as Butler, above).

Some critics argue that the loss of concepts such as identity mean marginalized groups may not be heard. However, thinkers such as Spivak ensure that a focus on marginalized groups is maintained. More generally, some critics question whether feminisms necessarily ought to rely on some concept of "woman." Without drawing on some notion of "woman" (or "women"), it is difficult to talk about oppression based on sex and difficult to organize collectively against oppression. Some critics also lament the loss of thinking about bodies and material effects. This is disputed by some postmodern feminists who discuss language and social practices together (e.g., Flax, above), and by thinkers such as Grosz who argue for a "corporeal feminism." To address these critiques, some feminists view it as useful to combine elements of modernism and postmodernism, with attention to material, social, and political issues (Bryson 2003, 242).

Other critiques focus on the inaccessibility, including the writing style(s), of postmodern feminist theories (e.g., see the critique of Butler by Nussbaum 1999). While these issues vary depending on the postmodern feminist approach, critics have argued that postmodern feminisms are too abstract, inaccessible, and elite, and are only able to be understood by other academics. Postmodern feminist writing can be difficult to read, thus creating barriers for readers and reducing possibilities for these texts to be used politically.

Ironically, postmodernism, including postmodern feminisms, has been critiqued as a grand narrative itself. Postmodernism may be viewed as a discourse of power which suggests universality while coming from particular perspectives and influencing which knowledges are legitimated and excluded. Postmodern feminists would argue that they draw on specific postmodern theories where useful, and actively critique and engage with them, including a focus on breaking down universal tenets in the form of gender and other social categories such as race, class, and sexuality.

SEE ALSO: Feminism and Postmodernism; Feminism, Poststructural; Gender Development, Feminist Psychoanalytic Perspectives on; Gender Performance; Language and Gender; Postmodern Feminist Psychology; Queer Theory; Social Constructionist Theory; Strategic Essentialism

REFERENCES

Beauvoir, Simone de. 1972. *The Second Sex*, trans. H. M. Parshley. London: Jonathan Cape. First published 1949.
Bryson, Valerie. 2003. *Feminist Political Theory: An Introduction*, 2nd ed. Basingstoke, UK: Palgrave Macmillan.
Butler, Judith. 1990. *Gender Trouble: Feminism and the Subversion of Identity*. New York: Routledge.
Cixous, Hélène, and Catherine Clément. 1986. *The Newly Born Woman*, trans. Betsy Wing. Minneapolis: University of Minnesota Press.
Derrida, Jacques. 1976. *Of Grammatology*, trans. Gayatri Chakravorty Spivak. Baltimore, MD: Johns Hopkins University Press.
Flax, Jane. 1987. "Postmodernism and Gender Relations in Feminist Theory." *Signs: Journal of Women in Culture and Society*, 12: 621–643. DOI: 10.1086/494359.
Foucault, Michel. 1980. *Power/Knowledge: Selected Interviews & Other Writings 1972–1977*, edited by Colin Gordon. New York: Vintage.
Freud, Sigmund. 1965. *New Introductory Lectures on Psychoanalysis*, edited and translated by James Strachey. New York: Norton.
Grosz, Elizabeth. 1994. *Volatile Bodies: Toward a Corporeal Feminism*. Bloomington: Indiana University Press.
Irigaray, Luce. 1985. *This Sex Which Is Not One*, trans. Catherine Porter and Carolyn Burke. Ithaca, NY: Cornell University Press.
Kristeva, Julia. 1986. *The Kristeva Reader*, edited by Toril Moi. New York: Columbia University Press.
Lacan, Jacques. 1977. *Écrits: A Selection*, trans. Alan Sheridan. New York: Norton.
Lyotard, Jean-François. 1984. *The Postmodern Condition: A Report on Knowledge*, trans. Geoff Bennington and Brian Massumi. Minneapolis: University of Minnesota Press.
Nussbaum, Martha. 1999. "The Professor of Parody." *The New Republic*, February 22.
Spivak, Gayatri Chakravorty. 1988. "Can the Subaltern Speak?" In *Marxism and the Interpretation of Culture*, edited by Cary Nelson and Lawrence Grossberg, 271–313. Urbana: University of Illinois Press.

Feminist Activism

CHRISTINE WALSH, LIZA LORENZETTI, and CARI GULBRANDSEN
University of Calgary, Canada

Feminism, often referred to with a singular moniker, encompasses diverse, fluid, and at times, conflicting practices. "Feminisms," defined in terms of philosophy, ideology, critique, methodology, standpoint, identity(ies), practice, and movement "arise from an understanding that women, in all our diversity, face some form of oppression and exploitation" with the goal of working "collectively in everyday life to end all forms of oppression, to challenge and transform the systems, structures, and relationships that sustain oppression in its many forms" (Maguire 1987, 28).

Feminist herstories, found within multiple geographies, race, ethnocultural and class realities, and various lived experiences of dominance and oppression, have given rise to multiple and emerging interpretations of feminisms. Intersectionality, a term coined by Crenshaw (1991), has been offered to account for these multiple forms of oppression within and outside the struggle for gender equality. Feminisms as ideologies, stances, and activism emerged from multiple sociopolitical and economic grievances that included a common feature of contesting gender oppression, androcentrism, sexism, and patriarchy (Maguire 1987).

Like feminism, feminist activism is multiple and contested. Feminist activism promotes social, political, economic, or environmental change through the use of various strategies, actions, or initiatives enacted within micro, mezzo, and macro contexts. Although feminist activism is frequently associated with visible social or political movements such as equal pay for equal work, LGBTQ (lesbian, gay, bisexual, transgender/transsexual, queer) rights, or gender-based violence prevention, Bhattacharjya et al. (2013) clarified how the mere participation of women in social movements cannot necessarily be equated with feminist activism; feminist activism differs from other forms of activism in the centrality of gender. Feminist activists, equated here with gender justice activists, have been instrumental in championing a strategic focus on gender justice, and a reinforcement of the significance of eradicating gender inequalities within social movements, thereby cultivating awareness of feminist concerns and priorities. Feminist activism is also concerned with the way in which gender is interconnected to other marginalized identities and the personal and political realities that ensue from those identities (i.e., race, sexual identity, ability, etc.).

Premised on a gender-based lens, multiple and emerging forms of feminist activism have arisen from a legion of feminist ideologies including, among others: decolonizing feminism, anti-racist feminism, black American/black Canadian feminism, Asian American feminism, radical feminism, socialist feminism, multicultural feminism, liberal feminism, and postmodern feminisms.

Feminist activism is conceptualized as politicized collective and individual actions, social movement organizing and development, advocacy, leadership, praxis, and everyday actions (Bhattacharjya et al. 2013). Feminist activism is the interrelationship between feminisms and women's lived experiences, or praxis, defined as the "realization of feminist goals in women's daily lives" (Nasser et al. 2010, 64).

Feminist activism includes pedagogy and knowledge generation. Feminist pedagogy, a form of critical pedagogy, is grounded in feminist theory and promotes the importance of social change (Brown 1992; Luke and Gore, 1992).

Feminist activism is embodied in feminist action research, which incorporates and is guided by theoretical frameworks comprised of interrelated feminist principles. As an example, Reid (2004) created a cohesive framework of feminist research principles that identified (a) inclusion: valuing women's experiences as crucial to understanding issues; (b) participation: shared decision-making and collaboration; (c) reflexivity: concerned with power and its role in relationships; (d) individual and collective action: learning about one's own and others' capacity for action and emancipation; and (e) social change: a desired, yet elusive and poorly understood outcome.

The following examples illustrate the diversity of feminist activism globally. As a consequence of complex interrelated social and her/historical factors, Aboriginal women in Canada are vulnerable to violence; official sources identify 1186 cases of murdered and missing indigenous women over the past 30 years (Royal Canadian Mounted Police 2014). Multi-level organizing, led by the Native Women's Association of Canada and the Sisters in Spirit Campaign, is recognized by the National Day of Action for Murdered and Missing Indigenous Women. This grassroots feminist activism has led to international calls for a national public inquiry into the issue of missing and murdered indigenous women and girls (i.e., Amnesty International, Inter-American Commission on Human Rights, The United Nations Committee on the Elimination of Discrimination Against Women, The United Nations Special Rapporteur on Indigenous Rights, UN Committee). Thus far, these calls have not been heeded by the conservative government of Canada.

Malala Yousafzai's stand for education rights for girls and women catalyzed an international human rights and advocacy movement. From her home in northwest Pakistan, Malala advocated for the education of girls, which was banned by the local Taliban. Although she does not describe herself as a feminist, her activism fostered the launch of the United Nations Special Envoy for Global Education "I am Malala" Fund, which demands education for all children by 2015 (http://www.malala.org/).

Mexico is home to a multi-billion dollar industry comprised of primarily American-owned "maquiladora" corporations. These self-authorizing entities have a pervasive record of abuse against women workers and the negation of governmental labor standards (Human Rights Watch 1996). Women have adopted leadership roles in labor rights organizing, protests, and efforts to unionize to protect the rights of workers within this growing industry.

The conscious and coordinated efforts of feminists to include women in the rebuilding of post-genocide Rwanda resulted in a Rwandan Parliament that has a greater proportion of women than anywhere else in the world (Munyaneza 2013). As of 2013, Rwanda remains the only country in the world with a female-dominated parliament, having first achieved this status in 2008, when women garnered 56 percent representation in the House of Representatives – a world-leading figure.

Claiming public space for women, creating political, environmental, or social justice campaigns, conducting research, coalition building, and creating communities to support and enable activism are aspirations inherent to feminist activism.

SEE ALSO: Backlash; Feminist Pedagogy; Intersectionality; Lesbian and Gay Movements

REFERENCES

Bhattacharjya, Manjima, Jenny Birchall, Pamela Caro, David Kelleher, and Vinita Sahasranaman. 2013. "Why Gender Matters in Activism: Feminism and Social Justice Movements." *Gender & Development*, 21(2): 277–293.

Brown, Julie. 1992. "Theory or Practice – What Exactly is Feminist Pedagogy?" *The Journal of General Education*, 41: 1–63.

Crenshaw, Kimberle. 1991. "Mapping the Margins: Intersectionality, Identity Politics, and Violence Against Women of Color." *Stanford Law Review*, 43: 1241–1299.

Human Rights Watch. 1996. "Mexico's Maquiladoras: Abuses Against Women Workers." Accessed September 12, 2015, at http://www.hrw.org/news/1996/08/17/mexicos-maquiladoras-abuses-against-women-workers.

Luke, Carmen, and Jennifer Gore. 1992. *Feminisms and Critical Pedagogy*. New York: Routledge.

Maguire, Patricia Ann. 1987. *Developing a Framework for Feminist Participatory Research: A Case and Assessment with Former Battered Women in Gallup, New Mexico*. Doctoral dissertation, University of Massachusetts. UMI Dissertations Publishing, 8710480.

Munyaneza, James. 2013. "Rwanda: Women Take 64 Percent Seats in Parliament." AllAfrica.com, *The New Times*, September 19, 2013. Accessed September 12, 2015, at http://allafrica.com/stories/201309190110.html.

Nasser, Randa, Fidaa Barghouti, and Janan Mousa. 2010. "Feminist Attitudes and Praxis Among Palestinian Women Activists." *Feminist Formations*, 22(3): 146–175.

Reid, Colleen. 2004. "Advancing Women's Social Justice Agendas: A Feminist Action Research

Framework." *International Journal of Qualitative Methods*, 3(3): 1–20.

Royal Canadian Mounted Police. 2014. *Missing and Murdered Aboriginal Women: A National Operational Overview*. Cat. No. PS64-115/2014E-PDF. Ottawa: Government of Canada Publications.

FURTHER READING

Calliste, Agnes, and George J. Sefa Dei. 2000. *Antiracist Feminism: Critical Race and Gender Studies*. Halifax, NS: Fernwood Publishing.

Collins, Patricia Hill. 2000. *Black Feminist Thought: Knowledge, Consciousness and the Politics of Empowerment*. New York: Routledge. First published 1990.

hooks, bell. 1990. *Yearning: Race, Gender, and Cultural Politics*. Boston, MA: South End Press.

hooks, bell. 1994. *Teaching to Transgress: Education as the Practice of Freedom*. New York: Routledge.

Jiwani, Yasmin. 2006. *Discourses of Denial: Mediations of Race, Gender, and Violence*. Vancouver: UBC Press.

Luke, Carmen, and Jennifer Gore. 1992. *Feminisms and Critical Pedagogy*. New York: Routledge.

Massaquoi, Notisha, and Njoki Nathani Wane, eds. 2007. *Theorizing Empowerment: Canadian Perspectives on Black Feminist Thought*. Toronto: Inanna Publications and Education.

Mohanty, Chandra Talpade. 2006. *Feminism Without Borders: Decolonizing Theory, Practicing Solidarity*. Durham, NC: Duke University Press.

Naples, Nancy A., ed. 1998. *Community Activism and Feminist Politics: Organizing Across Race, Class and Gender*. New York: Routledge.

Naples, Nancy A., and Manisha Desai, eds. 1998. *Women's Activism and Globalization: Linking Local Struggles with Transnational Politics*. New York: Routledge.

Feminist Art

CHRISTINA MORRIS PENN-GOETSCH
Cornell College, USA

Feminist art is an evolving descriptive term with permeable boundaries, as is the very word "feminism." Harmony Hammond's assertion represents a defining statement for feminist art during the second wave: "If art and life are connected, and if one is a feminist, then one must be a feminist artist – that is, one must make art that reflects a political consciousness of what it means to be a woman in patriarchal culture." There is no single "aesthetic" to feminist art (Hammond 1984, 99). Although this is still an accurate commentary, Hammond's definition neither reflects the sole criteria for determining what is feminist art nor the work of artists categorized as such in the wake of the movement of the late 1960s and the identity politics of the early 1990s. These dates frame that of second-wave feminism, a social movement that identified with the suffragists of the first wave and addressed the subjugation of women in the contexts of home and workplace during a period of struggle for greater civil rights on a broader hegemonic stage; this context fostered an awareness of the distinct effects of age, race, class, and gender and gave birth to the phrase "the personal is political." Hammond's designation, taken from the 1980 journal *Heresies*, was tied to artistic intent or an art – equals life – paradigm that lies at the core of how feminist art is still defined. The definition itself began with a focus on recovering the historical existence of women artists left out of a patriarchal canon as well as an exploration of biological and gender binaries; however, contemporary feminist art is rarely addressed in such a limiting way today. Rather categories have shifted to a focus on an intersectionality that addresses multiple and fluid identities and may also embrace masculinity as a construct. Furthermore, such art is not necessarily made by those who identify as feminist. In order to address the subtle shifts in classification, one must examine how art historians and curators have defined artists and their work during the 1970s and the decades that followed as well as the close relationship of the art historian or critic to the *construct*.

Hammond cofounded A.I.R. gallery, the first women's cooperative gallery in New York, in 1972. Her comments reflect much of the struggle faced by women artists then and in the decade that followed. This artist's characterization was, in part, a response to Lawrence Alloway's 1976 criticism of feminist art's lack of a single comprehensive manifesto to assist in linking the theory to practice (Alloway 1976, 104). The label "feminist" itself locates most easily in work coming out of this period and extends into the 1980s. The United Nations named 1975 the first International Women's Year and fostered a number of related exhibitions in the following years on an international stage. The feminist art movement often focused on three topics that helped form the term "feminist art": new media, embracing women's personal experience as a legitimate subject and a recovery of the history of women, including artists.

Overt feminist programs for artists in New York and California (Women Artists in Revolution (WAR), California State University at Fresno and later at the California Institute of the Arts, Valencia) started to explore what it meant to be a woman during the second wave. In this context, artists employed media outside modernism's narrow focus on formalism in painting and sculpture in favor of media financially more accessible or associated with craft. Performance art, video, photography, and fiber arts became a norm and commented on the lives and roles of women. Performance artists Ana Mendieta, Adrian Piper, Carolee Schneemann, Howardina Pindell, Martha Rosler, and Yoko Ono offered work that addressed gender along with other identities. Hammond's *Floorpieces* of 1973 mimicked domestic rag rugs. Faith Ringgold employed West African or African-inspired fabrics pieced into a sculpture entitled *Mrs. Jones and Family* in 1973, as a commentary on the positive and central role of the African American mother. Both performance and textile arts found a home under the direction of Miriam Schapiro and Judy Chicago, who led a group of students through consciousness-raising sessions and the creation of the Los Angeles *Womanhouse* installation space of 1972 with the express purpose of exploring their own experiences and challenging popular culture's view of a woman's role.

Schapiro and Chicago searched through their own work and that of others to find that which was "female" and discovered "central core" imagery as a recognizable feature of art by women. This awareness began after observing abstract circular forms and cavities, unconscious metaphors for that which was unique to women's bodies, in their work and that of other women artists (Schapiro and Chicago 1973). Chicago then transformed these initial observations into a new language that celebrated an active female sexuality that thwarted the male gaze through muscular vulvar forms. The concept of the gaze was made popular through the accessible 1972 BBC series and book, *Ways of Seeing*, where John Berger (1972) states, "men act and women appear" – that is, men are active agents whereas women are objects in Western art and advertising (Berger 1972, 47). Laura Mulvey's (2003) "Visual Pleasure in Narrative Cinema" followed a similar binary approach to the depiction of women in film through psychoanalytic theory. Central core imagery, however, would later earn the derogatory label "essentialism," thus suggesting that a woman's visual expression could be reduced to a body part. The one work of art that responds most directly to recovering the past, women's craft, and "central core" imagery remains Judy Chicago's *Dinner Party* of 1979 that celebrates the names of 999 women from history, often the lone work illustrating feminism in the standard introductory art history textbook.

Art historians expanded what qualified as feminist art in the 1970s and 1980s. Linda Nochlin's (1971) article "Why Have There Been No Great Women Artists?" had inspired contemporary artists like Chicago to reclaim women's history with the *Dinner Party* and, at the same time, art historians further blurred the boundaries of what art fits this categorization by identifying the work of artists who did not participate in the feminist movement of the 1970s or existed long before the second wave as feminist. The other result of this effort was the creation of new feminist or proto-feminist icons through the writing of monographs and articles on women artists like Artemisia Gentileschi, Mary Cassatt, Georgia O'Keeffe, and Frida Kahlo. Such texts gave feminist supporters new heroines that were missing from patriarchal histories. Mónica Mayer, who had worked with Chicago at the Feminist Arts Workshop, also described her experiences at the Escuela Nacional de Artes Plásticas in Mexico City similarly to those in the United States where the works of women artists were largely invisible in the art history classroom (Mayer 2010, 5). The need to recognize the contributions of women to the visual arts explains why the National Museum for Women in the Arts in Washington, DC, was founded in 1987 and why the museum still devotes attention only to work by women artists.

Shifts in how identity was defined had occurred by 1989 and this, in turn, moved the discussion of what methodologies feminist art historians should or should not employ. One critical shift gained prominence with Mary Garrard's analysis of the paintings and life of Artemisia Gentileschi and her methodology. Here she employs the premise "that women's art is inescapably, if unconsciously, different from men's, because the sexes have been socialized to different experiences of the world" (Garrard 1989, 5). Griselda Pollock would later see this approach as a binary line of questioning that privileges the normative and fails to truly re-vision the patriarchal canon (1999, 103–108). The zeitgeist was ripe for a new vocabulary, and Judith Butler introduced the notion of gender as a "masquerade" in *Gender Trouble* (1990, 25). Nevertheless, the door was left open for a study of the simultaneous intersection of race and gender that came to the forefront with the work of legal theorist, Kimberlé Williams Crenshaw (1989). Despite the criticism, Garrard's work represents the first major shift from women's to gender studies in art history.

Textbooks and exhibitions specifically devoted to feminist art after 1990 often employ the late 1960s and 1970s as a springboard for a discussion of artists influenced by this early movement. Norma Broude and Mary Garrard's introduction to the first major textbook, *The Power of Feminist Art*, relies heavily on Lucy R. Lippard's view that feminist art is a movement akin to Dada or Surrealism, where there are multiple styles linked to political strategies (Broude and Garrard 1994, 10). Such a definition implies an intentionality or consciousness on the part of the artist that does not agree with how art work is actually identified as feminist. Although the *Power of Feminist Art* touches on art that addresses multiple identities, it was not until Amelia Jones curated *Sexual Politics* (1996) that the question of how the focus on gender alone had left out the experiences of many was brought to the forefront just as cultural critics like bell hooks, Cherríe Moraga, Gloria Anzaldúa, Coco Fusco, and Trinh T. Minh-ha were calling out for change. Judy Chicago, whose work was a centerpiece for *Sexual Politics*, then participated in the 1997 exhibition *Lord of the Rim: In Herself/for Herself* in Hsin Chuang, China. Although influenced by the desire to recover women's history and employ materials associated with women's work, these artists from Taiwan, Korea, and Japan as well as the west coast of North America chose to focus on the anonymous women of the local textile industry instead of the more famous figures from history celebrated in Chicago's *Dinner Party* (Chien 2004). One of the more politically confrontational Asian exhibitions that considered feminism and gender stereotypes appeared in 2005, *Zen-ei no Josie* (Japanese Women Artists: Avant-garde Movements), 1950–1975. Elsewhere, the 2007 exhibition *Wack! Art and the Feminist Revolution* further defined the contribution of Latin American feminism and managed to expand our knowledge of a broader spectrum of women who already were a part of the feminist art movement from the beginning. The documentation of the feminist art movement in the United States was then further expanded with an exhibition of works by artists on both sides of the Atlantic by Xabier Arakistain's *Kiss Kiss Bang Bang: 45 Years of Art and Feminism* at Bilbao's Museum of Fine Art in 2007.

The one major transnational exhibition of 2007 that ventured outside of the realm of second-wave feminism was the Brooklyn Museum's *Global Feminisms: New Directions in Contemporary Art*, curated by Maura Reilly and Linda Nochlin. This exhibition set the stage for much of how feminist art is defined in the twenty-first century. The chronological starting point for the show was art work created after 1990 and the criteria for feminist art was "wide ranging, flexible and broad" in order to allow for feminisms from different racial, ethnic, political, and cultural contexts that might not see gender as the most urgent of questions to be considered. The curators did not propose a single definition, but they did embrace a multiplicity of identities that recalls Crenshaw's intersectionality. The exhibition opened at the same time as the Elizabeth A. Sackler Center for Feminist Art which maintains a "Feminist Art" database of work by women artists – whose work may or may not easily be recognized as feminist or, much less, by an artist claiming a specific or dominant feminist outlook. Although the database includes work that addresses masculinities, the artists appear to be biologically female. This is also true of "The Feminist Art Project" database at the Institute for Women and Art at Rutgers which specifically opens its database to women and transgender artists. Yet, in both cases, the categorization of these artists in a feminist archive for art suggests this categorization. There are practical reasons for documenting art that is not by identified feminists in these databases. Some artists avoid the use of the term in a world where many have become uncomfortable with its implied political stance. This struggle daunted curators such as Marina Loshak and Nataliya Kamenetskaya in their attempt to garner funding to mount a feminist exhibition for International Women's Month at Moscow's Manezh Museum and Exhibition Center in 2013 within the context of the controversial feminism of Pussy Riot (Turkina 2013).

The initial embrace of transnational feminisms in the United States did more than expand a knowledge base; Judith Kegan Gardiner and Gayatri Reddy argued that global feminism re-visions our very definitions and theoretical approaches (2007, 7). At the core of curator Maura Reilly's approach to the *Global Feminisms* exhibition was the theoretical work of Chandra Talpade Mohanty (Reilly 2010, 157). Her goal was to explore Mohanty's call for "common differences" that allowed for the recognition of intersections as well as contextual differences across cultures, races, and sexualities. Despite this lens, *Tiger by the Tail! Women Artists of India Transforming Culture* of 2007 responded to *Global Feminisms* with a call for greater cultural specificity that avoids the specter of imperialism (Reinharz 2007, 8). Although *Tiger by the Tail!* made the work of 17 women more visible, the text fails to mention that one featured artist, Mumbai-based Nalini Malani, was one of the organizers of the first exhibition of art by Indian women in 1985 (Rajgopal 2014). The evidence suggests that the burgeoning transnational scholarship or history has "gaps" yet to be filled.

A call for a better understanding of situating feminism within a specific cultural context allows for a better understanding of how intersectionality functions. Fran Lloyd argues that one must negotiate roles of gender, race, class, religion, and colonialism when examining the work and geographies of Arab women today – whose art and image become markers of political identity beyond gender alone (Lloyd 1999, 21). Lisa Aronson (2014) further argues that related issues with colonialism's past coupled with the effects of "racially based injustices" and apartheid in South Africa took precedence over feminist subjects in the art world until the 1980s. In the 1990s, the door was open to a broader definition of gender along with culture, race, and sexuality (Aronson 2014, 4).

The most recent textbooks on feminist art are anthologies that follow a similar path to those of feminist databases and argue for the continuing need for focusing on work by women artists. They examine individual contemporary artists from an intersection of national, racial, and sociopolitical backgrounds, but the space is not confined to a discussion of art by women who necessarily identify as sharing the same political position (Heartney et al. 2007, 2013). But the presence of work solely by female artists in both anthologies seems to be explained by the inclusion of statistical information about the current underrepresentation of art by women in galleries and museums. The need to establish a lost history of art by women also still seems apt. When the Pompidou Center opened with curator Camille Moirneau's *elles@centrepompidou* in 2009 with approximately 500 works all by women, the curator saw the show as "a revolutionary gesture of affirmative action" (quoted in Muchnic 2009).

Gender identity may be itself only a construction, but the lived experience of that identity remains a critical element in most definitions of feminist art, including that of Hammond in 1978. Identity is linked to the art/life model that is inherent to a Western understanding of art. Amelia Jones's more recent analysis in *Seeing Differently* summarizes the situation when she states, "we cling … to anachronistic Renaissance to modern modes of interpretation that occlude or veil our dependence on identification" (Jones 2012, 218). Nevertheless, Jones is arguing for a multiplicity of fluid identities and, in this sense, her work expands on Hammond's definition of feminist art as limited to women with a distinct feminist agenda and introduces a definition that is a clearer reflection of contemporary feminisms with one potential contradiction. The door of feminist art remains open to men whose work addresses such content through other identities; however, in a world that still privileges the male artist, it is only slightly ajar.

SEE ALSO: Consciousness-Raising; Essentialism; Feminisms, First, Second, and Third Wave; Gaze; Intersectionality; Visual Culture

REFERENCES

Alloway, Lawrence. 1976. "Women's Art in the '70s." *Art in America*, 64: 64–70, 72.
Aronson, Lisa. 2014. "Gender and South African Art." *African Arts*, 45: 3–5.
Berger, John. 1972. *Ways of Seeing*. London: Penguin Books.
Broude, Norma, and Mary D. Garrard, eds. 1994. *The Power of Feminist Art: The American Movement of the 1970s, History and Impact*. New York: Harry Abrams.

Butler, Judith. 1990. *Gender Trouble: Feminism and the Subversion of Identity*. New York: Routledge.
Chien, Ying-Ying. 2004. "Marginal Discourse and Pacific Rim Women's Arts." *Signs*, 29: 663–677.
Crenshaw, Kimberlé Williams. 1989. "Demarginalizing the Intersection of Race and Sex: A Black Feminist Critique of Antidiscrimination Doctrine, Feminist Theory, and Antiracist Politics." *University of Chicago Legal Forum*, 139: 139–167.
Gardiner, Judith Kegan and Gayatri Reddy. 2007. "Preface: Women's Resistance in Global Perspective." *Feminist Studies*, 33: 7–232.
Garrard, Mary D. 1989. *Artemisia Gentileschi: Image of the Female Hero in Italian Baroque Art*. Princeton: Princeton University Press.
Jones, Amelia. 2012. *Seeing Differently: A History and Theory of Identification and the Visual Arts*. London: Routledge.
Hammond, Harmony. 1984. "Horseblinders." In *Wrappings: Essays on Feminism, Art, and the Martial Arts*. New York: TSL Press.
Heartney, Eleanor, Helaine Posner, Nancy Princenthal, and Sue Scott. 2007. *After the Revolution: Women Who Transformed Contemporary Art*. Munich: Prestel.
Heartney, Eleanor, Helaine Posner, Nancy Princenthal, and Sue Scott. 2013. *The Reckoning: Women Artists of the New Millennium*. Munich: Prestel.
Lloyd, Fran. 1999. *Contemporary Arab Women's Art*. London: Women's Art Library.
Mayer, Mónica. 2010. "Art and Feminism: From Loving Education to Education through Osmosis." *n.paradoxa*, 26: 5–16.
Muchnic, Suzanne. 2009. "At Paris' Pompidou Center, The Year of the Women." *Los Angeles Times*, May 24. Accessed October 3, 2014, http://www.latimes.com/entertainment/arts/la-ca-elles24-2009may24-story.html#page=1.
Mulvey, Laura. 2003. "Visual Pleasure and Narrative Cinema." In *The Feminism and Visual Culture Reader*, edited by Amelia Jones, 44–53. New York: Routledge. First published 1975.
Nochlin, Linda. 1971. "Why Have There Been No Great Women Artists?" *ARTnews*, 69: 22–39, 67–71.
Pollock, Griselda. 1999. *Differencing the Canon: Feminist Desire and the Writing of Art's Histories*. New York: Routledge.
Rajgopal, Ambika. 2014. "Indian Artist Nalini Malani Talks Myth, Metaphor and Women – Interview." *Art Radar: Contemporary Art Trends and News from Asia and Beyond*, March 21. Accessed January 3, 2015, at http://artradarjournal.com/2014/03/21/artist-nalini-malani-talks-myth-metaphor-and-women-interview/.
Reilly, Maura. 2010. "Curating Transnational Feminisms." *Feminist Studies*, 36: 156–173.
Reinharz, Shulamit. 2007. *Tiger by the Tail! Women Artists of India Transforming Culture*. Waltham: Brandeis University.
Schapiro, Miriam, and Judy Chicago. 1973. "Female Imagery." *Womanspace Journal*, 1: 11–14.
Turkina, Olesya. 2013. "The F-word: Why is the Art World So Afraid of Feminism?" *The Calvert Journal: A Guide to Creative Russia*, March 13. Accessed January 3, 2014, at http://calvertjournal.com/comment/show/545/turkina-feminism-exhibition.

Feminist Art Practice

ALEXIS L. BOYLAN
University of Connecticut, USA

Feminist art practice is the attempt, by both artists and audiences, to articulate political and social spaces for feminisms through art. Feminist art practice has likewise been informed by, shaped, aided, and resisted attempts to construct and define a cohesive feminist aesthetic.

Two divergent understandings of feminist art practice must be considered in defining the term. The first is founded on the premise that in patriarchal societies in which women are systemically denied access to equal opportunities in regard to education, funding, exhibition space, publishing and performance spaces, job opportunities and security because of their gender, all art produced by women is an act of feminist art practice. This logic suggests that in such a society where women are not given equal footing intellectually, socially, or materially, any art practice is an act of resistance, should be understood as political, and is reflective of identity and creativity inherently tied to gender. This broad definition therefore allows for artists and art produced outside of historical feminist movements to be considered as actively engaging with feminist art practice (an example might be Artemisia Gentileschi, an Italian Baroque painter, born centuries before Western European feminism was a cohesive social or political paradigm). This understanding of feminist art practice can also accommodate art produced by women who reject the term feminist as part of their own political and social identity, philosophy, or art production (for example, painter Georgia O'Keeffe and pop singer Katy Perry) but whose work still resonates with others as espousing and reflecting feminist ideals. In other words, this definition does not limit feminist art production to artists who understand their work as feminist and instead places the power of interpreting feminist meaning on the object or the larger societal context as signifiers of practice.

The other, and perhaps more commonly understood definition of feminist art practice reflects an artist's embrace of feminism as a social, political, and creative identity that inspires art production and is reflected in the object itself. In this understanding it is the practice, and the desire through practice to reflect and reproduce an artist's feminist positioning, that is crucial. Feminist practice is a political, social, and personal act that is at once about expanding paradigms of art and creativity and also about challenging patriarchal structures. Therefore, feminist art practice is often understood as activism, and a position of resistance. Critics have often accused this kind of feminist art practice as privileging the idea over the object or the propagandistic potential over the product; yet the critique itself reveals a system of judging art and creativity that many feminists would argue is rooted in exclusionary practice and misogyny.

Feminist art practice is by its very nature diverse, but there are some recurrent themes and strategies evidenced in art. This practice often looks to challenge definitions of art that have privileged male artists and their work. Likewise, feminist art practice expands and/or deconstructs canons that reinforce traditional production. Feminist art practice also reimagines materials and form; spoken word, textiles, experimentation with film, language, and performance, for example, have all inspired feminist production. Using forms, materials, iconography, and symbols that have been traditionally dismissed as outside of art production because of their association with women and women's creativity aids in articulating feminisms and shifting definitions of art. As theorist and poet Gloria Anzaldúa and others have argued, art and theory can shift in form, language can be written and used in new and expansive ways, and art itself can move beyond narrow placement and positioning, all offering radical political and social possibilities for liberating bodies from oppression. This pressure to reconsider and change artistic relationships to form and materials necessarily impacts aesthetics. Feminist art practice confronts the limitations of traditional aesthetics and art criticism and demands a shift in critical language and criteria for judging the value and worth of art and art practice.

The diversity of feminist art practices makes predictions about future trends specious, yet there are several areas of rich potential. For example, feminist art practice will continue to grapple with the effects of technology on gender, race, equality, activism, and art. Artists must confront the impact of technology that at once has the potential to connect and inspire feminist art production by expanding and democratizing avenues of contact and access and yet also facilitates the proliferation of imagery and texts that denigrate women's bodies and intellectual, social, and political potential. Queer and trans art practice will also continue to shape and challenge what constitutes feminist art practice. Feminism is not a static category, and just as multicultural and global feminist art practices have necessarily reframed dialogues about bodies, art, politics, and identity, so too will new theories of sexual identity and creativity reimagine the potential for and limitations of feminist art practice. Finally, feminist aesthetics and the potential for reframing concepts such as "beauty," "ugliness," "success," or "failure" will inspire feminist art practice. Renewed interest in these terms has artists and theorists revisiting the potential of aesthetics to transform culture.

SEE ALSO: Feminist Activism; Feminist Art; Feminist Literary Criticism; Images of Gender and Sexuality in Advertising; Lesbian Performance; Performance Art; Representation; Women as Cultural Markers/Bearers; Women as Producers of Culture

FURTHER READING

Anzaldúa, Gloria. 1987. *Borderlands/La Frontera: The New Mestiza*. San Francisco: Aunt Lute Books.

Brand, Peg Zeglin, ed. 2013. *Beauty Unlimited*. Bloomington: Indiana University Press.

Gerhard, Jane F. 2013. *The Dinner Party: Judy Chicago and the Power of Popular Feminism, 1970–2007*. Athens, GA: University of Georgia Press.

Hein, Hilde, and Carolyn Korsmeyer, eds. 1993. *Aesthetics in Feminist Perspective*. Bloomington: Indiana University Press.

Lippard, Lucy R. 1995. *The Pick Glass: Selected Feminist Essays on Art*. New York: The New Press.

Mark, Lisa Gabrielle, ed. 2007. *WACK! Art and the Feminist Revolution*. Cambridge, MA: The MIT Press/Los Angeles: The Museum of Contemporary Art.

Various Authors. 1995. "A Conversation on Recent Feminist Art Practices." *October*, 71 (January): 49–69.

Feminist Christology

ROSEMARY RADFORD RUETHER
Claremont School of Theology and Claremont Graduate University, USA

Christology is a field of study that is concerned with the being of Jesus Christ as a person, as well as how he relates to God the Father. Those familiar with feminist theology are more acquainted with a patriarchal or sexist Christology, a Christology that claims a normative male representation of God and Christ. For example, Thomas Aquinas drew on Aristotle's view that women were defective human beings, lacking full capacity for reason, moral will, and physical strength, to claim that Jesus had to be incarnated as a male because only the male represented the fullness of human nature. This meant that women could not represent Christ as a priest. Women are considered ontologically incapable of being ordained, a view the Roman Catholic magisterium still maintains (Aquinas, *Summa Theologica*, pt. 1, q. 92, art. 1).

The historical Jesus was unquestionably a Jewish male, although no Christians would insist that priests and ministers must be Jewish in order to represent Christ. Yet maleness has been seen as more normative to represent Christ, not only because of the historical maleness of Jesus as a human, but also because Jesus is seen as incarnating the Logos of God, symbolized as male. Images of the crucified Christ as female are rare, and when such images were created they evoked negative responses. While a mostly naked male on a cross is seen as representing redemptive suffering, a similar image of a female may provoke a pornographic response (Ruether 1985, 104).

Yet Christianity has always affirmed that salvation in Christ included women as well as men. Paul's Letter to the Galatians states that "As many of you as were baptized into Christ have clothed yourself with Christ. There is no longer Jew or Greek, there is no longer slave or free, there is no longer male and female, for all of you are one in Christ Jesus" (3:27–28). Baptism has always been offered to all humans, male and female equally.

Some Christians have experimented with gender-inclusive images of Christ to express this vision of oneness in baptismal and eschatological redemption. This was facilitated by the identification of Christ with divine Wisdom, a concept that was female-identified in the biblical tradition. Thus Priscilla, one of the second-century Montanist prophets, claimed, "Christ came to me in the likeness of a woman, clad in a bright robe, and planted wisdom in me and revealed that this place is holy and that here Jerusalem comes down from heaven" (Stevenson 1975, 113).

The fourteenth-century English mystic Julian of Norwich created a gender-inclusive vision of God as Trinity:

> Furthermore I saw that the second Person who is our mother substantially, that same dear person is now become our mother sensually … the second Person of the Trinity is our mother in kind, in our substantial making, in whom we are grounded and rooted, and He is our Mother of mercy in taking our sensuality … Thus Jesus Christ who does good against evil is our very Mother. We have our being of him, where every grounds of Motherhood begins, with all the sweet keeping of love that endlessly follows. As truly as God is our Father so truly is God our Mother. (Walsh 1961, 159–161)

Several Protestant mystics, such as Jacob Boehme in the sixteenth to seventeenth centuries, drew on Wisdom imagery to insist that the Trinity was both male and female, the Second person of the Trinity being the female component (Ruether 2005, 226–236).

Several medieval mystical groups suggested that Christ in the last days would reappear as a female and the church would become female led, to overcome male domination. The more developed form of this view appeared in the Shaker movement in England and America (eighteenth to nineteenth centuries). Shakers believed that God was both male and female, and the incarnation of God into Jesus was incomplete since it revealed only the male aspect of God. God has now been incarnated in their foundress, Mother Ann Lee, thus completing the revelation of God in its female aspect. "[T]he second Adam [could not be] complete in the order of spiritual regeneration, without the second Eve, who of course would be manifested … in the line of the female, and become the first mother of the redeemed, the children of the kingdom of Promise" (Ruether 2005, 226–236).

Few Christians in the nineteenth century or today have been interested in claiming Mother Ann Lee is the second incarnation of Christ. Yet the belief that redemption in Christ is gender inclusive continues to be basic to the Christian message today. Feminist liberation theologies have reaffirmed the message of the New Testament gospels that Christ is liberator of all people and this means overcoming all forms of domination, slavery as well as sexual and racial discrimination. Redemption overturns all social hierarchies. The last shall be first and the first last.

Although Jesus favored the term "Abba" for his view of God, this is an intimate nurturing view of parenting, not a "father" to be translated as "King" or "Lord." In the Gospel of Matthew Jesus is quoted as rebuking forms of religion that created heavy burdens on the followers and set up hierarchical leaders. Church leaders should be characterized as servants of all, not vehicles of dominating power: "And call no one your father on earth, for you have one Father – the one in heaven.

Nor are you to be called teachers, for you have one teacher, the Messiah. The greatest among you will be your servant. All who exalt themselves will be humbled and all who humble themselves will be exalted" (23:9–12).

In his ministry Jesus embraced many marginalized and lower-class women, such as Samaritan women and prostitutes, as those who better understood his message, while criticizing the dominant Jewish religious leaders whose burdensome prescriptions for salvation excluded the poor and lowly, especially women. Thus there is ample basis in the heritage of Jesus' teaching for a redemption that not only overcomes patriarchal oppression, but also creates a redemptive community in which women equally with men are included in the liberated but also speak for the Christ, the liberator. This is the core of a feminist Christology.

SEE ALSO: Christianity, Gender and Sexuality; Creation Stories; Feminine and Masculine Elements; Feminist Theology; Mysticism; Religious Fundamentalism; Shaker Religion

REFERENCES

Aquinas, Thomas. *Summa Theologica*. Accessed June 19, 2015, at http://www.ccel.org/ccel/aquinas/summa.toc.html.

Ruether, Rosemary R. 1985. *Womenguides*. Boston: Beacon Press.

Ruether, Rosemary R. 2005. *Goddess and the Divine Feminine: A Western Religious History*. Berkeley: University of California Press.

Stevenson, James, ed. 1975. *A New Eusebius: Documents Illustrating the History of the Church to* AD *337*. New York: Macmillan.

Walsh, James. 1961. *The Revelations of Divine Love of Julian of Norwich*. New York: Harper and Row.

FURTHER READING

Brock, Rita N. 1988. *Journeys by Heart: A Christology of Erotic Power*. New York: Crossroads.

Ruether, Rosemary R. 1983. *Sexism and Godtalk: Toward a Feminist Theology*. Boston: Beacon Press.

Ruether, Rosemary R. 2012. *Women and Redemption: A Theological History*, 2nd ed. Minnesota: Fortress Press.

Feminist Consciousness in Historical Perspective

LINDA KIERNAN
Trinity College, Republic of Ireland

The term "feminist consciousness" is distinct from feminism, the term coined in the nineteenth century to designate a self-aware, politically active, and increasingly pervasive cultural idea that sought to address the inequalities that women faced in the political, legal, social, and familial spheres. In contrast to feminism, feminist consciousness was a recognition of the inequities of gender roles, either by an individual or by a small group in the pre-modern age, but a consciousness that lacked concerted political or social action. Feminist consciousness acknowledges the privately held thoughts of women whose writings went unpublished in their lifetimes; in this respect letters, diaries, testimonies, and memoirs serve as a means to understand the frustrations, hopes, desires, and wishes of individual women.

HISTORIOGRAPHY

The subject of women's history has grown enormously since the 1960s inspired by the work of numerous historians, most notably Gerda Lerner and Joan Scott. The issue of gender has been explored in a variety of ways; in conjunction with colonial, racial, legal, and labor history among others. It has also borrowed from other academic topics reflecting a wide and inclusive interdisciplinary approach in terms of both theory and methodology. As such literary, official, personal, philosophical, and political sources have all been utilized in uncovering the hitherto concealed, disguised, or undiscovered voices of women and men who sought to address gender imbalance and inequalities. Varieties of feminist consciousness have been identified by the vast research undertaken by gender historians, particularly in the past 30 years. In breaking away from the histories of "great women," scholars such as Olwen Hufton, Bonnie Smith, Merry Wiesner-Hanks, Renate Bridenthal, Georges Duby, Michelle Perrot, and others, have uncovered the lives of ordinary women, as well as enriching our understanding of women's roles and expectations in the medieval, early modern, and modern periods. Out of this research has emerged a more expansive and inclusive picture of women at all levels, gleaned from an ever-widening range of source materials from legal documents to personal papers to professional memberships. In almost all categories it is possible to find kernels of feminist consciousness.

In contrast to the history of "great women," that of feminist consciousness is very much a hidden history, one that challenges the scholar in a number of ways. First, assessing the idea that women, as either individuals or as part of a collective, had a sense of their own oppression, or of ideas of how to improve their status, roles, and independence, in many ways relies upon the written record of such sentiments. In this respect the history of feminist consciousness is dependent upon literacy. As such, given our knowledge of premodern literacy rates, feminist consciousness is (in most cases) restricted to those classes with access to education, thus limiting our opportunities to observe feminist consciousness at the lower levels of society. Within the period in question literacy rates improve, as do the educational opportunities of women, thus enriching the record of feminist consciousness. Second, when women did write, particularly prior to the seventeenth century, they were prohibited, either by traditions or societal norms, from deviating from suitable subjects for their sex. As Lerner notes, women were faced with a number of challenges, not least in "proving their right and their ability to think at all in opposition to traditional gender-roles they were expected to fill" (Lerner 1993, 57). Third, writers in general remained relatively isolated from like-minded thinkers, and certainly from their readers, in the centuries prior to the printing revolution. Finally, the absence of a history of women was not simply a relegation of women's contributions to life, both public and private, it designated a lack of worth to the endeavors, experiences, and expectations of women over time; in the absence of "a history of their own" or "herstory," the message to women was that their efforts were not worthy of record, nor were they expected to perform in the same spheres as men.

MEDIEVAL PERIOD

At the turn of the seventh century, Christianity was the most pervasive and influential source of ideas on the status of women in Europe. Christian writers were equally influenced by prevailing traditions across Europe in the first millennium, and indeed early formal Christian concepts were based on the philosophies of the Greeks, Romans, and Jews, as well as Celtic, Germanic, Gallic, and Anglo-Saxon beliefs. The views of the church remained entrenched in the story of Adam and Eve, seeing the feminine as the source of evil and sin. The stories of early female martyrs and saints such as St. Perpetua of Carthage or St. Brigid of Kildare did little to counteract the decrees of church fathers, including Tertullian, John Chrysostom, St. Augustine, and St. Jerome, whose works all attested to the dangers posed by women and femininity. The Aristotelian view that women were imperfect men was combined with Christian thought by the Scholastic movement in the twelfth century forming a potent condemnation of women as corrupt and deficient. According to the works of St. Thomas Aquinas and others in the Scholastic tradition, Eve was not inferior because of her sin, she had always been so.

Given the contemporary state of education, literacy, and written records for men, as well as women, for the early Middle Ages, up to the twelfth century, we are left with a small but significant number of examples of female authorship, feminist consciousness, and educated women; surveys of women in the Middle Ages battle against the "silence of the sources." Women who did, or could not write, may still have had their voices recorded, whether in confession or in legal testimony; however, these sources can mask the subject with the interpretation of the scribe. For those who could commit their work to paper it was most likely that they came from a religious standpoint; the majority of female writing that survives from the ninth to the twelfth centuries originates in religious congregations and communities, usually from professed women or beguines. Men also wrote on the proper roles for women, influenced by Christian theology, classical literature, and barbarian tradition. Hagiographies of female saints, as well as biographies of female rulers and warriors, in the seventh to eleventh centuries demonstrated the roles that exceptional women could fulfill, but for most women, the roles of mother, wife, and domestic laborer remained the standard models of womanhood.

Prior to the printing revolution and the extension of elementary education to women, an increasing number of women nonetheless made their mark in publishing original work beyond the confines of religious life. Nuns, abbesses, and canonesses could exert a degree of intellectual freedom unavailable to their secular sisters; however, they were much more likely to direct their thought to the issues of women in relation to the church, to religious life, and to the scripture's view of their sex. Their usually high social status combined with financial security and spiritual calling gave added weight to their contributions whether to the local community or on paper. Notable exceptions include one of the first examples of historical biography, the *Life of St. Radegund* by the nun Baudovinia, written in the seventh century. Hrotswith of Gandersheim (d. 1000) was a particularly active abbess who produced poetry, drama, history, and classical studies, and whose work provides scholars with examples of feminine spiritual scholarship. One of the most active religious women in this early medieval period was Hildegard of Bingen (1098–1179), whose work encompassed medicine, natural sciences, cosmology, theology, ethics, mystical revelations, and poetry. While she carried on extensive correspondence with church and secular leaders, she maintained that women were the weaker sex, though given her output and confidence in communicating her faith, this sentiment seems rather modest in comparison. Her works were circulated in her lifetime, but also in the following centuries. During the Renaissance her work was published, and continued to be read in the sixteenth and seventeenth centuries, providing not only a window to her scholarship, but also offering a notable precedent and role model for women who wished to follow suit.

As the opportunities for education expanded so too did the scope for women who could express themselves beyond the religious sphere. Often identified as the first feminist, Christine de Pizan (1365–c. 1430), began her writing career out of necessity as much as vocation. Widowed at 25, Christine was lucky to secure influential patronage through her late father's connections to the court of Charles V of France. While she undertook a variety of literary tasks, including copying, illustrating, and acting as a notary, she is remembered most for her work *The Book of the City of Ladies* (1405), in which she constructs a history of women and asks why women are denied an education. She developed these ideas in *Le livre des trois vertus*, in which she outlined the ideal education for girls. Her vision was of a practical but wide training for girls, in skills they would need as domestic managers. This would later form the basis of many debates in the sixteenth and seventeenth centuries; in many respects de Pizan's work initiated the "woman question" or *querelle des femmes* which persisted into the eighteenth century. In the seventeenth century the question of whether girls should be educated was replaced by the dilemma about which subjects to educate them in. Throughout the following three centuries an increasing number of both male and female writers were drawn into the debate about what precisely women should be allowed to do in the political, economic, education, and professional spheres.

EARLY MODERN PERIOD

The fourteenth century also saw the beginnings of a slow recognition of the contributions of women to society. In the 1370s, Giovanni Boccaccio completed *De mulieribus claris*, a compendium of women from biblical sources and mythology. As the first work devoted to female virtues and achievements it inspired Christine de Pizan and later writers such as Heinrich Cornelius Agrippa von Nettesheim, author of *De nobilitate et praecellentia foeminei sexus ... declamatio* (1529), and Thomas Elyot, author of *Defence of Good Women* (1540). By the seventeenth century the *querelle des femmes* formed a major part of the discussion of women's roles in both philosophical and literary genres, from Cartesian writers to playwrights like Molière. On the side of women the "fors" included Erasmus, Martin Franc, Heinrich Cornelius Agrippa, François de Billon, Hélisenne de Crenne, Marguerite de Navarre, Antoine Heroet, and the poet Louise Labé; the "againsts" counted Gratian du Pont, Valens Acidalius, and Rabelais among their number. Both male and female writers tackled the question of gender equality; however, it was in works by women where the ordinary issues of female life, such as the experiences of marriage and motherhood, were much more likely to be found. Two of the first "proto-feminist" tracts of the seventeenth century were the work of Marie de Gournay (1565–1645), the protégée of Montaigne. In *The Equality of Men and Women* (1622) and *The Ladies' Grievance* (1626), de Gournay presented her idea of a perfectly equal society, and argued that only by maintaining equality in the private sphere could one expect the state to follow equally high standards; abuse of power in the home she contended had naturally led to abuse of power in the state. In Germany, Anna Maria van Schurman published *The Learned Maid or, Whether a Maid May Be a Scholar* (1641) advocating education for women, but only for those who remained unmarried, without the responsibility of a family. This view was common among thinkers, indeed de Gournay, who was widely read, remained unmarried like van Schurman. Whether women could combine traditional duties as wives and mothers with the educational prospects enjoyed by their male counterparts remained unresolved.

By the 1670s more forceful works, influenced in many ways by the issues Cartesian and Neo-Platonist philosophy had raised with regard to the gendered mind and roles, began to appear. In his works, *On the Equality of the Two Sexes* (1673) and *On the Education of Ladies* (1674), Poulain de la Barre offered his central argument, inspired by his devotion to Descartes, that "the mind has no sex." He stated that women were not at a loss mentally, they were disadvantaged by cultural and legal prejudices. Poulain de la Barre's philosophy valued reason above tradition, and his work is representative of the growing strength and pervasiveness of Cartesian thought at this juncture. The impact of this debate can be measured no less than in the literary works that sought to counteract the educational and intellectual ambitions of women, the best known of these is perhaps Molière's *Les Femmes Savantes*. Poulain de la Barre falls within a wider canon of works by men on the roles of women in society; similar works included Jacques du Bosc's *L'Honneste Femme* (1632), Louis Machon, *Discours, Sermon Apologetique En Faveur des Femmes* (1641), Anon, *La Femme Généreuse* (1643), Jacquette Guillaume, *Les Dames Illustres* (1665), Abbé Fénélon, *Treatise on the Education of Girls* (1687), and Daniel Defoe, *The Education of Women* (1719).

Throughout the century, English women such as Margaret Cavendish (c.1623–1673), Frances Boothby (fl. 1669–1670), and Elizabeth Polwhele (c.1651–1691) as well as more prolific writers like Aphra Behn (1640–1689) and Mary Astell (1666–1731), produced works that addressed feminist concerns both directly and indirectly. While writers like Behn, Haywood, and Delarivier Manley expressed their views in the form of plays, novels, and short stories, others like Astell grappled with the issues of women's rights, tackling questions head-on. In her *Serious Proposal to the Ladies, Part II. Wherein a Method is Offer'd for the Improvement of Their Minds* (1694, 1697), Astell instructed women on how to pursue a program of self-education for as long as they were excluded from formal instruction.

Unlike the male sphere of formal schooling and university education, female thinkers and thought faced the challenge of finding continuity and community. Outside religious orders no female intellectual collectives existed and, as such, the gains made by each generation were easily lost to the next. Women were discouraged by the relative absence of a feminist heritage and the record of female writings in comparison to the dominant male view. With the slow emergence of literary salons in the seventeenth century some consistency was given to the hitherto nebulous *querelle des femmes*.

While literary and philosophical genres offer a rich seam of information on feminist consciousness, gender historians have endeavored to add to this from a number of different vantage points. For example, female testimonies in legal proceedings provide details about lower class women who would otherwise have left behind no evidence of their views and opinions. In religious, civil, and criminal cases the voices of women (questioned and transcribed by men it should be noted) emerge showing both acquiescence and resilience to structures of patriarchal authority. Cases regarding religious toleration show the roles played by women in maintaining or challenging religious practice. Family law cases show how women defended their rights to their dowries, their property, and their financial and physical security when dealing with an unreasonable spouse. Family disputes also reflect how women protected their rights as mothers, or sought to counteract threats to their family unit.

In the professional sphere, sources such as guild memberships, notarial records, and police files can reveal telling details regarding feminist consciousness further down the social scale. While guild membership was a predominantly male domain, women did participate in businesses on behalf of their families, as well as entering some of the female-only guilds that emerged in the medieval and early modern period. By the early eighteenth century women had to fight hard to retain the rights they had held; indeed attacks on the guild system as a whole started with the erosion of women's place within it. Notarial records can demonstrate the independence which women strove to maintain in their legal affairs; in this sense a woman's "feminist consciousness" may only ever have been recorded in her official correspondence, rather than in any polemical or personal writings. Police records too can show the lengths women went to in order to protect their rights, their property, and their lives, in circumstances determined largely by their gender. Details of marital separations, testimonies of physical attacks, and patterns of arrest records and crimes of women, can all reveal the gendered responses and reposts to the status quo.

While the subject of feminist consciousness challenges the scholar in terms of both methodology and theory, it is clear that historians, literary critics, and gender theorists alike have gleaned telling detail on the issue of women's rights, and their accompanying debates (however limited in terms of authorship and audience) in the medieval and early modern period. The ever-widening consideration of source material has led to the emergence of traces of feminist consciousness in previously untapped resources, doing much to inform the histories of women, gender, and feminism.

SEE ALSO: Feminism, Cultural; Feminism, Eighteenth-Century Britain; Gender, Politics, and the State in Western Europe; History of Women's Rights in International and Comparative Perspective; Women's and Feminist Activism in Western Europe

REFERENCES

de Pizan, Christiane. 1405. *The Book of the City of Ladies* (various editions).
Lerner, Gerda. 1993. *The Creation of Feminist Consciousness: From the Middle Ages to 1870.* Oxford: Oxford University Press.

Poulain de la Barre, François. 1673. *On the Equality of the Two Sexes* (various editions).

FURTHER READING

Scott, Joan. 1988. *Gender and the Politics of History.* New York: Columbia University Press.

Feminist Design in Computing

SHAOWEN BARDZELL and JEFFREY BARDZELL
Indiana University, USA

Feminist design in computing refers to IT design practices that are substantially informed by feminist thought and activism. The specifically feminist contribution to IT design can entail any of the following: feminist goals, methods, theories, histories, critiques, and so forth.

BACKGROUND AND CONTEXT

Feminist design approaches in computing have two key motivations. One is feminism's ongoing and heterogeneous efforts to achieve equal social, political, and economic rights for women, a struggle that is increasingly mediated by information technologies, from the workplace to the home, and from wealthy Western nations to the Global South.

Another is the specific gender problems attending to IT, which include unequal access to IT systems, skills, benefits, and professions, which are often consequences of poverty and lack of education and/or due to certain features of women's institutional, cultural, and political environments (UNESCO 2007). According to results published in 2009 by the Organization for Economic Cooperation and Development, in most of North America, Europe, and East Asia, women earn less than 20 percent of all tertiary degrees awarded in computing (OECD 2009). Women's access to computing is worse in the Global South, which not only has consequences for gender equality, but also adversely affects national economic development (Intel 2013).

Several concepts and research agendas have emerged to confront these issues. They include cyberfeminists (Haraway 1991; Hayles 1999), gender human–computer interaction (HCI) (Beckwith and Burnett 2004), feminist HCI (Bardzell 2010), feminist design histories and cultural studies (Buckley 1989; Sparke 1995; Goodall 1996), and female interaction (design-people 2012), among others. Common to each of these is that gender issues are seen as a central area of concern for design and IT. It is important to note that some of them, such as gender HCI, are tightly coupled with IT design practices but do not explicitly identify themselves with feminism, while others, such as feminist technology studies, are openly feminist but are not directly engaged in IT design practices.

Feminist design studies show how design contributes to the gendered status quo. Research explores the construction of the modern housewife and other "feminine" consumer subjectivities (Sparke 1986, 1995; Attfield 1989; Buckley 1989; de Grazia and Furlough 1996), accounts that focus specifically on technology's roles in constructing and perpetuating gender (Bødker and Greenbaum 1988; Cockburn 1992; Green, Owen, and Pain 1993; Lerman, Mohun, and Oldenziel 1997; Berg 1999), and accounts of the often-overlooked contributions of female designers in design history (Kirkham 2000; Gomez-Palacio and Vit 2008). Researchers such as Henwood (1993) seek to respond to questions such as: How did it come about that women and men hold the positions they do in relation to technology and technological work? How have these positions changed over time and what factors are responsible for these changes? Feminist design histories and cultural studies are thus crucial to motivating feminist design in computing and to helping frame the discourse by identifying relationships between design choices and gendered sociocultural outcomes, but they stop short of initiating or engaging directly with ongoing IT design processes.

GENDER AND COMPUTING

In the computer sciences, which obviously are much more tightly coupled with the design of IT interfaces and infrastructures, gender has been an ongoing concern, but openly feminist perspectives have been relatively scarce until recently. The topic is commonly framed in terms of "gender and computing," and its goal is to increase the number of women in computing fields. It is both an academic and an administrative agenda. Administratively, gender and computing programs seek to recruit and retain female university students and professionals, establishing groups, events, scholarships, and mobilizing other resources. Academically, gender and computing researchers conduct critical and empirical inquiries to theorize about and to discover facts about women in relation to computing disciplines and professions and also to design software systems that are responsive to the needs and desires of female users.

One formulation of gender and computing is "women in computing," an earlier formulation that investigates the number and nature of women in computer science, including undergraduate enrollment, participation in professional fields, and participation in computer science research, scholarship, and teaching. The primary strength of this agenda is that it is often backed by significant leadership and financial resources, manifesting a will to effect direct institutional change, carrying both a practical force (through its creation of targeted recruiting, events, groups, and other opportunities) and also a symbolic force. Yet this agenda can also be criticized for limiting itself to improving women's attitudes, self-confidence, and pre-collegiate academic experiences to prepare them better for computer science, as if the problem were the women themselves, rather than the men or even something about the discipline. Another aspect of the women in a computing approach is that it is often intentionally apolitical, which is administratively advantageous and helps with government funding (bearing in mind that many universities are state institutions), but which can also lead to strategic blind spots concerning underlying causes of the gender gap, including deep-seated misogynistic stereotypes about women's technical abilities and the effects of dominating "boy's club" cultures of interaction in both academic and professional computer science institutions and especially upper management. Thus, well-known problems about gender equity and tenure, management and leadership opportunities, teaching evaluations, and so on can be difficult to change, because of the ways that "women in computing" sometimes circumscribes itself as a women's initiative.

Another formulation of gender and computing is "gender in science and technology studies (STS)," which is a research domain whose overriding concern is to present and critique traditional scientific representations of gendered states of affairs. Relying on a social constructionist theory of gender, STS scholars observe how assumptions about the genders shape the development of science and technology, such that those assumptions are inscribed within the resulting technologies and thereby reproduce those assumptions. The inscribing of gender assumptions – including conscious and unconscious gendered identity claims, structural and institutional roles, and ideologies – into designs marginalizes women and thereby helps explain at least one underlying cause of the comparatively low representation of women in computing and by doing so expose opportunities to intervene in the field – its discourses and practices – directly (as opposed to seeking to improve gender representation by improving women). Gender STS studies often focus on groupings of individuals, skilled practices, and particular technologies as a way of surfacing the deep effects of gender, including studies on household technologies (Cowan 1983), everyday technologies (Cockburn and Ormrod 1993), and communication technologies (Lerman, Mohun, and Oldenziel 1997), among others. Other studies have focused on women in the contemporary computing industry, including inequities in career path between genders in HCI (Churchill 2010), and trends and influences on women's authorship of computing conference papers (Cohoon et al. 2011). A core assumption of STS in general is that society and the development of technologies are co-implicated, that is, social structures and ideologies shape how, why, and where technologies are designed, while designs in turn help shape social formations, practices, and identities.

The strength of the gender STS approach, especially coming from within the computer sciences, is that it reveals design interventions for the way in which the field itself operates – its institutional structures, collaborative practices, methodologies, and modes of legitimation. In doing so, gender STS offers direct benefits to women in computing. At the same time, it offers comparatively indirect benefits to women users of digital technologies, because not unlike the design historians, gender STS is typically not directly connected to particular design activities but stands more as a meta-criticism of the field.

A third major formulation of gender and technology is "gender HCI," which directly orients its attention to the design of technologies and systems that foregrounds gender as a primary axis of design inquiry. Gender HCI investigates "the ways software supports or inhibits male and female problem solvers" with a specific effort to "take gender differences into account in the *design of software*" (Gender HCI Project 2012). Examples of this work include research on gender differences and the design and development of interactive systems (Cassell 2002); gender and end-user programming (Beckwith et al. 2005); women's work as the focus in the design and use of home organizing systems (Taylor and Swan 2005); attitudinal and behavioral differences between men and women in perception and acceptance of interactive technologies (de Angeli and Bianchi-Berthouze 2006); gender and virtual world navigation (Czerwinski, Tan, and Robertson 2007); and the role of gender in domestic computing (Bell and Dourish 2006).

Collectively, gender HCI is strong at accounting for the behavioral, attitudinal, and professional differences between men and women with regard to computer use. A key strength of this work is its tight coupling with design – many of these papers articulate specific and actionable implications for design and are recognized widely in the field as an important part of the scientific literature supporting design. Another strength is that the empirical dimension of gender HCI helps ensure that women's experiences and voices are (often very directly) represented in design-oriented research. There are also two conceptual weaknesses of gender HCI as it is commonly formulated. First is that it seems predicated on dated assumptions of gender essentialism (i.e., that there are exactly and only two genders, that they are fundamentally different from one another, and that the experiences of one group of women are transferable to another group of women insofar as they are all women, etc.). There is little evidence that these views have been critically examined in much of this research, and with few exceptions there is minimal acknowledgment of gender theory, queer theory, and body theory, which problematizes gender essentialism as a workable assumption. The other weakness is that most of this research is framed in apolitical terms, so the sorts of underlying causes of gender inequity that feminists often point to – patriarchal ideologies, institutional structures, and social practices in particular – are tacitly, if at all, activated in this work.

The three formulations of gender and computing can thus be summarized as an administrative and academic effort to improve women's access to technology and its professions (women in computing); to critique, explain, and reveal opportunities to intervene against gender inequalities in IT (gender in STS); and to discover and accommodate gender differences to support the development of more accessible and usable software (gender HCI). Whereas gender HCI is strongly coupled with design practice but is thin on theory, gender in STS is strong on theory but more indirectly aligned with design practice. Neither is directly coupled with the deployment of institutional resources to change computing institutions, but "women in computing" is.

FEMINIST DESIGN IN COMPUTING

As noted earlier, an explicitly feminist approach to design in computing is a relatively recent phenomenon. Several reasons can be offered to account for this, including the self-perception of many computer scientists – albeit challenged from within by STS scholars – that gender is not relevant to their work. For professionals engaged in common computational tasks, which might include the design of mathematically efficient algorithms, database structures optimized to handle very specific needs, or encryption algorithms to improve cybersecurity infrastructure, this view is intuitively understandable, though problematic.

Nonetheless, all of the pieces needed for a feminist design in computing have been extant for years, beyond the foundational supports of feminist theory and social science: a historical sensibility that motivates gender as a key axis of inquiry in design research and practice, by demonstrating how design choices link to sociocultural consequences; the will and the ability to effect direct institutional change; a sophisticated theoretical basis to interrogate and propose interventions based on the underlying causes of gender inequity; and a body of research to support the (re-)design of both technologies and professional practices to acknowledge and work with a more diverse set of needs and desires than were possible in gender-blind practices.

A primary goal of feminist design and computing is to bring these threads more explicitly together, especially to integrate feminist theory into actual design practices to effect change in both design processes and products. This move entails recognizing the underlying politics that cause gender inequities in computing as their effects. It also entails the following consequences: first, that gender difference is not merely a problem to be solved (i.e., by accounting for how women versus men experience a technology), but is also an epistemological opportunity (i.e., obtaining gendered perspectives can contribute a more dialectic account of a use situation, potentially yielding more critical insights than can be achieved through a more homogeneous perspective); second, that "female" should not merely be a variable controlled for in empirical studies, but should also be a data source, namely, individuals' own spatially, physically, and historically situated accounts of how they as embodied individuals perform and become through their experiences with technology; and third, that "woman" does not become the privileged marginal other at the expense of other marginalized others, given that IT is a thoroughly globalized industry that draws resources (professionals, minerals, lucrative contracts) from all over the world and which also delivers IT infrastructures and end-user systems to the entire world. Specifically, in research and design areas such as information communication technologies for development (ICT4D), which often engage individuals in the Global South, indigenous groups, and others distinctive and/or marginalized from West-dominated globalism, it is vitally important to avoid reifying individuals as generic marginalized others.

Feminist design in computing is not surprisingly emerging as a heterogeneous discourse. Several research projects have attempted to build a theoretical base for it, including Rode and Bødker (2009), who proposed and sought to build explicit links between gender theory and computer-supported cooperative work (CSCW, a domain of computing that focuses on collaborative and location-specific forms of computing). Bardzell (2010) argued for a "feminist HCI," proposing feminist design practices that sought to live up to the following six qualities: pluralism, participation, advocacy, ecology, embodiment, and self-disclosure. In a follow-up, Bardzell and Bardzell (2011) developed linkages between feminist epistemological positions and HCI/design user research methods. Light (2011) criticized the apoliticization of computing and turned to the work of Judith Butler to propose ways to "queer" the formalization of identity in computer systems, offering users much more nuanced ways to represent themselves. Dimond, Fiesler, and Bruckman (2011) brought feminist activism into HCI in their research on the roles of information communication technologies among survivors of domestic violence.

In addition to scholarship on theory, methods, and individual design studies, there are also a number of feminist designs that are of interest. Many of these are "critical designs," that is, designs developed and publicly released not as commercially available commodities but as works to be exhibited and contemplated for their critical effects. Hiromi Ozaki's (aka Sputniko!'s) Menstruation Machine (Ozaki 2010) is a chastity belt-like device that fits around the waist and uses electrodes to stimulate the lower abdomen and a blood-dispensing system to simulate the pain and bleeding of menstruation; the design was motivated in part to raise awareness about how technological systems favor men. Amisha Gadani's series of Defensive Dresses embed protective biomimicry in everyday cocktail dresses to protect the bodies of the women who wear them, including Porcupine Dress, which raises dozens of sharp quills when the wearer bends into a protective fetal position; Skink Dress, comprised of hundreds of pieces that easily tear off making it difficult to grab hold of the wearer by her clothes; and Blowfish Dress, which rapidly inflates to prevent an attacker from getting near the wearer's body (Gadani 2008). Jill Magid's Surveillance Shoe is a high-heel shoe with an upskirt camera attached that keeps the leg bound within the frame, about which the designer writes, "By bringing surveillance technology closer in and attaching it to the body, I have been able to personalize a form of technological mirroring through which subjectivity and the body are reconstructed. Inside the field of view of this reconfigured vision, the wearer/user is open to create and explore the erotic formation of fluid identities and their potential transgressive relationships" (Magid 2000).

An avowedly feminist approach to computing offers the benefits of leveraging feminist and gender theory in actual design processes and products, offering a direct means for feminists to enact social change through the powerful force of IT design. Less positively, it remains a comparatively marginal practice for a number of reasons. The antifeminist backlash, combined with the apolitical and/or libertarian stance so common in computing fields, makes many researchers, designers, administrators, leaders, and funding agencies reluctant to embrace any project that explicitly aligns itself with feminism. Many, especially in the computer sciences, individually align themselves with feminist values and rely on gender theory, but they suppress this alignment in their public work and presentations, self-censoring to less controversial formulations. Many of the feminist designs themselves, such as Menstruation Machine and Porcupine Dress, are viewed as "art" and often relegated in the public imagination to an "art world" seen as cut off from the "real world." That said, the rise of research papers in computing that explicitly embrace the term "feminist" is creating some cover for computing researchers and designers who want to pull this aspect of their work forward.

SEE ALSO: Feminist Activism; Feminist Methodology; Gendered Innovations in Science, Health, and Technology; Queer Methods and Methodologies; Queer Theory; Women in Science

REFERENCES

Attfield, Judy. 1989. "Inside Pram Town: A Case Study of Harlow House Interiors." In *A View from the Interior: Feminism, Women and Design*, edited by Judy Attfield and Pat Kirkham, 1951–1961. London: The Women's Press.

Bardzell, Shaowen. 2010. "Feminist HCI: Taking Stock and Outlining an Agenda for Design." In *Proceedings of CHI2010*. New York: ACM.

Bardzell, Shaowen, and Jeffrey Bardzell. 2011. "Towards a Feminist HCI Methodology: Social Science, Feminism and HCI." In *Proceedings of CHI2011*. New York: ACM.

Beckwith, Laura, and Margaret Burnett. 2004. "Gender: An Important Factor in End-User Programming Environments?" In *Proceedings of Visual Languages and Human-Centric Computing Languages, IEEE* 2004, 107–114.

Beckwith, Laura, et al. 2005. "Designing Features for Both Genders in End-User Software Engineering Environments." In *IEEE Symposium on Visual Languages and Human-Centric Computing*, 153–160.

Bell, Genevieve, and Paul Dourish. 2006. "Yesterday's Tomorrows: Notes on Ubiquitous Computing's Dominant Vision." *Personal and Ubiquitous Computing*, 11(2): 133–143.

Berg, Anne-Jorunn 1999. "A Gendered Socio-Technical Construction: The Smart House." In *The Social Shaping of Technology*, 2nd ed., edited by Donald A. MacKenzie and Judy Wajcman, 301–313. Buckingham: Open University Press.

Bødker, Susanne, and Joan Greenbaum. 1988. "A Feeling for Systems Development Work." In *Women, Work and Computerization*, edited by Kea Tijdens, M. Jennings, I Wagner, and M. Weggelar. Amsterdam: North-Holland.

Buckley, Cheryl. 1989. "Made in Patriarchy: Toward a Feminist Analysis of Women and Design." In *Design Discourse: History, Theory, Criticism*, edited by Victor Margolin, 251–264. Chicago: University of Chicago Press.

Cassell, Justine. 2002. "Genderizing HCI." In *The Handbook of Human–Computer Interaction* edited by Julie A. Jacko and Andrew Sears, 402–411. Mahwah: Lawrence Erlbaum.

Churchill, Elizabeth. 2010. "Sugared Puppy-Dog Tail." *ACM interactions*, 17(2): March–April.

Cockburn, Cynthia. 1992. "The Circuit of Technology: Gender, Identity, and Power." In *Consuming Technologies: Media and Information in Domestic Spaces*, edited by Roger Silverstone and Eric Hirsch, 32–47. London: Routledge.

Cockburn, Cynthia, and Susan Ormrod. 1993. *Gender and Technology in the Making*. London: Sage.

Cohoon, J. McGrath, Sergey Nigai, and Joseph "Jofish" Kaye. 2011. "Gender and Computing Conference Papers." *Communications of the ACM*, 54(8): 72–80.

Cowan, Ruth Schwartz. 1983. *More Work for Mother: The Ironies of Household Technology from the Open Hearth to the Microwave*. New York: Basic Books.

Czerwinski, Mary, Desney S. Tan, and George G. Robertson. 2002. "Women Take a Wider View." In *Proceedings of CHI2002*, 195–202. New York: ACM,.

de Angeli, Antonella, and Nadia Bianchi-Berthouze. 2006. Presented at "Gender and Interaction: Real and Virtual Women in a Male World," AVI 2006 Workshop.

de Grazia, Victoria, and Ellen Furlough, eds. 1996. *The Sex of Things: Gender and Consumption in Historical Perspective*. Berkeley: University of California Press.

design-people. 2012. "Female Interaction." Accessed June 1, 2014, at http://www.femaleinteraction.com/.

Dimond, Jill, Casey Fiesler, and Amy S. Bruckman. 2011. "Domestic Violence and Information Communication Technologies." In Special Issue on *"Feminism and HCI: New Perspectives,"* edited by Shaowen Bardzell and Elizabeth Churchill. *Interacting with Computers*, 23(5): 413–421.

Gadani, Amisha. 2008. "Defensive Dresses." Accessed June 1, 2014, at http://www.amishagadani.com/Work/.

Gender HCI Project. 2012. "Gender HCI Project of the End Users Shaping Effective Software Consortium." Accessed June 18, 2005, at http://eusesconsortium.org/gender/.

Gomez-Palacio, Bryony, and Armin Vit, eds. 2008. *Women of Design*. Cincinnati: How Books.

Goodall, Philippa. 1996. "Design and Gender." In *The Block Reader in Visual Culture*, edited by Jon Bird, Barry Curtis, Melinda Mash, Tim Putnam, George Robertson, and Lisa Tickner, 187–208. London: Routledge.

Green, Eileen, Jenny Owen, and Den Pain, eds. 1993. *Gendered by Design? Information Technology and Office Systems*. London: Taylor & Francis.

Haraway, Donna. 1991. "A Cyborg Manifesto: Science, Technology, and Socialist-Feminism in the Late Twentieth Century." *Simians, Cyborgs, and Women: The Reinvention of Nature*, 149–181. New York: Routledge.

Hayles, N. Katherine. 1999. *How We Became Posthuman: Virtual Bodies in Cybernetics, Literature, and Informatics*. Chicago: University of Chicago Press.

Henwood, Flis. 1993. "Establishing Gender Perspectives on Information Technology: Problems, Issues, and Opportunities." In *Gendered by Design? Information Technology and Office Systems*, edited by Eileen Green, Jenny Owen, and Den Pain, 31–49. London: Taylor & Francis.

Intel. 2013. "Women and the Web: Bridging the Internet Gap and Creating New Global Opportunities in Low and Middle-Income Countries." Accessed June 18, 2015, at http://tinyurl.com/ban7odr.

Kirkham, Pat, ed. 2000. *Women Designers in the USA 1900–2000*. New Haven: Yale University Press.

Lerman, Nina, Arwen Palmer Mohun, and Ruth Oldenziel. 1997. "Versatile Tools: Gender Analysis and the History of Technology." *Technology and Culture*, 38: 1–8.

Light, Ann. 2011. "HCI as Heterodoxy: Technologies of Identity and the Queering of Interaction with Computers." In Special Issue on *"Feminism and HCI: New Perspectives,"* edited by Shaowen Bardzell and Elizabeth Churchill. *Interacting with Computers*, 23(5): 430–438.

Magid, Jill. 2000. "Monitoring Desire." Accessed June 18, 2015, at http://dspace.mit.edu/handle/1721.1/76084?show=full.

OECD. 2009. "Indicators of Gender Equality in Education." Accessed June 18, 2015, at http://www.oecd.org/gender/data/education.htm.

Ozaki, Hirome. 2010. "Menstruation Machine." Accessed June 1, 2014, at http://www.di10.rca.ac.uk/hiromiozaki/menstruation-machine.html.

Rode, Jennifer, and Susanne Bødker. "Considering Gender in ECSCW." *Extended Abstracts of the European Conference on Computer-Supported Cooperative Work* 2009. New York: ACM.

Sparke, Penny. 1986. *An Introduction to Design and Culture*. London: Unwin Hyman and Design Council.

Sparke, Penny. 1995. *As Long As It's Pink: The Sexual Politics of Taste*. London: Pandora.

Taylor, Alex S., and Laurel Swan. 2005. "Artful Systems in the Home." In *Proceedings of CHI'05*, 641–650. New York: ACM.

UNESCO. 2007. "Science, Technology, and Gender: An International Report. Executive Summary." Accessed June 1, 2014, at http://unesdoc.unesco.org/images/0015/001540/154027e.pdf.

Feminist Disability Studies

MICHAEL GILL
Syracuse University, USA

Feminist disability studies (FDS) is the interdisciplinary exploration of the intersections between categories of disability and gender. FDS shares the feminist commitment to addressing how women are excluded and discriminated due to interlocking systems of oppressions and how gender operates as a regulatory system, and disability studies' commitment to challenging discrimination and oppression that disabled individuals experience and how disability is socially constructed. Calls for attention to race, ethnicity, class, sexuality, and culture as well as other markers of identity have been made by many of its practitioners. FDS examines how categories of identity mark some individuals as "deviant" or "inferior," while others are assumed to be "normal." FDS centers the body, bodily difference, and systems of discrimination and oppression, including ableism, racism, and sexism, in its analyses, and how these various systems of oppression create inequality and exclusion. Western FDS emerged out of physically disabled women narrating their experiences and struggles, seeking to improve material and structural realities that shape disabled women's lives and to change ableist and sexist spaces of society, which include feminist and disability communities.

Michelle Fine and Adrienne Asch's edited collection, *Women with Disabilities* (1988), is a foundational text that uncovers disabled women's voices and perspectives. The text provides a feminist intervention to disability studies literature by examining how disabled women navigate sexist and ableist spaces and how feminist disability perspectives can revise policies including employment, social supports, and reproductive rights. As Kim Q. Hall argues in the introduction to *Feminist Disability Studies* (2011), FDS is not just about adding disabled women's perspectives to feminism or gender to disability studies, but rather is an effort to transform both feminism and disability studies to attend to the varying registers of disability and gender, as well as other categories of analysis. FDS is also multidisciplinary as many of the foundational texts come from traditions ranging from literature, sociology, history, and philosophy. FDS challenges feminist thinkers to engage with the category and theories of disability, in the same ways that other strands of feminism, such as indigenous feminism or transfeminism, demand intersectional examinations beyond additive models of analysis. FDS also challenges disability studies scholars to adopt a gender analysis in discussing various issues related to disability. FDS expands methodological approaches in both feminist and disability studies inquiries, by not only seeking out analyses of how gender matters to disability and disability matters to gender, but also by transforming how each discipline constructs personhood, identities, and abilities.

In an essay published in 1994, literary scholar Rosemarie Garland-Thomson called upon feminist scholars to critically engage with concepts of disability, defining FDS as a central feature of feminism. As examples of FDS, she offers feminist critiques of beauty, "normalization of the female body through cosmetic surgery," "representations of the 'grotesque,'" and "the cultural production of race or gender as forms of ostensible corporeal aberrance" (1994, 587). Similarly, in 1997, Barbara Waxman Fiduccia and Marsha Saxton, in *New Mobility*, penned "Disability Feminism: A Manifesto," which calls for disabled women's sexuality to be accepted, equal access to reproductive health, elimination of the Social Security Insurance "marriage penalty," support for disabled mothers, freedom to choose abortion without coercion, and welcoming spaces for disabled children.

Disability studies challenges conventional medical or rehabilitative approaches to disability as a deficit or pathology and finds new meanings of disability as human variation. Separating impairment and disability in the same way that feminists initially identified sex as biological and gender as culturally constructed, the social model of disability examines how individuals are disabled, not because of impairments, but through inaccessible environments, stereotypes, discrimination, and limited opportunities. Disability studies proffers disability as a minority or cultural identity, focusing on the collective and their ability to narrate experiences of exclusion and to demand rights and access. Material conditions, including but not limited to employment, accessible housing, and state-funded benefits, are also important facets to a disability studies examination. Additionally, disability studies in the humanities addresses how disability is imagined and represented in literature and film as well as in other cultural representations. Disability studies also actively engages in many fields of studies including legal and policy studies, history, medicine, sociology, anthropology, social welfare, and education, all of which affect the lives of people with disabilities. Disability studies also addresses discrimination against disabled faculty, students, and scholars in formal and informal systems of knowledge production.

One of the most important interventions FDS offers to feminism and disability studies is adding an emphasis on embodiment, including experiences of pain and dependence on medical interventions. The social model of disability has been criticized as focusing on ableist environments and exclusions at the expense of experiences of pain and living with impairments, which may not solely be mitigated by social changes. FDS theorists, including Liz Crow, Carol Thomas, and Janet Price, have criticized the social model (and its most vocal proponents) as masculinist and for not accurately addressing experiences of pain or impairment. In line with feminist analyses of the constructed nature of both sex and gender systems, FDS extends disability studies conceptions about how impairment is also constructed along with disability. FDS emphasizes the need to continue the vital work of narrating experiences of living with pain and impairment in order to transform the social model of disability. One such example is Alison Kafer's political/relational model of disability that refuses a separation of disability from impairment and a rejection of the role of medicine.

Connected to reforming the social model, FDS challenges independence, autonomy, and self-determination as standards to be upheld in disability rights frameworks and independent living movements at the expense of interdependence. Disabled feminist philosopher Susan Wendell, in *The Rejected Body* (1996), provides a sustained philosophical discussion of interdependence. She challenges the feminist ideal of hardworking, healthy, and strong women as it devalues women with pain, low energy, and chronic illnesses. FDS's focus on interdependence complicates not only feminist but also disability activist ideals of independence and agency. Wendell also discusses the limitations of feminist ethics of care, such as assuming disabled women only as recipients and not as givers of care labor, or failing to examine the conditions and power relations within care labor. Wendell argues that by attending to the ways in which individuals depend upon others, we can reclaim mutuality and shared purpose that will ultimately improve the status of those seen as dependent, including children, disabled individuals, and the elderly, while transforming ethics of care.

Often the discourse around abortion in feminist circles remains centered on access to abortion and other reproductive health services. Similar to the important challenges made by black feminists, FDS addresses the fact that the choice framework does not attend to how some women, because of disability, levels of poverty, or racism, are not able to access abortion services, because the services are unaffordable, physically inaccessible, or not available in areas heavily populated with racial and ethnic minorities. Scholars including Shelley Tremain, Marsha Saxton, and Adrienne Asch seek to complicate feminist positions on abortion and reproductive rights. They highlight that efforts to selectively abort disabled fetuses have to be understood as connected to material conditions of disability management and ableist views on disability. Potential parental views of disability might be based on stereotypical understandings of disabled lives. While FDS scholars generally do not negate women's right to abortion, including the right to abort disabled fetuses, they also advocate that women should have the right to choose to raise disabled children and to access unbiased information for decision-making. Some FDS scholars draw a parallel to sex- or race-based abortion and how problematizing such practice does not necessarily mean compromising women's rights to choose abortion, but points to the need for a reproductive justice analysis. Lastly, as more technological advancements allow for increased screening of impairments prenatally, FDS encourages increased partnership between disabled people, ethics boards, and parents to explore decisions on a case-by-case basis.

FDS also challenges the rhetoric of ableist stereotypes in discussions of motherhood and disabled children. Disabled children, especially girls, are assumed to be unproductive and draining on their family resources, often warranting isolation and limited access to education. Women and girls with labels of intellectual or cognitive disabilities have historically been seen as fecund and highly sexual, while physically disabled women are often assumed not to be interested in sexuality, forcing them to claim sexuality. In general, scholars point out that disabled women are also not seen as "fit" mothers and their reproductive capacity might be controlled through segregation in residential facilities, forced prescription of birth control, or eugenic sterilization practices. Women of color and non-Western women share these experiences of reproductive control, barriers to marriage, and parenthood. FDS deepens reproductive justice and intersectional feminist analyses by attending to the ways ability status impacts discussions of parenting and reproduction.

There is a particular strand of FDS that also seeks to complicate queer and sexuality studies with a disability focus. Queer, crip, and feminist disability theories challenge conceptions that focus solely on productivity, desire for cure, and what counts as a valid future. The special issue of GLQ (2003) on queer disability studies edited by Robert McRuer and Abby Wilkerson and Robert McRuer and Anna Mollow's edited collection, Sex and Disability (2012), further enrich the archive of feminist, queer, and disability studies.

FDS also addresses issues of pedagogy and inclusion within classroom spaces. Kristina Knoll (2009) addresses how FDS pedagogy "practices interdependency" and ensures complete access by deploying principles of universal design in partnership with accommodations to reflect the intersections of diverse learners and identities in the classroom space. FDS continues to question which bodies and experiences are able to access feminist classrooms, publishing, conferences, and events, and which bodies are excluded because of inaccessible spaces, discounted experiences, or other modes of segregation.

Important texts such as Anne Finger's *Past Due: A Story of Disability, Pregnancy, and Birth* (1990), Jenny Morris's *Pride Against Prejudice* (1991), and the edited collection *Encounters with Strangers: Feminism and Disability* (1996), also by Morris, demand an examination of the unique ways that disabled women experience oppression and discrimination by offering theoretically rich personal narratives. The topics in these texts, including issues around reproduction, parenting, employment, and sexuality, have remained central to FDS theorizations. Nancy Mairs's essays also diversify perspectives on gender, care labor, and independence. Diane Price Herndl's *Invalid Women: Figuring Feminine Illness in American Fiction and Culture, 1840–1940* (1993) traces out how representations of invalidism depended upon constructions of disability and gender. Rosemarie Garland-Thomson's 2005 essay on FDS that appeared in *Signs* offers wide-ranging examples of texts such as Lucy Grealy's *Autobiography of a Face* (1994), Simi Linton's *Claiming Disability* (1998), and her own *Extraordinary Bodies* (1997) that are included in the archive of FDS.

Other texts that expand FDS beyond Western-centered theories include the 2007 *Wagadu: A Journal of Transnational Women's and Gender Studies* special issue on gender, disability, and postcolonialism, edited by Pushpa Parekh. This thread discusses how disabled women are important stakeholders in addressing issues related to poverty, economic neoliberalism, and histories of colonialism. There have been three special issues on feminism and disability in the feminist philosophy journal *Hypatia*: two issues in 2001 and 2002 edited by Eva Kittay, Anita Silvers, Susan Wendell, and Alexa Schriempf, and an issue published in 2015 edited by Kim Q. Hall. In 2002, the *NWSA Journal* published a special issue on FDS, edited by Kim Q. Hall. Shelley Tremain edited a special issue of *Disability Studies Quarterly* (2013) on the ways in which feminist philosophy and theory can address ableism and how academic disciplines, including philosophy, continue to exclude disabled students, faculty, and scholars.

The growth of FDS goes hand in hand with the emergence of activist organizations of disabled women that forward unique agendas internationally. The DisAbled Women's Network Canada (DAWN) was established in 1985. DAWN fights to end poverty, discrimination, and violence against disabled women and advocates for disabled women's self-determination and empowerment. Equally important is the visibility of disabled women on the international stage. More than 200 disabled women from over 25 nation-states attended the 1995 Fourth World Conference on Women at Beijing, China, which marked the first collective presence of disabled women as a constituency at World Conferences on Women. The day before the NGO forum started, the delegates held an international symposium on various issues that disabled women faced. The symposium and gathering of disabled women attempted to influence the development of the platform for action. Disabled women protested the lack of access at Beijing. The conference space had significant access constraints, such as the lack of elevators and sign language interpretation, which limited the participation of delegates with physical, cognitive, and sensory impairments. In 2006, international disability rights communities celebrated the adoption of the United Nations Convention on the Rights of Persons with Disabilities. Throughout the negotiation processes, disabled feminists, especially from non-Western countries, worked to include gender-conscious perspectives into the document. As a result, the convention contains a separate article addressing disabled women and girls. Inclusion of this article reflects the need to address the gendered impacts of disability in patriarchal societies, including limited access to education, healthcare, and employment opportunities and discriminatory practices based on stereotyped gender roles and reproduction.

Many feminist theories and texts that can be described as FDS reflect the centrality of disability analyses as valid modes of inquiry. Kafer and McRuer argue that the archive of what counts as "feminist disability studies" should be expanded to include feminist thinkers with disabilities even if they do not claim the identity of disabled women. Their lived experiences with disability and illness impacted their scholarship and activism. McRuer (2006) calls Gloria Anzaldúa a crip theorist and Kafer (2013) discusses Bernice Johnson Reagon as such. Included in this list of FDS scholars would be Audre Lorde, Adrienne Rich, and Alice Walker. FDS will further claim and uncover historical examples of disabled women, adding to the works about Helen Keller, Jane Addams, and Frida Kahlo. Additionally, while this entry draws heavily on the work of scholars and activists in the United States, Canada, and Western Europe writing in English, practitioners of FDS are located throughout the globe, evidenced by the presence of activists at the UN.

As more university courses are offered on FDS coupled with the expansion of scholarship, the somewhat marginal and tenuous relationship between various strands of feminism and disability needs to be made clearer. FDS can complicate the role of disability identity and meanings of able-bodiedness and deepen intersectionality by attending to the various ways in which ability, able-bodiedness, disability, and impairment intersect and interlock experiences of gender, sexuality, race, ethnicity, indigeneity, class, language, citizenship, religion, and nationality. Through building coalitions with other critical studies, such as queer theory, sexuality studies, critical race studies, ethnic studies, and postcolonial studies, FDS can form mutually transformative relationships. FDS can expand understandings of disabled masculinity, femininity, and expressions of gender identities. The coalitional and intersectional work between transgender studies, fat studies, and neurodiversity studies with FDS will help transform queer theory, sexuality studies, critical race studies, ethnic studies, and postcolonial studies understandings of how diverse bodies are regulated, through medicine, science, law, and culture. Nirmala Erevelles (2011) argues that FDS needs to deepen its engagement with material concerns, through partnership with third world feminism, by examining how capitalism, economic exploitation, war, and legacies of colonialism produce disability. FDS can continue to explore the intersections between environmental justice, critical animal studies, and the conditions that produce disability. The intersections between prison abolition movements and FDS are also an important area of inquiry because disabled people are increasingly incarcerated in various systems including medical institutions, care facilities, nursing homes, and prison. Including disabled women as partners in reproductive justice analyses by addressing how ability/disability impacts parenting and reproduction will further deepen coalitional politics. Greater attention to how disabled people resist ableist and patriarchal systems and generate knowledge can continue to change conventional registers of disability.

SEE ALSO: Assisted Reproduction; Disability Rights Movement; Ethic of Care; Eugenics, Historical and Ethical Aspects of; Feminist Theories of the Body; Intersectionality; Queer Theory; Reproductive Justice and Reproductive Rights in the United States

REFERENCES

Erevelles, Nirmala. 2011. *Disability and Difference in Global Contexts: Enabling a Transformative Body Politic*. New York: Palgrave Macmillan.

Fine, Michelle, and Adrienne Asch, eds. 1988. *Women with Disabilities: Essays in Psychology, Culture, and Politics*. Philadelphia: Temple University Press.

Garland-Thomson, Rosemarie. 1994. "Redrawing the Boundaries of Feminist Disability Studies." *Feminist Studies*, 20(3): 583–595.

Garland-Thomson, Rosemarie. 2005. "Feminist Disability Studies." *Signs*, 30(2): 1557–1587.

Hall, Kim Q. 2011. *Feminist Disability Studies*. Bloomington: Indiana University Press.

Kafer, Alison. 2013. *Feminist, Queer, Crip*. Bloomington: Indiana University Press.

Knoll, Kristina. 2009. "Feminist Disability Studies Pedagogy." *Feminist Teacher*, 19(2): 122–133.

McRuer, Robert. 2006. *Crip Theory: Cultural Signs of Queerness and Disability*. New York: New York University Press.

McRuer, Robert, and Anna Mollow. 2012. *Sex and Disability*. Durham, NC: Duke University Press.

Morris, Jenny, ed. 1996. *Encounters with Strangers: Feminism and Disability*. London: Women's Press.

Waxman Fiduccia, Barbara, and Marsha Saxton. 1997. "Disability Feminism: A Manifesto." *New Mobility* (October): 60–61.

Wendell, Susan. 1996. *The Rejected Body: Feminist Philosophical Reflections on Disability*. New York: Routledge.

Feminist Economics

DRUCILLA K. BARKER
University of South Carolina, USA

Economics is a prestigious and influential social science. Professional economists exercise enormous influence on public policies that have far-reaching consequences for people's lives. While it purports to be gender-neutral, feminist scholars argue otherwise. In the absence of feminist analysis, economics results in a biased and incomplete account of economic phenomena. It is an account that rationalizes and naturalizes income inequality, poverty, and other social hierarchies based on gender, race, ethnicity, class, and nationality. Although there are several schools of economics, this entry will concentrate mainly on the feminist critique of the neoclassical school because it is without question the predominant school of contemporary economic theory. For most economists, neoclassical economics *is* economics, the standard to which all others are compared. Thus it can be referred to as mainstream economics.

Although economics is not homogeneous, there are a few assumptions that all mainstream economists share. First is the assumption that resources are scarce and human wants are unlimited, which leads to the definition of economics as the science of choice: the study of how societies allocate scarce resources among alternative uses. In this view, economics is an objective, gender-neutral, and value-free science that seeks to articulate the laws of economics in the same way that physicists seek to articulate the laws of physical phenomena. It assumes an economic reality the laws of which may be apprehended through the use of the scientific method. However, feminist science scholars have shown that scientific knowledge claims are inevitably saturated with a variety of contextual values that reflect the gender, class, culture, and social location of their practitioners (Harding 1993; Strassmann 1993; Barker and Feiner 2004). Feminist economists bring similar insights to an examination of neoclassical economics and provide a critique of the gender, race, and class bias in its theory and methodology. This entry examines the early feminist critique, draws the broad outlines of neoclassical economic theory, and concludes with a discussion of the contemporary feminist critique.

THE EARLY FEMINIST CRITIQUE

Progressive intellectuals have been critical of economists' treatment of women since at least the mid-nineteenth century (Dimand, Dimand, and Forget 1995). The political economists of the day, all of whom were men, did not consider women as independent adults, capable of choice and agency, but as part of families headed by men (Pujol 1992). Not only were they not independent adults, they were in fact the property of men and their economic roles were circumscribed to the domestic realm. For upper-class women who were unfortunate in marriage and family this meant finding employment as governesses and ladies' companions. For working-class women, this meant either entering "service" or, as the industrial revolution progressed, working in factories. Their wages were lower than men's and most economists considered this only right and proper since women worked only for "pin" money (Barker and Feiner 2004). Although women were mainly excluded from universities, learned societies, and so forth, a few were able to gain the necessary education to critique the prevailing views of women's economic and legal positions during the nineteenth and early twentieth centuries, and not surprisingly one of the most distinctive things about their writing was that it made abstract political economic concepts and ideas concrete and realistic (Kuiper 2010). They argued that treating women as property was fundamentally unjust and that educating women would work for the betterment of the human condition, particularly for the poor. The theme that women's education, economic independence, and political independence would work for the betterment of all society runs through this early work and continues in the contemporary critique.

During the 1920s and 1930s, women were making some headway in the academy. Their work questioned the strict separation between the household (consumers) and the market (firms), analyzed consumption, and argued for the importance of household production (cooking, cleaning, caring for children, and so forth) to economic well-being (Kryk 1923; Reid 1934). Their work was underappreciated at best. During the 1960s, the New Home Economics took up the question of household production and used standard supply and demand models to analyze household production and the division of labor within the family. This work was, however, decidedly not feminist and served to rationalize women's subordinate roles in the household and labor markets.

NEOCLASSICAL ECONOMICS

Economics underwent a significant change between the 1930s and 1950s as efforts were under way to establish it as a real science on a par with the physical sciences. To do so required that economics be expressed in the precise language of mathematics, formal models, and stylized facts. Instead of relying on empirical observations, which can be considered messy collections of facts and observations, economics was to be deduced from a series of first principles. These first principles are universal truths known through introspection. Economics was defined as the science of choice, and its methodology could be applied to any economy regardless of the political, technological, or cultural context (Robbins 1984). In a very short time, this methodological prescription came to be the accepted truth. Economics is the science of choice and studies how societies allocate scarce resources – land, labor, and capital – among competing uses. Some version of this definition can be found in all mainstream economics textbooks in use in US universities and colleges today.

Rational choice theory is central to mainstream economics. Rational choice simply refers to the ability of individuals to order their preferences (their likes and dislikes) in a manner that is logically consistent and then, given that preference structure, to make choices that maximize their self-interest. Within this framework, individuals are assumed to have no contingent obligations or responsibilities, prefer more consumption or less, and interact contractually with one another only when it is in their self-interest to do so. The neoclassical framework assumes away personal, familial, and communitarian responsibilities. This is an abstraction free from the specific legal, political, sociological, and cultural contexts of the actual economy and the individuals within it. In this abstract world, individual actors are rational economic agents and economic outcomes such as prices, incomes, interest rates, types of consumption, and so forth are the results of consumer choice and market interactions. If markets are perfectly competitive, then government intervention will only distort the market and lead to more bureaucracy and higher costs. Of course, most markets are not perfectly competitive, but nonetheless this is the paradigm with which economists begin. Moreover, markets, as conceived by the mainstream, bear little resemblance to the actual economy (Robinson 1981).

CONTEMPORARY FEMINIST CRITIQUE

Feminist economists have been critical of the assumption of self-interested individualism and the lack of any interactions, except those organized according to the principles of self-interested contractual exchange in markets, because these excluded all other motivations for human interactions such as obligation, altruism, and care (England 1993; Strassmann 1993; Nelson 1996). This renders invisible a wide variety of economically significant relationships that do not fit into the rubric of rational maximization, particularly motherhood and caring labor, i.e., that part of household labor that is undertaken out of affection or a sense of responsibility for other people (Hartsock 1983; Folbre 1995). Just as mainstream economics ignores the importance of all unpaid household labor, it also ignores the importance of caring labor, both paid and unpaid, that is crucial to the functioning of any society. In a world where families are under increasing pressure to generate market incomes, the demands of paid employment squeeze the supply of caring labor. A "care deficit" emerges as women (and men) devote increasing numbers of hours to paid employment purchase services such as childcare and eldercare in the market. However, the result of leaving caring labor to the vagaries of the market, or the altruistic behavior of families, will further the care deficit and ensure that care work is low status and poorly paid. In order to ensure a sufficient supply of caring labor, it needs to be well paid and well regulated. This suggests that governments have a significant role to play vis-à-vis care work (Standing 2001). But this notion of government intervention goes against the neoclassical dictum that governments should not interfere in markets.

The neoclassical conception of economic agents is also subject to feminist critique. Contrary to the claims of the mainstream, this is not a gender-neutral category, rather it is the unmarked category that describes the social position of an abstract rational subject devoid of context. Feminists point out that this abstract subject cannot exist with the other who exists in the realm of contingency, necessity, and obligation, and the activities of the other allow economic theory to posit an abstract realm removed from the contingencies and particularities of everyday life (Strassmann 1993). Likewise, the economic agent does not bear any markers of gender, race, or class. Women, poor people of color, and immigrants, are rendered invisible, as are the structural barriers that maintain social hierarchies. Markets alone cannot solve the structural effects of discrimination, poverty, and other forms of social exclusion.

An examination of the history of economic thought shows that questions concerning economic well-being, the ethics of poverty, unequal distribution of incomes, and so forth have always been important to the discipline of economics. Although the positive-normative distinction is considered necessary in economics, there is a long-standing tension between the economist as a detached scientist, concerned with explaining and predicting matters of fact, and the economist as an advocate of specific economic policies. Today, the prevailing orthodoxy is that although the positive-normative distinction should be maintained, it is equally within the purview of economists to offer policy advice based on their scientific expertise. The notion of economic efficiency, or optimality, is the key to this balancing act.

Economic efficiency is purportedly an objective way of judging economic outcomes: if there is no way to make anyone better off without making another one worse off, then an outcome is economically efficient. This does not mean that the outcome is fair or equitable. This criterion is contingent on a given distribution that may be quite unequal. Economists often talk about the tradeoffs between equity and efficiency. However, the feminist critique goes a step further and shows that economic efficiency implicitly assumes that measures of economic well-being can be collapsed into a single metric, that all values are commensurable, and that all human needs can be met through a species of market exchange. These are shared assumptions and values that, in practice, privilege market activities and diminish the significance of non-market activities, most of which have traditionally been considered women's work (Barker 1995).

Maintaining the positive-normative distinction in economics expunges explicit values but leaves in place implicit assumptions and values shared by the research community. This is particularly true in economics, where its practitioners remain largely white men. According to the Committee on the Status of Women in the Economics Profession, only 11.6 percent of tenured full professors at PhD-granting institutions were women in 2012 (McElroy 2012). The need for extensive mathematical expertise means that entry barriers are high and lay people are excluded from policy debates. Economics is a profession that is coded masculine, and women and minorities often receive subtle signals that their presence is unwelcome. Those who do stay have to prove themselves capable of doing the same sort of mathematically sophisticated research that men do. This leaves little room for dissenting views about the problems inherent in the neoclassical approach. The consequences of this closed epistemological community can be devastating for the people whose lives are affected.

Economic and financial models of both national and international economic systems are, like all mainstream models, abstract mathematical representations of real-world phenomena. As such, they miss some things and highlight others. One of the things they miss is the working of political power and influence. Beginning in the 1980s and continuing until today, many countries in the world experienced serious problems with their international debt obligations. These obligations were the results of international bankers and brokers loaning money to nation-states to finance large-scale development projects or to speculate on real estate and other financial assets. When these became bad debts and the countries were at risk of defaulting, various strategies were devised to make sure that the wealthy lenders were paid off, even if not in full. These were first called structural adjustment policies and today austerity policies. They are the same. Their stated intent was to make countries more competitive by decreasing government interventions and letting markets set the prices. The results were disastrous, but this disaster never showed up in the economists' models because they were constructed from the perspective of men's lives. Government cutbacks on spending for healthcare, education, and food and water supplies appeared to be efficient, cost-saving measures. It took feminist economists to point out that these cutbacks were not really savings, but merely turned paid work into unpaid work that was mostly done by women and children (Elson 1991; Benería and Feldman 1992). Moreover, generating the income necessary to pay the international debt likewise fell on the backs of women who went to work in export production factories sewing clothes, assembling electronics, making toys, and migrating, both legally and illegally, to the wealthy countries to work as nannies, maids, or sex workers (Peterson 2003; Barker and Feiner 2010; Runyan and Peterson 2014). While the world's powerful economic policymakers have taken note, their prescriptions remain squarely inside the neoliberal economic model (Bergeron 2006).

Neoclassical economics retains a firm hold on both the wealthy and powerful but also on the imaginations of the poor and disenfranchised. That its promise of freedom, of agency, and of the power of markets to work toward the social good leaves out the realities of most people's lives does not change the ideological power of this story. It is a gendered, raced, and classed narrative that needs to be continually challenged.

SEE ALSO: Androcentrism; Class, Caste, and Gender; Economic Determinism; Family Wage; Feminization of Poverty; Gender Inequality and Gender Stratification; Structural Adjustment

REFERENCES

Barker, Drucilla K. 1995. "Economists, Social Reformers and Prophets: A Feminist Critique of Economic Efficiency." *Feminist Economics*, 1(3): 26–39.

Barker, Drucilla K., and Susan F. Feiner. 2004. *Liberating Economics: Feminist Perspectives on Families, Work, and Globalization*. Ann Arbor: University of Michigan Press.

Barker, Drucilla K., and Susan F. Feiner. 2010. "As the World Turns: Globalization, Consumption, and the Feminization of Work." *Rethinking Marxism*, 22(2): 246–252.

Benería, Lourdes, and Shelley Feldman. 1992. *Unequal Burden: Economic Crises, Persistent Poverty, and Women's Work*. Boulder: Westview Press.

Bergeron, Suzanne. 2006. "Colonizing Knowledge: Economics and Intersectionality in Engendering Development." In *Feminist Economics and the World Bank: History, Theory and Policy*, edited by Edith Kuiper and Drucilla K. Barker, 127–141. Abingdon: Routledge.

Dimand, Mary Ann, Robert W. Dimand, and Evelyn L. Forget. 1995. *Women of Value: Feminist Essays on the History of Women in Economics*. Aldershot: Edward Elgar.

Elson, Diane. 1991. "Male Bias in Macro-Economics: The Case of Structural Adjustment." In *Male Bias in the Development Process*, edited by Dianne Elson, 164–190. Manchester: Manchester University Press.

England, Paula. 1993. "The Separative Self: Androcentric Bias in Neoclassical Assumptions." In *Beyond Economic Man: Feminist Theory and Economics*, edited by Marianne A. Ferber and Julie A. Nelson, 37–53. Chicago: University of Chicago Press.

Folbre, Nancy. 1995. "Holding Hands at Midnight: the Paradox of Caring Labor." *Feminist Economics*, 1(1): 73–92.

Harding, Sandra G. 1993. *The Science Question in Feminism*. Ithaca: Cornell University Press.

Hartsock, Nancy C. 1983. "The Feminist Standpoint: Developing the Grounds for a Specifically Feminist Historical Materialism." In *Discovering Reality: Feminist Perspectives on Epistemology, Metaphysics, Methodology, and Philosophy of Science*, edited by Sandra G. Harding and Merrill B. Hintikka, 283–310. Dordrecht: Kluwer.

Kuiper, Edith. 2010. "Introduction." In *Feminist Economics (Critical Concepts in Economics)*, edited by Drucilla K. Barker and Edith Kuiper, vol. 1, 1–22. Abingdon: Routledge.

Kyrk, Hazel. 1923. *A Theory of Consumption*. Boston: Houghton Mifflin.

McElroy, Marjorie B. 2012. "Report of the Committee on the Status of Women in the Economics Profession." *CSWEP: Annual Reports*. Accessed June 15, 2014, at http://www.aeaweb.org/committees/cswep/annual_reports/2012_CSWEP_Annual_Report.pdf.

Nelson, Julie A. 1996. *Feminism, Objectivity and Economics*. London: Routledge.

Peterson, V. Spike. 2003. *A Critical Rewriting of Global Political Economy: Integrating Reproductive, Productive and Virtual Economies*. Abingdon: Routledge.

Pujol, Michael A. 1992. *Feminism and Anti-Feminism in Early Economic Thought*. Aldershot: Edward Elgar.

Reid, Margaret G. 1934. *Economics of Household Production*. New York: John Wiley & Sons.

Robbins, Lionel R. 1984. *An Essay on the Nature and Significance of Economic Science*. New York: New York University Press. First published 1932.

Robinson, Joan. 1981. *What Are the Questions? And Other Essays: Further Contributions to Modern Economics*. Armonk: M. E. Sharpe.

Runyan, Anne Sisson, and V. Spike Peterson. 2014. *Global Gender Issues in the New Millennium*, 4th ed. Boulder: Westview Press.

Standing, Guy. 2001. "Care Work: Overcoming Insecurity and Neglect." In *Care Work: the Quest for Security*, edited by Mary Daly, 15–31. Geneva: International Labour Office.

Strassmann, Diana. 1993. "Not a Free Market: The Rhetoric of Disciplinary Authority in Economics." In *Beyond Economic Man: Feminist Theory and Economics*, edited by Marianne A. Ferber and Julie A. Nelson, 54–68. Chicago: University of Chicago Press.

Feminist Epistemology

IRIS VAN DER TUIN
Utrecht University, The Netherlands

The phrase feminist epistemology refers to the feminist engagement with questions of truth and knowledge. Under its scope fall the theoretical foundations of women's and gender studies. The key question in this field of inquiry involves the epistemic status of the knowledge produced by privileged versus marginalized subjects. Where to draw the line between knowledge and prejudice? Whose knowledge counts as valid and universal? What knowledge and what modes of knowing are disqualified from the dominant realms of social power and reality? In short, feminist epistemology interrogates the intersection of knowledge and social power.

Feminist epistemology entered the academy when Lorraine Code (1981) first raised the question whether the sex of the knower is epistemologically significant. The publication of *Discovering Reality: Feminist Perspectives on Epistemology, Metaphysics, Methodology, and Philosophy of Science* (1983), edited by Sandra Harding and Merrill B. Hintikka, marked the next step in the field's development. Harding's subsequent book *The Science Question in Feminism* (1986) identified various strands of feminist modes of knowing, designated "feminist empiricism," "feminist standpoint theory," and "feminist postmodernism," respectively. The first of these strands is associated with pro-science feminism (i.e., feminists who hold on to established scientific norms and methods, and apply them to resolve problems of gender bias in scientific research). Feminist standpoint theory, often considered the most radical strand of feminist epistemology, problematizes "science-as-usual" (i.e., science dominated by male perspectives and serving patriarchal purposes), and aims at inventing an alternative form of science by and for women. Postmodern feminist epistemological approaches, finally, depart from feminist standpoint theory by calling into question any "one true story," and by taking people's socially complex, "fractured" identities as a starting point to emphasize and foreground the inevitable partiality of any knowledge claim.

Donna Haraway and Mary E. Hawkesworth point out flaws in Harding's tripartite schema of feminist epistemology, Haraway claims that feminist epistemology is caught in a trap because of its inability to formulate an-*other* objectivity, a mode of objectivity that moves away from both universalism (characteristic of some forms of feminist empiricism), and from relativism (associated with feminist postmodernism). She suggests that "[f]eminist objectivity means quite simply *situated knowledges*" (Haraway, 1988, 581) and that "only partial perspective promises objective vision" (1988, 583). Hawkesworth (1989) argues that feminist epistemology can only move forward if it attends to the known rather than to the (gender) of the knower, because immediate or unmediated rational, sensory, embodied, or intuitive methods of knowing do *not* exist as such – whether for feminist or other knowledge producers. More important than the (gender) identity of the knower are the concrete situations of knowledge production, which bring their own complexities and specificities to the task of knowing (anything at all).

Code (1998) similarly rejects claims to a single feminist epistemology, by arguing that "doing" feminist epistemology in a variety of contexts requires a descent into concrete situations of knowing, even if such situations must be understood in the broadest possible term (i.e., from the laboratory to the literary text). The problem is that marginalized people everywhere continuously struggle for the legitimacy of their experiential knowledges. In order to validate such knowledge, feminist epistemology needs to move beyond postmodernist approaches that disconnect epistemological reflection from concrete situations of lived experience, as well as beyond its adherents' exclusive focus on text and textuality. Elizabeth Potter (2007) suggests that some form of feminist empiricism is, in fact, making a comeback, now that postmodernist relativism has been variously called into question. This more recent incarnation of feminist empiricism deals explicitly with the concrete interaction of fact and value in contextual explorations of sites of knowledge production. Code mentions feminist scholars such as Alison Wylie, Helen Longino, Lynn Hankinson Nelson, and Elizabeth Anderson as exemplary for this move towards empiricism. Miranda Fricker's *Epistemic Injustice: Power and the Ethics of Knowing* (2007) must be added to this list. This influential book revives the field of the epistemology of testimony.

Another significant trend in contemporary feminist epistemology is "feminist new materialism." New materialists wish to undo feminism's reduction of biology to biological determinism and aim to avoid the associated issue of the nature–culture split (Frost 2011; van der Tuin 2011). Feminist theorists such as Karen Barad (2007) and Vicki Kirby (2011) argue that the body is not only formed by discourse, as maintained by feminists ranging from Simone de Beauvoir to Judith Butler, but that bodies actively participate in processes of signification. The body or biology are not mute, but active agents. New materialism follows in the footsteps of feminist science studies that analyze the agency of instruments in laboratories and furthermore finds inspiration and resources in French philosophies working from "posthuman" perspectives (Braidotti 2013).

New materialism assumes that the world is an agential reality, and thus shifts human agency and intentionality to a more modest place in theories of knowledge. Subjectivities, materialities, and environments are considered to be "co-responsive," which is not to say that all agencies (human and non-human) must "correspond," but rather that they emerge together and in inter-relation. A correspondence theory of truth presupposes a gap between word and world, and implies that both operate independently of each other. Co-respondence theories draw attention to the fact that such separation (or "atomism") does not exist for either knower, known, or knowledge. Feminist new materialism does not entail an apolitical stance or a move away from inquiries into the intersection of knowledge and (social) power. Rather, the distinctive features of feminist new materialism are its commitment to beginning from within a material reality that is open to difference.

Epistemology is a prescriptive field of philosophical inquiry, which is to say that most epistemological positions translate into specific methodological strategies and requirements. Feminism's sensitivity to hierarchical power–knowledge systems prevents the relation between feminist epistemology and concrete research practices from becoming a one-way model: research practices may feed back into feminist epistemology and impact theoretical reflection as much as epistemological claims may inform research practices (Alcoff and Potter 1993; Lennon and Whitford 1994; Tanesini 1999).

Methodologically speaking, feminist empiricist approaches inform gender studies research that adheres to recognized investigative practices, from statistical analysis to hermeneutics. Feminist standpoint theorists reject standardized models of analysis and encourage semi-structured and open-ended interviewing, extensive fieldwork research, and (auto-)ethnography, seeking relations of equality between researcher and researched. In the humanities, this type of feminist standpoint scholarship has led to research into marginalized literary and media genres, such as romantic fiction or domestic photography and to the adoption of empirical methodologies such as reader-response theory.

SEE ALSO: Feminist Standpoint Theory; Scientific Sexism and Racism; Women in Science

REFERENCES

Alcoff, Linda Martín, and Elizabeth Potter, eds. 1993. *Feminist Epistemologies*. New York: Routledge.
Barad, Karen. 2007. *Meeting the Universe Halfway: Quantum Physics and the Entanglement of Matter and Meaning*. Durham and London: Duke University Press.
Braidotti, Rosi. 2013. *The Posthuman*. Cambridge: Polity Press.
Code, Lorraine. 1998. "Epistemology." In *A Companion to Feminist Philosophy*, edited by Alison M. Jaggar and Iris Marion Young, 173–184. Malden: Blackwell.
Fricker, Miranda. 2007. *Epistemic Injustice: Power and the Ethics of Knowing*. Oxford: Oxford University Press.
Frost, Samantha. 2011. "The Implications of the New Materialisms for Feminist Epistemology." In *Feminist Epistemology and Philosophy of Science: Power in Knowledge*, edited by Heidi E. Grasswick, 69–83. Dordrecht, Springer.
Haraway, Donna. 1988. "Situated Knowledges: The Science Question in Feminism and the Privilege of Partial Perspective." *Feminist Studies*, 14(3): 575–599. DOI: 10.2307/3178066.
Harding, Sandra. 1986. *The Science Question in Feminism*. Milton Keynes: Open University Press.
Harding, Sandra, and Merrill B. Hintikka. 1983. *Discovering Reality: Feminist Perspectives on Epistemology, Metaphysics, Methodology, and Philosophy of Science*. Boston: Kluwer.
Hawkesworth, Mary E. 1989. "Knowers, Knowing, Known: Feminist Theory and Claims of Truth." *Signs: Journal of Women in Culture and Society*, 14(3): 533–557.
Kirby, Vicki. 2011. *Quantum Anthropologies: Life at Large*. Durham, NC and London: Duke University Press.
Lennon, Kathleen, and Margaret Whitford, eds. 1994. *Knowing the Difference: Feminist Perspectives in Epistemology*. London and New York: Routledge.
Potter, Elizabeth. 2007. "Feminist Epistemology and Philosophy of Science." In *The Blackwell Guide to Feminist Philosophy*, edited by Linda Martín Alcoff and Eva Feder F. Kittay, 235–253. Malden: Blackwell.
Tanesini, Alessandra. 1999. *An Introduction to Feminist Epistemologies*. Malden: Blackwell.
van der Tuin, Iris. 2011. "New Feminist Materialisms: Review Essay." *Women's Studies International Forum*, 34(4): 271–277.

Feminist Ethnography

SANJUKTA T. GHOSH

Castleton State College, Vermont, USA

Though the phrase "feminist ethnography" emerged only in the late 1980s, the discipline had existed long before then. At its most fundamental level, feminist ethnography is a qualitative research methodology emerging out of anthropology – a discipline that examines the lived experiences of a community "in its natural habitat." It is a data-gathering approach that has been used not just in anthropology, but also in cultural studies, women's and gender studies, geography, education, and sociology, among other disciplines. This entry discusses the historical roots of feminist ethnography and the crisis that has plagued each of its three main parts: data collection, interpretation, and presentation of that data. The critiques of each of these three parts, from feminist, poststructuralist, and postcolonial theorists, for their androcentric and Eurocentric perspectives, have shaped the contours of what we today call "feminist ethnography."

ACADEMIC ANTECEDENTS

One of the main challenges in thinking about feminist ethnography is that it does not have a single coherent definition or universal research canons. It refers to the intersection of the multitudes of feminist theories and the plurality of ethnographic practices and therefore it has a myriad of methodological routings, objects, and inquiries. As an academic discipline, the emergence of feminist ethnography can be traced back to the perceived androcentric bias of mainstream anthropology.

At the most elemental level, anthropology examines the origins, development, and characteristics of social customs and cultures. It is concerned with uncovering the social order of everyday activities and practices in both mainstream societies and subcultures that make up the larger social formation. Thus, anthropologists have studied remaking of personal identities among migrant Filipino nurses in the United States. They have examined the corporate ethics and labor hierarchies in large multi-national businesses. Other anthropologists have given us vivid accounts of the Bedouin community in Egypt. Still others have examined the development of different femininities among women's roller derby participants. What all of these have in common is the use of qualitative methods to get to the root of their research inquiries.

The most common of these methods is the use of ethnography, an analytic technique that allows researchers to collect cultural data directly from the community by being embedded in it. Like many qualitative investigative tools, ethnography is less concerned with testing a set hypothesis and generalizing the results to a whole population than examining a social phenomenon from the inside. Thus, ethnographers record perceptible as well as imperceptible material goods, behaviors, ideas, and ritualistic practices through two major techniques: participant observation and key informant interviewing. Participant observation gives the ethnographer a chance to tease out the complexities of a culture through a process of cultural immersion and through forging and maintaining relationships with community members. Interviewing some key members of the community under study gives the researcher a chance to collect data in a structured and systematic way. These key community members become pivotal to the process of both knowledge gathering and construction and have been called research collaborators or even "native informants." It is these characteristics of ethnography – an immersion into the culture being examined, collaborating with the researched community, and the use of interpretive analytics rather than statistics – that make it particularly attractive to feminist researchers.

In fact, there are several reasons why feminists think ethnography is consonant with their own goals and objectives. First, ethnography rejects the false dualisms found in much of positivist research in that it refuses to categorize people and cultures using preset and axiomatic taxonomies. Second, ethnography repudiates the notion of objectivity found in quantitative, statistics-based research. This rejection is seen by feminists as being akin to their own recognition of the close links between the personal and the political. Third, ethnography seeks to understand "lived experience" in all its intricacies and specificities. This mirrors feminist researchers' insistence that the exploration of knowledge be grounded in the concrete realities of people's lives. Fourth, ethnography attempts to give voice to its subjects. Often fieldworkers collaborate with the subjects in producing the final report. This feature, a veering away from the strict social science practice of third-person narrative to collaboratively produced research documents, is an aim of feminist research too. Finally, good self-conscious ethnography is capable of yielding complex, multilayered interpretations that help to understand multiple identities and positionalities. This has led feminist researchers to acknowledge ethnography as a politically viable research method.

However, despite these parallels, feminist scholars have systematically critiqued ethnography's masculinist biases. It is through these critiques – of data gathering, interpreting, and writing – that feminists have made the most profound contributions to mainstream ethnography and challenged its widely held canons.

HISTORICAL ROOTS

Historically, scholars have identified three conceptual periods in feminist ethnography. The first period, 1850–1920, simply sought to include women's voices in ethnography which, up to that point, was usually undertaken by men using male informants. Inclusion of women's voices in ethnography opened up a new space in social science research. Not only were women conducting the research, they were also centering women's concerns and experiences and giving voice to other women. In other words, this period opened up a completely new perspective, as male ethnographers generally only had access to male informants. Some key figures in feminist ethnography during this period are Americans Elsie Clews Parsons and Alice Fletcher, and British anthropologist Phyllis Kayberry, whose book *Women of the Grassfields* (1952) examined women's work and rural development.

The second period, 1920–1980, was influenced by theoretical developments within feminist theory. The distinction between biological sex and the cultural category of gender enabled feminist ethnographers to rethink the boundaries of the public and private spheres and the power relationships embedded in those distinctions. Specifically, during this period, feminist ethnography attempted to uncover the asymmetries of power in social relations and community arrangements. While these ethnographers acknowledged that gender was socially constructed, they used "woman" as a universalizing category. In other words, feminist ethnographers of this period assumed that all women had the same experiences and problems. A key figure in this period is Margaret Mead and her classic works *Coming of Age in Samoa* (1928) and *Sex and Temperament* (1950). Another significant figure here is Betty Friedan, whose much-heralded book, *The Feminine Mystique* (1963), is based on an ethnography of middle-class suburban women who reflected on their roles as wives and mothers. Towards the end of this period, Gayle Rubin formally linked feminist theory, Marxism, and anthropology in her landmark essay "The Traffic in Women" (1975).

In the third period, which began in the 1980s, feminist ethnography widened its concerns and approaches, moving from a study of just women to a diversity of analytical approaches including a greater attention to discourse and more self-conscious as well as meditative modes of writing. Incorporating ideas from poststructuralism, postmodernism, and postcolonialism, these accounts acknowledged the androcentric and Eurocentric biases of anthropology in general and of ethnography in particular, and the asymmetries of power.

Contemporary feminist ethnographers reject "womanhood" as a universalizing category focusing instead on differences around class, race, ethnicity, religion, and identity politics. Thus, current feminist ethnographic research examines how power operates in the construction of both individual and community identities and how their stories are narrated and disseminated. Furthermore, it holds that discourse is formative of the very contexts being researched. Thus, issues of representation, positionalities, location, and the production and reproduction of social identities surface as the crucial questions for feminist ethnographers today. The works and theoretical writings of Lila Abu-Lughod, Judith Stacey, Kamala Visweswaran, and Radhika Parameswaran, among others, are very influential here.

FEMINIST CHALLENGES

By many accounts, feminist ethnography emerged as a reaction to androcentric as well as imperialist tendencies within the discipline. In fact, many scholars who have been blind to their own masculinist tilt have still characterized ethnography as the most imperialistic of all the Western social science methods. A remarkable number of early ethnographic accounts appeared at the height of European colonialism and were used as imperial tools. From the late sixteenth to mid-nineteenth century, scholars produced detailed ethnographic studies – of Native Americans, of Arab, Persian, and Turkish "harems," of widows in India, and so on. Essentially, these records sought to explore and establish the "other" and the "exotic" within the colonial empire. Scholars such as Edward Said (1978) have shown that colonialism was not simply a matter of winning on the battlefields with superior technology but was also an intricate system of scholarly traditions in art, philosophy, philology, historiography, literature, and anthropology. Said demonstrates in his book *Orientalism* that orientalist art or travelogues, ethnographic accounts written by European colonizers, defined cultures, named people, and told them who they were and were not. Thus, essentially ethnography paralleled and supported the master discourse of colonization.

Following Said and other postcolonial theorists, feminist scholars contested ethnography's claim to produce authentic, empirical, and "real" knowledge, asserting that knowledge and representations of the third world were replete with gross inaccuracies and stereotypes such as the presumed cultural, intellectual, and artistic inferiority of this "other." These researchers argued for a feminist ethnography that not only challenged hegemonic ethnographic knowledge, but also engaged with peoples of the Global South in a way that acknowledged their struggles and viewed them as capable of self-knowledge. The resulting new, more self-conscious ethnography, then, involved itself in issues of migration, identity, location, ideology, diaspora, representation, and resistance.

Janice Radway's (1984) ethnography of women romance readers, Elisabeth Enslin's (1994) account of women's literacy classes in Nepal, and Irma McClaurin's (1996) ethnography of women in Belize are just a few examples of introspective, responsive, polyphonic, and ethical feminist ethnographies.

DATA COLLECTION

Ethnography is predicated on the acquisition of rich experiential data that is reflexive and dialogic. Such data collection is possible only through the establishment of strong connections between researcher and subject. But what characterizes this relationship between the fieldworker and the subject? Can the relationship ever be on equal grounds? Is there any reciprocity in this relationship? Or is it forever and inevitably doomed to be exploitative? Does the ethnographer affect the very field she is studying merely by her presence? How does power already embedded in social structures affect the relationship between the scholar and those who are the subject of the scholarship? Given the extended period of engagement of the researcher with the research site and the intensity of the relationship with the community, how ethical is ethnographic research? It is feminist ethnographers who brought these questions to the forefront and problematized these relationships which once went unnoticed.

One of the first scholars to put the ethics of fieldwork under the ethical microscope was Judith Stacey. In an essay titled "Can There Be a Feminist Ethnography?" (1988), now considered a milestone in feminist ethnographic theory, she wondered whether the relationship between the researcher and the research subject could ever be a reciprocal and an equal one. For her, the appearance of greater respect for and equality with research subjects in the ethnographic approach masked a deeper, more dangerous form of exploitation. Given that good ethnography relied on good relationships with key informants, Stacey held that such relationships could easily give way to manipulation. Furthermore, the privileged position of the ethnographer made a mockery of ethnography's egalitarian promise. Thus, Stacey reached the troubling conclusion that despite its democratic pretentions ethnographic research was never collaborative.

In 1990, in an article also titled "Can There Be a Feminist Ethnography?," Lila Abu-Lughod reiterated Stacey's position that because of the differential class positions occupied by the privileged ethnographer and her research subject, feminist ethnographers were in danger of replicating the very androcentric ideas that they were attempting to critique. Using poststructuralist theories of gender subjectivity, Abu-Lughod argued against assuming a universal "women's experience" that erases power differentials. Despite commonalities of women's oppression under patriarchy, differences along vectors such as race, class, and education level, made global sisterhood (using Robin Morgan's phrase) only a dream, she argued. Thus, the emphasis on women's essential identities as "women" and their common oppressed state was criticized as an ethnocentric worldview that privileged white, middle-class, Western women. Moreover, power relations between the researcher and the subject, also called an informant or even consultant, made accountability to the subject an impossibility given that it was blocked by the very structure and organization of knowledge.

An ethical dilemma facing feminist anthropologists was the issue of motivations for employing ethnography in the first place. Postcolonial theorists have pointed out that the formative years of early ethnography was wrapped up with colonialism. The production of knowledge about the colonized "other" and the civilizing mission of Christianity were, after all, prompted by the colonizer's practical political need to maintain power and hegemony. Because of this history, feminist ethnographers feel the imperative to make overt their motivations and always aim for social change. However, this too is fraught with complications as feminists define this change in various ways.

The current cohort of feminist ethnographers argues that for qualitative fieldwork to be truly feminist, the collection of data as well as its presentation must be embedded within discourses of power. It must explore the multiple positionalities occupied by the researcher in relation to people encountered in the field and it must include an ethical critique of the unequal power relations. They argue that despite the contradictions and the near impossibility of an egalitarian relationship during data collection, feminists must not give up on ethnography but instead strive to do better anthropological work by being conscious of the way power impacts all relationships, and challenge the Manichean dichotomies such as self/other, native/Westerner, and insider/outsider.

NARRATIVE VOICE

The concept of power is also critical to the way ethnographic research is interpreted and shared. Here feminist ethnographers ask a whole host of questions. Who is writing about whom? Whose language is used? Who is the intended audience for the analysis? Whose terms define the discourse? Who translates whose concepts? What kind of institutions under Western control do these scholars belong to? Whose interests does the research ultimately serve?'

Here feminist ethnographers find Michel Foucault's notions of discourse and discursive formations very useful. Postcolonial theorists have already made links between knowledge produced by colonial ethnographers about the "natives" and the imperial endeavor to dominate and subordinate. Feminist ethnographers have taken this notion further using Foucault to understand the role of "authority" in mediating the relationship between knowledge – which is discursively produced – and power. In keeping with the canons of traditional anthropology, ethnographic accounts are usually presented in the form of a text (print and audiovisual media) authored by the researcher/fieldworker. Feminist ethnographers posit that because authorship invests the ethnographer with a power that is disproportionate and troubling, these texts, always historically situated, provide us with a colorful but colored way of thinking about the social actors and their culture.

Commenting on this, Judith Stacey (1988) says that ethnography is always finally a written document structured by the researcher's purposes, giving the researcher's interpretations and registered in the researcher's voice; therefore, inequality, exploitation, and even betrayal are endemic to ethnography. In fact, there are many ethnographies that have come under attack by key informants precisely because of this feeling of betrayal. Diane Bell's study (1983) of intra-racial rape in Australia's Aboriginal communities is an example of this.

Kamala Visweswaran (1998) takes this idea of a subject's consent further and says that a feminist ethnography should always be cognizant of who finally agrees to be a participant in the fieldworker's project, what she is willing to divulge and what she is not. She says an ethnography that is truly feminist would investigate when and why women do talk and assess what structures are placed on their speech. Like Stacey, she cautions that what women can and will say about themselves and their society can never be taken as direct evidence of what they know and do not know, or of women's status. One key element that demarcates feminist ethnography from masculinist accounts of a community would be the special attention given to the silence of the female subjects. Visweswaran says that often silence is seen as a marker of cultural barriers or a lack of knowledge, when it could indicate resistance and even an astute assault on the fieldworker's actions. Therefore, feminist theories of language and communication should inform anthropologies of women for them to be feminist ethnographies.

One way in which feminist ethnography attempts to give voice to its subjects is by producing collaborative accounts. In partnership with the native informants, many ethnographers have produced films, plays, songs, and other performance pieces, eschewing social scientific traditional practices. This textual turn away from conventional narratives is not new and has led to a recuperative endeavor on the part of feminists who now recognize the work of many women authors as feminist ethnographies. Some examples of these are Zora Neale Hurston's book *Their Eyes Were Watching God*. Hurston was trained as an anthropologist, yet her writings are mainly celebrated as fictions. Similarly, Paula Gunn Allen's work *The Woman Who Owned the Shadows* was once seen as a work of "mere fiction" but now is acknowledged as a study of the author's self-awakening and of her culture.

There also has been another recuperative project – one that revisits works of early anthropologists, especially works of heterosexual couples. Referring to the works of such couples, historians of ethnography have noted that often two separate monographs were produced on the same project – one an academic monograph and the other a more personal narrative that included the ethnographer's own reflections. This second piece of writing, often a work of fiction, was produced by the wife of the "academic anthropologist." Today, feminists recognize that these more personal narratives are ethnographies in their own right. They hold that women's writing within ethnography has been traditionally undervalued or dismissed simply for its more reflective, meditative, and personal tone; however, these works merit being marked as feminist ethnographies too and being recognized as authentic voices of the writers rather than of the women in the communities being studied.

Feminist ethnographers then not only encourage narratives that are collaborative and reflective of the form as well as the content of their informants, but also narratives that may depart from positivist research traditions. They hold that the plurality of subject positions women inhabit can be studied in multiple ways and may ultimately need multiple forms. The idea is to make the subject a participant and an author, not merely the "object," of study. It is an attempt to be accountable to people's own struggles for self-determination.

INTERPRETATION AND REPRESENTATION

Discussions of the power–knowledge nexus has inevitably brought feminist ethnographers to offer a rigorous critique of the very concept of representation, not only in ethnographic accounts but in academic discourse in general. Ethnography's claim to "realism" has led to overwhelmingly distorted representations of the third world. Feminist ethnographers have found Gayatri Chakravarty Spivak's (1988) insights on the problematic relation between representation and re-presentation invaluable for questioning ethnography's potential to reflect "reality." Additionally, they have also found other theorists of third world representations useful in redrawing the boundaries of feminist ethnography.

In 1991, Chandra Talpade Mohanty argued that using colonial knowledge practices Western feminists constructed third world women as a monolithic group, as hapless and helpless victims of their own patriarchal cultures and traditions. This representation of third world women as the victimized "other" served as a comparison for Western feminists, who could then see themselves as more actualized human beings in comparison with their non-Western counterparts. This kind of binary representation, Mohanty noted, led to the emergence of rescue narratives where ethnographies and other "invasive" research methods could help Western feminists save their third world sisters from their barbaric cultures. Mohanty did not rule out the possibility of women working collaboratively and collectively across difference, but cautioned against Western feminist discourses that simply reinforced colonial binaries.

Given that Western academic discourse is replete with essentialized representations of women in the Global South, Mary John (1996) asks if there can ever be a postcolonial feminist ethnography and what alternative forms this might take. Chiding ethnographers for their inattentiveness to the asymmetries of locations, John hopes for feminist ethnographies in the future that will focus on third world citizens who are scholars and producers of feminist knowledge. Most ethnographies, even those produced by feminists, she says, assume two worlds in their representations: the Western one and another where women are *not* feminist. Why not an ethnography about being a feminist in other places, she asks.

Aihwa Ong (2001) argues that Western "feminist" ethnographies produce linear narratives of development that represent third world women as living in a pre-modern era. These ethnographies also construct "development" and "modernity" as magical tools capable of being able to emancipate women from oppressive gender roles. She advocates the use of native informants' understanding of development and liberation for ethnographies to be "feminist" in principle and practice.

However, the question still remains as to how to represent women ethnographic subjects that do not reinforce old dichotomies and also give them a voice. Spivak pessimistically states academics simply cannot "give voice" to the subaltern others. By seeking to bring in those who have been historically silenced, intellectuals will always already co-opt and subjugate the subaltern's voice, according to Spivak. Echoing her, Vietnamese artist and theorist Trinh Minh-ha says that a "conversation of 'us' about 'them' is a conversation in which 'them' is silenced." She argues that an ethnographer's gaze can serve to preserve the current status hierarchy, rather than to dislodge or interrupt it. In her own work, she attempts to challenge and block the colonialist's gaze through experiments with representational form but admits that these attempts may be only partially successful.

Despite their critiques of past discourses about the third world "other," these postcolonial theorists exhort feminists to continue to undertake transnational ethnographic projects. They say that fraught though the linkages are between representational practices and knowledge formation, ethical and political dilemmas should not keep feminist ethnographers from continuing to search for ways in which to tell the stories of the voiceless. However, rather than see subjects of their fieldwork as inert objects of knowledge, they should be recognized as sources of real, connected, and grounded knowledge. This shift would be tantamount to a shift in casting third and fourth world peoples as passive objects with no control over their histories to active producers of and authorities on knowledge. While these feminists acknowledge that there is a critical need to interrogate the processes that produce "knowledge" and the "knowledge" itself, they also recognize that not speaking for others is dangerous and that "partial truths and understandings" may be preferable to all-encompassing theories (Ong 2001).

In the final analysis then, what makes an ethnography feminist? It is one that produces alternative knowledge and assigns a central place to the self-knowledge of the informants. It understands that the everyday lives of subaltern peoples is a primary site where power is negotiated and therefore recognizes "ethnographies of everyday lives" as political praxis. Feminist ethnography is a careful, politically focused analysis that empowers and allows for self-definition. It brings up questions of asymmetry, revealing the relations of power between the researchers and those being studied. In doing so, it also complicates the notion of "ethnographic authority" leading to shared and collaborative authorships. Finally, it understands the complex and complicated connections between "representation," "knowledge," and "power."

SEE ALSO: Colonialism and Gender; Discursive Theories of Gender; Empowerment; Feminism, Aboriginal Australia and Torres Strait Islands; Feminism, Postcolonial; Feminism, Poststructural; Subaltern; Third World Women

REFERENCES

Abu-Lughod, Lila. 1990. "Can There Be a Feminist Ethnography?" *Woman and Performance: A Journal of Feminist Theory*, 5(1): 7–27.
Bell, Diane. 1983. *Daughters of the Dreaming*, 3rd ed. Melbourne: McPheeGribble/Sydney: Allen and Unwin.
John, Mary. 1996. *Discrepant Dislocations: Feminism, Theory, and Postcolonial Histories*. Berkeley: University of California Press.
Mohanty, Chandra Talpade. 1991. "Under Western Eyes: Feminist Scholarship and Colonial Discourses." In *Third World Women and the Politics of Feminism*, edited by Chandra Talpade Mohanty, Ann Russo, and Lourdes Torres, 51–80. Bloomington: Indiana University Press.
Ong, Aihwa. 2001. "Colonialism and Modernity: Feminist Re-Presentations of Women in Non-Western Societies." In *Feminism and "Race,"* edited by Kum-Kum Bhavnani, 108–118. Oxford: Oxford University Press.
Spivak, Gayatri Chakravorty. 1988. "Can the Subaltern Speak?" In *The Post-Colonial Studies Reader*, edited by Bill Ashcroft, Gareth Griffiths, and Helen Tiffin, 24–28. New York: Routledge.
Stacey, Judith. 1988. "Can There Be a Feminist Ethnography?" *Women's Studies International Forum*, 1: 21–27.
Visweswaran, Kamala. 1994. "Defining Feminist Ethnography." In *Fictions of Feminist Ethnography*. Minnesota: University of Minnesota Press.

FURTHER READING

Abu-Lughod, Lila. 1993. *Writing Women's Worlds: Bedouin Stories*. Berkeley: University of California Press.
Abu-Lughod, Lila. 2000. "Locating Ethnography." *Ethnography*, 1(2): 261–267.
Bell, Diane, Pat Caplan, and Jahan Karim Wazir, eds. 1993. *Gendered Fields: Women, Men, and Ethnography*. London: Routledge.
Enslin, Elizabeth. 1994. "Beyond Writing: Feminist Practice and the Limitations of Ethnography." *Cultural Anthropology*, 9(4): 537–568.
McClaurin, Irma. 1996. *Women of Belize: Gender and Change in Central America*. Brunswick: Rutgers University Press.
Parameswaran, Radhika. 2001. "Feminist Media Ethnography in India: Exploring Power, Gender, and Culture in the Field." *Qualitative Inquiry* 7(1): 69–103.
Radway, Janice. 1984. *Reading the Romance: Women, Patriarchy, and Popular Literature*. Chapel Hill: University of North Carolina Press.

Feminist Family Therapy in the United States

LOUISE BORDEAUX SILVERSTEIN
Yeshiva University, USA

THE GOLDEN YEARS: 1978–1995

The feminist critique of family therapy is virtually invisible outside the United States (see Silverstein 2003 for a detailed historical overview). In a literature search of the Web of Knowledge database from 1985 to 2013, several of the 162 citations reviewed work done in the United States. However, only two articles reflecting original work in this field appeared in a non-US (Australian) journal. These were later included in a book that analyzed how governmental family policies either empowered or weakened women, and thus should be considered by feminist family therapists (Prouty Lyness 2005).

The US critique began in the late 1970s and was most influential in family therapy throughout the 1980s and mid-1990s. The early years of the critique transformed family therapy by arguing that the larger social context constructed gendered power differences within the family, and by addressing the need to work with men from a feminist perspective. The virulent tone of Haley's (2010) "satiric" article, "How Should a Gentleman Talk to a Feminist Therapist?," illustrates the defensive flavor of the white male establishment's response.

In the 1980s, feminists also began to focus on lesbian and gay couples, and on differences in race, class, ethnicity, and sexual orientation. In the 1990s, literature on race/ethnicity expanded, while the feminist critique constricted from a general emphasis on gendered power differences to focus primarily on intimate violence. The traditional approach had conceptualized both members of the couple as equally responsible. The feminist approach acknowledged that both men and women contribute to the cycle of violence, but held men primarily responsible for their violent behavior.

This shift to a focus on holding men accountable led to an emphasis on working with men from a feminist perspective. Many therapists responded to this theme as "male bashing," and developed the "gender-sensitive approach" to working with couples. Hare-Mustin and Goodrich (see Silverstein 2003) have termed this "feel good feminism," an approach that avoided ruffling male feathers, emphasizing the reciprocal nature of couple interactions, while ignoring power differences.

This focus on men from a feminist perspective occurred in tandem with the emergence of a new theoretical framework for conceptualizing men's behavior, the gender role strain paradigm (GRS) (see Silverstein and Brooks 2010). Just as feminism had deconstructed femininity, GRS identified the ways that traditional masculine socialization stressed men by prescribing negative behaviors, such as an emphasis on achievement and aggression, emotional stoicism, and excessive risk taking.

In summary, the feminist critique was at its strongest in the 1980s and early 1990s. It transformed family therapy and contributed to the social deconstruction of traditional masculinity.

MARGINALIZATION: MID-1990s TO 2013

Although a large body of literature on feminist theory and research has emerged since the 1970s (see, for example, the journals *Feminism and Psychology*, *Gender & Society*, *Psychology of Women Quarterly*), that literature has had relatively little impact on mainstream family studies and family therapy. Silverstein and Brooks (2010) and a review conducted for this entry searched mainstream family studies, family psychology, and family therapy journals (*Family Issues*, *Family Process*, *Family Relations*, *Journal of Family Psychology*, *Journal of Marriage and Family*, *Journal of Marriage and Family Therapy*, *Journal of Marital and Family Therapy*) for the keyword "feminist." The reviews identified the *Journal of Marital and Family Therapy* as an exception in mainstream journals, in that 23 percent of its articles addressed feminist principles between 2000 and 2013. In the other mainstream journals from 1972 to the present, the percentage of articles that explicitly referenced a feminist perspective ranged from 5 percent to 11 percent.

The journal that has regularly published articles on feminist family therapy is the *Journal of Feminist Family Therapy*. *Women and Therapy*, also focused on feminist issues, does not contain many articles on family therapy. A small number of specialized books and chapters (e.g., Silverstein and Goodrich 2003) have introduced feminist principles to couple and family therapy.

Just as feminism remains cloistered in specialized publications, scholars using the gender role strain paradigm have not been embraced in mainstream journals. They publish primarily in the journals *Psychology of Men and Masculinity* and *Masculinities*. Similarly, feminist therapy with lesbian couples remains marginalized, representing 3 percent of articles in mainstream family studies journals between 2002 and 2008.

Even in the *Journal of Feminist Family Therapy*, only 14 (11 percent) of the 127 articles published during that time period focused on lesbian and gay families, seven of which were in a single special issue (volume 18). In response to this invisibility in mainstream journals, the *Journal of GLBT Family Studies* was launched in 2005. This journal has dramatically increased the number of articles focused on research with lesbian and gay couples and families. However, fewer than 10 percent of articles in this journal used a feminist conceptual framework. In summary, these specialized journals, books, and chapters illustrate the trend of marginalizing all things relating to gender.

In summary, if one were to focus on the degree to which feminism has been marginalized in family therapy, one might conclude, "The feminist revision of family therapy … in the first decade of the 21st Century … is practically on life support" (Silverstein and Brooks 2010, 253).

THE CONTINUING PROBLEM OF WHITE, HETEROSEXUAL PRIVILEGE

Another factor contributing to the marginalization of feminist scholarship is the failure of white feminist family therapists to address race, ethnicity, and social class. Rather than integrating these multiple aspects of identity, the vast majority of white feminists have focused on either race/ethnicity or gender (Silverstein and Brooks 2010). An exception to this was Michele Bograd (1999), one of the first white feminist family therapists to reflect publicly on her failure to consider the multiple oppressions in the lives of women of color, poor women, and immigrant women. She acknowledged that her social location as a white, middle-class, heterosexual woman led her to privilege gender over other aspects of experience.

A second expression of white privilege is the evidence-based therapy (EBT) movement dominated primarily by white men (see Silverstein and Brooks 2010 for a review of the absence of gender, power, and race/ethnicity in EBT couple therapy). The need to provide empirical validation for family and couples therapy is an authentic concern. However, to date, most of the EBT models in couple therapy do not address the ways that gendered power and diverse social locations construct relationships in couples and families.

Rampage (2002) addressed this failure in her comment on three articles evaluating the state of marriage in the twentieth century. She proposed that, although the authors in this genre recognized that gender is relevant, these main(male)stream family therapists did not understand its significance, or how to apply feminist principles to the practice of couple therapy in order to redress power inequities.

THE FUTURE: WHERE DO WE GO FROM HERE?

Deconstructing gendered power in relationships has always been at the core of feminist family therapy. In order to remain relevant, feminist family therapy must move beyond gender and white, heterosexual, middle-class families to address marginalized groups of women.

Feminist women of color and a small number of white women have embraced an intersectionalities perspective that examines women's lives in terms of classism, racism, sexism, and homophobia. Monica McGoldrick (McGoldrick and Hardy 2008) and Elaine Pinderhughes (2002) are at the forefront of developing an intersectionalities model of family therapy. Rhea Almeida, Kenneth Dolan-Del Vecchio, and Lynne Parker (2008), as well as Teresa McDowell and Pilar Hernandez (2010) have gone beyond an intersectionalities perspective to address social justice issues directly in their model of family therapy.

Prouty Lyness (2005) and Feree (2010) have advocated an even broader expansion of feminism beyond individuals and families to include an examination of the ways that societal institutions perpetuate intersectional inequalities in families. For example, police profiling and incarceration disrupt young black men's family relationships. Similarly, women's family relationships are stressed by unequal pay in the public world of work, and unequal responsibility for childcare and housework in the private world of the family. This inter-institutional analysis expands feminism's early focus on the personal as political. The intersectionalities and social justice perspectives represent the future of mainstream, as well as feminist, family therapy.

Addressing these interpersonal and multi-institutional inequalities would require white men to give up power to women and men of color, and white women to share their power with women of color. It is rare for human beings to give up power and privilege voluntarily. Until the current white majority in the United States becomes just another minority group, it is unlikely that feminist family therapy will be integrated into the mainstream.

SEE ALSO: Gender Analysis; Intersectionality

REFERENCES

Almeida, Rhea V., Kenneth Dolan-Del Vecchio, and Lynne Parker. 2008. *Transformative Family Therapy: Just Families in a Just Society*. New York: Peterson, Allyn and Bacon.

Bograd, Michele. 1999. "Strengthening Domestic Violence Theories: Intersections of Race, Class, Sexual Orientation and Gender." *Journal of Marital and Family Therapy*, 25: 275–289.

Feree, Myra Marx. 2010. "Filling the Glass." *Journal of Marriage and Family*, 72: 420–439. DOI: 10.1111/j.1741-3737.2010.00711.x.

Haley, Jay. 2010. "How Should a Gentleman Talk to a Feminist Therapist?" In *Jay Haley Revisited*, edited by John Carlson, 235–254. New York: Routledge.

McDowell, Teresa, and Pilar Hernandez. 2010. "Decolonizing Academia: Intersectionality, Participation, and Accountability in Family Therapy and Counseling." *Journal of Feminist Family Therapy*, 22: 93–111. DOI: 10.1080/08952831003787834.

McGoldrick, Monica, and Kenneth Hardy, eds. 2008. *Re-Visioning Family Therapy: Race, Culture, and Gender in Clinical Practice*, 2nd ed. New York: Norton.

Pinderhughes, Elaine B. 2002. "African American Marriage in the 20th Century." *Family Process*, 41: 269–282. DOI: 10.1111/j.1545-5300.2002.41206.x.

Prouty Lyness, Anne M., ed. 2005. *The Politics of the Personal in Feminist Family Therapy: International Examinations of Family Policy*. New York: Haworth Press.

Rampage, Cheryl. 2002. "Marriage in the 20th Century: A Feminist Perspective." *Family Process*, 41: 261–268. DOI: 10.1111/j.1545-5300.2002.41205.x.

Silverstein, Louise B. 2003. "Classic Texts and Early Critiques." In *Feminist Family Therapy: Empowerment in Social Context*, edited by Louise B. Silverstein and Thelma Jean Goodrich, 17–35. Washington, DC: American Psychological Association Books.

Silverstein, Louise B., and Gary R. Brooks. 2010. "Gender Issues in Family Therapy and Couples Counseling." In *Handbook of Gender and Research in Psychology*, edited by Joan C. Chrisler and Donald R. McCreary, 253–277. New York: Springer. DOI: 10.1007/978-1-4419-1467-5_11.

Silverstein, Louise B., and Thelma Jean Goodrich, eds. 2003. *Feminist Family Therapy: Empowerment in Social Context*. Washington, DC: American Psychological Association Books.

Feminist Film Theory

ANNEKE SMELIK
Radboud University Nijmegen, The Netherlands

Feminist film theory came into being in the early 1970s with the aim of understanding cinema as a cultural practice that represents and reproduces myths about women and femininity. Theoretical approaches were developed to critically discuss the sign and image of woman in film as well as open up issues of female spectatorship. Feminist film theory criticized on the one hand classical cinema for its stereotyped representation of women, and discussed on the other hand possibilities for a women's cinema that allowed for representations of female subjectivity and female desire. The feminist wave in film studies was prompted by the emergence of women's film festivals. Feminist film studies in general had a wider, often more sociological approach in studying female audiences and the position of women in the film industry, ranging from actresses, producers, and technicians to directors.

Informed by a (post)structuralist perspective, feminist film theory moved beyond reading the meaning of a film to analyzing the deep structures of how meaning is constructed. The main argument is that sexual difference – or gender – is paramount to creating meaning in film. Using insights from a Marxist critique of ideology, semiotics, psychoanalysis, and deconstruction, feminist film theory claims that cinema is more than just a reflection of social relations: film actively constructs meanings of sexual difference and sexuality. Into the late 1980s psychoanalysis was to be the dominant paradigm in feminist film theory, producing pertinent readings of many Hollywood genres like melodrama, film noir, horror, science fiction, and the action movie. In the 1990s feminist film theory moved away from a binary understanding of sexual difference to multiple perspectives, hybrid identities, and possible spectatorships. This resulted in an increasing concern with questions of ethnicity, masculinity, and queer sexualities. In the first decade of 2000 feminist film theory made room for new theoretical approaches, ranging from performance studies and phenomenology to Deleuzian studies. Feminist film theory was highly influential in the 1970s and 1980s, making a lasting impact on the wider fields of visual culture and cultural studies, especially with the study of woman-as-image and the male gaze.

Early feminist criticism in the 1960s was directed at sexist images of women in classical Hollywood films. Women were portrayed as passive sex objects or fixed in stereotypes oscillating between the mother ("Maria") and the whore ("Eve"). Such endlessly repeated images of women were considered to be objectionable distortions of reality, which would have a negative impact on the female spectator. Feminists called for positive images of women in cinema and a reversal of sexist schemes. With the advent of (post)structuralism, the insight dawned that positive images of women were not enough to change underlying structures in cinema. Hollywood cinema with its history of sexualized stereotypes of women and violence against women demanded a deeper understanding of its pernicious structures. Theoretical frameworks drawing on critiques of ideology, semiotics, psychoanalysis, and deconstruction proved more productive in analyzing the ways in which sexual difference is encoded in the visual and narrative structure of the film.

From semiotics, feminist film theory drew the insight that Hollywood cinema veils its ideological construction by hiding its means of production. Cinema film passes off the sign "woman" as natural or realistic, while it is in fact a structure, code, or convention carrying an ideological meaning. In patriarchal ideology the image of woman can only signify anything in relation to men. The sign "woman" is thus negatively represented as "not-man," which means that the "woman-as-woman" is absent from the film.

While semiotics moved feminist film theory away from a naïve understanding of stereotypes of women to the structures of gendered representation in visual culture, it was psychoanalysis that introduced the famous notion of the male gaze. In her groundbreaking article "Visual Pleasure and Narrative Cinema" (1975/1989), Laura Mulvey takes from Freud the notion of scopophilia, the pleasure of looking, to explain the fascination of Hollywood cinema. Films stimulate visual pleasure by integrating structures of voyeurism and narcissism into the story and the image. Voyeuristic visual pleasure is produced by looking at another, whereas narcissistic visual pleasure can be derived from self-identification with the figure in the image. Mulvey's analysis shows how both voyeurism and narcissism are gendered. Within the narrative of classical film male characters direct their gaze toward female characters. The spectator in the theater is made to identify with the male look, because the camera films from the optical, as well as libidinal, point of view of the male character. There are thus three levels of the cinematic gaze – camera, character, and spectator – objectifying the female character and turning her into a spectacle. Narcissistic visual pleasure works through identification: the spectator identifies with the perfected image of a human figure on the screen, usually the male hero. Both the voyeuristic gaze and narcissistic identification depend for their meaning upon the controlling power of the male character as well as on the objectified representation of the female character.

The account of "the male gaze" as a structuring logic in Western visual culture became controversial in the early 1980s, as it made no room for the female spectator or for a female gaze. Within the dichotomous categories of psychoanalytic theory it was virtually impossible to address female spectatorship; the female viewer could only identify with the male gaze. Hollywood's women's movies of the 1970s and 1980s allowed the female character to make the male character the object of her gaze, but her desire carried no power. Such films involved a mere reversal of roles in which the underlying structures of dominance and submission are still intact (Kaplan 1983). Some alternatives to identifying with a male gaze were theorized. The female spectator could adopt the masochism of overidentification or the narcissism entailed in becoming one's own object of desire. In this view, both the female character and the female spectator had to turn their active desire into a passive desire to be the desired object (Doane 1987).

The question of female spectatorship and the female look circles around the issue of subjectivity and desire. Subjectivity is understood as a constant process of self-production rather than as a fixed entity. Cinema, or visual culture at large, is considered an important means of constructing certain positions for female subjectivity by inscribing desire into the codes and conventions of the imagery and the narrative. In the 1980s feminist film theory considered the female subject in cinema an impossibility. In Hollywood movies "woman" functioned as a sign within an Oedipal narrative in which she could not be the subject of desire; instead she could only be represented as representation (de Lauretis 1984). The female character and through identification the female spectator are "seduced" into femininity.

Feminist film theory in the 1980s is then built on the very paradox of the unrepresentability of woman as subject of desire. Several feminist film critics have tried to theorize possible paths to female desire, still within the psychoanalytic framework, by a bisexual identification with the mother as love object which would then function as a potential, yet masochistic, source of visual pleasure. The female spectator could enjoy identification with the image of female beauty on the screen, for example in the figure of the autonomous vamp or the powerful femme fatale. Kaja Silverman (1988) drew attention to the auditory register rather than the visual regime to make room for a cultural fantasy of maternal enclosure. The acoustic voice created an opening for female desire within discourse and the symbolic order.

From these accounts it becomes clear that feminist film theory was much dominated by the discourse of both Freudian and Lacanian psychoanalysis. Although feminists have not always agreed about the usefulness of psychoanalysis, there has been general agreement about the limitations of an exclusive focus on sexual difference. One such limitation is the reproduction of a dichotomy, male/female, that needs to be deconstructed. Another limitation is the failure to focus on other differences such as class, race, age, and sexual preference.

Lesbian feminists were among the first to raise objections to the heterosexual bias of psychoanalytic feminist film theory, which seemed initially unable to conceive of representation outside heterosexuality. The shift away from the restrictive binary oppositions of psychoanalytic feminist film theory resulted in a more historical and cultural criticism of cinema by gay and lesbian critics. This involved re-readings of Hollywood cinema, for example of the implicit lesbianism of the female buddy film. The argument was advanced that the female spectator is quite likely to encompass erotic components in her desiring look, while at the same time identifying with the woman-as-spectacle. The homoerotic appeal of female Hollywood stars has been widely recognized.

Persistent critique of psychoanalytic film theory has also come from black feminism, which rebuked its exclusive focus on sexual difference and its failure to deal with racial difference. An inclusion of black feminist theory and of a historical approach into feminist film theory was necessary in order to understand how gender intersects with race and class in cinema (Gaines 1988; Young 1996). The influential feminist critic bell hooks (1992) argued that black viewers have always critically responded to Hollywood, allowing for an oppositional spectatorship for black women. Richard Dyer (1993) put forward that cinema constructs whiteness as the norm, by leaving it unmarked. The eerie property of whiteness to be nothing and everything at the same time is the source of its representational power.

In the 1990s masculinity studies addressed questions about the eroticization of the male body as erotic object. The image of the male body as the object of a – male or female – look is traditionally fraught with ambivalences, repressions, and denials. The notion of spectacle has such strong feminine connotations that for a male performer to be put on display threatens his very masculinity. In the last two decades other or new realms of visual culture, such as advertising and videoclips, have adopted objectification of the male body, which fed back into cinema. The eroticization of the male body is one of the profound changes in the visual culture of today.

Feminist film theory was not only concerned with a critique of Hollywood – or sometimes European – cinema, but was also interested in the question of a feminist cinema. In the wake of the revolutionary 1960s, feminists called initially for a counter-cinema that was rooted in avant-garde film practice. The idea was that only a deconstruction of classical visual and narrative codes and conventions could allow for an exploration of female subjectivity, gaze, and desire. Many films by women filmmakers were produced within an experimental mode, which received a lot of attention from feminist film theorists (Kuhn 1982). Gradually, women filmmakers started to develop women's films within the framework of popular cinema, trying to create new forms of visual and narrative pleasure (Smelik 1998).

The same development occurred for gay and lesbian cinema: from experimental films to more realist or romantic films for a more mainstream audience. Postmodernist cinema of the 1980s and 1990s brought campy strategies of gay subcultures into the mainstream. As of the 1990s, lesbians and gay men identify their oppositional reading strategies as "queer." Away from the notions of oppression and liberation of earlier gay and lesbian criticism, queerness is associated with the playful self-definition of homosexuality in non-essentialist terms. Not unlike camp, but more self-assertive, queer readings are fully inflected with irony, transgressive gender parody, and deconstructed subjectivities.

Feminist film theory lived through its heyday in the 1980s, after which it became less of a coherent corpus of thought by opening up to adjacent fields such as television, new media, visual culture, performance studies, and fashion studies. While the semiotic and psychoanalytical frameworks have long inspired film studies, they no longer have the explanatory force of understanding the complexity and paradoxes of contemporary visual culture, which has changed rapidly because of styles like postmodernism, developments in digital technology, and the advent of new media. New forms of cinematic aesthetics are breaking through the classic ("Oedipal") structures of representation and narration. Changes in cinema and developments in cultural theory asked for a new focus on experience, body, and affect. Important new sources for revitalizing feminist film theory are performance studies, new media theory, phenomenology, and a Deleuzian body of thought. These are theoretical frameworks that move beyond the semiotic preoccupation with meaning, representation, and interpretation. The focus on the sensory and emotional experience of the audiovisual medium of cinema operates away from the purely visual that often exclusively determined the orientation of film theory (Marks 2000). A Deleuzian approach allows for a less negative outlook on desire, subjectivity, and identity, opening up readings of film as embodying many forms of desire and creating experiences of affirmation for the spectator (Lin Tay 2009). Deleuze and Guattari refer to this process as a radical "becoming." In this way feminist film theory returns once again to the revolutionary attitude that started it all in the 1960s, creating space for the multiple becomings of the female character and the female spectator.

SEE ALSO: Camp; Feminism and Psychoanalysis; Gaze; Gender Stereotypes; Popular Culture and Gender; Visual Culture and Gender; Women as Producers of Culture

REFERENCES

de Lauretis, Teresa. 1984. *Alice Doesn't: Feminism, Semiotics, Cinema*. Bloomington: Indiana University Press.

Doane, Mary Ann. 1987. *The Desire to Desire: The Woman's Film of the 1940s*. Bloomington: Indiana University Press.

Dyer, Richard. 1993. *The Matter of Images: Essays on Representations*. London: Routledge.

Gaines, Jane. 1988. "White Privilege and Looking Relations: Race and Gender in Feminist Film Theory." *Screen*, 29(4): 12–27.

hooks, bell. 1992. *Black Looks: Race and Representation*. Boston: South End Press.

Kaplan, E. Ann. 1983. *Women and Film: Both Sides of the Camera*. New York: Methuen.

Kuhn, Annette. 1982. *Women's Pictures: Feminism and Cinema*. London: Routledge.

Lin Tay, Sharon. 2009. *Women on the Edge: Twelve Political Film Practices*. Basingstoke: Palgrave Macmillan.

Marks, Laura U. 2000. *The Skin of the Film: Intercultural Cinema, Embodiment, and the Senses*. Durham, NC: Duke University Press.

Mulvey, Laura. 1989. "Visual Pleasure and Narrative Cinema." In *Visual and Other Pleasures*,

14–26. London: Macmillan. First published 1975.

Silverman, Kaja. 1988. *The Acoustic Mirror: The Female Voice in Psychoanalysis and Cinema.* Bloomington: Indiana University Press.

Smelik, Anneke. 1998. *And the Mirror Cracked: Feminist Cinema and Film Theory.* Basingstoke: Palgrave Macmillan.

Young, Lola. 1996. *Fear of the Dark: "Race," Gender and Sexuality in the Cinema.* London: Routledge.

FURTHER READING

Dyer, Richard. 1990. *Now You See It: Studies on Lesbian and Gay Film.* London: Routledge.

Smelik, Anneke. 2009. "Lara Croft, *Kill Bill*, and Feminist Film Studies." In *Doing Gender in Media, Art and Culture*, edited by Rosemarie Buikema and Iris van der Tuin, 178–192. London: Routledge.

Feminist Jurisprudence

JILL MARSHALL
University of Leicester, UK

WOMEN AND LAW

Law has traditionally been associated with justice. However, what justice means and how it relates to law are disputed. At the same time, those working within the legal profession are commonly perceived as upholding its traditions and often the status quo, making it seem inherently conservative. Law is supposed to be neutral, objective, and impartial, blind to bias, with everyone equal before it.

Historically, like many professions, men have dominated it: indeed, women have been excluded from it. Perhaps as a consequence of the women's liberation movement of the 1960s and 1970s, women have been drawn to the profession so that the volume of women lawyers has significantly increased globally (Michelson 2013). Within this changing legal world, questions are increasingly asked about the way in which different types of people are viewed, reflected, and protected by and through law. Some work began to question different areas of the law to see how girls and women were legally perceived and treated. For example, in criminal law, what are the experiences of girls and women with rape allegations? How are sex workers treated? In employment law, how have women who are pregnant, or sexually harassed, been protected by law? Why are women and men not paid the same amount of money for work of equal value?

Despite women globally entering higher education, the legal profession, and its community in increasing numbers (UNESCO Institute for Statistics 2014), the proportion of women partners at large global law firms has not significantly increased, and the difference in salaries largely remains, in the legal profession and elsewhere. Women have the equal right to vote but are not equally represented in political or legal life. Women across the world continue to suffer from gender-based violence and unequal life chances (see in general www.un.org). In law, as a subject of study at university, academics in legal theory modules question the structure and underlying purpose of law. Some within this subject seek to investigate whether it is gendered in some way. Could questioning the *structure* of law show that it is somehow arranged to favor men's existence? As a generic form, feminist jurisprudence seeks to highlight such a gendered nature and the content of law in general, legal theory and the structure of law in particular.

THE GENDER OF LAW

Law seeks to encapsulate how people should be and/or are regulated in society. Some theorists seek to separate law analytically from other disciplines whereas others say this cannot be done. Feminist legal theorists vary in their approaches but more generally take an interdisciplinary approach, showing law's role in reflecting, creating, and sustaining an unfairly gendered world that is arranged to women's disadvantage. They often take an interpretive approach: while criticizing the law for its male bias, they seek to reconstruct it in some way to women's advantage. It is often claimed that the aim is gender equality and women's individual freedom. Yet these concepts are often interpreted in ways that pull in different directions.

Before elaborating further, it is highlighted and explained briefly that the term "feminist jurisprudence" is itself contested by some feminists working in this field.

One of the best-known feminist legal theorists, Professor Catharine MacKinnon, describes radical feminism, "feminism unmodified," as *the* Feminist Jurisprudence (with capital F and J) (MacKinnon 1987). In this view, as its focus examines structural patriarchy that exists in society globally, there is only one feminist theory of law. This concentrates on the way in which such structural patriarchy is reflected, enabled, and perpetuated in law. MacKinnon's early work on this compares feminism to Marxism: that which is most one's own, is that which is most taken away. In patriarchy, that "most one's own" and most taken away for women is our sex[uality]. As is explained more in what follows, many feminists take issue with the perspective that there is only one Feminist Jurisprudence, as such a view conveys any other perspective as wrong or untrue. They prefer to use the label "feminist legal theories," which they see as more pluralistic and inclusive (see, for example, Jackson and Lacey 2002).

DIFFERENT ORIENTATIONS OF FEMINIST JURISPRUDENCE

Feminist analysis of law takes on different forms. These have been described as "political orientations" (Jackson and Lacey 2002), or classifications of responses to legal life. In the latter, Roger Cotterrell categorizes feminist jurisprudence as one type of "jurisprudence of difference" (Cotterrell 2003). He analyzes liberal, radical, cultural, and anti-essentialist movements within feminist legal theory. Often these are instead labeled sameness, dominance, ethic of care, and postmodern feminism, respectively. These classifications are useful as an introduction to feminist jurisprudence. However, they can overlap and intermingle and often theorists are not easily classified into them. They are used here as an introductory tool.

LIBERAL FEMINIST LEGAL THEORY

Liberal feminism aims to ensure that women are included in the universal, in the human, so that justice, equality, and freedom are something of meaning to women as well as to men, to girls just as much as to boys. It seeks to include women within the existing paradigms of liberal thought to provide equality of opportunity and fairness to all equally.

For many, this is a practical feminism, one that works within existing structures while trying to transform them. It is based on the idea that we are all individual persons with lives to lead. It implies that an underlying personal freedom exists so that we should be enabled to live our own lives as we wish. For many women, this holds a great attraction as it is something that has eluded us throughout history. With this underlying individualism and personal freedom, this approach can fit into the existing worldview and into the world of law and rights. So, for example, feminists highlight how international human rights have not traditionally protected women from violence or harms happening to them *as women*. However, it has been and can continue to be reinterpreted in ways that do protect them. Such interpretations have occurred so that, for example, domestic violence and rape can now be classified as violations for which a state is held responsible under international human rights law.

Liberal feminism in law has been criticized as presenting a sameness approach: women may obtain some benefits if their lives are very similar to men's. The problem is highlighted that this perspective "allows" women admission to a "world already constituted" (Dalton 1988) and one that is suited to men's ways of living and being. If this is so, maybe women do not want to be so admitted, and maybe it is always going to mean that they will never be successful in obtaining equality if the comparator is a man's life. Liberal theory structures our lives into the public world of work and politics and the private world of the family and personal space. Carole Pateman provides a carefully crafted critique of this public/private divide, arguing that the division is dependent on women's "sexual contract" (Pateman 1988; see also Olsen 1995).

CULTURAL FEMINISM IN LAW

Instead of admission to a world already constituted, some argue that a "woman-centered" subject is the way forward. Based on the ethic of care work of psychologist Carol Gilligan, this type of feminist jurisprudence advocates for the recognition of a different voice by the legal system. In this view, this "voice" ought to be recognized, on at least equal terms to what is seen as the traditional image of legality, the ethic of justice: of balancing rights, of independent, abstract reasoning (Gilligan 1982). Gilligan had questioned a previous categorization of moral reasoning that appeared to show women and girls as lower in the scale from men and boys, as if the former were not reasoning properly when they were presented with a set of moral dilemmas.

The ethic of care, the different voice, is concerned with particular others, with looking at people in their actual contexts, in seeing that we exist in networks of relationships, and acknowledging our interconnection to and with others. Because women have traditionally been viewed as carers (of children and men), this has been criticized by Claudia Card as a "slave morality" (Card 1988) and as "morality in a higher register" by MacKinnon (1987). Rather than celebrating women's difference, is this an acceptance of oppression? Do more women traditionally think and feel in this caring and connected way because it suits men's interests for us to do so?

Whilst acknowledging the criticisms, many feminists caution against throwing out care. Is it not a good thing to care? (see, for example, Nussbaum 1999). Indeed, care ethics do not need to be gendered at all. Many use the theory without the emphasis on this being a "women's way of thinking" (see, for example, Herring 2013). This approach has been used in a variety of legal fields, including international relations (Held 2006), to produce more creative and imaginative ways of thinking about our world.

MULTICULTURALISM AND FEMINIST JURISPRUDENCE

In recent years, there have been calls from some feminist quarters to question the sympathetic move toward multiculturalism that is evident in many political and legal theories. This has sparked debates as to whether multiculturalism is bad for women (Okin 1999). After 9/11, much of the focus of these debates appears to be on Islam as some form of religion and/or producer of cultural practices that are said to oppress girls and women. However, we all come from and live within a culture and many feminists point out that most if not all of them are sexist. Feminists, often working in different parts of the world and from anti-neocolonial perspectives, seek to highlight that feminism needs to be careful not to patronize and judge people, including women who do not agree with their approaches and views.

RADICAL AND SOCIALIST FEMINISM

Radical feminism is strong in law. Following on from MacKinnon's early comparison between it and Marxism already mentioned, it focuses on the structural and social constructionist form of global patriarchy. This needs to be changed so that women are freed from oppression to be truly themselves. As in Marxism, our true essence will be revealed through history. The methodology for doing this is consciousness raising and the transformation of societies worldwide. With this view, celebrating difference is celebrating powerlessness (MacKinnon 1987). Law is a tool that can help aim toward this transformative end goal of gender equality. Although different from radical feminism, socialist feminism is Marxist, seeking to apply Marxism to women's lives as well as to men's to obtain the end goal of communism. Law is again instrumental to this goal.

ANTI-ESSENTIALISM IN FEMINIST JURISPRUDENCE

Radical and cultural feminist legal theories have a strong version of woman as a subject. Liberal and socialist feminism too remains in the modernist tradition with a strong sense of a universal subject aiming to achieve freedom. However, anti-essentialist feminists warn against the potential for authoritarian judgment in these other feminist theories. "Grand Theory" produces its own new "truths" that could end up being just as constraining as the male straightjacket it is aiming to replace (Smart 1989).

Instead of focusing on equality, difference, or dominance in a structural sense, how about following Foucault to focus on the way we are produced by and through power and technologies of the self? If gender is created then "gender trouble" can be too (Butler 1990). We could also show, like Derrida, that we need to deconstruct subjectivity, to find the "utopian moment" in finding an ethical way forward (see in particular Cornell 1992).

In this view, any authoritarian tendency needs to be avoided. In recent times, this has led some to call for us to "take a break from feminism" (Halley 2006). If we do this, as Janet Halley argues, theories can be used as and when appropriate, to produce the best results from a critical legal theory perspective. In doing this and "taking a break from one argument," we might be exposed to others, enabling new insights into power. Hence we face the "split decision," as in the title of Halley's book, about what to think and do.

In terms of the political unity and strength needed to be able to change the lives of real people for the better, some feminists are wary of taking a break from feminism when we live in a hierarchically gendered, unequal, violent, and dangerous world. They question such theories' potential to enable and strengthen feminist movements for change, and challenge the anti-essentialist "turn" which can fracture and lessen political activism (see, for example, Conaghan 2000). At the same time, though, many postmodern feminists *are* activists seeking political dynamic change. For these activists, context is important, and political activism does not need to depend on *one* view of feminism being the "best" or "true" or "real."

Aiming to make the lives of women better *now* can sometimes make reforms to overhaul and transform society and legal control in the *future* more difficult. For example, focusing on the present distribution of power and securing protection for women legally in this form can entrench stereotypes and existing ways of living which many may want to change. Feminist jurisprudence often runs into difficulties in somehow aiming for a more just and fair society for all, while at the same time some perceive these efforts as dictating to people how to "correct" their "bad" behavior.

SEE ALSO: Gender Justice; Gender, Politics, and the State: Overview

REFERENCES

Butler, Judith. 1990. *Gender Trouble: Feminism and the Subversion of Identity*. New York: Routledge.
Card, Claudia. 1988. "Review Essay: Women's Voices and Ethical Ideals: Must We Mean What We Say?" *Ethics*, 99(1): 125–135.
Conaghan, Joanne. 2000. "Reassessing the Feminist Theoretical Project in Law." *Journal of Law and Society*, 27(3): 351–385.
Cornell, Drucilla. 1992. *The Philosophy of the Limit*. New York: Routledge.
Cotterrell, Roger. 2003. *The Politics of Jurisprudence: A Critical Introduction to Legal Philosophy*, 2nd ed. Oxford: Oxford University Press.
Dalton, Clare. 1988. "Where We Stand: Observations on the Situation of Feminist Legal Thought." *Berkeley Women's Law Journal*, 3: 1–13.
Gilligan, Carol. 1982. *In a Different Voice: Psychological Theory and Women's Development*. Cambridge, MA: Harvard University Press.
Halley, Janet. 2006. *Split Decisions: How and Why to Take a Break from Feminism*. Princeton: Princeton University Press.
Held, Virginia. 2006. *The Ethics of Care: Personal, Political and Global*. Oxford: Oxford University Press.
Herring, Jonathan. 2013. *Caring and the Law*. Oxford: Hart.
Jackson, Emily, and Nicola Lacey. 2002. "Introducing Feminist Legal Theory." In *Jurisprudence and Legal Theory: Commentary and Materials*, edited by James E. Penner, David Schiff, and Richard Nobles, 779–853. Oxford: Oxford University Press.
MacKinnon, Catharine A. 1987. *Feminism Unmodified: Discourses on Life and Law*. Cambridge, MA: Harvard University Press.
Michelson, Ethan. 2013. "Women in the Legal Profession, 1970–2010: A Study of the Global Supply of Lawyers." *Indiana Journal of Global Legal Studies*, 20: 1071–1137.
Nussbaum, Martha C. 1999. *Sex and Social Justice*. Oxford: Oxford University Press.
Okin, Susan M. 1999. "Is Multiculturalism Bad for Women?" In *Is Multiculturalism Bad for Women? Susan Moller Okin with Respondents*, edited by Joshua Cohen, Matthew Howard, and Martha C. Nussbaum, 7–26. Princeton: Princeton University Press.
Olsen, Frances. 1995. "The Family and the Market: A Study of Ideology and Legal Reform, Part I." In *Feminist Legal Theory I: Foundations and Outlooks*, edited by Frances Olsen, 107–138; "Part III." In *Feminist Legal Theory II: Positioning Feminist Theory Within the Law*, edited by Frances Olsen, 509–527. New York: NYU Press.
Pateman Carole. 1988. *The Sexual Contract*. Cambridge: Polity Press.
Smart, Carol. 1989. *Feminism and the Power of Law*. New York: Routledge.
UNESCO Institute for Statistics. 2014. Women in Higher Education. Accessed June 13, 2014, at www.uis.unesco.org/Education/Pages/women-higher-education.aspx.

Feminist Literary Criticism

ERIN BELL
Wayne State University, Detroit, USA

Feminist literary criticism is a method for the analysis and interpretation of literary texts and other cultural productions through the lens of feminist theories. Just as the feminist political agenda has numerous objectives, the intentions of feminist literary theory are manifold; there is not a singular theory of feminist literary criticism, but numerous modes of intervention for textual analysis.

Feminist literary criticism engages in a number of consequential undertakings. While feminist literary critics may locate and explore the presence of feminist ideologies in literary texts, they may also expose how patriarchal ideologies are incorporated within representations. The literary canon, that is, the list of exceptional works of literature, was influenced by gender bias so that female writers were often overlooked or ignored, therefore feminist literary critics continue to revise this register by introducing female authors.

Feminist literary criticism also uncovers how the structure of literature can reveal a patriarchal impulse through the traditional narrative schema which moves from the exposition towards climax and resolution. Additionally, scholars in the field have demonstrated sexist language practices at the level of the word itself, belying latent male-centered textual practice in Western thought. Viewpoints that emphasize or privilege the male point of view are defined as phallocentric. Just as the feminist movement is often categorized into first, second, and third waves, feminist literary criticism is also organized into several iterations. Feminist literary criticism can be traced back as early as the work of English writer Mary Wollstonecraft, who critiqued inequalities between the sexes in the eighteenth century as well as in the literary works of her time.

By the mid-nineteenth century, women's suffrage was underway and the changing political climate of the first wave of feminism is reflected in the female literary criticism of the time. Many literary historians cite American author Margaret Fuller as a key figure in the development of American feminist literary criticism. Fuller was affiliated with the American Transcendental Movement and published *Women in the Nineteenth Century* in 1845, a short text which proposed equality between genders and critiqued sexist practices in American society.

Though some studies also cite British author and journalist Rebecca West as an early feminist literary critic, arguably the most significant scholar and feminist literary critic of the early twentieth century is Virginia Woolf (1981). A prolific writer of fiction and criticism, Woolf's *A Room of One's Own* remains a canonical text in feminist studies. In this extended essay Woolf argues that the emotional and physical burdens of maternity combined with a lack of financial freedom negatively impact women's ability to write great fiction. Woolf also elucidates how male writers have not always adequately represented the female experience. In addition, *A Room of One's Own* also includes an account of noteworthy female authors, thereby establishing a women's literary history.

While Woolf's text stands as an important touchstone, many of the concepts that became the groundwork for feminist literary studies as we understand it today sprang from French feminists of the second wave. Simone de Beauvoir's *Le Deuxième Sexe* or *The Second Sex* (1949) is considered a seminal text in contemporary feminist literary studies. Here, de Beauvoir critiques women's position in society as inferior as mandated by patriarchy, arguing that: "One is not born, but rather becomes, a woman." de Beauvoir also critiques representations in *The Second Sex*, claiming that most representations – literary and otherwise – are the work of men, and therefore skewed toward a phallocentric point of view. As such, de Beauvoir's claim became an important point of intervention to study literary texts in order to uncover how literary representations have been written from the male point of view.

French feminists Luce Irigaray, Hélène Cixous, and Julia Kristeva also greatly influenced and developed feminist literary criticism by focusing on how language itself is an instrument of patriarchal dominance. Cixous's essay "The Laugh of the Medusa" (1976) argues that women have been repressed throughout history, and so they may either remain trapped within a phallocentric system of representation or work toward using the female body as a mode of unique communication. For Cixous, such a mode of expression is *écriture féminine*, or female/feminine writing. Psychoanalytic and cultural theorist Luce Irigaray explores similar conceptions of writing from the body, likewise gesturing toward the conception of a distinct, feminine mode of expression in her *The Speculum of the Other Woman* (1974) and *This Sex Which is Not One* (1977). Julia Kristeva published her *Semiotike* in 1969. Kristeva writes extensively about the maternal body as well as the pre-oedipal stage of human development in relationship to female subjectivity. Her theoretical conceptions of women's time as well as of the abject are both frequently cited in feminist literary critiques.

In the 1970s and 1980s, North American feminist literary critics evaluated texts through close readings and analysis in order to expose latent and overt misogynistic themes in texts while others practiced "gynocriticism" in order to determine how women write about women. Annette Kolodny (1975), however, explored how a unified theory of feminist literary criticism had yet to be defined. Elaine Showalter (1981) continued to explore this subject as well as the ramifications of feminist literary critique. Though second-wave feminist theory offered numerous modes for engaging with texts, by the 1980s feminist literary criticism itself was critiqued for a number of reasons, particularly that many examples of such criticism privileged a white, middle-class, heterosexual point of view and that some critics relied upon the idea of a universal or essential feminism which suggests women are similar based on biology alone.

Just as third-wave feminism works toward thinking about feminism within a global context, third-wave and contemporary feminist literary theory moves beyond conceptualizing feminism in terms of white, heterosexual women. Gloria Anzaldúa (2007) explores the ramifications of bilingual discursive modes through the voices of mestiza women, and African American feminist theorists such as Barbara Christian, Alice Walker (1983), bell hooks, and Audre Lorde (1984) locate the role of race in discursive practices and in feminist theory. Materialist feminist and radical lesbian Monique Wittig (1992) demonstrates the flaws in assuming that feminism is contingent upon heterosexuality, arguing that the term "women" is defined by men. Wittig also suggests that lesbians are not women, as the current definition of women is defined only through a heterosexual schematic.

Considering the numerous points of view in feminist literary criticism, there is not necessarily a uniform or singular feminist literary theory. Instead, feminist literary critics continue to locate and explore numerous ways in which gender has a role in epistemologic practices and representations, locating a plurality of points of interventions with texts.

SEE ALSO: Cognitive Critical and Cultural Theory; Discursive Theories of Gender; Feminism, French; Feminism and Psychoanalysis; Feminisms, First, Second, and Third Wave; Gender Bias; Gynocriticism; Phallocentrism and Phallogocentrism; Structuralism, Feminist Approaches to; Women's Writing

REFERENCES

Anzaldúa, Gloria. 2007. *Borderlands/La Frontera: The New Mestiza*. San Francisco: Aunt Lute Books.

Cixous, Hélène. 1976. "The Laugh of the Medusa," translated by Keith Cohen and Paula Cohen. *Signs*, 1: 875–893.

de Beauvoir, Simone. 1993. *The Second Sex*, translated and edited by H. M. Parshley. New York: Alfred A. Knopf. First published 1949.

Kolodny, Annette. 1975. "Some Notes on Defining a 'Feminist Literary Criticism.'" *Critical Inquiry*, 2: 75–92.

Lorde, Audre. 1984. "The Master's Tools Will Never Dismantle the Master's House." *Sister Outsider: Essays and Speeches*, 110–114. Berkeley: Crossing Press.
Showalter, Elaine. 1981. "Feminist Criticism in the Wilderness." *Critical Inquiry*, 8: 179–205.
Walker, Alice. 1983. *In Search of Our Mother's Gardens*. Orlando: Harcourt.
Wittig, Monique. 1992. *The Straight Mind and Other Essays*. New York: Harvester Wheatsheaf.
Woolf, Virginia. 1981. *A Room of One's Own*. New York: Harcourt. First published 1929.

FURTHER READING

Christian, Barbara. 1988. "The Race for Theory." *Feminist Studies*, 14: 67–79.
Moraga, Cherríe, and Gloria Anzaldúa. 1981. *This Bridge Called My Back: Writings by Radical Women of Color*. Watertown: Persephone Press.

Feminist Magazines

ELIZABETH GROENEVELD
Old Dominion University, USA

Feminist magazines have been part of the feminist and women's rights movement from the 1850s onwards. These publications have been used to influence government policy, attract new supporters, and document the movement. Each upsurge of feminist activism has been accompanied by a rise in magazine publishing by feminists. The magazines may introduce readers to feminism and keep readers up-to-date with the debates and events within the various strands of the movement, and can help to engender momentum or growth. The generic conventions of magazines – the editorial voice, the use of the collective "we," and the "letters to the editor" section – help cultivate a sense of community.

Classic feminist scholarship has analyzed magazines in terms of the ideological messages conveyed to readers, while other scholars have built on these studies through either discursive analyses or ethnographic sociological approaches that engage more directly with readers' responses to periodical texts. Other scholars engage with the important role that economic formations play in the lives of feminist magazines.

The first women's rights magazines were established in the nineteenth century, often in conjunction with the suffrage movement. In addition to suffrage, these periodicals discussed a variety of topics, including women's education, divorce, property rights, dress reform, and domesticity. Some of the major publications from this era in the United States were *The Lily* (1849–1858); *The Woman's Advocate* (1855–1858/1860); *The Una* (1853–1855); *The Genius of Liberty* (1851–1853); *The Revolution* (1868–1870); *The Queen Bee* (1882–1895); *The Agitator* (1869); *The Woman's Journal* (1870–1931); *The Woman's Chronicle* (1888–1893); *The New Northwest* (1871–1887); and *The Woman's Tribune* (1883–1909). In the United Kingdom, women's rights magazines included the *English Woman's Journal* (1858–1864); the *Englishwoman's Review* (1866–1910); and *The Woman's Signal* (1894–1899). Additional publications established during the nineteenth century were the Norwegian publication *Nylænde* (1887–1927); Denmark's *Kvinden and Samfundet* (1885–); Australia's *The Dawn* (1888–1950); and the Egyptian *Al Fatat* (1892–1994). In the late nineteenth and early twentieth centuries, developments in the magazine industry offered both new opportunities and new challenges for these publications. Late nineteenth- and early twentieth-century publications were often more geographically diverse than their predecessors and carried national and international news stories pertaining to the women's movement.

The second feminist "wave" in the 1960s and 1970s again saw a burgeoning of feminist publications. Cynthia Ellen Harrison's sourcebook of feminist periodicals, including newsletters of various feminist organizations, lists almost 200 Canadian and American publications in circulation in 1975 alone. This was a period of major growth for independent media, a change due in part to increasingly easy access to the technologies of mass production.

Second-wave periodicals were as numerous in their foci as their number. Feminist publications ranged from lesbian magazines, such as *Amazon Quarterly* (1972–1975) and *Sinister Wisdom* (1976–1994); to publications for women over age 40, including *Broomstick* (1978–1993) and *Primetime* (1971–1977); to periodicals for women of color, such as *Revista Mujeres* (1984–?), *Sage: a Scholarly Journal on Black Women* (1983–), and *Third Woman* (n.d.); to professional publications such as *Medica* (n.d.), and *Harvard Women's Law Journal* (n.d.); to political magazines such as *Second Wave* (n.d.) and *Woman: a Journal of Liberation* (1969–); to radical feminist publications *off our backs* (or *oob*) (1970–), *No More Fun and Games* (1968–1973), and *Notes from the First Year* (1968–1971). While these publications emerged from a US context, *Opzij* (1972–), *Spare Rib* (1972–1993), *Herizons* (1979–), and *Emma* (1977–) began publishing from The Netherlands, the United Kingdom, Canada, and Germany, respectively, during the same period.

Most of the scholarly work on periodicals from this era is centered on *Ms.* magazine, which was the first openly feminist magazine that entered the marketplace with the dual goal of competing directly with non-feminist women's magazines and reforming the magazine industry from within. *Ms.* is the longest running feminist magazine and has had many incarnations – from commercial to not-for-profit publication; from its initial acceptance of non-sexist advertisements, to its metamorphosis into an advertisement-free publication.

One of the major subgenres of feminist magazines is arts, literature, and culture publications. In the United States, examples of this genre include the literary journal *Aphra* (1969–1975), the *Feminist Art Journal* (1972–1977), *Blatant Image* (1981–1983), and *Calyx* (1976–). Publications outside the United States include Canada's *Makara* (1975–1978), Sweden's *Bang* (1991–), Austria's *An. Schlage* (2000–), Japan's *Image and Gender* (2000–2007), and the UK-based women writers' magazine *Mslexia* (1999–).

Beginning in the early 1990s, a new kind of feminist publication appeared: the "third-wave" feminist magazine. These periodicals – *BUST* (1993–), *Bitch* (1996–), *HUES* (1992–1999), *Venus Zine* (1994–2010), and *ROCKRGRL* (1995–2006) – began as independently produced small-scale zines and were also inspired by the mass circulation girls' magazine *Sassy* (1988–1996). *Sassy* was not an overtly feminist publication, but it did run content that was inflected by feminism, and was generally considered more socially progressive than the other teen magazines that were its contemporaries. Third-wave feminist magazines cover topics ranging from popular culture to fashion, to domesticity, to the arts. There were other late twentieth-century feminist magazines that neither started as zines nor fit into a Western-based "wave" framework: these include Iran's *Zanan* (1992–2008) and *Bad Jens* (2000–2004) and the UK-based *Harpies and Quines* (1992–1994).

The early twentieth century saw the emergence of a new cohort of feminist magazines, such as Canada's *Shameless* (2004–), the US-based *RookieMag* (2010–), and the UK-based *Mookychick* (2005–), which are all published for teenage girls, and also the US-based *Make/Shift* (2007–), *The Vagenda* (2012–) in the United Kingdom, and *GUTS Canadian Feminist Magazine* (2013–). Whereas *Shameless* and *Make/Shift* publish both in print and online, *RookieMag*, *Mookychick*, and *The Vagenda* publish exclusively online. With little exception, all currently publishing feminist magazines are hybrids of print and online content.

SEE ALSO: Feminist Activism; Popular Culture and Gender

FURTHER READING

Butcher, Patricia S. 1989. *Education for Equality: Women's Rights Periodicals and Women's Higher Education, 1849–1920*. Contributions in Women's Studies. Westport: Greenwood Press.
Endres, Kathleen L., and Therese L. Lueck, eds. 1996. *Women's Periodicals in the United States: Social and Political Issues*. Historical Guides to the World's Periodicals and Newspapers. Westport: Greenwood Press.
Farrell, Amy E. 1998. *Yours in Sisterhood: Ms. Magazine and the Promise of Popular Feminism*. Chapel Hill: University of North Carolina Press.
Groeneveld, Elizabeth. 2015. *Making Public Cultures: Feminist Magazines on the Cusp of the Digital Age*. Waterloo, ON: Wilfred Laurier University Press.
Harrison, Cynthia E. 1975. *Women's Movement Media: a Sourcebook*. New York: Bowker.

Feminist Methodology

NANCY A. NAPLES
University of Connecticut, USA

Feminist methodology is the approach to research that has been developed in response to concerns by feminist scholars about the limits of traditional methodology to capture the experiences of women and others who have been marginalized in academic research. Feminist methodology includes a wide range of methods, approaches, and research strategies. Beginning in the early 1970s, feminist scholars critiqued positivist scientific methods that reduced lived experiences to a series of disconnected variables that did not do justice to the complexities of social life. Feminists were also among the first scholars to highlight the marginalization of women of color in academic research and to offer research strategies that would counter this trend within academia (Baca Zinn 1979; Collins 1990). Feminist scholars also stress the importance of intersectional analysis, an approach that highlights the intersection of race, class, gender, and sexuality in examining women's lives (Crenshaw 1993). Some of the earliest writing on feminist methodology emphasized the connection between "feminist consciousness and feminist research," which is the subtitle of a 1983 edited collection by Stanley and Wise. Over the years, feminist methodology has developed a very broad vision of research practice that can be used to study a wide range of topics, to analyze both men's and women's lives, and to explore both local and transnational or global processes.

Feminist sociologists like Dorothy Smith (1987) pointed out that the taken-for-granted research practices associated with positivism rendered invisible or domesticated women's work as well as their everyday lives. She argued for a sociology for women that would begin in their everyday lives. Feminist philosopher Sandra Harding (1987, 1998) has also written extensively about the limits of positivism and argues for an approach to knowledge production that incorporates the point of view of feminist and postcolonial theoretical and political concerns. She stresses that traditional approaches to science fail to acknowledge how the social context and perspectives of those who generate the questions, conduct the research, and interpret the findings shape what counts as knowledge and how data is interpreted. Instead, she argues for a holistic approach that includes greater attention to the knowledge production process and to the role of the researcher. Harding and Smith both critique the androcentric nature of academic knowledge production. They argue for the importance of starting analysis from the lived experiences and activities of women and others who have been left out of the knowledge production process rather than start inquiry with the abstract categories and a priori assumptions of traditional academic disciplines or dominant social institutions.

In 1991, sociologists Mary Margaret Fonow and Judith A. Cook published a collection of essays in a book titled *Beyond Methodology: Feminist Scholarship as Lived Research*. The authors in this collection discussed how different methodological techniques could be used to capture the complexities of gender as it intersects with race, sexuality, and class. The authors also explored the ethical dilemmas faced by feminist researchers, such as: How does a researcher negotiate power imbalance between the researcher and researched? What responsibilities do researchers have to those they study? How does participatory research influence analytic choices during a research study? Feminist scholars have consistently raised such questions, suggesting that if researchers fail to explore how their personal, professional, and structural positions frame social scientific investigations, researchers inevitably reproduce dominant gender, race, and class biases (see Naples 2003).

Fonow and Cook (2005) revisited the themes that were prevalent when they wrote *Beyond Methodology* and highlighted the continuity and differences in the themes that dominate discussions of feminist methodology at the beginning of the twenty-first century. They found that the concerns about reflexivity of the researcher, transparency of the research process, and women's empowerment remained central concerns in contemporary feminist methodology. They also point out the continuity in the multiple methods that are utilized by feminist researchers, which include participatory research, ethnography, discourse analysis, comparative case study, cross-culture analysis, conversation analysis, oral history, participant observation, and personal narrative. However, they note that contemporary feminist researchers are more likely to use sophisticated quantitative methods than they were in the 1980s and 1990s.

Another important text that provides an overview of feminist methods in the social sciences is that of Reinharz (1992). Following a comprehensive review of feminist methods with illustrations from diverse feminist studies, Reinharz identifies 10 features that appear in efforts by feminist scholars to distinguish how their research methods differ from traditional approaches. These include the following: (1) feminism is a point of view, not a particular method; (2) feminist methodology consists of multiple methods; (3) feminist researchers offer a self-reflective understanding of their role in the research; and (4) a central goal of feminist research is to contribute to social changes that would improve women's lives. The themes of reflexivity and research for social change are two of the most important aspects of feminist methodology that distinguishes it from other modes of research.

REFLEXIVITY

Reflective practice and reflexivity include an array of strategies that begin when one first considers conducting a research project. Reflective practices can be employed throughout the research process and implemented on different levels, ranging from remaining sensitive to the perspectives of others and how we interact with them, to a deeper recognition of the power dynamics that infuse ethnographic encounters. By adopting reflective strategies, feminist researchers work to reveal the inequalities and processes of domination that shape the research process. Wolf (1996) emphasizes that power is evident in the research process in three ways: first, the differences in power between the researcher and those she or he researches in terms of race, class, nationality, among other dimensions; second, the power to define the relationship and the potential to exploit those who are the subjects of the research; and third, the power to construct the written account and therefore shape how research subjects are represented in the text. Feminist researchers argue that dynamics of power influence how problems are defined, which knowers are identified and are given credibility, how interactions are interpreted, and how ethnographic narratives are constructed. Feminist researchers stress that if researchers fail to explore how their personal, professional, and structural positions frame social scientific investigations, researchers inevitably reproduce dominant gender, race, and class biases.

Harding (1987) argues for a self-reflexive approach to theorizing in order to foreground how relations of power may be shaping the production of knowledge in different contexts. The point of view of all those involved in the knowledge production process must be acknowledged and taken into account in order to produce what she terms "strong objectivity," an approach to objectivity that contrasts with weaker and unreflective positivist approaches. In this way, knowledge production should involve a collective process, rather than the individualistic, top-down, and distanced approach that typifies the traditional scientific method. For Harding, strong objectivity involves analysis of the relationship between both the subject and object of inquiry. This approach contrasts with traditional scientific method that either denies this relationship or seeks to achieve control over it. However, as Harding and other feminist theorists point out, an approach to research that produces a more objective approach acknowledges the partial and situated nature of all knowledge production (see Collins 1990). Although not a complete solution to challenging inequalities in the research process, feminist researchers have used reflective strategies effectively to become aware of, and diminish the ways in which domination and repression are reproduced in the course of their research and in the products of this work. Furthermore, feminist researchers argue, sustained attention to these dynamics can enrich research accounts as well as improve the practice of social research (Naples 2003).

Feminist ethnography and feminist work with narratives are two of the methods in which feminist researchers have been the most concerned with processes of reflexivity. Examining work that utilizes both of these methods, the range of approaches that count as feminist is especially evident. For example, Chase's (1995) approach to oral narratives includes attention to the way women narrate their stories. Rather than treat the narratives as "evidence" in an unmediated sense of the term, Chase is interested in exploring the relationship between culture, experience, and narrative. Her work on women school superintendents examines how women use narrative strategies to make sense of their everyday life experiences as shaped by different cultural contexts. In contrast, Bloom (1998) adopts a "progressive-regressive method" derived from Sartre's notion of "spirals" in a life to examine how the individual can overcome her or his social and cultural conditioning, "thereby manifesting what he calls 'positive praxis.'" Drawing on Dorothy Smith's institutional ethnographic method, DeVault (1999) utilizes narratives she generates from ethnographic interviews to explore how relations of ruling are woven into women's everyday lives such that they are hidden from the view of those whose lives are organized by these processes of domination. The institutional and political knowledges that DeVault uncovers illustrate the link between institutional ethnography and feminist activism. In the context of activist research, feminist analysts using Smith's approach explore the institutional forms and procedures, informal organizational processes, as well as discursive frames used to construct the goals and targets of the work that the institution performs. This approach ensures that a commitment to the political goals of the women's movement remains central to feminist research by foregrounding how ruling relations work to organize everyday life. With a "thick" understanding of "how things are put together" it becomes possible to identify effective activist interventions.

POSTCOLONIAL AND POSTMODERN CHALLENGES

The call for reflective practice has also been informed by the critiques of third world and postcolonial feminist theorists who argue for self-reflexive understanding of the epistemological investments that shape the politics of method (Alexander and Mohanty 1997). Postmodern and postcolonial critiques of the practice of social scientific research raise a number of dilemmas that challenge feminist researchers as they attempt to conduct research that makes self-evident the assumptions and politics involved in the process of knowledge production in order to avoid exploitative research practices. Postmodern feminist scholars emphasize the ways disciplinary discourses shape how researchers see the worlds they investigate. They point out that without recognition of disciplinary metanarratives, research operates to reinsert power relations, rather than challenge them. Many feminist researchers have grappled with the challenges posed by postmodern critics. Wolf (1996) explains that for some feminist scholars postmodern theories provide opportunities for innovation in research practices, particularly in the attention they pay to representation of research participants or research subjects and to the written products that are produced from a research study. However, many other feminist scholars are concerned that too much emphasis on the linguistic and textual constructions decenters those who are the subjects of our research and renders the lives of women or others whom we study irrelevant.

Postmodern analyses of power have destabilized the practice of research, especially research that involves human subjects. If power infects every encounter and if discourse infuses all expressions of personal experience, what can the researcher do to counter such powerful forces? This dilemma is at the heart of a radical postmodern challenge to social scientific practice in general, but has been taken up most seriously in feminist research. Naples (2003) argues that one partial solution to this dilemma is to foreground praxis, namely, to generate a materialist feminist approach informed by postmodern and postcolonial analyses of knowledge, power, and language that speaks to the empirical world in which one's research takes place. For example, in her work, by foregrounding the everyday world of poor women of different racial and ethnic backgrounds in both the rural and urban United States and by exploring the governing practices that shape their lives, she has worked to build a class-conscious and anti-racist methodological approach (see also Alexander and Mohanty 1997).

While postmodern and postcolonial feminist scholars point to the myriad ways relations of domination infuse feminist research, they also offer some guidance for negotiating power inherent in the practice of fieldwork. For example, Mohanty (1991) calls for "focused, local analyses" to counter the trend in feminist scholarship to distance from or misrepresent third world women's concerns. Alexander and Mohanty (1997) recommend "grounding analyses in particular, local feminist praxis" as well as understanding "the local in relation to larger, cross-national processes."

RESEARCH FOR SOCIAL CHANGE

A consistent goal expressed by those who adopt feminist methodology is to create knowledge for social-change purposes. The emphasis on social action has influenced the type of methods utilized by feminist researchers as well as the topics chosen for study. For example, feminists have utilized participatory action research to help empower subjects of research as well as to ensure that the research is responsive to the needs of specific communities or to social movements (Reinharz 1992; Naples 2003; Fonow and Cook 2005). This approach to research is also designed to diminish the power differentials between the researcher and those who are the subjects of the research. In an effort to democratize the research process, many activist researchers argue for adopting participatory strategies that involve community residents or other participants in the design, implementation, and analysis of the research. Collaborative writing also broadens the perspectives represented in the final product.

A wide array of research strategies and cultural products can serve this goal. Yet such strategies and cultural products can be of more or less immediate use for specific activist agendas. For example, activist research includes chronicling the history of activists, activist art, diverse community actions, and social movements. Such analyses are often conducted after the completion of a specific struggle or examine a wide range of different campaigns and activist organizations. This form of research on activism is extremely important for feminists working toward a broadened political vision of women's activism and can help generate new strategies for coalition-building. However, these studies may not answer specific questions activists have about the value of certain strategies for their particular political struggles. Yet these broad-based feminist historical and sociological analyses do shed new light on processes of politicization, diversity, and continuity in political struggles over time.

On the one hand, many activists could be critical of these apparently more "academic" constructions of activism, especially since the need for specific knowledges to support activist agendas frequently goes unmet. The texts in which such analyses appear are often not widely available and further create a division between feminists located within the academy and community-based activists. On the other hand, many activist scholars have developed linkages with activists and policy arenas in such a way as to effectively bridge the so-called activist/scholar divide. Ronnie Steinberg brought her sociological research skills to campaigns for comparable worth and pay equity. She reports on the moderate success of the movement for comparable worth and the significance of careful statistical analyses for supporting changes in pay and job classifications. As one highlight, she reports that in 1991 systematic standards for assessing job equity developed with her associate Lois Haignere were translated into guidelines for gender-neutral policies incorporated by the Ontario Pay Equity Tribunal. In another example of feminist activist research, Roberta Spalter-Roth and Heidi Hartmann testified before Congress and produced policy briefs as well as more detailed academic articles to disseminate their findings about low-income women's economic survival strategies. Measures of a rigid positivism are often used to undermine feminists' credibility in legal and legislative settings. Even more problematic, research generated for specific activist goals may be misappropriated by those who do not share feminist political perspectives to support anti-feminist aims. For example, proponents of "workfare" programs for women on public assistance could also use Spalter-Roth and Hartmann's analysis of welfare recipients' income-packaging strategies to further justify coercive "welfare to work" measures.

Some feminist scholars working directly in local community actions have also brought their academic skills to bear on specific community problems or have trained community members to conduct feminist activist research. Terry Haywoode (1991) worked as an educator and community organizer alongside women in her Brooklyn community and helped establish the National Congress of Neighborhood Women's (NCNW) college program, a unique community-based program in which local residents can earn a two-year Associates degree in neighborhood studies. By promoting women's educational growth and development within an activist community organization, NCNW's college program helped enhance working-class women's political efficacy in struggles to improve their neighborhood.

CONCLUSION

Feminist methodology was developed in the context of diverse struggles against hegemonic modes of knowledge production that render women's lives, and those of other marginal groups, invisible or dispensable. Within the social sciences, feminist researchers have raised questions about the separation of theory and method, the gendered biases inherent in positivism, and the hierarchies that limit who can be considered the most appropriate producers of theoretical knowledge. Feminist reconceptualizations of knowledge production processes have contributed to a shift in research practices in many disciplines, and require more diverse methodological and self-reflective skills than traditional methodological approaches. However, some feminist scholars question whether or not it is possible to develop a reflexive practice that can fully attend to all the different manifestations of power (Stacey 1991). However, since feminist methodology is open to critique and responsive to the changing dynamics of power that shape women's lives and those of others who have been traditionally marginalized within academia, feminist researchers often act as innovators who are quick to develop new research approaches and frameworks.

ACKNOWLEDGMENT

This entry is based in part on a previously published entry by Nancy Naples: N. A. Naples, "Feminist Methodology," in G. Ritzer (ed.), *Blackwell Encyclopedia of Sociology*, Blackwell Publishing, UK, 2007. Reproduced with permission.

SEE ALSO: Black Feminist Thought; Consciousness-Raising; Feminism, Postcolonial; Feminist Standpoint Theory; Intersectionality; Matrix of Domination; Outsider Within; Strong Objectivity; Subaltern; Third World Women

REFERENCES

Alexander, M. Jacqui, and Chandra T. Mohanty. 1997. "Introduction: Genealogies, Legacies, Movements." In *Feminist Genealogies, Colonial Legacies, Democratic Futures*, xiii–xlii. New York: Routledge.

Baca Zinn, Maxine. 1979. "Field Research in Minority Communities: Ethical, Methodological, and Political Observations by an Insider." *Social Problems*, 27: 209–219.

Bloom, Leslie R. 1998. *Under the Sign of Hope: Feminist Methodology and Narrative Interpretation*. Albany: State University of New York Press.

Chase, Susan E. 1995. *Ambiguous Empowerment: The Work Narratives of Women School Superintendents*. Amherst: University of Massachusetts Press.

Collins, Patricia Hill. 1990. *Black Feminist Thought: Knowledge, Consciousness, and the Politics of Empowerment*. Boston, MA: Unwin Hyman.

Crenshaw, Kimberlé. 1993. "Mapping the Margins: Intersectionality, Identity Politics, and Violence against Women of Color." *Stanford Law Review*, 43: 1241–1299.

DeVault, Marjorie. 1999. *Liberating Method: Feminism and Social Research*. Philadelphia, PA: Temple University Press.

Fonow, Mary M., and Cook, Judith A., eds. 1991. *Beyond Methodology: Feminist Scholarship as Lived Research*. Bloomington: Indiana University Press.

Fonow, Mary M., and Cook, Judith A. 2005. "Feminist Methodology: New Applications in the Academy and Public Policy." *Signs: Journal of Women in Culture and Society*, 30(4): 221–236.

Harding, Sandra P., ed. 1987. *Feminism and Methodology*. Bloomington: Indiana University Press.

Harding, Sandra P. 1998. *Is Science Multicultural? Postcolonialisms, Feminisms, and Epistemologies*. Bloomington: Indiana University Press.

Haywoode, Terry. 1991. "Working Class Feminism: Creating a Politics of Community, Connection, and Concern." PhD dissertation, City University of New York.

Mohanty, Chandra T. 1991. "Under Western Eyes: Feminist Scholarship and Colonial Discourses." In *Third World Women and the Politics of Feminism*, edited by Chandra T. Mohanty, Ann Russo, and Lourdes Torres, 51–80. Bloomington: Indiana University Press.

Naples, Nancy A. 2003. *Feminism and Method: Ethnography, Discourse Analysis, and Activist Research*. New York: Routledge.

Reinharz, S. 1992. *Feminist Methods in Social Research*. New York: Oxford University Press.

Smith, Dorothy E. 1987. *The Everyday World as Problematic: A Feminist Sociology*. Toronto: University of Toronto Press.

Spalter-Roth, Roberta, Heidi Hartmann, and Linda Andrews. 1992. *Combining Work, and Welfare: An Anti-Poverty Strategy*. Washington, DC: Institute for Women's Policy Research.

Stacey, Judith. 1991. "Can There Be a Feminist Ethnography?" In *Women's Words*, edited by Sherna Gluck and Daphne Patai, 111–119. New York: Routledge.

Stanley, Liz, and Sue Wise, eds. 1983. *Breaking Out: Feminist Consciousness and Feminist Research*. London: Routledge and Kegan Paul.

Wolf, Diane L. 1996. "Situating Feminist Dilemmas in Fieldwork." In *Feminist Dilemmas in Fieldwork*, edited by Diane L. Wolf, 1–55. Boulder, CO: Westview Press.

Feminist Movements in Historical and Comparative Perspective

ANNULLA LINDERS
University of Cincinnati, USA

Women have long critiqued the social order that prevents them from participating fully in public and intellectual life, but what we today refer to as the feminist movement has its origins in the late eighteenth century. It paralleled and intersected in various ways with the revolutionary movements for democracy and equality that swept Western Europe and North America but distinguished itself early on for its focus on women's lives. As the movement has grown and spread over the past two centuries, both socially and geographically, its character has changed, its members have diversified, and its goals and ambitions have multiplied.

At its core, however, it has remained committed to improving the social conditions that bring hardship to women and prevent women from determining the contours of their own lives. This observation does not suggest that adherents to the feminist movement are always in agreement concerning either the problems to be addressed or the solutions to fight for – on the contrary. For this reason, it is best to think of the feminist movement as a series of loosely connected networks of organizations, groups, and individuals that pursue a range of issues that do not always align with each other and sometimes are in direct conflict with each other. Nonetheless, it does mean that, whatever the particular issues and goals, women play significant roles both in formulating them and enacting them. In this sense, the most enduring and defining characteristic of the feminist movement is precisely that it is pursued by women, originates in women's lives, and targets women as the primary beneficiaries of social transformation. The emphasis on the necessary link between situated knowledge, experience, and activism is generally termed "feminist praxis" (Stanley 1990).

Another defining characteristic of the feminist movement is the blurring of the lines between activism and scholarship. Not only is women's entry into institutions of higher learning preceded by women's demands to get such access but also the scholarship they pursue once on the inside is not only inspired by women's lives but is also aimed at filling the big voids in scholarship that the omission of women and their experiences as both targets and generators of research has produced. Theoretically, this means that knowledge about women generally and the feminist movement specifically cannot be entirely separated from feminist activism. In this view, then, knowledge is never neutral but always produced from a particular perspective (Harding 2004).

After a brief summary of the historical development of the feminist movement, some of the tensions and diversity that have pervaded the feminist movement since its inception are discussed and then more recent developments of scholarship and activism are addressed, some of them linked to processes of globalization and some to new coalitions and novel forms of activism. The definition of feminist movements that guides the discussion is broad and encompassing, aimed at capturing a wide range of women's activism, whether or not that activism is always self-consciously feminist.

I. THE HISTORY AND DEVELOPMENT OF THE FEMINIST MOVEMENT

Although women have long recognized and resisted the constraints placed on their lives due to their gender, the feminist movement as we know it was born in the late eighteenth and early nineteenth century. From its inception, the movement was marked by differences and conflicts among women, both within and across particular social contexts. This means that there is neither a single trajectory of a coherent feminist movement nor a stable set of issues and concerns that characterize a uniform movement. Instead, the movement has always been comprised of a diverse set of networks, organizations, individuals, actions, and collaborations – spanning time and place – that emerge in response to particular concerns in particular contexts, whether local, national, or global in scope (Rowbotham 1992). Sometimes these networks have coalesced around common goals, but at many other times the differences in terms of power and privilege that mark women's lives have generated divergent concerns and hence strained collaborative efforts.

Although the emergence and development of feminist movements are as diverse as the contexts in which they arise, it is nonetheless possible to identify a few core and recurrent themes in feminist mobilization across the globe. Here the focus is on concerns for women's rights, on women's opportunities for self-determination, and on social justice more generally that has always been part of feminist movements but is particularly pronounced among contemporary groups and coalitions.

Women's rights

Late eighteenth- and early nineteenth-century feminists in Europe and North America pointed to a wide range of issues that impaired women's ability to live productive and happy lives, among them women's lack of education, their inability to support themselves in employment, their inability to escape bad marriages, and their legal position, somewhere between man and child, which made it difficult for them to manage their own affairs. Mary Wollstonecraft's *Vindication of the Rights of Woman* (1792) is one of the best known and most widely read of these early statements of liberal feminism. As democracy spread, however, and more and more men gained the right to vote, the burgeoning movement for women's rights increasingly came to focus on suffrage as the immediate goal and the most significant mechanism for accomplishing change. From the beginning, the middle-class standpoint that helped define early feminist goals and mobilizing strategies inevitably, whether from neglect or exclusionary practices, led to the marginalization of the concerns that other groups of women (working class, racial and ethnic minorities, religious minorities, immigrants) mobilized around (DuBois 1998).

In many of the Western democracies, the first generation of feminist mobilization culminated in the achievement of suffrage during the first few decades in the twentieth century. However, extensive variations in the timing of the adoption of unrestricted suffrage for women in otherwise democratic nations point to the complex patterns of power relations, political structures, cultural practices, religious forces, and a range of shifting coalitions, working both for and against expanded rights for women, that everywhere have influenced the process whereby women have gained the right to participate fully in the political process and move freely across the institutional landscape. The development in other parts of the world, although sharing some aspects with that of the West, diverges in important ways. Long histories of colonial abuses and continued exploitation and/or interference by external capitalist and political forces after independence have influenced women's mobilization for freedom and equality in numerous ways, as is discussed further below (Nouraie-Simone 2005). Most significantly, perhaps, are the many ways in which women have been implicated in nationalist projects which, more or less directly, inspire new forms of feminisms and introduce new forms of tensions among feminists, both within and across nations (Jayawardena 1986). Although most democratic societies now recognize women's right to vote, it is a very recent development in several parts of the world. Moreover, the extent to which suffrage is an effective means of sociopolitical change is variable, which means that few contemporary movements for women's rights are focused exclusively on suffrage.

The quest for self-determination

The early assumption among Western feminists that the achievement of political rights would end the impetus for feminist mobilization has long since been abandoned in the nations that won such rights early. In other nations, especially where democratic institutions are fragile or wholly absent, the pursuit of women's suffrage as a goal apart from other concerns has almost never been a priority for feminist organizations. In addition to, or in lieu of, political rights, women activists everywhere have pursued a range of projects, from various standpoints and in relation to a spectrum of institutional settings, aimed at removing barriers to self-determination. The term self-determination is used here to capture a number of feminist movement goals, ranging from the kind of individual-level rights-based projects that characterize the liberal feminist project in the West to community projects within and across impoverished regions where women's concerns cannot be divorced from those of the communities in which they work.

The distinctions between these different forms of feminism have driven both scholarship and activism in somewhat different directions. The resulting multiplicity in theorizing and activism notwithstanding, most feminist groups support the elimination of the numerous policies, regulations, and practices that place both formal and informal obstacles in the way of women. Particularly important here is reproductive self-determination. According to the World Health Organization, almost 300,000 women died in 2013 from complications associated with pregnancy and birth. The majority (more than 85 percent) of these women lived in sub-Saharan Africa and southern Asia, thus signaling persistent and vast inequalities regarding opportunities for maternal health and well-being. Women's ongoing mobilization around reproductive issues includes efforts to both limit childbearing – through women's access to effective contraceptives and safe and legal abortion services – and to enhance women's ability to have children – health services, maternal leave, child support and, not the least, the prevention of forced sterilization.

Even though feminists disagree on the root causes of women's inequality, on what basis women should mobilize, and the sociopolitical changes that would make things better, they generally agree that women should not be prevented from living the kinds of lives they want just because they are women. That said, there are extensive disagreements over how to understand and conceptualize women's freely chosen life paths in more or less patriarchal societies, as is illustrated in thorny feminist debates over issues such as the veil, abortion, pornography, polygamy, genital cutting, and women's lives as mothers (Nouraie-Simone 2005).

The pursuit of social justice

Looking back in time, feminist movements everywhere have placed the quest for women's equality in a larger context of social justice. Not only have feminists argued that women's rights, however defined, are themselves a matter of social justice, but also that feminism, as a guiding principle for action, requires a deep engagement with social justice issues. However, the extent to which the pursuit of social justice by feminist organizations reaches beyond the concerns of women as women has varied extensively, across both time and place. Moreover, the conceptualization of social justice that guides feminist organizations has also varied extensively (and still does). At least some of the tensions and conflicts among individual feminists and feminist organizations are rooted precisely in the question of how to understand social justice and how far-reaching feminist movements should be in their quest for it.

Feminist organizations have always and everywhere been more or less directly involved in a wide range of issues that have clear social justice implications, including slavery, human rights, class inequality, workplace safety, poverty, national independence, environmental degradation, sustainability, civil rights, consumer rights, health inequalities, child welfare, sexual exploitation, human trafficking, sexual freedoms, criminal justice, and a host of community-based justice movements. The involvement of feminist groups in such a wide array of justice projects signals the breadth of feminism as a social justice ideology. Moreover, given the complexity of such large-scale issues in terms of both institutional involvement (business, law, politics, religion, and family) and geographic reach, they often demand cooperation across national borders and sometimes give rise to transnational networks and international mobilization efforts (Moghadam 2005).

II. HOW TO UNDERSTAND DIVERSITY AND CONFLICT IN FEMINIST MOVEMENTS

Rather than approaching the feminist movement as a single coherent "movement," it is more accurate to view it as a composite of multiple movement strands and diversely situated actors that are committed to feminist goals and pursue a range of social justice projects, whether or not they identify with or are recognized by the dominant Western, white, middle-class women's movement. When Sojourner Truth, who escaped slavery a few decades earlier, posed the question "Ain't I a Woman?" to a Women's Rights convention in Akron, Ohio, in 1851, she forced her listeners to confront at least temporarily the differences between her and their lives. Although some of the nineteenth-century women's rights activists that Truth addressed were cognizant of the vast differences among women, the movement as a whole mostly focused on issues affecting primarily the middle class and hence was inhospitable to the concerns that affected women from other social locations. Among the most significant, if overlapping, differences among women are those related to economic conditions (class), social status (race, ethnicity, caste), and nation/region. Such differences are significant not simply because they capture different life experiences among women, but also because they propel different kinds of political action, identity different kinds of sociopolitical obstacles, inspire different visions of a good society, and introduce sources of tension and conflict among women (Rowbotham 1992).

This also means that the theoretical models developed to understand gendered inequality need to be significantly elaborated to capture and account for all this variety. One of the most important theoretical tools that aid contemporary scholarship is intersectionality (Collins 1990). As a concept, intersectionality is based on the fundamental insight that women are not only women; that is, in addition to gender, women (and everyone else) also occupy positions of race, class, sexuality, age, nationality, and a host of other socially structured roles, statuses, and positions. In order to understand gendered inequality and oppression, in other words, it is necessary to recognize that gender is always lodged in a matrix of other social positions that vary in terms of the advantages and disadvantages they confer upon the women who occupy them. A critical implication of this insight, moreover, is that neither scholars nor activists can assume that gender is always the social location that is the most salient to particular groups of women.

Another theoretical approach that has produced important insights to scholars trying to understand and explain both gendered inequality and diversity in feminist mobilization is that of standpoint theory (Harding 2004). As a theoretical tool, this one also rests on the fundamental assumption that social location matters, but in this case the focus is more on the process of knowledge production than on documenting and understanding difference. Originally used by feminist scholars to critique the notion of objectivity in the production of male scholarship, the notion of standpoint has subsequently been used as a challenge to the feminist perspectives generated by white, middle-class women in the United States. In short, the notion of standpoint directs our attention to the numerous ways in which the production of knowledge is not, and cannot be, formally objective; that is, knowledge, like any other way of seeing and understanding, is always socially positioned. This means that different people, because they have different vantage points, not only see different things but also see things differently. Hence knowledge will always be incomplete, if not altogether wrong, as long as its practitioners are drawn from only a limited number of social vantage points (e.g., male, middle class, Western). Viewed from the perspective of feminist praxis, moreover, it is readily evident that feminist knowledge produced by privileged women in wealthy nations is insufficient at best to tackle the problems facing women in nations characterized by armed conflict, exploitation, poverty, and political instability.

These and other theoretical approaches have inspired a wide range of scholarship that takes seriously not only the many variations that characterize women's lives, but also the wide range of sociopolitical concerns that define women's activism, whether or not conducted under a self-conscious feminist umbrella. The following sections discuss first, variations in experiences and feminist activism among women who live within the same national context, and second, variations among women across national contexts.

Same nation, different experiences

The frequent claims by middle-class feminists in the West to universality when it comes to women's grievances have always been greatly exaggerated. Although nominally true in the sense that no other women have access to the resources that the middle-class women are fighting for, such claims nonetheless serves to render invisible the divergent grievances of women in other social locations. That is, poor women, immigrant women, women of color, and enslaved women and their descendants have always had such different life experiences in relation to the white middle class that their concerns and priorities diverge in important ways. This also means that their relationships to the dominant movement for women's rights have always been tenuous at best, both because they are less implicated in the concerns of that movement and because their own concerns are not fully recognized by the dominant movement. This is not to suggest that women at the margins have no gendered grievances – on the contrary – but rather to highlight that their own experiences with oppression and inequality are such that the concerns of white middle-class women can appear foreign. It is also true that working-class women and especially women of color were long excluded more or less directly from the white feminist organizations that dominated the quest for women's liberation in the past. Although contemporary feminist organizations are generally much more alert to questions of difference and exclusion, the privileges of white Western feminists still haunt feminisms at the global level (Eisenstein 2004).

In order to understand different patterns of mobilization and political action, then, it is necessary to examine the different experiences of oppression and injustice, at both the individual and communal levels, that characterize the lives of different groups of women. For example, one of the most significant differences between early women's rights activists in the West and their counterparts outside the white middle class and in other regions relates to their experiences with work. If women from the middle classes lamented the limitations, both legal and cultural, placed on their abilities to pursue productive and meaningful work, women from the working classes experienced considerably fewer constraints on their ability to work. On the contrary, they often worked, and worked hard, under similar dismal conditions as men (albeit often with less pay). This and many similar tensions between the experiences of middle- and working-class women still characterize the relationships between more or less privileged feminists. For poor women everywhere, their encounters with inequality and oppression are much more similar to those of the men in their own class and community than Western women in the middle classes. This does not mean that their experiences and activism as workers are gender neutral – far from it – but only that their global class location produces a very different set of gendered constraints and injustices than those experienced by more privileged women. As another example, although black women have long had a presence in the white-dominated movement for women's rights in the United States, the bulk of their activism has always been reserved for black-dominated groups and organizations, ranging from women's civic organizations to mixed-gender radical protest organizations. Although gendered class distinctions have pervaded black communities just as they have white communities, the persistence of racism, including in the white-led organizations devoted to women's rights, has been a consistent source of mobilization into black-led organizations. Rather than suggesting that black women prioritize race over gender, their pattern of activism illustrates clearly how gender works through race and race through gender.

Different nations, different experiences

The national context in which women's political actions are formulated matters for a number of interrelated reasons. First, the particular issues that women mobilize around are bound in various ways by the nation, that is, women face different problems and challenges in different nations. Second, both the nature and trajectory of women's sociopolitical actions and the development of feminism as a political ideology are deeply entangled in nationalist projects. This means that women's political actions are always implicated in the larger power struggles that play out at the level of the nation state. Third, because nations occupy different positions in the larger world system, their ability to withstand pressures from without varies extensively across both regions and nations (Jayawardena 1986).

It is for reasons such as these that the models of feminist organizing and theorizing that characterize Western democracies generally, and the United States in particular, have not been, and cannot be, fully embraced by women who live outside the democratic West. This is so not because women across the globe are less subject to gendered constraints and injustices – on the contrary – but instead because the assumption of gendered universalism that was long an unmistaken subtext in Western feminism is clearly insufficient as an organizing principle in diverse global contexts. For many women grassroots activists across the globe, this Western bias may not matter very much, especially if they mobilize and act locally. But in so far as international funding agencies, non-governmental organizations, and sociopolitical priorities are informed by and committed to mostly Western conceptions of women's concerns and actions, then it could matter considerably (Christensen, Halsaa, and Saarinen 2004). Moreover, from the perspective of scholarship, the omission until the last few decades of non-Western women's perspectives and activism led to incomplete and impoverished understandings of the conditions of women's existence in many parts of the world and the circumstances that facilitate or constrain mobilization and protest. More recently, however, this picture has changed dramatically. Now there is a rich literature documenting the full diversity of women's activism in all regions of the world (Naples and Desai 2002; Lindio-McGovern and Wallimann 2009).

One inevitable consequence of the recognition of the varieties of women's sociopolitical engagements is precisely the erosion of the notion of a universal womanhood. Rather than abandoning the idea of a global feminist movement, however, women activists are trying to find new ways to combine and mobilize. The dream of a movement that links women across the globe is a longstanding one, formulated in the late nineteenth century by feminist activists in the West. It originated in the assumption that womanhood, at its most fundamental level, is a shared experience with enough commonalities to justify both a notion of global sisterhood and a program of joint actions. For the first generation of transnational activists, in other words, it was taken as self-evident not only that women were different from men, but also that the distinctions between men and women provided enough of a foundation to build a set of common goals upon and hence warrant transnational organization building (Rupp 1997). During and after the world wars of the twentieth century, it was the desire for peace that served as a recurrent source of mobilization. In later years, issues such as women's bodily integrity, health and safety, and the right to self-determination have taken on greater importance. While the idea of a common womanhood has not been entirely abandoned, as the many international and transnational women's initiatives are testaments to, the diversity in women's experiences across nations has nonetheless brought challenges to the dream of a unified global feminist movement (Moghadam 2005).

III. CONTEMPORARY FEMINIST MOVEMENTS

Although the issues have changed and the diversity has increased, historically there has always been an assumption that womanhood is a meaningful identity to mobilize a movement around even long after ideas of gender essentialism were abandoned. As already discussed, the history of the feminist movement is one of exceptional diversity in terms of goals, actions, and coalition building. However, whether women have mobilized for women specifically or for the greater community of which they are a part, they have for the most part acted *as* women, that is, their identity as women has been a critical organizing principle and an important source of knowledge and experience (Prince, Silvia-Wayne, and Vernon 2004). Although womanhood still serves as an important status for women to mobilize around, contemporary feminist movements are so diverse and dynamic that they defy easy description and categorization. In fact, in many ways it is precisely this very diversity and dynamism that best describe contemporary feminisms, including scholarship aimed at documenting and understanding this field of social action.

Although both scholars and activists disagree about how to define contemporary feminism, they typically share the assumption that the context of feminist activism has changed in such a way that new theorizing and new practices are called for. This is so for several different reasons. First, the issues of importance to feminist activists worldwide are ever more diverse. Second, as the sociopolitical environment becomes increasingly fragmented and social locations destabilized, the notion that womanhood connotes a simple shared experience is no longer sustainable, if it ever were. Further, the issues that affect women are no longer confined or defined by the boundaries of nation states but instead reach across the globe in complicated ways (Naples and Desai 2002).

Drawing on the wave metaphor that has often been applied to the middle-class women's rights movement in the West, some scholars find the term third-wave feminism useful for capturing the diversity of contemporary feminist concerns and actions (Reger 2005). The first wave, in this framework, refers to the mobilization around suffrage in the nineteenth and early twentieth century and the second wave to the push for gender-based equal rights in the 1960s and 1970s. Given the limited geographic scope and fairly narrow focus on feminist activism that characterize the wave metaphor, other observers have concluded that it obscures and misrepresents as much as it describes and clarifies (Gillis, Howie, and Munford 2007). Moreover, it reinforces the mistaken notion of the women's movement as a single, coherent movement that both unfolds sequentially over time and represents the concerns of all women. For the purposes of this essay, it is not necessary to try to resolve this and other scholarly debates about how best to characterize and distinguish feminist movements and actions from other types of movements and protest actions. Rather, the aim is to be as inclusive as possible. Given the multitude of activism across the globe, however, it is not possible to catalogue and address everything that could be included in this discussion. Instead, the focus is on three of the most significant points of divergence between feminist movements of the past and contemporary movement activity: first, a move away from the goal of rights-based gender equality; second, the emergence of transnational feminism; and third, feminist projects aimed at deconstructing gender as a coherent category.

The limitations of equal rights as a goal of feminism

The goal of rights-based equality between women and men has been on the forefront of the feminist movement since its inception. Regardless of the fact that there have always been disagreements among women's rights activists about how best to achieve equality, until recently few Western feminists have challenged the idea that equality in this sense is one, if not *the*, primary goal of the feminist movement. The main issue here is not that women no longer want or demand equal rights – they do – but instead that the assumptions that have always guided the equal rights project are increasingly challenged, albeit in somewhat different ways.

For many feminists, especially those who live and work outside the Western democracies, the greatest problems they encounter, such as oppressive work conditions, environmental degradation, and the destruction of traditional communities, are often such that they cannot be resolved or addressed via individual rights in the Western sense. More specifically, the notion of individual rights, such critics point out, originates in the particular political ideology referred to as liberalism. In its contemporary form, neoliberalism is enmeshed with capitalism to such an extent that the two are mutually constitutive. This means not only that the distinction between citizen and consumer has faded, but also that rights and obligations apportioned out at the individual level cannot solve the problems that neoliberalism, as both an ideology and a set of practices, has produced in many parts of the world. It is for this reason that women activists across the developing world draw on much more expansive and communal definitions of rights, justice, and freedom from oppression when they mobilize for social and political change and the protection of the commons (Alexander and Mohanty 1997). Moreover, the geopolitical instabilities in many parts of the world, due to war, imperialism, and the ravages of global capitalism, bring particularly urgent challenges to the forefront of feminist movements (Eisenstein 2004; Cheldelin and Eliatamby 2011).

Transnational feminisms

One of the most persistent and pervasive aspects of feminism, as both an ideology and a set of practices, has always been, and continues to be, a concern with social justice. It is certainly true that there always has been, and still is, extensive disagreement about what kinds of activism this concern should inform and motivate, but it is also true that the commitment to social justice has inspired any number of novel projects and productive alliances. This is also the commitment that has propelled women activists, across time and place, to join forces and work for goals that spill over national boundaries. During the past century, mobilization against war has been one of the most prominent issues that have inspired the formation of cross-national initiatives and organizations among women (Rupp 1997).

During the last few decades of the twentieth century, however, transnational feminist initiatives and networks have grown exponentially (Moghadam 2005). Globalization and massive economic restructuring have brought new challenges to the lives of women worldwide – rising inequality, poverty, reproductive health concerns, environmental destruction, violence against women, militarization, religious conflict – and these challenges have inspired new projects and new forms of mobilization and alliances. Some of this new organization building has been facilitated by the United Nation's world conferences on women in Mexico City (1975), Copenhagen (1980), Nairobi (1985), and Beijing (1995). These conferences have facilitated the coming together of women's groups, feminist activists, and non-governmental organizations devoted to improving the lives of women, but they have also brought enduring differences among women to the forefront of the global conversation and, importantly, helped expose the inequities among feminists and especially the problems associated with the persistent domination of Western ideologies and practices (Christensen, Halsaa, and Saarinen 2004). Other transnational work, at both the theoretical and activist levels, focus on the connections between global processes and women's everyday struggles (Naples and Desai 2002). This work is inspired by the recognition that the large-scale problems identified worldwide always have local expressions and consequences. It is at this level that many women take action, trying to improve labor conditions, protect environmental resources, prevent violence and human rights violations, and sustain local communities in the face of destructive global forces.

Challenging gender

Influenced by queer, postmodern, and poststructural theorizing, some contemporary feminist movements approach gender categories as something to deconstruct rather than reconstitute by gender-based activism, that is, they target the categories themselves and with their actions aim to trouble and destabilize the categories (Butler 1990). There is no shortage of terms used to define this new landscape of feminist action, including postfeminism, hip-hop feminist, do-it-yourself (DIY) feminism, queer feminism, ecofeminism, and even girlie feminism (Reger 2005). Although often self-designated as feminist projects, the feminism that activists both draw on and produce is as varied as the projects they engage in. Activists and practitioners see womanhood differently, see gender differently, see the past differently, and see the future differently. It is not surprising, therefore, that there are extensive debates in scholarly circles about what, if anything, holds all this together as forms of feminism. If not a relatively stable notion of womanhood, what then provides the feminist glue? On the surface, much contemporary activism can appear fleeting and impatient, and more focused on temporarily transgressing the various barriers and boundaries that inspire action than on developing and pursuing more long-term sociopolitical goals that could redraw some of those boundaries and destroy some of the barriers. At a deeper level, however, and taken together, this kind of activism reflects the increasing instability of social life, the continuous fracturing of the social contract, and a justified disillusion with the institutions charged with protecting social welfare and pursuing social justice (Nicholson 1990).

IV. PROSPECTS FOR THE FUTURE

The prospects for a modern feminist movement that resembles its historical antecedents in coherence, scope, and womanist focus have, if they were ever bright, dimmed considerably. Rather than being a cause for concern, however, the multitude of contemporary feminist-inspired and feminist-aligned activism across the globe suggests that feminism, in all its forms, will continue to have a significant impact on social life. The forces of globalization – economic, cultural, political – that have caused so much disruption in the world have not only prompted new forms of activism but also provided new opportunities for mobilization and coalition building, linking struggles at the local level with transnational networks of activists. In all parts of the world, women are on the forefront of movements to redress injustices and develop new forms of sustainable life. Many of these women activists are inspired by feminism and call themselves feminists while many others do feminist work under different guises. What all this means, in short, is that feminism itself is a malleable and dynamic source of social action that, far from weakening, is strengthened the more it is used in the service of social justice.

SEE ALSO: Economic Globalization and Gender; Feminisms, First, Second, and Third Wave; Feminism, Multiracial; Feminist Activism; Gender, Politics, and the State: Overview; History of Women's Rights in International and Comparative Perspective

REFERENCES

Alexander, M. Jacqui, and Chandra Talpade Mohanty, eds. 1997. *Feminist Genealogies, Colonial Legacies, Democratic Futures*. New York: Routledge.

Butler, Judith. 1990. *Gender Trouble*. New York: Routledge.

Cheldelin, Sandra I., and Maneshka Eliatamby, eds. 2011. *Women Waging War and Peace: International Perspectives on Women's Roles in Conflict and Post-Conflict Reconstruction*. New York: Continuum International Publishing.

Christensen, Hilda Rømer, Beatrice Halsaa, and Aino Saarinen, eds. 2004. *Crossing Borders: Re-mapping Women's Movements at the Turn of the 21st Century*. Odense: University Press of Southern Denmark.

Collins, Patricia Hill. 1990. *Black Feminist Thought: Knowledge, Consciousness, and the Politics of Empowerment*. New York: Routledge.

DuBois, Ellen Carol. 1998. *Woman Suffrage and Women's Rights*. New York: New York University Press.

Eisenstein, Zillah R. 2004. *Against Empire: Feminism, Racism, and the West*. Melbourne: Spinifex Press.

Gillis, Stacy, Gillian Howie, and Rebecca Munford, eds. 2007. *Third Wave Feminism: a Critical Exploration*. New York: Palgrave Macmillan.

Harding, Sandra, ed. 2004. *The Feminist Standpoint Theory Reader: Intellectual and Political Controversies*. New York: Routledge.

Jayawardena, Kumari. 1986. *Feminism and Nationalism in the Third World*. London: Zed Books.

Lindio-McGovern, Ligaya, and Isidor Wallimann, eds. 2009. *Globalization and Third World Women: Exploitation, Coping and Resistance*. Farnham: Ashgate Publishing.

Moghadam, Valentine M. 2005. *Globalizing Women: Transnational Feminist Networks*. Baltimore: Johns Hopkins University Press.

Naples, Nancy A., and Manisha Desai, eds. 2002. *Women's Activism and Globalization: Linking Local Struggles and Transnational Politics*. New York: Routledge.

Nicholson, Linda J. ed. 1990. *Feminism/Postmodernism*. New York: Routledge.

Nouraie-Simone, Fereshteh, ed. 2005. *On Shifting Ground: Muslim Women in the Global Era*. New York: The Feminist Press at the City University of New York.

Prince, Althea, Susan Silva-Wayne, and Christian Vernon eds. 2004. *Feminisms and Womanisms. A Women's Studies Reader*. Toronto: Women's Press.

Reger, Jo, ed. 2005. *Different Wavelengths: Studies of the Contemporary Women's Movement*. New York: Routledge.

Rowbotham, Sheila. 1992. *Women in Movement: Feminism and Social Action*. New York: Routledge.

Rupp, Leila J. 1997. *Worlds of Women: the Making of an International Women's Movement*. Princeton: Princeton University Press.

Stanley, Liz. 1990. *Feminist Praxis: Research, Theory, and Epistemology in Feminist Sociology*. New York: Routledge.

Feminist Objectivity

KRISTEN INTEMANN
Montana State University, USA

Feminist conceptions of objectivity arose, in part, out of the identification biases in scientific reasoning and methods that were previously considered "objective." The dominant conception of "objective knowledge" that arose in the twentieth century was "knowledge that bears no trace of the knower" or claims that were true independently of humans. Scientific knowledge was thought to be the paradigm example of objective knowledge because of its methods, which, if correctly employed, would arrive at the same conclusions regardless of who was employing them. Scientists, then, were objective insofar as they employed scientific methods and norms appropriately. Moreover, to do so, individual scientists should distance themselves from all of their non-epistemic values and interests (including social, personal, moral, and political values). Thus, the traditional conception of objectivity was associated with a "god's eye view of the world" that could be discovered by disinterested and value-neutral scientists who were distinct from the subjects of their investigations. The historical successes of science were taken to be evidence not only that this conception of objectivity was accurate, but also that scientists were generally successful in achieving objective knowledge.

Despite this, feminist scientists and feminist theorists began to uncover sexist, heteronormative, racist, and other biases in cases of what had otherwise been considered to be good science. In biology, for example, feminists identified cases where gender stereotypes influenced the languages and models used to describe the natural world (Fausto-Sterling 1985). Gender norms were also found to have influenced and limited the sorts of explanations considered. As more women began to enter fields such as primatology, anthropology, and archaeology, many began to notice the ways in which gendered assumptions shaped observation, as well as the collection and interpretation of evidence (Wylie 1997). Moreover, such biases occurred in cases where standard scientific norms and practices were followed and had been previously regarded as "objective." Finally, postcolonial theorists identified biases not only in the content of scientific reasoning, but also in assumptions about what constituted "science" itself. In particular, non-Western knowledge traditions were often dismissed as "superstition," or "non-science," and were assumed to be incapable of producing reliable knowledge claims (Narayan 1997). Feminist scholars showed that indigenous knowledge traditions are not only often reliable, but crucial to producing the kind of knowledge likely to benefit those affected by the science.

In response to these concerns, some concluded that "objectivity" is not a useful concept for thinking about science or knowledge more generally. Other feminist scholars, however, argued that cases of bias reveal not that objectivity is impossible, but that the particular conception of objectivity that had guided both scientists and philosophers of science was flawed. Despite serious problems with the traditional view, they maintained that some alternative conception of objectivity could offer promising epistemological and political resources. Such a conception might be useful for explaining how and why, for example, certain forms of biases (such as racist or sexist biases) can limit and hinder the production of knowledge. This would have the potential to help guide and improve science, without rejecting scientific successes. Feminist conceptions of objectivity, then, arose from critiques of traditional assumptions about what it is to be objective and how objectivity is achieved. The aim is to produce alternative accounts of objectivity that are not only theoretically superior, but that can also be used to prevent and identify bias, as well as challenge, rather than reinforce, systems of oppression.

Broadly speaking, there have been three main alternative accounts of objectivity offered by feminist scholars: procedural objectivity, strong objectivity, and virtue-based objectivity.

PROCEDURAL OBJECTIVITY

Procedural accounts of objectivity (PO) reject the assumption that objectivity requires individual scientists to be "value neutral" or "disinterested." First, many have argued that such an ideal is impossible for scientists to attain. Humans cannot strip away all of their values and interests, nor are they very good at recognizing when their values and interests may be influencing their reasoning. Second, and perhaps more importantly, it is not clear that it would be desirable for scientists to do so, even if they could. Some values and interests may play important and positive roles in science. That is, many feminists have argued that scientists ought to be more directed by equalitarian values or important social aims in order to produce science that is more just and responsive to social needs. Some have argued that although *individuals* cannot be impartial in the sense of being value-neutral or disinterested, scientific *communities* can achieve impartiality by establishing procedures or mechanisms that balance or minimize the negative effects of individual interests (Longino 1990). Longino, for example, argues that objective scientific communities are best comprised of inquirers with diverse values and interests, but who have equal intellectual authority to challenge and scrutinize scientific research. If adequate mechanisms for scrutinizing research exist, such as methodological transparency and peer review, then scientific decision-making influenced by idiosyncratic values or interests is more likely to be caught and corrected by others in the community who have different values and interests. Thus, on this account, while researchers are not *individually objective*, the scientific community as a whole can be *procedurally objective*. To the extent that scientific communities have historically failed to be diverse, to recognize the intellectual authority of women, or to allow underrepresented groups opportunities to raise criticisms and have those criticisms taken seriously, they have been less objective than they could be.

STRONG OBJECTIVITY

The term "strong objectivity" was originally developed by Harding and has been most associated with standpoint feminism and postcolonial feminism (Harding 1991). Proponents of strong objectivity (SO) maintain that objectivity requires a critical reflection on the ways that systems of oppression have shaped and limited what we know, as well as the epistemic practices that produce knowledge. Early standpoint theorists focused on gender as a category of analysis and examined the ways in which sexism and the gendered division of labor produced different experiences crucial to identifying problematic assumptions in the theories and frameworks widely held by those in power who likely benefit from justifying existing social inequalities (Hartsock 1983). Yet, as many critical race theorists and postcolonial theorists later argued, this seemed to falsely assume that women share some universal experiences in virtue of being women (Mohanty 1991). Thus, SO evolved to recognize the ways in which race, ethnicity, nationality, and history of colonization intersect with other categories of difference (Hill Collins 1991; Narayan 1997). SO requires conscious reflection on the ways in which multiple systems of oppression interact to shape and limit what we know.

Achieving SO thus requires communities of inquirers to be comprised of individuals from diverse social positions (e.g., different races, classes, genders, nationalities) who share a normative commitment to pursue science in ways that challenge, rather than reinforce those systems of oppression. Thus, although both PO and SO maintain that objectivity increases in diverse communities, the type of diversity that SO requires is diversity of social locations rather than of values or interests. Moreover, although both PO and SO reject the idea that objectivity requires individuals to be disinterested or value free, SO also rejects the idea that communities or procedures should be neutral toward ethical and political values. SO requires the endorsement of particular ethical and political values; specifically, that oppression is morally unjust and ought to be abolished. Within the context of science, this may involve a commitment to reveal the ways in which gender, for example, shapes and limits scientific inquiry as well as what we take to be scientific knowledge. It requires understanding and revising our epistemic practices so as to identify, understand, and ultimately abolish the ways in which systems of oppression direct knowledge production. Communities that achieve this will be more likely to produce knowledge that is "strongly objective," or less partial and distorted.

VIRTUE-BASED ACCOUNTS OF OBJECTIVITY

A third conception will be referred to as a *virtue-based account* of objectivity. Such accounts maintain that objectivity is best understood in terms of some virtue, such as responsibility or trustworthiness, as opposed to some set of procedures or features of the individuals that comprise epistemic communities. For example, Scheman argues that a scientific institution or community is objective insofar as it can be rationally trusted. If a scientific community (or, for example, the educational system that helps to constitute it) is unjust or oppressive, the less rational it is for those who are oppressed to trust it and, hence, the less objective it will be (Scheman 2001). In this view, scientific inquiry is objective to the extent that participants acknowledge and fulfill the responsibilities of inquiry, including the responsibilities to other inquirers, those who may be objects of inquiry, and those who may be affected by inquiry (such as the public). Bhavnani, for example, has urged that objectivity be understood in terms of responsibilities to refrain from reinscribing dominant stereotypes onto research subjects, adequately to account for the differences among human subjects, and to contextualize our understanding of phenomena within the cultural, historical, and political contexts in which they occur.

Despite their differences, all virtue-based accounts of objectivity take scientific inquiry to be a process that occurs in a larger social context. Inquiry is influenced by the social context in which it occurs and the social context is ultimately influenced by the production of knowledge. Such accounts emphasize the extent to which participants must then depend on each other. Biases, on this sort of view, become understood as threats to undermining the kinds of relationships that are necessary for producing knowledge.

While these three approaches disagree about the best way to understand objectivity, they share many of the same concerns about the traditional view. In particular, they all argue that the traditional conception of objectivity problematically assumes that objectivity is a property of individuals and that it requires freedom from all social and political values. Moreover, they reject the idea that objective scientific inquiry is independent of the social context in which it occurs or that it makes no difference *who* participates in inquiry. Finally, feminist accounts do not take "objectivity" to be an "all or nothing" property in opposition to "subjectivity." Rather, all three approaches take objectivity to come in degrees, so that scientific communities can be more or less objective. What makes these alternatives feminist is that they have been developed with an eye toward certain feminist aims. In particular all three accounts aim to identify and reduce biases that result from systems of oppression, to explain why the participation of women and other historically underrepresented groups is important in science, and to promote science that is more responsive to the needs of marginalized groups.

SEE ALSO: Feminist Standpoint Theory; Gender Bias; Strong Objectivity

REFERENCES

Bhavnani, Kum Kum. 1993. "Tracing the Contours: Feminist Research and Feminist Objectivity." *Women's Studies International Forum*, 16(2): 95–104.

Fausto-Sterling, Anne. 1985. *Myths of Gender: Biological Theories about Women and Men*. New York: Basic Books.

Harding, Sandra. 1991. *Whose Science? Whose Knowledge? Thinking From Women's Lives*. Ithaca: Cornell University Press.

Hartsock, Nancy. 1983. "The Feminist Standpoint: Developing the Ground for a Specifically Feminist Historical Materialism." In *Discovering Reality*, edited by M. B. Hintikka and S. Harding, 283–310. Dordrecht: Kluwer.

Hill Collins, Patricia. 1991. "Learning from the Outsider Within." In *Beyond Methodology: Feminist Scholarship as Lived Research*, edited by Mary Margaret Fonow and Judith A. Cook, 35–59. Bloomington: Indiana University Press.

Longino, Helen. 1990. *Science as Social Knowledge: Values and Objectivity in Scientific Inquiry*. Princeton: Princeton University Press.

Mohanty, Chandra Talpade. 1991. "Under Western Eyes: Feminist Scholarship and Colonial Discourse." In *Third World Women and the Politics of Feminism*, edited by Chandra Talpade Mohanty, Ann Russo, and Lourdes Torres, 51–80. Bloomington: Indiana University Press.

Narayan, Uma. 1997. *Dislocating Cultures: Identities, Traditions, and Third World Feminism*. New York: Routledge.

Scheman, Naomi. 2001. "Epistemology Resuscitated: Objectivity as Trustworthiness." In *Engendering Rationalities*, edited by Nancy Tuana and Sandra Morgan, 23–52. Albany: SUNY Press.

Wylie, Alison. 1997. "The Engendering of Archaeology: Refiguring Feminist Science Studies." *Osiris*, 12: 80–99. Special issue: *Women, Gender, and Science: New Directions*, edited by Sally Gregory Kohlstedt and Helen Longino. DOI: 10.1086/649268.

FURTHER READING

Fox Keller, Evelyn, and Helen Longino. 1998. *Feminism and Science*. Oxford: Oxford University Press.

Feminist Organizations, Definition of

MELINDA A. LEMKE
The University of Texas at Austin, USA

Feminist organizations are characterized by divergent organizational foci, geographical location, and historical moment. Based on but not limited to these factors, feminist organizations may acquire either a singular or multifocal theoretical bent including for example, Asian, Black, Chicana, eco, Indígena, lesbian, liberal, Marxist, multicultural, Muslim, postmodern, radical, or socialist feminist perspectives. Although various typologies exist, feminism and respective organizations generally aim to problematize sociopolitical, economic, and cultural forces that privilege males while simultaneously disempowering and oppressing females.

In promoting feminist values and goals, feminist organizations create unique organizational identities. Unlike other organizations, feminist organizational identity is focused on challenging mainstream and hegemonic societal constructions. Concerned with the influence patriarchy has on organizational structuring, representation, and voice, feminist organizations within the United States have formed in response to mainstream treatment of female issues. To this end, early organizations often refused public funding viewed to be non-consonant with the goals of feminist organizing. Feminist organizations, therefore, are known to face organizational constraints like limited staffing, resource constraints, and institutional hostility to feminist organizational ethos not witnessed in traditional, often male-dominated organizations.

Such problems can be mitigated by working both within and across class, ethnic, racial, sexual orientation, age, education, and geographic boundaries. By doing so, feminist organizations develop unique histories, orientations, and support structures to assist policy agenda setting, creation, and implementation. Despite varying degrees of internal organizational conflict, transnational, international, national, and local grassroots feminist organizations are held to be the major force in maintaining feminism's legacy of commitment to personal and collective change.

HISTORICAL AND POLITICAL DIMENSIONS

Historically, feminist organizations have been organized around the amelioration of female inequality, discrimination, and oppression. National feminist organizational efforts on issues like sanitation, abolition of slavery, suffrage, child labor, and healthcare date to the eighteenth and nineteenth centuries. Certain major national organizations, such as the Women's International League for Peace and Freedom (WILPF), which focused on military conflict, economic justice, and women's rights, date to 1915. Yet, the growth of feminist organizations primarily is linked with mid-twentieth-century sociopolitical and economic movements. In the United States, these organizations focused on problems like educational opportunity and access, equal pay for equal work, reproductive freedom, harassment, global conflict, domestic violence, and rape culture.

Alongside anti-war, civil rights, and labor activism, feminist collectives and organizations emerged globally. By the 1970s feminist organizations were split between those that were national and international versus smaller local coalitions. The former were connected to existent policy work done, for example, by the United Nations Convention on the Elimination of Discrimination against Women (CEDAW, 1979) and United States

Presidential Commission on the Status of Women (1963). The latter often comprised student and non-student advocates committed to local feminist consciousness-raising and activism. While major national and international feminist advocacy and policy institutions exist today, from the 1970s onward localized organizations proliferated in the form of women's shelters, rape crisis centers, family planning clinics, prison projects, environmental entities, local educational groups, feminist book stores, poetry clubs, radio shows, and media campaigns.

Despite changing the face of organizational structures, as well as accomplishing major feats within the global women's movement, the history of feminist organizing is not without blemish. Similar to debates within feminist theory and research, queer and women of color faced exclusionary organizational practices by Western feminist organizations. In research and public form, Asian, Black, Chicana, and Indígena feminists railed against US feminist organizations for failing to address the intersections of racism and classism within the movement. Accused of representing a "Lavender menace" to mainstream feminism and respective organizing, lesbian feminists also pushed back through major critiques of heterosexism. Finally, Third World feminists criticized Western organizations for neglecting issues like health, military expansionism, and political instability in formerly colonized nations.

Thus, myriad feminist organizations aimed at increasing the representation of marginalized female groups emerged in the United States including the Third World Women's Alliance (TWWA, 1968–1979), Combahee River Collective (1975–1980), and the Chicana/Latina Foundation (1977). Beginning in the 1980s, national non-Western feminist organizations increased with the development of Salud Integral para la Mujer (SIPAM) in Mexico (1987), Zimbabwe Women Writers (1990), and Al-Zahraa in Palestine (1997), among other organizations. Contemporary development of transnational feminism, which is attentive to intersections of sex, sexuality, class, race, nationhood, and global exploitation, also prompted the formation of transnational feminist organizations such as Madre (1983), Asian Pacific Forum on Women, Law and Development (1985), and the Global Alliance Against Traffic in Women (1994).

CONTEMPORARY ISSUES

Feminist organizations proved to be prolific at local, national, international, and transnational levels, garnering multiple successes in the areas of educational representation, reproductive freedom, as well as sexual assault, domestic violence, and rape jurisprudence. Yet, these are limited successes in light of continued inequality in governmental representation, lack of equal wages, cuts to social programming, prevalence of sexual violence, economic exploitation, and conservative backlash. Feminist organizations, therefore, face tangible challenges in the twenty-first century.

One of the primary issues faced by feminist organizations today is the dilution of feminist values, messaging, and non-hierarchical structures. Contemporary organizations face pressure to deny they are feminist due to conservative backlash. Unlike organizations of the past that resisted public funding, new collaborative financial relationships with public and state entities threaten feminist organizational identity. The acceptance of public dollars is known to reduce political activism and lead to more bureaucratic, hierarchical organizational structures. This reality is exacerbated by a globalized neoliberal marketplace that demands constant access to organizational functioning while simultaneously co-opting feminist language associated with choice and equity. Thus, contemporary feminist organizing stands to benefit from empirical research on feminist organizational structures, alliance building, historic connections to the women's movement, sustainability, and overall impact on female empowerment.

SEE ALSO: Consciousness-Raising; Feminist Activism; Feminist Movements in Historical and Comparative Perspective; Feminist Theories of Organization; Women's Movements: Modern International Movements

FURTHER READING

Duŕan, Lydia A., Noël Payne, and Anahi Russo, eds. 2007. *Building Feminist Movements and Organizations: Global Perspectives*. New York: Zed Books.

Ferree, Myra M., and Patricia Y. Martin, eds. 1995. *Feminist Organizations: Harvest of the New Feminist Movement*. Philadelphia: Temple University Press.

Martin, Patricia Y. 2005. *Rape Work: Victims, Gender, and Emotions in Organization and Community Context*. New York: Routledge.

Moraga, Cherríe L., and Gloria Anzaldúa. 2002. *This Bridge Called My Back: Writings by Radical Women of Color*, 3rd ed. Berkeley, CA: Third Woman Press.

Naples, Nancy A., ed. 1998. *Community Activism and Feminist Politics: Organizing across Race, Class, and Gender*. New York: Routledge.

Springer, Kimberly. 2005. *Living for the Revolution: Black Feminist Organizations, 1968–1980*. Durham, NC: Duke University Press.

Feminist Pedagogy

MICHELLE SAN PEDRO
University of Connecticut, Storrs, USA

Feminist pedagogy is an approach to teaching concerned with gender injustice and other inequalities. Education is a site of empowerment and social change. Pedagogy is an emancipatory process that cultivates political awareness. Teachers facilitate the development of critical knowledge and inquiry through consciousness-raising techniques. Students construct valuable knowledge based on their lived experiences. Teachers and students reflect on processes of oppression in daily life. Together, they act as empowered agents of social change (hooks 1994). Feminist pedagogy explores expressions of difference. It is a movement against educational practices that accept or reproduce oppressive social orders. The philosophy and practices of feminist teaching highlight a shifting power dynamic between educators and learners.

Feminist pedagogy challenges an old paradigm of teaching. In classic lecture-based classrooms, teachers transmit knowledge to students. Students are passive consumers, who simply memorize and recall fixed information. In this model, education is a transactional, impersonal process (Freire 1970). Students are valued for their performance on a test. Rather than perpetuate these roles and power dynamics, feminist teachers recognize that students actively create knowledge and reconstruct meaning. Feminist pedagogy affirms the place of passion, desire, and emotions in the educational process. Contrary to the traditional notion of emotional distance between educators and students, love is critical to democratic participation. When an educator is fully committed, the student feels validated as a holistic person. The connection between educators and students, then, is vital in their passion for truth and justice (hooks 1994).

Feminist pedagogy includes voices traditionally excluded from power structures (Fisher 2001). Individuals do not simply occupy a privileged or disadvantaged status; feminists argue that an individual has multiple social identities. Each identity carries a differently positioned status in a social structure. Feminist pedagogy acknowledges the complex dynamics of privilege and oppression. The identity of students shifts across different contexts (Maher and Tetreault 2001). Influenced by postmodern thought, feminist pedagogy addresses histories of sexism, racism, imperialism, and homophobia. Students learn about perspectives of others with lives different from their own. Feminist pedagogy offers different frameworks to examine the variation in gender, class, ethnicity, culture, language, sexual orientation, and belief systems (Macdonald and Sanchez-Casal 2002).

Students may resist feminist pedagogy through silence and other forms of expression (Bell and Tastsoglou 1999). Due to exposure to the old paradigm of teaching, some students are socialized as spectators in the classroom. Students struggle to integrate contradictory information from their personal experiences with polarizing ideas. They consider their privileges, identity, and oppressions and how these beliefs and structures affect others. As they confront inequality, they attempt to understand the mechanisms that contribute to oppression (Freire 1970). They negotiate their sense of self and the world. One fundamental component of feminist pedagogy is applying theory to practice, then changing based on those lessons (Bignell 1996). Praxis is the interrelationship between critical theory, reflection, and practice and focuses on the development of knowledge through engagement with practice.

Feminist scholars continue to start with women's experience to teach feminist praxis through an experiential approach. Naples (2002) argues for "a critical feminist pedagogy that is open to self-reflexivity about the processes by which we produce knowledge for and with our students" (Naples 2002, 16). Praxis unfolds with participatory activities within and beyond the feminist classroom. For example, service learning projects or internships through feminist organizations encourage reflection on actions taken to counter inequality in dialogue with insights from feminist theory. Students explore their thoughts and feelings about their experiences and reactions to feminist analysis with journal writing. During group exercises, students compare and contrast their views. Students question oppression in circumstances that they once considered normal. Teachers may serve as mentors, guiding students in their journey towards personal growth, feminist inquiry, and social responsibility. Teachers and students engage with and model forms of self-assessment, intellectual engagement, and evaluation. Praxis continually improves to support classroom equity. The classroom transforms into a collaborative, learning community of committed scholars (Naples and Bojar 2002; Enns and Sinacore 2005).

SEE ALSO: Empowerment; Feminist Theories of Experience; Gender Inequality in Education

REFERENCES

Bell, Sandra, M. Morrow, and Evangelis Tastsoglou. 1999. "Teaching in Environments of Resistance: Toward a Critical Feminist and Antiracist Pedagogy." In *Meeting the Challenge: Innovative Feminist Pedagogies in Action*, edited by Maralee Mayberry and Ellen Cronan Rose, 23–48. New York: Routledge.

Bignell, K.C. 1996. "Building Feminist Praxis out of Feminist Pedagogy: The Importance of Students' Perspectives." *Womens Studies International Forum*, 19: 315–325.

Enns, Carolyn Zerbe, and Ada L. Sinacore. 2005. *Teaching and Social Justice: Integrating Multicultural Feminist Theories in the Classroom*. Washington: Association Psychological Association.

Fisher, Berenice Malka. 2001. *No Angel in the Classroom: Teaching Through Feminist Discourse*, revised edition. Lanham: Rowman & Littlefield.

Freire, Paulo. 1970. *Pedagogy of the Oppressed*, translated by M.B. Rams. New York: Seabury Press.

hooks, bell. 1994. *Teaching to Transgress: Education as the Practice of Freedom*. New York: Routledge.

Macdonald, Amie and Susan Sanchez-Casal. 2002. *Twenty First Century Feminist Classrooms: Pedagogies of Identity and Difference*. New York: Palgrave Macmillan.

Maher, Frances A., and Mary Kay Thompson Tetreault. 2001. *The Feminist Classroom: Dynamics of Gender, Race, and Privilege*, revised edition. Lanham: Rowman & Littlefield.

Naples, Nancy A. 2002. " The Dynamic of Critical Pedagogy, Experiential Learning and Feminist Praxis in Women's Studies." In *Teaching Feminist Activism: Strategies from the Field*, edited by Nancy A. Naples and Karen Bojar, 9–21. New York: Routledge.

Naples, Nancy A., and Karen Bojar, eds. 2002. *Teaching Feminist Activism: Strategies from the Field*. New York: Routledge.

FURTHER READING

Byrd, Deborah, et al., eds. 2010. *Teaching the "isms": Feminist Pedagogy Across the Disciplines*. Institute for Teaching and Research on Women. Baltimore: Ridge Print Corporation.

Crabtree, Robbin, David Sapp, and Adela Licona. 2009. *Feminist Pedagogy: Looking Back to Move Forward*. Baltimore: Johns Hopkins University Press.

Ellsworth, Elizabeth. 1992. "Why Doesn't This Feel Empowering? Working Through the Repressive Myths of Critical Pedagogy." In *Feminisms and Critical Pedagogy*, edited by Carmen Luke and Jennifer Gore, 90–119. New York: Routledge.

Feminist Perspectives on Whiteness

LUCY F. BAILEY
Oklahoma State University, USA

The critical investigation of "whiteness" as an interdisciplinary area of study developed in the 1980s from critical race, labor, and legal studies. Feminist scholars have contributed to the anti-racist practice of theorizing whiteness through casting their critical gaze on its gendered, historical, social, legal, corporeal, and economic dimensions. Their analysis of race as a social construct and structural force in white women's lives and white feminists' complicity in racism have offered important insights for activists committed to social justice and theoretical contributions to both feminist scholarship and the field of whiteness studies. Across the last two decades, feminists have variously conceptualized whiteness in individual, intersectional, structural, and epistemological terms (as a way of knowing). While studies of whiteness continue to develop, feminists have also detailed the limits of this theoretical and emancipatory endeavor.

Scholars who theorize the concept of whiteness investigate its varied expressions and implications as well as the facets of people identified as white. In contrast to white supremacist groups organized to champion and protect the "white race," scholars in whiteness studies trace racial processes of whiteness in various contexts to critique and undermine its hegemony. Although the category "white" is a common racial designation for people of European descent, feminist scholars reject the idea that whiteness is a biological or genetic entity – a racial essence that is constitutive of a particular group of people. Instead, they argue that whiteness is a malleable and socially constructed concept deployed in varied ways to maintain white economic, social, and political power. The category is relational, accruing meaning only in relation to other concepts such as "blackness" or "indigeneity." A key feminist contribution to theorizing whiteness is examining how local and global forces, as well as gender, sexuality, nationality, ethnicity, language, and class (among other forces), shape the fluid and relational meanings of whiteness, its contours, and its effects on embodied beings.

Interdisciplinary feminist studies of whiteness have been undertaken by white scholars and scholars of color in the United States, and recently, postcolonial and indigenous scholars in England and Australia. The turn to scrutinizing whites, rather than subjects of color, is a key characteristic of whiteness studies. However, a critical stance toward whiteness accompanied its development as a racial category during the seventeenth and eighteenth centuries and throughout the nineteenth century as colonialism and migration transformed local and global relations and scientific theories justified racial hierarchies. Indeed, scholars of color have argued that analyzing whiteness has been essential to the survival of colonized and enslaved peoples. The theoretical work of African American scholar W. E. B. Du Bois in the early 1900s advanced a critical stance toward whiteness in the United States that continues to influence critical and feminist work today. The field also developed through research analyzing nineteenth-century labor patterns and diverse classifications of ethnic groups into "white" and "non-white," such as Allen's research into the "invention of the white race" that began in the 1960s (Allen 1994, 1997), and other studies tracing whiteness as a system of practices that produces "unearned" social, legal, and economic "assets" for those who appear white. Feminist analyses have offered key insights into the centrality of whiteness in American racial discourse.

Feminist studies helped expand the theoretical reach of whiteness studies beyond a homogeneous (male) white subject common in early critical studies through analyzing its gendered aspects. An important force in the development of contemporary feminist analysis of whiteness in the United States dates to the second wave of the women's movement (late 1960s and 1970s) and the critiques women of color brought to bear on white feminists' racism and solipsism about their racial positioning. Activists of color argued that white women too often assumed their concerns were universal and ignored key differences among women. Some white activists focused on gendered subordination rather than the multiple systems of oppression and axes of identity, particularly race and ethnicity, shaping women's experiences (the term "intersectionality" developed in the 1980s to refer to such intersecting aspects of identity). In response to charges of racism, some white feminists considered how white privilege had shaped their relationships, perspectives, and opportunities. Through reflexive autobiographical essays, research, and dialogue, feminists worked to raise their own critical consciousness of their racial positioning to assist in forging coalitions that better serve the interests of all women.

Minnie Bruce Pratt's (1984) and Peggy McIntosh's (1988) theorizing of their individual experiences were important contributions to this body of work. Pratt's "Identity: Skin, Blood, Heart" traced her journey to critical consciousness of her whiteness and to feminist anti-racist activism while McIntosh's well-known essay, "White Privilege and Male Privilege" (1988) detailed her process of coming to understand how whiteness accrues certain benefits neither readily available to people of color nor typically visible to whites. She crafted a list of examples of "assets" – an invisible "knapsack" of supports – that structure whites' daily experiences, such as the opportunity for whites to be viewed primarily as individuals rather than as members of a group; to choose to be in the company of their majority group most of the time; or even to purchase bandages in a shade resembling their skin color (McIntosh 1988). Those who appear white may take these daily benefits for granted, attributing their comfort, choices, and accomplishments to their individual actions rather than as an outcome of systemic benefits of whiteness. Some white feminists have not engaged in this reflective labor because they do not feel privileged, do not recognize the ways race has shaped their lives, or, given the gendered or class subordination they face, do not experience their whiteness as a personal "advantage" when comparing their gendered structural positioning to the higher social status of white men. Yet this body of work suggests that reflecting on individual privilege can facilitate awareness of structural privilege.

The invisible, or selectively visible, ways that whiteness operates in whites' lives also characterizes its structuring of broader social, economic, and political relations. Its fluid and unmarked character sustains its power. People of color, rather than whites, are often thought to "have" race, just as women, rather than men, are thought to "have" gender. Literature by Native and African American women is marked as raced and gendered, while literature written by white men is not. In this sense, whiteness is considered a normative, raceless category against which people of color appear racialized. Such patterns structure daily interactions and resources. For example, a white manager's decision to hire a qualified applicant who appears white rather than an equally qualified person of color is an unearned benefit the white applicant garners from her perceived membership in a racial group. The applicant does not necessarily have to "do" anything differently from others to benefit from the manager's racial allegiances, attitudes, or actions. Yet the manager's conscious or unconscious preferences advantage her as a white applicant. Similar daily practices among landlords, teachers, doctors, and so forth, are cumulatively woven into the fabric of institutional practices and sustain white economic privilege.

During the 1990s, fueled in part by Pratt and McIntosh's work, feminists expanded whiteness studies through scrutinizing how whiteness operates alongside and through other axes of structural positioning. Pointing to differing subject positions – a white working-class lesbian, for example, inhabits a different structural position in relation to "whiteness" than her wealthy heterosexual male counterpart – feminist scholars considered how social locations intersect and shape access to racial power. Those who benefit from white privilege may simultaneously negotiate structural disadvantages on the basis of their sexuality, religion, citizenship status, or class. For example, the term "white trash," a disparaging label sometimes used to refer to poor, rural whites, indicates how class is central to normative understandings of whiteness. Poverty fractures the homogeneity of the category and exposes its variegated meanings. Similarly, the 1790 Naturalization Act tied citizenship rights to "white" persons residing in the country for a designated period to gender and sexuality as well as race. For white women, this right was granted only through marriage because their citizenship status was linked to that of their husbands. Inscribing the word "white" into national policy initially denied citizenship to anyone deemed "non-white," rendered invisible the gendered, classed, and heterosexual nature of that whiteness, and forced diverse immigrants to advocate for legal status as whites. First Lady Abigail Adams was acutely aware of gendered white legal vulnerabilities when in 1776 she urged her Presidential husband, John, to "remember the ladies" in his political endeavors.

Intersectional analyses have also surfaced on how whiteness functions in diverse cultural processes and sites such as film, history, literature, pedagogy, politics, popular culture, research, institutional practices, and beauty culture, among others. For example, feminists have analyzed how popular culture, media, toys, and other cultural artifacts reflect and perpetuate ideologies of white heterosexual middle-class femininity that serve to regulate race, sexuality, and gender norms that fuel corporate power. Authors and producers, regardless of their race, often assume a white audience when creating their texts and toys (Morrison 1992). Dolls with "white" features, "white" characters in books, and "white" celebrities have been assumed uncritically to have universal appeal, sustaining Eurocentric aesthetics at odds with the affinities and diversity of the world's women. Companies market "white" middle-class standards of beauty internationally as a form of cultural capital women can attain through surgery, skin lighteners, hair dyes, diet products, and makeup. For customers with sufficient resources, the body is a malleable canvas that offers through cosmetics the potential to alter corporeal signifiers of race. Bodies pass, destabilizing race, while also reflecting and nourishing racial ideals, consumerism, women's bodily self-regulation, and surveilling other women's bodies that cumulatively sustains hegemonic and subordinated expressions of racialized femininity.

Feminist perspectives of whiteness also recognize its dynamic, relational character. Analyses of white masculinity reflect that vigilance to context and change, dissecting multiple, shifting hegemonic masculinities (Connell and Messerschmidt 2005) to which conceptions of race, class, and sexuality are central. Scholars have focused on "white heterosexual men" as a locus of power around which rights and benefits accrue and the social forces and institutions – from slavery and colonialism to contemporary media, policy, and sports – cultivating and enforcing damaging forms of masculinity. White power, violence, control, and entitlement have been integral to such constructions, defined against women and non-hegemonic (e.g., men of color, gay, working-class) masculinities. Class complicates access to white masculine power. While working-class labor embodies hegemonic masculine physicality, its social status is lower than middle-class work. However, in the wake of 1990s economic shifts, white men across class protested what they perceived as reverse discrimination on the basis of race affecting access to jobs. Given the fundamental role work plays in constructions of productive masculinity, economic vulnerability threatens a key source of male identity. These dynamics have resulted in a new expression of white masculinity as victimized and a backlash against affirmative action, women, immigrants, and people of color as threatening a livelihood to which they feel entitled.

More recent feminist perspectives theorize whiteness as a particular epistemological (a way of knowing) and ontological stance (a way of being in the world) that transcends the specific identity or attributes of a given individual. This is an important theoretical contribution. The standpoint of whiteness shapes how people perceive the world and their place within it. In this perspective, whiteness is not an individual attribute but a set of assumptions, practices, and habits that diverse people can acquire. The gendered metaphor of whiteness is suffused with notions of goodness, purity, civilization, innocence, and superiority that has variously signified "Europeans" or "the West," or more broadly, "humanity." Conceptualizing whiteness as a way of thinking and being suggests a cyclical process in which particular beliefs of whiteness as moral, civilized, and innocent, are structured into individual (white) psyches as normal, fueling the processes by which racialized benefits are structured into social, and then, individual practices. In this view, the status of whiteness shapes whites' fundamental orientation to the world: whose lives are of most value, one's vision for one's life, one's concepts of womanhood, one's research trajectories, and the life patterns that feel natural.

The conception of whiteness as a way of thinking and being has informed feminist analysis of colonial operations. Colonialism, the practice of one territory invading and occupying another, was justified in part through a masculine white logic that assumed people indigenous to colonized territories were feminine subjects, inferior to Europeans, in need of guidance, and incapable of self-rule. Western nations drew gendered links among the concepts of "whiteness," "rationality," and "civilization" to justify their colonial mission. Both the symbolic role of idealized white womanhood and white women's daily work were instrumental to white supremacy and colonialism. Constructions of white femininity functioned to police race and gender relations. As symbols of nationalism, white women embodied for colonial subjects the new nation's promise and the purity, respectability, civility, and morality to which they should aspire. Middle-class white women benefited from their expanding opportunities during colonialism and affirmation of their white moral goodness as agents of civilization.

Constructions of idealized white womanhood served a similar regulating function in the United States. Perceived threats to white women's safety, chastity, and roles as moral and civilizing agents also threaten nationalist projects. Both nineteenth-century resistors to abolition and white supremacists today have manufactured racist myths of the black male rapist as a threat to white women's purity to regulate race, gender, and race relations. Protecting white women's capacity to reproduce future generations of citizens has stirred particular anxieties, enduring today in the racialized politics of motherhood in which mothers are not valued equally. The philosophy of eugenics, a term that refers to efforts to improve human genetic traits, was shaped by beliefs about the racialized superiority of whiteness. Feminists have detailed the history of white supremacy and racial politics shaping reproductive and mothering rights, including birth control, surrogacy, adoption, and in vitro fertilization, that reflect fears of declining white birth rates, patterns of idealizing white motherhood, and stigmatizing and devaluing women of color.

Feminist perspectives include the awareness that focusing on whiteness, even from a critical stance, serves to codify and re-center it. In this view, well-intentioned efforts can reinforce rather than undermine white privilege by centering "whiteness" in investigation or mistakenly imply that analysis releases whites from moral complicity. Westerners may not recognize imperialist legacies in their training and assume their ideas have universal application. Such studies may also displace needed analysis of racial relations, racial processes, and marginalized groups. Additionally, detailed chartings of whiteness may not necessarily interrupt its power because its epistemological stance is not tied to specific bodies – anyone can perpetuate white ways of knowing and being. Whites and whiteness are thus relational but not synonymous. Examining white complicity in racial inequities is insufficient to interrupt deeply entrenched systems of thought, and one cannot simply shed his/her "white" identity, as some suggest, as an anti-racist act. If whiteness is a set of practices and assumptions rather than something one "has" or "is," the category cannot be cast aside at will.

Despite salient critiques, theorizing of whiteness persists from convictions that tracing how racial process are conceptualized, created, and maintained in specific contexts remains a critical anti-racist act. Whiteness is a contested, dynamic, and fiercely protected status with material benefits. Feminist, postcolonial, and indigenous perspectives have expanded and complicated whiteness studies, considering new racial processes emerging from shifting global relations and outside

US contexts, the effects of colonialism and white supremacy on whites and whiteness, white anti-racist identities and activism, pedagogy, affect studies, and virtual spaces and social media. While such analyses are increasingly complex, so too are the ways the elastic and relational concept of whiteness is sustained and reconfigured, even as many white/Western subjects perceive their subject positions as raceless. If, as some scholars suggest, whiteness has accrued a universalizing quality sometimes associated with the state of being human, examining new approaches and sites of inquiry remain valuable.

SEE ALSO: Critical Race Theory; Eurocentrism; White Supremacy and Gender

REFERENCES

Allen, Theodore W. 1994, 1997. *The Invention of the White Race*, vol. 1 and 2. New York: Verso.

Connell, R. W., and James W. Messerschmidt. 2005. "Hegemonic Masculinity: Rethinking the Concept." *Gender & Society*, 19(6): 829–859.

McIntosh, Peggy. 1988. *White Privilege and Male Privilege: A Personal Account of Coming to See Correspondences through Work in Women's Studies*. Wellesley: Wellesley College Center for Research on Women.

Morrison, Toni. 1992. *Playing in the Dark*. New York: Random House.

Pratt, Minnie B. 1984. "Identity: Skin Blood Heart." In *Yours in Struggle: Three Feminist Perspectives on Anti-Semitism and Racism*, edited by Elly Bulkin, Minnie B. Pratt, and Barbara Smith, 11–63. New York: Long Haul Press.

FURTHER READING

Feminist Theory. 2007. 8(2).

Frankenberg, Ruth. 1993. *White Woman, Race Matters: The Social Construction of Whiteness*. Minneapolis: University of Minnesota Press.

Moreton-Robinson, Aileen. 2000. *Talkin' Up to the White Woman: Indigenous Women and Feminism*. St Lucia: University of Queensland Press.

Painter, Nell I. 2011. *The History of White People*. New York: Norton.

Ware, Vron. 1992. *Beyond the Pale: White Women, Racism, and History*. London: Verso.

Feminist Psychotherapy

ELLYN KASCHAK
San Jose State University, USA, and the University for Peace, Costa Rica

EARLY HISTORY

Feminist psychotherapy came into existence in the late 1960s and early 1970s as a direct outgrowth of the second wave of the women's liberation movement. Women in the United States and other Western countries had begun organizing consciousness-raising groups based on the Speak Bitterness groups of the Chinese revolution. These groups were rooted in a life-changing idea that "The personal is political," initially popularized by Carol Hanisch in her article of the same name and quickly adopted by feminists everywhere.

In these groups, women gathered to speak of the troubling personal issues in their lives and to make the connection between these issues and the politics of society, to name the personal pain and transform it into political change. Such concerns as anxiety and fear, depression, body image and eating disorders among women, hidden and unspoken experiences of childhood sexual abuse, and the incidence of rape began to be discussed and named in these groups Previously, these experiences of abuse and molestation of girls and women were believed by the professions of psychology and psychiatry to be extremely rare; the number of women slowly but surely coming to consciousness and speaking out overwhelmingly demonstrated that this supposition was erroneous and unfounded.

For psychotherapists, the prevalence of these experiences, along with many other forms of distress, revealed the inadequacy of then contemporary models of treatment. From behaviorism to humanism to Freudianism, all the contemporary forms of psychotherapy ignored or distorted the actual experiences of girls and women in context.

Prominent among these was Freudian theory and practice, soon revealed to be biased by the perspective of Freud himself, whose ideas were being applied to demonstrate the inferiority and second-class status of women (Chodorow 1978; Kaschak 1992; Lerman 1996). As a result of belief in such phallocentric concepts as the Oedipal complex, women's memories of childhood abuse had been considered, by most therapists of the time, to be the product of wish and fantasy. Kaschak eventually deconstructed and reconstructed the Oedipal conflict within a gendered and societal context and replaced it for women only with her Antigone complex, also a consideration of the female self in context. Through this lens, men could also be treated in a feminist context.

BIAS IN PSYCHOLOGY AND PSYCHOTHERAPY

Naomi Weisstein (1968) published her classic article *Psychology Constructs the Female*, in which she stated, "Psychology has nothing to say about what women are really like, what they need and what they want, especially because psychology does not know" (1971, 197). Psychological theories and models continued to be unmasked as based almost entirely on male experience. In *Women and Madness* (1972), Phyllis Chesler presented a scathing and incisive analysis of the patriarchal nature of the psychological professions. There followed an outpouring of theoretical, clinical, and empirical studies demonstrating the biases of pre-feminist psychology in its understanding and treatment of women. A groundbreaking study by Broverman et al. (1972) demonstrated that therapists held women and men to entirely different standards of mental health. The healthy normal individual was considered by researchers and therapists alike to be a white male. The practice of more frequently diagnosing African American patients as psychotic was also being revealed. The sexism and racism that pervaded society was equally present in all aspects of the field of psychotherapy.

At the same time, as a result of Title IX and other federal legislation, an entire generation of women was admitted into the graduate and professional schools of the United States in previously unprecedented numbers. Having arrived, these students instantly discovered that not only had they not been part of the academy or the professions themselves, but they were similarly absent from models or theories of psychology except as inferior versions of males. This generation set about changing all that by challenging subjective theories, the use of only white, male subjects in research, and other related biases and practices. Psychotherapy was revealed to be an enterprise that needed complete revision and many female therapists and trainees set about the task (Kaschak 1976; Miller 1976; Walker 1979).

FEMINIST MODELS OF PSYCHOTHERAPY

Having participated in time-limited consciousness-raising (CR) groups, women also began to search for deeper psychological understanding and a therapeutic experience necessary to deal with these newly developed insights. Many who were already studying to become psychotherapists and the few already in the field began to turn their efforts toward this problem. Some untrained women, as well, began of necessity to counsel the many women who had discovered that they had been abused in some way. The latter effort resulted in many of these "grassroots" counselors enrolling in graduate programs and becoming licensed counselors and therapists. Both groups, with a great deal of overlap in membership, became the founders of the field of feminist psychotherapy.

Feminist therapy set about equalizing the power differential in therapy by encouraging self-disclosure by the therapist, sliding scale fees, and the idea that the personal is always also political. Lesbian and bisexual women were treated as normal in every way, considerations of gender and ethnicity/race were noted as central to any effective approach, and, perhaps most revolutionary of all, therapists would believe that what women said they had experienced had really happened and was not merely a wish or a fantasy. This was the first time women clients/patients were considered by their own psychotherapists to be telling the truth unless otherwise indicated.

Feminist therapists simultaneously began to develop models of psychotherapy that took into consideration the social and political contexts of women's lives, as well as their real lived experiences (Brodsky 1973; Kaschak 1976; Chodorow 1978). During the first decade of feminist psychotherapy, analysis and treatment were developed almost exclusively by collectives of feminist psychotherapists who had organized themselves in a few major urban centers, such as Boston, New York, Philadelphia, San Francisco, and Los Angeles. There was also an analytically oriented group that created the Women's Therapy Center in London in 1976. Most members were young women who were themselves still students or early career professionals and had become involved in the feminist critique of psychotherapy. These groups developed the principles of feminist therapy and eventually formed into a national group known as the Feminist Therapy Institute. Many, in fact most, of the ideas and principles introduced by these early feminists are now considered pro forma in virtually all psychotherapeutic approaches – first and foremost the acknowledgment of gender as a centrally important construct and acknowledging thereby the lived experiences of women.

Feminist psychotherapy soon produced its own ethical code that paid particular attention to "boundary violations" and the imposition of sex on clients and patients by some male therapists, who defended the practice as therapeutic. The treatment of the various abuses that girls and women experience, sexually and otherwise, expanded to become the separate field of trauma, now deemed a specialty within psychology with its own experts, journals, conferences, and APA (American Psychiatric Association) division.

Feminist psychology was rapidly adopted by feminist practitioners of family therapy, which had been dealing with issues of power and control inside the family without dealing clearly with issues of gender in that same area. While they met as much resistance as had the individually oriented group, they persevered and eventually their analysis could no longer be resisted.

Feminist psychologists and psychiatrists also undertook a profound critique of the holy grail of diagnosis, the then third edition of the Diagnostic and Statistical Manual (DSM-3) of the American Psychiatric Association. Partially in response to these early feminists, the DSM has undergone several revisions in the ensuing years and many of the gender-biased diagnoses have been removed or radically revised. Nevertheless, many feminist practitioners consider the entire enterprise of psychiatric diagnosis to be unscientific, culturally biased, and based in the service of the American insurance industry rather than of the professions.

CONTEMPORARY FEMINIST PSYCHOTHERAPY

Originally, the nascent field of feminist psychotherapy organized itself into three groups: radical feminist therapy, liberal feminist therapies, and non-sexist therapy. The most significant differences were that radical therapists maintained that society had to be changed at the roots; liberal feminists believed that equal rights and other modifications were sufficient change; and non-sexist therapists felt that they could make therapy non-sexist without having to adhere to feminist principles. The radical faction often included lesbians, women of color, and other marginalized individuals in their ranks. The more liberal faction emphasized the importance of women's relationships and, after many years of suffering criticism as essentialist, has acknowledged the crucial importance of the cultural context. In recognition of this shift in emphasis, the group responsible for the development of Self in Relation therapy officially changed its name to Cultural Relational Therapy (CRT). The majority of the more radical group had practiced Self in Context approaches (Kaschak 1992; Brown 1994; Worrell and Remer 2003) and cultural complexity from inception.

Feminist therapy became multicultural and global and can be found in such diverse countries as Russia, Poland, Costa Rica, Israel, Palestine, Bosnia, Serbia, Egypt, the Philippines, Japan, most of Western Europe, England, New Zealand, and Australia.

In the United States, Crenshaw introduced the concept of intersectionality, which was enthusiastically adopted by practitioners of feminist and multicultural approaches. Kaschak (1992) soon after discussed the inclusion of the entire cultural frame in understanding multiple cause and effects, including, race, class, ethnicity, and a multitude of other influences and characteristics. She named that approach the Mattering Map (Kaschak 1992). McIntosh (1998) presented the issue of white privilege in her forceful article that added significantly to the paradigm. It became clearer than ever that women suffer from many gender, ethnicity, class, and sexual orientation related disorders originating in societal discrimination as much as in personal experience. Precisely, there is no purely personal experience, according to feminist therapy.

In 1978, the American Psychiatric Association voted on a new diagnostic category, which they called post-traumatic stress disorder (PTSD), to be applied to returning Vietnam veterans. Feminist psychiatrists and psychologists were able, through political pressure, to have "women's issues," such as surviving rape, domestic violence, and abuse, included in the description of the disorder. As the incidence of abuse of women and girls was revealed, this aspect of feminist therapy morphed into an entire "field" now known as trauma-based treatment (Herman 1992). As well, there is a separate field dealing with eating disorders that grows larger all the time.

The field of feminist therapy continues to thrive in the twenty-first century, with many books and articles published every year, annual meetings of the Association for Women in Psychology (AWP), and an active division (35) of the American Psychological Association, among other organizations. The journal *Women and Therapy* was founded in 1983 and other journals, such as *Feminist Family Therapy, Psychology of Women Quarterly, Sex Roles,* and *Feminism & Psychology* are also published regularly. Sadly, the fields of trauma and eating disorders have also grown exponentially and continue to thrive in their own right. A liberation movement created a cultural revolution that, in turn, has resulted in the development of many new tools, prominent among them an entirely new profession, feminist therapy.

SEE ALSO: Consciousness-Raising; Intersectionality; Oedipal Conflict; Patriarchy; Post-Traumatic Stress Disorder; Psychological Theory, Research, Methodology, and Feminist Critiques

REFERENCES

Brodsky, Annette M. 1973. "The Consciousness-Raising Group as a Model for Therapy with Women." *Psychotherapy: Theory, Research & Practice*, 10(1): 24–29.

Broverman, Inge K., Donald M. Broverman, Frank E. Clarkson, Paul S. Rosenkrantz, and Susan R. Vogel. 1970. "Sex-role Stereotypes and Clinical Judgements of Mental Health." *Journal of Consulting and Clinical Psychology*, 34(1), 1–7.

Brown, Laura. 1994. *Subversive Dialogues*. New York: Basic Books.

Chesler, Phyllis. 1972. *Women and Madness*. Garden City, NY: Doubleday.

Chodorow, Nancy. 1978. *The Reproduction of Mothering: Psychoanalysis and the Sociology of Gender*. Berkeley: University of California Press.

Herman, Judith L. 1992. *Trauma and Recovery*. New York: Basic Books.

Kaschak, Ellyn. 1976. "Sociotherapy: An Ecological Model for Psychotherapy with Women." *Psychotherapy: Theory, Research and Practice*, 13(1): 61–63.

Kaschak, Ellyn. 1992. *Engendered Lives*. New York: Basic Books.

Lerman, Hannah. 1996. *A Mote in Freud's Eye: From Psychoanalysis to the Psychology of Women*. New York: Springer.

McIntosh, Peggy. 1998. "White Privilege: Unpacking the Invisible Knapsack." In *Re-visioning Family Therapy: Race, Culture and Gender in Clinical Practice*, edited by Monica McGoldrick, 147–152. New York: Guilford Press.

Weisstein, Naomi. 1971. "Psychology Constructs the Female." *Journal of Social Education*, 35: 362–373.

Worrell, Judith, and Pamela Remer. 2003. *Feminist Perspectives in Therapy: Empowering Diverse Women*, 2nd ed. New York: Wiley.

FURTHER READING

Brodsky, Annette M., and Rachel Hare-Mustin, eds. 1980. *Women and Psychotherapy*. New York: Guilford.

Greenspan, Miriam. 1983. *A New Approach to Women and Therapy*. New York: McGraw-Hill.

Hare-Mustin, Rachel. 1978. "A Feminist Approach to Family Therapy." *Family Process*, 17(2): 181–194.

Miller, Jean B. 1976. *Toward a New Psychology of Women*. Boston: Beacon Press.

Sharratt, Sara, and Ellyn Kaschak, eds. 1999. *Assault on the Soul: Women in the Former Yugoslavia*. New York: Haworth Press.

Walker, Lenore E. 1979. *The Battered Woman Syndrome*. New York: Harper and Row.

Feminist Publishing

SUSAN HAWTHORNE
James Cook University, Cairns, Australia

INTRODUCTION

Feminist publishing bounces into existence whenever there is a movement of women to free themselves from oppression, and in the late decades of the twentieth century until now, it has brought about the distribution of many new, challenging, creative, and controversial ideas through books and other media. Indeed, the understanding of the world would be poorer without the work of feminist publishers. This entry is about the contemporary feminist publishing scene, which started its resurgence in the 1960s followed by a flowering of feminist publishing in the early 1970s.

The most ancient attributable writing in the world is by the Sumerian poet Enheduanna (c.2300 BCE). There are also the Akkadian poet Eristi-Aye (c.1790–1745 BCE); the Greek poet Sappho (c.630 BCE), known as the Tenth Muse; and in Japan Murakami Shikibu (974–1031 CE), author of *The Tale of Genji*, the first novel ever written. Modernists Virginia Woolf, Gertrude Stein, and HD (Hilda Doolittle) all published books privately and in limited editions. Women have long fought for ways to express themselves, and in prehistoric times – before writing – women's storytelling was the key method of passing on cultural knowledge.

It took people of a radical turn of mind to publish Mary Wollstonecraft's *A Vindication of the Rights of Woman* (1792), which was her response to the French Revolution. Almost a century later in the United States, Elizabeth Cady Stanton and 25 other women were writing and publishing *The Woman's Bible* (1895, 1898), while in what is currently known as Bangladesh, Rokeya Sakhawat Hossain, a Muslim feminist and reformer, published her novella *Sultana's Dream* (1905).

FEMINIST SMALL PRESSES IN THE ENGLISH-SPEAKING WORLD

The world of publishing changed massively in the last century. It has shifted from shilling thrillers and hardcover copies to paperbacks and e-books and other forms of digital publishing. Feminist publishers have played an important role in the changing face of publishing.

When Virginia Woolf set type for the Hogarth Press, this was an art form several hundred years old and required her to become a type compositor. Woolf was engaged in taking over the means of production and today would be seen as a self-published writer. She and her husband Leonard also published many other innovative and exciting modernist writers. The benefit of being on the inside of this process is that you are not beholden to the quirks of fate and fashion that can make or break a writer. Indeed, Woolf said of herself that she was "the only woman in England free to write what I like" (Woolf 1953, 83).

Feminist publishers have engaged in self-publishing and taking over the means of production in some instances as well as setting up publishing houses that range from the very small to significant global players.

Feminist publishing experienced a resurgence in the early 1970s when works like Judy Grahn's *Edward the Dyke* and *A Woman is Talking to Death* were published along with new, sometimes subversive books from United States-based Persephone Press and Diana Press, not to mention the large number of mimeographed and photocopied single articles that did the rounds of the women's movement. In Australia, a group called Radicalesbians published a pirated edition of Robin Morgan's poetry collection, *Monster* (1972). These publishers and writers changed the outlook on the world of a generation of readers alongside the mainstream published works of Germaine Greer, Kate Millett, Shulamith Firestone, Ti-Grace Atkinson, Jill Johnston, and others.

EXPERIMENTATION TO MAINSTREAM

In Australia, the feminist newspaper *The Dawn* was founded in 1888 by Louisa Lawson and ran for 17 years. It was the first journal in Australia to be produced solely by women. In the next feminist generation, Bessie Guthrie founded the Viking Press in Sydney in 1939, mostly publishing women poets.

In 1976, the Non-Sexist Children's Book Collective was formed in Melbourne. The group took on four short manuscripts, which were eventually published, and soon changed its name to Sugar and Snails. Feminist publishing in Australia branched out in the 1970s with, in Melbourne, Sisters in 1979 and Sybylla Press in 1982. Poetry and anthologies were important elements in these ventures. Sisters drew on a more mainstream audience and its publishers were already running their own companies, while Sybylla's anthologies, novels, and autobiographies were decidedly experimental. Sybylla initially set up as a printer, hiring out its services for bread and butter and publishing one or two titles a year. Also in Melbourne, Dykebooks set up as an alternative self-publishing venture to publish lesbian fiction, poetry, and in recent years documentary "herstories" of the women's liberation movement. In Sydney, Women's Redress Press, which existed throughout the 1980s, published important anthologies of poetry, short fiction, novellas, and work by migrant women writers, including bilingual editions. Gorgon's Head Press has published lesbian feminist theory. Meanwhile in Adelaide, from 1986, Tantrum Press produced feminist books by South Australian women, including cassette recordings. In Melbourne in the early 1990s two presses started. Artemis Publishing, founded by Jocelynne Scutt, published anthologies of autobiographies by Australian women and crime fiction. Spinifex Press, founded by Renate Klein and Susan Hawthorne in 1991, was established to publish innovative and controversial international feminist books with an optimistic edge. Spinifex was the first feminist press in Australia to make the move to e-books in 2006. In more than two decades, Spinifex Press has published thousands of writers from every continent and has a list of around 250 titles, most of which are available as e-books.

In New Zealand, *Broadsheet* magazine had an impact inside the country similar to *Ms Magazine* in the United States or *Spare Rib* in the United Kingdom. While *Courage* in Germany lasted from 1978 to 1984, *Emma* still continues to this day. Book publishers in New Zealand included New Women's Press run by publisher Wendy Harrex. Bridget Williams Books published non-fiction books for and about women, and Daphne Brassel published fiction and non-fiction for the trade and was instrumental in setting up the Māori-run Huia Press. Spiral Press made a big splash by publishing Keri Hulme's *The Bone People* (1984), which went on to win the Booker Prize and the Pegasus Prize for Literature in 1985 and subsequently was made available in a mainstream edition from Hodder and Stoughton in 1985.

The United States was a hive of feminist publishing activity from the early 1970s until the mid-1990s. The Feminist Press based at the City University of New York was founded in 1970 and released long-out-of-print works by Zora Neale Hurston and Charlotte Perkins Gilman. Founder Florence Howe, with her international outlook, led the press to publish some extraordinary books by writers from around the world. Three series in particular – the anthologies *Women Writing in India*, *Women Writing in Africa*, and *Women Writing in the Middle East* – have brought many writers previously unknown in the mainstream English market to world attention. *The Defiant Muse* series brings parallel texts from European women's poetry in Italian, German, French, Hispanic, Hebrew, Dutch, and Flemish languages. Alongside these anthologies sit original works by wry and humorous Ghanian writer Ama Ata Aidoo and by Grace Paley, in whose works one can hear the rhythms of New York Jewish speech. The Feminist Press continues to publish new titles and must be congratulated for its longevity.

Daughters Press and Diana Press were two very small presses with impressive publications by first-rate writers and thinkers. *Ruby Fruit Jungle* (1973) by Rita Mae Brown was passed around lesbian communities at the speed of light (in much the same way that the LP *Lavender Jane Loves Women* did in music). Daughters went on to publish a number of writers, including Elana Dykewomon and June Arnold. Diana Press published a series of small books with titles such as *Lesbianism in the Women's Movement* and *Class in the Women's Movement*. They were short books with readily accessible, punchy essays by young radical lesbian feminists. Many of these titles have since become classics.

A number of presses have specialized in spirituality and archaeology. Among them Knowledge, Ideas and Trends (KIT) in Connecticut has published books by and about the work of radical archaeologist Marija Gimbutas and books on goddess religions, as has Astarte Shell Press in Portland, Oregon.

In Canada, Inanna Publications specializes in these subjects as well as in women's studies titles and poetry. (Feminist spirituality and archaeology are areas of specialty for a number of mainstream publishing houses such as Beacon, Shambalah, and HarperSanFrancisco.)

There was a huge growth in feminist, lesbian, and women's presses in this period across the United States and Canada. Among them are, on the West Coast: Aunt Lute/Spinsters Ink, Calyx, Seal Press, Cleis Press, HerBooks, Conari Press, Red Letter Press, Papier-Mache Press, and Shameless Hussy. Aunt Lute's multicultural publishing has been especially successful with its backlist because its books are widely used in courses. Aunt Lute author Judy Grahn won the 2013 American Book Award for her memoir, *A Simple Revolution: The Making of an Activist Poet*; Calyx's literary publishing has been groundbreaking, and Seal's translations brought new work into the English-language readership. Further east are Persephone Press, Crossing Press, Kitchen Table: Women of Color Press, New Victoria, and Firebrand. Firebrand published Alison Bechdel, Dorothy Allison, Audre Lorde, Jewel Gomez, and many others. In Florida, Naiad Press had huge success in publishing lesbian books, both new and out-of-print lesbian romances by writers like Katherine V. Forrest and Claire McNab through to classics such as Gertrude Stein's poem, *Lifting Belly*. The Naiad imprint has been taken over by Bella Books. Kitchen Table: Women of Color Press brought important works to publication, including the classic anthologies *This Bridge Called My Back*, *Home Girls*, and *Cuentos*. There are too many small magazines to list but important ones that publish both fiction and non-fiction (that are not university- or mainstream-owned) include, in the United States: *Quest*, *Trivia*, *Sinister Wisdom*, *Heresies*, and *Conditions*; in the United Kingdom: *Trouble and Strife*; in Australia: *MeJane*, *Refractory Girl*, *Hecate*, *Poetrix*, and *Lip*; and in Canada: *Tessera*. These magazines gave voice to new writers, new themes, and new kinds of writing.

The explosion of publishing inspired by the women's movement is shown by the 300-page book *Guide to Women's Publishing* (1978), which not only lists and describes the publishers active at that time, but also includes articles on journals and newspapers, distribution companies, and booksellers.

Feminist publishing flourished in Canada also. These presses were mainly small and many published books that were experimental in nature. Among them are Press Gang, Women's Press, Sister Vision, Gynergy, Sumach, Ragweed, and Second Story. Press Gang, set up in 1975, publishes lesbians, First Nation writers, and women of color. French-speaking Canada created Les Éditions du Remue-Ménage in 1975, which published the work of Nicole Brossard and other francophone writers. As one example, Brossard's book *La lettre aérienne* was subsequently published in English as *The Aerial Letter* by the Women's Press, Canada. Currently the Women's Press has become less radical and its website states that it publishes Canadian writers. Sister Vision was the first publishing house run by black women and women of color in Canada. Second Story has had a huge success with children's books and young adult fiction, in addition to trade fiction and non-fiction, and has a very active schedule of publishing.

The United Kingdom and Ireland has quite a different history of feminist publishing and feminist publishers have come from every part of the British Isles. Three publishers had significant international market clout outside of the US market: Virago, The Women's Press, and Pandora. Unusually, all had women from the former British colonies at their head: Carmen Callil (Australia) at Virago;

Stephanie Dowrick (New Zealand) and Ros de Lanerolle (Zimbabwe) at The Women's Press; while the idea for Pandora was inspired by Dale Spender (Australia). Perhaps with their outsider status, these women could see ways around the rather stultifying world of British publishing. Whatever the reason, all three of these publishers sold many books by many authors. No feminist household (in the UK publishing territory) is likely to have been without at least some books from these three publishers.

Virago started by bringing out-of-print classics back into print. The writers they published had been household names in previous eras. It was also an astute business decision, with lower costs of production than books by living authors. But it was not long before the list expanded into contemporary writing. The Women's Press made quite a statement with its logo of the iron on its striped spine. It published an incredible range of writers from around the world, including Africa, Turkey, India, and South America. Here was an education in international feminist writing. It also published radical writing by feminists such as Mary Daly, Jane Caputi, Sheila Jeffreys, and others. Pandora found a space between these two publishers that included new fiction and out-of-print works, political works such as those on reproductive technologies (*Test-Tube Women*) and women's studies (*Theories of Women's Studies*), and a significant number of titles around the history of women's writing, including Dale Spender's *Mothers of the Novel*.

Both Virago and The Women's Press started young adult lists under the names Upstarts (Virago) and Livewire (The Women's Press). Virago is now owned by Little, Brown and continues to publish. The others remain publishers only in name and are not currently publishing new titles. The Women's Press (UK) was the publisher of Alice Walker's *The Color Purple*, and when the book was turned into a film, it was a great success. But success creates expectations, and The Women's Press could not maintain either the momentum or the sales in the following years. Managing director Ros de Lanerolle said that it was the beginning of the end for them.

Elsewhere in the United Kingdom, Myriad Editions in Brighton is run by former *Women's Studies International Forum* editor Candida Lacey. Scotland has brought us the Edinburgh-based Linen Press, a relative newcomer that prides itself on working closely with authors every step of the way. This is one way a small press can do things differently from mainstream publishers. And from Wales comes Honno, established in 1986 by volunteers. It publishes books in English and Welsh by women writers.

These are not the only feminist publishers in the British Isles. From Ireland came Attic Press, which published the works of Irish feminists and had a series of political pamphlets as well as some important anthologies. Sheba Feminist Publishing was a small radical press that published the first edition of Suniti Namjoshi's classic, *Feminist Fables*. The short-lived Open Letters had a great initial list but failed early because of the ill health and premature death of its co-founder, Ros de Lanerolle. Onlywomen published radical and lesbian writing, the most famous of which is probably *For Lesbians Only: A Separatist Anthology*, a book that could not find a publisher in North America.

INTERNATIONAL FEMINIST BOOK FAIRS AND THE MARKETING OF FEMINIST BOOKS

In 1984, feminist publishing was thriving in the United Kingdom and Silvermoon Bookstore in London's Charing Cross Road was a meeting place for women from around the world. Sisterwrite bookshop in Islington carried an exhaustive range of international publications, while Compendium in Camden had a substantial feminist stock. In this year, the First International Feminist Book Fair was held in London. The event brought together feminist writers, publishers, booksellers, and readers from around the world. From the beginning it was both international and multicultural, a space for lesbians and heterosexual feminists alike. Over the next decade the International Feminist Book Fair, with its advisory committee headed by Carole Spedding, would travel to Oslo (1986), Montreal (1988), Barcelona (1990), Amsterdam (1992), and Melbourne (1994). Each country put its own stamp on the event but it also became a way for women working in the publishing industry to meet one another every two years. Some strong friendships and business relationships emerged out of this, and feminist publishers began to co-publish works across territories and have newly discovered works translated into other languages. The Women's Press (UK), Kali for Women (India), The Feminist Press (USA), Spinifex Press (Australia), and Frauenoffensive (Germany) talked about how feminist presses in different regions and even different languages might work together in joint publishing ventures simultaneously. These discussions happened before it was possible to instantaneously share files, jointly edit in Dropbox, or do instant messaging. The destruction of feminist publishing in North America, the United Kingdom, and Europe has temporarily reduced these ventures occurring. But feminist publishers in India, Australia, New Zealand, South Africa, Turkey, and the United States are continuing to engage in co-publishing arrangements.

Out of the International Feminist Book Fairs grew another phenomenon: the book fortnights. A Feminist Book Fortnight was run in London from the 1980s to 1990s as an annual two-week period in which a catalogue of feminist books was distributed to bookshops. Twenty titles were listed as Feminist Book Fortnight Favourites, which formed the basis of window displays. Bookshops were encouraged to host readings and events by authors in the catalogue. In Australia, two Feminist Book Fortnights were held in 1989 and 1991, with more than 200 events around the country from Burnie in Tasmania to Broome in the far northwest. In New Zealand, the Listener Women's Book Festival ran annually for about a decade in the 1990s, and the United States had a *Summer Feminist Reading Catalog*.

Women in Publishing was started in the United Kingdom in 1979 and among its earliest members were the women running feminist presses. It was established to promote the status of women in the industry and to help them develop their careers. It has chapters in the United Kingdom, United States, Hong Kong, Ireland, India, the Philippines, Australia, and Germany. In Germany, the organization Bücherfrauen has been active since 1990, each year naming a particular woman whose work in the book industry has made a difference; they have included publishers, writers, booksellers, magazine editors, translators, librarians, and agents. There are 16 branches in cities across Germany and numerous activities throughout the year culminate in the annual awards at the Frankfurt Book Fair in October. In other countries, Women in Publishing has existed but with less success than in Germany because it lost its radical edge and the word "feminist" was hardly ever used. Instead of being an organization for women who had something to give to the community for political reasons, it became a get-ahead organization with very little analysis of the reasons why women working in publishing remained underpaid and underrecognized.

The giving of prizes has increased across the publishing world. The Feminist Book Fortnights attempted to avoid the star phenomenon by spreading the prize across 20 titles. In recent years the Women's Prize for Fiction (formerly the Orange Prize) in the United Kingdom and the Stella Prize in Australia have highlighted the ways in which women's writing is sidelined in mainstream publishing. The Orange Prize came into existence in 1992 following all-male shortlists of the Booker Prize in the United Kingdom, and the Stella Prize in 2013 after recognition that in its 54-year history only 10 women had won the Miles Franklin Prize. Both prizes put out a longlist as well as a shortlist that helps to promote all the books included on these lists.

INTERNATIONAL FEMINIST PUBLISHING

Feminist publishers have flourished in many different language markets. The German-language market has had a number of very successful feminist publishers, among them the earliest (originally part of the left-wing publisher Trikont Verlag), Frauenoffensive, independent since 1975 with its international bestseller, *Shedding* by Verena Stefan. Frauenoffensive publishes trade fiction and non-fiction and has translated many well-known works from English, including books by Janice Raymond, Betty McLellan, and Dale Spender. Orlanda Verlag (which was originally called sub rosa) made new inroads into publishing black women writers from Germany, Jewish voices like Adrienne Rich, and several works by Audre Lorde. Ulrike Helmer started to publish classical works by and about women and continues to this day with topical non-fiction and lesbian fiction. Argument Verlag (a left-wing publisher) began a crime imprint called Ariadne, which has existed for over 25 years. Verlag Krug and Schadenberg have published a strong list of literary lesbian writing, while Aviva Verlag, which was founded in 1997, specializes in books by and about forgotten women authors and artists of the 1920s and 1930s. The literary review magazine *Virginia Frauenbuchkritik* is still being published twice a year after more than 27 years. In Austria, Milena Verlag (formerly Weiner Frauenverlag) used to be a feminist publisher. Brigitte Ebersbach, one of the founding members of eFeF Verlag in Switzerland, founded editions ebersbach in 1990. Her main focus is on discovering older publications, especially about textiles, and literary wall calendars.

Other presses include Weismann Verlag – Frauenbuchverlag, now known as Antje Kunstmann, and Lilith Verlag, which grew out of one of the three women's bookshops of the same name in Berlin. In Germany, as in the United Kingdom, several large mainstream houses picked up on feminist publishing in the 1980s; among them were rororo neue frau from Rowohlt, begun by Angela Praesent, Die Frau in der Gesellschaft, an imprint of Fischer, and Die Frau in der Literatur, a list from Ullstein. None of these exists any longer.

The Netherlands had two publishers. Feministische uitgeverij Sara (1977–1987) published Dutch and international fiction and non-fiction and was taken over by Uitgeverij An Decker specializing in literature and poetry. In 1993, it was taken over by Feministische uitgeverij Vita with its lesbian imprint, Furie, and continued until 1998. In 2004, a new publisher of lesbian writers arrived on the scene, La Vita Publishing, a nice play on the name of Vita Sackville-West.

France has struggled to maintain a lively feminist publishing scene in spite of an active women's movement. The copyrighting of the words "Mouvement de Libération des Femmes" by publisher Des Femmes was correctly seen as an appropriative move, one that attempted to privatize what in other countries represented a collective movement. Éditions Tierce was active in France for many years around the same time as Des Femmes and was more identified with the feminist movement, although it was not as well known or as long-lived. It was followed by côté-femmes, which later became integrated as the feminist collection in well-known alternative publisher L'Harmattan. More recently, Editions iXe have emerged as a new independent feminist publisher.

The first feminist publishing house in Italy came out of Milan in 1975. It was Tartaruga Edizione, set up by Laura Lepetit, and its first publication was a translation of *Three Guineas* by Virginia Woolf. The publishing house became well known throughout Italy and continues to publish. Other feminist publishing houses in Italy include Essedue Edizione, which works in conjunction with the University of Verona and publishes books on ancient history and religion. In Florence, Estro Editrice focuses on books by women and on lesbian culture. In Rome, Firmato Donna was founded in 1988 to promote women's writing. Cooperative Libera Stampa publishes trade books on current affairs, fiction, and poetry. Palermo in Sicily has Luna Edizione, which runs an annual prize, and Dharba Editrice. In Syracuse there is Ombra Editrice, and in Sardinia, Tarantola Edizioni.

Indian feminist publishers have brought important works into the market in both English and Indian languages. Delhi-based Kali for Women, founded and run by Urvashi Butalia and Ritu Menon, began publishing in 1984. They were among the publishers participating regularly in the International Feminist Book Fairs and have published significant historical documents, feminist theory, histories, fiction, and poetry, focusing on the voices of minorities. They were the publishers of Vandana Shiva's first book, *Staying Alive*, in 1989. In 2003, Kali for Women became two presses. One is Zubaan, which has a big children's and young adult list as well as trade fiction and non-fiction; it works with Penguin Books India in the distribution of its books. The second press to come out of Kali is Women Unlimited, run by Ritu Menon, which has a more academic edge to its publishing output and also publishes poetry and fiction. Streelekha in Calcutta publishes non-fiction titles including women's studies and politics. Tulika Books in Delhi publishes academic titles in history, art, and social sciences, while the unrelated Tulika Books in Chennai has a strong children's list, including works by feminist poet Suniti Namjoshi. The publishers at Tara Books in Chennai, V. Geeta and Gita Wolf, work with many Indian tribal peoples and produce handmade books as well as picture books for children and a line of beautiful stationery.

In Bangladesh, Farida Akhter's Narigrantha Prabartana publishes activist books, in particular books on globalization, women's health, farming, critiques of population control, as well as pamphlets for international organizations such as the Food and Agriculture Organization (FAO). Farida Akhter's *Women and Trees* is a fine example of small press publishing that challenges Western assumptions. It has also published books by German feminist Maria Mies.

South Africa has a number of presses that publish feminist books. Jacana publishes political books – both anti-apartheid and feminist – while Modjaji Books, a relative newcomer, is publishing some very fine fiction and poetry by women, including lesbian fiction. The most recent feminist press to emerge is Huza Press in Rwanda, founded by Louise Umutoni, which will be publishing a collection of short stories in late 2015.

Feminist publishing companies have also existed in Scandinavia, Eastern Europe, Turkey, and the Middle East. Among the very small publishers at the 6th International Feminist Book Fair in 1994 were Nour Arab Women's Publishing (Egypt), JoJo Workshop for Women (Japan), Women Living Under Muslim Law (France), Blackbooks

(Vanuatu), Daphne Brasell Associates (Aotearoa/New Zealand), and Gorgon's Head Press (Australia).

THREATS TO FEMINIST PUBLISHING

In the early 1990s, the American book fair (now called BEA) had an aisle specifically for feminist, lesbian, and gay publishers. Before the fair started, feminist booksellers and publishers would have separate day-long meetings to strategize, get to know one another, and share information. With around 100 feminist booksellers and 50 feminist publishers, it was a rich and exciting atmosphere. Carole Seajay, through her monthly publication *Feminist Bookstore News*, helped booksellers and publishers alike to know what was going on, what was cutting edge, and what were the threats facing feminist publishing.

At the US book fair meeting in 1994, Nancy Bereano of Firebrand warned that the Borders chain of bookstores was threatening feminist publishing. It had started in 1992 when Borders was bought by K-Mart and the Borders brand had become a by-word for superstore. In 1994, there were more than 100 feminist bookstores around the United States. Borders began to sweep through the nation, setting up new outlets across the street, around the corner, and next door to good independent bookstores, many of which were feminist and some gay and lesbian. This coincided with the computerization of the industry and inventories. The low-profit independents struggled to keep pace with Borders, which made sure it had all the same specialist stock, and furthermore could afford to fly in high-selling authors for events. Feminist presses benefited briefly from the increase in sales, but soon discovered that the habit of over-ordering by Borders was a calamity for them. Publishers thought they had run out of stock, put in place a reprint, and were then faced with massive returns from the superstores. This crippled a number of feminist publishers. In Australia, Borders followed a similar pattern of setting up close to independent bookshops, but it did not count on a certain Australian loyalty to its own shops. When Borders was sold to Pacific Equity Partners, the knowledge base of book lovers was lost and it was not long before it went into receivership in 2009.

The combined forces of superstores, the depoliticization of feminism with postmodernist anything-goes philosophies, and globalization wrecked the feminist bookselling and publishing industry in the United States and Canada. By the late 1990s and early 2000s, only a handful of feminist presses remained. Amazon.com also has had a deleterious effect, and stole the name Amazon Bookstore, which was originally the name of an excellent feminist bookstore based in Sacramento, California. The bookstore sued Amazon.com, but never recovered from the poaching of its name and went out of business. The Feminist Press continues to publish and has gone more commercial. Cleis Press turned to publishing books about sex. The Crossing Press was sold to Crown Publishing Group. Aunt Lute has a small output each year and continues to reprint its substantial backlist, among which are a number of high sellers including works by Alice Walker, Audre Lorde, Gloria Anzaldúa, and Paula Gunn Allen. In Canada, Inanna and Second Story are both very active.

The International Alliance of Independent Publishers, based in Paris, has become a new meeting place for some feminist presses and independent publishing houses with feminist lists. Publishers from India, Turkey, South Africa, the United States, and Australia have worked together to produce books with international markets. Among the titles co-published in this way are *The World According to Monsanto* by French journalist

Marie-Monique Robin; *Making Peace with the Earth* by Indian physicist Vandana Shiva; and *My Grandmother* by Turkish lawyer Fethiye Çetin.

CONCLUSION

It is impossible to name all the feminist publishers working around the world in a huge range of languages. In 1996, Spinifex Press set up a network of feminist publishers in the Asia Pacific region. The result was a website (sadly now out of date) that offers a glimpse of what was happening in the region at that time (Spinifex Press 1997). Similar networks exist elsewhere, even if they remain unknown outside their publishing territories. Keeping feminist publishing alive is vital yet difficult. Presses are established, some flourish, some produce incredibly important books, some publish work that would never see the light of day without feminist inspiration and effort.

Feminist publishing is important to the history of the world. Some writers become veritable publishing industries (examples include Virginia Woolf, HD). But few were able to claim such a likely future during their most active years. Perhaps this is because feminist publishers are part of the conceptual minority, whose ideas and taste frame what the next generation sees as standard. But always predating that shift means that it is difficult to sustain those small groups or companies long enough for them to become mainstream. And if they did, perhaps they would no longer be interesting or innovative.

Many of the most significant books for feminists since 1970 have been published first by feminist presses. Without the feminist presses, the more mainstream publications would not exist. There is a dance that occurs in publishing. The smallest presses are the most innovative; they publish risky books. These books might be creatively innovative or politically controversial, and they open the way for others. Some 50 years later some of these risky books make it into the mainstream, and in the meantime new publishers and new writers are producing new works at the new risky edge.

SEE ALSO: *A Vindication of the Rights of Woman*; Feminist Literary Criticism; Feminist Magazines; Feminist Methodology; Feminist Utopian Writing; Gynocriticism; Language and Gender; Women's Writing

REFERENCES

Spinifex Press. 1997. "Feminist Publishing in Asia and the Pacific." Accessed July 15, 2015, at http://www.spinifexpress.com.au/Feminist_Publishing/.

Woolf, Virginia. 1953. *A Writer's Diary*, edited by Leonard Woolf. London: Hogarth.

FURTHER READING

Sixth International Feminist Book Fair Programme: *Indigenous, Asian and Pacific Writing and Publishing*. 1994. Melbourne: 6th IFBF.

Aubet, María José, ed. 1991. *Débats, Debates, Dibattiti, Panel Discussions, Besprechungen: IV Fira Internacional del Libre Feminista, Barcelona 19–23 de juny de 1990*. Barcelona: Ajuntament de Barcelona.

Bellamy, Suzanne. 1996. "Guthrie, Bessie Jean Thompson (1905–1977)." *Australian Dictionary of Biography*, vol. 14. Melbourne: MUP. Accessed July 15, 2015, at http://adb.anu.edu.au/biography/guthrie-bessie-jean-thompson-10382.

Brown, Diane, and Susan Hawthorne. 2006. "Feminist Publishing." In *Paper Empires: A History of the Book in Australia, 1946–2005*, edited by Craig Munro and Robyn Sheahan-Bright, 263–268. St. Lucia: University of Queensland Press.

Feminist Bookstores Fall Catalog. 1994. San Francisco: Feminist Bookstore News.

Joan, Polly, and Andrea Chesman. 1978. *Guide to Women's Publishing*. Paradise, CA: Dustbooks.

Listener Women's Book Festival. 1994. *Catalogue*. Wellington: Booksellers New Zealand.

Svendsen, Jessica. 2010. "Hogarth Press." Modernism Lab at Yale University. Accessed July 15, 2015, at http://modernism.research.yale.edu/wiki/index.php/Hogarth_Press.

Feminist Sex Wars

CARISA R. SHOWDEN
University of North Carolina at Greensboro, USA,
and University of Auckland, New Zealand

The phrase "feminist sex wars" refers to debates about both sexual orientation – specifically the role of lesbians and lesbianism in the feminist movement – and sexual practices, especially whether prostitution, pornography, and sado-masochism (S/M), are examples of violence against women or instead can be part of a "sex-positive" feminist practice. Although the arguments about lesbianism were fierce during the second wave of the feminist movement (roughly 1960s through early 1990s), these have largely been resolved. Conflicts over sexual practices, however, are still being fought.

All sides in the sex wars agree that sexuality is socially constructed rather than essential or biologically driven and that sexuality is important in women's self-development. Disagreement arises over how women can best undo patriarchal definitions of women's "proper" sexual expression and how women can gain greater control over their sexuality. In particular, feminists debate whether prostitution and pornography constitute violence against women, a type of labor like many others, with harms that feminists should try to minimize, or a potentially liberating form of behavior that can allow women to free themselves from patriarchal expectations that define and constrain women's sexual identities and practices. In short, feminists continue to debate whether to focus on the "pleasures" or "dangers" of sex and sex work (Vance 1984).

Tensions over the role of lesbians and lesbianism in the feminist movement were most palpable during the second wave; in 1969, Betty Friedan, then president of the US National Organization of Women, famously referred to lesbians as a "lavender menace" that threatened the focus on women's shared issues (Jackson and Scott 1996, 13). (Not all heterosexual women shared Friedan's view; some allied themselves with "gay liberation" groups in a show of solidarity.) Partly in response to views like Friedan's, the Radicalesbians group wrote the political manifesto *The Woman Identified Woman* (1970), arguing that heterosexual women were collaborating with the enemy by using women's energy to support men's needs and power. While this split was most pronounced in the United States, it also existed in women's liberation movements across Europe (Jackson and Scott 1996; Rowland and Klein 1996). Calls for women-only spaces and lesbian separatism were one result, as were calls for heterosexual women to re-examine their heterosexual privilege, which functions as a pillar of patriarchy (Rich 1978; Clarke 1981; Pharr 1988). Today, lesbians are part of the mainstream feminist movement, and heterosexism is regularly included in analyses of the nexus of power supporting patriarchy.

In the feminist sex wars over sexual practices, there are two primary groups. The first is "abolitionist" or "anti-pornography" radical feminists – erroneously labeled "anti-sex feminists" by some critics – who argue that prostitution and pornography are forms of violence against women (MacKinnon 1987; Jeffreys 1990). Robin Morgan summed up this view with her claim that "pornography is the theory, and rape the practice" (Morgan 1978, 169). Activist organizations adopting this view include Women Against Pornography, WHISPER (Women Hurt in Systems of Prostitution Engaged in Revolt), and, more recently, the Coalition Against Trafficking in Women. In their account, women's sexuality is socially constructed by and through male domination. Under patriarchy, prostitution and pornography are the ultimate forms of men's perceived right to women's bodies. Abolitionist feminists have tried to get laws passed outlawing pornography, with limited and short-lived success. They have also, more successfully, been influential in state policies to end demand for prostitution by criminalizing "johns." This "Nordic model" of prostitution policy has been adopted by Sweden, Norway, Iceland, and (in a non-binding resolution) the European Parliament.

The other primary group in this debate is generally labeled "pro-sex" or "sex positive." These feminists argue that when women embrace their sexuality, they are undoing the binary of male dominance/female submission. In the view of sex-positive feminists, the anti-pornography argument that sexuality is fundamental to women's oppression amounts to a claim that all sexuality victimizes women. In contrast, sex-positive feminists believe that even when sexuality is infused with dominance and power, its meanings can be contested and it can be an essential site of women's agency. Sex-positive feminists argue that women have a range of desires, and that making and distributing pornography, or engaging in sex work or BDSM, can be ways for women to claim sexual agency. Consequently, abolitionist feminists accuse them of conspiring with patriarchy, echoing the charges lesbian separatists leveled against heterosexual women years ago.

The sex wars over pornography, prostitution, and sexual practices have also spurred theoretical debates between feminism and queer theory (Weed and Schor 1997) and between second- and third-wave feminisms. "Third wave" refers to a range of positions within feminism, but it is often used to signify more libertarian or individualistic versions of feminist theory and activism that embrace women's individual sexual agency and are skeptical of "victim feminism." Some sex-positive and third-wave feminists align their argument that women have a right to enjoy sexual expression and action with central claims of queer theory, e.g., that sexuality is performative rather than an expression of identity, and that sexuality and sexual practices can be used to challenge dominant notions of gender (Franke 2001). In contrast, abolitionist feminists want to reconstruct sexuality within an egalitarian framework and believe that erotic relations of power cannot be separated from forms of dominance and subordination in spheres such as politics and the economy.

Future sex wars are likely to be fought primarily over prostitution and trafficking. Lesbians and lesbianism are now embraced by mainstream feminism, and arguments about the meaning and value of S/M practices have been folded into the sex work/prostitution debates. Although anti-pornography feminists continue to write and speak about the harms of making and viewing pornography (Boyle 2010), in the United States pornography is well protected by free speech jurisprudence. And with the advent of the Internet and the ability to distribute all kinds of pornography with little public scrutiny, sex-positive feminist pornographers, alongside other pornographers, continue to reach broad, international audiences with minimal regulation.

Conversely, in the United States, the United Nations, and most of Europe, "anti-sex work" feminists have greater political visibility and viability around the issue of prostitution than sex-positive feminists do. Anti-prostitution feminists have successfully combined arguments against prostitution with international arguments and policies against human trafficking, whereas "sex-positive" feminists argue that trafficking and prostitution are separate problems, not all women who cross borders to engage in sex work are trafficked, and women who engage in prostitution for a variety of reasons should not be penalized by anti-trafficking laws.

SEE ALSO: Feminism, Radical; Human Trafficking, Feminist Perspectives on; Pornography, Feminist Legal and Political Debates on; Prostitution/Sex Work; Queer Theory; Sex-Radical Feminists

REFERENCES

Boyle, Karen, ed. 2010 *Everyday Pornography*. New York: Routledge.
Clarke, Cheryl. 1981. "Lesbianism: an Act of Resistance." In *This Bridge Called My Back: Writings by Radical Women of Color*, edited by Cherríe Moraga and Gloria Anzaldúa, 128–137. New York: Kitchen Table: Women of Color Press.
Franke, Katherine M. 2001. "Theorizing Yes: an Essay on Feminism, Law, and Desire." *The Columbia Law Review*, 101(January): 181–208.
Jackson, Stevi and Sue Scott. 1996. "Sexual Skirmishes and Feminist Factions: Twenty-Five Years of Debate on Women and Sexuality." In *Feminism and Sexuality: a Reader*, edited by Stevi Jackson and Sue Scott, 1–31. New York: Columbia University Press.
Jeffreys, Sheila. 1990. *Anticlimax: a Feminist Perspective on the Sexual Revolution*. Washington Square: New York University Press.
MacKinnon, Catharine A. 1987. *Feminism Unmodified: Discourses on Life and Law*. Cambridge, MA: Harvard University Press.
Morgan, Robin. 1978. *Going Too Far: the Personal Chronicle of a Feminist*. New York: Random House.
Pharr, Suzanne. 1988. *Homophobia: a Weapon of Sexism*. Little Rock: Chardon Press.
Rich, Adrienne. 1978. *Blood, Bread, and Poetry*. London: Virago.
Rowland, Robyn, and Renate Klein. 1996. "Radical Feminism: History, Politics, Action." In *Radically Speaking: Feminism Reclaimed*, edited by Diane Bell and Renate Klein, 9–36. North Melbourne: Spinifex Press.
Vance, Carole S., ed. 1984. *Pleasure and Danger: Exploring Female Sexuality*. Boston: Routledge and Kegan Paul.
Weed, Elizabeth, and Naomi Schor, eds. 1997. *Feminism Meets Queer Theory*. Bloomington: Indiana University Press.

Feminist Standpoint Theory

IRIS VAN DER TUIN
Utrecht University, The Netherlands

Feminist standpoint theory privileges thinking from the position of the marginalized, including women. Standpoint theorists consider these positions privileged because those in the margins of society have a better view on the center than those at the center themselves. The working hypothesis of feminist standpoint theory can hence be summarized as follows: a social disadvantage implies an epistemological advantage. Since knowledge and power are indissolubly connected, feminist standpoint theory problematizes the intersection of everyday practices of power and the production of knowledge.

Theorists such as Nancy M. Hartsock, Sandra Harding, and Patricia Hill Collins argue that the epistemic value of a knowledge claim increases when the location of the knowing subject is consciously acknowledged. Such an increase is even more marked when the knowledge is generated from a nondominant (white, heterosexual, middle-class male) position. However, the question as to which positions are underprivileged and in what ways is not easy to answer.

Feminist standpoint theory finds its origins in the 1970s and 1980s, in the wake of the practice of "consciousness raising," and served as the epistemological backbone of women's studies. Women's studies arose simultaneously with African American studies at North American universities. Both fields of study were the direct offshoot of the liberalization of higher education that started in the United States, Western Europe, and Australia in the late 1960s. Upon entering academia, women, and black people, did not find a theory of knowledge commensurate with their insights into themselves and the world, insights they had acquired in the women's and black liberation movements rather than in the sterile context of academia. Women had made important steps toward a feminist theory of knowledge in consciousness-raising groups in which they discussed their personal experiences and discovered that what they had presumed to be individual problems were shared by many others, and hence had to be recognized as social and political problems stemming from systemic sexism. The personal thus became not only political, but also theoretical.

An important model of thought to account for the political and theoretical nature of knowledge and to open up a space for feminist epistemologies was Marxism, as Alison M. Jaggar pointed out as early as 1983. However, feminists needed to move beyond Marxism in order to postulate the special class position of women: the *standpoint* of women.

The working hypothesis of feminist standpoint theory can be traced back to the so-called master–slave dialectics of Georg Wilhelm Friedrich Hegel, one of Karl Marx's main sources of inspiration. In his *Theses on Feuerbach* (1845), the text in which he begins to fold out the main ideas of *Capital*, co-authored with Friedrich Engels, Marx reflects upon the complex nature of "praxis." In the *Theses*, Marx reformulates rationality as a practical phenomenon and truth as something that is produced in practice by agents other than individuals. The individual, autonomous subject characteristic of the Enlightenment does not do the knowing, Marx insists, because the smallest epistemological unit can be defined as the sum of social relations. Marx thus follows the German philosopher Ludwig Feuerbach in turning the Cartesian *cogito* ("I think therefore I am") upside down in order to claim that thought results from being, not the other way around. This opens up possibilities for change: if thinking is an embodied human activity, this activity of thought needs to be lived instead of contemplated from a distance.

In the 1960s, a focus on knowledge production in terms of praxis), and taking on a Marxist or, rather, a *socialist* stance, entailed that objectivity was exchanged for subjectivity. The first cohort of women's studies scholars needed more than just a theory about the value of the knowledge produced by women outside of academia. They also needed to provide the epistemic rationale for their own observations, for example on the ways in which the university was organized, and their own everyday praxis within it. The discipline of history, for instance, was, even in its Marxist incarnation, said to deal with dead, white, and privileged men, while male professors were argued to favor a biased objectivity. Feminists critiqued "science-as-usual" and agreed on the need to change syllabi, the foci of research, and academic policies. The status of such observations was established by theorizing "experience" as a basis for knowledge, and therewith, the installation of a *feminist* epistemology. In addition to Marxism, feminists in the 1970s began to embrace psychoanalysis. For, as theorists such as Jane Flax and Hillary Rose pointed out, the feminist reliance on Marxism might lead to a renaturalization of women's labor on the basis of economic parameters. By foregrounding the gender division of labor in both society and the academy, feminists were able to sharpen the concept of praxis.

In her article, "The Feminist Standpoint: Developing the Ground for a Specifically Feminist Historical Materialism" (1983), Nancy M. Hartsock builds on Iris Marion Young's argument that class and sex/gender are not parallel but intertwining tracks. In order to overcome the gender blindness of historical materialism, Hartsock appropriates Marxist categories for understanding not capitalism but "phallocratic domination" and for envisioning a future beyond "abstract masculinity." Divisions of labor, defined by both class and gender, put limitations on knowledge production. Hartsock aims at developing a "feminist" standpoint – rather than a "female" one – which must be achieved, has to be communal, and may be liberatory. The basis of a feminist standpoint is a sexual division of labor that is both social and biological. By calling the division "sexual," Hartsock hopes to engage with social bias as well as with the bodily dimensions of human activity (most importantly labor and reproduction). She thus uses the "standpoint" as a mediating device, affirming the socially constructed nature of all aspects of the lives of embodied humans.

Despite its broad sway, Hartsock's argument is not a universalizing one. Even though she develops *one* feminist standpoint and thus ostensibly ignores differences between women, abstract masculinity and the proposed feminist standpoint are not the same. Indeed, Hartsock's model serves to expose the universalizing effects of abstract masculinity and opens up space for the specificities of lived female experience by allowing for a focus on specific (groups of) women. A difference should nonetheless be made between universalist feminist standpoint theories, addressing the lives of all women), and particularist ones that single out the lives of a certain group of women as epistemologically advantageous. An example of the latter is Patricia Hill Collins's (1991) concept of "black feminist thought" which rests on the idea of the "outsider within" (i.e., the standpoint of the woman in the margin of the margin). Collins argues that black women experience the effects of what Hartsock calls abstract masculinity as well as the effects of white privilege. Black women's experiences of gendered and racialized marginalization, especially in labor situations and as a result of their interactions with both white men and white women, gives them privileged insights into racism and sexism alike. Collins identifies "black women intellectuals" for recording these insights.

A central figure in feminist standpoint theory is Sandra Harding. Her influential book *The Science Question in Feminism* (1986) introduces a threefold classification of feminist epistemology, defined as "feminist empiricism," "feminist standpoint theory," and "feminist postmodernism," respectively. Harding's founding role and continuing influence on feminist epistemology notwithstanding, the field has also been subject of critique. Another important figure, Donna Haraway, argues (in "Situated Knowledges: *The Science Question in Feminism* and The Privilege of Partial Perspective," 1988) that whereas feminist standpoint epistemology seeks to make way for knowledge production based on the diverse experiences of different groups of women, it ultimately relies on a foundational notion of gender dualism. This cannot but result in a decided and problematical universalism.

Despite their differences, Haraway and Harding have been working in tandem on situated forms of knowledge and towards a concept of "strong objectivity" (Harding 1993). Haraway's main intervention has been to self-identify as a feminist standpoint theorist by arguing that the need to classify and taxonomize feminist epistemic positions is the problem, not the content of the theories. She posits: "What boundaries provisionally contain remains generative, productive of meanings and bodies. Siting (sighting) boundaries is a risky practice" (Haraway 1988, 594).

Given the gendered organization of the academy in which women's studies were forced to develop, standpoint theory has been a driving force behind the attempt at democratizing the relation between the knowing subject and the object of knowledge.

Before the liberalization of higher education, women, and black people, were the objects of research, not the researching subjects. Feminist standpoint theorists have successfully democratized the subject–object relation in knowledge production, by working with semi-structured or open-ended questionnaires, by doing extensive fieldwork, and by trying to write in such a way that the researched communities can easily access the outcomes of research.

Since 1997 there has been no sustained debate about the theory of the feminist standpoint, even if Harding published *The Feminist Standpoint Theory Reader: Intellectual and Political Controversies* in 2004. Standpoint theory was further referred to in debates about the decline of social constructivism (see, for example, Haraway 1997; Barad 2003). Ultimately, feminist standpoint theory is a *materialist* theory. The theory deals with embodied subjects, subjects marked by sexism, racism, ethnocentrism, classism, and heterosexism. Hartsock argued: "As embodied humans we are of course inextricably both natural and social, though feminist theory to date has, for important strategic reasons, concentrated attention on the social aspect" (Hartsock 1983, 283–284). This statement underlines that the critical reflection on social constructivism is in fact part and parcel of even the earliest forms of feminist standpoint theory, and may be the reason why the theory keeps on being attractive to both feminist scholars and students.

SEE ALSO: Class, Caste, and Gender; Division of Labor, Gender; Epistemology of the Closet; Scientific Motherhood

REFERENCES

Barad, Karen. 2003. "Posthumanist Performativity: Toward an Understanding of How Matter Comes to Matter." *Signs: Journal of Women in Culture and Society*, 28(3): 801–831. DOI: 10.1086/345321.

Collins, Patricia Hill. 1991. *Black Feminist Thought: Knowledge, Consciousness, and the Politics of Empowerment*. New York: Routledge.

Haraway, Donna. 1988. "Situated Knowledges: The Science Question in Feminism and the Privilege of Partial Perspective." *Feminist Studies*, 14(3): 575–599. DOI: 10.2307/3178066.

Haraway, Donna. 1997. *Modest_Witness@Second_Millennium.FemaleMan©_ Meets_OncoMouse™: Feminism and Technoscience*. New York: Routledge.

Harding, Sandra. 1986. *The Science Question in Feminism*. Milton Keynes: Open University Press.

Harding, Sandra. 1993. "Rethinking Standpoint Epistemology: What is 'Strong Objectivity'?" In *Feminist Epistemologies*, edited by Linda M. Alcoff and Elizabeth Potter, 49–82. New York: Routledge.

Harding, Sandra, ed. 2004. *The Feminist Standpoint Theory Reader: Intellectual and Political Controversies*. New York: Routledge.

Hartsock, Nancy C. M. 1983. "The Feminist Standpoint: Developing the Ground for a Specifically Feminist Historical Materialism." In *Discovering Reality: Feminist Perspectives on Epistemology, Metaphysics, Methodology, and Philosophy of Science*, edited by Sandra Harding and Merrill B. Hintikka, 283–310. Boston: Kluwer.

Jaggar, Alison M. 1983. *Feminist Politics and Human Nature*. Totowa: Rowman & Allanheld.

FURTHER READING

Harding, Sandra. 1991. *Whose Science? Whose Knowledge? Thinking From Women's Lives*. Milton Keynes: Open University Press.

Smith, Dorothy E. 1987. *The Everyday World as Problematic: A Feminist Sociology*. Boston: Northeastern University Press.

Feminist Studies of Science

LETITIA MEYNELL
Dalhousie University, Canada

While a case can be made that there were feminist studies of science long before the

1980s, it is with the second wave of the women's movement and the growth of a self-identified feminist community in academia that this area really blossomed. Roughly, feminist studies of science can be thought of as coming from four disciplinary orientations: a philosophy of science orientation (informed primarily by Anglo-American philosophy); a science and technology studies orientation (informed primarily by continental and postmodernist philosophies as well as sociology and anthropology); a historical orientation; and an insider's orientation in which scientists bring feminist analyses to their own disciplines. However, the boundaries between these approaches are more honored in the breach than the observance. Key works are familiar to all and many authors fit more or less into multiple orientations.

The tensions and cross-fertilizations between these approaches render feminist studies of science particularly complex and fertile in ways that are less common among their non-feminist equivalents (i.e., philosophy of science, history of science, and science and technology studies). This ongoing interaction is fed by feminist commitments, including a critical stance on traditional mainstream work, attentiveness to insights from non-traditional sources, and an unwillingness to simply ignore or otherwise silence other feminist and particularly women's voices. Awareness of the politics of knowledge, concerns about sex differences, gender identities, sexual practices and their many intersections, and a sensitivity to the effects of science and technology on women and members of various vulnerable or oppressed groups are never far from the surface.

Several themes run throughout feminist studies of science: the struggles and successes of women scientists; scientific research on sex differences; the character of science itself; and the connection of science with applied, especially environmental and biomedical, issues. Although each topic is addressed separately below, they are all interlinked and early works in particular tended to draw them all together. Carolyn Merchant's *The Death of Nature: Women, Ecology and the Scientific Revolution* (1980) is a case in point. Here Merchant challenges the traditional view of the Scientific Revolution as a time of unparalleled human progress, instead relating it to ecological devastation, urbanization, the concomitant alienation from nature, and the exploitation of the poor. Crucial to her account is the idea that modern science replaced an organismic view of the cosmos, which emphasized the interdependency of life and community, with a mechanistic and reductionist view, which treated nature as something to be dominated and controlled to serve human ends. Moreover, this conceptual framework was imbued with sexist ideology, associating men with science, culture, and rationality and women with nature, unruliness, emotionality, and submission (albeit with resistance). Merchant's account was controversial and various aspects have been rejected or amended. Nonetheless, many feminist thinkers agree that the interrogation and correction of mainstream histories and accounts of the contemporary character of science help to show how the stories told about men, women, and nature are often neither well evidenced nor value-neutral. Moreover, many of the conceptual frameworks and background assumptions behind these mainstream views have been implicated in current injustices and the environmental crisis.

THE STRUGGLES AND SUCCESSES OF WOMEN SCIENTISTS

Accounts of the experiences of women in the sciences often seek to explain the ways in which the institutions of science have functioned to exclude women. While scientists themselves have done much of the work on the contemporary status of women in science, historians have shown how the current situation is rooted in a history of exclusion and struggle as well as important and often forgotten successes. Some authors have addressed the lives of particular women, such as Evelyn Fox Keller's (1983) biography of Nobel Prize-winning geneticist Barbara McClintock. Others have woven the histories of individual women together with histories of the institutions of science, exemplified by Margaret Rossiter's three-volume history, *Women Scientists in America* (1984, 1995, 2012). A number of theorists have taken a more synoptic view, weaving together the stories of particular women scientists and scientific institutions with the other prominent themes in feminist studies of science (e.g., Haraway 1989; Schiebinger 1989). Because of a tendency to focus on the development of science since the Scientific Revolution, the majority of this literature has focused on white European and North American women, leaving an important lacuna concerning women of color, the role of women in the global history of science, current cross-cultural comparisons, and the many constructive cross-cultural interactions that have produced scientific knowledge. This omission is singular as the Scientific Revolution was contemporaneous with European imperialism, in which technologies were appropriated and various scientific practices and insights circulated. Feminists increasingly recognize that their studies of science must engage postcolonial perspectives or risk repeating a Eurocentricity that mirrors the sexism of traditional mainstream science studies (Harding 1998). Happily there is exciting new work starting to fill this important gap (e.g., Subramaniam 2015).

SCIENTIFIC RESEARCH ON SEX DIFFERENCES

The character, contingency, and extent of the differences between men and women is a fraught issue for feminists. Early in the second wave of the women's movement two distinct views formed. Some invoked a kind of female essence in their celebration of the traditionally female and feminine. Others totally rejected sex essentialism and biologically given sexual dimorphism in all but the most basic reproductive functions, seeing the many behavioral and psychological differences between men and women as a function of a historically contingent gender ideology. Yet others have sought to explain the differences between men and women through Marxist accounts of labor or psychoanalytic theory. Nonetheless, sex essentialism, whether couched in terms of innate biological differences or psychosocial development, has become increasingly difficult to maintain in the face of the widespread acceptance among feminists that the intersectionality of various identities is crucial to understanding the real lives of women of all different classes, ethnicities, cultures, and abilities (see, for example, Fausto-Sterling 2000). This, in addition to the increasing acceptance of trans identities and intersexuality as normal human variation, makes it implausible to maintain that there is one women's voice, perspective, psychological or behavioral profile, or oppression.

As feminists have wrestled with the question of essentialism, research programs devoted to establishing the evolutionary, psychological, and neurological basis of sexual dimorphism have flourished, seemingly immune to feminist critique. Rather than investigating the diversity of morphology and behavior within human and non-human populations, this research has focused on investigating two distinct kinds – the male and the female. Much of this research and especially its uptake among the general populace seems to be predicated on a conceptual slip from findings of incomplete dimorphism – average differences between male and female populations with considerable overlap – to discussions that imply complete dimorphism, where there are two discrete kinds with no ambiguous or intermediate cases.

Though some feminists have attempted to employ these research programs for various ends (e.g., feminist proponents of evolutionary psychology), many others have roundly criticized them. Feminists have found fault with the simplifying assumptions, reductionism, and the urge to quantify the seemingly unquantifiable in much of this research. Historians have shown the connections between current research and earlier projects devised to show the intellectual inferiority of women and their fitness for traditional feminine roles, while a number of scientific insiders have shown that by ordinary scientific standards much of this research is simply bad science (e.g., Jordan-Young 2010). By employing traditional standards in their critiques they make a point about the power of sexist ideology to distort scientific practices and the interpretation of scientific results. Nonetheless, even as they employ these traditional standards, many acknowledge that there are deeper problems rooted in the traditional understanding of the character of science itself.

THE CHARACTER OF SCIENCE

Along with those feminists who endorse or employ traditional scientific methods and standards are those who critically investigate the character of science itself. In the 1980s and early 1990s, when these different approaches – most notably, feminist empiricism, feminist standpoint theory, and feminist postmodernism – were first being articulated, they were seen as competitors. In recent years they have come to be thought of as more complementary. Although in this early period some feminists argued that science is inherently corrupt – nothing more than a tool for those in power to assert their will – few hold this view anymore. Even feminist authors who are associated with postmodernist approaches have typically retained a certain degree of optimism that science can successfully tell us about natural processes, and they warn against treating science as simply one more socially constructed narrative with no more claim to authority than any other political or metaphysical view (e.g., Haraway 1989; Harding 1998). Any extreme relativism about knowledge is now widely recognized as counterproductive to feminist ends as it implicitly locates feminist claims about the existence of sex (and other) oppression (and the psychological and sociological studies that reveal oppression's existence and effects) as one more vested interest vying for power, rather than claims about real states of affairs. The majority of feminists who study science support a critically pro-science view: they accept that the sciences are powerful and effective ways of finding out about the world, while at the same time acknowledging the troubled history of the sciences of the Global North in facilitating atrocities and perpetuating inequality. Behind this is the conviction that science, like any other human endeavor, is prone to distortions by ideology, vested interests, metaphysical assumptions, and the limitations of the scientists themselves as well as a commitment to reforming the sciences to make them as accurate, effective, and just as possible, given these distorting tendencies.

According to the traditional view of science developed since the Scientific Revolution, the privileged status that it has been accorded is based on scientists' relentless pursuit of mind-independent fact and indifference to questions of value, which are associated with ethics, politics, and aesthetics. Against this view, feminists have been at pains to show the ways that values and subjective interests inevitably shape science. In the early days this was taken by some anti-feminist scientists and philosophers of science as a sign that feminists failed to really understand the logic of science (or, indeed, epistemology). In recent years, however, the epistemological role of values in the sciences has increasingly been accepted by non-feminist theorists also, though often the feminist pedigree of this insight goes unacknowledged.

There has been a wide variety of different projects within feminist studies of science elucidating how values and subjective interests influence the sciences and suggesting how scientific methods and institutions should be rethought and reformed in light of these influences. These projects can provisionally be classified on the basis of whether they focus on the character of the knower or on the character of the known. In the 1980s some feminists drew on Marxist theory to develop standpoint theory. The basic idea is that the perspectives of subjects located in marginal political positions that are typically excluded from the production of scientific knowledge – for instance, women in a patriarchal society – are more objective and better positioned to produce relevant knowledge. When standpoint theory was developed in the 1980s theorists tended to focus on standpoint determined by gender (and later by race, class, etc.), but in the 1990s the focus shifted somewhat to the standpoint produced by political commitment, in other words, the feminist perspective. Some scholars have been leery of privileging one perspective over others, preferring the idea that knowers are situated and that every perspective is partial, both in the sense of being limited and being interested. Another approach is to see objectivity as the achievement of a group of scientists, rooted in the process of rigorous evaluation of scientific claims by a diverse community of experts (Longino 2001). All are agreed that the traditional idea of objectivity as a position of disinterested observation that is equally available to all knowers is not only false but dangerous, tending toward both dogmatism and conservatism, reifying the views of the most powerful. Moreover, it is now widely recognized that we all have various identities – typically associated with ethnicity, race, sex, sexuality, ability status, indigeneity, or other politically and socially salient positions – and that the ways that people suffer oppression or enjoy privilege by virtue of association with any of these groups are not additive. Rather, it is an open question how the intersection of any given set of identities informs both the social position and epistemic perspective of a given knower.

Many feminist theorists take pluralist approaches not just to knowers but to the content of knowledge itself. Against the theoretical excesses of an "anything goes" relativism, this approach suggests that there may be many accounts of a given phenomenon or system that are equally consistent with the observational evidence. A number of feminists have used W. V. O. Quine's insight that theory choice is inevitably underdetermined by data to argue that which of the set of empirically adequate theories should be preferred is a contextual matter, properly driven by the interests and resources of the researchers, but also concerns for justice and equality. Intriguingly, a new interest in pluralism and mechanism in mainstream philosophy of science is influencing this discussion, with some authors challenging early feminist critiques of mechanistic approaches to science (like Merchant's, discussed earlier), maintaining that mechanistic analyses can be both anti-reductionist and pluralist.

In a similar vein, Karen Barad (2007) has introduced an influential pluralist ontology – agential realism. Barad draws from early twentieth-century physicist Niels Bohr's ideas about the ways in which the act of observation both alters the observed object and determines the content of the observation. According to Barad, the phenomena studied by physics emerge as a result of the dynamic relations among experimental instrumentation, observed, and observer. Rather than a passive given, the object of knowledge is reconceived as an agent, of sorts, that is in constant interaction with other objects including the observer. How an observer specifies the object of knowledge – how one makes the cut between knower and known – then becomes a contingent matter, chosen by the knower rather than given in the world.

THE CONNECTION WITH ENVIRONMENTAL AND BIOMEDICAL ETHICS

This reconsideration of the fundamental character of science extends to questions about the human relationship with the non-human world. Though this interest has been present from the beginning, over time its character has changed. Early work, like Merchant (1980), married the analysis of science with ecofeminism, looking to characterize how the abstract image and practice of science derogated both women and the environment. More recent work tends to identify the failings of particular scientific research programs or practices, in terms of environmental damage or injustice, using feminist analyses. Postcolonial feminisms, perhaps by virtue of their relation to international development studies, have frequently engaged the way the global knowledge economy exploits the people and ecologies of the Global South (Shiva 1997). Currently, the science of anthropogenic climate change is enjoying considerable feminist attention. Feminist thinkers are well positioned to interrogate the ways in which the politics of knowledge have shaped debate and produced a democratic deficit on this topic. Recent work on epistemologies of ignorance seems ideally suited to explaining how so much uncertainty and misinformation could be produced about such an important and, scientifically speaking, fairly uncontroversial issue. Another strand of feminist studies of science draws from the behavioral sciences to interrogate the human relationship with non-human animals. Some of the work by scientific insiders on this topic is, in effect, unsayable in traditional scientific contexts and some of these researchers have looked to more feminist-friendly spaces to recount their personal experiences and moral awakenings that have evolved from their study of non-human others (e.g., Birke 1994).

Just as environmental considerations have been a constant companion to feminist studies of science throughout its development, so have biomedical issues. *Our Bodies Ourselves* (Boston Women's Health Book Collective 1979) was one of the earliest attempts to empower ordinary women by presenting them with specialized scientific knowledge about their own bodies – information which had traditionally been controlled by a medical establishment dominated by men. First published in the 1970s and informed by pro-choice politics, the sexual revolution, and a growing lesbian consciousness, the many editions of *Our Bodies Ourselves* implicitly recognized the relationship between medical science and technology and personal and political power. Feminist bioethics continues to engage questions of patient autonomy and medical authority as well as the challenges raised by scientific research and new technologies. The focus remains on understanding the ways in which medical practices and interventions affect women, especially for conditions and procedures unique to women (e.g., reproductive issues), and placing medical interventions and industries within larger contexts of social justice and equality.

SEE ALSO: Biological Determinism; Cognitive Sex Differences, Debates on; Ecofeminism; Environment and Gender; Essentialism; Feminist Epistemology; Feminist Objectivity; Feminist Standpoint Theory; Feminist Theories of the Body; Gender Bias in Research; Gender Difference Research; Nature–Nurture Debate; Sex Difference Research and Cognitive Abilities; Strong Objectivity

REFERENCES

Barad, Karen. 2007. *Meeting the Universe Halfway: Quantum Physics and the Entanglement of Matter and Meaning.* Durham, NC: Duke University Press.

Birke, Lynda. 1994. *Feminism, Animals and Science: The Naming of the Shrew.* Buckingham: Open University Press.

Boston Women's Health Book Collective. 1979. *Our Bodies, Ourselves: A Book By and For Women,* 2nd ed. New York: Simon and Schuster.

Fausto-Sterling, Anne. 2000. *Sexing the Body: Gender Politics and the Construction of Sexuality.* New York: Basic Books.

Haraway, Donna. 1989. *Primate Visions: Gender, Race and Nature in Modern Science.* New York: Routledge.

Harding, Sandra. 1998. *Is Science Multi-Cultural? Postcolonialisms, Feminisms and Epistemologies.* Bloomington: Indiana University Press.

Jordan-Young, Rebecca. 2010. *Brain Storm: The Flaws in the Science of Sex Differences.* Cambridge: Harvard University Press.

Keller, Evelyn Fox. 1983. *A Feeling for the Organism: The Life and Work of Barbara McClintock.* New York: W. H. Freeman.

Longino, Helen. 2001. *The Fate of Knowledge.* Princeton: Princeton University Press.

Merchant, Carolyn. 1980. *The Death of Nature: Women, Ecology and the Scientific Revolution.* New York: HarperCollins.

Rossiter, Margaret. 1984. *Women Scientists in America: Struggles and Strategies to 1940.* Baltimore: Johns Hopkins University Press.

Rossiter, Margaret. 1995. *Women Scientists in America: Before Affirmative Action, 1940–1972.* Baltimore: Johns Hopkins University Press.

Rossiter, Margaret. 2012. *Women Scientists in America: Forging a New World Since 1972.* Baltimore: Johns Hopkins University Press.

Schiebinger, Londa. 1989. *The Mind Has No Sex: Women in the Origins of Modern Science.* Cambridge, MA: Harvard University Press.

Shiva, Vandana. 1997. *Biopiracy: The Plunder of Nature and Knowledge.* Boston: South End Press.

Subramaniam, Banu. 2015. *Ghost Stories for Darwin: The Science of Variation and the Politics of Diversity.* Champaign: University of Illinois Press.

Feminist Theology

ROSEMARY RADFORD RUETHER
Claremont School of Theology and Claremont Graduate University, USA

Feminist theology developed out of the Christian theological tradition because the theological systems in Christianity were shaped to express and enforce elite male dominance. Patriarchal societies divide society between a system of dominance by ruling-class males and subordinate groups of dependent women and slaves who lack legal, economic, and political rights and are often excluded from education. This means that the official culture is shaped by and for the ruling-class males. Male generic language makes the male human the normative human being. Foundational Judeo-Christian creation stories make God create males first, as rulers. Philosophical theories position males on top with women as inferior. For example, Christian theology incorporates the teaching of the Greek philosophers, Plato and Aristotle, who defined women as secondary, lacking full humanness and rationality, and needing to be under the rule of the ruling-class male, who alone is fully human.

These theories, and the practices they express, are incorporated over the centuries into the teaching of the Christian church. Women are thereby excluded from leadership. The church teaches that women are incapable of being ordained, since Christ is a male and cannot be represented by a female. They cannot preach in church or represent God or Christ.

Feminist theology thus represents a process of criticism of these patterns of thought and practice as wrong, as contrary to the authentic message of Christian thought of equality of men and women in the image of God and their redemption as equals. They dismantle these patterns of thought and seek alternative language about God, Christ, the creation and humans, male and female, their redemption and roles in the church.

Feminist theology begins with the critique of misogyny. Reading scripture and theological tradition, one notes passages that inferiorize women and forbid their leadership, such as 1 Timothy 2:12: "I permit no woman to teach or to have authority over men, she is to keep silence." One examines the argument for this teaching, namely, that men were created first and were not deceived, but women are both secondary in the order of creation and were the deceivers that brought sin into the world (1 Timothy 2:13–14). Feminist theology begins to critique this tradition, to question whether it is in fact valid and to disaffiliate from it. This critique includes the questioning of androcentrism, the assumption that the elite male is the normative human and all other humans are invisible.

The second stage of feminist theology explores alternative traditions in the history of Christianity. One discovers that there were foundational teachings that affirmed a gender equality that should be seen as more normative. These alternatives are expressed in biblical texts that affirm that God created humanity, "male and female, in the image of God" (Genesis 1:27), and St. Paul taught that in Christ, "there were neither male and female, for you are all one in Christ" (Galatians 3:28). God can be imaged as female, as in the Wisdom tradition.

The third stage of feminist theology is a process of reconstruction of theological symbols. One redefines how we should speak of God, of Christ, of humans, male and female, of the nature of good and evil, redemption, and the ministry of the church in ways that include women and men as equals. This means we redefine how we tell the story of the tradition, showing that equality in creation and redemption is the normative vision, and patriarchy is a distortion that we should reject. This leads to reforms that affirm women's leadership and new practices of egalitarian redemptive practice.

Feminist theology is not simply a process of transformation that is done by only women and affects only women. Feminism as a critique of sexism and patriarchy in church and society includes women and men who have been shaped to play their roles in the patriarchal system, and both have to be converted to a new vision and new practice in church and society. Men too have been distorted by sexism and the roles they have been taught to play, and need to learn to affirm a new, more holistic identity, even as they learn to sympathize with women's suffering and to oppose the ways women have been subjugated in this system. The goal of feminism is a new system of relations of equality and mutuality of both men and women.

Feminism includes a critique of class and race hierarchies. Men and women do not exist in the abstract. They have been shaped to fit into class and race roles, as well as gender roles. Ruling-class males were socialized to belong to ruling-class and economic hierarchies, and white ruling-class women also shared in the advantages of class and race privileges, even as they were told their place as women. Likewise men and women of impoverished and racially discriminated groups suffered these subjugations, even if differentiated as male and female. Thus feminist theology must question and reconstruct the way men and women have been shaped by class and race.

Over time, feminist theology has become increasingly inter-faith and global. Jews, Muslims, Buddhists, and other religious groups have been led to question how their religious traditions have been shaped by patriarchy and how to retrieve equalitarian traditions that affirm the liberation and equality of men and women in their histories. This process of transformation is happening not just in the West, but in Eastern Europe, Asia, Africa, and Latin America. It is leading groups of Christians, Jews, Muslims, and others in third world countries to examine how sexism has been interconnected with racism, colonialism, and class hierarchy in their histories, both ancient and modern.

Thus feminist theory, theology, and transformative practice is a global revolution that is being contextualized in different ways in societies all over the world.

SEE ALSO: Feminist Christology; Woman-Centeredness; Womanist Theology; Women-Church

FURTHER READING

Adler, Rachel. 1997. *Engendering Judaism: An Inclusive Theology and Ethics*. Philadelphia: Jewish Publication Society.
Badran, Margot. 2009. *Feminism and Islam: Secular and Religious Controversies*. Oxford: One World.
Coleman, Monica. 2008. *Making a Way Out of No Way: A Womanist Theology*. Minneapolis: Fortress Press.
Gross, Rita. 1993. *Buddhism after Patriarchy: A Feminist Analysis and Reconstruction of Buddhism*. Albany: SUNY Press.
Heyward, Carter. 1989. *Touching Our Strength: The Erotic as Power and Love*. San Francisco: Harper and Row.
Isasi-Diaz, Ada Maria. 1996. *Mujerista Theology: A Theology for the 21st Century*. Maryknoll: Orbis Press.
Ruether, Rosemary R. 1983. *Sexism and God-Talk: Toward a Feminist Theology*. Boston: Beacon Press.

Feminist Theories of the Body

KRYSTAL CLEARY
Indiana University, USA

To discuss feminist theories of the body is in some ways to discuss feminist theory as a whole, for "feminism has long seen its own project as intimately connected to the body, and has responded to the masculinist conventions by producing a variety of oftentimes incompatible theories which attempt to take the body into account" (Shildrick and Price 1999b, 1). Dominant Western intellectual tradition regards the body suspiciously as a source of unwieldy and base desires and functions. Feminist theorists' contention with the mind/body dichotomy, however, has been not only with its insistence upon disembodied thought but also the devalued body's persistent correlation with femininity. While many first-wave feminist thinkers in the eighteenth and nineteenth centuries and even more contemporary liberal feminists have similarly devalued or ignored the body in attempts to demonstrate women's capacity for reason and advocate for equality, others reclaim and rejoice in the body as a site of valuable knowledge production.

Feminist theory of the body as a collection of literatures is a complex tapestry of interwoven thought traditions rather than a monolithic, linear analytical thread. Indeed, the several notable volumes that have taken up the project of sketching the literatures' contours, such as Shildrick and

Price's *Feminist Theory and the Body: A Reader* (Shildrick and Price 1999a), each map different genealogical histories and include a diversity of voices. In tracing the historical development of feminist theories of the body, Elizabeth Grosz outlines three camps (Grosz 1994). The first, egalitarian feminism, includes "figures as diverse as Simone de Beauvoir, Shulamith Firestone, Mary Wollstonecraft, and other liberal, conservative, and humanist feminists, even ecofeminists" (Grosz 1994, 15). The female body in this category is regarded by some as a barrier to women's access to the power afforded to men in a patriarchal culture and by others more positively as a unique site of knowledge; both iterations of egalitarian feminism, in Grosz's view, "have accepted patriarchal and misogynistic assumptions about the female body as somehow more natural, less detached, more engaged with and directly related to its 'objects' than male bodies" (Grosz 1994, 15). Social constructionists, Grosz's second category, include those who, like Julia Kristeva, Nancy Chodorow, Marxist feminists, and psychoanalytic feminists, view bodies as "the raw materials for the inculcation of and interpellation into ideology but are merely media of communication rather than the object or focus of ideological production/reproduction" (Grosz 1994, 17). Through this theoretical thread's insistence that it is not biology but rather the ways in which that body has been imbued with meaning that is oppressive to women, the body becomes fixed, naturalized, and ahistorical. The last position, sexual difference, includes thinkers such as Luce Irigaray, Hélène Cixous, Gayatri Spivak, Monique Wittig, and Judith Butler. In this camp, "the body is crucial to understanding women's psychical and social existence, but the body is no longer understood as an ahistorical, biological given, acultural object" (Grosz 1994, 17–18). The body is instead "interwoven with and constitutive of systems of meaning, signification, and representation"; this category, in which I include Grosz herself, is generally wary of sex/gender distinctions and "less interested in the question of the cultural construction of subjectivity than in the materials out of which such a construction is forged" (Grosz 1994, 18).

Menstruation, reproduction, the medicalization of women's bodies, motherhood, body image, beauty practices, disordered eating, cosmetic surgery, sexuality, sexual assault, women's health, media representations, and countless other thematics animate feminist attention to the body. Although not academic in nature, the Women's Health Movement of the 1970s and onward marks an important moment in the history of feminist discourse about the body in that it sought to disseminate accurate health information to women and encourage them to become experts on their bodies, health, and sexualities. Similarly resisting individualistic and medical models that pathologize disordered eating, in her book *Unbearable Weight: Feminism, Western Culture, and the Body*, Susan Bordo contends that disorders such as anorexia nervosa and bulimia must be understood in relation to the specific cultural contexts from which they emerge (Bordo 2003). She asserts that seemingly extreme and gendered disciplinary body practices such as restrictive eating and cosmetic surgery should not be viewed as "bizarre or anomalous, but, rather, as the logical (if extreme) manifestations of anxieties and fantasies fostered by our culture" (Bordo 2003, 15). In the same vein, Sandra Lee Bartky employs a Foucauldian analysis of women's disciplinary body practices in her essay "Foucault, Femininity, and the Modernization of Patriarchal Power" (Bartky 2003). The docile body is often a feminized body wherein women have internalized a patriarchal male gaze through which they view their own bodies, monitor their behaviors, and measure the success of their femininity. Arguing that feminist preoccupation with cosmetic surgery expand beyond the internalized male gaze theory, Victoria Pitts-Taylor's book *Surgery Junkies: Wellness and Pathology in Cosmetic Culture* urges us to resist the binary of cosmetic surgery as oppressive/empowering and elucidates "how in cosmetic surgery the body becomes a zone of social conflict, coded on the one hand as a sign of interior wellness and self-enhancements and on the other hand as a sign of moral, politics, or mental weakness" (Pitts-Taylor 2007, 7).

One of the early fundamental contributions of feminist theory that remains central to discussions of the body is the distinction between sex and gender. This unhinging of sex from gender enabled feminist theorists to assert that sex has a frequently neglected political aspect and that women's subordination is the product of unequal social, political, and economic relations rather than inferior embodiment. Cleaving sex and gender, although it has been analytically useful, can falsely fix sex as a self-evident biological truth. However, sex is not a precultural fact but, like gender, a construction of cultural, political, and scientific discourses that is ideologically informed by the very gender norms it serves to naturalize. Far from being natural truths unearthed by objective methodologies, feminist analyses elucidate how the information generated by the positivist, empiricist tradition of scientific knowledge production about the body is actually socially constituted and situated. For instance, in her piece "The Egg and the Sperm," Emily Martin analyzes the ways in which heteronormative conventions of sexuality and gender inform both scientific and popular understandings of reproduction and fertilization (Martin 1991). In a survey of science textbooks, Martin finds that the egg is described as passive "damsel in distress" while sperm are imagined as active and aggressive in ways that obscure the complex biological processes at work. Moreover, Anne Fausto-Sterling's important scholarship illuminates how scientific knowledge about gender, sex, and sexuality is not only constructed but has also become naturalized in our cultural environment (Fausto-Sterling 2000). "The truths about human sexuality created by scholars in general and by biologists in particular," she insists, "are one component of political, social, and moral struggles about our cultures and economies. At the same time, components of our political, social, and moral struggles become, quite literally, embodied, incorporated into our very physiological being" (Fausto-Sterling 2000, 5). Fausto-Sterling's argument that scientific knowledge is both culturally constructed and naturalized in the social milieu is perhaps most clearly demonstrated in her discussions of intersexuality. She discusses the arbitrary distinctions between properly sexed and abnormally configured genitals, as well as the heterosexist assumptions that inform the surgical "correction" of intersexed infants. Scientific and cultural knowledge about sexual difference is therefore socially constructed and, in the case of intersexed infants, literally landscaped on and in turn naturalized through the materiality of the body.

The arrival of postmodern theory in the 1990s unsettled and expanded upon early feminist sex/gender distinctions and examined the relationship between discourse and materiality. Judith Butler's work on gender performativity has profoundly shaped feminist theory's understanding of gender as a discursive production. Butler notoriously argues in *Gender Trouble* that gender "has no ontological status apart from the various acts that constitute its reality" (Butler 1990, 185). Resisting the notion that one harbors a core gender identity, she employs the example of drag to illuminate how gender is "the repeated stylization of the body, a set of repeated acts within a highly rigid regulatory frame that congeal over time to produce the appearance of substance, of a natural sort of being" (Butler 1990, 45). Gender, then, is a *verb* – a series of acts and reenactments of learned behaviors, dress, mannerisms, and so on that only in their ongoing repetition come to feel and appear to us as natural. In response to critiques that her theory of gender performativity fell into the postmodernist trap of focusing on the discursive at the expense of seriously considering lived, embodied experience, in *Bodies that Matter* she elaborates that "the regulatory norms of 'sex' work in a performative fashion to constitute the materiality of bodies and more specifically, to materialize the body's sex, to materialize sexual difference in the service of the consolidation of the heterosexual imperative" (Butler 1993, 2). Much of Butler's text is in conversation with other feminist theorists such as Fausto-Sterling as she argues that sex has been gender all along in so far as the materiality of the body and its sex difference are always already inscribed with gendered meaning. In *Bodies the Matter*, Butler also contributes the concept of the heterosexual matrix, which outlines the appropriate binaristic categories of sex, gender, and sexuality as well as the socially acceptable combinations of the aforementioned, and determines who is within the realm of intelligibility. Those who fall outside this realm of intelligibility are the objects of heteronormativity. The fear of the abject prompts a distancing from it and therefore a reaffirmation of gender/sexed/sexual normalcy for those who are within the heterosexual matrix. Moreover, those who occupy the social location of abjection have difficulty accessing what Butler calls a livable life, which includes social and political recognition, the support of loved ones, access to employment, and so forth.

Postmodern feminist theorizations of the body and their preoccupation with discourse, however, have been both widely embraced and fiercely challenged. In *Material Feminisms*, editors Stacy Alaimo and Susan Hekman argue that the body occupies an absent presence in contemporary postmodern theory. "Ironically," the editors observe, "although there has been a tremendous outpouring of scholarship on 'the body' in the last twenty years, nearly all of the work in this area has been confined to the analysis of discourses *about* the body" (Alaimo and Hekman 2008, 3). This volume argues that feminist theory has also been captured and constrained by postmodernism's rejection of materiality. Material feminism seeks to combat the linguistic turn without throwing the discursive baby out with the postmodern bathwater. Instead, material feminist thinkers in this collection seek to forge a rejuvenated attention to materiality and nature while still recognizing the importance of language, representation, and discourse. The authors collectively insist that "The new settlement we are seeking is not a return to modernism. Rather, it accomplishes what the postmoderns failed to do: a deconstruction of the material/discursive dichotomy that retains both elements without privileging either" (Alaimo and Hekman 2008, 6).

Whereas much attention is often paid to postmodern feminist theory, the contributions of women of color to foundational feminist theories, particularly those of the body, are often forgotten. The insistence that feminist theory not be a monofocal project can be traced to the interventions made by feminists of color who have demanded (and continue to stress) that feminist scholarship examine the ways in which gender intersects with other systems of domination and is therefore experienced differentially among women across race, class, and sexuality. In Cherríe Moraga and Gloria Anzaldúa's collection *This Bridge Called My Back: Writings by Radical Women of Color*, the editors state, "What began as a reaction to the racism of white feminists soon became a positive affirmation of the commitment of women of color to our own feminism" (Moraga and Anzaldúa 2002, 1ii). The feminist thinkers, activists, and artists in this original 1981 collection reject not only the expectation that women of color take on the burden of bridging racial differences in feminist spaces but also the reproduction of disembodied knowledge production in feminist theory. This germinal collection unabashedly proclaims the body as a site of knowledge in its focus on "the ways in which Third World women derive a feminist political theory specifically from our racial/cultural background and experience" (Moraga and Anzaldúa 2002, 1iii). Similarly, Patricia Hill Collins's identifies black feminist thought as "specialized knowledge created by African American women which clarifies a standpoint of and for black women. In other words, black feminist thought encompasses theoretical interpretations of black women's reality by those who live it" (Hill Collins 2000, 22). Collins' *Black Feminist Thought*, originally published in 1990, reclaims black women's intellectual tradition and articulates an afrocentric feminist epistemology that is rooted in everyday experiences and resists Eurocentric, masculinist knowledge validation. Queer of color critique, such as that pursued by E. Patrick Johnson and Mae G. Henderson, continues this work of destabilizing static and binaristic conceptualizations of identity and rejuvenates intersectional analyses where the complex embodied experiences of race and sexuality have been undertheorized.

In the same spirit of challenging feminist theory to think intersectionally, a myriad of fields such as the aforementioned queer of color critique, and also transgender studies and feminist disability studies, have emerged that make vital contributions to and profoundly transform feminist theorizations of corporeality. For example, pioneering transgender studies scholar Susan Stryker's 1994 essay "My Words to Victor Frankenstein Above the Village of Chamounix: Performing Transgender Rage" argues that trans people possess a queer relation to nature; "while doctors landscape the aesthetic of naturalness on their skin, their very existence highlights that the 'natural' itself is a fabrication" (Stryker 2006). The lesson that trans people have to share, Stryker insists, is that nature and the body are constructed and technological products for all people. Feminist disability studies attempt to challenge, expand, and transform the ableism of feminist theory and feminist philosophy more specifically by putting it into conversation with the emergent field of disability studies and the lived embodied experiences of people with physical disabilities. In *The Rejected Body*, Susan Wendell writes, "The more I learned about other people's experiences of disability and reflected upon my own, the more connections I saw between feminist analyses of gender as socially constructed from biological differences between females and males, and my emerging understanding of disability as socially constructed from biological differences between the disabled and the non-disabled ... It was clear to me that this knowledge did not inform theorizing about the body by non-disabled feminists and that feminist theory of the body was consequentially both incomplete and skewed toward healthy, non-disabled experience" (Wendell 1996, 5). Echoing Wendell's call, Rosemarie Garland-Thomson's essay "Integrating Disability, Transforming Feminist Theory" arguably inaugurated the field of feminist disability studies in 2005 when it was published in the *NWSA Journal* (Garland-Thomson 2011). Garland-Thomson critiques disability studies' reinvention of the wheel through its failure to engage with feminist theory as it developed its own study of identity. In addition to disability studies' failure to engage meaningfully with concepts of gender and feminist theory, feminist theory fails to recognize disability. Feminist disability studies, as Garland-Thomson asserts, are not simply an additive endeavor; instead, feminist disability studies not only draw from and critique both fields, but also emphasize that the integration of disability can and should transform and expand feminist theorizing on representation, the body, identity, and activism.

SEE ALSO: Body Politics; Cosmetic Surgery in the United States; Eating Disorders and Disordered Eating; Feminist Disability Studies; Gender Performance; Mind/Body Split; Sex Versus Gender Categorization

REFERENCES

Alaimo, Stacy, and Susan Hekman. 2008. In *Material Feminisms*, edited by Stacy Alaimo and Susan Hekman, 1–22. Bloomington: Indiana University Press.

Bartky, Sandra Lee. 2003. "Foucault, Femininity, and the Modernization of Patriarchal Power." In *The Politics of Women's Bodies: Sexuality, Appearance, and Behavior*, edited by Rose Weitz, 25–45. New York: Oxford University Press.

Bordo, Susan. 2003. *Unbearable Weight: Feminism, Western Culture, and the Body*, 10th anniversary ed. Berkeley: University of California.

Butler, Judith. 1990. *Gender Trouble: Feminism and the Subversion of Identity*. New York: Routledge.

Butler, Judith. 1993. *Bodies That Matter: On the Discursive Limits of "Sex."* New York: Routledge.

Fausto-Sterling, Anne. 2000. *Sexing the Body: Gender Politics and the Construction of Sexuality*. New York: Basic Books.

Garland-Thomson, Rosemarie. 2011. "Integrating Disability, Transforming Feminist Theory." In *Feminist Disability Studies*, edited by Kim Q. Hall, 13–47. Bloomington: Indiana University Press. First published 2005.

Grosz, Elizabeth. 1994. *Volatile Bodies: Toward a Corporeal Feminism*. Bloomington: Indiana University Press.

Hill Collins, Patricia. 2000. *Black Feminist Thought: Knowledge, Consciousness, and the Politics of Empowerment*. New York: Routledge. First published 1990.

Martin, Emily. 1991. "The Egg and the Sperm: How Science Has Constructed a Romance Based on Stereotypical Male–Female Roles." *Signs*, 16(3): 485–501.

Moraga, Cherríe, and Anzaldúa, Gloria, eds. 2002. *This Bridge Called My Back: Writings by Radical Women of Color*, 3rd ed. Berkeley: Third Woman Press. First published 1981.

Pitts-Taylor, Victoria. 2007. *Surgery Junkies: Wellness and Pathology in Cosmetic Culture*. New Brunswick: Rutgers University Press.

Shildrick, Margrit, and Janet Price, eds. 1999a. *Feminist Theory and the Body: A Reader*. New York: Routledge.

Shildrick, Margrit, and Janet Price. 1999b. "Openings on the Body: A Critical Introduction." In *Feminist Theory and the Body: A Reader*, edited by Margrit Shildrick and Janet Price, 1–14. New York: Routledge.

Stryker, Susan. 2006. "My Words to Victor Frankenstein Above the Village of Chamounix: Performing Transgender Rage." *The Transgender Studies Reader*, edited by Susan Stryker and Stephen Whittle, 244–256. New York: Routledge. First published 1994.

Wendell, Susan. 1996. *The Rejected Body: Feminist Philosophical Reflections on Disability*. New York: Routledge.

Feminist Theories of Experience

CARYL NUÑEZ
University of Connecticut, USA

Feminist theories that locate experience as legitimate knowledge have historically provided a strong dimension of empowerment in feminism. Experience has come to mean evidence as a strong component of data for many feminist scholar-activists because women's perceptions, ways of knowing, and experiences are valued on ontological and epistemological levels. Over time, the focus on women subjectivities constructed as normative shifted to also include those on the margins of race, class, gender, sexuality, and ability. The inclusion of diverse perspectives is in part attributed to the rise in specific sub-disciplines and the creation of new paradigms of study, including but not limiting to area studies, cultural studies, disability studies, gender and sexuality studies, memory studies, and postcolonial studies. Making the invisible visible has been the project of feminist inquiry but the subjects that can be counted among the "invisible" has been evolving and widening. Interdisciplinary scholarship from and about individuals along a broad continuum of identity and their familiarity with patriarchal, misogynistic, homophobic, racist, ablest, and classist systems of oppression is a powerful testament to experience as evidence. Experience creates a consciousness that analytically shifts both ontological and epistemological assumptions dominated by white, male, Western thinkers.

There are feminist theories that arose during the second wave of feminism, specifically challenging the status quo by calling upon experience to be heard and applied to a variety of social issues such as white privilege, hegemonic masculinities, trauma and survival, sexuality and trans*activism, and postcolonial violence. These theories worked to legitimate experience by pushing against the mind–body divide. First is the umbrella theory known as standpoint. Standpoint theory has its roots in Hegelian and Marxist tradition and evolved toward a focus on women's sociopolitical positions as epistemic opportunity. For theorists such as Nancy Hartsock, Dorothy Smith, and Patricia Hill Collins, standpoint theory promotes personal knowledge as authentic knowledge in order to question the nature of oppression. Theory is generated from the individual place one originates their perspective about the world or, in literal terms, the point from where an individual stands. Epistemologically, this means how one comes to *know* is predicated on one's position in relationship to their social setting. For Sandra Harding this is also a crucial component in research about the entire social order since standpoint should account for the experiences of both men and women. Standpoint draws from the sense of engagement one feels, interacts, and negotiates from their interested position.

Second is a critical perspective on theories like standpoint. For example, Joan W. Scott crafted a pivotal critique of experience as evidence in 1991. While acknowledging the importance of making experiences visible, the act alone does not question how one is rendered invisible through oppressive structures. She proposes historically contextualizing experiences in order to analyze the logic of repression that "positions subjects and produces their experiences" (Scott 1991, 779). If subjects are created through experience then experience is not the origin of explanation, rather scholars need to historicize the identity the evidence of experience produces. Judith Butler also echoes Scott's sentiments, arguing that cultural context is not created by experience, rather cultural context is always already in the process of the subject's creation (Butler and Scott 1995). This perspective reverberates with a number of feminist methodological interventions including critical race theory, legal studies, and poststructuralist debates that responded to perceived failures of second-wave feminism such as the following perspectives in this entry, both national and global.

Intersectionality is a feminist theory that accounts for concurrent modes of difference – US women's activism and scholarship beginning in the 1970s responded to the exclusionary politics of the women's movement. As a result, black women crafted a number of documents to theorize their personal experience. The creation of the

Combahee River Collective statement of 1976 (Smith 1983), Kimberlé Crenshaw's (1991) seminal article on identity politics and violence against women of color, and Patricia Hill Collins's (1999) book on black feminist theory are crucial to the development of intersectionality. Intersectionality centers on the ways women experience discrimination along multiple axes of identity including race, gender, and class. In this regard, there is no hierarchy of oppressions, rather all aspects of their identity work in tandem and intersect and overlap one another. A paradigm of intersectionality is black feminist theory, which argues that the experience of black women in America interacts with additional cultural categories such as sexuality and class. Oftentimes the prejudice and discrimination black women face is a result of the interactions of multiple fronts of difference, which reinforce one another. Black women's experience with the law and social justice is often a reflection of the failures of legal structures and representation to capture the complexity of these identity politics.

Chicana feminists both critique and contribute to intersectionality by bringing their experiences to bear in prominent works like *This Bridge Called My Back: Writings by Radical Women of Color* (Moraga and Anzaldúa 1981), *Borderlands/La Frontera: The New Mestiza* (Anzaldúa 1987), and *Methodology of the Oppressed* (Sandoval 2000). Centering on a woman of color feminism that accounts for sexuality and heritage, these perspectives highlight the dimension of experience born from difference and the creation of new language to combat oppression. Drawing on colonial histories and the complexity of identities and representation, radical women of color feminism carries experience side by side with modes of resistance. Experience is the basis for the creation of new words and phrasing, poetry, and speeches. For example, Cherríe Moraga and Gloria Anzaldúa speak from their experiences as Chicana lesbians. Gloria Anzaldúa theorizes "speaking in tongues" as an extension of mestiza consciousness and mode of relating to fellow third world women. For these feminists and others such as June Jordan, Michelle Cliff, and Clenora Hudson-Weems, poetry is a means of survival. It is an artistic response to the experiences that are a consistent reminder of systemic violence.

In addition, Cherríe Moraga, Michelle Cliff, Anita Valerio and others crafted "theory in the flesh," or entering the lives of others. It is a prerogative that takes perspectives on the margins seriously to broaden the scope of what feminism is, who it is for, and envisioning transcultural solidarity. This is the practice of silencing one's own experience for the sake of understanding and sympathizing with the experiences of others on the margins. It is both a method and mode of practice on closing the eyes so as not to locate experience on what one sees, but to amplify one's ability to meaningfully listen to the other. This reflects what some African and Africana womanists express in problematizing the way the body is an exaggerated presence in the West, claiming that feminism is still caught up in the visual logic of Western thought that keeps one from affirming sex similarities over difference (Oyewumi 1997; Nnaemeka 1998). These theories breathe life into feminist movements within and beyond the United States by demanding women embrace a language of their own and engage in self-naming, self-definition, and self-care. They also widen feminist methodological frames of modes of resistance based on experiences.

There are a variety of non-Western woman of color feminists such as Chandra Talpade Mohanty, Kandice Chuh, and Gayatri Spivak who articulate a postcolonial perspective of feminism. Postcolonial theory adds the element of reflective engagement with the experience of colonization and the legacy that remains and shapes the lives of others. Postcolonial feminist scholars locate experience in relationship to colonial configurations of power such as the legal, economic, political, and educational structures. Additionally, they problematize the way the idea of the third world is construed through Western knowledge and history to represent individuals as subjects of underdevelopment. For example, this theory is applied through a critical analysis of the ways late capital creates poor subjects and in turn targets them through development initiatives such as economic empowerment programs for women. The perverse logic of postcoloniality functions through local culture, nationalistic rhetoric, and international policies that acutely affect third world women. Chandra Talpade Mohanty (2004) confronts Western feminist writings of third world women and the notion of "women" as a stable category of analysis that assumes ahistorical sisterhood and dismisses how women are complicit in the oppression of other women. Postcolonial feminist theory aims to include the voices and experiences of third world women who have been historically rendered invisible. Furthermore, M. Jacqui Alexander theorizes that the construction of specific bodies as legal or illegal subjects based on race, gender, and sexuality is a reflection of colonial desires of control and exceptionalism. By bringing the colonial history together with the experiences of the third world, new links are uncovered between women's struggles and geopolitical location.

There are a number of additional theories such as performance studies and affect that theorize specific experience and the influence on self. For example, Sara Ahmed (2004) theorizes about the formation of bodies shaped by the contact they have with others and objects that are ridden with emotions of pain, hate, fear, disgust, queer, love, shame, and attachments. In addition, the focus on experience from feminist perspectives of trauma and memory studies, for example, are noteworthy and represent other directions in which this interrogation of experience as self branches. They are made possible by earlier inquiries specified in this entry. Finally, theories of experience influence feminist pedagogies in the classroom. Though they vary immensely in nature, oftentimes these pedagogies center on student's experiences with several "isms," gender and performance, critique of social norms, and draw on experience to address larger structural and systemic oppressions. Its purpose is to unsettle the myth of objectivity in the creation of strategy and praxis of feminism and to apply new frames to theory, method, and being.

SEE ALSO: Feminist Theories of the Body; Intersectionality; Womanist; Women as Producers of Culture; Women's Ways of Knowing

REFERENCES

Ahmed, Sara. 2004. *The Cultural Politics of Emotion*. New York: Routledge.

Anzaldúa, Gloria. 1987. *Borderlands/La Frontera: The New Mestiza*. San Francisco: Aunt Lute.

Butler, Judith, and Joan Wallach Scott, eds. 1995. *Feminists Theorize the Political*. New York: Routledge.

Collins, Patricia Hill. 1999. *Black Feminist Thought: Knowledge, Consciousness and the Politics of Empowerment*. New York: Routledge.

Crenshaw, Kimberlé. 1991. "Mapping the Margins: Intersectionality, Identity Politics and Violence Against Women of Color." *Stanford Law Review*, 43(6): 1241–1299.

Mohanty, Chandra Talpade. 2004. *Feminism Without Borders. Decolonizing Theory, Practicing Solidarity*. Durham, NC: Duke University Press.

Moraga, Cherríe, and Gloria Anzaldúa. 1981. *This Bridge Called My Back: Writings by Radical Women of Color*. New York: Kitchen Table: Women of Color Press.

Nnaemeka, Obioma. 1998. *Sisterhood Feminisms & Power: From Africa to Diaspora*. Asmara, Eritrea: Africa World Press.

Oyewumi, Oyeronke. 1997. *The Invention of Women: Making African Sense of Western*

Gender Discourses. Minneapolis: University of Minnesota Press.

Sandoval, Chela. 2000. *Methodology of the Oppressed*. Minneapolis: Minnesota University Press.

Scott, Joan. 1991. "The Evidence of Experience." *Critical Inquiry*, 17(4): 773–797.

Smith, Barbara. 1983. "The Combahee River Collective." In *Home Girls: A Black Feminist Anthology*, edited by Barbara Smith, 272–281. New York: Kitchen Table: Women of Color Press.

FURTHER READING

Alexander, M. Jacqui. 2005. *Pedagogies of Crossing: Meditations on Feminism, Sexual Politics, Memory and the Sacred*. Durham, NC: Duke University Press.

Foss, Karen A., and Sonja K. Foss. 1994. "Personal Experience as Evidence in Feminist Scholarship." *Western Journal of Communication*, 58, 39–43.

Gilman, Laura. 2010. *Unassimilable Feminisms: Reappraising Feminist, Womanist, and Mestiza Identity Politics*. New York: Palgrave Macmillan.

Hartstock, Nancy. 1983. "The Feminist Standpoint: Developing Ground for a Specifically Feminist Historical Materialism." In *Discovering Reality*, edited by Sandra Harding and Merrill B. Hintikka. Dordrecht: D. Reidel.

Irigary, Luce. 1993. *An Ethics of Sexual Difference*, trans. Carolyn Burke and Gillian C. Gill. Ithaca: Cornell University Press.

Turcotte, Heather. 2014. "Feminist Asylums and Acts of Dreaming." *Feminist Theory*, 15(2): 141–160.

Feminist Theories of Organization

MARTA B. CALÁS and LINDA SMIRCICH
University of Massachusetts Amherst, USA

Over the years scholars in organization and management studies have been building on the conceptual innovations of feminist theorizing, using various feminist epistemological approaches to contribute alternative understandings of various topics. Often they have engaged with concerns where gender is readily apparent, such as sex differences in management, and work–family issues in organizations. In other instances, they have made visible gendered premises and practices behind topics conventionally represented as gender neutral; for example, in reconceptualizations of the stakeholder concept, organization structuring, and social networks. This scholarship draws, explicitly or implicitly, from feminist theoretical perspectives as analytical lenses to discern gendered aspects of organizational topics. These are derivative approaches which would seldom qualify as feminist theories of organization in their own right, but there are exceptions which will also be addressed.

This entry presents a broad outline of how feminist theorizing has contributed to organization and management studies, also considering its prospect to continue doing so. It highlights the contributions that five feminist theoretical tendencies – *liberal, radical, psychoanalytic, socialist*, and *poststructuralist* – have made to understanding gendered aspects of organization and management studies scholarship. It also illustrates changes in this scholarship as the literature has ranged from concerns with women's *access* to participation in organizations, to concerns about the *gendering* of organization processes and practices, and to further concerns for organization and management theorizing regarding the *stability of categories* such as "gender," "masculinity," "femininity," and "organization" (Calás and Smircich 2006). The ending acknowledges emerging tendencies in feminist theorizing engaging with *transnationalism, neoliberalism*, and *new materialisms*, considered relevant for the future of organization and management studies as a domain of theory and practice.

LIBERAL FEMINISM AND ITS INFLUENCE ON WOMEN-IN-MANAGEMENT SCHOLARSHIP

From the early 1970s, the second-wave women's movement and associated legislative and cultural changes brought in a greater presence and influence of women in the economy and in the academy. In this period researchers in organization studies, in particular those affiliated with the newly minted Women in Management division of the US Academy of Management, directed their attention to a new focus of study, "the woman manager." This line of research – with an added emphasis on diversity since the 1990s – continues to be motivated by knowledge of women and minorities' disadvantage in organizations, exploring issues related to their status including, in particular, their underrepresentation at higher levels.

The original influence of liberal feminism in this literature has also become more loose and uneven as tensions between the political stances of feminism and managerialism have become more marked. Organizations and management as institutions of liberal political and economic systems are assumed to be by definition sex/gender neutral, where individuals have equal access insofar as they are equally meritorious. The pursuit of *equity* – fostering the exercise of all people's individual rights – is a consistent goal, rather than the elimination of *inequality* – that is, acknowledging fundamental institutional problems which disadvantage particular groups. Despite the importance and influence of Kanter's (1977) sociological work, and its frequent appearance as a citation of choice in this literature, sociological-based research examining structural inequalities in organizations is not usual in the US women-in-management literature. Thus, the individualist pursuit of equity and inattention to inequality leads to several other premises distancing the women-in-management research from the original interests of liberal feminism.

This research is commonly conducted in US business schools and is primarily informed by social psychological approaches tending to locate the problem of women's inequality in flawed cognitive judgment processes, including overreliance on outdated stereotypes and their association with normative gender roles. Suggested remedies for unequal workplace outcomes imply that solutions to inequality can be found inside the heads of people rather than in reforming the organizational system. To this day expectations for change fall more often than not on individual women's capabilities to enact tactics for navigating hostile circumstances. As well, highly favored research topics, such as leadership, the glass ceiling, and even work–family issues, are oriented to understanding women's limitations for accessing higher management and organizational levels, and tend to ignore the conditions of work at lower organizational levels where most women are found. Altogether, women-in-management research mostly documents the persistence and endurance of sex segregation in management and organizations.

RADICAL FEMINISM AND FEMINIST ORGANIZATIONS

Concurrent with the appearance of women-in-management research, another organizational literature, in this case influenced by radical feminism, was also emerging. This research was primarily done in sociology departments and focused on *feminist organizations*: small organizations seeking to organize in ways consistent with feminist values emphasizing community, equality, and participation, and exhibiting a separatist intent to create womenspaces. They also rejected what was understood as male forms of power, including those inherent in conventional modes of organizing such as bureaucracies (Ferree and Martin 1995).

Radical feminists created a variety of alternative organizations and institutions such as book shops, women's health centers, banks, rape crisis centers, auto repair and carpentry shops, among others, but they were rarely subjects of analysis within organization and management studies even when they could have been considered excellent examples of entrepreneurship. Their absence in the management literature, in the United States in particular, can be attributed to being associated with anti-patriarchal and in some cases anti-capitalist values, considered antagonistic to business school values. Meanwhile, sociological research over time has also shown the precariousness of these organizations, documenting the transformation and even co-optation of their ideals. Yet, as discussed next, some radical feminist premises about "women's values" were eventually incorporated into the women-in-management literature.

WOMEN'S WAYS OF MANAGING: RADICAL AND PSYCHOANALYTIC FEMINIST INFLUENCES

Psychoanalytic theory applied to women-in-management research appeared in the late 1970s and focused on feminine character traits to explain women's subordinate economic status. Later, a popularized organizational scholarship added a "women's different ways of management" argument also, combining some versions of radical feminism with views from liberal feminisms.

Applications of psychoanalytic theory included associations of Freudian analyses of males' and females' socialization experiences, and their differing resolutions of the Oedipal complex, with their subsequent managerial behavior. Accordingly, most women were socialized to be passive, to see themselves as victims rather than agents, and lacked men's drive for mastery. Thus, most women fell short in the corporate culture because the rules, norms, and ethos of modern business reflected male developmental experiences. The corollary was that women would have to change if they were to succeed, but, unlike the women-in-management literature which addressed women's success as a personal issue, this literature addressed psychosexual development as *both* a personal *and* a societal issue, with cultural and historical roots.

Later, mostly during the early 1990s, organization and management research combined feminist "women's difference" arguments, including radical-cultural, psychoanalytic, and psychomoral, to contend that women's different "voices" should not be seen as a lack of managerial capabilities but as beneficial for both organizations and women. However, this style of argument depoliticized much of the feminist edge from their original sources to be able to enter into the women-in-management literature, and also cross over to the popular press. Lacking recognition of debates over essentialism, and mostly ignoring developmental and epistemological issues articulated in the sources from which they drew, these works claimed, for instance, that women's unique sex-role socialization, and different character traits, including an ethics of care, were not deficiencies, but *advantages* for corporate effectiveness, well suited to conditions in the contemporary economy, and making women a non-traditional but increasingly valuable and skillful resource for global competition.

However, this period also experienced the emergence of critical management scholarship, including the influence of feminist theorizing in scholarship which highlighted limitations and contradictions in the "female advantage" literature. For instance, some questioned if such research would actually advantage women or whether it further entrenched gender stereotypes. Others called attention to the dangers inherent in the instrumental positioning of women's supposedly "essential" qualities for coming to the rescue of corporations. Eventually these potential problems have become clearly demonstrated in recent research documenting a perverse dynamic where women are overrepresented in high-risk, precarious leadership positions, and confront a "glass cliff" when they fail and are singled out for criticism and blame.

SOCIALIST FEMINIST THEORIZING AND THE GENDERING OF THE ORGANIZATIONAL

With its emphasis on power relations and historical and material conditions, socialist feminism has had very productive connections with organization studies. Since the mid-1990s a substantial body of scholarship, both conceptual and in particular empirical, has advanced a field of research now named as "gendered organizations." Guided by Joan Acker's (1990) theory of gendered organizations as well as others' work on gendering practices in organizations, much of this research is well known in the United States within organizational sociology but less noted within business schools; it is nonetheless abundant in management and organization studies in Europe, Australia, and New Zealand.

Standing in clear contrast with the women-in-management research, instead of asking whether women's differences make a difference in organizations – which in some ways justify women's inequality – this literature asks, how is it possible that gender differences have become an explanation for sex-/gender-based inequality in organizations? What ongoing practices and processes produce and sustain organizations as gendered spaces? Here organizations are seen as *inequality regimes* interconnecting organizational processes and practices that produce and maintain racialized and gendered class relations. These arguments are now further articulated through analyses of *intersectionality*, focusing on the simultaneity of gender, race, class, sexuality, and other social categories in the production of social inequality, and strengthening understanding of the complexity of hierarchical differentiation in organizations. Altogether, studies taking a "gendered organization" perspective illuminate how changing organizations is much more than a matter of bringing in more female bodies. The focus of analyses becomes instead practices and relationships reinscribing structures of domination, which cut across organizational levels.

As conceptualized by Acker, persistent structuring of organizations along gender lines is reproduced in a number of ways including ordinary, daily procedures and decisions that segregate, manage, control, and construct hierarchies in which gender, class, and race are involved. For instance, a vicious cycle of job segregation is played out in recruiting and promoting practices. Gender structuring persists through wage setting practices and job evaluation schemes with embedded gender assumptions, resulting in the undervaluing of the interpersonal dimensions of work, such as nurturing and listening. Gendering, racializing, and sexualizing of organizations also occurs through symbols, images, and ideologies that legitimate inequalities and differences, including in intersections of race and gender in the labor market. Researchers' attention also focuses on *men as a social category*, examining relationships between masculinities, management, and organization.

Gender structuring, embodiment, and embeddedness are produced as well through social interactions that enact dominance and submission. Identity-making processes – for example, the choice of appropriate work, use of language, style of clothing, and the presentation of self as a gendered member of an organization – also contribute to structuring along gendered lines. Finally, all of these processes maintain the persistent structuring of organizations along gender lines and are supported, sustained by, and constitutive of a gendered substructure of organizations, also contributing to the extra-organizational reproduction of organizational members. In short, in these arguments "doing" organization and management, whether practicing or theorizing, implies *doing gender*.

FEMINIST POSTSTRUCTURALISMS AND STUDIES OF MANAGEMENT AND ORGANIZATION

From the mid-1990s to the present, applications of various strands of feminist poststructuralism have proliferated in this field, particularly in Europe, contributing to rethinking what constitutes knowledge in organization studies, and to whose advantage it works. Collectively these approaches to inquiry have demonstrated how the texts/language producing *organizational knowledge* are not naïve or innocent, but rather engaged in a politics of representation that can gender organizations. They examine, for instance, how masculinity is the unstated but very present norm in organizational knowledge construction. While seldom strictly "deconstructive," these writings often challenge dualistic thinking that underlies gender hierarchies of domination/subordination, making suspect the proclaimed objectivity and universality of organizational knowledge and asserting the possibility that it could be otherwise.

Foucault's influence is prominent in analyses examining discursive formations of gendered organizational subjectivities as well as practices of resistance to these formations. For instance, some works stress the dimension of resistance in the care of the self, interpreting it as a queer practice that turns a spatial politics of (sexual) difference into one of queering the spaces of management and organization. More broadly, Judith Butler's influence in this research ranges from her contributions to queer theory, for instance in arguments where gender and leadership are caught within the heterosexual matrix, to her notion of performativity in analyses of management recruitment activities which articulate reciprocal relationships between the social and the material, and further to interests in learning how gender gets done and (un)done in organizations and with what consequences. Other works, also often inspired by Butler, consider the meaning and potentiality of the body as a focus of analysis. For instance, the potential of transgender subjects for causing "gender trouble" in organizations is analyzed to address the importance of taking into account the materiality and subjectivity of transgender people, as well as the context in which gender crossing occurs. Transgender workers are usually a vulnerable population economically who therefore must balance political desires to shake up gender with concerns for job security.

EMERGING TENDENCIES

After the "discursive turn" from poststructuralism, emerging tendencies in feminist theorizing exhibit some commonalities: a return to materialism; recognition that attention to gender is no longer enough and the question of the subject of feminism must be redefined; and recognition that theory/practice engagements must attend to broader global issues. These common threads show up in otherwise distinct theoretical approaches: *transnational feminism*; *critiques of neoliberalism*; and *new materialisms*, as their concerns intersect in unveiling contradictions of global capitalism. Such intersections and concerns speak directly to organization and management studies. This field may be seen as an accomplice of global capitalism while it creeps into every crevice of socioeconomic life, with disparate consequences according to the social location of those affected. At present, thus, critical management and organization studies is poised to gain strength from these newer areas of feminist theorizing.

SEE ALSO: Discursive Theories of Gender; Gender as a Practice; Gender Inequality and Gender Stratification; Intersectionality

REFERENCES

Acker, Joan. 1990. "Hierarchies, Jobs, Bodies: A Theory of Gendered Organizations." *Gender & Society*, 4(2): 139–158.

Calás, Marta B., and Linda Smircich. 2006. "From the 'Woman's Point of View' Ten Years Later: Towards a Feminist Organization Studies." In *Sage Handbook of Organization Studies*, 2nd ed., edited by Stewart R. Clegg, Cynthia Hardy, Thomas B. Lawrence, and Walter R. Nord, 284–346. London: Sage.

Ferree, Myra Marx, and Patricia Y. Martin, eds. 1995. *Feminist Organizations: Harvest of the New Women's Movement* Philadelphia: Temple University Press.

Kanter, Rosabeth M. 1977. *Men and Women of the Corporation*. New York: Basic Books.

FURTHER READING

Acker, Joan. 2006. *Class Questions Feminist Answers*. Lanham, MD: Rowman & Littlefield.

Calás, Marta B., Linda Smircich, and Evangelina Holvino. 2014. "Theorizing Gender-and-Organization: Changing Times … Changing Theories?" In *Oxford Handbook of Gender in Organizations*, edited by Savita Kumra, Ruth Simpson, and Ronald Burke. Oxford: Oxford University Press. DOI: 10.1093/oxfordhb/9780199658213.013.025.

West, Candace, and Don H. Zimmerman. 1987. "Doing Gender." *Gender & Society*, 1(2): 125–151.

Feminist Theories of the Welfare State

NAAMA NAGAR
University of Wisconsin–Madison, USA

The welfare state is a form of state relations between state, citizens, and markets under capitalism, designed to provide a living safety net to protect and promote citizens' economic and social well-being, compensating for market inefficiencies. The welfare state operates two major types of redistributive interventions. First, the regulation of markets for commodities and services – importantly labor markets. Second, state spending on public services, investments in infrastructure, and cash transfers for social security, insurance or assistance programs.

Feminist theories of welfare states emerged in several areas of research, primarily: history, sociology, social work and social welfare, political science, policy and government studies, and economics. They responded to what was – especially before the 1990s and to some extent until today – a gender-blind body of knowledge. Mainstream welfare theory had understood welfare in terms of class power, and had conceptualized welfare primarily as a set of relations between state and market, both of which seemed to operate at the public sphere. It therefore neglected questions of gendered impact and the entire "private" sphere of family relations. Feminist critique, on the other hand, maintains that welfare programs are based on ideas regarding social relations, including ideas about femininity and masculinity, sexuality, and family structure. These ideas cannot be captured in terms of political or economic relations. Rather, relations of political or economic entitlement, privilege, dependency, or disadvantage in welfare states have specific gendered character. The state profoundly shapes gender relations by regulating both the public and the private spheres, and in turn gender relations profoundly shape welfare states (Orloff 1996). For example, early feminist scholarship on welfare noted the gender dichotomies in welfare design. In most Western states, social citizenship initially followed a contractual model between men, as workers, and the state. Both labor markets and welfare provisions were tailored to the "male breadwinner" model (Lewis 1992). Employers endorsed the "family wage" for male workers – a wage level high enough to provide for dependants, based on the assumption that upon marriage women would not seek paid employment but rather depend on their husbands for living. Similarly, public services and provisions often distinguished between insurance, which was available to men pending on their status as workers, and assistance, which was granted to women based on their familial status as wives and mothers.

Feminist scholarship on welfare states nowadays has two main lines of research. The first looks at the mechanisms of material redistribution – mainly public services, welfare benefits and cash transfers – through a gendered lens. The questions asked include: what populations are impacted by different welfare policies or included in different benefits programs, what types of opportunities they are awarded, what types of protection they are granted from either market or patriarchal relations, and whether it is the responsibility of the state, the market, or both to guarantee social rights. This line of research renders itself in particular to cross-national comparisons of the variations among welfare states, in addition to historical or case studies. The second line of inquiry considers gendered processes of distinction-making that drive welfare regulation and provision. Feminist scholars look at the ways in which welfare state discriminates among different populations. Feminist scholars often use methods of discursive and content analysis to examine gendered assumptions, values, and priorities that shape welfare policy; the identification, signifying, and classification of different populations in welfare design; and the articulation of needs and framing of policy solutions. In other words, feminists ask how different programs and policies are tailored along gender lines – in addition to class, race, nationality, religion or other salient categories – and to what effect. Both lines of inquiry complement each other.

FEMINIST COMPARATIVE WELFARE REGIME ANALYSIS

The single most influential work on the welfare state in the past quarter-century has been Gösta Esping-Andersen's (1990) theory of "welfare regimes," in which he examined the degree to which social rights permit people to have a livelihood independent of market forces, and created a typology of states, based on historical developments in the relations between the organized working class, states, and elites. Esping-Andersen uses the concept of "regime" to explain how and why different states followed different models for redistributing wealth, the types of regulations they placed on markets, the extent of their direct transfers to populations, and the normative basis for their policies and provisions. He distinguished between three main regimes. A "liberal" regime characterizes the United States, Canada, and Australia for example. These states grant only modest benefits or insurance. The "conservative" regime in states like Germany or Austria ties social rights with status, linking insurance to employment and benefits to families. Finally, the social democratic regime, characteristic of Scandinavian states, is the most generous in governmental spending, the most inclusive in its coverage, and promotes full employment. It provides universal healthcare, childcare, and eldercare, among other benefits.

For feminist scholars engaging with Esping-Andersen's model, a comparative analysis that focuses on labor and class relations ignores important elements of welfare states in relation to women's political and economic power, such as women's access to education and paid work, women's earnings level, and any income support they get. More importantly, however, not only states but families, too, are providers of welfare, and through policies and provisions states shape gender relations and family relations. Therefore any regime classification must consider the gendered burden of domestic and care work, assess all aspects of women's work, including unpaid work, and account for women's ability to sustain autonomous households. The capacity to live independently of familial care responsibilities is referred to as "de-familization" (e.g., Lewis 1992; Orloff 1993; Sainsbury 1994).

Looking at OECD countries – the subject of most comparative studies through a feminist lens – several patterns of gender regulation are observed. Women are viewed as "earners," not "caregivers." While equal opportunity in the labor market is promoted, in the lack of family-friendly policies, they find it hard to balance work and family. Consequently, there are wide gaps between mothers and other workers in the workforce, and women – particularly mothering women – are over-represented among the poor in general, and the working poor in particular. Whatever poor assistance schemes exist in this regime have strict entitlement criteria, modest transfers, and a stigmatizing effect. Most conservative states provide only modest caregiving services, but more generous and inclusive cash benefits to families. They are, however, also more religious states which reinforce a traditional gender labor division between men as breadwinners and women as caregivers; through the granting of paid maternal leave but no, or limited, right for paternal leave. Combined with relatively high wages, there is little demand for low-wage private sector services. Consequently, women's labor force participation is lower than in other OECD states, and gender pay gaps are large. Finally, social-democratic states, which rely on full employment, raise women's employment and wages through large spending on public sector services. High labor force participation of women is combined with provision of subsidized childcare, extensive parental leave policies for both mothers and fathers, and a system of individual (rather than familial) benefits, so the state encourages a family model of "dual-earner/dual carer": both parents are expected to do their equal share of wage labor and caregiving. These policies result in high levels of gender equality both in the labor market and within families (Orloff 1993). Feminist models of welfare regimes thus offer a multidimensional analysis of the redistributive practices of states, revealing how regimes differ not only in their impact on class relations, but also in their gender effect.

Moreover, feminist theories challenge the concept of "regime" and offer more nuanced distinctions between the various stratifying policy effects in each state. First, including gender complicates the "regime" map because there are actually great commonalities across regimes and significant differences among states within the same regime. For example, in all regimes, women are the majority among recipients of welfare transfer payments, and usually the majority among welfare state professionals. In all countries, working women take on a larger share of the housework (although the extent of this gender gap varies) and are also more likely than men to take parental leave (where it is provided). Differences in gender policies among states within each regime are likewise numerous; for example, social-democratic states differ in their support for employed mothers, conservative states differ in their support for women's paid employment, and liberal regimes differ in pay gap, in mothers' employment, and in their support for mothers who are sole heads of households. Second, gendered elements in welfare regimes change with time in multiple, even contradictory directions, depending on what domains one looks at: political representation, labor force participation, or other. Third, models of the welfare state need to include factors that greatly shape social policy, and in particular women's lives, in non-Western countries, such as religion and religious institutions, or a culture of political clientelism, and also take into account the greater role played by international aid agencies and non-governmental organizations (NGOs) in middle and low income economies. Even within Europe scholars argue that a separate "southern European" model should be considered for the more familial religious countries. Finally, feminist theorists argue that, regardless of state expenditure, the differences in the qualitative effects of welfare policies influence women's economic status, through the formation of gendered identities and interests. As part of that, the different strategies and demands made by women's movements shape the gendered character of welfare provisions. Attention to the formative, constructive power of the state led some scholars to argue that women's access to social benefits has been shaped by gender assumptions and family relationship more than affiliation with a welfare regime (O'Connor, Orloff, and Shaver 1999; Martínez-Franzoni 2008; Razavi and Staab 2012; Sung and Pascall 2014).

PRODUCTIVE PROCESSES OF SOCIAL PROVISION

Influenced by Marxian attention to ideology, as well as by the constructionist turn in many disciplines since the 1990s, feminist scholars came to view the state not only as a source of regulation and provision, but also a site of ideological battles – over gender meanings, sexual possibilities and norms, as well as race relations, religious practices, ethnic identities, and more. Welfare policies in particular define who needy people are and what it is they need. In so doing, they rely on, reinforce, and/or manipulate gender ideologies. Many gender-centered studies look not only at the material investment of welfare states, but also weigh in the criteria with which investments are made. Studies analyzing the ideologically productive nature of welfare states usually employ qualitative methods and focus on the discursive level of state actions and public demands, from problem definition and the classification of population groups, through claims making and the articulation of needs, to the framing of policy programs and the language used in implementation. Whereas regime studies are helpful in mapping policy discourses, a focus on the discursive development of political frames provides an understanding of where categories emerge from and how they develop (Fraser 1987; Bacchi 1999).

In most cases, gender stereotypes are used to define criteria of merit, in relation to moral and social norms. For example, a discourse of "dependency" in liberal regime states encourages middle-class women to depend economically on their husbands and not on state support. Such discourse fosters the separation between the public realm of paid labor and the private sphere of care, between the category of "husband" as breadwinner and "wife" as homemaker. Not only does this discourse strengthen heterosexuality and the patriarchal institution of marriage, it also stigmatizes poor women – married or not – who draw on state welfare, such as child support. These women are portrayed as passive and non-contributing subjects, and are encouraged to become "independent" from the state. They are deemed incapable or irresponsible enough to manage their own financial and domestic affairs, and often must accept close state scrutiny of their family life as a condition to receiving provisions (Fraser and Gordon 1994). Social policies thus provide recognition and support to some models of family organization and forms of caregiving while sanctioning others (Orloff 1996).

Most mainstream analyses of welfare states tend to adopt institutional/state-centered lens or a conflict approach, focusing on formal policies and programs and the operations of high-ranking administration officials, as well as on organized interest groups and debates at the decision-making levels. Feminist theorists – because they stress the private sphere – pay special attention to women's daily lives: to women as welfare recipients, to women who work as providers within the welfare system, to women policymakers, and to women who may be invisible in welfare legislation, such as homemakers. For example, a major site for feminist research is the welfare office, where social workers – themselves usually women – apply gender, race, class, and other criteria and assumptions in the assessment of needs, sorting of claimants into recipient groups, distribution of provision and other processes of resources allocation. The welfare office is also a venue for gender disciplining through the sanctioning of certain parental practices and ideas of motherhood or fatherhood, gendered and sexual conduct, and so on. The interaction between social workers and other welfare professionals and clients/beneficiaries at that level has an important, even determining, role in shaping women's social citizenship (Korteweg 2006).

The home perspective is also important in assessing redistribution outcomes. Receipt of welfare benefits is not an automatic guarantor of economic independence, as women and elderly in particular may lack decision power over spending in their household. This in turn has implications for intervention methods, and the implementation of state policies (Hassim 2005).

INTERSECTING PROCESSES AND SITES

Feminist scholarship on welfare during the 1970–1990s tended to subscribe to either a structural (specifically socialist) analysis of state relations or a more institutional emphasis on state agency. Consequently, scholars place emphasis either on particular domains of state activity – for instance, labor regulation, childcare services, provision for eldercare – and/or on one area of impact, such as class stratification or gender oppression. Scholars' capacity to encompass the mutually influencing connections among these processes was limited. Recent conceptualizations of intersectionality have shifted the emphasis to intertwining processes of allocation and signification (Bacchi 1999).

Theorists of the state nowadays account for the multiple ways in which processes of gendering intersect with other processes of categorization and stratification in order to account for the differentiated symbolic and material aspects of welfare states. For one, scholars combine gender analysis with processes of racialization which have shaped labor relations, welfare entitlements, and venues for claiming and exercising citizenship. The legacies of lingering racial or ethnic conflicts, and conflicts around immigration or religion continue to shape the possibilities of state–family–market constellations. For example, they influence the cost of labor and in particular of paid care work. At the same time, racial motivations often underpin the allocation of different services and provisions to different populations. Together these processes influence the employment choices and mobility venues open to different women (Orloff 1996). Sexuality is similarly an important axis of normative regulation intersecting with gender. Feminists study the discriminatory practices against population groups identified as homosexuals or lesbians, and beyond that – processes of "sexualization," that is, the constitution of gay subjects through state regulation. Welfare systems in the United States, for example, allocated benefits unevenly, not only between men and women, but also among men and women, in ways that excluded certain gender traits and sexual behaviors that were classified as perverse, crystalizing them as separate identities (Canaday 2009). Furthermore, racialization and sexualization are themselves mutually constitutive, and formative in other dimensions of the welfare state, such as criminalization, incarceration, and violence against women, for instance.

SOUTHERN PERSPECTIVES ON WELFARE STATES

Scholars studying social policies in states with developing, rather than developed, economies, have called to question some northern assumptions regarding the relationship among states, markets, and families, which are fundamental to the main theories in the field. Feminist scholars of the Global South offer different perspectives on each of the questions that are central to feminist theory of welfare states: the formation and transformations of welfare states, the gendered nature of welfare regimes, the effect of social policy on gender relations and how it can be used effectively to improve them, and implications for theories of the state and citizenship.

On the topic of the historical formation of welfare states, developing states have had different trajectories of state building and economic development than most Western countries, and correspondingly their welfare regimes are influenced by mixed legacies: colonial and postcolonial; customary, religious, and secular; national, tribal and ethnic; and in some cases that of military and/or racist regimes. The different agendas of previous administrations not only left a mark on social stratification, but still echo in shaping redistribution policies today (Martínez-Franzoni 2008). In postcolonial nations, for instance, social provisions reflect Eurocentric views of gender relations – as well as race/ethnic relations. Under apartheid South Africa, for example, the welfare system was tailored for European-style nuclear families, with the assumption that each household is comprised of two generations (parents and children), two adults and a division between male breadwinner and female housewife. In reality, many Africans had no access to the racialized labor markets, and many workers had responsibilities for more than one household (Hassim 2005).

As far as the gendered nature and effect of social policies, in mainstream theories of modernization, development is often linked to improvement in women's status and life chances, wherein women's welfare is usually seen not as a goal in and of itself but as a means to a broader societal end. Feminists critique this logic, which makes women expedient to development, and refute the assumption that economic progress necessarily improves women's lives. More specifically, feminist scholars have demonstrated that familialism (reliance on families for care provision) does not disappear with economic development. Rather, global economic structures coexist with traditional arrangements that assign care responsibilities to women. In fact, in large parts of Africa, Asia, and Latin

America, modern welfare is embedded in family relations, hence people's well-being is more dependent on women's unpaid labor than on public policy (Razavi and Staab 2012). Developing countries are not necessarily more "familial" than developed ones – as many industrialized states also rely heavily on families and women's unpaid work for care provision – but they may be familial in different ways: less individualized and organized around traditional patriarchal forms of authority, such as extended kinship circles or tribes. In addition, an informal welfare sector (e.g., religious organizations) and community support networks are crucial for care provision and societal well-being (Martínez-Franzoni 2008). While women may feel more respectfully treated by community-based charity workers than by state officials, this places the burden of care on women's unrecognized and unpaid work not only within families but also in their larger communities (Hassim 2005).

Contemporary transformations of welfare regimes also differ greatly between the Global North and the Global South. The latter tend to be inflicted by war, military regimes, nature disasters, humanitarian crises, and global debt inequalities. In particular, international pressures to prioritize fiscal restraint over governmental spending limit states' ability to address poverty comprehensively and impacts poor women's welfare in particular. For instance, between 1975 and 2000 Argentina has gone from an extensive – albeit stratified – social security coverage to a "dualist regime" in which half the workforce is informally employed, and about half of women in paid jobs have no entitlement to provisions such as workplace-based childcare or paid maternity leave. These changes forced poor women in particular to rely more heavily on public services and social assistance (Razavi and Staab 2012).

As for the gendered effect of welfare, developing countries are not necessarily more "familial" than developed ones. As noted, some industrialized states rely heavily on families – on women's unpaid work – for care provision. That said, many developing states are less individualized than the West, and organized around traditional patriarchal forms of authority: extended kinship circles, tribes, and so on. Informal welfare sector (e.g., religious organizations and NGOs) and community support networks are crucial for care provision and societal well-being (Martínez-Franzoni 2008). This places the burden of care on women's unrecognized and unpaid work not only within families but also in their larger communities (Hassim 2005). At the same time, women may feel more respectfully treated by community-based charity workers than by state officials.

Making social provisions effective for the welfare and status of women therefore requires adjusted thinking to the context of developmental states. Many developing states face governability difficulties and poor management, and their administration and infrastructure fall short of delivering services and implementing programs fully. Often, welfare budgets are underspent, less money reaches women and families, and future planning may be misinformed. In addition, developmental states further face non-conventional challenges to their population's life chances – like the HIV/AIDS epidemic – which have gendered effects (more women carry the virus, and from a younger age than men), and which call for specific national priorities in healthcare and public assistance programs (Hassim 2005).

NEW REALITIES

Processes related to caregiving are central to welfare debates not only in terms of gender relations, but also because of their broader importance for population reproduction and the economy at large. Rapid changes to family structures create new realities for welfare states to accommodate, including an increase in premarital cohabitation, in divorce rates, and in the number of women-headed households, a rise in the percentage of married women working in paid employment, legalization of gay and lesbian marriages and unions, a growth in men's share of care duties, and more. Today more than ever it is important to de-link the question of care from normative ideas about family structure and gendered responsibilities. For example, new theories of welfare states pay greater attention to questions of masculinity and fatherhood, and also to children; whereas in the past mothers were taken as proxies for children's best interests and needs, states and scholars show greater concern for children as welfare subjects in and of themselves.

The inclusion of southern perspectives is particularly important for understanding the interaction of mutually influencing global care systems, which today shape welfare policies and gender regimes in national economies. In developed economies, the revolution in women's employment, declining fertility and increased longevity are sources of pressing demands for care. Neoliberal policies and economic crises brought about a welfare recession and retrenchment of care services. As the major workers in welfare institutions and recipients of their services, women have been disproportionately impacted by the retreat of the state and in particular from the care deficit. Many postindustrial states turn to immigration as an answer to their domestic care labor demand. On the supply side, in developing economies, access to paid jobs is lacking and weak states leave families with little provisions, pushing women to seek work abroad in the growing paid care sector. Migration from the Global South to the Global North creates new constellations of states, global markets, and families, and fosters profound changes in family relations and in the status of women in immigration-receiving as well as immigration-sending states. South European states, for example, traditionally encouraged a "male breadwinner" family pattern, relying on women's unpaid work at home for reproductive labor, and therefore offered little benefits to families. In recent decades these states have been shifting from a "conservative-familial" regime to a a "migrant in the family" model (Bettio, Simonazzi, and Villa 2006). Migrant women's status in their countries of origin also changes as a result of the power of their remittances in local economies. These global transformations create new dilemmas and new political opportunities for action for feminist movements and welfare reformers.

CONCLUSIONS

The welfare state should be understood not only in the narrow sense of social assistance or poverty relief, but broadly as a system redistributing wealth through the provision of reproductive services by investing in care, education, health and other public services, and through the regulation of markets and labor, immigration, taxation, and property ownership policy – all of which are designed utilizing gender distinctions, and shape gender and family relations. "Malestream" gender-blind theories used to portray the welfare state as a protective mechanism against market failure, focusing on male workers while ignoring or under-theorizing women's activities.

Feminist scholarship demonstrated that while the welfare state has an important role in providing economic opportunities and protecting women from market inequalities, it is constituted upon gendered ideology, which in many cases restricts women by confining them to patriarchal relationships and keeping them at an inferior position to men. Feminist theories stress the need for protection from a failure of care, due to the gender division of reproductive labor and devaluation of women's work. Feminist scholars of the welfare state therefore study different areas of regulation and provision pertaining in particular to care provision and care work. Feminist studies highlight not only central welfare administration, but also the power of day-to-day workings of welfare services to shape gender relations. Importantly, scholars engage with symbolic and cultural dimensions of the welfare state, analyzing the constitutive processes that are instrumental to policy and program-making. From a constructionist perspective, the recognition of policy problems, the definition and characterization of target populations, and the framing of solutions are all gendered processes. Furthermore, welfare states developed along exclusionary lines of race, ethnicity, nationality, religion, sexuality, and immigration, as well as gender. The impact of welfare policies is consequently not simply gender bifurcated but complex and intersectional.

Beyond a simplistic view of the state as either friend or foe, feminist theorists today hold a view of state as a complex system with multiple operating mechanisms and dimensions of influence. The state regulates many areas – from labor and taxation to the provision of social services – with multiple effects that are not always consistent. The welfare state operates at many different levels, from policy-makers to the daily interactions at the welfare office. The balance between states, markets, families, and other communal forces (religious communities, non-profit institutions) varies across states, cultures, and regimes. This complexity shapes people's experiences and social citizenship, and opens different venues for action for feminist movements and welfare reformers in every context. Feminist researchers thus no longer ask "Should women look to the state for protection?" Rather, they problematize different ways in which women may exercise their agency vis-à-vis state agencies and programs.

SEE ALSO: Feminist Theories of Organization; Immigration and Gender; Private/Public Spheres; Work–Family Balance

REFERENCES

Bacchi, Carol Lee. 1999. *Women, Policy and Politics: The Construction of Policy Problems*. London: Sage.

Bettio, Francesca, Annamaria Simonazzi, and Paola Villa. 2006. "Change in Care Regimes and Female Migration: The 'Care Drain' in the Mediterranean." *Journal of European Social Policy*, 16(3): 271–285.

Canaday, Margot. 2009. *The Straight State: Sexuality and Citizenship in Twentieth-Century America*. Princeton: Princeton University Press.

Esping-Andersen, Gösta. 1990. *The Three Worlds of Capitalism*. Princeton: Princeton University Press.

Fraser, Nancy. 1987. "Women, Welfare and the Politics of Need Interpretation." *Hypatia, Special Issue: Philosophy and Women Symposium*, 2(1): 103–121.

Fraser, Nancy, and Linda Gordon. 1994. "A Genealogy of Dependency: Tracing a Keyword of the US Welfare State." *Signs*, 19(2): 309–336.

Hassim, Shireen. 2005. *Gender, Welfare and the Developmental State in South Africa*. United Nations Research Institute for Social Development (UNRISD).

Korteweg, Anna. 2006. "The Construction of Gendered Citizenship at the Welfare Office: An Ethnographic Comparison of Welfare-to-Work Workshops in the United States and the Netherlands." *Social Politics: International Studies in Gender, State and Society*, 13(3): 314–340.

Lewis, Jane. 1992. "Gender and the Development of Welfare Regimes." *Journal of European Social Policy*, 3(2): 159–173.

Martínez-Franzoni, Juliana. 2008. "Welfare Regimes in Latin America: Capturing Constellations of Markets, Families, and Policies." *Latin American Politics and Society*, 50(2): 67–100.

O'Connor, Julia, Ann Shola Orloff, and Sheila Shaver. 1999. *States, Markets, Families: Gender, Liberalism and Social Policy in Australia, Canada, Great Britain, and the United States*. Cambridge: Cambridge University Press.

Orloff, Ann Shola. 1993. "Gender and the Social Rights of Citizenship: The Comparative Analysis of Gender Relations." *American Sociological Review*, 58(2): 303–328.

Orloff, Ann Shola. 1996. "Gender in the Welfare State." *Annual Review of Sociology*, 22: 51–78.

Razavi, Shahra, and Silke Staab. 2012. "Introduction." In *Global Variations in the Political and Social Economy of Care: Worlds Apart*, edited by Shahra Razavi and Silke Staab, 1–28. New York: Routledge.

Sainsbury, Diane. 1994. *Gendering Welfare States*. Sage.

Sung, Sirin, and Gillian Pascall. 2014 "Introduction: Gender and Welfare States in East Asia." In *Gender and Welfare States in East Asia: Confucianism or Gender Equality?* edited by Sirin Sung and Gillian Pascall, 1–28. New York: Palgrave Macmillan.

Feminist Utopian Writing

SALLY L. KITCH
Arizona State University, USA

Many US feminists have been attracted to the idea of envisioning, or even inhabiting, a utopian or ideal society designed along feminist principles. In the 1980s and 1990s, for example, theorists such as Frances Bartkowski (1989), Drucilla Cornell (1991), and Lucy Sargisson (1996) argued that feminism itself depended on utopian thinking, on considering the "not-yet as the basis for feminist practice, textual, political, or otherwise" (Bartkowski 1989, 12).

A long history of Western feminist utopian writing precedes such declarations, going back at least to Christine de Pisan's fifteenth-century *Book of the City of Ladies*, in which wealthy, educated women could experience aesthetic, intellectual, and sensual pleasure without male interference (Capasso 1994, 44–47). In the United States, utopian fiction by women began appearing in the 1840s, several decades before the term *feminist* was coined. One motif in such works, such as Mary E. Bradley Lane's *Mizora: A Prophecy* (1880–1881) and Charlotte Perkins Gilman's *Herland* (1915), is an all-female society flourishing after men's elimination by various means. In such societies, motherhood is typically the highest calling and defining ethos, and asexual or parthenogenetic reproduction prevails (Kitch 2014, 504–505).

Other texts from that period offered more reformist advances. They envisioned enlightened social programs designed to eliminate the inequities of marriage and traditional family life, based on positive assumptions about women's capabilities, in recognizable, sexually integrated societies (Lewes 1995, 44). In many such works, including M. Louise Moore's *Al Modad* (1892) and Martha Bensley Bruère's *Mildred Carver, USA* (1919), new career opportunities were identified as crucial to improving gender relations and eliminating gender hierarchy throughout society (Kitch 2014, 507).

The 1960s and 1970s brought texts that were more focused on communitarian values, androgyny, or female separatism, including Ursula Le Guin's *The Left Hand of Darkness* (1969) and *The Dispossessed* (1974); Marge Piercy's *Woman on the Edge of Time* (1976); Mary Staton's *From the Legend of Biel* (1975); and Suzy McKee Charnas's *Motherlines* (1978). Many works produced throughout the 1980s de-emphasized motherhood's centrality to women's identities, including lesbian feminist utopian novels such as Monique Wittig's *Les guérillères* (1969), Sally Gearhart's *The Wanderground* (1979), Katherine Forrest's *Daughters of a Coral Dawn* (1984), and Jewelle Gomez's *The Gilda Stories* (1991). Lesbian utopian novels were linked to some earlier texts to the extent that they identified transformed visions of sexuality and sexual practices as pivotal to elevating women's social status (Kitch 2014, 509).

Toward the end of the twentieth century, something of a crisis erupted in feminist *speculative* fiction, a term writers began using to challenge the automatic connection of feminism with utopian visions and thought. Newer texts highlighted the internally contradictory aspects of *utopia*, a term coined in 1516 by Sir Thomas More to convey the idea that an ideal place (*eutopia*) is also an impossible place (*outopia*). One aspect of *utopia*'s impossibility is its close connection to *dystopia*, because defining ideals work for all, even all feminists, is treacherous business. Margaret Atwood's *The Handmaid's Tale* (1985) struck many readers as the epitome of that ironic danger. The novel depicts a dystopian world that has ostensibly fulfilled certain feminist dreams but with chilling results. As she suffers in a gender dictatorship, in which handmaids like herself must bear children for sterile commanders' wives in all-female birthing circles, the novel's narrator, Offred, asks, "Mother … Wherever you may be. Can you hear me? You wanted a women's culture. Well, now there is one" (Atwood 1985, 164). Writers recognized that even the term *women* can be utopian, if it imposes coherent identities and distinct gender boundaries upon the wide variety of people it purports to signify (Kitch 2000, 119, 123, 132–133, 139).

As the twenty-first century approached, feminist writers redefined *utopia* as a means of exploring fragmentations, impossibilities, and inconsistencies as creative forces. Using a postmodern, neofeminist lens, writers celebrated parts rather than wholes, desire as well as politics. They employed heterogeneity, contradiction, diversity, and playful juxtapositions in their *heterotopian* speculative fiction (Siebers 1994, 7). Some invented fictional worlds in which literary and social conventions are disrupted and fantasy and reality intertwine. Instead of definitive places, *utopias* became *no-places* of disjointed possibilities (Wagner-Lawlor 2013, 13–14, 23, 60). Novels adopting this postmodern, speculative, neofeminist perspective contemplated unresolved, open-ended worlds of re-gendered possibilities, where even the past can be reimagined. Examples of this form include Toni Morrison's *Paradise* (1998), Octavia Butler's *Parable* series (1993, 1998), Susan Sontag's *In America* (2000), Ursula Le Guin's *The Telling* (2000), Doris Lessing's *The Cleft* (2007), Jeanette Winterson's *The Stone Gods* (2009), and Margaret Atwood's *The Year of the Flood* (2009). Lesbian feminist writers also embraced utopia as a feminist tool of possibility and critique (Kitch 2014, 518). Post-millennial nonfiction writers embraced the idea of discovering "utopian moments" that can point to, if not fully describe, feminist possibilities even in fields like economics (Schönpflug 2008).

Although feminist utopian writing has transformed over centuries, the idea of *utopia* remains in the feminist toolbox for spurring thought about future possibilities. Instead of full-blown utopian visions that cannot accommodate a diversely gendered, raced, and embodied world, however, such writing serves transformative purposes by tantalizing and provoking.

SEE ALSO: Celibacy; Chastity; Cognitive Critical and Cultural Theory; Ecofeminism; Environment and Gender; Feminist Literary Criticism; Gender as Institution; Sex-Related Difference Research

REFERENCES

Atwood, Margaret. 1985. *The Handmaid's Tale*. London: Vintage Books.

Bartkowski, Frances. 1989. *Feminist Utopias*. Lincoln: University of Nebraska Press.
Capasso, Ruth Carver. 1994. "Islands of Felicity: Women Seeking Utopia in Seventeenth-Century France." In *Utopian and Science Fiction by Women*, edited by Jane L. Donawerth and Carol A. Kolmerten, 35–53. Syracuse: Syracuse University Press.
Cornell, Drucilla. 1991. *Beyond Accommodation: Ethical Feminism, Deconstruction, and the Law*. London: Routledge.
Kitch, Sally. 2000. *Higher Ground: From Utopianism to Realism in Feminist Thought and Theory*. Chicago: University of Chicago Press.
Kitch, Sally. 2014. "Utopia." In *Critical Terms for the Study of Gender*, 487–526. Chicago: University of Chicago Press.
Lewes, Darby. 1995. *Dream Revisionaries: Gender and Genre in Women's Utopian Fiction, 1870–1920*. Tuscaloosa: University of Alabama Press.
Sargisson, Lucy. 1996. *Contemporary Feminist Utopianism*. New York: Routledge.
Schönpflug, Karin. 2008. *Feminism, Economics and Utopia: Time Travelling through Paradigms*. New York: Routledge.
Siebers, Tobin. 1994. "Introduction: What Does Postmodernism Want? Utopia." In *Heterotopia: Postmodern Utopia and the Body Politic*, edited by Tobin Siebers, 1–38. Ann Arbor: University of Michigan Press.
Wagner-Lawlor, Jennifer A. 2013. *Postmodern Utopias and Feminist Fictions*. Cambridge: Cambridge University Press.

FURTHER READING

Bryson, Valerie. 2007. *Gender and the Politics of Time: Feminist Theory and Contemporary Debates*. Bristol: Policy Press.

Feminization of Labor

ANGELA DZIEDZOM AKORSU
University of Cape Coast, Ghana

Among the several reports of the negative effects of economic globalization, particularly in developing countries, feminization of labor emerges as ubiquitous. In view of this, the importance of knowledge-building about the feminized nature of labor cannot be overemphasized. Conceptually, feminization of labor has two dimensions. The first dimension refers to the quantitative increases in the number and proportion of females engaged in paid work over the last 20 or so years. The second dimension refers to flexible work forms such as home-based work, subcontracting, and part-time work, which, though not necessarily targeted at women and not necessarily bad, have attracted an increased number of women and have meant insecurity and precariousness of labor. This entry seeks to highlight the trends and/or patterns, the context of the phenomena, the implication for women and for policy, and the future direction of such discourses.

Twenty-seven million people, 90 percent of them women, are reported to be working in the export processing zones worldwide. These are free trade zones established in developing countries by their governments to promote industrial and commercial exports and are often characterized by exemptions from certain taxes and business regulations. For the past 20 years, the participation of women in the labor force, particularly in paid employment, has increased more than that of their male counterparts everywhere in the world with the exception of Africa, where the majority of women continue to eke out a living in the still invisible traditional sectors (International Labour Organization 1999). It appears that the traditional barriers to formal employment in Africa, such as marriage and childbearing, remain strong. Notably, however, the upward trend in women's participation in paid employment is due to the proliferation of more flexible and informal work forms.

The single most important contextual factor that has culminated in the increasing feminization of labor is neoliberal economic globalization, with its associated free trade. This has meant a greater quest for cheap labor, which in turn has led to all kinds of flexibility, especially in the transfer of production to economies where labor costs are relatively cheaper, as well as flexibility in fragmenting production and reorganizing employment forms from regular full-time employment to part-time, casual, temporal, and home-based work. Since women have been traditionally marginalized into domestic, informal, and casual work, this development seems to offer them some form of freedom to earn income and still hold on to their domestic responsibilities. For the capitalists, certain qualitative features of "female" work in the traditional sectors have become more desirable and have transformed women into a strategic pool of labor (Morini 2007). For instance, Standing (1999) reported that, among the several possible reasons why women's wages are lower than men's, their preparedness to work for less and their having lower wage aspirations stand out and are enough to induce capitalists to substitute men with women. Unlike their male counterparts, women tend not to complain or agitate about their exploitation at work. Indications are that they either tend to be somewhat timid and loyal to their employers, or they are unaware of their labor rights in view of their limited education and background. Women's adroitness and malleable nature, which are so often cited as desirable to modern capitalists, especially those in the textile and technology industries, are a reflection of women's socialization and gendered position in society. Thus, feminization of labor is driven by a complex combination of demographic, cultural, and economic elements.

The implications of the feminization of labor for women are enormous. Granted, women who are absorbed into flexible work forms have the opportunity to earn income, take decisions, have a greater voice in their family and community life, and enjoy mobility (Choudhry, 1997). That notwithstanding, most of the world's working women continue to experience insecurity and precariousness that cannot be ignored. Female workers continue to receive lower wages than their male counterparts for work of equal value. Just as flexible work forms have meant easy entry into paid employment, it has also meant easy exit for most women. Most women tend to be dismissed from work easily on the basis of marriage and childbirth. Many young, unskilled, or semi-skilled women who are employed in the export processing zones by multinational corporations receive hardly any training. Other detrimental consequences include poor labor standards and conditions. Deteriorating health and in some cases deaths are also reported among such women. Thus, for women, feminization of labor means opportunities for some economic freedom as well as for more exploitation, with the ultimate beneficiaries being their employers.

It is noteworthy that the same neoliberal factors that have feminized work have also worked to erode the protective role of labor legislation and unionization. Capitalists' aversion to state intervention and unionization is common. As a result, there has been a proliferation of firm-specific codes of conduct for labor market governance, monitoring, and regulation. Though the firm-specific codes of conduct technically reflect the ILO's labor standards to a large extent, employers seem to prefer them. The fact that these are often voluntary and not legally binding has been a source of concern, since capitalist employers cannot be relied on to remedy the consequences of their own strategic decisions.

The future direction of women's work is obviously confronted with two main factors, namely, the uncontrolled economic and political leverage of global capitalists, and the traditional male-dominated character of labor unions. With regard to the former, it seems that the political commitment of world leaders and their supporting institutions such as the International Monetary Fund (IMF) and the World Bank is crucial. This is in view of the fact that so much research has been conducted to critique neoliberal economics as the driving force of the world economy. As regards the latter, the empowering potential of women's own agency can be helpful. If trade unions provide women more opportunities within their own male-dominated structures, and if civil society organizations do the same, women can and will pursue an agenda to address their particular needs. Undoubtedly, the protectionist role of the state, trade unions, and civil society organizations continue to be necessary for all workers, and particularly for vulnerable working women.

SEE ALSO: Feminization of Poverty; Gender Wage Gap

REFERENCES

Choudhry, Saud. 1997. "Women Workers in the Global Factory: Impact of Gender Power Asymmetries." In *The Political Economy of Globalization*, edited by Satya Dev Gupta, 216–236. Boston: Kluwer.
International Labour Organization (ILO). 1999. *World Employment Report 1998–99*. Geneva: ILO Publications.
Morini, Cristina. 2007. "The Feminisation of Labour in Cognitive Capitalism." *Feminist Review*, 87: 40–59.
Standing, Guy. 1999. "Global Feminization Through Flexible Labor: A Theme Revisited." *World Development*, 27(3): 583–602.

FURTHER READING

Standing, Guy. 1989. "Global Feminization Through Flexible Labor." *World Development*, 17(7): 1077–1095.

Feminization of Migration

DONNA R. GABACCIA
University of Toronto, Canada

Since the mid-1980s, scholars, journalists, and advocates have pointed to the growth of female migration worldwide; increasingly, experts measure this so-called feminization of migration with a sex or gender ratio that describes the proportion of females relative to males in migration streams. Although many scholars assumed that globalization drove the recent feminization of migration (Castles and Miller 1993), demographers at the United Nations showed that international migrations have been gender balanced since 1960 (Zlotnik 2003). Subsequent studies have pushed the onset of feminization back to the early twentieth century (Donato and Gabaccia 2015). Across disciplines, scholars have nevertheless agreed that variations in the migrant gender composition hold important clues to how gender relations shape emigration and immigration for men and women alike.

Study of the feminization of migration began when statisticians in the US Department of Labor first documented female majorities among American immigrants (Houstoun et al. 1984). By the early 1990s, the United Nations had compiled preliminary census data on immigrant gender ratios worldwide; in 2006, they reported that gender balance or slight female majorities were common worldwide (UNFPA 2006). Many studies of feminization pointed toward the dangers of migration for women, in the form of abusive labor conditions for female domestic workers and sex trafficking; advocates discussed feminization in order to call for enhanced policies and programs to assist endangered women. Advocates and scholars portrayed contemporary migrations as significantly different from those of the past, when male predominance had presumably been the norm. Some world historians agreed (Manning 2004). Viewed from this perspective, globalization threatened to upend gender relations that may have been based on inegalitarian gender ideology but that had nevertheless protected families, traditional communities, and their local cultures by rendering women less mobile than men.

Over the past decade, historical and social scientific studies have significantly revised scholars' understanding of the feminization of migration by pointing to several long-term shifts in the gender composition of international migrants and toward considerable variations in sex ratios among migrants before and after 1960. Historically, for example, Indian Ocean, North African, and Middle Eastern slave trades were heavily female; there, domestic slavery worked mainly to expand lineage political and economic power through reproduction. The Atlantic slave trade – the largest coerced migration of the early modern era – remained relatively gender balanced compared with the heavily male migrations of European indentured servants traveling at the same time, but both became more male by the eighteenth century, especially in areas of plantation labor. With the industrialization and the expansion of European empires in the nineteenth century, international labor migrations grew and became more masculine, with the female proportion falling to only one quarter of all migrants and to even lower levels among Asian and European contract laborers. Temporary and circulatory migrations were the most heavily male. Even during the nineteenth century, however, female-majority and gender-balanced migrations existed, for example among the Irish (with high numbers of female domestic servants), among refugees (e.g., Jews fleeing to the Americas), and among imperial schemes for settler colonization, for example to Australia in the 1830s.

Evidence for an early twentieth-century onset of the feminization of migration can be found in migration data compiled in the twentieth century by the International Labour Office and the United Nations and in ships lists for Asian ports. From 1930 to 1970, the United States received many more female than male immigrants: it privileged family unification during a period of international warfare that facilitated international marriages between soldiers and foreign brides. Guest worker programs in Europe and the United States before 1970 and in the oil-exporting countries after 1970 still produced heavily male migrations. Refugee movements since World War II were typically gender balanced whereas asylum seekers, lacking a guaranteed right to enter another country, were more male. Contemporary demand for care workers in Europe, parts of Asia such as Hong Kong, and parts of Latin America have encouraged female-predominant migrations. Although more countries in the twenty-first century send and receive gender-balanced migrations than 100 years ago, census data provide firm evidence of periods of both masculinization (the United States after 1980) and feminization, and also of variation among immigrants from diverse backgrounds living in a single country. No one factor can explain all these shifts and variations; scholars must attend to the particularities of policies, education, labor markets, marriage, and family and gender ideologies in both sending and receiving societies to explain them.

Although scholars have succeeded in describing shifts in gender ratios and tracing the causes of their variations in migrant gender composition, documenting and explaining the consequences of variations in gender composition have remained elusive. Few existing studies document any negative consequences of feminization. At most they suggest that sexually unbalanced migrant populations may modestly influence rates of immigrant female employment, rates of intermarriage among immigrants and natives, and marital fertility among immigrants.

SEE ALSO: Economic Globalization and Gender; Immigration and Gender

REFERENCES

Castles, Stephen, and Mark Miller. 1993. *The Age of Migration*. New York: Guilford Press.

Donato, Katharine, and Donna Gabaccia. 2015. *Gender and International Migration: From the Slavery Era to the Global Age*. New York: Russell Sage Foundation Press.

Houstoun, Marion F., Roger J. Kramer, and Joan Mackin Barrett. 1984. "Female Predominance of Immigration to the U.S." *International Migration Review*, 18(4): 908–963.

Manning, Patrick. 2004. *Migration in World History*. London: Routledge.

UNFPA. 2006. *State of World Population 2006: A Passage to Hope: Women and International Migration*. New York: United Nations Population Fund. Accessed September 10, 2015, at http://www.unfpa.org/publications/state-world-population-2006#sthash.JHMBS0i5.dpuf.

Zlotnik, Hania. 2003. "The Global Dimensions of Female Migration." *Migration Information Source*, March 1, 2003. Accessed September 10, 2015, at http://www.migrationpolicy.org/article/global-dimensions-female-migration.

FURTHER READING

Donato, Katharine M., J. Trent Alexander, Donna Gabaccia, and Johanna Leinonen. 2011. "Variations in the Gender Composition of Immigrant Populations: How and Why They Matter." *International Migration Review*, 45(3): 495–525.

Eltis, David, and Stanley L. Engerman. 1993. "Fluctuations in Sex and Age Ratios in the Transatlantic Slave Trade, 1663–1864." *The Economic History Review*, 346: 308–323.

Gabaccia, Donna R., and Elizabeth Zanoni. 2012. "Transition in Gender Ratios Among International Migrants, 1820–1930." *Social Science History*, 36(2): 197–222.

Feminization of Poverty

SARAH H. ABERCROMBIE and SARAH L. HASTINGS
Radford University, USA

The feminization of poverty is a phenomenon commonly understood as the general disproportionate over-representation of women in poverty globally. This burden of poverty is especially predominant in developing countries although it is still quite visible in affluent Western and Eastern societies. The term "feminization of poverty" was originally coined in 1978 by Diana Pearce as she observed distinct patterns of poverty in the United States and globally. At that time, Pearce lamented an observable irony of both increased opportunities of employment and education for women with, relative to men, an increased likelihood of living in poverty.

Since the term's introduction, its use has become quite widespread in academic literature. Trends across time have been documented both in the United States and internationally. Poverty is a complex area of study with many variables of interest. Women's and men's poverty and poverty in the general population of a country are highly associated. Countries with high levels of overall poverty tend to have high women's as well as high men's poverty. Research does indicate that women are at an absolute greater risk of poverty than men, and mother–child families experience much higher poverty levels than two-parent families. However, with respect to qualified correlates and patterns in the feminization of poverty, there are significant complexities.

Feminization of poverty seems to be a systemic, social problem. While the subject has been given a substantial amount of attention in academia, governmental and fiscal action was meager, if non-existent until the 1990s. The fourth UN World Conference on Women ignited significant conversation when it was asserted there that 70 percent of the world's poor were female. However, Sylvia Chant (2008), a strong proponent in the conversation on feminization of poverty, argues that since this surge of activity, various methodological and analytical problems developed in terms of translation of problem to policy. Chant (2008) argues that in order to enact effective change we must first accurately understand the correlates of the issue.

While income is an important privilege to protection against poverty, it does not seem to be the single factor at play in the feminization of poverty. Much more significant is the disadvantaged status of women's social positions in the world perpetuated by patriarchal practices. In general, women are still plagued globally by legal, political, cultural, and religious discrimination. Lack of income seems to be an important byproduct of the vicious cycle of inadequate access to resources; although low income is not discrimination's sole manifestation. Women also share a lack of political rights, lack of opportunity to command and allocate resources within their households, limited social options, and greater vulnerability to risks and crises (Rodenberg 2004). Most societies are dominated by masculine culture, resulting in the assignment of gender roles whereby men are the head of households, and women are responsible for the upbringing of children. The social worth of these endeavors by women tends to be undervalued in many cultures, robbing them of prestige and satisfaction generally associated with these tasks. In households, men typically make decisions while women implement the decisions (Kang'ethe and Munzara 2014). Women's needs and priorities are often not considered, resulting in women having less control over decisions that affect them. In some cultures, patriarchy is codified, with laws and cultural practices written to prevent women from managing money, owning land, or accessing education. Males in the household may have the power to dictate women's health options and their ability to socialize with friends and family. Limitations in women's freedom of mobility impact their range of options to provide for their own needs and the needs of their children through employment.

In impoverished households, women seem to be taking up much of the responsibility for coping with poverty. Women more often seek jobs through the informal economy, making and selling goods at markets or festivals, cleaning for others, mending clothes, or begging. However, this form of work can render women vulnerable to abuses associated with unregulated employment. Employment opportunities are generally classified into two categories, formal and informal. Formal employment tends to be regulated by government affording workers greater protections. Informal employment lacks these wage and benefit advantages. Some women do actively choose household headship as a means by which they are able to increase the quality of their well-being and take more control over their own lives. Thus, by understanding the inequality of opportunities, it is important not to overemphasize the idea that a woman being alone in a household is the direct cause of her poverty.

Solutions to remedy disparities in economic opportunities for women are complex and multifaceted. By examining and targeting sociocultural factors associated with the feminization of poverty, governments and policy makers may spur changes that will ultimately curtail practices trapping women and their children in a state of economic disadvantage. Targeting health services, employment opportunity, education, and social power are means of combating poverty that disproportionately affects women. Poor health contributes to poverty in several ways.

Individuals afflicted with health conditions are less able to work. Women who cannot access healthcare are at greater risk for disease including HIV/AIDS. Patriarchy interferes with women's ability to negotiate sexual relationships with male partners, making them vulnerable to contracting HIV/AIDS. Women, as the primary custodians of children, are more affected by their children's health status given that caring for a sick child limits a woman's ability to work outside the home. Thus, providing adequate healthcare to women and their families is critical to addressing poverty among women. Assuring access to quality education is another means of addressing disparity. Some cultures prohibit girls from receiving education. Families, when faced with limited resources, may prioritize boys' education over girls'. Education, however, enables girls to participate more fully in society, to make informed decisions, and to take advantage of employment opportunities available only to those who have achieved a specified level of education. Access to employment allows one to make choices about one's environment and to engage in work that is both financially rewarding and personally enriching. Ensuring that girls and women have access to education and to employment opportunities is generally viewed as an essential means to help reduce poverty for women and their children. Finally, addressing laws and cultural practices that limit women's abilities to live independently and to exercise control over resources is necessary to address the feminization of poverty.

SEE ALSO: Governance and Gender; Patriarchy; Universal Human Rights

REFERENCES

Chant, S. 2008. "The 'Feminization of Poverty' and the 'Feminization' of Anti-Poverty Programmes: Room for Revision?" *Journal of Development Studies*, 44(2): 165–197. DOI: 10.1080/00220380701789810.

Kang'ethe, S. M., and M. Munzara. 2014. "Exploring an Inextricable Relationship between Feminization of Poverty and Feminization of HIV/AIDS in Zimbabwe." *Journal of Human Ecology*, 47(1): 17–26.

Rodenberg, B. (2004). "Gender and Poverty Reduction: New Conceptual Approaches in International Development Cooperation," Reports and Working Papers 4/2004. Bonn: German Development Institute.

Femocrat

MARIAN SAWER
Australian National University, Australia

"Femocrat" is a term invented in Australia in the 1970s to describe feminists taking up newly created women's policy positions in government. Originally, it was a term of abuse, whether used by conservatives critical of feminist influence on government or by those in the women's movement critical of feminists "selling out" to patriarchy. It was used in a self-deprecating way by femocrats themselves, conscious of how little power they actually exercised. Later it was used internationally in a more neutral sense to describe feminists in government, whether in women's policy agencies or elsewhere.

From the beginning of the 1990s, feminist scholars began systematically to explore the nature of feminist interventions in the state, rejecting the idea that the state was monolithic in nature and instead viewing it as an arena for contestation. Previously, many had assumed that "feminism" and "the state" were a contradiction in terms, but around the world there had been increased entry of feminists into policy positions. This followed acceptance by United Nations (UN) member states of the idea that dedicated government machinery was necessary to promote the status of women. The Plan of Action adopted in 1975 at the UN First World Conference on Women at Mexico City was reinforced at the subsequent UN World Conferences on Women, particularly the Fourth World Conference at Beijing in 1995.

Early research on femocrats focused on the structures and processes they were initiating to ensure government considered the gender impact of policy; the women's services and women's advocacy they were helping to fund; and their sometimes uneasy relationship with the women's movement outside government as well as with more traditional bureaucrats inside (Sawer 1990). While from outside femocrats might be seen as apologists for government, from inside femocrats had to overcome suspicion of their radical intent or potential for creating political embarrassment. For femocrats to be effective in policy bargaining they needed allies within government, whose goals might differ and be more conservative than theirs, as well as external pressure from a radical and noisy women's movement to make their own advice appear reasonable and moderate (Levi and Edwards 1990).

A classic study by US scholar Hester Eisenstein (1996), who like Sawer and Edwards had experience as an Australian femocrat, presented a vivid picture of the difficulties involved in trying to sustain a feminist culture within government, particularly within governments increasingly influenced by neoliberal ideology. Femocrats were left trying to achieve "least worst outcomes" from policies designed to reduce public provision in favor of market provision of services.

Meanwhile, Dorothy E. McBride and Amy G. Mazur were developing a framework to compare what they called "state feminism" in a range of European and North American countries. Following a first book in 1995, McBride and Mazur established the international Research Network on Gender Politics and the State (RNGS), which, over the next 15 years, involved some 40 researchers and produced eight books. The project used the term femocrat in a neutral way to refer to those who staffed women's policy agencies. The aim was to explore whether such agencies function as significant allies for women's movements. The key question was whether women's policy agencies bring women's movement framing of issues into government – either through ensuring access for women's movement actors to government or through their own policy advice.

The overall finding of the RNGS project, summed up in the capstone book *The Politics of State Feminism* (McBride and Mazur 2010), was that women's policy agencies could help achieve more favorable responses to women's movement demands, even in the context of globalization and state reconfiguration. However, there was significant variation in effectiveness across policy sectors: for example, economic portfolios were characteristically resistant to demands for gender-disaggregated analysis.

To address such resistance, in 1984, Australian femocrats initiated a "women's budget program," requiring all portfolios to provide gender breakdowns of policy and program impact in the budget context. Thanks to policy diffusion through international institutions and transnational advocacy networks, gender budgeting was subsequently adopted in some form in at least 90 countries and was regarded as a good practice model of "gender mainstreaming." This example also illustrates the role of transnational femocrats within institutions such as the UN and the European Union in developing and disseminating gender equality norms and practices and engaging in "insider" advocacy.

While the RNGS project was a huge step forward in the comparative analysis of feminist interventions in government, there have been subsequent critiques of its starting point – the judging of women's policy agencies by how effectively they mediate issue frames generated by an autonomous women's movement. This poses a problem for adequate analysis of femocrats because it gives ontological priority to the activity of feminists outside government. Recent studies, such as that of Lee Ann Banaszak (2010), have rejected such privileging of an "autonomous" women's movement. Banaszak found that feminists working within government institutions were women's movement actors in their own right and not necessarily deradicalized by their location. This is not a finding that is universally accepted; in particular, scholars of Latin American social movements argue that feminist institutionalization has weakened women's movements. So, after 40 years, femocrats remain the subject of lively debate and disputation.

SEE ALSO: Gender Budget; Gender Mainstreaming; Gender, Politics and the State: Overview

REFERENCES

Banaszak, Lee Ann. 2010. *The Women's Movement Inside and Outside the State*. Cambridge: Cambridge University Press.
Eisenstein, Hester. 1996. *Inside Agitators: Australian Femocrats and the State*. Philadelphia: Temple University Press.
Levi, Margaret and Meredith Edwards. 1990. "The Dilemmas of Femocratic Reform." In *Going Public: National Histories of Women's Enfranchisement and Women's Participation Within State Institutions*, edited by Mary F. Katzenstein and Hege Skjeie, 141–172. Oslo: Institute for Social Research.
McBride, Dorothy E., and Amy G. Mazur. 2010. *The Politics of State Feminism: Innovation in Comparative Research*. Philadelphia: Temple University Press.
Sawer, Marian. 1990. *Sisters in Suits: Women and Public Policy in Australia*. Sydney: Allen & Unwin.

Fertility Rates

SUSAN E. SHORT and JENNIFER W. BOUEK
Brown University, USA

Fertility rates are common measures of fertility. The two most common measures are the *crude birth rate* (CBR) and the *total fertility rate* (TFR). The CBR is the number of live births per 1,000 people in the population. The TFR is an average number of births for a hypothetical cohort of 1,000 women, and is often presented as the number of children who would be born per woman if this woman were to pass through the childbearing years giving birth to children according to a current schedule of age-specific fertility rates. Unlike the CBR, the TFR takes into account childbearing patterns by age. Fertility rates, such as TFR, are most often calculated for women, although paternal fertility rates can be calculated. The replacement fertility rate is the rate necessary to sustain the population at current levels. Replacement calculations take into account the need for girls to survive to reproductive age to be able to give birth, and also a sex ratio at birth that advantages boys. In the United States and many industrialized countries, the replacement TFR is about 2.1.

Fertility rates vary across populations. In 2013, the CBR in the United States was 13; in low-fertility countries, such as Germany and Japan, the CBR was 8, whereas in high-fertility countries the CBR was estimated to be over 45, with a high of 50 in Niger (Population Reference Bureau, 2014). The TFR in the United States in 2013 was 1.9. Internationally, it ranged as high as 7.6 in Niger and as low as 1.1 or 1.2 in several countries in East Asia and Europe, including South Korea, Portugal, and Poland (Population Reference Bureau, 2014). Historically, despite substantial variations, fertility rates on average were higher than they are today. While TFR worldwide today is about 2.5, as recently as 1970 it was estimated at 4.7 (Population Reference Bureau, 2014).

In the United States, fertility patterns vary by demographic, social, and economic factors as documented by the National Center for Health Statistics (Brady, Martin, and Ventura 2013). Women who give birth now are older and less likely to be married than in the recent past. Birth rates for women 30–34 years of age increased substantially between 1980 and 2012, from 62 to 97 per 1,000 women. Over the same period, birth rates to women 20–24 years of age declined from 115 to 83 per 1,000 women. Women aged 25–29 years have the highest birth rates in the United States, 107 per 1,000 in 2012. Consistent with these trends, mean age at first birth has risen substantially, from 21 years in 1970 to 26 years in 2012. The link between marriage and childbearing has been weakening. In 2012, 41 percent of all births were to women who were not married at the time of the birth. This figure has more than tripled since 1970, when it was 11 percent.

Fertility rates influence and are influenced by social institutions. Social institutions most widely recognized as relevant to fertility behavior include religious organizations, the education system, the healthcare system, political organizations, and the economy. Economic downturns and high unemployment, for example, have been linked to postponements and reductions in fertility as couples delay childbirth in anticipation of an improved economy (Kohler, Billari and Ortega 2002). Fertility similarly influences social institutions. Declining or rising fertility rates at the aggregate level affect the size and growth of a population. A rapidly growing population may lead to overcrowded schools as children age or strain a country's natural and social resources (Lam and Marteleto 2008). Conversely, a declining population may result in a smaller workforce unable to replace retiring workers, potentially restricting economic growth.

The gender organization of society is strongly tied to a woman's fertility behavior. The degree of gender equality within the public sphere and the private home may shape a woman's fertility and inhibit or encourage her engagement with family planning methods (McDonald 2000; Torr and Short 2004). The freedom and ability to decide on the number, timing, and spacing of births, often referred to as reproductive rights, can affect the health, income, and educational attainment of the mother and her children, as well as that of the father. Women's education is consistently tied to fertility behavior (Greene, Joshi, and Robles 2012). Although the relationship varies across settings and time periods, often higher levels of education are associated with later childbearing and lower completed fertility. Reproductive rights are therefore inherently associated with other basic human rights that may be tied to a country's broader development goals, such as improved education and health standards. Despite the benefits of family planning, the United Nations reported that, as of 2012, approximately 222 million women in developing countries did not have access to modern contraception (Greene, Joshi, and Robles 2012).

Governments concerned with population sometimes intervene with public policy. Countries with low fertility implement policies intended to increase fertility, ranging from tax breaks or childbearing incentives to regulations stipulating more generous maternity and paternity leaves. France encourages multiple births using direct cash transfers, known as family allowance, to families with more than one dependent child, and significant tax incentives for large families (Boling 2015). High-fertility countries may attempt to lower fertility by improving access to contraception or restricting the number of children per couple. China discouraged fertility in recent decades with a series of population control efforts that have included fines and penalties for unsanctioned births and rewards for those with only one child (Short and Zhai 1998). Finally, governments sometimes intervene to influence fertility when sex ratios at birth (SRBs) are atypical. Strong son preference and an excess of male births in many South and East Asian countries have prompted government campaigns promoting the benefits of daughters.

Interventionist population policies, however, can reflect ethno-nationalist and gendered ideologies and, as such, reinforce existing inequalities in social organization. For example, child benefits or subsidies can be targeted at special groups. In the recent past, these have included citizens or voters (France) and those who have served in the military (Israel) (King 2002). Pro-natalist messaging can promote ideology assigning reproductive responsibilities to women, and access to fertility control can be restricted (e.g., Romania) (King 2002). In some cases, ethno-nationalist ideologies result in discriminatory fertility limiting practices. For example, cases of forced and coerced sterilization among Roma women have been brought to national-level courts in the Czech Republic and Slovakia in recent decades (Zampas and Lamačková 2011). For related reasons, governments may also refuse to issue full citizenship rights to immigrants. Without full citizenship, immigrants are unable to access employment opportunities and social and health services, which also indirectly influence a population's fertility rates.

SEE ALSO: Contraception and Contraceptives; Family Planning; Gender Equality; Population Control and Population Policy; Reproductive Justice and Reproductive Rights in the United States; Sex Selection

REFERENCES

Boling, Patricia. 2015. *The Politics of Work–Family Policies: Comparing Japan, France, Germany and the United States*. Cambridge: Cambridge University Press.

Brady E. Hamilton, Joyce A. Martin, and Stephanie J. Ventura. 2013. Births: Preliminary Data for 2012. *National Vital Statistics Reports*, vol. 62, no. 3, 1–20. Hyattsville: National Center for Health Statistics.

Greene, Margaret, Shareen Joshi, and Omar Robles. United Nations Population Fund, Information and External Relations Division. 2012. *State of the World Population 2012: By Choice, Not By Chance: Family Planning, Human Rights and Development*. New York: United Nations Population Fund, Information and External Relations Division.

King, Leslie. 2002. "Demographic Trends, Pronatalism, and Nationalist Ideologies in the Late Twentieth Century." *Ethnic and Racial Studies*, 25: 367–389.

Kohler, Hans-Peter, Francesco C. Billari, and Jose Antonio Ortega. 2002. "The Emergence of Lowest-Low Fertility in Europe During the 1990s." *Population and Development Review*, 28: 641–680.

Lam, David, and Leticia Marteleto. 2008. "Stages of the Demographic Transition from a Child's Perspective: Family Size, Cohort Size, and Children's Resources." *Population and Development Review*, 34: 225–252.

McDonald, Peter. 2000. "Gender Equity in Theories of Fertility Transition." *Population and Development Review*, 26: 427–439.

Population Reference Bureau. 2014. *2014 World Population Data Sheet*. Washington, DC: Population Reference Bureau.

Short, Susan E., and Fengying Zhai. 1998. "Looking Locally at China's One-Child Policy." *Studies in Family Planning*, 29: 373–387.

Torr, Berna Miller, and Susan E. Short. 2004. "Second Births and the Second Shift: A Research Note on Gender Equity and Fertility." *Population and Development Review*, 30: 109–130.

Zampas, Christina, and Adriana Lamačková. 2011. "Forced and Coerced Sterilization of Women in Europe." *International Journal of Gynaecology and Obstetrics*, 114(2): 163–166.

FURTHER READING

Livi-Bacci, Massimo. 2012. *A Concise History of World Population*, 5th ed. Chichester: Wiley-Blackwell.

Ringheim, Karin, James Gribble, and Mia Foreman. 2011. *Integrating Family Planning and Maternal and Child Health Care: Saving Lives, Money, and Time*. Washington, DC: Population Reference Bureau.

United Nations, Department of Economic and Social Affairs, Population Division. 2013. *World Fertility Report: 2012*. New York: United Nations.

Fetal Alcohol Syndrome

CAROLINE L. TAIT
University of Saskatchewan, Canada

The diagnosis fetal alcohol syndrome grew out of a research study conducted in France that described a cluster of features observed in children born to alcoholic women (Lemoine et al. 1968). American researchers Kenneth Jones and David Smith (1973) subsequently found similar anomalies in infants born to alcoholic women, which led them to formally describe *fetal alcohol syndrome* (FAS) in 1973. FAS is marked by pre- and/or postnatal growth deficiency (low birth weight and height), central nervous system (CNS) dysfunction, and facial abnormalities (short palpebral fissures, flat upper lip, smooth philtrum, and flat mid-face) (Chudley et al. 2005). The diagnosis is most commonly associated with maternal alcohol dependency and/or binge-drinking patterns of alcohol consumption, and is more frequently diagnosed in offspring of women who experience other alcohol-related health problems, have poor nutrition, are older, and have given birth to previous children. Women who have given birth to a child with FAS are at highest risk of giving birth to subsequent children with FAS if they continue to drink alcohol (Abel 1998).

An American study of 80 women who gave birth to children with FAS found high rates of psychiatric comorbidities in this population, with alcohol use often beginning after the women experienced psychiatric problems (Astley et al. 2000). The significance of this study's findings points toward the need for further investigation across different countries to determine whether this finding holds true globally in mothers of FASD children, and if so, what the appropriate intervention strategies are for this population.

In recent years the term fetal alcohol spectrum disorders (FASD) has been used to describe the continuum of mild to severe health problems resulting from in utero alcohol exposure. However, controversy has persisted in areas of diagnosis, including determining the boundaries of the diagnosis and the bio-markers that should be used to define those boundaries. In 2005, Chudley and colleagues put forward clinical guidelines for FAS and argued that accurate assessments of patients required a multidisciplinary team approach to diagnosis. This approach outlines diagnostic guidelines in seven categories comprising screening and referral, physical examination, neurobehavioral assessment, treatment and follow-up, maternal alcohol history in pregnancy, diagnostic criteria for FASD, and the harmonization of two influential American-designed diagnostic approaches: the Institute of Medicine nomenclature (Stratton, Howe, and Battaglia 1996) and the 4-Digit Code diagnostic tool (Astley 2004).

Over recent decades the diagnosis of FAS has generated much needed global attention to the problem of female addictions (May et al. 2007; Drabble et al. 2011; Vagnarelli et al. 2011; Chersich et al. 2012; Tait 2014). However, while attention to prevention has resulted in improved women-centered treatment and aftercare supports in some countries, most countries have either ignored the problem or turned to punitive approaches that use either the legal system (e.g., mandatory detainment of pregnant women known to be drinking alcohol) or the child welfare system (e.g., coercing women into treatment through the threat of having their baby taken into state care at birth) to prevent FASD (Greaves and Poole 2004; Drabble et al. 2011). Such measures and surveillance of maternal behaviors have largely been directed toward women who are poor, of color, unemployed, and single. Qualitative research has found that in women who are most at risk, punitive measures result in women concealing their pregnancies from service providers, and not seeking prenatal care and other supports for fear of the consequences (Tait 2000). The most common public health message reduces the cause of FASD to a pregnant woman's choice to use or not use, despite the known complexities of alcohol abuse, and thus resulting in widespread stigma and judgment of pregnant women who consume alcohol (Drabble et al. 2011; Poole 2011).

The diagnostic challenges and expense associated with diagnosing FASD have hindered determination of accurate incidence and prevalence rates (Abel 1998; Ceccanti et al. 2007; May et al. 2007; Drabble et al. 2011; Vagnarelli et al. 2011). Estimated rates across different countries vary from less than 1/1,000 to as high as 1/100 in some subpopulations. Cognitive and behavioral problems are the most significant disability of the syndrome, with patients experiencing short- and long-term memory problems, attention-deficit disorder, hyperactivity, problems understanding causal links and consequences, and mental illness. Secondary disabilities (those resulting from interaction of primary disabilities and environmental influences) include dropping out of school, unemployment, trouble with the law, incarceration, sexual deviancy, and substance abuse (Streissguth and Kanter 1999). The estimated lifelong financial costs to society of caring for and supporting a person with FASD are significant; however, the human costs are much greater, including the difficulties faced by the patient, premature deaths of mothers who are unable to access treatment or recover from alcohol dependency, and the intergenerational impact upon families.

SEE ALSO: Fetal Rights; Stigma

REFERENCES

Abel, Ernest L. 1998. "Fetal Alcohol Syndrome: The 'American Paradox'." *Alcohol and Alcoholism*, 33: 195–201.

Astley, Susan J. 2004. *Diagnostic Guide for Fetal Alcohol Spectrum Disorders: The 4-Digit Diagnostic Code*. Seattle: University of Washington Publication Services.

Astley, Susan J., Diane Bailey, Christina Talbot, and Sterling K. Clarren. 2000. "Fetal Alcohol Syndrome (FAS) Primary Prevention through FAS Diagnosis: II. A Comprehensive Profile of 80 Birth Mothers of Children with FAS." *Alcohol and Alcoholism*, 35: 509–519.

Ceccanti, Mauro, et al. 2007. "Clinical Delineation of Fetal Alcohol Spectrum Disorders (FASD) in Italian Children: Comparison and Contrast with Other Racial/Ethnic Groups and Implications for Diagnosis and Prevention." *Neuroscience and Biobehavioral Reviews*, 31: 270–277.

Chersich, Matthew F., et al. 2012. "Universal Prevention is Associated with Lower Prevalence of Fetal Alcohol Spectrum Disorders in Northern Cape, South Africa: A Multicentre Before–After Study." *Alcohol and Alcoholism*, 47(1): 67–74.

Chudley, Albert, et al. 2005. "Fetal Alcohol Spectrum Disorder: Canadian Guidelines for Diagnosis." *Canadian Medical Association Journal*, 172: S1–S21.

Drabble, Laurie A., et al. 2011. "Conceiving Risk, Divergent Responses: Perspectives on the Construction of Risk of FASD in Six Countries." *Substance Use & Misuse*, 1–16.

Greaves, L., and N. Poole. 2004. "Victimized or Validated? Responses to Substance-Using Pregnant Women." *Canadian Woman Studies*, 24(1): 87–92.

Jones, Kenneth. L., and David W. Smith. 1973. "Recognition of the Fetal Alcohol Syndrome in Early Infancy." *Lancet*, 302(7836): 999–1001.

Lemoine, Paul, H. Harousseau, J. P. Borteyru, and J. C. Menuet. 1968. "Les enfants de parents alcooliques. Anomalies observées. A propos de 127 cas" [Children of Alcoholic Parents: Abnormalities Observed in 127 Cases]. *Paris, Ouest Medical*, 21: 476–482.

May, Philip A., et al. 2007. "The Epidemiology of Fetal Alcohol Syndrome and Partial FAS in a South African Community." *Drug and Alcohol Dependence*, 88(2–3): 259–271.

Poole, Nancy. 2011. "Bringing a Women's Health Perspective to FASD Prevention." In *Fetal Alcohol Spectrum Disorder: Management and Policy Perspectives of FASD*, edited by Edward P. Riley, Sterling Clarren, Joanne Weinberg, and Egon Jonsson, 161–174. Weinheim, Germany: Wiley-Blackwell.

Stratton, Kathleen, Cynthia Howe, and Frederick Battaglia, eds. 1996. *Fetal Alcohol Syndrome: Diagnosis, Epidemiology, Prevention, and Treatment*. Washington, DC: National Academy Press.

Streissguth, Ann, and Jonathon Kanter, eds. 1999. *The Challenge of Fetal Alcohol Syndrome: Overcoming Secondary Disabilities*. Seattle: University of Washington Press.

Tait, Caroline L. 2000. *A Study of the Service Needs of Pregnant Addicted Women in Manitoba*. Winnipeg: Prairie Women's Health Centre of Excellence.

Tait, Caroline L. 2014. "Fetal Alcohol Spectrum Disorder and Indigenous Peoples of Canada." In *Journey to Healing: Aboriginal People with Addictions and Mental Health Issues: What Health, Social Services and Justice Workers Need to Know*, edited by Peter Menzies and Lynn F. Lavallee, 217–230. Toronto: Center for Addictions and Mental Health.

Vagnarelli, F., et al. 2011. "A Survey of Italian and Spanish Neonatologists and Paediatricians Regarding Awareness of the Diagnosis of FAS and FASD and Maternal Ethanol Use during Pregnancy." *BMC Pediatrics*, 11:51. At http://www.biomedcentral.com/1471-2431/11/51.

Fetal Rights

CARL WELLMAN
Washington University in Saint Louis, USA

Article 6.1 of the International Covenant on Civil and Political Rights asserts that "Every human being has the inherent right to life," but it is unclear whether a fetus qualifies as a human being. Among the regional human rights conventions, only Article 6.1 of the American Convention on Human Rights states explicitly that "Every person has the right to have his life respected. This right shall be protected by law and, in general, from the moment of conception." National legal systems provide this protection in a variety of ways. Both the Irish and German constitutions recognize a right to life from the moment of conception, but although Irish courts have decided that this renders abortions (except to save the life of the mother) illegal, German courts have permitted abortions under a number of conditions. Article 21 of the Constitution of India includes the right to life, but although this extends to children it does not include fetuses. Chapter Two of the Constitution of the People's Republic of China confers a variety of fundamental rights, but not the right to life, and forced abortions are used to limit population growth in China. The United States Supreme Court has refused to apply the constitutional right to life to the fetus; and although Article 7 of the Canadian Charter of Rights and Freedoms asserts that everyone has the right to life, section 222 of the Criminal Code of Canada specifies that the fetus becomes a human being only when it has completely proceeded, in a living state, from the body of the mother. Therefore, the constitutional right to life may or may not deny a pregnant woman the right to abort her fetus.

Moreover, courts in the United States and other countries have recognized a number of other fetal rights. John Salmond (1920) reports that the English common law has traditionally recognized the right of a fetus to inherit property. And in *Bonbrest v. Kotz* a United States court recognized the right of a fetus not to be wrongfully injured before birth. This right has been interpreted in some cases to impose a duty upon a pregnant woman not to smoke, consume alcoholic beverages, or use illicit drugs. John A. Robertson (1983) explains that the fetus also has a right to medical treatment necessary to protect its life or health. This could impose on a pregnant woman a legal duty to submit to a blood transfusion or *in utero* surgery. In African nations where AIDS is common, this would require pregnant women infected with the HIV virus to take medication to protect their fetus from infection. Barry R. Furrow et al. (1991) report that a few courts have recognized the right of a fetus not to be born seriously defective. This sometimes imposes upon a pregnant woman a duty to abort her unborn child or, in rare cases, a duty not to become pregnant.

Philosophers disagree about whether fetuses do, or even could, have any moral or legal rights. H. L. A. Hart's theory (1982) that at the center of every right is a choice implies that it would be idle and misleading to ascribe any right to fetuses because they lack the capacity to choose. Carl Wellman argues (2005) that because rights confer freedom and control upon the right-holder, fetuses that cannot exercise freedom or control cannot possess rights. Joel Feinberg (1980) maintains that to have a right is to be in a position to claim a corresponding duty. Since fetuses lack the linguistic and psychological abilities necessary to make claims, this seems to imply that fetuses cannot have any rights. But Feinberg insists that fetuses can and do have rights, rights that their parents or guardians can claim on their behalf. This is because what qualifies any being as a right-holder is the possession of interests. Since fetuses do have interests in continuing to live and in their future well-being, they can and do have rights. Mary Anne Warren (1973) insists that only persons or human beings can have moral rights. Because fetuses have not yet developed the traits, such as consciousness and the capacity to reason, that define personhood or humanity in the morally relevant sense, they cannot have any moral rights. However, Francis C. Wade replies (1975) that because fetuses already have the active potentiality for becoming rational human beings they already have moral rights. Finally, Annette Baier (1981) holds that it is being a member of the moral community that confers rights on one, and unborn children have rights because they are members of the moral community even before birth.

While lawyers agree that fetuses have a variety of legal rights, philosophers such as H. L. A. Hart and Carl Wellman argue that fetuses cannot possibly possess any rights. Although one might side with the lawyers and conclude that the legal realities disprove the speculative philosophical theories, a sounder conclusion would be that the language of rights is highly ambiguous. In the legally relevant sense, fetuses can and do have rights. However, Hart and Wellman may be correct when they argue that to say that fetuses have rights is misleading and that the legal realities can be explained more accurately in other terms.

SEE ALSO: Abortion, Legal Status in Global Perspective on; Pro-Choice Movement in the United States; Pro-Life Movement in the United States; Universal Human Rights

REFERENCES

Baier, Annette. 1981. "The Rights of Past and Future Persons." In *Responsibilities to Future Generations*, edited by Ernest Partridge, 171–185. Buffalo, NY: Prometheus Books.

Bonbrest v. Kotz, 65 F. Supp. 138 (1946).
Feinberg, Joel. 1980. *Rights, Justice, and the Bounds of Liberty*. Princeton, NJ: Princeton University Press.
Furrow, Barry R., Thomas L. Greaney, Sandra H. Johnson, Timothy Stoltzfus Jost, and Robert L. Schwartz. 1991. *Health Law: Cases, Materials and Problems*, 2nd ed. Saint Paul, MN: West Publishing Co.
Hart, H. L. A. 1982. *Essays on Bentham: Studies in Jurisprudence Political Theory*. Oxford: Clarendon Press.
Robertson, John A. 1983. "Procreative Liberty and the Control of Conception, Pregnancy, and Childbirth." *Virginia Law Review*, 69: 444.
Salmond, John. 1920. *Jurisprudence*, 6th ed. London: Sweet and Maxwell.
Wade, Francis C. 1975. "Potentiality in the Abortion Discussion." *Review of Metaphysics*, 29: 239–255.
Warren, Mary Anne. 1973. "On the Moral and Legal Status of Abortion." *The Monist*, 57: 43–61.
Wellman, Carl. 2005. *Medical Law and Moral Rights*. Dordrecht: Springer.

Fictive Kin

ANNA MURACO
Loyola Marymount University, Los Angeles, USA

The concept of kinship is commonly discussed in social science disciplines, most notably in anthropology and sociology. Fictive kin, also known by the terms fictive kinship, voluntary kin, and chosen family, connotes a relationship that exists outside of the normative definitions of families, both biological and legal, unless actions are taken to formalize the bond; thus, the concept of fictive kinship theoretically relies upon a social constructionist framework (Braithwaite et al. 2010). Ibsen and Klobus, for example, state that fictive kinship "encompasses the adoption of non-relatives into kin-like relationships" (Ibsen and Klobus 1972, 615). Fictive kin relationships are a long-standing relationship form present in many cultures (Ebaugh and Curry 2000; Braithwaite et al. 2010). Some research about fictive kin focuses on the discursive processes or development of stories to identify voluntary kin as part of their family networks (Gubrium and Holstein 1990). Jacob characterizes kinship as performative "without an ontological existence except for the various acts that constitute its reality" (Jacob 2009, 119).

Fictive kin expand resources for oppressed or marginalized communities and fulfill the functions more traditionally served by family networks. For example, fictive kin provide immigrants to the United States with social and economic capital that helps them adapt to a new social context (Ebaugh and Curry 2000).

One of the most notable uses of the concept of fictive kin occurred in Carol Stack's book, *All Our Kin: Strategies for Survival in a Black Community* (1974). In this ethnographic study, Stack addressed poor black women's reliance on social networks of kin for instrumental assistance with maintaining households and childrearing. Stack observed that kin were defined not simply by biological or legal connection, but also by those who were trustworthy and reciprocated support in the manner of kin that resembled a sisterly or cousin-like relationship. These fictive kin networks, rather than members of households or biological family members, constituted a web of support. Subsequent research findings also support the importance of fictive kin in black and Latino communities (Chatters, Taylor, and Jayakody 1994).

Fictive kin was also a central concept in anthropologist Kath Weston's book, *Families We Choose: Lesbians, Gays, Kinship* (1997). In this qualitative study of San Francisco Bay Area lesbian and gay communities in the 1980s, Weston focuses on the concept and function of chosen families, which are kinship ties that deemphasize the differences between blood and non-blood relations. Chosen families include biological kin, as well as current partners, friends, former partners and lovers, business and community contacts, co-parents, and other significant relationships. Lesbians and gay men in Weston's study construct networks and households from chosen family members and recognize these important relationships through mutual celebrations of birthdays and holidays, as well as in shared and reciprocal assistance when needed. Other researchers have confirmed Weston's findings about the significance of chosen family members in gay male and lesbian communities (Nardi 1999; Moore 2011), as well as for straight people who have close ties with gay men and lesbians (Tillmann-Healy 2001; Muraco 2006, 2012).

Fictive kin also exists in broader social contexts. People often expand their available connections by incorporating fictive kin into their support networks. Prior research has illustrated the significance of fictive kin in networks of older adults (MacRae 1992; Allen, Blieszner, and Roberto 2011), homeless individuals (McCarthy, Hagan, and Martin 2002), nursing homes (Dodson and Zincavage 2007), new immigrants to the United States (Ebaugh and Curry 2000), and international adoptee families (Traver 2009). Conceptions of family have historically been intertwined with policies of US immigration, which over time, prompted the creation of fictive kin ties in order facilitate migration (Lee 2013).

Theorizing about fictive kin also occurs in biomedical and legal scholarship. Central to these discussions are the tensions between biological definitions of kinship and kinship construction through actions and medical technologies. Jacob (2009), for example, examines the differences in legal and practical processes of surrogacy in Israel, where biological family members are prohibited from participation and kidney donation, where biological relation is downplayed in favor of the development of emotional bonds with strangers. Historically, organ donation primarily occurred between biologically and genetically close relatives; with technological advances that lessened the possibility of physical rejection of organs, non-related others became donors. Jacob highlights the limitations of biological family in these biomedical processes. Parents revere biological ties with children, yet often will accept organs from unrelated others and not from children. According to Jacob, through the organ transplant process, people form a kinship relation called "transplant relatedness" because they share history and material (bodily) substance (Jacob 2009).

Kinship processes also emerge in surrogacy, sperm donor selection, and other forms of reproductive technologies. In commercial gestational surrogacy in India, surrogates create new bases and substance of kinship in their focus on alternative means to relatedness; because they carry the fetus and give birth to the child, surrogates view their labor and blood as creating an enduring kinship with the baby and its mother (Pande 2009). The selection of sperm from a donor bank also is a site of kinship building. Through the selection of sperm, women and couples (in this case, lesbian couples) seek "affinity ties," or sperm from donors that are similar to one or both of the mothers (Mamo 2005). "Affinity ties" is a kinship device that potential parents use to envision their connectedness to the imagined child in ways that privilege the biological (nature) over the cultural (nurture) through selection of sperm from donors with shared ancestry or other similarities to the parent(s) (Mamo 2005). In so doing, the potential parents both disrupt and reinforce hegemonic norms of family and kinship.

SEE ALSO: Community Other Mothers; Extended Families; Families of Choice; Household Livelihood Strategies; Lesbians as Community Other Mothers; Same-Sex Families

REFERENCES

Allen, Katherine R., Rosemary Blieszner, and Karen A. Roberto. 2011. "Perspectives on Extended Family and Fictive Kin in the Later Years: Strategies and Meanings of Kin Reinterpretation." *Journal of Family Issues*, 32(9): 1156–1177.
Braithwaite, Dawn O., et al. 2010. "Constructing Family: A Typology of Voluntary Kin." *Journal of Social and Personal Relationships*, 27(3): 388–407.
Chatters, Linda M, Robert J. Taylor, and Rukmalie Jayakody. 1994. "Fictive Kinship Relations in Black Extended Families." *Journal of Comparative Family Studies*, 25(3): 297–313.
Dodson, Lisa, and Rebekah M. Zincavage. 2007. "'It's Like a Family': Caring Labor, Exploitation, and Race in Nursing Homes." *Gender and Society*, 21(6): 905–928.
Ebaugh, Helen R., and Mary Curry. 2000. "Fictive Kin as Social Capital in New Immigrant Communities." *Sociological Perspectives*, 43(2): 189–209.
Gubrium, J.F., and J.A. Holstein. 1990. *What is Family?* Mountain View: Mayfield Press.
Ibsen, Charles A., and Patricia Klobus. 1972. "Fictive Kin Term Use and Social Relationships: Alternative Interpretations." *Journal of Marriage and Family*, 34(4): 615–620.
Jacob, Marie-Andree. 2009. "The Shared History: Unknotting Fictive Kinship and Legal Process." *Law and Society Review*, 43(1): 95–126.
Lee, Catherine. 2013. *Fictive Kinship: Family Reunification and the Meaning of Race and Nation in American Migration.* New York: Russell Sage Foundation.
MacRae, Helen. 1992. "Fictive Kin as a Component of the Social Networks of Older People." *Research on Aging*, 14(2): 226–247.
Mamo, Laura. 2005. "Biomedicalizing Kinship: Sperm Banks and the Creation of Affinity-Ties." *Science as Culture*, 14(3): 237–264.
McCarthy, Bill, John Hagan, and Monica J. Martin. 2002. "In and Out of Harm's Way: Violent Victimization and the Social Capital of Fictive Street Families." *Criminology*, 40(4): 831–866.
Moore, Mignon. 2011. *Invisible Families: Gay Identities, Relationships, and Motherhood Among Black Women.* Berkeley: University of California Press.
Muraco, Anna. 2006. "Intentional Families: Fictive Kin Ties Between Cross-Gender, Different Sexual Orientation Friends." *Journal of Marriage and Family*, 68(5): 1313–1325.
Muraco, Anna. 2012. *Odd Couples: Friendship at the Intersection of Gender and Sexual Orientation.* Durham, NC: Duke University Press.
Nardi, Peter M. 1999. *Gay Men's Friendships: Invincible Communities.* Chicago: University of Chicago Press.
Pande, Amrita. 2009. "'It May Be Her Eggs But It's My Blood': Surrogates and Everyday Forms of Kinship in India." *Qualitative Sociology*, 32: 379–397.
Stack, Carol. 1974. *All Our Kin: Strategies for Survival in a Black Community.* New York: Harper and Row.
Tillmann-Healy, Lisa M. 2001. *Between Gay and Straight: Understanding Friendship Across Sexual Orientation.* Walnut Creek: Alta Mira Press.
Traver, Amye E. 2009. "Toward a Theory of Fictive Kin Work: China Adoptive Parents' Efforts to Connect their Children to Americans of Chinese Heritage." *International Journal of Sociology of the Family*, 35(1): 45–67.
Weston, Kath. 1997. *Families We Choose: Lesbians, Gays, Kinship.* New York: Columbia University Press.

Footbinding

SARAH D'ANDREA
The Graduate Center, CUNY, USA

Footbinding is the practice of wrapping a young girl's feet in a cotton or silk cloth to prevent growth and transform their natural shape. Binding usually began between the ages of five and seven, though six was best given that feet were still composed of prebone cartilage and more easily molded. The practice left the big toe unbound, but folded and wrapped the remaining four toes toward the sole. The cloth was also wrapped to bring the front and back of the foot closer together. Ideally, bound feet, also called "golden lotuses" or "golden lilies" because they were to resemble unopened lotus flower buds, measured only three inches in length. Binding was intensely painful, as bones were broken, feet were inflamed, and flesh deteriorated. Pain came not only from the binding itself, but the subsequent walking necessary to facilitate the bone breaking process. The practice also came with great risk. Foot infections were the most common malady, but blood poisoning, paralysis, low back problems, and even gangrene could result.

The specific origin of footbinding is unclear. It is commonly thought to have begun among the court and royal families in the tenth or eleventh century, eventually trickling down to the lower classes in the seventeenth and eighteenth centuries. In exploring the beginnings of the practice, a variety of accounts prove instructive, including some from Chinese folklore. One speaks of a fox taking the guise of an empress, wholly transforming except for its paws. To conceal its still animalistic appendages, it wrapped them in silk bandages, starting a palace trend. Another account states that an empress of the Shang dynasty had a clubfoot. Self-conscious about her deformity, she encouraged her spouse to require the binding of young girls' feet to transform her abnormality to the standard of beauty (Levy 1992; Jackson 1997). The most popular tale centers around Yao Niang, a dancer in the court of Li Yu. The story goes that the southern Chinese ruler had a six-foot golden lotus constructed, adorned with precious stones and ribbons. Yao Niang was told to wrap her feet in cloth, which she bound to resemble a new moon. She then danced in the middle, whirling like a rising cloud. Others then sought to emulate her slim, arched feet (Ping 2000).

Scholars have also put forth several possible theories as to why the practice was perpetuated, many revolving around issues of sex and marriage. Throughout Chinese culture, bound feet were believed to signal high status, promote female chastity, enhance marriageability, and sexually arouse men. If a man's wife had bound feet, rendering her physically unable to stand and walk without difficulty, it signaled a man's prosperity. Her feet symbolized his wealth being enough to sustain the family without spousal assistance (Jackson 1997). Severely restricting her movement also kept her primarily confined to the home. Keeping women sequestered, it was believed, encouraged chastity and moral behavior. A folk ditty from the Hopei Province reaffirms this sentiment: "Bound feet, bound feet, past the gate can't retreat" (Levy 1992). In addition, bound feet were seen as essential to a bride's desirability. If a young girl's feet were unbound, she would not be seen as a viable spouse. In a patriarchal society, alienating prospective suitors negatively affected a woman's means of support, identity, and social status (Ping 2000). Bound feet were also central to sexual relations; men were said to find the sight, touch, and smell of the golden lotus extremely erotic. Foreplay included kissing, sucking, and nibbling the foot. Further, men would press the bound feet against various parts of their bodies. The erotic nature of footbinding extended beyond the foot itself, in that bound feet impacted other parts of the female form. Foot-bound women had an altered gait and moved with a sway, referred to as the "golden lotus limp" or the "lotus gait." This walk enlarged the buttocks, and tightened the flesh and skin of the legs and vagina (Levy 1992).

Footbinding was performed for centuries. However, it garnered criticism and opposition from a variety of sources. In the seventeenth century, Emperor Kangxi of the Qing Dynasty banned the practice. He threatened harsh punishment if any girl was discovered binding her feet, but overturned the regulation only four years later. During the eighteenth century and beyond, footbinding came under further attack. Liberal scholars, writers, and poets openly condemned the practice. Chinese intellectuals called for reform, concerned that footbinding subjected their country to international ridicule. Christian missionaries were also opposed to the practice, discouraging footbinding by making natural or unbound feet a requirement for admission into boarding schools or the church, though it was not until 1949 that footbinding officially ended under Chinese Communist rule.

Much of the scholarship on footbinding depicts it as cruel, misogynistic, and inhumane, but Dorothy Ko (2001) advocates for the viewing of footbinding through the eyes of foot-bound women. To accomplish this, she shifts attention from the act of binding to the lotus shoes produced. Footbinding then becomes intertwined with the lotus shoes and how creating them reflected women's pride and craftsmanship, especially as citizens within a culture that valued female domesticity and handwork. While this is a minority view, it does highlight agency within a practice almost exclusively depicted as barbaric and forcefully imposed on Chinese women.

SEE ALSO: Fashion; Patriarchy; Sex and Culture; Sexual Fetishism

REFERENCES

Jackson, Beverly. 1997. *Splendid Slippers: A Thousand Years of an Exotic Tradition*. Berkeley: Ten Speed Press.

Ko, Dorothy. 2001. *Every Step a Lotus: Shoes for Bound Feet*. Berkeley: University of California Press.

Levy, Howard. 1992. *The Lotus Lovers: The Complete History of the Curious Erotic Custom of Footbinding in China*. New York: Prometheus Books.

Ping, Wang. 2000. *Aching for Beauty: Footbinding in China*. Minneapolis: University of Minnesota Press.

FURTHER READING

Gao, Xionagya. 2003. "Women Existing for Men: Confucianism and Social Injustice against Women in China." *Race, Gender and Class*, 10: 114–125.

Hong, Fan. 1997. *Footbinding, Fetishism and Freedom*. London: Frank Cass & Co.

Yung, Judy. 1999. *Unbound Voices: A Documentary History of Chinese Women in San Francisco*. Berkeley: University of California Press.

Free Trade Zones

SAMANTHI J. GUNAWARDANA
Monash University, Australia

Free trade zones (FTZs) are territorially delineated spaces where historically, goods could be stored, processed, or serviced before redistribution around the world. They are distinct from free trade agreements. FTZs have attracted attention owing to their use and dispersion across the world as a tool of economic development pursued under neoliberal, open-market economic policy. However, they are also found in high-income advanced economies. The International Labour Organization (ILO) reported that in 1986 there were 176 zones in 47 countries; by 2006 there were approximately 35,000. Alongside attempts to evaluate their effectiveness in stimulating economic development and growth, they have also attracted critique for the working conditions found within FTZ enterprises. Weaving through these narratives has been a sustained focus on gender and sexualities not only in terms of noting the gendered division of labor found in zone employment systems, but also the way in which gender identities are constituted, mobilized, and reconstituted in global spaces of production, and the connections between violence, economic policy, and gender.

Zones are deemed to be "free" in the sense that they are tax-free or tax-reduced spaces for capital investment. Historic antecedent forms signal the continuity of this idea, tied to the growth of international trade and capitalism. Historical forms include sixteenth-century free ports in cities such as Genoa, or entrepot cities such as Gibraltar, Hamburg, and Singapore. Post-1940s, FTZs were linked to domestic economic development via development policies promoted by the World Bank and International Monetary Fund, particularly in Structural Adjustment Programs (SAPs). According to the World Bank, zones are established by states to attract foreign investment, alleviate mass unemployment, support economic reform in particular diversifying exports, and serve as laboratories for new policies. The last goal has been underscored by economic development prescriptions that promote export-oriented development, free trade, and privatization, a common policy bundle associated with neoliberal economic reform. FTZs were often treated as the entry point for shifting to export-oriented development and global economic integration.

Encompassing the production of services such as business processing operations, the form and purpose of FTZs have evolved over time to encompass both a geographical area in the form of a cordoned off zone or economic estate, or a single enterprise granted special status, which accounts for their rapid proliferation. Although established by states, FTZs can be managed by either an independent quasi-state authority or owned and managed by private owners. A variety of zones have emerged, including Export Processing Zones in Haiti, Special Economic Zones (SEZs) in China, and maquiladoras in Mexico. Evidence continues to be assessed to determine the impact of FTZs on local economies, converging upon export-oriented development strategy that promised employment and income growth, and the transfers of skills, knowledge, and technology.

FTZs have been critiqued by human rights advocates, pro-people development activists, and labor movements for contributing to the violation of human rights, including labor rights. Connected to a broader critique of economic globalization and neoliberalism, Aihwa Ong characterized FTZs as a space of economic neoliberal exception from existing regulation (Ong 2006). States have modified or amended taxation, customs, and, in some cases, labor laws to attract foreign investment. David Harvey outlined how spaces such as FTZs represented a form of dispossession associated with predatory capitalism whereby profits and investment are valued higher than people's human or land rights (Harvey 2005).

A particular focus of critique has been on working conditions. According to Fröbel et al.'s early thesis on the New International Division of Labour, FTZs were implicated in a "race to the bottom" by large Western-based corporations who sought to bypass home-based labor laws and rising wages by relocating manufacturing activities to such sites (Fröbel, Heinrichs, and Kreye 1980). Indeed, the World Bank concluded that in 2011 zones generally housed labor-intensive manufacturing industries and a key challenge was to diversify such activities to promote further growth and develop backward linkages into the local economy. In 2008, the ILO noted that there continued to be a lack of "decent work" – a term used by the ILO to denote universal minimum acceptable standards of employment – in FTZs. Workers rarely received a living wage, were subject to weak labor inspection practices, had fewer rights than workers outside the zone, faced restrictions on trade unions, completed excessive working hours, including mandatory overtime, had lax health and safety standards, and had greater work intensity. Owing to this, FTZ workplaces and FTZs have become the focus of research on regulation in the global economy; a key debate has focused on the potential and weaknesses of voluntary corporate regulation in the form of corporate social responsibility initiatives.

Moreover, as the majority of FTZs employ primarily women in their unskilled or semi-skilled positions, although FTZs opened up formal employment opportunities for women workers, increasing their economic empowerment, FTZs became noted for the way in which they helped to recreate or reinforce gender and often racial hierarchies. Ethnographic study of the labor process in FTZs has demonstrated that gender is vital for the labor process as a preemptive measure of control, owing to expected feminized behaviors such as acquiescence in the workplace, or the mobilization of productive femininity. Early studies noted employer gendered preference for young, often neophyte, female labor. Once recruited, women faced employment conditions that interacted with, and were deeply embedded in, assumptions concerning womanhood and manhood within labor markets, communities, and households. Job segregation persisted, as did gender wage gaps in the zone.

Gender impacted the experience of work and outcomes, and also ascribed worker identities. In Sri Lanka, anthropologist Caitrin Lynch demonstrated how FTZ women workers were depicted as victims of an exploitative work environment, but wider social critique was made on the basis on cultural anxieties about womanhood (Lynch 2007). The objectifying social designation "Juki Girls" became a recognized social category denoting poor migrant women workers, laden with a variety of sexualized critiques and meanings. In India, Jamie Cross found that young Telugu men with secondary-level technical qualifications employed in the Vishakhapatnam SEZ were faced with pressure to be providers for their families but were confronted with devaluation of their education, their failure to realize local visions of masculine success, and the prospects of their future marginality.

The mobilization of gender and sexualities has been found to be important within the labor process. In China, supervisors faced with non-docile workers resorted to invoking sexualized bodies, ascriptions of feminine behaviors such as docility, to assert control, reinforced by gender segregation in job roles. In Mexico, gendered discourses were used as a primary mechanism of workplace control. Leslie Salzinger's study of maquiladora factories demonstrated how male fantasies about productive femininity sexually objectified women for greater productivity, while women workers enjoyed this desiring gaze, and dated supervisors to gain power (Salinger 2003). In a plant making disposable hospital garments, a newly hired Mexican manager symbolically changed the meaning of assembly work from feminine to masculine by altering gendered rules around attire; heels and make-up were banned, and hair was to be kept covered. At a wire harness plant implementing lean technologies, femininity was cast as independence, assertiveness, and the capacity to make decisions to match the principles of lean production. Yet women workers had limited access to promotions. At another wire harnessing factory, the masculinity of men who took low-paid feminized assembly jobs was censured. The male workers tried to redefine work as masculine, which involved considering women workers in sexualized terms.

FTZ employment also led to the creation of subaltern identities, complicating the picture of victimhood prevalent in anti-sweatshop discourse. Sandya Hewamanne explored the emergence of subaltern worker identities in

Sri Lanka, which involved the production of working-class critiques and the assertion of distinct tastes in dress, reading materials, and speech patterns and also "disrespectful" public behaviors (Hewamanne 2008). Across Asia and Latin America, FTZ workers have been engaged in various forms of opposition, including attempts at union organizing and involvement in non-governmental organization activities. A key trend has been the emergence of transnational networks of labor solidarity and advocacy.

SEE ALSO: Anti-Globalization Movements

REFERENCES

Fröbel, Folker, Jürgen Heinrichs, and Otto Kreye. 1980. *The New International Division of Labour: Structural Unemployment in Industrialised Countries and Industrialisation in Developing Countries*. Cambridge: Cambridge University Press.

Harvey, David. 2005. *A Brief History of Neoliberalism*. New York: Oxford University Press.

Hewamanne, Sandya. 2008. *Stitching Identities in a Free Trade Zone: Gender and Politics in Sri Lanka*. Philadelphia: University of Pennsylvania Press.

Lynch, Caitrin. 2007. *Juki Girls, Good Girls: Gender and Cultural Politics in Sri Lanka's Global Garment Industry*. Ithaca: Cornell University Press.

Ong, Aihwa. 2006. *Neoliberalism as Exception: Mutations in Citizenship and Sovereignty*. Durham, NC: Duke University Press.

Salzinger, Leslie. 2003. *Genders in Production: Making Workers in Mexico's Global Factories*, Berkeley: University of California Press.

FURTHER READING

Boyenge Jean-Pierre Singa. 2007. *ILO Database on Export Processing Zones (Revised)*. Geneva: International Labour Organization.

Egels-Zandén, Niklas, and Peter Hyllman. 2007. "Evaluating Strategies for Negotiating Workers' Rights in Transnational Corporations: the Effects of Codes of Conduct and Global Agreements on Workplace Democracy," *Journal of Business Ethics*, 76(2): 207–223.

Elias, Juanita. 2005. "The Gendered Political Economy of Control and Resistance on the Shop Floor of the Multinational Firm: a Case-Study from Malaysia." *New Political Economy*, 10(2): 203–222.

Farole, Thomas, and Gokhan Akinci, eds. 2011. *Special Economic Zones: Progress, Emerging Challenges, and Future Directions*. Washington, DC: World Bank Publications.

Gunawardana, Samanthi. 2007. "Perseverance, Struggle and Organization in Sri Lanka's Export Processing Zones: 1978–2003." In *Global Unions: Challenging Transnational Capital Through Cross-Border Campaigns. Frank W. Pierce Memorial Lectureship and Conference Series No. 13*, edited by Kate Bronfenbrenner, 78–98. Ithaca: Cornell University Press.

Mendez, Jennifer Bickham. 2005. *From the Revolution to the Maquiladoras: Gender, Labor, and Globalization in Nicaragua*. Durham, NC: Duke University Press.

Milberg, William, and Matthew Amengual. 2008. *Economic Development and Working Conditions in Export Processing Zones: a Survey of Trends*. Working Paper No. 3. InFocus Initiative on Export Processing Zones. Geneva: International Labour Office.

Ngai, Pun. 2005. *Made in China: Women Factory Workers in a Global Workplace*. Durham, NC: Duke University Press, and Hong Kong: Hong Kong University Press.

Fundamentalism and Public Policy

TIMOTHY J. DEMY
US Naval War College, USA

The resurgence of global religious fundamentalism in all religions since the 1970s has been accompanied in many countries by political promotion and legal enforcement of gender roles that are restrictive and detrimental to women's rights and contemporary sexual values. Religious fundamentalism is a worldwide phenomenon not limited to specific countries, populations, or religious traditions. Particular doctrines, values, and individual and community practices derived from the fundamentalist's theological and social views are frequently understood as contrary to modern and postmodern secular standards, especially in the West. In the realm of gender, sexuality, and women's rights and concerns of public policy advocacy and/or implementation, there are specific legal and political challenges. Among the debated issues are: sexual orientation, sartorial requirements, marriage and divorce practice, education for girls and women, reproductive rights, healthcare, economic opportunity and independence, workforce and labor practices, social independence, and military and public service. However, given the varied social worlds and histories in which fundamentalism occurs globally, the results are far from uniform and they are not always conservative or reactive. Published research on the topic was abundant in the 1980s and 1990s, but has waned significantly since 2000.

Use of the term fundamentalism is itself contested and has a specific history tied to early twentieth-century Protestantism in the United States and social and theological divisions within it. The term is derived from a series of essays affirming conservative Protestant theology that were published in 12 volumes from 1910 to 1915 that were anonymously funded by brothers Lyman and Milton Stewart, who were businessmen and philanthropists. Though initially used by advocates in a positive sense of representing individuals and groups wanting to return to and represent what they considered to be the basics or "fundamentals" of conservative Protestant Christianity, the term was quickly adopted by opponents and journalists to represent any group of religious faithful who opposed broader theological interpretations and who were seen as being opposed to science and modernity. In the 1980s pejorative usage of the term became common in journalistic presentations and political debates in the United States. Critics of the term claim that there is often a failure to understand and distinguish between conservative theology and fundamentalist theology. In the 1940s in the United States, Protestant conservatives made an intentional break with the Christian fundamentalism of the 1920s and 1930s, adopting the term "evangelical." In subsequent public policy matters there have been distinct differences between the two groups. While they share some theological interpretations of sexuality and gender, there has been a broader acceptance, with debate, of the political and policy affirmations of women's rights, sexual orientation, and economic opportunity for women. Internationally, evangelicals have been instrumental in promoting the combating of AIDS in Africa and slavery and sex trafficking in Asia. However, evangelical activism in Africa has also drawn criticism for its opposition to homosexuality and support of legislation against it.

With respect to gender issues, the focal point of the debate about fundamentalism and public policy, historically, was abortion and the Equal Rights Amendment (ERA). After the Islamic revolution in Iran in 1979, the term fundamentalism came into wide use in a global context referring to individuals or groups within any religious tradition who were seen to display narrow, ultra-conservative, or anti-modern political and social values. The results of the search for a more representative alternate term such as "religious extremism" or "religious fanaticism" have not gained universal acceptance, with the result that usage of "fundamentalism" or "fundamentalist" remains widespread in spite of the pejorative and distinctively Christian connotations and history. However, as a religious, political, and social phenomenon the rise of religious fundamentalism since the 1970s has been well documented.

Fundamentalism is a spectrum of political activity, and not all religious groups deemed to be fundamentalists participate in the civic and political realm. Whether or not a faith community participates in the political process is rooted in religious convictions regarding the relationship between the sacred and the secular. However, those who do participate tend to promote restrictive policies. Public policies promoted by religious fundamentalists are understood by adherents as being derived directly or indirectly from religious texts and norms, usually viewed as divinely given or divinely inspired and inerrant such as the Torah, Bible, Qur'an, or Guru Granth Sahib. From these texts arises the codification of religious law for the religious community and, when pursued through public policy, for the larger society. Whether it is the Hindu *dharma*, the Islamic *sharia*, the Jewish *torah*, or the Christian *logos*, religious values are applied to all aspects of life.

Fundamentalism is not easy to define and this has led many more accurately to speak of "fundamentalisms." Lawrence (1995) defines it as: "the affirmation of religious authority as holistic and absolute, admitting of neither criticism or reduction; it is expressed through the collective demand that specific creedal and ethical dictates derived from scripture be publicly recognized and legally enforced."

Helpful understanding of fundamentalism as a phenomenon can be found in the work of Hadden (1992), who identified four kinds of fundamentalism: theological, political, cultural, and global. Theological fundamentalism is the theological and philosophical effort that attempts to defend traditional religious doctrine over and against contemporary values. Political fundamentalism is a combination of theological fundamentalism with personal commitments of religious adherents to combat what are understood to be socially accepted vices and values contrary to religious values of the fundamentalists. Theological and political fundamentalism can converge to form cultural fundamentalism, which is a broader acceptance of what is deemed by those outside of fundamentalism as being anti-scientific, against progress, and culturally unenlightened. The political activity engaged in by fundamentalists invites comparison to other religiously motivated groups around the world from either the same religious perspective or another one. It is in this macro-comparative framework that one speaks of global fundamentalism, which is a linked network of religiously motivated, politically active groups that exist in a variety of religious traditions. An example of global fundamentalism is the study of the control of female sexuality through language and sartorial coding such as distinctive clothing and veiling or covering of women through hats, chadors, hijab, niqab, and burqas – practices that blend religious, political, and cultural fundamentalism. This may be from religious traditions as diverse and disparate as those practiced by the Taliban in Afghanistan and the Fundamentalist Church of Jesus Christ of Latter-Day Saints (FLDS Church) in the United States. When viewing such practices and making sociological comparisons, the religious component of the practice is normally grounded in interpretations of religious texts and the personal and corporate application of those texts to the individual, gender, and community. It then crosses into public policy when such practices are codified or permitted in the public and civic domains.

Frequently tied to political conservatism and authoritarian policymaking, the political strategy of fundamentalists, if and when they engage in politics and public policy, tends to reject political accommodation or policy compromise. The ultimate goal of policy implementation is the construction of a society grounded upon political theology and belief in a utopian or theocratic society. Within fundamentalist religion there is a belief in a divinely ordained social order that strongly segregates social roles between genders. For those traditions that engage in political discourse and activity, combined with this belief of a gender-structured society is the belief that law and public policy should reflect and enforce the theological interpretation of gender and sexuality. While diverse religious traditions resist comparison, contrast, and clustering of common sociological and religious themes identified with the fundamentalist phenomenon, there are similarities.

The response of women within religio-cultural, gender-stratified boundaries has not been fully understood or researched. This has led to assumptions about women in ultraconservative religious groups as being uniformly victimized and instances otherwise as being anomalies. Yet ethnographic research has shown that there is a more complex reality wherein some women actively advocate restrictive ideologies and practices while others are rendered passive. Since the 1970s there are notable instances of women being vocal and active in conservative public policy endeavors and organizations. In the United States and from within US Christian fundamentalism, constitutional attorney Phyllis Schafley founded the Eagle Forum and gained national attention for efforts to block the ERA, civil unions, and same-sex marriage. Similarly, Anita Bryant campaigned against homosexuality and gay rights in Florida and Beverly LaHaye, in 1979, founded the nation's largest women's political action group, Concerned Women for America, as a conservative alternative to the National Organization for Women. Another contemporary example is Hindu political activist Uma Bharti and her anti-Muslim rhetoric and policy views on behalf of the Bharatiya Janshakti Party (BJP).

Within orthodox Judaism gender segregation, boundaries, and expectations are centuries old, as are sexual values. These are rooted in the Levitical laws of the Torah and subsequent rabbinic interpretations. Outside of Israel public policy engagement by ultra-orthodox Jews is not promoted.

In Latin America the significant growth of evangelical and Pentecostal communities, both of which have strong patriarchal theology, has led to increased opportunities for women in a geographic region where men often abandon their children. Though not translated into public policies, such a phenomenon demonstrates the complexities of religion, sociology, and gender. Likewise, Japanese New Religions, some of which were founded by female prophets and espouse patriarchal values, have allowed more active and participatory roles for women than often found in traditional Buddhism and Shinto.

Studies of how women negotiate their agency, identity, and status within a religious community reveal diversity that does not easily fit secular assumptions. The studies also show that the difficulties of confronting political and cultural practices and policies that are understood as being derived from divine revelation, inspired religious texts, or authoritarian religious leaders present formidable legal and political challenges.

With respect to gender and sexuality in relation to fundamentalism, there is not a single controversy that can be framed. Rather, one finds a series of overlapping debates that often involve different local and national cultures, histories, and constituencies. A narrow or conservative position on one issue does not necessarily mean a similar position on another topic, though there often is such alignment.

Broadly speaking, religious, legal, and sociological studies of religious fundamentalism demonstrate the existence of public policies that reject legal steps ensuring equality of gender and sexuality. The fundamentalist framework also creates strict boundaries of gender activity, and bases religious norms and public policy on gender and sexual identities understood to be God-given at birth and restricted to male–female sexual activity within the bounds of marriage (or polygamy in some religious traditions).

Among the public policies enacted by nations where there is political activism by religious fundamentalists, one finds a wide array of laws and practices that range from corporal punishment and execution for adultery and homosexuality to prohibition of abortion, education, and opportunities for economic independence. Fundamentalist public policies often succeed where secular and authoritarian governments have held power and failed and thrive in conditions of economic and social crisis and in countries on the global periphery. Fundamentalism is also prevalent in countries where there is strong central authority or monarchy. In democratic countries fundamentalism exists where there is both the political opportunity to promote religiously based public policy and the freedom to abstain from political activity and confine sexuality and gender mores to practices within the religious communities. Fundamentalism remains an important religious, social, and political phenomenon. It has not disappeared as in the last century many thought it would, and its appeal of certitude, truth, hierarchy, and structure in times of personal, social, and global change means that it will be an active and formidable force across the public policy spectrum.

SEE ALSO: Abortion and Religion; Abortion, Legal Status in Global Perspective on; Human Rights, International Laws and Policies on; Religious Fundamentalism

REFERENCES

Hadden, Jeffrey. 1992. *Secularization and Fundamentalism Reconstructed*. New York: Crossroad.

Lawrence, Bruce B. 1995. *Defenders of God: The Fundamentalist Revolt Against the Modern Age*. Columbia: University of South Carolina Press.

FURTHER READING

Blaydes, Lisa, and Drew Linzer. 2008. "The Political Economy of Women's Support of Fundamentalist Islam." *World Politics*, 60(4): 576–609.

Brink, Judy, and Joan Mencher, eds. 1997. *Mixed Blessings: Gender and Religious Fundamentalism Cross Culturally*. New York: Routledge.

Burkhalter, Holly. 2004. "The Politics of AIDS: Engaging Conservative Activists." *Foreign Affairs*, 83: 8–14.

Davidman, Lynn, and Janet Stocks. 1995. "Varieties of Fundamentalist Experience: Lubavitch and Hasidic and Fundamentalist Christian Approaches to Family Life." In *Ethnographic Studies of Hasidic Jews in America*, edited by Janet S. Belcove-Shalin, 107–134. Albany: SUNY Press.

Gerami, Shahin. 1996. *Women and Fundamentalism: Islam and Christianity*. New York: Garland.

Hawley, John Stratton, ed. 1994. *Fundamentalism and Gender*. New York: Oxford University Press.

Howland, Courtney W. 1999. *Religious Fundamentalisms and the Human Rights of Women*. New York: Palgrave Macmillan.

Marty, Martin E., and R. Scott Appleby, eds. 1993. *Fundamentalisms and Society: Reclaiming the Sciences, the Family, and Education*. Chicago: University of Chicago Press.

Saha, Santosh C., and Thomas K. Carr, eds. 2003. *Islamic, Hindu, and Christian Fundamentalism Compared – Public Policy in Global Perspective*. Lewiston: Edwin Mellen Press.